# Mountain Bike
## AMERICA™

# COLORADO

# Contact

Dear Readers:

Every effort was made to make this the most accurate, informative, and easy-to-use guidebook on the planet. Any comments, suggestions, and/or corrections regarding this guide are welcome and should be sent to:

**Outside America™**
c/o Editorial Dept.
300 West Main St., Ste. A
Charlottesville, VA 22903
*editorial@outside-america.com*
**www.outside-america.com**

We'd love to hear from you so we can make future editions and future guides even better.

Thanks and happy trails!

# Mountain Bike AMERICA™

# COLORADO

An Atlas of Colorado's Greatest
Off-Road Bicycle Rides

**by Stephen Hlawaty**

The Globe Pequot Press

Guilford, Connecticut

Published by
**The Globe Pequot Press**
P.O. Box 480
Guilford, CT 06437
www.globe-pequot.com

Produced by
**Beachway Press Publishing, Inc.**
300 West Main St., Ste A
Charlottesville, VA 22903
www.beachway.com

Mountain Bike America is a trademark of Beachway Press
Publishing, Inc.

**Cover Design**  Beachway Press

**Photographers**  Stephen Hlawaty, Amanda Williams, John
Gray, Jeremy Moore, Peter Boniface

**Maps** designed and produced by Beachway Press

Find Outside America™ at **www.outside-america.com**

Cover Photo: An autumn ride along Deep Creek Trail near
Telluride, Colorado. Wilson Peaks in the background. Photo by
Amanda Williams

**Library of Congress Cataloging-in-Publication Data**
is available

ISBN: 0-7627-0697-X

Manufactured in the United States of America
**First Edition/First Printing**

# Acknowledgments

Nil Sine Numine ("*Nothing Without Providence*"—Colorado state motto)

**A**s with any creation, this book is borne of the workings of many hands, and I remain forever grateful.

Papa, you're a proud, hard-working cabinetmaker and father, and a craftsman of both. "I'm better than most and just as good as some," you'd say—an understatement which has always inspired me to do my best. When book deadlines were freaking me out, you volunteered to relocate from New York City to Colorado to chauffeur me from ride to ride, just to ease the burden of constant driving and then riding. Mama, you're the epitome of good-heartedness. Your support and kindness is forever expressed in your gleaming eyes and loving smile, a vision which will forever brighten my dimmest days. So to my parents, know that any successes I may achieve remain uniquely your own, as is the love with which you've raised me. Thank you.

To Roland and Ingrid, your life-long achievements have always challenged me. This book testifies to the good that occurs when one is flanked on either side by the greatness that is my older brother and younger sister.

I may never have had the opportunity to write this book had it not been for my mountain biking mentor and good friend John Gray. Always the defender of the struggling artist, John sent me the classified ad for this assignment, enabling my life-long dream to be realized. Rave on John Gray.

Amber Beyer, you opened your home to me when I was on the road and opened my eyes to the benefits of rice milk and whole grains. Thanks for the meals: they were all nutritious, delicious, and they made me feel so ambitious.

A special thank you goes to Dave Herz, my boss when I worked as a hod for his stucco crew, for understanding when I had to quit midseason to pursue this project full bore. Facing five inches from the wall, you'll never know the world you've shown me.

Much thanks goes out to the city-slicker boys back home—Mark Reinstadler, Paul Iovane and Michael Iovane—who came to visit me with sea-level lungs, but hung tough on some grueling Rocky Mountain rides.

John Barnes, Curtis Church, Jeremy Moore and Peter Boniface, you guys are tough stuff. Thanks for all the good vibes through a lot of these rides. Pete, after your bout with the La Sals on the hut trip, I really do believe you can take on a bolt of lightning. Thanks also goes to Kelly Keim. How 'bout them BV bears?

During the course of my research, I've met many unique individuals who've dedicated themselves to their passions. Thank you Michael Whiting of Wildernet and Team Phoenix for opening my eyes to the bigger picture. Thank you Richard Fischer of Extreme Snow Bikes and the Alpine Snow Bicycle Association for that windy snow ride atop Berthoud Pass. Tim Blumenthal of the IMBA, thank you for all your help and insights into the future of Colorado mountain biking. Thank you Grant Lamont, race-coordinator extraordinaire, for helping me out with the Howelsen Hill map.

I'd like to thank all the strangers that I've met on the trails who, offering to pose for the camera and wait while I diligently took notes, reminded me that a good time shared makes friends of us all.

Thanks to all at Sore Saddle Cyclery in Steamboat Springs who kept my bicycle in great shape.

A respectful bow goes to both my rallynugen—211,000+ miles and going strong—and my old Stumpy—steel is real—for taking me where I needed to go.

Thank you Scott Adams and Ryan Croxton of Beachway Press for polishing the blood, sweat, and tears I offered as a finished manuscript.

Of course, my life, and all that it may accomplish, has been forever blessed by the presence of my beautiful fiancé, Amanda Williams. From the scorching desert sands of Picket Wire Canyonlands to soaked sleeping bags in an early Autumn snowstorm in Telluride, your confidence and patience during the harried summer of 1998 were only equaled by your sense of humor. Thanks for the laughs; your smile will always offer my present unbridled promise for the future.

Lastly, thank you readers and riders for choosing Mountain Bike Colorado. I hope you find it to be as good as some and better than most.

# Contents

# Preface

**G**rowing up in New York City, my friends and I took to the streets, the cemeteries and the railroad tracks with our 3- and 5-speed Ross, Schwinn and Huffy bicycles. We'd set up ramps of brick and plywood before trains of old metal garbage cans and clear as many of those rusted "cars" as we could. In hindsight, those cemeteries were anything but eternal resting places, and train tracks, nothing more than modified singletrack. One thing was certain, we had inherited the earth, albeit of stone and steel, and knew enough to enjoy what had been given to us.

That single truth remained steadfast throughout my years growing up: through weekends camping as a Boy Scout in the cold rain and snow of the Mid-Atlantic states, through timeless hours spent chopping wood for the Clubhouse in Hawley, Pennsylvania, through many a star-filled night, staring aimlessly into campfires ablaze with the hope and the understanding of my many years to come and of the few that have already. And as the flames of my childhood forged the frame of my life, my inheritance took shape and began to grow in the embers of my eyes.

It wasn't until moving to Colorado that I realized the sheer magnitude of this inheritance. Standing in awe before the Rocky Mountains, absorbed in the cool darkness of a 14,000-foot mountain shadow (one of 54), I welcomed Colorado as my new home. And Colorado, for its part, had welcomed me as its newest inheritor, offering me verdant forests larger than the entire state of Maine, three hundred miles of Rocky Mountain highs, champagne powder, crashing rivers, lonesome deserts, sprawling grasslands and the sweetest cantaloupes in the world. But what's always to be remem-

bered, however, is that this is a shared inheritance. And due courtesy should be given to those who have come before us.

As mountain bikers, we owe much to the original "clunkers" who in 1974 took their modified Schwinn Excelsiors to the top of Mount Tamalpias in Marin County, California and descended with news of the next great and future king in the way of outdoor recreation. Mountain biking had been born. But although mountain biking was born in California, its soul lives in Colorado. That's not to say, however, that mountain biking is dead. Far from it. Mountain biking has only found itself a heaven on earth in which to lay its tracks.

And nowhere in Colorado do these tracks sink deeper than in the hallowed hills of Crested Butte. As local lore has it, after the summer's forest fire season had ended, local firefighters would return from their mountain posts via their town bicycles, careening down mountain dirt roads at break-neck speeds. One such road led to the top of 12,705-foot Pearl Pass. In the summer of 1976, a crew of motorcyclists from Aspen roared over Pearl Pass and descended upon Crested Butte, commencing to boast about their

achievement. Viewing the incident as a cultural invasion and a challenge to their bravado, the firefighters decided to do their Aspen neighbors one better. On a cold September morning, about 15 of Crested Butte's finest smoke eaters began their climb of Pearl Pass to Aspen on their town bikes. The tour ended at Aspen's Hotel Jerome, and Colorado mountain biking had been born. Interestingly enough, the same spirit that sparked the birth of mountain biking in Colorado also fueled the flames of the birth of the state.

"Gold! Gold!! Gold!!! Gold!!!! Hard to Get and Heavy to Hold!" read the headlines in 1858 when the valuable metal was discovered along the Platte River at the base of the Rocky Mountains. Within a year, 50,000 emigrants forced settlers old and new to consider establishing an organized government on the Colorado frontier. "Government of some kind we must have," hailed one new Coloradan, "and the question narrows itself down to this point: Shall it be the government of the knife and the revolver, or shall we unite in forming here in our golden country . . . a new and independent state?"

It is this spirit of independence, and at the same time, a willingness to get along with each other that define the character of the Colorado people. From Colorado's most recent mountain bikers to its earliest settlers, the people of Colorado have learned to adopt and adapt to their changing environments, reinventing what it means to be a Coloradan. It is this spirit that connects Colorado mountain biking irrevocably to the history of this land. And it is this land that invites mountain bikers to share the spirit and accept their inheritance.

Since coming to Colorado, I've past through many centuries, collecting the inheritances of the ages along the way. I've journeyed through a single dinosaur print, one step in North America's longest recorded set of pre-Cambrian dinosaur tracks impressed upon the desert sands of Picket Wire Canyon. I've marveled at the thousands-years-old ancient Anazazi cliff dwellings carved meticulously within the walls of Sand Canyon and. I've past pioneering homesteads of sod and timber in the dusty, rocky foothills of the Front Range, conscious of why these sod house doors all open inward. I've sat entranced around a farmer's kitchen table, listening to stories of Colorado's strange, and sometimes, macabre beginnings. I've stopped to spy a bull moose take his drink from the cool waters of a glacial runoff, and I've bathed nude in the healing hot waters of a natural thermal spring on the western slope.

And now, having accepted my rightful place among the riches of our world, I hope to pass this inheritance on to you, making mountain biking the portal through which to feel the power, admire the beauty and revere the majesty that is Colorado.

*Stephen Hlawaty*

## A note from the folks behind this endeavor...

*We at Outside America look at guidebook publishing a little differently. There's just no reason that a guidebook has to look like it was published out of your Uncle Ernie's woodshed. We feel that guidebooks need to be both easy to use and nice to look at, and that takes an innovative approach to design. We want you to spend less time fumbling through your guidebook and more time enjoying the adventure at hand. At any rate, we hope you like what you see and enjoy the places we lead you. And most of all, we'd like to thank you for taking an adventure with us.*

*Happy Trails!*

# Introduction

**W**elcome to the new generation of bicycling! Indeed, the sport has evolved dramatically from the thin-tired, featherweight-frame days of old. The sleek geometry and lightweight frames of racing bicycles, still the heart and soul of bicycling worldwide, have lost much ground in recent years, unpaving the way for the mountain bike, which now accounts for the majority of all bicycle sales in the U.S. And with this change comes a new breed of cyclist, less concerned with smooth roads and long rides, who thrives in places once inaccessible to the mortal road bike.

The mountain bike, with its knobby tread and reinforced frame, takes cyclists to places once unheard of—down rugged mountain trails, through streams of rushing water, across the frozen Alaskan tundra, and even to work in the city. There seem to be few limits on what this fat-tired beast can do and where it can take us. Few obstacles stand in its way, few boundaries slow its progress. Except for one—its own success. If trail closure means little to you now, read on and discover how a trail can be here today and gone tomorrow. With so many new off-road cyclists taking to the trails each year, it's no wonder trail access hinges precariously between universal acceptance and complete termination. But a little work on your part can go a long way to preserving trail access for future use. Nothing is more crucial to the survival of mountain biking itself than to read the examples set forth in the following pages and practice their message. Then turn to the maps, pick out your favorite ride, and hit the dirt!

## WHAT THIS BOOK IS ABOUT

Within these pages you will find everything you need to know about off-road bicycling in Colorado. This guidebook begins by exploring the fascinating history of the mountain bike itself, then goes on to discuss everything from the health benefits of off-road cycling to tips and techniques for bicycling over logs and up hills. Also included are the types of clothing to keep you comfortable and in style, essential equipment ideas to keep your rides smooth and trouble-free, and descriptions of off-road terrain to prepare you for the kinds of bumps and bounces you can expect to encounter. The major provisions of this book, though, are its unique perspectives on each ride, it detailed maps, and its relentless dedication to trail preservation.

Without open trails, the maps in this book are virtually useless. Cyclists must learn to be responsible for the trails they use and to share these trails with others. This guidebook addresses such issues as why trail use has become so controversial, what can be done to improve the image of mountain biking, how to have fun and ride responsibly, on-the-spot trail repair techniques, trail maintenance hotlines for each trail, and the worldwide-standard Rules of the Trail.

Each of the 50-plus rides is complete with maps, photos, trail descriptions and directions, local history, and a quick-reference ride information guide including such items as trail contact information, park schedules, fees/permits, local bike stores, dining, lodging, entertainment, alternative map resources and more. Also included at the end of each regional section is an "Honorable Mentions" list of alternative off-road rides (60-plus rides total).

1

It's important to note that mountain bike rides tend to take longer than road rides because the average speed is often much slower. Average speeds can vary from a climbing pace of three to four miles per hour to 12 to 13 miles per hour on flatter roads and trails. Keep this in mind when planning your trip.

## MOUNTAIN BIKE BEGINNINGS

It seems the mountain bike, originally designed for lunatic adventurists bored with straight lines, clean clothes, and smooth tires, has become globally popular in as short a time as it would take to race down a mountain trail.

Like many things of a revolutionary nature, the mountain bike was born on the west coast. But unlike Rollerblades, purple hair, and the peace sign, the concept of the off-road bike cannot be credited solely to the imaginative Californians—they were just the first to make waves.

The design of the first off-road specific bike was based on the geometry of the old Schwinn Excelsior, a one-speed, camel-back cruiser with balloon tires. Joe Breeze was the creator behind it, and in 1977 he built 10 of these "Breezers" for himself and his Marin County, California, friends at $750 apiece—a bargain.

Breeze was a serious competitor in bicycle racing, placing 13th in the 1977 U.S. Road Racing National Championships. After races, he and friends would scour local bike shops hoping to find old bikes they could then restore.

It was the 1941 Schwinn Excelsior, for which Breeze paid just five dollars, that began to shape and change bicycling history forever. After taking the bike home, removing the fenders, oiling the chain, and pumping up the tires, Breeze hit the dirt. He loved it.

His inspiration, while forerunning, was not altogether unique. On the opposite end of the country, nearly 2,500 miles from Marin County, east coast bike bums were also growing restless. More and more old, beat-up clunkers were being restored and modified. These behemoths often weighed as much as 80 pounds and were so reinforced they seemed virtually indestructible. But rides that take just 40 minutes on today's 25-pound featherweights took the steel-toed-boot- and-blue-jean-clad bikers of the late 1970s and early 1980s nearly four hours to complete.

Not until 1981 was it possible to purchase a production mountain bike, but local retailers found these ungainly bicycles difficult to sell and rarely kept them in stock. By 1983, however, mountain bikes were no longer such a fringe item, and large bike manufacturers quickly jumped into the action, producing their own versions of the off-road bike. By the 1990s, the mountain bike had firmly established its place with bicyclists of nearly all ages and abilities, and now command nearly 90 percent of the U.S. bike market.

There are many reasons for the mountain bike's success in becoming the hottest two-wheeled vehicle in the nation. They are much friendlier to the cyclist than traditional road bikes because of their comfortable upright position and shock-absorbing fat tires. And because of the health-conscious, environmentalist movement of the late 1980s and 1990s, people are more activity minded and seek nature on a closer front than paved roads can allow. The mountain bike gives you these things and takes you far away from the daily grind—even if you're only minutes from the city.

## MOUNTAIN BIKING INTO SHAPE

If your objective is to get in shape and lose weight, then you're on the right track, because mountain biking is one of the best ways to get started.

One way many of us have lost weight in this sport is the crash-and-burn-it-off method. Picture this: you're speeding uncontrollably down a vertical drop that you realize you shouldn't be on—only after it is too late. Your front wheel lodges into a rut and launches you through endless weeds, trees, and pointy rocks before coming to an abrupt halt in a puddle of thick mud. Surveying the damage, you discover, with the layers of skin, body parts, and lost confidence littering the trail above, that those unwanted pounds have been shed—*permanently*. Instant weight loss.

There is, of course, a more conventional (and quite a bit less painful) approach to losing weight and gaining fitness on a mountain bike. It's called the workout, and bicycles provide an ideal way to get physical. Take a look at some of the benefits associated with cycling.

Cycling helps you shed pounds without gimmicky diet fads or weight-loss programs. You can explore the countryside and burn nearly 10 to 16 calories per minute or close to 600 to 1,000 calories per hour. Moreover, it's a great way to spend an afternoon.

No less significant than the external and cosmetic changes of your body from riding are the internal changes taking place. Over time, cycling regularly will strengthen your heart as your body grows vast networks of new capillaries to carry blood to all those working muscles. This will, in turn, give your skin a healthier glow. The capacity of your lungs may increase up to 20 percent, and your resting heart rate will drop significantly. The Stanford University School of Medicine reports to the American Heart Association that people can reduce their risk of heart attack by nearly 64 percent if they can burn up to 2,000 calories per week. This is only two to three hours of bike riding!

Recommended for insomnia, hypertension, indigestion, anxiety, and even for recuperation from major heart attacks, bicycling can be an excellent cure-all as well as a great preventive. Cycling just a few hours per week can improve your figure and sleeping habits, give you greater resistance to illness, increase your energy levels, and provide feelings of accomplishment and heightened self-esteem.

## BE SAFE—KNOW THE LAW

Occasionally, even the hard-core off-road cyclists will find they have no choice but to ride the pavement. When you are forced to hit the road, it's important for you to know and understand the rules.

Outlined below are a few of the common laws found in Colorado's Vehicle Code book.

- **Bicycles are legally classified as vehicles in Colorado.** This means that as a bicyclist, you are responsible for obeying the same rules of the road as a driver of a motor vehicle.
- **Bicyclists must ride with the traffic—NOT AGAINST IT!** Because bicycles are considered vehicles, you must ride your bicycle just as you would drive a car—with traffic. Only pedestrians should travel against the flow of traffic.

- *You must obey all traffic signs.* This includes stop signs and stoplights.
- *Always signal your turns.* Most drivers aren't expecting bicyclists to be on the roads, and many drivers would prefer that cyclists stay off the roads altogether. It's important, therefore, to clearly signal your intentions to motorists both in front and behind you.
- *Bicyclists are entitled to the same roads as cars (except controlled-access highways).* Unfortunately, cyclists are rarely given this consideration.
- *Be a responsible cyclist.* Do not abuse your rights to ride on open roads. Follow the rules and set a good example for all of us as you roll along.

## THE MOUNTAIN BIKE CONTROVERSY

*Are Off-Road Bicyclists Environmental Outlaws? Do We have the Right to Use Public Trails?*
Mountain bikers have long endured the animosity of folks in the backcountry who complain about the consequences of off-road bicycling. Many people believe that the fat tires and knobby tread do unacceptable environmental damage and that our uncontrollable riding habits are a danger to animals and to other trail users. To the contrary, mountain bikes have no more environmental impact than hiking boots or horseshoes. This does not mean, however, that mountain bikes leave no imprint at all. Wherever man treads, there is an impact. By riding responsibly, though, it is possible to leave only a minimum impact—something we all must take care to achieve.

Unfortunately, it is often people of great influence who view the mountain bike as the environment's worst enemy. Consequently, we as mountain bike riders and environmentally concerned citizens must be educators, impressing upon others that we also deserve the right to use these trails. Our responsibilities as bicyclists are no more and no less than any other trail user. We must all take the soft-cycling approach and show that mountain bicyclists are not environmental outlaws.

## ETIQUETTE OF MOUNTAIN BIKING

When discussing mountain biking etiquette, we are in essence discussing the soft-cycling approach. This term, as mentioned previously, describes the art of minimum-impact bicycling and should apply to both the physical and social dimensions of the sport. But make no mistake—it is possible to ride fast and furiously while maintaining the balance of soft-cycling. Here first are a few ways to minimize the physical impact of mountain bike riding.

- *Stay on the trail.* Don't ride around fallen trees or mud holes that block your path. Stop and cross over them. When you come to a vista overlooking a deep valley, don't ride off the trail for a better vantage point. Instead, leave the bike and walk to see the view. Riding off the trail may seem inconsequential when done only once, but soon someone else will follow, then others, and the cumulative results can be catastrophic. Each time you wander from the trail you begin creating a new path, adding one more scar to the earth's surface.
- *Do not disturb the soil.* Follow a line within the trail that will not disturb or damage the soil.

4

- *Do not ride over soft or wet trails.* After a rain shower or during the thawing season, trails will often resemble muddy, oozing swampland. The best thing to do is stay off the trails altogether. Realistically, however, we're all going to come across some muddy trails we cannot anticipate. Instead of blasting through each section of mud, which may seem both easier and more fun, lift the bike and walk past. Each time a cyclist rides through a soft or muddy section of trail, that part of the trail is permanently damaged. Regardless of the trail's conditions, though, remember always to go over the obstacles across the path, not around them. Stay on the trail.
- *Avoid trails that, for all but God, are considered impassable and impossible.* Don't take a leap of faith down a kamikaze descent on which you will be forced to lock your brakes and skid to the bottom, ripping the ground apart as you go.

**Soft-cycling** should apply to the social dimensions of the sport as well, since mountain bikers are not the only folks who use the trails. Hikers, equestrians, cross-country skiers, and other outdoors people use many of the same trails and can be easily spooked by a marauding mountain biker tearing through the trees. Be friendly in the forest and give ample warning of your approach.

- *Take out what you bring in.* Don't leave broken bike pieces and banana peels scattered along the trail.
- *Be aware of your surroundings.* Don't use popular hiking trails for race training.
- *Slow down!* Rocketing around blind corners is a sure way to ruin an unsuspecting hiker's day. Consider this—If you fly down a quick singletrack descent at 20 mph, then hit the brakes and slow down to only six mph to pass someone, you're still moving twice as fast as they are!

Like the trails we ride on, the social dimension of mountain biking is very fragile and must be cared for responsibly. We should not want to destroy another person's enjoyment of the outdoors. By riding in the backcountry with caution, control, and responsibility, our presence should be felt positively by other trail users. By adhering to these rules, trail riding—a privilege that can quickly be taken away—will continue to be ours to share.

## TRAIL MAINTENANCE

Unfortunately, despite all of the preventive measures taken to avoid trail damage, we're still going to run into many trails requiring attention. Simply put, a lot of hikers, equestrians, and cyclists alike use the same trails—some wear and tear is unavoidable. But like your bike, if you want to use these trails for a long time to come, you must also maintain them.

Trail maintenance and restoration can be accomplished in a variety of ways. One way is for mountain bike clubs to combine efforts with other trail users (i.e. hikers and equestrians) and work closely with land managers to cut new trails or repair existing ones. This not only reinforces to others the commitment cyclists have in caring for and maintaining the land, but also breaks the ice that often separates cyclists from their fellow trailmates. Another good way to help out is to show up on a Saturday morning with a few riding buddies at your favorite off-road domain ready to work. With a good attitude, thick gloves, and the local land manager's supervision, trail repair is fun and very rewarding. It's important, of course, that you arrange a trail-repair outing with the local land manager before you start pounding shovels into the dirt. They can lead you to the most needy sections of trail and instruct you on what repairs should be done and how best to accomplish the task. Perhaps the most effective means of trail maintenance, though, can be done by yourself and while you're riding. Read on.

## ON–THE–SPOT QUICK FIX

Most of us, when we're riding, have at one time or another come upon muddy trails or fallen trees blocking our path. We notice that over time the mud gets deeper and the trail gets wider as people go through or around the obstacles. We worry that the problem will become so severe and repairs too difficult that the trail's access may be threatened. We also know that our ambition to do anything about it is greatest at that moment, not after a hot shower and a plate of spaghetti. Here are a few on-the-spot quick fixes you can do that will hopefully correct a problem before it gets out of hand and get you back on your bike within minutes.

**Muddy Trails.** What do you do when trails develop huge mud holes destined for the EPA's Superfund status? The technique is called corduroying, and it works much like building a pontoon over the mud to support bikes, horses, or hikers as they cross. Corduroy (not the pants) is the term for roads made of logs laid down crosswise. Use small-and medium-sized sticks and lay them side by side across the trail until they cover the length of the muddy section (break the sticks to fit the width of the trail). Press them into the mud with your feet, then lay more on top if needed. Keep adding sticks until the trail is firm. Not only will you stay clean as you cross, but the sticks may soak up some of the water and help the puddle dry. This quick fix may last as long as one month before needing to be redone. And as time goes on, with new layers added to the trail, the soil will grow stronger, thicker, and more resistant to erosion. This whole process may take fewer than five minutes, and you can be on your way, knowing the trail behind you is in good repair.

**Leaving the Trail.** What do you do to keep cyclists from cutting corners and leaving the designated trail? The solution is much simpler than you may think. (No, don't hire an off-road police force.) Notice where people are leaving the trail and throw a pile of thick branches or brush along the path, or place logs across the opening to block the way through. There are probably dozens of subtle tricks like these that will manipulate people into staying on the designated trail. If executed well, no one will even notice that the thick branches scattered along the ground in the woods weren't always there. And most folks would probably rather take a moment to hop a log in the trail than get tangled in a web of branches.

**Obstacle in the Way.** If there are large obstacles blocking the trail, try and remove them or push them aside. If you cannot do this by yourself, call the trail maintenance hotline to speak with the land manager of that particular trail and see what can be done.

We must be willing to sweat for our trails in order to sweat on them. Police yourself and point out to others the significance of trail maintenance. "Sweat Equity," the rewards of continued land use won with a fair share of sweat, pays off when the trail is "up for review" by the land manager and he or she remembers the efforts made by trail-conscious mountain bikers.

## RULES OF THE TRAIL

The International Mountain Bicycling Association (IMBA) has developed these guidelines to trail riding. These "Rules of the Trail" are accepted worldwide and will go a long way in keeping trails open. Please respect and follow these rules for everyone's sake.

1. **Ride only on open trails.** Respect trail and road closures (if you're not sure, ask a park or state official first), do not trespass on private property, and obtain permits or authorization if required. Federal and state wilderness areas are off-limits to cycling. Parks and state forests may also have certain trails closed to cycling.

2. **Leave no trace.** Be sensitive to the dirt beneath you. Even on open trails, you should not ride under conditions by which you will leave evidence of your passing, such as on certain soils or shortly after a rainfall. Be sure to observe the different types of soils and trails you're riding on, practicing minimum-impact cycling. Never ride off the trail, don't skid your tires, and be sure to bring out at least as much as you bring in.

3. **Control your bicycle!** Inattention for even one second can cause disaster for yourself or for others. Excessive speed frightens and can injure people, gives mountain biking a bad name, and can result in trail closures.

4. **Always yield.** Let others know you're coming well in advance (a friendly greeting is always good and often appreciated). Show your respect when passing others by slowing to walking speed or stopping altogether, especially in the presence of horses. Horses can be unpredictable, so be very careful. Anticipate that other trail users may be around corners or in blind spots.

5. **Never spook animals.** All animals are spooked by sudden movements, unannounced approaches, or loud noises. Give the animals extra room and time so they can adjust to you. Move slowly or dismount around animals. Running cattle and disturbing wild animals are serious offenses. Leave gates as you find them, or as marked.

6. **Plan ahead.** Know your equipment, your ability, and the area in which you are riding, and plan your trip accordingly. Be self-sufficient at all times, keep your bike in good repair, and carry necessary supplies for changes in weather or other conditions. You can help keep trails open by setting an example of responsible, courteous, and controlled mountain bike riding.

7. **Always wear a helmet when you ride.** For your own safety and protection, a helmet should be worn whenever you are riding your bike. You never know when a tree root or small rock will throw you the wrong way and send you tumbling.

Thousands of miles of dirt trails have been closed to mountain bicycling because of the irresponsible riding habits of just a few riders. Don't follow the example of these offending riders. Don't take away trail privileges from thousands of others who work hard each year to keep the backcountry avenues open to us all.

## THE NECESSITIES OF CYCLING

When discussing the most important items to have on a bike ride, cyclists generally agree on the following four items.

**Helmet.** The reasons to wear a helmet should be obvious. Helmets are discussed in more detail in the *Be Safe—Wear Your Armor* section.

**Water.** Without it, cyclists may face dehydration, which may result in dizziness and fatigue. On a warm day, cyclists should drink at least one full bottle during every hour of riding. Remember, it's always good to drink before you feel thirsty—otherwise, it may be too late.

**Cycling Shorts.** These are necessary if you plan to ride your bike more than 20 to 30 minutes. Padded cycling shorts may be the only thing preventing your derriere from serious saddle soreness by ride's end. There are two types of cycling shorts you can buy. Touring shorts are good for people who don't want to look like they're wearing anatomically correct cellophane. These look like regular athletic shorts with pockets, but have built-in padding in the crotch area for protection from chafing and saddle sores. The more popular, traditional cycling shorts are made of skin-tight material, also with a padded crotch. Whichever style you find most comfortable, cycling shorts are a necessity for long rides.

**Food.** This essential item will keep you rolling. Cycling burns up a lot of calories and is among the few sports in which no one is safe from the "Bonk." Bonking feels like it sounds. Without food in your system, your blood sugar level collapses, and there is no longer any energy in your body. This instantly results in total fatigue and light-headedness. So when you're filling your water bottle, remember to bring along some food. Fruit, energy bars, or some other forms of high-energy food are highly recommended. Candy bars are not, however, because they will deliver a sudden burst of high energy, then let you down soon after, causing you to feel worse than before. Energy bars are available at most bike stores and are similar to candy bars, but provide complex carbohydrate energy and high nutrition rather than fast-burning simple sugars.

## BE PREPARED OR DIE

Essential equipment that will keep you from dying alone in the woods:

- **Spare Tube**
- **Tire Irons**—See the Appendix for instructions on fixing flat tires.
- **Patch Kit**
- **Pump**
- **Money**—Spare change for emergency calls.

8

- **Spoke Wrench**
- **Spare Spokes**—To fit your wheel. Tape these to the chain stay.
- **Chain Tool**
- **Allen Keys**—Bring appropriate sizes to fit your bike.
- **Compass**
- **First-Aid Kit**
- **Rain Gear**—For quick changes in weather.
- **Matches**
- **Guidebook**—In case all else fails and you must start a fire to survive, this guidebook will serve as excellent fire starter!

To carry these items, you may need a bike bag. A bag mounted in front of the handlebars provides quick access to your belongings, whereas a saddle bag fitted underneath the saddle keeps things out of your way. If you're carrying lots of equipment, you may want to consider a set of panniers. These are much larger and mount on either side of each wheel on a rack. Many cyclists, though, prefer not to use a bag at all. They just slip all they need into their jersey pockets, and off they go.

## BE SAFE—WEAR YOUR ARMOR

While on the subject of jerseys, it's crucial to discuss the clothing you must wear to be safe, practical, and—if you prefer—stylish. The following is a list of items that will save you from disaster, outfit you comfortably, and most important, keep you looking cool.

**Helmet.** A helmet is an absolute necessity because it protects your head from complete annihilation. It is the only thing that will not disintegrate into a million pieces after a wicked crash on a descent you shouldn't have been on in the first place. A helmet with a solid exterior shell will also protect your head from sharp or protruding objects. Of course, with a hard-shelled helmet, you can paste several stickers of your favorite bicycle manufacturers all over the outer shell, giving companies even more free advertising for your dollar.

**Shorts.** Let's just say Lycra™ cycling shorts are considered a major safety item if you plan to ride for more than 20 or 30 minutes at a time. As mentioned in *The Necessities of Cycling* section, cycling shorts are well regarded as the leading cure-all for chafing and saddle sores. The most preventive cycling shorts have padded "chamois" (most chamois is synthetic nowadays) in the crotch area. Of course, if you choose to wear these traditional cycling shorts, it's imperative that they look as if someone spray painted them onto your body.

**Gloves.** You may find well-padded cycling gloves invaluable when traveling over rocky trails and gravelly roads for hours on end. Long-fingered gloves may also be useful, as branches, trees, assorted hard objects, and, occasionally, small animals will reach out and whack your knuckles.

**Glasses.** Not only do sunglasses give you an imposing presence and make you look cool (both are extremely important), they also protect your eyes from harmful ultraviolet rays, invisible branches, creepy bugs, dirt, and may prevent you from being caught sneaking glances at riders of the opposite sex also wearing skintight, revealing Lycra™.

**Shoes.** Mountain bike shoes should have stiff soles to help make pedaling easier and provide better traction when walking your bike up a trail becomes necessary. Virtually any kind of good outdoor hiking footwear will work, but specific mountain bike shoes (especially those with inset cleats) are best. It is vital that these shoes look as ugly as humanly possible. Those closest in style to bowling shoes are, of course, the most popular.

**Jersey or Shirt.** Bicycling jerseys are popular because of their snug fit and back pockets. When purchasing a jersey, look for ones that are loaded with bright, blinding, neon logos and manufacturers' names. These loudly decorated billboards are also good for drawing unnecessary attention to yourself just before taking a mean spill while trying to hop a curb. A cotton T-shirt is a good alternative in warm weather, but when the weather turns cold, cotton becomes a chilling substitute for the jersey. Cotton retains moisture and sweat against your body, which may cause you to get the chills and ills on those cold-weather rides.

## OH, THOSE COLD COLORADO DAYS

If the weather chooses not to cooperate on the day you've set aside for a bike ride, it's helpful to be prepared.

**Tights or leg warmers.** These are best in temperatures below 55 degrees. Knees are sensitive and can develop all kinds of problems if they get cold. Common problems include tendinitis, bursitis, and arthritis.

**Plenty of layers on your upper body.** When the air has a nip in it, layers of clothing will keep the chill away from your chest and help prevent the development of bronchitis. If the air is cool, a Polypropylene™ or Capilene™ long-sleeved shirt is best to wear against the skin beneath other layers of clothing. Polypropylene or Capilene, like wool, wicks away moisture from your skin to keep your body dry. Try to avoid wearing cotton or baggy clothing when the temperature falls. Cotton, as mentioned before, holds moisture like a sponge, and baggy clothing catches cold air and swirls it around your body. Good cold-weather clothing should fit snugly against your body, but not be restrictive.

**Wool socks.** Don't pack too many layers under those shoes, though. You may stand the chance of restricting circulation, and your feet will get real cold, real fast.

**Thinsulate or Gortex™ gloves.** We may all agree that there is nothing worse than frozen feet—unless your hands are frozen. A good pair of Thinsulate™ or Gortex™ gloves should keep your hands toasty and warm.

**Hat or helmet on cold days?** Sometimes, when the weather gets really cold and you still want to hit the trails, it's tough to stay warm. We all know that 130 percent of the body's heat escapes through the head (overactive brains, I imagine), so it's important to keep the cranium warm. Ventilated helmets are designed to keep heads cool in the summer heat, but they do little to help keep heads warm during rides in sub-zero temperatures. Cyclists should consider wearing a hat on extremely cold days.

Capilene Skullcaps are great head and ear warmers that snugly fit over your head beneath the helmet. Head protection is not lost. Another option is a helmet cover that covers those ventilating gaps and helps keep the body heat in. These do not, however, keep your ears warm. Some cyclists will opt for a simple knit cycling cap sans the helmet, but these have never been shown to be very good cranium protectors.

All of this clothing can be found at your local bike store, where the staff should be happy to help fit you into the seasons of the year.

## TO HAVE OR NOT TO HAVE… (*Other Very Useful Items*)

Though mountain biking is relatively new to the cycling scene, there is no shortage of items for you and your bike to make riding better, safer, and easier. We have rummaged through the unending lists and separated the gadgets from the good stuff, coming up with what we believe are items certain to make mountain bike riding easier and more enjoyable.

**Tires.** Buying yourself a good pair of knobby tires is the quickest way to enhance the off-road handling capabilities of your bike. There are many types of mountain bike tires on the market. Some are made exclusively for very rugged off-road terrain. These big-knobbed, soft rubber tires virtually stick to the ground with unforgiving traction, but tend to deteriorate quickly on pavement. There are other tires made exclusively for the road. These are called "slicks" and have no tread at all. For the average cyclist, though, a good tire somewhere in the middle of these two extremes should do the trick.

**Toe Clips or Clipless Pedals.** With these, you will ride with more power. Toe clips attach to your pedals and strap your feet firmly in place, allowing you to exert pressure on the pedals on both the downstroke and the upstroke. They will increase your pedaling efficiency by 30 percent to 50 percent. Clipless pedals, which liberate your feet from the traditional straps and clips, have made toe clips virtually obsolete. Like ski bindings, they attach your shoe directly to the pedal. They are, however, much more expensive than toe clips.

**Bar Ends.** These great clamp-on additions to your original straight bar will provide more leverage, an excellent grip for climbing, and a more natural position for your hands. Be aware, however, of the bar end's propensity for hooking trees on fast descents, sending you, the cyclist, airborne.

**Fanny Pack.** These bags are ideal for carrying keys, extra food, guidebooks, tools, spare tubes, and a cellular phone, in case you need to call for help.

**Suspension Forks.** For the more serious off-roaders who want nothing to impede their speed on the trails, investing in a pair of suspension forks is a good idea. Like tires, there are plenty of brands to choose from, and they all do the same thing—absorb the brutal beatings of a rough trail. The cost of these forks, however, is sometimes more brutal than the trail itself.

**Bike Computers.** These are fun gadgets to own and are much less expensive than in years past. They have such features as trip distance, speedometer, odometer, time of day, altitude, alarm, average speed, maximum speed, heart rate, global satellite

11

positioning, etc. Bike computers will come in handy when following these maps or to know just how far you've ridden in the wrong direction.

**Water Pack.** This is quickly becoming an essential item for cyclists pedaling for more than a few hours, especially in hot, dry conditions. The most popular brand is, of course, the Camelback™, and these water packs can carry in their bladder bags as much as 100 ounces of water. These packs strap onto your back with a handy hose running over your shoulder so you can be drinking water while still holding onto the bars on a rocky descent with both hands. These packs are a great way to carry a lot of extra liquid on hot rides in the middle of nowhere.

## TYPES OF OFF-ROAD TERRAIN

Before roughing it off road, we may first have to ride the pavement to get to our destination. Please, don't be dismayed. Some of the country's best rides are on the road. Once we get past these smooth-surfaced pathways, though, adventures in dirt await us.

**Rails-to-Trails.** Abandoned rail lines are converted into usable public resources for exercising, commuting, or just enjoying nature. Old rails and ties are torn up and a trail, paved or unpaved, is laid along the existing corridor. This completes the cycle from ancient Indian trading routes to railroad corridors and back again to hiking and cycling trails.

**Unpaved Roads** are typically found in rural areas and are most often public roads. Be careful when exploring, though, not to ride on someone's unpaved private drive.

**Forest Roads.** These dirt and gravel roads are used primarily as access to forest land and are generally kept in good condition. They are almost always open to public use.

**Singletrack** can be the most fun on a mountain bike. These trails, with only one track to follow, are often narrow, challenging pathways through the woods. Remember to make sure these trails are open before zipping into the woods. (At the time of this printing, all trails and roads in this guidebook were open to mountain bikes.)

**Open Land.** Unless there is a marked trail through a field or open space, you should not plan to ride here. Once one person cuts his or her wheels through a field or meadow, many more are sure to follow, causing irreparable damage to the landscape.

## TECHNIQUES TO SHARPEN YOUR SKILLS

Many of us see ourselves as pure athletes—blessed with power, strength, and endless endurance. However, it may be those with finesse, balance, agility, and grace that get around most quickly on a mountain bike. Although power, strength, and endurance do have their places in mountain biking, these elements don't necessarily form the framework for a champion mountain biker.

The bike should become an extension of your body. Slight shifts in your hips or knees can have remarkable results. Experienced bike handlers seem to flash down technical descents, dashing over obstacles in a smooth and graceful effort as if pirouetting in Swan

Lake. Here are some tips and techniques to help you connect with your bike and float gracefully over the dirt.

## Braking

Using your brakes requires using your head, especially when descending. This doesn't mean using your head as a stopping block, but rather to think intelligently. Use your best judgment in terms of how much or how little to squeeze those brake levers.

The more weight a tire is carrying, the more braking power it has. When you're going downhill, your front wheel carries more weight than the rear. Braking with the front brake will help keep you in control without going into a skid. Be careful, though, not to overdo it with the front brakes and accidentally toss yourself over the handlebars. And don't neglect your rear brake! When descending, shift your weight back over the rear wheel, thus increasing your rear braking power as well. This will balance the power of both brakes and give you maximum control.

Good riders learn just how much of their weight to shift over each wheel and how to apply just enough braking power to each brake, so not to "endo" over the handlebars or skid down a trail.

## GOING UPHILL—*Climbing Those Treacherous Hills*

**Shift into a low gear** (push the shifter away from you). Before shifting, be sure to ease up on your pedaling so there is not too much pressure on the chain. Find the gear best for you that matches the terrain and steepness of each climb.

**Stay seated.** Standing out of the saddle is often helpful when climbing steep hills with a road bike, but you may find that on dirt, standing may cause your rear tire to lose its grip and spin out. Climbing requires traction. Stay seated as long as you can, and keep the rear tire digging into the ground. Ascending skyward may prove to be much easier in the saddle.

**Lean forward.** On very steep hills, the front end may feel unweighted and suddenly pop up. Slide forward on the saddle and lean over the handlebars. This will add more weight to the front wheel and should keep you grounded.

**Keep pedaling.** On rocky climbs, be sure to keep the pressure on, and don't let up on those pedals! The slower you go through rough trail sections, the harder you will work.

## GOING DOWNHILL—*The Real Reason We Get Up in the Morning*

**Shifting into the big chainring** before a bumpy descent will help keep the chain from bouncing off. And should you crash or disengage your leg from the pedal, the chain will cover the teeth of the big ring so they don't bite into your leg.

**Relax.** Stay loose on the bike, and don't lock your elbows or clench your grip. Your elbows need to bend with the bumps and absorb the shock, while your hands should have a firm but controlled grip on the bars to keep things steady. Steer with your body, allowing your shoulders to guide you through each turn and around each obstacle.

**Don't oversteer or lose control.** Mountain biking is much like downhill skiing, since you must shift your weight from side to side down narrow, bumpy descents. Your bike will have the tendency to track in the direction you look and follow the slight shifts and leans of your body. You should not think so much about steering, but rather in what direction you wish to go.

**Rise above the saddle.** When racing down bumpy, technical descents, you should not be sitting on the saddle, but standing on the pedals, allowing your legs and knees to absorb the rocky trail instead of your rear.

**Drop your saddle.** For steep, technical descents, you may want to drop your saddle three or four inches. This lowers your center of gravity, giving you much more room to bounce around.

**Keep your pedals parallel to the ground.** The front pedal should be slightly higher so that it doesn't catch on small rocks or logs.

**Stay focused.** Many descents require your utmost concentration and focus just to reach the bottom. You must notice every groove, every root, every rock, every hole, every bump. You, the bike, and the trail should all become one as you seek singletrack nirvana on your way down the mountain. But if your thoughts wander, however, then so may your bike, and you may instead become one with the trees!

## WATCH OUT!
### Back-road Obstacles

**Logs.** When you want to hop a log, throw your body back, yank up on the handlebars, and pedal forward in one swift motion. This clears the front end of the bike. Then quickly scoot forward and pedal the rear wheel up and over. Keep the forward momentum until you've cleared the log, and by all means, don't hit the brakes, or you may do some interesting acrobatic maneuvers!

**Rocks and Roots.** Worse than highway potholes! Stay relaxed, let your elbows and knees absorb the shock, and always continue applying power to your pedals. Staying seated will keep the rear wheel weighted to prevent slipping, and a light front end will help you to respond quickly to each new obstacle. The slower you go, the more time your tires will have to get caught between the grooves.

**Water.** Before crossing a stream or puddle, be sure to first check the depth and bottom surface. There may be an unseen hole or large rock hidden under the water that could wash you up if you're not careful. After you're sure all is safe, hit the water at a good speed, pedal steadily, and allow the bike to steer you through. Once you're across, tap the breaks to squeegee the water off the rims.

**Leaves.** Be careful of wet leaves. These may look pretty, but a trail covered with leaves may cause your wheels to slip out from under you. Leaves are not nearly as unpredictable and dangerous as ice, but they do warrant your attention on a rainy day.

**Mud.** If you must ride through mud, hit it head on and keep pedaling. You want to part the ooze with your front wheel and get across before it swallows you up. Above all, don't leave the trail to go around the mud. This just widens the path even more and leads to increased trail erosion.

## Urban Obstacles

**Curbs** are fun to jump, but like with logs, be careful.

**Curbside Drains** are typically not a problem for bikes. Just be careful not to get a wheel caught in the grate.

**Dogs** make great pets, but seem to have it in for bicyclists. If you think you can't out-run a dog that's chasing you, stop and walk your bike out of its territory. A loud yell to Get! or Go home! often works, as does a sharp squirt from your water bottle right between the eyes.

**Cars** are tremendously convenient when we're in them, but dodging irate motorists in big automobiles becomes a real hazard when riding a bike. As a cyclist, you must realize most drivers aren't expecting you to be there and often wish you weren't. Stay alert and ride carefully, clearly signaling all of your intentions.

**Potholes**, like grates and back-road canyons, should be avoided. Just because you're on an all-terrain bicycle doesn't mean you're indestructible. Potholes regularly damage rims, pop tires, and sometimes lift unsuspecting cyclists into a spectacular swan dive over the handlebars.

## LAST-MINUTE CHECKOVER

Before a ride, it's a good idea to give your bike a once-over to make sure everything is in working order. Begin by checking the air pressure in your tires before each ride to make sure they are properly inflated. Mountain bikes require about 45 to 55 pounds per square inch of air pressure. If your tires are underinflated, there is greater likelihood that the tubes may get pinched on a bump or rock, causing the tire to flat.

Looking over your bike to make sure everything is secure and in its place is the next step. Go through the following checklist before each ride.

- *Pinch the tires to feel for proper inflation.* They should give just a little on the sides, but feel very hard on the treads. If you have a pressure gauge, use that.
- *Check your brakes.* Squeeze the rear brake and roll your bike forward. The rear tire should skid. Next, squeeze the front brake and roll your bike forward. The rear wheel should lift into the air. If this doesn't happen, then your brakes are too loose. Make sure the brake levers don't touch the handlebars when squeezed with full force.
- *Check all quick releases on your bike.* Make sure they are all securely tightened.
- *Lube up.* If your chain squeaks, apply some lubricant.
- *Check your nuts and bolts.* Check the handlebars, saddle, cranks, and pedals to make sure that each is tight and securely fastened to your bike.
- *Check your wheels.* Spin each wheel to see that they spin through the frame and between brake pads freely.
- *Have you got everything?* Make sure you have your spare tube, tire irons patch kit, frame pump, tools, food, water, and guidebook.

## Liability Disclaimer

Neither the pubisher, the producer, nor the author of this guide assumes any liability for cyclists traveling along any of the suggested routes in this book. At the time of publication, all routes shown on the following maps were open to bicycles. They were chosen for their safety, aesthetics, and pleasure, and are deemed acceptable and accommodating to bicyclists. Safety upon these routes, however, cannot be guaranteed. Cyclists must assume their own responsibility when riding these routes and understand that with an activity such as mountain bike riding, there may be unforeseen risks and dangers.

# HOW TO USE THESE MAPS

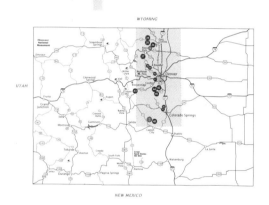 **Area Locator Map**

This thumbnail relief map at the beginning of each ride shows you where the ride is within the state. The ride area is indicated with a star.

**Regional Location Map**

This map helps you find your way to the start of each ride from the nearest sizeable town or city. Coupled with the detailed directions at the beginning of the cue, this map should visually lead you to where you need to be for each ride.

 **Profile Map**

This helpful profile gives you a cross-sectional look at the ride's ups and downs. Elevation is labeled on the left, mileage is indicated on the top. Road and trail names are shown along the route with towns and points of interest labeled in bold.

18

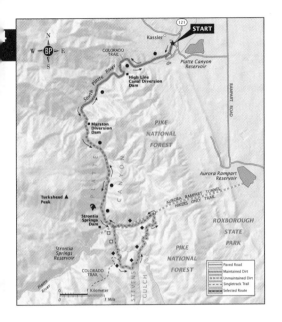

## 4 Route Map

This is your primary guide to each ride. It shows all of the accessible roads and trails, points of interest, water, towns, landmarks, and geographical features. It also distinguishes trails from roads, and paved roads from unpaved roads. The selected route is highlighted, and directional arrows point the way. Shaded topographic relief in the background gives you an accurate representation of the terrain and landscape in the ride area.

## Ride Information (Included in each ride section)

### 🌀 Trail Contacts:

This is the direct number for the local land managers in charge of all the trails within the selected ride. Use this hotline to call ahead for trail access information, or after your visit if you see problems with trail erosion, damage, or misuse.

### 🕐 Schedule:

This tells you at what times trails open and close, if on private or park land.

### 💲 Fees/Permits:

What money, if any, you may need to carry with you for park entrance fees or tolls.

### 🌑 Maps:

This is a list of other maps to supplement the maps in this book. They are listed in order from most detailed to most general.

Any other important or useful information will also be listed here such as local attractions, bike shops, nearby accommodations, etc.

# THE MAPS  Map Legend

We don't want anyone, by any means, to feel restricted to just the roads and trails that are mapped here. We hope you will have an adventurous spirit and use this guide as a platform to dive into Colorado's backcountry and discover new routes for yourself. One of the simplest ways to begin this is to just turn the map upside down and ride the course in reverse. The change in perspective is fantastic and the ride should feel quite different. With this in mind, it will be like getting two distinctly different rides on each map.

For your own purposes, you may wish to copy the directions for the course onto a small sheet to help you while riding, or photocopy the map and cue sheet to take with you. These pages can be folded into a bike bag, stuffed into a jersey pocket, or better still, used with the **BarMap** or **BarMapOTG** (see *www.cycoactive.com* for more info). Just remember to slow or even stop when you want to read the map.

| | |
|---|---|
| Interstate Highway | |
| U.S. Highway | |
| State Road | |
| County Road | |
| Township Road | |
| Forest Road | |
| Paved Road | |
| Paved Bike Lane | |
| Maintained Dirt Road | |
| Unmaintained Jeep Trail | |
| Singletrack Trail | |
| Highlighted Route | |
| Ntl Forest/County Boundaries | |
| State Boundaries | |
| Railroad Tracks | |
| Power Lines | |
| Special Trail | |
| Rivers or Streams | |
| Water and Lakes | |
| Marsh | |

✝ Airfield                 ♣ Golf Course
✈ Airport                  🚶 Hiking Trail
🚲 Bike Trail              ⛏ Mine
🚫 No Bikes               ✕ Overlook
🛶 Boat Launch           🌲 Picnic
)( Bridge                  🅿 Parking
🚌 Bus Stop               ✕ Quarry
▲ Campground            (((A))) Radio Tower
♨ Campsite                Rock Climbing
Canoe Access             School
Cattle Guard             Shelter
✝ Cemetery               Spring
Church                    Swimming
Covered Bridge           Train Station
Direction Arrows         Wildlife Refuge
Downhill Skiing          Vineyard
Fire Tower               ♦♦ Most Difficult
Forest HQ                ♦ Difficult
4WD Trail                □ Moderate
Gate                     ● Easy

UT          CO

AZ          NM

20

# MOUNTAIN BIKE COLORADO

## The Rides

1. Three Forks Trail
2. Chutes and Ladders
3. Troy Built Loop
4. Crag Crest Trail
5. Aspen to Buck Trail
6. Deep Creek Trail
7. Wasatch Trail
8. Hermosa Creek Trail
9. Log Chutes Trail
10. Sand Canyon Trail
11. Nipple Peak Loop
12. Diamond Park to Scott's Run
13. Bockman Campground Loop
14. Hot Springs to Mad Creek to Red Dirt Trails
15. Howelson Hill
16. Arapaho Ridge Trail
17. Base Camp Trail to Mountain View Trail
18. Muddy Slide/ Morrison Divide Trail
19. Tipperary Creek Loop
20. Grand Traverse and Cougar Ridge Trail
21. Searle and Kokomo Pass Trail
22. Wise Mountain/ The Colorado Trail

23. Deer Creek Trail
24. Deadman's Gulch
25. Dyke Trail
26. Mount Princeton to Rasberry Gulch
27. Bear Creek to Methodist Mountain
28. Hartman Rocks
29. Monarch Crest Trail
30. Wheeler Monument
31. Trout Creek Trail
32. Zapata Falls
33. Cat Creek Trail
34. Hewlett's Gulch
35. Young Gulch
36. Mill Creek Trail
37. House Rock to Pierson Park
38. Sourdough Trail
39. Walker Ranch Loop
40. White Ranch
41. The Hogback: Dakota Ridge and Red Rocks Trails
42. Waterton Canyon
43. Kenosha to Gerogia Passes
44. Baldey Trail to Gashouse Gulch Trail
45. Jackson Creek Trail

46. Rampart Reservoir Shoreline Loop
47. Waldo Canyon
48. Shelf Road
49. Picket Wire Canyonlands
50. Telluride to Moab Hut Trip
   • Day One
   • Day Two
   • Day Three
   • Day Four
   • Day Five
   • Day Six
   • Day Seven

## Honorable Mentions

A. Dinosaur National Monument
B. Tall Pines Trail
C. Portland Creek Trail
D. Ute Mountain Ute Tribal Park
E. Baker's Tank Loop
F. Old Midland Railroad Grade
G. Resevoir Hill
H. Crosier Mountain Loop
I. Deer Haven Ranch
J. Pawnee National Grasslands

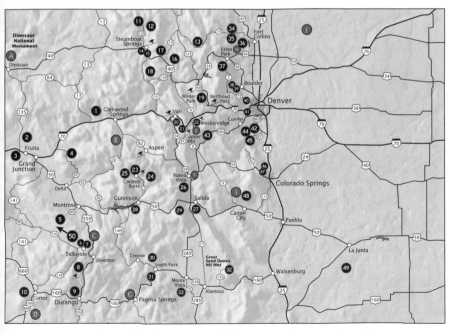

# COURSES AT A GLANCE

### 1. Three Forks Trail

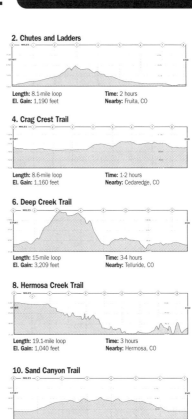

**Length:** 11.2 mile out-and-back    **Time:** 2-3 hours
**El. Gain:** 2,420 feet    **Nearby:** Rifle, CO

### 2. Chutes and Ladders

**Length:** 8.1-mile loop    **Time:** 2 hours
**El. Gain:** 1,190 feet    **Nearby:** Fruita, CO

### 3. Troy Built Loop

**Length:** 6.3-mile loop    **Time:** 2 hours
**El. Gain:** 1,395 feet    **Nearby:** Fruita, CO

### 4. Crag Crest Trail

**Length:** 8.6-mile loop    **Time:** 1-2 hours
**El. Gain:** 1,160 feet    **Nearby:** Cedaredge, CO

### 5. Aspen to Buck Trail

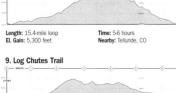

**Length:** 16.3-mile loop    **Time:** 3-4 hours
**El. Gain:** 1,801 feet    **Nearby:** Montrose, CO

### 6. Deep Creek Trail

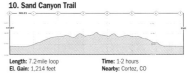

**Length:** 15-mile loop    **Time:** 3-4 hours
**El. Gain:** 3,209 feet    **Nearby:** Telluride, CO

### 7. Wasatch Trail

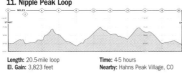

**Length:** 15.4-mile loop    **Time:** 5-6 hours
**El. Gain:** 5,300 feet    **Nearby:** Telluride, CO

### 8. Hermosa Creek Trail

**Length:** 19.1-mile loop    **Time:** 3 hours
**El. Gain:** 1,040 feet    **Nearby:** Hermosa, CO

### 9. Log Chutes Trail

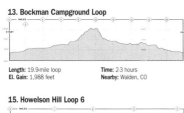

**Length:** 6.5-mile loop    **Time:** 1-2 hours
**El. Gain:** 1,532 feet    **Nearby:** Durango, CO

### 10. Sand Canyon Trail

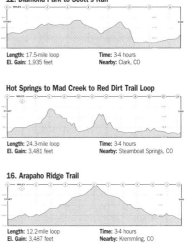

**Length:** 7.2-mile loop    **Time:** 1-2 hours
**El. Gain:** 1,214 feet    **Nearby:** Cortez, CO

### 11. Nipple Peak Loop

**Length:** 20.5-mile loop    **Time:** 4-5 hours
**El. Gain:** 3,823 feet    **Nearby:** Hahns Peak Village, CO

### 12. Diamond Park to Scott's Run

**Length:** 17.5-mile loop    **Time:** 3-4 hours
**El. Gain:** 1,935 feet    **Nearby:** Clark, CO

### 13. Bockman Campground Loop

**Length:** 19.9-mile loop    **Time:** 2-3 hours
**El. Gain:** 1,988 feet    **Nearby:** Walden, CO

### Hot Springs to Mad Creek to Red Dirt Trail Loop

**Length:** 24.3-mile loop    **Time:** 3-4 hours
**El. Gain:** 3,481 feet    **Nearby:** Steamboat Springs, CO

### 15. Howelson Hill Loop 6

**Length:** 4.1-mile loop    **Time:** 1-2 hours
**El. Gain:** 1,240 feet    **Nearby:** Steamboat Springs, CO

### 16. Arapaho Ridge Trail

**Length:** 12.2-mile loop    **Time:** 3-4 hours
**El. Gain:** 3,487 feet    **Nearby:** Kremmling, CO

# Ride Profiles

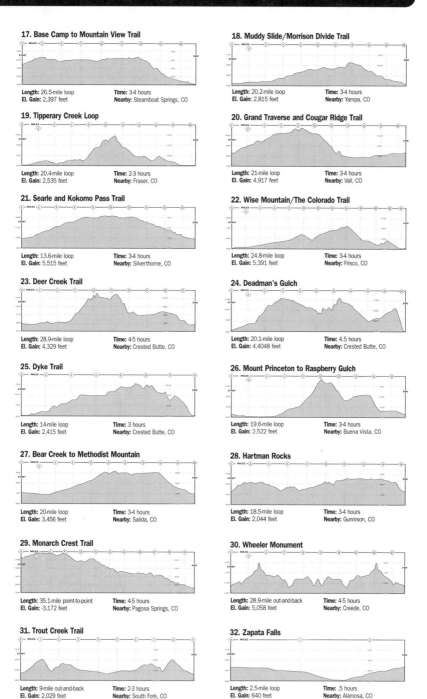

**17. Base Camp to Mountain View Trail**

**Length:** 26.5-mile loop
**El. Gain:** 2,397 feet
**Time:** 3-4 hours
**Nearby:** Steamboat Springs, CO

**18. Muddy Slide/Morrison Divide Trail**

**Length:** 20.2-mile loop
**El. Gain:** 2,815 feet
**Time:** 3-4 hours
**Nearby:** Yampa, CO

**19. Tipperary Creek Loop**

**Length:** 20.4-mile loop
**El. Gain:** 2,535 feet
**Time:** 2-3 hours
**Nearby:** Fraser, CO

**20. Grand Traverse and Cougar Ridge Trail**

**Length:** 21-mile loop
**El. Gain:** 4,917 feet
**Time:** 3-4 hours
**Nearby:** Vail, CO

**21. Searle and Kokomo Pass Trail**

**Length:** 13.6-mile loop
**El. Gain:** 5,515 feet
**Time:** 3-4 hours
**Nearby:** Silverthorne, CO

**22. Wise Mountain/The Colorado Trail**

**Length:** 24.8-mile loop
**El. Gain:** 5,391 feet
**Time:** 3-4 hours
**Nearby:** Frisco, CO

**23. Deer Creek Trail**

**Length:** 28.9-mile loop
**El. Gain:** 4,329 feet
**Time:** 4-5 hours
**Nearby:** Crested Butte, CO

**24. Deadman's Gulch**

**Length:** 20.1-mile loop
**El. Gain:** 4,4048 feet
**Time:** 4.5 hours
**Nearby:** Crested Butte, CO

**25. Dyke Trail**

**Length:** 14-mile loop
**El. Gain:** 2,415 feet
**Time:** 3 hours
**Nearby:** Crested Butte, CO

**26. Mount Princeton to Raspberry Gulch**

**Length:** 19.6-mile loop
**El. Gain:** 2,522 feet
**Time:** 3-4 hours
**Nearby:** Buena Vista, CO

**27. Bear Creek to Methodist Mountain**

**Length:** 20-mile loop
**El. Gain:** 3,456 feet
**Time:** 3-4 hours
**Nearby:** Salida, CO

**28. Hartman Rocks**

**Length:** 18.5-mile loop
**El. Gain:** 2,044 feet
**Time:** 3-4 hours
**Nearby:** Gunnison, CO

**29. Monarch Crest Trail**

**Length:** 35.1-mile point-to-point
**El. Gain:** -3,172 feet
**Time:** 4-5 hours
**Nearby:** Pagosa Springs, CO

**30. Wheeler Monument**

**Length:** 28.9-mile out-and-back
**El. Gain:** 5,058 feet
**Time:** 4-5 hours
**Nearby:** Creede, CO

**31. Trout Creek Trail**

**Length:** 9-mile out-and-back
**El. Gain:** 2,029 feet
**Time:** 2-3 hours
**Nearby:** South Fork, CO

**32. Zapata Falls**

**Length:** 2.5-mile loop
**El. Gain:** 640 feet
**Time:** .5 hours
**Nearby:** Alamosa, CO

# COURSES AT A GLANCE

### 33. Cat Creek Trail

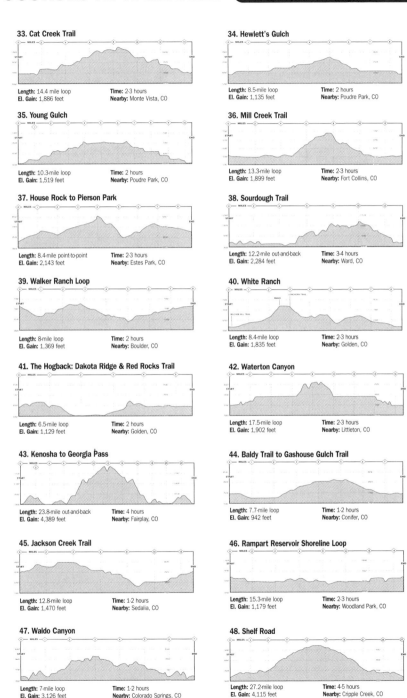

**Length:** 14.4 mile loop  **Time:** 2-3 hours
**El. Gain:** 1,886 feet  **Nearby:** Monte Vista, CO

### 34. Hewlett's Gulch

**Length:** 8.5-mile loop  **Time:** 2 hours
**El. Gain:** 1,135 feet  **Nearby:** Poudre Park, CO

### 35. Young Gulch

**Length:** 10.3-mile loop  **Time:** 2 hours
**El. Gain:** 1,519 feet  **Nearby:** Poudre Park, CO

### 36. Mill Creek Trail

**Length:** 13.3-mile loop  **Time:** 2-3 hours
**El. Gain:** 1,899 feet  **Nearby:** Fort Collins, CO

### 37. House Rock to Pierson Park

**Length:** 8.4-mile point-to-point  **Time:** 2-3 hours
**El. Gain:** 2,143 feet  **Nearby:** Estes Park, CO

### 38. Sourdough Trail

**Length:** 12.2-mile out-and-back  **Time:** 3-4 hours
**El. Gain:** 2,284 feet  **Nearby:** Ward, CO

### 39. Walker Ranch Loop

**Length:** 8-mile loop  **Time:** 2 hours
**El. Gain:** 1,369 feet  **Nearby:** Boulder, CO

### 40. White Ranch

**Length:** 8.4-mile loop  **Time:** 2-3 hours
**El. Gain:** 1,835 feet  **Nearby:** Golden, CO

### 41. The Hogback: Dakota Ridge & Red Rocks Trail

**Length:** 6.5-mile loop  **Time:** 2 hours
**El. Gain:** 1,129 feet  **Nearby:** Golden, CO

### 42. Waterton Canyon

**Length:** 17.5-mile loop  **Time:** 2-3 hours
**El. Gain:** 1,902 feet  **Nearby:** Littleton, CO

### 43. Kenosha to Georgia Pass

**Length:** 23.8-mile out-and-back  **Time:** 4 hours
**El. Gain:** 4,389 feet  **Nearby:** Fairplay, CO

### 44. Baldy Trail to Gashouse Gulch Trail

**Length:** 7.7-mile loop  **Time:** 1-2 hours
**El. Gain:** 942 feet  **Nearby:** Conifer, CO

### 45. Jackson Creek Trail

**Length:** 12.8-mile loop  **Time:** 1-2 hours
**El. Gain:** 1,470 feet  **Nearby:** Sedalia, CO

### 46. Rampart Reservoir Shoreline Loop

**Length:** 15.3-mile loop  **Time:** 2-3 hours
**El. Gain:** 1,179 feet  **Nearby:** Woodland Park, CO

### 47. Waldo Canyon

**Length:** 7-mile loop  **Time:** 1-2 hours
**El. Gain:** 3,126 feet  **Nearby:** Colorado Springs, CO

### 48. Shelf Road

**Length:** 27.2-mile loop  **Time:** 4-5 hours
**El. Gain:** 4,115 feet  **Nearby:** Cripple Creek, CO

## Ride Profiles

### 49. Picket Wire Canyonlands

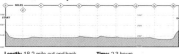

**Length:** 18.2 mile out-and-back
**El. Gain:** 1,098 feet

**Time:** 2-3 hours
**Nearby:** La Junta, CO

# The Great Escape
### Telluride to Moab Hut-to-Hut Adventure

### Day 1: Telluride to Last Dollar Hut

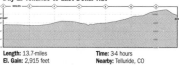

**Length:** 13.7-miles
**El. Gain:** 2,915 feet

**Time:** 3-4 hours
**Nearby:** Telluride, CO

### Day 2: Last Dollar Hut to Spring Creek Hut

**Length:** 27-miles
**El. Gain:** -878 feet

**Time:** 3-4 hours
**Nearby:** Montrose, CO

### Day 3: Spring Creek Hut to Columbine Hut

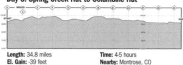

**Length:** 34.8 miles
**El. Gain:** -39 feet

**Time:** 4-5 hours
**Nearby:** Montrose, CO

### Day 4: Columbine Hut to Big Creek Cabin

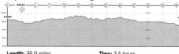

**Length:** 36.9 miles
**El. Gain:** 1,600 feet

**Time:** 3-4 hours
**Nearby:** Gateway, CO

### Day 5: Big Creek Cabin to Gateway Hut

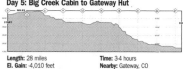

**Length:** 28 miles
**El. Gain:** -4,010 feet

**Time:** 3-4 hours
**Nearby:** Gateway, CO

### Day 6: Gateway Hut to La Sal Hut

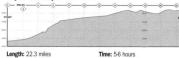

**Length:** 22.3 miles
**El. Gain:** 5,027 feet

**Time:** 5-6 hours
**Nearby:** Moab, CO

### Day 7: La Sal Hut to Moab

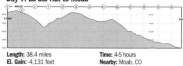

**Length:** 38.4 miles
**El. Gain:** -4,131 feet

**Time:** 4-5 hours
**Nearby:** Moab, CO

# Getting Around Colorado

## 🚌 AREA CODES

Colorado currently has four area codes: The Denver/Boulder metro area uses **303** and **720**. The **719** area code services the greater southeastern part of the state, including Colorado Springs, Pueblo, Buena Vista, and Alamosa. The **970** area code services the northern Front Range and Eastern Plains, as well as the western slope, extending north from Steamboat Springs to Durango and Cortez.

## 🚗 ROADS

For current information on statewide weather and road conditions and closures, contact the **Colorado Department of Transportation** (CDOT) at the toll free hotline 1-877-315-ROAD. Denver metro area and out-of-state callers can still access the hotline by calling (303) 639-1111. The same information can also be found by visiting CDOT's website at *www.dot.state.co.us*.

## ✈ BY AIR

**Denver International Airport** (DIA) is 23 miles northeast of downtown Denver. Along with servicing the majority of flights into Colorado, Denver International also links flights throughout the global village. For more information, contact its website at www.flydenver.com.

Roughly 60 miles south of Denver lies the Colorado Springs Airport. The **Colorado Springs Airport** (COS) services the southern half of the Front Range and Eastern Plains. For more information, contact its website at *www.flycos.com*.

Servicing the northwestern towns of Steamboat Springs and Hayden, the **Yampa Valley Airport** (HDN) can be reached by dialing (970) 276-3669.

The **Walker Field Airport** (GJT) in Grand Junction services Colorado and Eastern Utah. Walker Field Airport features commercial carrier service with over 20 daily departures to Denver, Phoenix, and Salt Lake City and over 500 one-stop connections to cities in the United States, Canada, Europe, and Central America. For more information, check out its website at *www.walkerfield.com*.

To the southwest lies the **Durango-La Plata County Airport** (DRO). The Durango-La Plata County Airport is located about 20 miles southeast of Durango and is served by three airlines: United Express, serving Denver with nine daily flights; America West Express, offering four daily non-stop flights to Phoenix; and Mesa Airlines, which offers five flights daily to Albuquerque. For more information, contact its website at *http://co.laplata.co.us/airport.html*.

To book reservations online, check out your favorite airline's website or search one of the following travel sites for the best price: www.cheaptickets.com, *www.expedia.com*, *www.previewtravel.com*, *www.priceline.com*, *http://travel.yahoo.com*, *www.travelocity.com*, or *www.Trip.com*—just to name a few.

Most major airlines will carry your bicycle for a fee that varies between $50 and $90.

## 🚆 By Rail

Amtrak has two routes that travel through Colorado daily. The **California Zephyr** travels between Chicago and Oakland via Fort Morgan, Denver, Winter Park, Granby, Glenwood Springs, and Grand Junction. The stations in Grand Junction, Glenwood Springs, and Denver have checked baggage service, and it's $12 to carry a bike. The **Southwest Chief** travels between Chicago and Los Angeles via Lamar, La Junta, and Trinidad.

For more details, call 1-800-872-7245 or visit *www.amtrak.com* for more information.

## 🚌 By Bus

**Greyhound** serves most cities in Colorado and the major ski resorts along Interstate 70 and U.S. Route 40. Greyhound will carry boxed bikes for $15, and boxes are available at most major terminals for $10. Call Greyhound at 1-800-231-2222 or visit *www.greyhound.com* for more information.

**Roaring Fork Transit** (RFTA) runs frequent service from Glenwood Springs to Aspen, making it a convenient connection with Amtrak and Greyhound. Each (RFTA) bus has a bike rack that carries four bikes. $2 per bike. For more information, check out the website at *www.rfta.com.*

**Denver/Boulder Regional Transportation District** (RTD) serves Boulder and Metro Denver from Downtown and the airport. There is a free permit for light rail trains, and no permit required for buses. All buses carry bicycles. Bikes are allowed on off-peak light rail trains, but a permit is required. There are bike lockers located at over 30 different locations. For more information contact Ken Epperson at (303) 299-2223. All RTD buses carry bicycles.

For more information, check out the website *www.bikemap.com/transit/co.htm* for links to local bus services that carry bikes.

## 🚐 Shuttles

From **Denver International Airport**, taxicabs, charters, and luxury limousines can deliver you to most any Colorado location by prior arrangements. Check the Denver International Airport website at *www.flydenver.com/z106.html* for a detailed listing of all available shuttle options.

## ❓ Visitor Information

For general information on Colorado, visit the official website of Colorado travel: *www.colorado.com.* The site contains a wealth of information vacation information.

Visitors to Colorado can find vacation information, free state maps and brochures, and clean restrooms at **Colorado's Welcome Centers**. Colorado's Welcome Centers are located near most of the major highways entering Colorado. For more information, contact their website at *www.state.co.us/data2/fs/welcome.htm.*

# Northwest Colorado

*WYOMING*

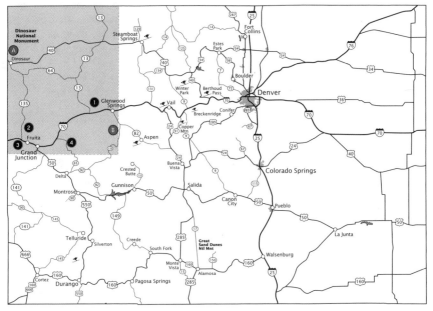

*NEW MEXICO*

olorado's northwest corner is distinguished by rolling, sage-filled ranchland, high desert plateaus and buttes, river-carved gorges, sandy deserts and green, mountainous forests. Since the northwest is Colorado's remotest region, it's no surprise that the area west of the town of Craig to the town of Dinosaur is home to some of the few remaining wild horse herds in the country. Here, the open, sage-filled meadows and rolling hills provide ample room to roam for horses and riders alike. Lying 3 miles east of the Colorado/Utah border, Dinosaur, Colorado is gateway to Dinosaur National Monument. The monument's Dinosaur Quarry building, located seven miles north of Jensen, Utah, allows you to observe real dinosaur bones extracted from a cliff face. The monument's 210,000 acres deliver spectacular canyon country views. The high-clearance, four-wheel drive road (Echo Road) which leads to Echo Park, confluence of the Green and Yampa Rivers, is a must ride, offering stellar canyon scenery.

Lying to the southeast of Dinosaur National Monument, White River National Forest offers this region its only high alpine relief. South of Glenwood Springs, home to the world's largest hot springs pool, the Tall Pines Trail travels from the town of Carbondale to the town of Redstone. These towns provide a down-to-earth atmosphere separate from the glitz and glitter of their neighboring town of Aspen. In the 1910s, Carbondale was a dominant producer of potatoes, whose legacy continues today in its annual Potato Festival, held each October. In the 1960s, Redstone's beehive-like brick ovens, once used to turn coal into coke, were used as living quarters for resident hippies.

As one travels west from Glenwood Springs along Interstate 70, one passes the little known town of Rifle. Just north of Rifle, on Colorado 325, lies the Rifle Gap State Recreation Area. Aside from the rugged Three Forks Trail, this area includes some of America's finest technical climbing routes. West of Rifle is the small town of Pallisade. Here local farmers sell some of the world's sweetest peaches along roadside stands. Continuing west, mountains give way to mesas, buttes and deserts.

The Grand Mesa, near Grand Junction, is one of the world's largest flat-topped mountains. In sharp contrast to the surrounding deserts below, the Grand Mesa boasts over 200 lakes. On the north side of Grand Junction, the town of Fruita delivers incredible singletrack along the moonscaped terrain of the Book Cliffs. John Wesley Powell, a Colorado River explorer, named these cliffs after he noticed that they looked like edges of a bound book. This geological library stretches over 150 miles to Price, Utah. While visiting Fruita, don't miss an opportunity to see the Colorado National Monument. This 20,000 acre landscape includes incredibly sculptured spires and crags which create a perfect backdrop to a day's bicycling tour on Rim Rock Drive. Rattlesnake Canyon, home to the world's second (to Moab) largest group of natural stone arches, is also a must see.

# Colorado National Monument

While visiting Fruita, don't miss an opportunity to see the Colorado National Monument. This 20,000 acre landscape includes incredibly sculptured spires and crags which create a perfect backdrop to a day's bicycling tour on Rim Rock Drive. Rattlesnake Canyon, home to the world's second (to Moab) largest group of natural stone arches, is also a must see.

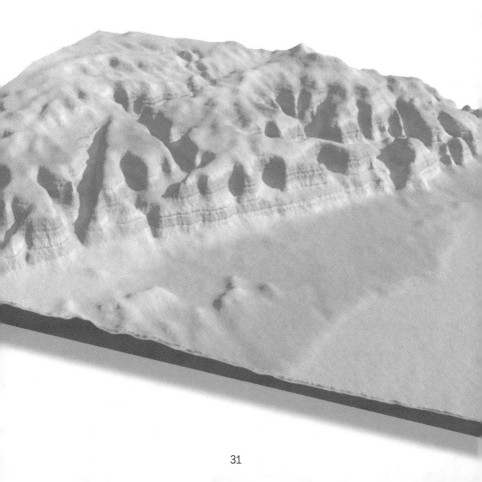

# Three Forks Trail

## Ride Summary

Since this is a very remote and seldom used trail, wildlife and signs of wildlife are abundant. Mule deer, elk, black bear, and beavers are all present. The trail parallels the mellow Three Forks Creek—though that's not to say these waters haven't seen their fare share of activity. There are over 30 beaver dams constructed along the creek. Enjoy excellent fishing, with brook trout averaging nine to 11 inches. Rainbow and brown trout can also be found. On your ride, you'll see aspen, sub-alpine fir, spruce, oak brush, serviceberry, and willows along the banks of the creek. The trail starts at 7,500 feet and rises to 9,257 feet.

## Ride Specs

**Start:** From the Three Forks Trail trailhead in Rifle Mountain Park

**Length:** 11.2-mile out-and-back – with options to extend into a loop

**Approximate Riding Time:** Advanced Riders, 1½–2 hours; Intermediate Riders, 2½–3 hours

**Technical Difficulty Rating:** Technically easy to moderate. Although most of this trail rolls over smooth singletrack, much of the singletrack, particularly as you near the top, is overgrown, making for a limited field of vision.

**Physical Difficulty Rating:** Physically moderate due to its elevation gain and steeper sections near the top.

**Terrain:** Singletrack. The trail rolls over hilly terrain, through dense conifer and aspen forests, and past many beaver ponds. The trail is remote and sees little traffic, owing primarily to its severely overgrown segments. With a variety of creeks in the area, there are a few muddy sections.

**Elevation Gain:** 2,420 feet

**Nearest Town:** Rifle, CO

**Other Trail Users:** Campers, hikers, anglers, hunters, and picnickers

**Canine Compatibility:** Dog friendly

## Getting There

**From Glenwood Springs:** Drive west on I-70 for 25 miles to Exit 90. Bear right onto CO 13, heading north. Drive through Rifle on CO 13 and continue out of Rifle for 0.75 miles before intersecting CR 325. Bear right onto CR 325 and follow the signs for Rifle State Park. Pass Rifle Gap Park and Rifle Falls State Park on your way to Rifle Mountain Park. After passing a large trout hatchery, CR 325 ends, becoming dirt FS 832. Cross a cattle guard and continue on FS 832 through Rifle Mountain Park. After turning onto CR 325, you will have driven 15.3 miles before entering into the White River National Forest. Once in the forest, FS 832 intersects with FS 825. Continue straight on FS 825. After 16.8 miles, FS 825 forks. The right fork leads through a narrow canyon to Triangle Park. Bear left and drive for another 0.25 miles before parking your vehicle at the Three Forks Campground. **DeLorme: Colorado Atlas & Gazetteer.** Page 34, B4

The town of Rifle received its name logically enough. In the mid 19th Century, a party of explorers traveled roughly 190 miles from Denver to Colorado's Western Slope. Upon reaching the junction of a small creek and the Colorado River (then called the Grand River), the party found an old rifle leaning against the trunk of a tree. The rest, as they say, is history. Located at the intersection of Interstate 70 and

Colorado 13, Rifle has somehow staved off the endless hordes of Colorado summer vacationers. Interstate 70 motorists, in their 80-mph dash to get to either Grand Junction or Vail or beyond, often shoot right past the little town. What they don't know is that rivers run deep in Rifle, rivers whose undercurrents have attracted serious high country players for some time.

Surrounded by the White River National Forest, Rifle is home to some first-class hunting—Rifle is home to the world's largest mule deer herd—fishing, spelunking, camping, rock climbing, and mountain biking. A 15-minute drive north of Rifle delivers you to the Rifle Gap Reservoir where gold-medal fishing takes center stage. The Harvey Gap Reservoir, east of the Rifle Gap, is one of the West's premier windsurfing destinations. Four miles north of the Rifle Gap is Rifle Falls State Park, which features a spectacular 60-foot triple waterfall. The fall's

## **Miles**Directions

**0.0 START** at the Three Forks Trail 2150 trailhead.

**0.4** Bear right. Cross the Three Forks Creek, via a wooden footbridge, and Stump Gulch. Climb from the creek and continue riding through a dense pine forest, with the creek to your left.

**1.4** The singletrack forks. Bear left and cross Garden Gulch.

**1.7** The trail cuts sharply to the north (right), around a rocky section of trail. Bear right here, crossing GV Creek and Irish Gulch.

**2.3** The Three Forks Trail 2150 intersects with the Coulter Lake/Guest Ranch Trail. Continue riding straight.

*[**Option:** Those interested in riding a shorter loop, can bear left onto the Coulter Lake/Guest Ranch Trail, which drops you past Coulter Lake and onto FS 832. Bear left onto FS 832 and ride to its intersection with FS 825 for a shorter, looped version of this ride.]*

**2.4** Cross Trappers Gulch and continue riding in a westerly direction, bushwhacking over severely overgrown trail.

**3.3** After crossing a small creek, Three Forks Trail 2150 intersects with the Tangle Gulch Trail. Bear right here, following signs for Three

Forks Trail and Hoover Gulch. Ride in an easterly direction through tall stands of pine.

**4.0** After passing the beaver ponds on your right and crossing a small creek, the trail forks again. The left fork is a game trail. Take the right fork, heading in an easterly direction. Climb steadily through the drainage and onto the crest of the mountain, Little Hill.

**4.7** The trail tops out into a large meadow, surrounded on all sides by tall stands of aspen. Head in a northerly direction through this meadow. The Flat Tops Wilderness Area should come into view.

**5.6** Three Forks Trail intersects with FS 211 (Bar HL Road). Turn around here and return the way you came.

*[**Option:** For a longer loop, bear right onto FS 211 and head to Triangle Park. From Triangle Park, descend down the 4WD road of FS 825 to its intersection with the Three Forks. Note: the longer, looped version of this ride can be done in the opposite direction as well, starting your ride by climbing FS 825 to Triangle Park and FS 211 to the Three Forks Trail. This option will have you descending the singletrack of the Three Forks Trail to your vehicle.]*

**11.2** Arrive at your vehicle.

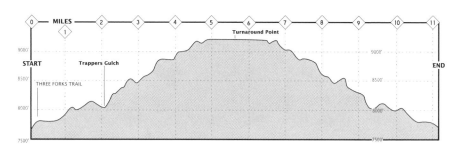

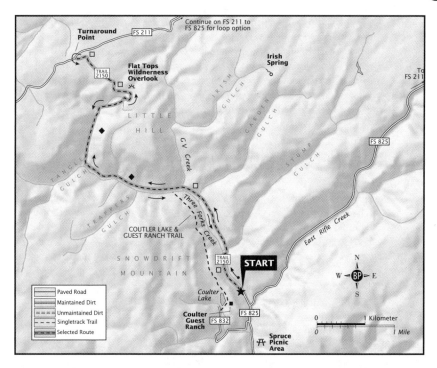

moss-covered limestone walls invite spelunkers to delve deep into the 90-foot cave behind its watery veil. But perhaps the most significant outdoor activity to emerge from Rifle in recent years is rock climbing.

Following County Road 325 east, past Rifle Falls State Park, you enter into Rifle Mountain State Park, a 400-acre, 2.5-mile long stretch of towering limestone canyon walls. Prior to 1991, Rifle Mountain Park was the locals' private stash. The park's riparian ecosystem provided cool relief from the summer temperatures of the Western Slope's lower elevations. Only a handful of climbers knew of the park's climbing potential. Rifle local Mark Tarrant and his Denver pal Richard Wright were among some of the first to climb the park's walls for sport. Together, Tarrant and Wright laid what many climbing faithfuls believe to be the first route in Rifle: "Rumor Has It…." Rumor had it, indeed, and word spread fast throughout Colorado climbing circles that Rifle was the hot new ticket.

Owing to its easy access, proliferation of climbing routes, and classic limestone features, Rifle Mountain State Park has quickly become one of America's premier climbing destinations. Although most of the park's climbing routes are reserved for top-level athletes, there are a number of moderate and easy routes to be had, most of which are located above the park's ice caves. With access into these caves provided by the "Ice Age Trail," Rifle climbers, hikers, and mountain bikers are never too far from staying cool.

Like the ice caves, Colorado's mystique depends, in large part, on its secret stashes, those places that, for one reason or another, remain hidden from the rest of the world. These climbing routes, powder fields, and mountain bike trails may never get used, except by the few who know where the stashes are kept. The Three Forks Trail is one such stash.

The hard-packed, smooth singletrack of the Three Forks Trail quickly gives way to the rough-and-tumble ways of a secret stash that has yet to be smoothed over by the masses. Heading in a northwesterly direction, the trail snakes its way through mixed conifer forests, meadows, aspen groves, and creeks on its way to the Forest Service Road 211. As the trail climbs steadily, you can't help but notice the disintegration of the singletrack. Nothing short of Jedi training could keep you from bonking once or twice on this severely overgrown trail. Once you arrive at the Three Forks and Tangle Gulch intersection, even the Force can't help you.

The remoteness of the trail is really made apparent after passing a variety of beaver ponds. These ponds mark the spot beyond which big game most likely frequent. Riding through a miniature berry bush forest, one recognizes the flattened vegetation of the forest. There seems to be no rhyme or reason as to why certain areas of the forest would be flattened—that is, until one realizes that these areas of forest are bedding for big game. Were it not for the trail's limited use, these big game animals would probably be more comfortable some distance from any trail, as opposed to directly beside it. After passing these beds of elk, mule deer, and bear, you begin your final push to the top through a magical stand of aspen. As you slowly crank through this stand, you should notice the "bear trees" among the aspen. "Bear trees" are those scarred by the teeth and claws of bears. These scars can be eight to 10 feet high (as high as a bear can reach standing on its hind legs) on any tree.

Using the Force to find the way on this all but invisible trail.

# Ride Information

## 📞 Trail Contacts:
**City of Rifle Parks and Recreation Department**, Rifle, CO; (970) 625-2151 • **Rifle Ranger District**, Rifle, CO; (970) 625-2371 • **Blanco Ranger District**, White River National Forest, CO; (970) 878-4039

## 🕐 Schedule:
Late June to October

## 💲 Fees/Permits:
$4 for daily entrance fee into Rifle Mountain Park; $10 for overnight camping

## ❓ Local Information:
**Rifle Area Chamber of Commerce and Information Center**, Rifle, CO; (970) 625-2085 or 1-800-842-2085 • **City of Rifle**, Rifle, CO; (970) 625-2121

## ❓ Local Events/Attractions:
**Flat Tops Trail Scenic Byway**, Meeker, CO; (970) 879-4039 • **The Roan Cliffs**, Rifle, CO; (970) 625-2085 or 1-800-842-2085 • **Rifle Gap State Park**, Rifle, CO; (970) 625-1607 or *www.dnr.state.co.us/parks* • **Rifle Falls State Park**, Rifle, CO; (970) 625-1607 or *www.dnr.state.co.us/parks* • **Glenwood Hot Springs**, Glenwood Springs, CO; (970) 945-7131 • **Rifle Rendezvous**, in May, Rifle, CO; (970) 625-2085 or 1-800-842-2085 – *providing a taste of the Old West with an old-fashioned shoot out, tribal dancing and other events* • **Garfield County Fair**, in August, Rifle, CO; (970) 625-2085 or 1-800-842-2085

## 🚲 Local Bike Shops:
**Alpine Bike Shop**, Glenwood Springs Mall, Glenwood, CO; (970) 945-6434 – *located 25 miles east of Rifle*

## Ⓝ Maps:
**USGS maps:** Triangle Park, CO • *Trails Illustrated* map: #125 • **White River National Forest Map** – *available at Blanco Ranger District, White River National Forest (970) 878-4039*

Having climbed through these aspens unscathed, take in the views of the Flat Tops Wilderness Area to the north, home to Colorado's largest herd of elk. After riding through the meadow, you'll arrive at a grouping of 12 aspens on your left—one of which will have "Alijandro" carved into it, beside the trail marker for 2150. From here the trail descends through another little ravine to its connection with Forest Service Road 211. From Forest Service Road 211, either return the way you came or bear right onto Forest Service Road 211 to Triangle Park, intercepting Forest Service Road 825 back to your vehicle.

Should you want to ride this as an out-and-back, the return descent from the meadow is very fast, bumpy and overgrown. Since the trail itself can hardly be seen in spots, the descent can be tricky. Many little bumps and holes in the trail are hard to detect at high speeds. One thing to be cautious of is the skewer to your front tire. Be sure that it's locked (folded) to the back of the bicycle, not toward the front, as thick vegetation, coupled with a speedy descent, may cause the skewer to open and release your front tire.

Once you intersect with the Coulter Lake/Guest Ranch Trail for the second time, you can either bear right onto the Coulter Lake/Guest Ranch Trail and include a mini loop into your out-and-back ride, or you can simply continue descending on the Three Forks Trail back to your vehicle.

# Chutes & Ladders

## Ride Summary

Chutes & Ladders is a long-time favorite of Fruita mountain bikers. Recalling the ups and downs of the old childhood board game, Chutes & Ladders offers a technically rolling romp over some of the best slickrock outside of Moab, Utah. The ride offers many short climbs and descents over slickrock and through sand. It delivers one of the smoothest and narrowest sections of singletrack in all of Colorado. After negotiating the rocky terrain of the Book Cliffs, the tireless rider is rewarded with a fast and straight singletrack shot through a cow pasture—smooth as butter.

## Ride Specs

**Start:** From the Chutes & Ladders trailhead
**Length:** 8.1-mile loop
**Approximate Riding Time:** Advanced Riders, 1 hour; Intermediate Riders, 2 hours
**Technical Difficulty Rating:** Technically challenging due to its steeper climbs and descents and a variety of switchbacks.
**Physical Difficulty Rating:** Physically moderate to challenging due to the variety of terrain: sometimes flat and rolling, other times steep.
**Terrain:** Singletrack. The terrain rolls over hilly slickrock and sand and through open pasture.
**Elevation Gain:** 1,190 feet
**Nearest Town:** Fruita, CO
**Other Trail Users:** Hikers and cows
**Canine Compatibility:** Dog friendly

## Getting There

**From downtown Fruita:** Drive east on Aspen Avenue, passing the Civic Center on your left. Turn north (left) onto Maple Street by two stone churches. Drive four miles north on Maple Street, which eventually turns into CR 17.5. Before arriving at a sharp left curve, turn right onto CR N&3/10. CR N&3/10 comes to a "T" intersection. At the "T," turn left onto CR 18. (The rides in this area are more commonly referred to as located in the "18 Road Area" and the "Book Cliffs"). Drive seven miles on CR 18, then notice a parking lot pull-out to your left. Park here and begin your ride on the singletrack located across the road. *DeLorme: Colorado Atlas & Gazetteer.* Page 42 C-3

For years, mountain bikers en route to Moab, Utah, would blaze right past Fruita (one of the last towns before entering Utah) without so much as a tip of the hat. What these slickrock and arch-crazed mountain bikers failed to realize is that Fruita has the second largest concentration of natural arches in the world, not to mention miles of boundless slickrock and access to one of the most incredibly beautiful high desert mountain biking trails. It's a wonder Fruita hasn't received the recognition Moab has. But the tides are beginning to turn for Fruita as mountain bikers are starting to "discover" the juicy rides that abound in the area.

Named after the fruit trees that William Pabor envisioned planting when he founded the town in 1884, Fruita, with its 5,000 residents, is a growing agricultural center and a gateway to a number of recreational adventures. From its noteworthy fossil discoveries to its designation as the main entrance to the Colorado National Monument, Fruita has earned its place in Colorado's rich recreational and historical heritage.

The Colorado National Monument, Fruita's leading attraction, superbly illustrates the effects of a billion years of erosion: spindrift of blasting tidal seas, spiraling sands, windswept fresh water lakes, sinking swamps, and quaking ground. The 4,000-vertical-foot drive from the valley floor through the sandstone strata via the Rim Rock Drive literally shows you the history of the earth. The Colorado National Monument offers the widest variety of color found in any desert: towering red sandstone, 12-million-year-old coke ovens, stands of green juniper and piñon, and blooming yellow cacti and red Indian paintbrush. It stands to reason that John Otto, fearing the arrival of settlers into the area, petitioned Congress in 1900 to preserve this venerable place. Congress would eventually concede, and in 1911 President Taft officially designated the 32-mile plot as a national monument.

In case you didn't realize it, this is dinosaur country, and the town of Fruita boasts one of the most interactive learning centers for the study of dinosaurs, the 26,000-square-foot Devil's Canyon Science and Learning Center. The annual Fat Tire Festival in late April is also bringing attention to Fruita. Riders from all over the country come to compete in the four-day event. The festival welcomes riders of all abilities. Commemorative t-shirts, guidebooks, pasta dinners, parties, live music, and prizes await festival goers. The event has become quite a hit among Fruitans, providing not only amusement but also a boon to the local economy. The festival is also another way of introducing cyclists to the mountain bike trails which abound in this "Grand Valley."

One such trail, Chutes & Ladders, is a favorite among Fruita locals and for good reason. The trail runs along the Grand Valley's northern edge, bordered entirely by the Book Cliffs. This continuous band of stark adobe cliffs and ridges runs west into Utah and bears a striking resemblance to books on a shelf. The first European settlers to the Grand Valley recognized the region's grazing potential. In the early days, cattleman had an almost exclusive hold on the land, but as word got out, sheepmen started to arrive. Having lost much of their lands to these newly-arrived sheep, the cattlemen decided to take action. The finer details of their action are still a matter of debate. Some say the cattlemen simply drove the sheep over the Book Cliffs, others say they clubbed and threw them over. Regardless, the sheep ended up dead at the bottom of the cliffs. A battle broke out between the cattlemen and the sheepmen. What resulted was legislation, the Rees-Odland Act, which permanently outlined the government's grazing rights. Today, cattle and sheep happily graze together—no hard feelings. As for the ranchers, today's herds are often managed by the same rancher.

Hanging it tight around some rocky singletrack.

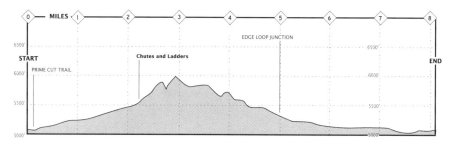

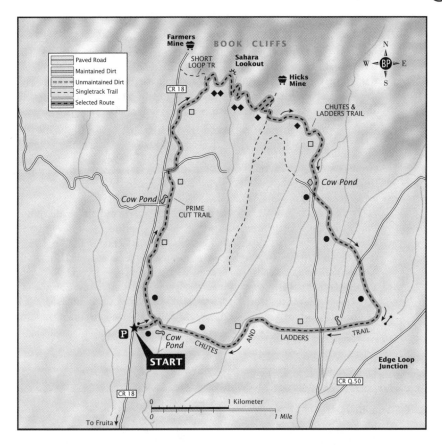

**Miles**Directions

**0.0 START** at the parking lot and the trailhead for Prime Cut, which eventually leads you to Chutes & Ladders.

**0.1** Arrive at a cow pond. The route ends here. Bear left and continue on the smooth and tight singletrack, as it winds its way along the west slope of a small drainage.

**1.3** Arrive at another cow pond. Ride right, around it, continuing on the singletrack.

**2.2** The trail forks. This marks the beginning of Chutes & Ladders, at the base of the Books Cliffs. (Bearing left here will lead you to the dirt road and back to your vehicles, the short loop of "Chutes & Ladders" or Prime Cut.) Bearing right delivers you to the main Chutes & Ladders trail. Before you lie three deceptively steep climbs. Now on Chutes & Ladders, the trail crosses four drainages. Stay left at any junctions.

**3.5** Sweet singletrack begins, running smooth and fast across a grassy knoll. Views of the Grand Mesa are to your left. Here's the place to hammer-down.

**5.0** Arrive at the Edge Loop junction. Don't ride beyond the fence. Bear right onto singletrack running parallel with the fence. This singletrack returns you to the first cow pond you passed and ultimately to your vehicle.

**8.1** Return to the parking lot.

Aside from this bit of historical controversy, what makes this area a great place to ride is its first rate singletrack. Chutes & Ladders offers mountain bikers continuous, fast, smooth-running singletrack, as well as rocky and sandy singletrack. The first two miles of the ride (Prime Cut) offer riders a chance to warm up. The smooth-running singletrack winds its way north, gradually ascending a small valley. With many ups and downs, the trail winds through a thick Juniper Forest. Visions of trolls and leprechauns come to mind as you wind your way through this Enchanted Forest. After ducking and dodging a number of low-lying branches, you come to your first real technical spot at mile 1.9. The singletrack swings right and immediately drops you into a small washout before a big rock. You have to climb out of the washout and over the rock to continue to the Book Cliffs. Here it's best that you keep your speed (as is usually the case) and pick the line directly in the center of the rock. Avoid the line to the left, as a tricky juniper branch waits to close-line.

By the end of the two miles, your heart rate has melded with the rhythm of the trail, vacillating from highs to lows—just in time to climb a series of three pitches. Atop these pitches you'll gain a better insight as to how Chutes & Ladders derived its name. Look to the west and you'd swear you were in the Sahara. From here, a singletrack descent awaits, as you plunge into rocky valleys via even rockier and tight singletrack. The slope of the trail is very precipitous. Pedal against the adverse camber of the trail as you try to negotiate some tight switchbacks. Once out of the "Book Cliffs," you're treated to some sweet singletrack, described in some riding circles as "like butta." Don't knock it 'till you mock it. From here it's more of the same.

## Ride Information

### ● Trail Contacts:
**Over the Edge: Cycling & Adventure Sports,** Fruita, CO; 1-800-873-3068 or visit them at *www.gj.net/~edge*

### ● Schedule:
April to November

### ● Local Information:
**Bureau of Land Management,** Grand Junction Resource Area, Grand Junction, CO; (970) 244-3050 • **Colorado Welcome Center,** Fruita, CO; (970) 858-9335

### ● Local Events/Attractions:
**The Annual Fruita Fat Tire Festival,** late April, Fruita, CO – *contact Over the Edge* • **Colorado National Monument,** Fruita, CO; (970) 858-3617 • **Devil's Canyon Science/Learning Center,** Fruita, CO; (970) 858-7282

### ● Organizations:
**The Colorado Plateau Mountain Bike Trail Association (COPMOBA),** Grand Junction, CO; (970) 241-9561

### ● Local Bike Shops:
**Over the Edge: Cycling & Adventure Sports,** Fruita, CO; (970) 858-7220 or *www.gj.net/~edge*

### ● Maps:
**USGS maps:** Ruby Lee Reservoir, CO • *Trails Illustrated map:* #208 • **Fruita Fat Tire Guide map** – *available at Over the Edge*

## Composition of "America the Beautiful"

*America the Beautiful*

*"We stood at last on that gait-of-heaven summit [Pike's Peak] . . .and gazed in wordless rapture over the far expanse of mountain ranges and sea-like sweep of plain. It was then and there that the opening lines of 'America the Beautiful' sprang into being."*

*Katherine Lee Bates*

In the summer of 1893, Katherine Lee Bates braved the wild, open prairies of the United States' interior on her way to Colorado. A renowned professor of English Literature at Wellesley College in Massachusetts, Bates was invited by her cross-continent colleagues to spend the summer as a visiting professor at Colorado College in Colorado Springs.

No sooner than she arrived, friends urged Bates to summit the 14,110-foot Pikes Peak—a must-see for first-time visitors to Colorado Springs. Just 35 years prior, Pikes Peak had been the focus of one of Colorado's most famous gold rushes. Though gold was never found, the magnificent mountain still drew visitors. Since 1891 the Pikes Peak Cog Railway had been ferrying visitors to the summit, and so, Bates' trip to the top wasn't of the lung-busting and scree-scrambling order.

Once Bates reached the summit of Colorado's most famous mountain, she found herself in the middle of a lover's kiss, overcome with poetic inspiration. There lay glittering Denver 70 miles to the north, a vast ocean of green prairies to the east, towering jagged peaks of the Sangre de Cristo Mountains and the Spanish Peaks to the south, and the imposing granite mammoths of the Sawatch and Mosquito ranges due west. The dramatic contrast of the flat prairie oceans crashing against the towering peaks of the Rockies seemed a striking metaphor not just for the west, but for the nation as a whole. Inspired, she penned these inspirational words:

> *Oh beautiful for spacious skies,*
> *For amber waves of grain:*
> *For purple mountain majesties*
> *Above the fruited plain—*
> *America, America, God shed his grace on thee,*
> *And crown thy good with brotherhood*
> *From sea to shining sea . . .*

*The poem "America the Beautiful" did not appear in print until 1911, when Bates featured it in one of her many books of poetry. But as soon as the poem reached the public, it was set to music. The rest, as they say, is history. Today, many a patriot considers "America the Beautiful" (the song) America's real national anthem.*

# 3

# Troy Built Loop

## Ride Summary

The Troy Built Loop, named in honor of its builder, is the newest addition to the famed Kokopelli Trail, which links Grand Junction, Colorado, to Moab, Utah, via a mountain bike trail. This loop delivers some tough climbing on narrow and rocky singletrack. Views of the Grand Valley are spectacular. Some of the riding involves speedy descents along the edge of Rabbit Valley—one hell-of-a-long-way down. Once at the top of Mack Ridge, however, it's a speedy wide doubletrack back to your vehicle. The views atop Mack Ridge offer distant sights of Utah, the Grand Mesa, and the entire Grand Valley.

## Ride Specs

**Start:** From parking lot, just one mile west of Exit 11, off of I-70 on dirt road
**Length:** 6.3-mile loop
**Approximate Riding Time:** Advanced Riders, 1 hour; Intermediate Riders, 2 hours
**Technical Difficulty Rating:** Technically moderate to challenging due to its rocky and narrow climbs and fast and open descents
**Physical Difficulty Rating:** Physically challenging due to its steeper, rocky climbs
**Terrain:** Singletrack, doubletrack, jeep road, and some slick rock. The trail travels over arid and rocky terrain, skirting, at times, to precipitous canyon edges.
**Elevation Gain:** 1,395 feet
**Nearest Town:** Fruita, CO
**Other Trail Users:** Motorcyclist, hikers, four-wheelers, campers, and equestrians
**Canine Compatibility:** Dog friendly. Although short in terms of mileage, this trail can get very hot, so bring plenty of water for the pooch.

## Getting There

**From Fruita:** Drive 8.3 miles west on I-70 to the town of Mack, Exit 11. From the exit ramp in Mack, make a left under I-70 and head for the steep dirt road straight ahead. Cross the cattle guard and bear right, now heading west. You will immediately notice a parking lot. Here is where most descriptions of this ride will suggest that you start. I suggest otherwise. Continue driving west along the dirt road, passing this parking lot, for approximately one mile. After driving about one mile on this dirt road, you will notice a parking lot pull off. Park here. **DeLorme: Colorado Atlas & Gazetteer.** Page 42, C-1&2

Doing the right thing for Pooh in the Colorado desert.

The Troy Built Loop is the newest in a series of loops along the Kokopelli Trail. Its completion marks the final leg of the 26.9-mile Grand Loop, which along with the Troy Built Loop includes Lion's Loop (7.8 miles) and Mary's Loop (12.8 miles). The Grand Loop is a chain of three trails whose highest points intersect with the Kokopelli Trail. The route is a tribute to the hard working mountain biking community of the Grand Valley. Of the three loops, the Troy Built Loop, due to its quality singletrack and incredible Colorado River views, is quite possibly the best. Located in the Grand Loop's northernmost section, the Troy Built Loop offers dazzling views and technical singletrack.

Although most descriptions of this trail will advise you to ride in a clockwise direction—beginning by climbing 560-foot Mack Ridge and riding down the incredible singletrack—this description advises you to begin counter clockwise. The singletrack is such that you can be challenged by its climb without being frustrated by its futility. In other words, although very challenging, the singletrack climb is ridable. All to often, trail descriptions overlook the challenges of a technical singletrack climb, opting rather to describe a trail's technical singletrack descent. The singletrack to the Troy Built Loop offers lovers of the climb a chance to strut their stuff, while allowing those who'd rather do down to see the world as others see it.

Beginning with a short singletrack descent, the trail soon transforms itself into a rigorously rocky climb. Scrambling over loose rock and dirt for three miles, you'll eventually arrive at the trails trickiest section. Here the singletrack enters a short, technical descent into a sandstone creek bottom. Be patient here. Keep your speed, as this section of trail requires a couple of swift moves before hitting the last big drop off. If at first you don't succeed, give it another shot—that is, as long as *you're* not shot. Cairns mark the way of the trail along this creek bottom.

After this section, the toughest part of the climb begins, before reaching a doubletrack at 4.0 miles. After having reached the rim, which overlooks Crow Bottom and the junction of Salt Creek and the Colorado River, relish in the thought of your technical climb accomplished.

From the top of Mack Ridge, notice the rise of the 11,234-foot Grand Mesa to the east and its smaller neighbor of the Colorado Plateau, Mount Garfield. Though the Grand Mesa looms toweringly over this "Grand Valley," its 11,234-foot shadow isn't what enshrouds Mount Garfield in mysterious darkness. Rather, it's the tales told by weary locals of the deaths that have occurred in its toxic gas-filled mines of old. Like lemmings, curious adventurers and miners have succumbed to the noxious fumes emanating from this one-time coal mine.

Before spooking yourself for too long, rip down the remaining 1.3 miles to your vehicle, rounding off the Troy Built Loop and part of the Kokopelli Trail. All told, the Kokopelli Trail includes 140 miles of isolated, backcountry 4WD roads, slickrock and singletrack. Running from Loma, Colorado, to Moab, Utah, the Kokopelli Trail was originally used by the Anasazi Indians ("Ancient Ones") as a migration route through the Colorado Plateau. It wasn't until 1989 that the Kokopelli Trail officially opened for recreational use.

## **Miles**Directions

**0.0 START** from the parking lot. Head west along the doubletrack.

**0.1** The doubletrack will "T." Most descriptions of this ride will suggest you take the left route of the "T," climbing the steep jeep road to the summit of Mack Ridge (560 feet); whereupon, you get to descend the tricky 4 miles of singletrack. For our purposes, bear right behind the interpretive sign and continue heading west to ascend the tricky singletrack, whereupon, you get to race down the steep and rocky jeep road.

**0.2** You'll arrive at a map outlining the Kokopelli Trail, of which the Troy Built Loop is a part. A tight and rocky singletrack begins to the right and just beyond this map, descending for a while before beginning its gradual, southern ascent.

**1.5** The singletrack once again "Y's." Bear left to climb, continuing on the Troy Built Loop. The right will lead you to the main Kokopelli Trail, which heads on across Salt Creek and toward Rabbit Valley, offering incredible views of the Colorado River.

**3.6** Begin the steepest and most technical part of the climb.

**4.0** The singletrack reaches a doubletrack, which also marks the junction with Lion's Loop. From here, bear left. Both Lion's and Troy Built Loops share this section of trail. Be sure not to take any right-handed offshoots.

**5.0** Reach the summit of Mack Ridge. Take in the sights and begin your fast and furious race to the bottom.

**6.3** Arrive at the parking lot.

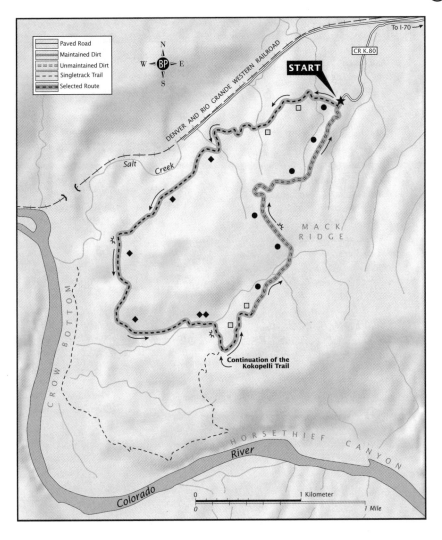

Troy Built Loop

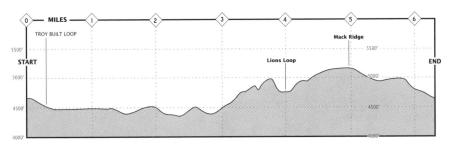

# Ride Information

## Trail Contacts:

**Over The Edge:** Cycling & Adventure Sports, Fruita, CO; 1-800-873-3068 or www.gj.net/~edge

## Schedule:

April to November

## Local Information:

**Bureau of Land Management,** Grand Junction Resource Area, Grand Junction, CO; (970) 244-3050 • **The Colorado Plateau Mountain Bike Trail Association (COPMOBA),** Grand Junction, CO; (970) 241-9561 • **Colorado Welcome Center,** Fruita, CO, 970-858-9335

## Local Events/Attractions:

**The Annual Fruita Fat Tire Festival in late April,** Fruita, CO – contact Over the Edge: Cycling & Adventure Sports at (970) 858-3068 • **Colorado National Monument,** Fruita, CO; (970) 858-3617 **Devil's Canyon Science/Learning Center,** Fruita, CO; (970) 858-7282 • **Colorado National Monument,** Fruita, CO; (970) 858-3617

## Local Bike Shops:

**Over The Edge:** Cycling & Adventure Sports, Fruita, CO; (970) 858-3068

## Tours:

**Adventure Quest Expeditions,** Grand Junction, CO; (970) 245-9058 or 1-888-AD-Quest

## Organizations:

**The Colorado Plateau Mountain Bike Trail Association (COPMOBA),** Grand Junction, CO; 970-241-9561

## Maps:

**USGS maps:** Ruby Canyon, CO • **Trails Illustrated map:** # 208. • **Fruita Fat Tire Guide** – available at Over the Edge: Cycling & Adventure Sports • **Kokopelli's Trail: Grand Junction/Fruita Area Loops Map** – available at the Colorado Welcome Center, Fruita, CO; (970) 858-9335

The Kokopelli Trail takes its name from a mythical figure recognized by many Native American tribes of the Colorado Plateau. Usually associated with the flute playing Hopi Indians, this humped back flute player could drive back winter with his flute playing. According to legend, Kokopelli would wander from village to village with a bag of songs tucked under his arm. A symbol of fertility, Kokopelli was always welcome among villages, particularly during the spring planting season.

Although the Kokopelli Trail was originally named out of respect for Native American heritage, today's mountain bikers have adopted this legend as their own, viewing the Kokopelli as a symbol for the network of trails throughout the Colorado Plateau. Who knows which other paths of the Kokopelli's wanderings cross other area bike trails? All that is certain is that where the two meet, there is song, dance, and good rides.

## The RTD's Bike-n-Ride Program

Part of Colorado's appeal to cyclists is its bicycle-friendly attitude. Even Denver, Colorado's capital, boasts a healthy attitude toward its lycra-wearing residents.

In a city as beautiful as Denver, with its Rocky Mountain backdrop and over 300 days of sunshine a year, it makes sense to commute on your bicycle—which is why Denver has reserved cycling lanes alongside its car lanes. The Greater Colorado Transit Authority goes to great lengths to secure this healthy alternative to commuting.

Commuting via cycle does have its unexpected obstacles: rainy weather, flat tires, and lack of leg power. For this reason, the Regional Transportation District (RTD) developed its Bike-n-Ride program. As a service to commuters and cyclists alike, the Boulder and Longmont local, numbered buses provide bicycle mounts, should a commuting cyclist find him or herself in need of an alternate mode of transportation. Fort Collins' buses are all equipped with bicycle mounts. The Denver local, limited and express busses also offer bicycle racks for distressed cyclists.

As if this weren't enough, the RTD permits bicycles inside luggage compartments on its regional buses. The cost for such convenience? Nil. Light rail trains also welcome bicycles. Although there's no fee for bringing your bicycle on a light rail train, you are required to obtain a permit.

With Colorado's population ever-growing, many commuters are taking advantage of the many Park-n-Rides throughout the RTD's six-county district. Free bicycle lockers and racks are provided at many Park-n-Ride locations. With a $25 refundable deposit, lockers can be leased for up to six months.

For further information on the RTD's Bike-n-Ride program, contact the RTD's telephone information center at (303) 299-6000, and then press 140. For those of you outside the Denver-Boulder metro area, call 1-800-388-7433, and then press 140.

Bike racks on buses are also available in Aspen/Glenwood Springs (Roaring Fork Transit), Avon/Vail (ECO Transit), Summit County (The Summit Stage) and in Colorado Springs (Springs Transit).

Heading home from atop Mack Ridge.

# Crag Crest Trail

## Ride Summary

The Crag Crest Trail is located on Colorado's Grand Mesa. With 300 lakes to its credit, the Grand Mesa is truly "Land o' Lakes" country. The entire 10-mile loop of the Crag Crest Trail passes a number of these lakes and was designated a National Recreation Trail on March 14, 1978, by Forest Service Chief John McGuire. Very rarely used by mountain bikers, the trail features smooth and tacky, hard-packed terrain over exposed roots and rocks. This trail combines lake-views with wild-flowering hillside meadows set between mixed aspen and conifer forests. The Crag Crest Trail can be divided into two sections: the crest portion and the lower loop. This ride concerns itself strictly with the lower loop, as mountain bikes are not allowed on the crest portion. You should, however, make it a point to hike the upper crest portion of the trail, as it offers insight into the geological history of the Grand Mesa. During the height of the summer months, the mosquitoes in this area are some of the most bothersome in the state. September is usually a great time to visit.

## Ride Specs

**Start:** From the Grand Mesa Visitors Center
**Length:** 8.6-mile loop
**Approximate Riding Time:** Advanced Riders, 45–60 minutes; Intermediate Riders, 1½–2 hours
**Technical Difficulty Rating:** Technically moderate due to some rockier sections
**Physical Difficulty Rating:** Physically moderate due to some elevation gain at higher elevations
**Terrain:** Paved state road, paved forest road, improved gravel road, and singletrack. This route passes a number of lakes, as it makes its way through the forests of the Grand Mesa. Although not particularly technical, there are some short rock and root sections, as well as a few switchbacks with which to contend.
**Elevation Gain:** 1,160 feet
**Nearest Town:** Cedaredge, CO
**Other Trail Users:** Hikers, picnickers, and anglers
**Canine Compatibility:** Dog friendly

## Getting There

**From Montrose:** Drive west on U.S. 50 for 20 miles to Delta. Bear right onto CO 92, by the Conoco and Diamond Shamrock stations. Drive for four miles on CO 92 before turning left onto CO 65, following signs for the Grand Mesa. After approximately 14.5 miles, come to the town of Cedaredge. Continue on CO 65, passing the old Grand Mesa Road to your right, and enter into Grand Mesa National Forest. At 54 miles, arrive at the Grand Mesa Visitors Center, to your right. Park your vehicle here. *DeLorme: Colorado Atlas & Gazetteer:* Page 44, D-2

According to tradition, when the Ute Council Tree (located in Delta, Colorado) loses a branch, Indian medicine men are to dispatch from the reservation and hold blessing rights. They then make ceremonial drums from the wood.

The Crag Crest Trail runs through the Grand Mesa National Forest—the second forest reserve to be set aside in Colorado. One of the world's largest flattop mountains, the Grand Mesa reaches as high as 11,234 feet atop Leon Peak. Framed in by the converging valleys of the Colorado and Gunnison rivers, the Grand Mesa has over 300 stream-fed alpine lakes—an angler's paradise. The lakes beautifully mirror the surrounding Engelmann spruce, sub-alpine fir, and aspen. Dubbed

Land's end atop the Grand Mesa.

"Thunder Mountain" by early Ute Indians, the Grand Mesa is a rare find in Colorado. When you visit for the first time, you'll marvel at how few people there are milling around. The Grand Mesa is definitely a sight to see, so enjoy the peace and solitude while you can.

The Grand Mesa formed 70 to 100 million years ago, the result of a series of volcanic eruptions, glaciation, and uplifts. At one time or another, a beach, a sea, and a large swamp occupied the area. The sand, silt, clay, and low-grade oil shale that were deposited some 50 million years ago when the area was a lake basin, all hardened to form sedimentary rock. It is this sedimentary rock that is responsible, in part, for the crest's craggy appearance. Views from the Crag Crest tell the geological story of the Grand Mesa.

A series of lava flows starting 50 million years ago and ending 10 million years ago poured from cracks in the earth's crust onto the flat and wide sedimentary surface. Repeated lava flows poured over the surface, in turn cooling and hardening. Eventually, the sedimentary rock became completely covered by layers of volcanic rock—layers in excess of 400 feet thick. Due to underground turmoil, this entire area reached its present elevation about 10 million years ago, exposing its lava cap (basalt rock) and the finer sedimentary rocks below the cap to wind and erosion.

Views of Twin Lakes and the distant Uncompahgre Plateau.

The actual Crag Crest is a narrow, rocky ridge at the top of the Grand Mesa. It was formed as wind and water slowly eroded the softer sedimentary rock from its volcanic cap. Consequently, "slip surfaces" (large vertical cracks) were left in the rock. These cracks would, in effect, separate portions of smaller rock from the larger whole. These smaller portions would then slip down the sides of the opposing larger rock and tilt backward, forming large cavities that in time would fill with water. If viewed from the top of the Crag Crest Trail, Upper Eggleston Lake makes a shimmering example of such slumping. Butts Lake offers an even clearer picture of how these smaller portions of rock could have slipped and tilted to form the present lake. As these separate portions of smaller rock slipped from its larger whole, what remained was a larger hole whose sides were considerably steeper than before. As this process continued, the sides grew ever steeper, as its volcanic cap grew narrower. This constant slumping has given rise both to the Crag Crest and the Grand Mesa's numerous lakes. Since this slumping is a continual process, eventually the narrow ridge of the Crag Crest will be destroyed.

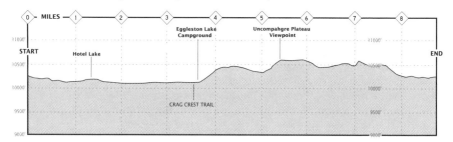

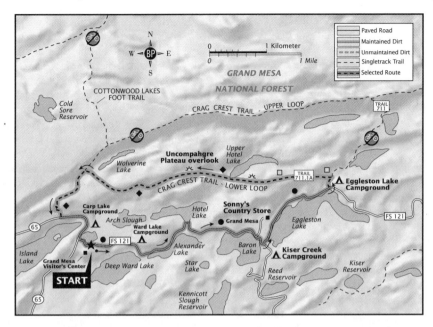

## **Miles**Directions

**0.0 START** riding from the Grand Mesa Visitors Center on the paved FS 121 (Trickel Park Road) east, climbing gradually through the pines.

**0.3** Begin descending. Expansive views of Ward Lake are to your right.

**0.4** Pass Alexander Lake on your right.

**1.4** Pass Sonny's Country Store on your left—burgers and drinks available.

**2.0** Pass Baron Lake.

**2.4** The pavement ends and FS 121 turns into an improved gravel road.

**2.5** Eggleston Lake is to your right.

**3.5** FS 121 intersects with the Crag Crest East Trailhead (711.1A). Bear left onto the singletrack of the Crag Crest Trail. The sign here reading "Foot and Horse Traffic Only" is in reference to the upper portion of the Crag Crest Trail (711). You are allowed to ride on the lower looped portion of the Crag Crest Trail.

**3.6** After a short climb through a meadow, arrive at the Crag Crest Trail intersection and a sign reading "West trailhead via crest – 6 ½, via lower loop – 4." Bear left (west) onto the lower loop of the Crag Crest Trail.

**4.9** Cross a tributary of Forrest Lake. Just after crossing the creek, cross a 4WD road. You'll notice a trail sign to your right pointing in a westerly direction. Continue heading west on the Crag Crest Trail.

**5.3** Reach a hilltop meadow with expansive views of the Uncompahgre Plateau and the Hotel Twin Lake.

**7.0** Pass through a rock field and again intersect with the trailheads of the Crag Crest Trail's upper and lower loops. Continue riding straight, passing the Visitor Center sign.

**7.1** Signs reading "West Trailhead – 0.4" and "Visitor Center – 0.8" mark another trail intersection. Bear right here, and follow the sign for the "West Trailhead – 0.4."

**7.5** Reach the west trailhead for the Crag Crest Trail where toilet facilities are available. Bear left onto the paved CO 65 and head east back to the Grand Mesa Visitor Center, passing Island Lake to your right.

**8.6** Arrive at the Visitor Center and your vehicle.

Delta, Colorado, is home to the one-time brick thrower turned world champion boxer Jack Dempsey.

Immediately after beginning the ride, you're offered views of Cobbett Lake, which lies directly to the north and through the pines. Harry Cobbett who lends his name to the lake, moved to the Delta Valley in 1892 from England. Enamored by the valley's beauty and the Grand Mesa's silent dominion over it, he persuaded his fiancée Lilian to follow him in 1895. Harry and Lilian settled in a dirt-roofed cabin by the Gunnison River near the town of Delta. A short time after moving in, Harry led Lilian to view the Grand Mesa. It didn't take long before Lilian realized why her husband had been so insistent that she join him.

Harry started building dams for several of the mesa's lakes, and by the early 1900s, he was employed as a ditch rider—a person who releases water from the reservoirs into the creeks and irrigation ditches to help irrigate the crops below the mesa. Eventually, the Cobbett's would move to Cedaredge, the town located directly below the beginning of the mesa's steepest rise, where Harry became postmaster. Due to his vigilant work clearing trails between the lakes and reservoirs and his contributions to the town of Cedaredge, Cobbett Lake is named in Harry's honor.

The ride to the singletrack of the Crag Crest Trail passes no less than six of these sapphire lakes. The going is lazy but very scenic. Once you've connected with the singletrack of the Crag Crest's lower loop, the trail heads west and is highlighted by wide, smooth singletrack over soft earth. After passing through meadows and mixed conifer and aspen forests, the trail starts climbing moderately, at about mile 3.5. Rocks and roots offer a technically moderate challenge, before they relent to the more commanding views of Eggleston Lake to the south. After descending through a dense lodgepole pine forest, the singletrack becomes especially tacky—nice cornering potential—as you blaze the flatter sections and across south-facing hillsides awash with bluebells, daisies, and sunflowers.

Once you've crossed the tributary of Forrest Lake, the trail again starts to ascend moderately. After reaching the hilltop meadow with views of the Uncompahgre Plateau, you begin to descend into a thick pine and aspen forest. The trail forks at 5.8 miles. Be sure to take the high fork, following the trail marker sign. From the west-

Original wooden silos in Pioneer Town, Cedaredge, CO.

# Ride Information

## ⓒ Trail Contacts:

**Grand Mesa Visitor Center**, Intersection of CO 65 and FS 121 (Trickel Park Road), CO; (970) 856-4153 • **Grand Mesa National Forest**, Supervisor, Delta, CO; (970) 874-6600

## ⓢ Schedule:

June to October

## ❓ Local Information:

**Delta County Tourism**, Delta, CO; 1-800-436-3041 • **Delta Chamber of Commerce**, Delta, CO; (970) 874-8616 **Cedaredge Chamber of Commerce**, Cedaredge, CO; (970) 856-6961 • **Grand Junction Ranger District**, Grand Junction, CO; (970) 242-8211 • **The Grand Mesa Scenic Byway News**, Cedaredge, CO; (970) 856-3100

## ⓠ Local Events/Attractions:

**Lands End Road:** From milepost 29 on CO 65, the Lands End Road, as part of the Grand Mesa Scenic and Historic Byway, follows the rim of the mesa for roughly 10 miles to the Land's End Overlook. Incredible views of the La Sal Mountains in Utah and the San Juan mountains in Colorado are offered. For information, contact the Grand Mesa Visitor Center at (970) 856-4153. • **Council Tree Pow-wow**, in September, Delta, CO; (970) 874-8616 • **Fort Uncompahgre**, Delta, CO; (970) 874-8349 • **Pioneer Town**, Cedaredge, CO; (970) 856-7554 • **Applefest**, in October, Cedaredge, CO; (970) 856-6961

## ⓘ Restaurants:

**Cozy Corner Café**, Delta, CO; (970) 874-3116 • **The Apple Shed Fruit Stand**, Cedaredge, CO; (970) 856-3877 or (970) 856-7007

## ⓣ Tours:

**Tour de Gold**, in September, Montrose, CO; (970) 249-8055 – for tour coordinator Bill Harris • **Bicycle Outfitter Touring Adventures**, Grand Junction, CO; (970) 245-2699

## ⓞ Organizations:

**Montrose Mountain Bike Club**, Montrose, CO Contact Cascade Bicycles, Montrose, CO; (970) 249-7375 • **The Colorado Plateau Mountain Bike Trail Association (COPMOBA)**, Grand Junction, CO; (970) 241-9561

## ⓑ Local Bike Shops:

**KC's Cycles**, Delta, CO; (970) 874-1563 • **Cascade Bicycles**, Montrose, CO; (970) 249-7375 • **Grand Mesa Cyclery Inc.**, Montrose, CO; (970) 249-7515

## Ⓝ Maps:

**USGS maps:** Grand Mesa, CO • **Grand Mesa National Forest Map** – available at the Grand Mesa Visitor Center (970) 856-4153 • **Crag Crest National Recreation Trail Map** – available at Grand Mesa National Forest Office (970) 874-6600 • **Grand Mesa Recreation Trails Map** – available at Grand Mesa National Forest Office (970) 874-6600

ern intersection of the Crag Crest Trail's upper and lower loops, the trail descends rapidly on some tight, rocky singletrack—the most difficult segment of the ride. There is an immediate left-hand switchback that you'll want to keep in mind before arriving at the Crag Crest's west trailhead. From the west trailhead, bear left onto Colorado 65 and ride back to your vehicle.

# Honorable Mentions

## Northwest Colorado

Compiled here is an index of great rides in the Northwest region that didn't make the A-list this time around but deserve recognition. Check them out and let us know what you think. You may decide that one or more of these rides deserves higher status in future editions or, perhaps, you may have a ride of your own that merits some attention.

### (A) Dinosaur National Monument

Located roughly 140 miles west of Steamboat Springs and 190 miles east of Salt Lake City, Dinosaur National Monument is far from being a destination resort. In fact, it's just plain far. It is, however, close to many a traveler's heart, as it offers boundless surprises in an area all too often overlooked.

Dinosaur National Monument sits on the border of Colorado and Utah, atop a high plains desert. Its seemingly barren plateau, alive with sagebrush, greasewood, and saltbrush, turns away most quick-to-judge travelers, while the canyons of the Green and Yampa rivers invite those who are more patient.

Named for the fossil bone deposits first unearthed on here in August of 1909 by Earl Douglass, a paleontologist from the Carnegie Museum in Pittsburgh, Pennsylvania, the Monument proudly boasts the Dinosaur Quarry building, an in-place museum centered around large fossil walls. The Monument's other attractions include its canyons. Access the to canyon floors are by a variety of paved, well-graded, and 4WD roads. Although Dinosaur National Monument doesn't have trails reserved strictly for mountain biking, mountain bikes are allowed on all roads.

Leading farther into the backcountry is the rugged but spectacular Echo Park Road. This road begins atop Harper's Corner Self-guiding Scenic Drive and runs a fast and rocky 12.3 miles to Echo Park, the confluence of the Green and Yampa rivers.

After passing red-cliffed buttes and a maze of meadows, exploring mountain bikers will come upon the remains of the Jack and Rial Chew Ranch (1910-1970). Not far from the ranch, the prehistoric Fremont people carved elaborate drawings into the canyon walls, circa 1000 AD. Here the sagebrush, greaswood, and saltbrush give way to piñon pine, juniper, cottonwoods, and boxelders, a veritable oasis in this otherwise brutal landscape. And if the sight of green doesn't immediately cool your jets, try spending a moment in the nearby "Whispering Cave," a cave that's temperatures runs approximately 30° cooler than the ambient temperatures outside.

At journey's end, Echo Park, mountain bikers will enjoy a refreshing dip in either the Green or the Yampa River, or both. The park offers the perfect idyllic surprise to a day in the sun. What you need to keep in mind, however, is that your 12.3-mile descent to Echo Park, must now be returned. The last four-mile climb to the top of Harper's Corner Self-guiding Scenic Drive is a killer. Be prepared with food and water.

For more information on Dinosaur National Monument contact the Dinosaur Area Chamber of Commerce in Dinosaur, Colorado, at 1-800-864-4405 or visit *www.colorado-go-west.com*. To reach Dinosaur, drive west on U.S. 40, 90 miles from Craig, Colorado. **DeLorme: Colorado Atlas & Gazetteer:** Page 22, B-1

# (B) Tall Pines Trail

The Tall Pines Trail is an incredibly beautiful ride through one of Colorado's most pristine places. Beginning roughly six miles west of Carbondale, which is about 10 miles south of Glenwood Springs, the Tall Pines Trail leads you through some gorgeous wooded terrain to its end in Redstone. The trail weaves its sinewy course over open meadows, along a number of creeks, and through sections of forest that can only be described as enchanting, The trail combines smooth-running, well-marked singletrack with tougher climbs and rockier sections, made all the more tough by being at the trail's end. If you're doing the ride as a 17-mile point-to-point, plan on leaving a shuttle in Redstone.

Lying roughly 22 miles west of Aspen, beyond the ski resort town of Snowmass Village, Redstone should be as popular as its neighbors. But with a population of only 92, it's far from an Aspen. While offering all the amenities of a "civilized" mountain town—champagne Sunday brunches and gourmet dinners at the Redstone Inn and Redstone Castle—Redstone has retained a certain authenticity. The original coal-mining cottages that line the banks of the Crystal River recall a time of lost craftsmanship. The Crystal River has the distinction of being the last undammed river in Colorado. Registered a National Historic District, Redstone enjoys its beautiful setting, backed by the Maroon Bells Snowmass Wilderness, and invites others to do the same.

To reach the trail's terminus at Redstone for your shuttle vehicle, drive south on Colorado 133 from Carbondale for 18 miles. Park your vehicle near the intersection of Colorado 133 and Forest Service Road 307. To reach the Tall Pines Trailhead, drive west on Main Street through Carbondale, as it turns into County Road 108 and crosses the Crystal River. Notice the jeep road off to the left (east) at roughly seven miles from Carbondale. Park your vehicle off of County Road 108 and take the road marked County Road 1C. For more information, contact Life Cycles at 0902 Colorado 133, Carbondale, Colorado, (970) 963-1149. *DeLorme: Colorado Atlas & Gazetteer:* Page 45, B-7

# Southwest Colorado

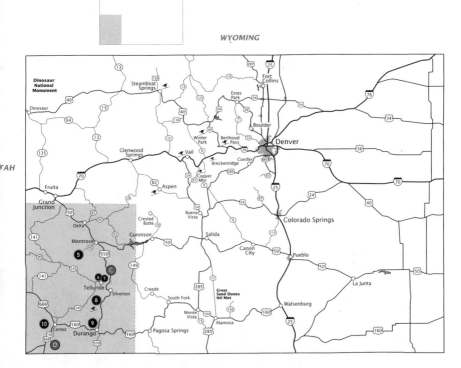

NEW MEXICO

S outhwest Colorado offers, by far, some of the most dramatic scenery and varied landscapes in the state. From Grand Junction, south to the towns of Telluride and Cortez, and then east to Durango, and all points in between, southwest Colorado is the shining jewel of all of Colorado's regions.

Included within the southwest are the high mesas and deserts of the Uncompahgre Plateau, a provincial block of land stretching from Colorado into Utah, New Mexico and Arizona. Here the desert canyons below the plateau meld with the lush forests atop the plateau. One of Colorado's best kept secrets is the superb mountain biking opportunities atop the Uncompahgre Plateau. A ride not to be missed is the Aspen to Buck Trail. When visiting the area, take time to explore the Black Canyon of the Gunnison National Monument. Gouged by the Gunnison River, the somber countenance of this gorge combines charcoal-pink cliffs half a mile high with widths shrinking to forty feet.

Considered to be the Switzerland of America, the town of Ouray lies just to the southeast of the plateau. The area surrounding Ouray is dotted with natural hot springs, the perfect compliment to a day in the saddle. In the winter, Ouray features the country's only ice climbing park. Centrally located, the Portland Creek Trail offers a beautiful look at this would-be Switzerland.

To the south of Ouray, rise the granite peaks of Telluride's San Juan Mountains. Known to early Ute Indians as the "land of the shining mountains," the San Juans are Colorado's most striking range. The onetime mining town of Telluride sits snugly within a box canyon, surrounded on all but one of its sides by these towering monoliths. Today, Telluride boasts some of the most challenging mountain bike terrain in all of Colorado. With its annual Bluegrass and Jazz Festival, Telluride is considered to be the state's summer music festival capital.

Traveling farther south still, one enters the Four Corners area of the country, the only place in the nation where four states converge to share a border. You can literally stand in Colorado, Utah, Arizona, and New Mexico at the same time. Although this area of the country is marked by its arid deserts and blazing heat, it was once home to North America's oldest known inhabitants, the Anasazi Indians (Ancient Puebloans). The Sand Canyon Trail, just outside the town of Cortez, travels past a number of small Ancient Puebloan kivas (ceremonial shelters of brick and mortar). More of these pueblos may be found at Hovenweep National Monument, forty-three miles west of Cortez or at Mesa Verde National Park.

Animas River

Durango

To the east of Cortez lies Durango, the region's recreational and economic epicenter. As the undisputed mountain biking Mecca of Colorado, Durango is the southern terminus for the 470-mile Colorado Trail, was venue to the first ever World Mountain Bike Championships and features one of the nation's oldest bicycle races, the Iron Horse Bicycle Classic.

# Aspen to Buck Trail

## Ride Summary

This loop enlists the help of three individual trails: the Aspen Trail, the Dry Creek Cutoff Trail, and the Buck Trail. Each of the three delivers its own unique contribution to the whole ride. The Aspen Trail is easy and rolls beautifully over smooth singletrack and through dense aspen. The Dry Creek Cutoff Trail offers some great technical riding on loose, rocky terrain before dropping to Dry Creek. The Buck Trail includes a moderate ride over a variety of exposed roots, as it passes through meadows and forests of ponderosa pine—offering this route's best view at mile 12.6 miles. Situated high atop the Uncompahgre Plateau, this ride is nearly never crowded. It's a solo rider's dream.

## Ride Specs

**Start:** From the intersection of the north Buck Trail 115 trailhead and Colorado 90, ride in a southwesterly direction on Colorado 90

**Length:** 16.3-mile loop

**Approximate Riding Time:** Advanced Riders, 2–3 hours; Intermediate Riders, 3–4 hours

**Technical Difficulty Rating:** Technically moderate with some challenging sections. Although most of the trail is relatively smooth, there are a few sections that offer a good degree of exposed rocks and roots.

**Physical Difficulty Rating:** Physically moderate due to a couple of shorter climbs at elevations exceeding 9,000 feet

**Terrain:** Improved dirt roads, doubletrack, and singletrack. Most of the terrain is rolling, as it snakes atop the Uncompahgre Plateau. The trail is considerably forested, with only a couple of eye-catching vistas. In general, this ride runs over hard packed singletrack featuring the occasional exposed root or rock. Portions of the Buck Trail are considerably dusty.

**Elevation Gain:** 1,801 feet

**Nearest Town:** Montrose, CO

**Other Trail Users:** Hunters, hikers, anglers, and picnickers

**Canine Compatibility:** Dog friendly

## Getting There

**From Montrose:** Drive southwest on Main Street, which eventually turns into CO 90. Drive west on CO 90 toward the Uncompahgre Plateau. The pavement ends at 8.9 miles. At 20.7 miles, enter into the Uncompahgre National Forest and pass the south Buck Trail 115 trailhead to your right. After 22.8 miles, you'll reach the north Buck Trail 115 trailhead to your right. Park your vehicle here. ***DeLorme: Colorado Atlas & Gazetteer.*** Page 65, B-7

On Colorado's Western Slope, along the eastern flank of the Colorado Plateau Province lies the Uncompahgre Plateau, perhaps the most overlooked and underrated of any of Colorado's high mountain attractions. Its 100-mile length makes the Plateau look low, and its flat top makes it look smooth. "Low" and "smooth" are not about to draw attention in Colorado—I guaranty you that. But

Enjoying the Aspen Trail.

the Uncompahgre is neither low nor smooth. Topping out at 10,347 feet (Horsefly Peak), the Uncompahgre Plateau draws together a collection of steep canyons and drainages, particularly along its western rim, and so it could hardly be considered low or smooth. The fact that the Uncompahgre Plateau remains one of Colorado's greatest anomalies does not prevent it from hosting a variety of incredible singletrack—notably the Aspen and Buck trails.

The Aspen to Buck Trail loop features some of the area's finest singletrack, as it weaves its serpentine course through a territory the Utes' called "uncompahgre"—translated by some as "hot water spring" and by others as "rocks made red by water." The Utes, Colorado's oldest permanent residents, came into Colorado along the eastern slope of the Rocky Mountains, reaching the Uncompahgre Plateau between 1200 and 1400 AD. The Utes' powerfully built frames and bronze-colored skin identified them to other Native Americans as the "Black Indians." Until the Spanish introduced the horse to North America in the 1600s, these early Utes traveled solely on foot, relying on bow and arrow to replenish their stores.

The Ute's territorial home was the nearby San Juan Mountains, or as they called them, the "land of shining mountains." They would often winter in the low-lying areas and then move to the higher mountainous regions in the summer to hunt. The Utes so respected the land and life that should necessity dictate the killing of an ani-

# **Miles**Directions

**0.0 START** from the intersection of the north Trail 115 (Buck Trail) trailhead and CO 90. Begin riding in a southwesterly direction on CO 90.

**0.7** Reach the intersection of CO 90 and South Divide Road. Continue riding on CO 90.

**0.8** Reach the intersection of CO 90 and FS 549 (States Draw Road). Bear left onto FS 549 and pass through the fence.

**2.6** After passing a pond, FS 549 intersects with Trail 125 (Aspen Trail). Bear left onto Trail 125.

**3.1** The Trail 125 opens up onto a beautiful vista above Red Canyon. Looking to the south, one can see Lone Cone and the town of Naturita.

**3.6** Intersect an old logging road. Cross the logging road and continue on the singletrack on the other side through intermittent pine and aspen.

**5.3** The Trail 125 intersects with the Little Red Springs Trail. Bear left (west) here, continuing on the Trail 125 loop.

**5.6** Reach the intersection of the Trail 125 and the Dry Creek Cutoff Trail. Bear right onto the Dry Creek Cutoff Trail.

**5.8** The Dry Creek Cutoff Trail intersects with the Divide Road. Bear left onto the Divide Road and ride for roughly 25 feet before bearing right to rejoin the singletrack of the Dry Creek Cutoff Trail.

**6.8** A steep and rocky doubletrack spurs off to the right of the Dry Creek Cutoff Trail. Do not bear right onto this spur. It will only climb savagely back to the Divide Road. Instead, continue straight ahead on the Dry Creek Cutoff Trail, descending over rocks and roots, to Dry Creek.

**7.2** At Dry Creek, the trail forks again. Bear left here, crossing Dry Creek and continuing up the doubletrack of the Dry Creek Cutoff Trail to the power lines. The right fork begins the Dry Creek Trail (Pack), which eventually climbs steeply from the Dry Creek drainage to the Divide Road.

**7.7** Reach the power lines. Bear right, climbing underneath the power lines.

**7.9** Once you near the crest of the climb underneath the power lines, you'll be able to distinguish a singletrack trail veering off to the right into a stand of aspen and pine trees. Bear right (southeast) onto this singletrack. Descend through the aspens. The trail parallels a split-rail fence (the National Forest Boundary) to your right.

**8.8** Pass underneath the power lines again and continue straight ahead.

**9.0** Reach the intersection of the south Trail 115 (Buck Trail) trailhead and CO 90. Cross CO 90 and continue your ride on the south Trail 115.

*[**Option:** If you bear left onto CO 90, it will deliver you to your vehicle after 2.1 miles, cutting your ride by roughly five miles. In doing so, however, you miss roughly seven miles of awesome Trail 115 singletrack.]*

**11.8** Enter into a wide-open aspen glen where a number of singletrack spurs break from the main trail. Be careful to stay on the main trail, following the trail marker signs nailed to the trees.

**12.4** Exit the aspen glen, climb moderately through a meadow, and pass through fields of scrub oak.

**12.6** Arrive at a high plateau with panoramic views. From here, descend into the meadow below and then into another grouping of aspen trees.

**13.3** Pass a stock tank on your right and grind up a tough and steep section of trail.

**14.0** Pass another stock tank to your left. Cross a 4WD road and continue on the Trail 115 on the other side, passing a multiple-use trail marker sign.

**14.6** The singletrack turns into a rough dirt road. Continue riding on the road.

**16.2** Cross under the power lines.

**16.3** Arrive at your vehicle.

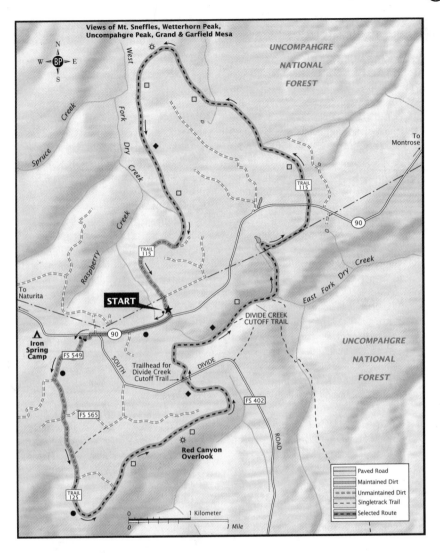

Views of Mt. Sneffles, Wetterhorn Peak,
Uncompahgre Peak, Grand & Garfield Mesa

UNCOMPAHGRE

NATIONAL

FOREST

West

Fork

Dry

Creek

Spruce Creek

Raspberry Creek

To Naturita

START

90

TRAIL 115

TRAIL 115

To Montrose

90

East Fork Dry Creek

DIVIDE CREEK CUTOFF TRAIL

Iron Spring Camp

FS 549

SOUTH

Trailhead for Divide Creek Cutoff Trail

DIVIDE

FS 402

ROAD

UNCOMPAHGRE

NATIONAL

FOREST

FS 565

Red Canyon Overlook

TRAIL 125

| | Paved Road |
| | Maintained Dirt |
| | Unmaintained Dirt |
| | Singletrack Trail |
| | Selected Route |

0        1 Kilometer

0                1 Mile

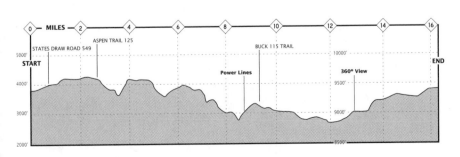

0    MILES    2        4        6        8        10        12        14        16

STATES DRAW ROAD 549

ASPEN TRAIL 125

BUCK 115 TRAIL

5000'

START

Power Lines

10000'

360° View

END

4000'

9500'

3000'

9000'

2000'

8500'

# Ride Information

## ◐ Trail Contacts:
**U.S. Forest Service, Ouray Ranger District**, Montrose, CO; (970) 249-3711 • **Cascade Bicycles**, Montrose, CO; (970) 249-7375 • **Colorado Plateau Mountain Bike Trail Association**, Grand Junction, CO; (970) 241-9561

## ◑ Schedule:
Late May to October

## ❓ Local Information:
**Montrose Visitors and Convention Bureau**, Montrose, CO; (970) 240-1429 • **Montrose Chamber of Commerce**, Montrose, CO; (970) 249-5000 or 1-800-923-5515 • **Visitor Information Center**, Montrose, CO; (970) 249-1726 • **Bureau of Land Management, Uncompahgre Resource Area**, Montrose, CO; (970) 249-6047

## 💡 Local Events/Attractions:
**Black Canyon of the Gunnison**, Montrose, CO; (970) 249-1915 – *for info call (970) 249-7036* • **American Handgunner World Shoot-off Championship**, *in July, Montrose, CO – contact the Montrose Visitors and Convention Bureau at (970) 240-1429.* • **Montrose County Historical Museum**, mid May to October, Montrose, CO; (970) 249-2085 • **Ute Indian Museum**, Montrose, CO; (970) 249-3098

## 🐾 Tours:
**Tour de Gold**, in September, Montrose, CO; (970) 249-8055

## 🍴 Restaurants:
**Sicily's Italian Restaurant**, Montrose, CO; (970) 249-9199 • **Daily Bread & Bakery**, Montrose, CO; (970) 249-8444 **Sakura**, Montrose, CO; (970) 249-8230

## 👥 Organizations:
**Montrose Mountain Bike Club**, Montrose, CO – *contact Cascade Bicycles at (970) 249-7375* • **The Colorado Plateau Mountain Bike Trail Association (COPMOBA)**, Grand Junction, CO; (970) 241-9561

## 🚲 Local Bike Shops:
**Cascade Bicycles**, Montrose, CO; (970) 249-7375 • **Grand Mesa Cyclery Inc.**, Montrose, CO; (970) 249-7515

## Ⓝ Maps:
**USGS maps:** Antone Spring, CO; Pryor Creek, CO • **Montrose Area Bicycling Trails** – *available at all bike shops* • **Uncompahgre National Forest Map** – *available from the U.S. Forest Service, Ouray Ranger District (970) 249-3711*

mal, they'd pray for it before releasing the arrow. The Utes believed they possessed an intuitive understanding of the inner workings of nature. This ability helped them to rouse the bear from hibernation with the "Bear Dance" in early spring—the awakening of bears marked the beginning of spring, which would allow for an early growing season.

Perhaps it seems fitting that the Uncompahgre Plateau should remain relatively hidden, untainted by the development that has since disrespected so much of Colorado's mountains. Undoubtedly the Utes would agree that that which is left pure is blessed with strength. Today, the Uncompahgre Plateau remains a natural, if not formidable, monument to the earliest Americans.

As you weave your course along the Aspen Trail, through thick stands of aspen and over impeccably smooth singletrack, you can imagine what it must be like to be in a Bev Doolittle painting. Herds of wapiti (American elk) stand motionless, almost invisible, in the whites, greens, and golds of the aspen trees. Although not very technical, the trail offers a beautiful ride, one that can be ridden fast without fear of high-speed impact. This fast ride lasts until you pass a vista on the right that looks out over the small town of Nucla. Soon thereafter, you reach the route's first technical climb, featuring many exposed rocks on tight singletrack.

This climb doesn't last long. The trail levels out again into another aspen glen. After five miles, the trail descends rapidly through a ponderosa and lodgepole pine forest. Once it connects with the Dry Creek Cutoff Trail, you'll intersect and cross the Divide Road, rejoining the Dry Creek Cutoff Trail on the other side. From here the riding gets considerably more technical—a definite wakeup call from the casual Aspen Trail. The trail descends quickly over loose rocky terrain to Dry Creek and the southern tip of the Buck Trail.

The Buck Trail begins as a rough looking dirt road. Travelling in a northerly direction through the aspens, the road eventually disintegrates to singletrack as it makes its speedy descent, paralleling the pole-worm fence of the national forest boundary. From atop the high plateau at 12.6 miles, you're offered southeasterly views of Mount Sneffels (14,686), Wetterhorn Peak (14,017), and Uncompahgre Peak (14,309); and northerly views of the Grand Mesa and Garfield Mesa. Like white caps on a sea of green, the San Juan range rolls quietly in the distance.

From here descend through the meadows and aspens to a stock tank at 13.3 miles. Just after passing the stock tank, you'll have to grind up a tough, steep climb on loose dirt. Alan Ardizone, resident bike guru and owner of Cascade Bicycles, calls this section of trail the "50 percenter hill"—meaning that riders, if lucky, make this climb only 50 percent of the time. From the top of this hill, it's a mellow cruise back to your vehicle.

Atop a high plateau with the Gunnison Range in the background.

# 6

# Deep Creek Trail

## Ride Summary

The Deep Creek Trail might be one of Telluride's best. Although there's a tough climb to the Deep Creek Trail intersection, the trail, itself, offers a fast romp through thick aspens and pine. The Deep Creek Trail runs a technically challenging descent over exposed rocks and roots before dumping you into a fast meadow. Views of the Wilson Peaks are outstanding. Riders will find the switchbacks down to the Deep Creek trailhead a delight. For those of you who like speed anyway you can get it, you'll enjoy the mad race down Last Dollar Road to its intersection with Colorado 145. Take care, though. The stop sign at the end of Last Dollar Road, right before the road meets with the highway, comes up quickly.

## Ride Specs

**Start:** From the clock tower in downtown Telluride
**Length:** 15-mile loop
**Approximate Riding Time:** Advanced Riders, 2–2½ hours; Intermediate Riders, 3–4 hours
**Technical Difficulty Rating:** Technically challenging due to the rocky terrain
**Physical Difficulty Rating:** Physically challenging to demanding due to the trail's steep grades and high elevations
**Terrain:** Paved road, paved bike path, dirt road, and singletrack. The terrain encountered is mountainous: slide areas, talus fields, thick-wooded forests, soft and tacky earth, steep climbs and descents, and creek crossings.
**Elevation Gain:** 3,209 feet
**Nearest Town:** Telluride, CO
**Other Trail Users:** Hikers and campers
**Canine Compatibility:** Dog friendly

## Getting There

**From downtown Telluride:** Pedal east on Colorado Avenue to the courthouse and clock tower in the middle of town by the Oak Street park. Begin your ride here. *DeLorme: Colorado Atlas & Gazetteer:* Page 76, A 2-3

Imagine a force so strong that it could wipe out a small town in seconds, leaving nothing but silent devastation in its wake. A force preceded by a thunderous boom, or sometimes no sound at all. A force that can reach speeds of over 100 mph and bear the weight of thousands of tons. Now imagine riding through the path of such a force. How about twice? Yes, the Deep Creek Trail passes through two avalanche paths, one below Campbell Peak and the other below Iron Mountain. Colorado is notorious for avalanches. In fact, Colorado has the highest reported avalanche rate in the country. And no one knows, with any real degree of accuracy, exactly how many avalanches actually occur in Colorado's vast backcountry. Many of Colorado's avalanches, therefore, go unreported.

Passing through Mount Campbell's Avalanche Path.

Avalanches have, quite curiously, reached somewhat of a celebrity-status in Colorado. A 50-mile stretch of U.S. Route 550 (between the Purgatory Ski Area north of Durango to Ouray) boasts over 100 regular avalanche paths. Most of these paths can be identified by name. The East Riverside Path, just five miles south of Ouray, is arguably one of Colorado's most dangerous. This section of U.S. Route 550 has taken a number of lives over the years. Because of the tremendous threat, a cement roof was constructed over the section of road to deflect debris into Canyon Creek.

Of all the mountain ranges in Colorado, the San Juan range of Southwest Colorado is perhaps the most noted for its high number of avalanches. The town of Telluride, home to the Deep Creek Trail, is tucked in the far, eastern end of a box canyon and surrounded on three sides by the sheer cliffs and soaring peaks of the San Juan Mountains. On average, Telluride receives somewhere in the vicinity of 300 inches of snow a year. The large temperature difference between the warmer, lower layers of snow and the colder surface layers create snow layer instability. Coupled with a heavy annual snowfall, this makes Telluride a prime avalanche location. And Telluride has endured its share of avalanche hardships.

## **Miles**Directions

**0.0 START** from the courthouse and clock tower in downtown Telluride on Colorado Avenue. Ride west on Colorado Avenue out of town and intersect the paved bicycle path.

**1.5** Just after passing the Texaco station, cross a cattle guard and bear right onto dirt FS 637. Begin riding up FS 637.

**2.2** FS 637 intersects with Eider Creek Trail, a gated doubletrack off to the left, near some camping sites. Bear left, passing through the gate, onto this doubletrack and continue climbing in a northerly direction. Soon thereafter, bear left again at another intersection and begin a steep and rocky climb on the doubletrack.

**3.0** Cross Eider Creek.

**3.5** Arrive at a short, but technically demanding rocky climb—probably a hike-a-bike for all but the most adept.

**3.7** Eider Creek Trail meets Trail 418 (Deep Creek Trail) at a "T" intersection. Trail 418 travels both left and right. Bear left here, continuing in a westerly direction. Note: there is no trail marker at this intersection.

**4.0** Pass the "Deep Creek" trail sign to your right.

**4.8** Cross an old logging road and continue on the singletrack. Descend quickly through a young aspen forest.

**5.0** Pass through an avalanche path of Campbell Peak.

**5.8** Pass through Iron Mountain's avalanche path, with breathtaking views of Wilson Peak.

**6.4** Arrive at a beautiful vista, offering expansive views of the Telluride ski resort and the San Juan Range. Intersect an old logging road that climbs sharply to the right into a stand of aspens. A sign facing in the opposite direction from which you came reads "Deep Creek Trail and Mill Creek – 4." Continue straight, however, descending on this old logging road in a southwesterly direction.

**6.6** This old logging road leads to a green, private property gate to the left. Bear right here, continuing on Trail 418 singletrack, passing a trail marker to the right.

**7.7** Reach the intersection of Trail 418 and Whipple Mountain Trail. Cross Sheep Creek and intersect a road marked with two trail signs. The sign on the left reads "Last Dollar Road" (FS 638) and "Deep Creek Trailhead – 0.5 mi." The sign on the right reads "Deep Creek Trail 418, Whipple Mtn Trail – 3, Mill Creek – 6." Bear left here onto this dirt road, following signs for "Last Dollar Road" (FS 638) and "Deep Creek Trailhead – 0.5 mi."

**8.2** The road forks. Bear right and pass through the barbwire fence and descend switchbacks through the meadow to the Deep Creek Trailhead.

**8.7** Reach the Deep Creek Trailhead. Bear left onto FS 638 (Last Dollar Road).

**9.8** FS 638 turns to pavement by the stop sign. Bear left onto the paved FS 638 and descend to Society Turn and CO 145.

**11.7** FS 638 intersects with CO 145 at Society Turn. Cross CO 145 and bear left onto the paved bike bath back to town.

**15.0** Arrive at the courthouse and clock tower in downtown Telluride.

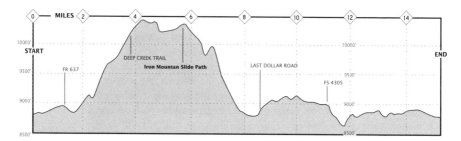

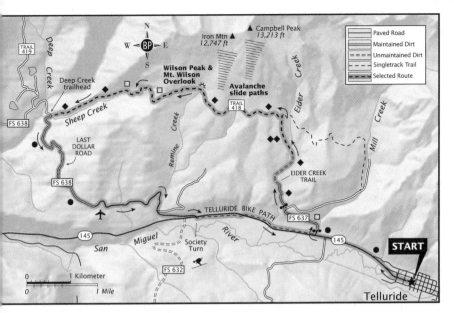

In 1902 an avalanche razed part of the Liberty Mine, located just outside of town, killing seven and injuring several more. Concussions created by the slide's thunderous roar shattered windows in Telluride. A second slide would hit the Liberty Mine's rescue team. Luckily, it hurt no one. However, while transporting some of the dead and injured back to Telluride, a third slide struck the team, killing an additional three and injuring five more. Another story tells of a home caught in the path of an avalanche. Two women on the first floor were crushed, while a baby in an upstairs room sustained only a minor scratch on the cheek. In Rico, a small town south of Telluride, a man woke to find himself sleeping under the stars. A slow-moving avalanche had slipped its way into the man's bedroom and pushed both him and his bed into the cold night sky. These and other stories could fill volumes. The key to our safety in avalanche country is understanding.

Avalanches range from thin to broad, slow to fast, dry to wet, and shallow to deep. The thinnest slide down a slope in slivers. The broadest take down whole mountainsides at a time. The slowest move at a rate of two miles an hour. The fastest can move in excess of 200 miles an hour. The drier avalanches usually move the quickest, while the wetter ones move more slowly. Some peel off only an inch of snow, while others can carry an entire winter's snowpack. Of the many varieties of avalanches, there are essentially two you should know: the *loose-snow avalanche* and the *slab avalanche*. A loose-snow avalanche usually begins at a specific point and flows down a mountainside like a visual current in the shape of an inverted "V." The slab avalanche includes a large cohesive section of snow, sliding down at one time. Of the two, slab avalanches are more dangerous, as they invariably involve large and heavy amounts of snow.

In assessing whether a slope may slide, you should consider three things: terrain, weather, and snowpack. Stay away from cornices that hang over ridges. Look for rocks, trees, shrubs, anything that may anchor snow better. Avalanches usually occur after big storms when the newly fallen snow slides off of the snowy base underneath. High winds and dramatic shifts in air temperature should also be duly noted. Finally, analyzing snowpack is essential, but involves digging into the snow and observing its layers. The *Life-Link Snow Pit Card* offers a template of important information in assessing snow type. Fredston and Fesler's *Snow Sense*, along with LaChapelle's *The ABCs of Avalanche Safety*, provide important further reading for avalanches and avalanche safety.

While traveling in avalanche country, look for paths of old slides (fallen trees) and listen for the snow settling. The unmistakable "whoompf" sound of snow settling means that air is being forced from underlying snow, indicating weak or unstable layers. When crossing exposed slopes, cross one at a time. A transceiver is a must for winter backcountry travelers, as is an avalanche shovel. If caught in a slide, transceivers transmit a signal that can be received by other members of your party. This signal, along with their shovels, can be used in locating the lost member. If you do get caught in an avalanche, try to "swim,"—much like body surfing—to stay on top. Keep your hands in front of your face, creating an air pocket, before being buried by the slide. Try to stay calm as you wait for help to arrive.

Prior to arriving at the Deep Creek Trail's two avalanche paths, you must climb some rocky doubletrack as you make your way through thick aspen stands with the Eider Creek to your left. Though the riding here is tough, this section is simply entrancing. Once on the Deep Creek Trail, climb a brief spurt before descending on soft forest earth carpeted with pine needles. After crossing an old logging road at mile 4.8, descend through a young aspen forest. You're dropped into the avalanche path of Campbell Peak (13,213 feet). A little farther up is Iron Mountain's (12,747 feet) avalanche path. Notice the deadfall. These torn paths are a good sign of avalanche activity.

Most slide paths lie on east and north-facing slopes, since they typically receive more snow and harsher weather. The path itself has three individual parts. The "starting zone," as the name implies, denotes where a slide begins. The "track" lies in the middle of the path. Here the avalanche is no longer accelerating but is keeping a constant speed. Generally, an avalanche doesn't "pick up" any additional snow once in the "track." Finally, the path ends, as does the avalanche, when it reaches the "runout zone." Most slope angles range from 30 to 45 degrees in the "starting zone." The "track" typically runs along a 20 to 30-degree pitch, while the "runout zone" has less than 20-degree slope.

After passing the beautiful vistas of the Wilson Peaks, you arrive at the private property gate at mile 6.6. From here the Deep Creek Trail descends steeply over rocky singletrack through tall stands of aspen before coming to a smooth and fast, hassle-free descent into a large meadow. Cross Sheep Creek and bear left onto the road. Descend the fun switchbacks to the Deep Creek Trailhead. Bear left again onto the Last Dollar Road. Intersect with Colorado 145, and slip, slide, and away back to Telluride.

Heading toward Deep Creek Trailhead, with the Wilson Peaks in the foreground.

# Ride Information

## 🌀 Trail Contacts:
**Paragon Ski & Sport**, Telluride, CO; (970) 728-4525

## 🕐 Schedule:
Mid June to October

## ❓ Local Information:
**Telluride Visitor Center and Chamber of Commerce**, Telluride, CO; (970) 728-6265 or 1-800-525-2717

## 💡 Local Events/Attractions:
**Telluride Bluegrass Festival**, in June, Telluride, CO – contact Telluride Visitor Center and Chamber of Commerce at (970) 728-6265 or 1-800-525-2717 • **Melee in the Mines Mountain Bike Races**, in July, Telluride, CO – contact Telluride Visitor Center and Chamber of Commerce at (970) 728-6265 or 1-800-525-2717 • **Wild Mushrooms Conference**, in August, Telluride, CO – contact Telluride Visitor Center and Chamber of Commerce at (970) 728-6265 or 1-800-525-2717 • **Film Festival**, in September, Telluride, CO – contact Telluride Visitor Center and Chamber of Commerce at (970) 728-6265 or 1-800-525-2717 • **Blues & Brews Festival**, in September, Telluride, CO – contact Telluride Visitor Center and Chamber of Commerce at (970) 728-6265 or 1-800-525-2717

## 🛏 Accommodations:
**Town of Telluride Park & Camp**, Telluride, CO; (970) 728-2173 – cost is $11 per night; camping, showers and toilet facilities; available, May 15 through October 15

## 🍴 Restaurants:
**La Cocina De Luz**, Telluride, CO; (970) 728-9355 – Mexican take-out and catering company • **Rustico Ristorante**, Telluride, CO; (970) 728-4046 • **Smuggler's**, Telluride, CO; (970) 728-0919 – Telluride's only brew pub

## 🚲 Tours Guides:
**Telluride Outside**, Telluride, CO; (970) 728-3895 or 1-800-831-6230 or www.tellurideoutside.com • **Back Country Biking**, Telluride, CO; (970) 728-0861 or cell (970) 519-0874 • **Telluride Sports/Adventure Desk**, Telluride, CO; (970) 728-4477 or 1-800-828-7547 • **Telski/Mountain Adventures**, Telluride, CO; (970) 728-6900

## 📖 Other Resources:
*The Avalanche Book*, by Betsy R. Armstrong and Knox Williams, Fulcrum Publishing, Golden, CO • *Snow Sense: A Guide to Evaluating Snow Avalanche Hazard*, by Jill Fredston and Doug Fesler, Alaska Mountain Safety Center, Anchorage, AK • *The ABCs of Avalanche Safety*, by Edward LaChapelle, The Mountaineers, Seattle, WA

## 🚲 Local Bike Shops:
**Paragon Ski & Sport**, Telluride, CO; (970) 728-4525 • **Easy Rider Mountain Sports**, Telluride, CO; (970) 728-4734 • **Telluride Sports**, Telluride, CO; (970) 728-4477 or 1-800-828-7547

## Ⓝ Maps:
**USGS maps:** Grayhead, CO; Telluride, CO • *Trails Illustrated* map: #504, Durango, Silverton, Telluride, Pagosa Springs and Cortez • **Map of the Mountains of Silverton, Telluride, and Ouray; Drake Mountain Maps** – available at select area outdoor shops • **Uncompahgre National Forest Map** – available at Telluride Visitor Center and Chamber of Commerce (970) 728-6265 or 1-800-525-2717

# Extreme Snow Bikes—Alpine Snow Bicycle Association

Berthoud Pass, which straddles the Continental Divide at 11,307 feet, traditionally has tempted only the best backcountry skiers and snowboarders to swoosh through its 400 to 500 inches of annual snowfall. Until now.

There's a new breed of adventurer on Colorado's winter mountains. He doesn't fall within the skier/snowboarder camp or the mountain biker camp, but rather, somewhere in between. Expanding the boundaries of what can be done on snow, snow bikers are taking to the hills in their modified BMX and vintage Laguna bicycles and ripping it up, smiling all the way.

"We were up here one day taking photos for ESPN," says Richard Fischer. "The wind blew so hard that it lifted my Ford 250's rear suspension four to five inches." Fischer owns and manages the Extreme Snow Bikes and Alpine Snow Bicycle Association.

According to Fischer, snow biking has been around since the mid 70s. Out of necessity, Coloradoans started studding their bicycle tires with screws as a way to get to and from work without having to contend with the hazards of driving in snowy conditions.

Today, thanks to the efforts of Fischer and Butch Bendele (creator of the Wake Board), snow biking has made its way to the X-Games, found a home among NORBA-sanctioned events, and been officially recognized by the Union Cyclist International (UCI), the world governing body for cycling.

For the past several years Colorado has held a variety of snow biking races. Extreme Snow Bikes has competed in Leadville, at Breckenridge, and Arapahoe Basin—to name just a few. Their proving grounds are the windswept mountains of Berthoud Pass, where speeds in excess of 70 mph are reached on bulletproof snow.

Racing is only part of the new snow bikers' paradigm. Unlike snowboarding, which began life at Colorado ski areas as a recreational vehicle, snow biking has emerged as a competitive vehicle. The goal of Fischer and the Alpine Snow Bicycle Association is to bring snow biking more into the mainstream—as snowboarding has since become.

Fischer admits: "Everything I've done since day-one—working with NORBA, creating a dialogue with ski areas, racing with Extreme Snow Bikes—has been for the ultimate goal of recreational snow biking at ski areas." In response to this single goal, the Alpine Snow Bicycle Association—a union of promoters and snow bikers from Alaska to Maine—was created in 1996 as a way to bring snow bikers together and exchange ideas. With no membership fee, the Alpine Snow Bicycle Association is intended for anybody.

Although the future of snow biking remains uncertain for now, no one can dispute the fact that it's an intriguing concept, not to mention a lot of fun. To Fischer's credit, people will never be able to look at a mountain bike quite the same way. With an air of boastful triumph, Fischer laughs, "...always that preconception of a bicycle as a summer vehicle, not any more."

**Extreme Snow Bikes**
Alpine Snow Bicycle Association
Richard Fischer, Owner/Operator
620 South Knox Court
Denver, CO 80218
(303) 935-8494

# Wasatch Trail

## Ride Summary

The Wasatch Trail offers a truly high alpine adventure. Its rugged terrain is not for the faint-hearted. No Van Trapps singing here. This trail is mountain biking's equivalent to skiing in Valdez, Alaska. If it doesn't kill you, it won't just make you stronger, it'll make you fearless. Steep climbs, rocky terrain, narrow switchbacks, huge drop-offs, and hanging canyon walls all attest to this trail's dominance over any other. Mountain biking at its most extreme. This is by far the hardest trail in the book and considered by many to be the hardest trail in Colorado—if not the country. Only expert riders in great physical shape should consider this trail. For a shorter ride which includes part of this route description, you can ride to the top of Bridal Veil Falls (Colorado's tallest waterfall at 365 feet) and return the same way.

## Ride Specs

**Start:** From Telluride's Town Park & Campground
**Length:** 15.4-mile loop
**Approximate Riding Time:** Advanced Riders, 3-4 hours; Intermediate Riders, 5-6 hours
**Technical Difficulty Rating:** Technically demanding due to the preponderance of rocks and large drop-offs, coupled with narrow singletrack and tight, steeply descending switchbacks.
**Physical Difficulty Rating:** Physically demanding due to the steep climbs at elevations exceeding 13,000 feet.
**Terrain:** Paved street, dirt road, 4WD road, and singletrack. The terrain of this trail includes loose rocks, tundra-like environments above timberline, steep grades, snowfields, hillside meadows, and deep-carved canyons.
**Elevation Gain:** 5,300 feet
**Nearest Town:** Telluride, CO
**Other Trail Users:** Hikers, backpackers, and sightseers
**Canine Compatibility:** Not dog friendly – due to vehicular traffic on the Bridal Veil Falls Road

## Getting There

**From downtown Telluride:** Pedal east on Colorado Avenue (heading toward Bridal Veil Falls) to Maple Street and the Town Park & Campground. Begin your ride from the Town Park & Campground, continuing in an easterly direction toward Bridal Veil Falls. *DeLorme: Colorado Atlas & Gazetteer:* Page 76, A-3

### "To Hell U Ride!"

- *To emphasize its remoteness, railroad conductors would announce "To-hell-you-ride" as they arrived in Telluride. A mining mecca in the late 1800s, Telluride's mining tunnels would sometimes stretch as far as a thousand feet underground. To light their way this far under the earth's surface, Telluride miners invented alternating current (AC)—which ultimately led to Telluride's distinction as being the first city in the world with electric streetlights.*

They say that the box canyon in which Telluride sits offers but one way out, west on Colorado 145. To the north, south, and east of town lie the impenetrable mountains of the San Juan Range. Where east Colorado 145 ends, the Bridal Veil Falls Road begins. At first glance, the monoliths of Mendota Peak, Telluride Peak, Ajax Peak, Ingram Peak, Ballard Mountain, and La Junta Peak form a seemingly impass-

The Lewis Mine. If you get here, you've come too far.

able barrier at the eastern end of this box canyon. Further inspection will reveal, however, the unremitting Bridal Veil Falls Road snaking its way to the top and beyond this canyon, eventually connecting with the Wasatch Trail. But like rushing the Denver Bronco's offensive line, expect to take your share of hits before breaking on through to the other side.

The route begins casually enough—riding east on Colorado Avenue to the historic Pandora Mill, located at the headwaters of the San Miguel River. Like Pandora's mythic box of evils, the Pandora Mill marks the entrance to what you might call the quintessential "To-Hell-U-Ride" ride. The cable lines you see overhead once toted ore, at the rate of 300 to 400 tons a day, from the Smuggler-Union Mine, located three miles above in Marshall Basin. Over 4 million ounces of gold, 21 million ounces of silver, and 12 million tons of lead, zinc, and copper were transported along this 6,700-foot aerial tramway to Pandora Mill.

In 1875 Marshall Basin was discovered to be rich in gold, silver, lead, zinc, copper, and iron. John Fallon, a prospector, opened the Sheridan Mine. Rather than develop the mine himself, Fallon leased it to other mining developers and then eventually sold it for $40,000. The Sheridan Mine became another addition to the portfolio of a group of English and Scottish bankers who were living in Shanghai at the time. Their other interests lay in the nearby Mendota, Union, and Smuggler mines.

Roughly one year after Marshall Basin unearthed its pay dirt to Fallon, a prospector by the name of J.B. Ingram found out that the Sheridan and Union claims exceeded the legal limits of their claim by roughly 500 feet. Staking a claim on the area between these two mines, Ingram's fortunate discovery led to the opening of the Smuggler Mine. From a single ton, the Smuggler Mine would yield 18 ounces of gold and 800 ounces of silver. The Smuggler Mine would eventually join with the Union Mine. Their combined claim would unearth a gold vein one mile long. By 1900, the Smuggler-Union Mine laid claim to over 35 miles of excavated tunnels.

From the Pandora Mill, riders continue up the Bridal Veil Falls Road (Lucky #13), as it switches back a number of times to the power plant. This road is simply a warm up for what lies ahead. As you climb through this rugged terrain, you can't help but marvel at the tenacity of Telluride's earliest miners. Once you pass the power plant, the trail becomes very rocky, offering even tougher climbs. Your only relief comes in the form of the cool trickle of the Bridal Veil Creek to your right. The moisture from the creek and spray from the waterfall allows for wildflowers to grow very late into the season, as late as mid September. Columbine (aquilegia caerules), roundleaf bluebell (campanula rotundifolia), Western monkshood (aconitum columbianum), and Explorer's Gentian (Gentiana calycosa) offer soft contrast to this otherwise brutal terrain.

## MilesDirections

**0.0 START** from the Telluride Town Park & Campground. Begin riding east on Colorado Avenue toward Bridal Veil Falls and the end of the canyon.

**0.3** Pass the Lone Tree Cemetery to your left—the final resting place of miners killed in a fire in the 1880s.

**1.4** The pavement ends and the Bridal Veil Falls Road 13 begins.

**4.3** Bear right as the Bridal Veil Falls Road 13 meets an intersection. (The left fork travels against one-way traffic.) Duck under a gate and continue climbing above and behind the power plant on the old and rugged 4WD road.

**6.2** Reach the intersection with the Blue Lake Road. The left fork leads to Blue Lake, while the right fork continues in a southerly direction, making its way around La Junta Peak (13,472 feet). Bear right here, heading toward La Junta Peak.

**6.8** Pass an old miner's cabin to your left. The rough 4WD road splits. Bear right here, following alongside the old rusted drainpipe to the right. Cairns begin to mark your route.

**7.8** The trail meets another intersection. Bear right (south) at this intersection on the more primitive looking road. Grind up this very

steep shell-rock road, heading toward the rim of Bridal Veil Basin. Continuing straight (east) will lead you to Bridal Veil Basin, passing the old Lewis Mine to your left as you make your way to Lewis Lake. If you've come to this Mine, you've gone too far.

**8.3** Reach the intersection of the road that cuts across the rim of Bridal Veil Basin. To your left is a trail sign for Bridal Veil Trail, pointing back in the direction from which you came. Bear left onto this road, continuing a more moderate ascent on an easier road to the saddle between Wasatch Mountain (13,555 feet) and Oscar's Pass.

**8.8** A Bear Creek Trail sign is to your right. Bear right here, following the Bear Creek Trail sign to the saddle and the beginning of Wasatch Trail 508.

**9.0** Arrive at the saddle (Blick's Pass) and the beginning of Wasatch Trail 508. A trail marker atop this saddle reads "Bridal Veil Basin" and "Wasatch Trail." Descend in a westerly direction on the singletrack of Wasatch Trail 508 through a talus field.

**10.4** Reach Bear Creek and the junction of Wasatch Trail 508, the East Fork Bear Creek, and Trail 513. Do not cross the creek at this point. Instead, bear right (north), following

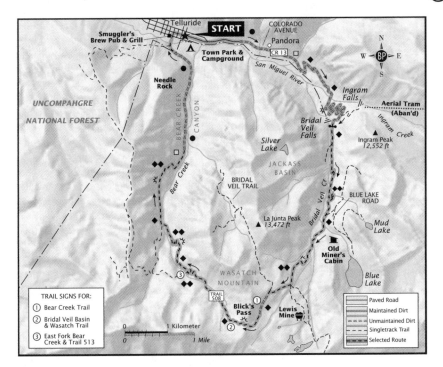

signs for East Fork Bear Creek and Trail 513, with Bear Creek to your left.

**10.8** Cross another talus field as you descend on remarkably tight and steep switchbacks.

**11.4** Cross Bear Creek and continue riding in a southerly direction along Wasatch Trail 508.

**11.9** Cross a footbridge pressed firmly against the canyon walls of the Bear Creek canyon.

**13.0** Intersect with the Bear Creek Trail. Bear left onto the Bear Creek Trail and head back to town.

**15.0** Reach the Bear Creek trailhead and South Pine Street. Intersect with the paved South Pine Street and ride north to Colorado Avenue.

**15.1** Pass Smuggler's Brew Pub & Grill to your left.

**15.2** Reach the junction of South Pine Street and Colorado Avenue. Bear right onto Colorado Avenue and ride east toward the Telluride Town Park & Campground.

**15.4** Arrive at the Town Park & Campground and your vehicle.

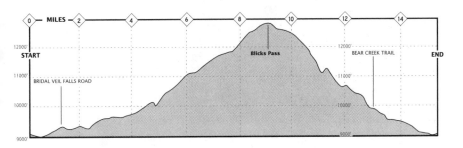

Scrap your way to the Blue Lake turnoff, after which you'll find a grueling loose rocky climb above timberline. This climb may last upward of one to two hours, so be prepared for unexpected weather patterns. Bear right again after roughly one mile from passing the abandoned miner's cabin and climb up this loose, shell-rock road. This is the most grueling climb of the day. Once you intersect with the road that bears the Bridal Veil Trail sign, the going gets considerably easier.

Once at the Bear Creek sign, give yourself a pat on the back. You've broken on through. From here you're offered stunning views of Bridal Veil Basin (the basin through which you just road), Lookout Peak, Ophir Pass, and Ophir. To enjoy a panoramic view of the surrounding San Juan Mountains, you can opt to take a 0.3-mile spur to the top of Oscar's Pass, dividing Telluride and the town of Ophir.

Once on the Wasatch Trail, the descent begins with a bone-jarring tour through a scree field, before dumping you into Lena Basin and the headwaters of Bear Creek. The hillside meadows of Lena Basin are laden with tight switchbacks over loose sand and rock. These first switchbacks eventually relent to offer you a straighter ride through a drainage, as the trail continues in a westerly direction. After about 10 miles, the trail falls precipitously to Bear Creek, which lies about 60 feet below. This section demands technical skill. Aside from the steep and large drop off, the trail is tight and rock-laden.

After the junction of the Wasatch Trail and the East Fork Bear Creek and Trail 513, the Wasatch Trail switches back a number of times down a steep hillside meadow to meet with Bear Creek again. These switchbacks are very tight and steep. As you near the second intersection with Bear Creek at mile 11.3, notice a snowfield over the creek. This field is usually frozen through the whole summer. Riders are ill advised to walk on this snowfield, since it could break, dropping you some 15 feet into the creek below. Cross the creek just below the snowfield.

After crossing the creek, the trail levels out for a bit, offering views of Telluride, before delivering you to the steep canyon walls of Bear Creek Valley. The Bear Creek Valley was once a sacred ceremonial ground for early Ute Indians. Here, prayers and vision quests were conducted. Riders alike, may also find comfort in prayer, since this section of trail skirts the steep hanging walls of the canyon some 80 to 100 feet above the creek. With big drops and large rocks, this is no place to make a mistake. After several dizzying drop-offs, ledges, and tight switchbacks, you eventually arrive at the Bear Creek Trail. Take the Bear Creek Trail to Pine Street and belly up to the bar at Smuggler's Brew Pub & Grill.

# Ride Information

## 📞 Trail Contacts:
**Paragon Ski & Sport**, Telluride, CO; (970) 728-4525

## 🕐 Schedule:
Mid July to mid September

## ❓ Local Information:
**Telluride Visitor Center and Chamber of Commerce**, Telluride, CO; (970) 728-6265 or 1-800-525-2717

## 💡 Local Events/Attractions:
**Telluride Bluegrass Festival**, in June, Telluride, CO – *contact Telluride Visitor Center and Chamber of Commerce at (970) 728-6265 or 1-800-525-2717* • **Melee in the Mines Mountain Bike Races**, in July, Telluride, CO – *contact Telluride Visitor Center and Chamber of Commerce at (970) 728-6265 or 1-800-525-2717* • **Wild Mushrooms Conference**, in August, Telluride, CO – *contact Telluride Visitor Center and Chamber of Commerce at (970) 728-6265 or 1-800-525-2717* • **Film Festival**, in September, Telluride, CO – *contact Telluride Visitor Center and Chamber of Commerce at (970) 728-6265 or 1-800-525-2717* • **Blues & Brews Festival**, in September, Telluride, CO – *contact Telluride Visitor Center and Chamber of Commerce at (970) 728-6265 or 1-800-525-2717*

## 🛏️ Accommodations:
**Town of Telluride Park & Camp**, Telluride, CO; (970) 728-2173 – *cost is $11 per night; camping, showers and toilet facilities; available, May 15 through October 15*

## 🍴 Restaurants:
**La Cocina De Luz**, Telluride, CO; (970) 728-9355 – *Mexican take-out and catering company* • **Rustico Ristorante**, Telluride, CO; (970) 728-4046 • **Smuggler's Brew Pub & Grill**, Telluride, CO; (970) 728-0919 – *Telluride's only brew pub*

## 🔧 Tours Guides:
**Telluride Outside**, Telluride, CO; (970) 728-3895 or 1-800-831-6230 or *www.tellurideoutside.com* • **Back Country Biking**, Telluride, CO; (970) 728-0861 or cell (970) 519-0874 • **Telluride Sports/Adventure Desk**, Telluride, CO; (970) 728-4477 or 1-800-828-7547 • **Telski/Mountain Adventures**, Telluride, CO; (970) 728-6900

## 🚲 Local Bike Shops:
**Paragon Ski & Sport**, Telluride, CO; (970) 728-4525 • **Easy Rider Mountain Sports**, Telluride, CO; (970) 728-4734 • **Telluride Sports**, Telluride, CO; (970) 728-4477 or 1-800-828-7547

## 🅝 Maps:
**USGS maps:** Telluride, CO; Ophir, CO • *Trails Illustrated* map: #504, Durango, Silverton, Telluride, Pagosa Springs, and Cortez • **Map of the Mountains of Silverton, Telluride, and Ouray; Drake Mountain Maps** – *available at select area outdoor shops* • **Uncompahgre National Forest Map** – *available at Telluride Visitor Center and Chamber of Commerce (970) 728-6265 or 1-800-525-2717*

# Hermosa Creek Trail

## Ride Summary

The Hermosa Creek Trail has long been considered as one of the country's top rides—and for good reason. It is nearly 20 miles of descending smooth-running singletrack beside the beautiful Hermosa Creek. While not overly technical, there are some off-camber sections of trail that look precipitously down to the creek. Complicated with roots and rocks, these sections lend an element of technicality not otherwise encountered. Those packing a collapsible fishing rod will find that the north half of this ride offers great access to the creek.

## Ride Specs

**Start:** From Hermosa Creek Trail's northern trailhead, off of FS 578
**Length:** 19.1-mile point-to-point
**Approximate Riding Time:** Advanced Riders, 2 hours; Intermediate Riders, 3 hours
**Technical Difficulty Rating:** Technically moderate due to some rocky and steep sections
**Physical Difficulty Rating:** Physically easy to moderate due to the fact that most of this ride descends with only a few climbs mixed in
**Terrain:** Singletrack. The trail follows the Hermosa Creek to the town of Hermosa. There are a number of creek crossings, as well as rocky sections to test your skills. Some of the terrain slopes precipitously to the creek at times, while at other times the trail delivers smooth and fast running singletrack.
**Elevation Gain:** 1,040 feet
**Nearest Town:** Hermosa, CO
**Other Trail Users:** Hikers, ATVs, hunters, picnickers, and anglers
**Canine Compatibility:** Dog friendly

## Getting There

**From Durango to Hermosa Creek Trail's northern trailhead:** Drive north on U.S. 550 for 22.8 miles to the Purgatory Ski Resort. Bear left into the resort by the Purgatory sign. The road into the ski resort splits immediately, so keep right. This will turn into FS 578 (San Juan CR 38). Pass the ski resort on your left. At mile 23.2, the pavement ends. At 26.1 miles, FS 578 intersects with FS 581. Bear right, continuing on FS 578. Follow signs for Sig Creek Campground and Hermosa Creek Trail. FS 581 bears left and leads to Elbert Creek Road and Trail. At 26.5 miles, FS 578 intersects with FS 579. Bear left here, continuing on FS 578 and follow signs for Sig Creek Campground and Hermosa Creek Trail. Pass Sig Creek Campground at mile 29.8. After the campground, FS 578 forks. Continue straight (to the right) at this fork. At mile 31.7, bear left into the Hermosa Creek's northern trailhead. *DeLorme: Colorado Atlas & Gazetteer.* Page 76, C-2

**Shuttle Point (Hermosa Creek Trail's southern trailhead):** From Durango drive north on U.S 550 for eight miles to Hermosa. Bear left onto La Plata CR 203 and immediately bear right onto CR 201 (Hermosa Creek Road), marked by a sign that reads "Hermosa Creek Trail – 4 miles." At mile 9.7, cross a cattle guard and enter into the San Juan National Forest. Once in the national forest, the road becomes FS 576. The pavement ends at mile 10.5. At mile 12.8, reach the Hermosa Creek's southern trailhead. *DeLorme: Colorado Atlas & Gazetteer.* Page 86, A 2-3

Hermosa Park and the San Juans in the background.

Durango's Hermosa Creek Trail is one of Colorado's classic rides. Located just 12.8 miles north of Durango, the trail spears directly through the heart of the San Juan National Forest. And that's no small feat considering the San Juan National Forest is 2,086,484 acres of volcanic domes, jagged aretes, and verdant forests. What this ride offers is a beautiful—that's "hermosa" in Spanish—tour through dense forests and alongside a resounding creek, all under the cover of densely grown plant life. It's absolute paradise.

Starting from behind the Purgatory Ski Resort, site of the 1990 World Mountain Bike Championships, the Hermosa Creek Trail runs for just under 20 miles along smooth-running singletrack to its southernmost terminus at Hermosa. Local riders like Ned Overend and Sara Ballantyne consider the Hermosa Creek Trail to be one of their all-time favorite rides and take pride in the area's World Mountain Bike Championships association. It seems that from its earliest beginnings, the entire Animas Valley has been imbued with an incredible sense of pride.

When the Denver & Rio Grande railroad first started making its way from the silver and gold resources in Silverton through the Animas Valley, circa 1879, it was met with a certain degree of resistance. Animas City, located approximately 2 miles north of the present-day Durango, had already established itself in the Animas Valley as a thriving farming and ranching community. In order for the Denver & Rio Grande to profit from the Silverton mines, it hoped to transport the ore to Animas City for smelting. Although the D&RG railroad offered to develop Animas City as a railroad center, the small community of farmers and ranchers who took such pride in their city's status as the region's trading center refused to be bought.

Undeterred by the town's pride, the Denver & Rio Grande threatened to establish a rival community to the south, bypassing Animas City altogether. That community would turn out to be Durango. Proving to be no match against the railroad's major investors, Animas City would eventually fold and become the north part of present-day Durango. The Denver & Rio Grande's William Bell and Alexander Hunt chose the site of the rival community. Hunt had been the railroad's liaison for some time, traveling as far as Mexico to rally for the rail. In fact, many speculate that Hunt chose the name Durango because of its territorial similarity to Durango, Mexico, from where he had just returned. By 1879, the Durango Trust was formed by wealthy developers from Denver & Rio Grande, whose interests included making Main Avenue, the wholesale street; Second Avenue, the retail section; and Third Avenue, the residential boulevard. Dubbed the "Denver of Southern Colorado," Durango boomed, as little Animas City became nothing more than a railroad stop on the way to Durango.

During Durango's rise to metropolitan proportions, the Denver & Rio Grande tried developing and promoting other satellite communities, which they hoped would mature as well as Durango had. Towns like Hermosa and Elbert City, which enjoyed short-lived successes, just didn't have the staying power of Durango. Though these towns may have been prosperous and home to many in the early years of the Animas Valley, there still remains a sense of pride and endurance in this valley. As years pass and people move in, this pride continues and transcends all aspects of Colorado's Southwest, including its mountain biking.

It's a dog's life.

## MilesDirections

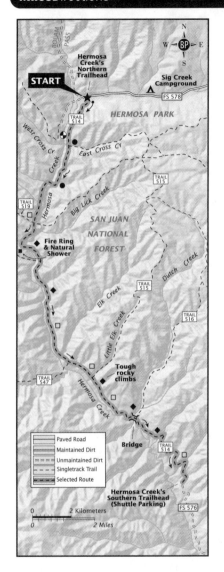

**0.0 START** at the Hermosa Creek Trail's (Trail 514) northern trailhead and begin riding in a southerly direction.

**0.7** Cross a cattle guard and continue riding in a southerly direction.

**1.7** Cross another cattle guard, as the trail meets Hermosa Creek. Cross the creek and continue descending on the trail.

**3.1** Pass Corral Draw Trail (Trail 519) to your right. Continue on the Hermosa Creek Trail.

**4.8** Cross Hermosa Creek via a footbridge and blaze through a large, open meadow surrounded by pine trees. Soon thereafter, the trail climbs up a short, east-facing hillside to the right.

**5.8** Cross Hermosa Creek again via another footbridge.

**6.5** The Hermosa Creek Trail intersects with the Salt Creek Trail (Trail 547). Pass the Salt Creek Trail and continue riding on the Hermosa Creek Trail.

**10.4** Descend a rocky and tight section and cross Little Elk Creek.

**14.0** Proceed down a rough, rocky descent

**14.5** Cross Dutch Creek via a footbridge and begin the first of two tough, but short, climbs to the finish.

**15.4** Pass the intersection with the Dutch Creek Trail and climb steadily into a beautiful stand of aspen.

**16.0** Here begins the second short and steep climb before the trail's end.

**18.0** Begin your final descent to the Hermosa Creek Trail's southern trailhead. Near the end of the trail, the route forks. Bear left and climb the 100 feet to the trailhead.

**19.1** Reach the end of Hermosa Creek Trail and your vehicle.

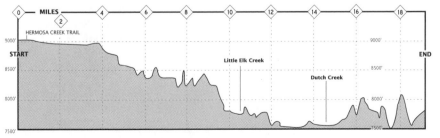

# Ride Information

## ● Trail Contacts:
San Juan Mountains Association (SJMA), Durango, CO; (970) 385-1210 • **Durango Cyclery**, Durango, CO; (970) 247-0747 • **San Juan-Rio Grande National Forests**, Columbine Ranger District, Bayfield, CO; (970) 884-2512

## ◐ Schedule:
June to October

## ● Local Information:
**Durango Area Chamber Resort Association**, Durango, CO; (970) 247-0312 or 1-800-525-8855 • **San Juan National Forest**, Supervisor's Office, Durango, CO; (970) 247-4874 • **Purgatory Resort**, Durango, CO; (970) 247-9000 or 1-800-525-0892 • **Durango**, CO – for information visit www.durango.com • **Animas Ranger District**, Durango, CO; (970) 385-1283

## ● Local Events/Attractions:
**Durango & Silverton Narrow Gauge Railroad**, Durango, CO; (970) 247-2733 or 1-888-872-4607 • **Iron Horse Bicycle Classic**, in May, Durango, CO – contact the Durango Area Chamber Resort Association at (970) 247-0312 or 1-800-525-8855 • **Trimble Hot Springs**, 6 miles north of Durango on U.S. 550, Trimble, CO; (970) 247-0111

## ● Accommodations:
**Strater Hotel**, Durango, CO; (970) 247-4431 or 1-800-247-4431 or www.strater.com

## ● Organizations:
San Juan Mountains Association (SJMA), Durango CO; (970) 385-1210 • **Trails 2000**, Durango, CO; (970) 259-4682

## ● Restaurants:
**Lady Falconburgh's Barley Exchange**, CO; (970) 382-9664 or www.falconburgh.com • **Stonehouse Subs**, Durango, CO; (970) 247-4882 • **Nature's Oasis**, Durango, CO; (970) 247-1988

## ● Tours:
**Fat Tire Downhill**, Durango, CO; (970) 385-1778 • **Southwest Adventures**, Durango, CO; (970) 259-0370 • **Durango Singletrack Tours**, Durango, CO; (970) 385-7489 or 1-888-336-8687

## ● Camps:
**Durango Mountain Bike Camp**, Durango, CO; (970) 259-0238 or (970) 259-0481

## ● Local Bike Shops:
**Durango Cyclery**, Durango, CO; (970) 247-0747 • **Pedal the Peaks**, Durango, CO; (970) 259-6880 or www.big-mountain.com/pedalpks • **Mountain Bike Specialists**, Durango, CO; (970) 247-4066 • **Hard Line Sports**, Durango, CO; (970) 259-9141 • **Hassle Free Sports**, Durango, CO; (970) 259-3874

## ● Maps:
**USGS maps**: Hermosa Peak, CO; Elk Creek, CO; Monument Hill, CO; Hermosa, CO • **Trails Illustrated map**: #504, Durango, Silverton, Telluride, Pagosa Springs, and Cortez • **Bicycle on Public Lands of Southwest Colorado Routes Map** – available at area bike shops

The Hermosa Creek Trail begins by entering into a large pine forest on smooth, wide singletrack. It heads south along the left side of the valley. Once the trail meets Hermosa Creek, it becomes a little rockier. At 3.5 miles, the trail passes underneath large cliffs, their sides covered in streaming moss and fern. Here the primeval forest offers one of the most beautiful sections of the trail. The terrain becomes increasingly muddy and rocky. Passing through an alpine meadow surrounded by large stands of Engelmann spruce, you cross Hermosa Creek and descend into Big Bend. At the intersection of the Hermosa Creek Trail and the Salt Creek Trail there lies a fire pit and picnic area. Here Hermosa Creek provides a small natural shower and bath. Fallen trees have blocked much of the creeks flow, allowing the water to pool atop the branches and letting soft curtains of water fall between the cracks in the limbs—thus, the perfect natural shower.

After passing the Salt Creek Trail, the Hermosa Creek Trail rises above the creek's eastern slopes, falling precipitously to it. This, added to some rocky sections and narrow singletrack, make for a moderately technical ride. Here, along the sweetest section of trail, the terrain gets really playful with tight switches, roots, rocks, and a whole lot of jazz.

From Little Elk Creek you're offered a technically advanced climb. Although short, the trail is narrow and steep and combines roots and rocks to make for a tough climb. Trees hug the sides of the trail tightly. After this section the trail mellows and begins a fast and smooth descent through a lodgepole pine forest. Once you cross Dutch Creek, the trail offers the most physically challenging section of the entire ride. A series of three short climbs tests a rider's staying power all the way to the finish line. Although this trail is mostly downhill, these short climbs challenge anyone who has already ridden 14 miles. After busting out two final miles of climbing, the trail descends speedily for another mile before delivering you to the Hermosa Creek Trail's southern trailhead and your vehicle.

Getting ready at Hermosa Park.

# Log Chutes Trail

## Ride Summary

Located just outside of Durango, the Log Chutes Trail provides an easily accessible ride for riders staying in town or camping near Junction Creek. The section of trail along the historic Neglected Mine Road has been used in the past for the Iron Horse Bicycle Classic downhill course. This section provides a fast and fun descent. The ride can be ridden as either a short or long loop. The short loop is designated an easy ride, while the long loop is more difficult. Featured here is the long loop. The Log Chutes Road is open to vehicles, so be aware.

## Ride Specs

**Start:** From the Log Chutes Trail parking lot
**Length:** 6.5-mile loop
**Approximate Riding Time:** Advanced Riders, 45–60 minutes; Intermediate Riders, 1–2 hours
**Technical Difficulty Rating:** Technically moderate due to some rocky and sandy sections
**Physical Difficulty Rating:** Physically moderate due to some shorter climbs
**Terrain:** Dirt forest road, old logging road, and singletrack. The terrain is very woodsy. There are patches of rock and sand with which to contend; however, most of the trail travels on soft forest earth among conifer trees and aspen.
**Elevation Gain:** 1,532 feet
**Nearest Town:** Durango, CO
**Other Trail Users:** Hikers
**Canine Compatibility:** Dog friendly

## Getting There

**From Durango:** Drive north on Main Avenue for 1.5 miles to 25th Street. Turn left onto 25th Street by the Texaco and Big O Tires. This street becomes Junction Creek Road (La Plata CR 204). Junction Creek Road intersects with La Plata CR 205 at 4.5 miles. Bear left here, continuing on Junction Creek Road, following the sign for the "Junction Creek Campground – 2 miles." Cross the cattle guard and enter into the San Juan National Forest at mile 5.1. Junction Creek Road turns into FS 171. Continue on the dirt FS 171, passing the Junction Creek Campground at 6.6 miles to your left. Bear right into the Log Chutes parking area at 7.4 miles.
***DeLorme: Colorado Atlas & Gazetteer:*** Page 86, B-2

With regard to mountain biking, not much can be said of Durango that hasn't already been said. Durango, more than any other town in Colorado, has had, and continues to have, the greatest influence on the sport of mountain biking. Pictures dating back to 1895 show the Durango Wheel Club (the area's first bicycling club) poised across Baker's Bridge, one of the area's favorite road loops. In 1990 Durango was home to the first-ever World Mountain Bike Championships. Such renowned World Mountain Bike Champions as Ned Overend, Juli Furtado, Lisa Muhich, John Tomac, Missy Giove, and Greg Herbold have called Durango home. Durango is also home to one of the country's 10 largest bicycle races, the Iron Horse Bicycle Classic (IHBC). It seems that with all the mountain biking mania going on in Durango, one would have a hard time finding a trail hidden from the hype. Well, the Log Chutes Trail comes as close as it gets.

Start of the IHBC Downhill Course.

Situated just outside of Durango, the Log Chutes Trail keeps a low profile among such trails as Hermosa Creek, the Colorado Trail, and Kennebec Pass. But even the Log Chutes Trail has had its brush with fame. Several years ago the Log Chutes Trail's historic Neglected Mine Road was included as part of the downhill course for the Iron Horse Bicycle Classic. Since the IHBC discontinued the downhill race, the Log Chutes Trail has slipped into virtual anonymity, unknown to all but the most connected members of Durango's mountain biking circle.

And so, how did Durango become Colorado's premier mountain bike playground? Curiously, both the town of Durango and its status as a mountain bike mecca owe their existence to the railroad. In 1879, a workman for the Denver & Rio Grande railroad laid the first in a long line of railroad stakes that would eventually pierce the heart of the San Juan mountains and connect Silverton with Durango. Intent on tapping the rich mining district of Silverton, the Denver & Rio Grande railroad established the town Durango in 1881 as depot. By 1882 the Denver & Rio Grande was hauling gold and silver unearthed in Silverton to Durango for smelting. In no time, Durango grew into the "City of the Silver San Juan."

The Denver & Rio Grande railroad conducted business as usual until the mining started to wane, shortly after World War II. As other lines pulled out of the area to save what money they could, the Durango to Silverton line was full steam ahead; only now, it was hauling tourists and train aficionados. The Durango & Silverton Narrow Gauge Railroad (as it's now called) has become such a part of Durango that residents are unwilling to give it up. That same steam-powered locomotive line would usher in Durango's mountain bike craze.

## **Miles**Directions

**0.0 START** from the Log Chutes parking area and begin riding up the Log Chutes Road in an easterly direction.

**1.1** The Log Chutes Road forks. Bear left at this fork, passing beyond the gate that bears a "Road Closed" sign. Continue climbing for 0.5 miles before leveling out. There's a bicycle-emblem signpost to the right.

**1.8** The road intersects with the "Short Loop" segment of the Log Chutes Trail to the left. Pass the "Short Loop" trailhead and continue riding up the road in a northerly direction. Just after passing the turnoff for the "Short Loop," bear left onto the more difficult, long loop.

**2.5** The singletrack trail leads into an old logging road, offering an overgrown, wide platform through which the trail travels. Follow this trail in a westerly direction, taking note of the occasional bicycle-emblem signpost pointing the way.

**4.1** Cross the dirt Junction Creek Road and immediately pick up the continuation of the singletrack on the other side. Follow this singletrack up for about 200 yards, heading in a southerly direction, before bearing left onto the old Neglected Mine Road, part of the IHBC downhill course.

**4.2** Bear left onto the old Neglected Mine Road and descend to the corrals.

**5.7** Pass the abandoned corrals to your right and ride approximately 200 yards past the corrals to a fork in the trail. Bear right at this fork, following trail marker signs.

**6.4** The singletrack descends to the Junction Creek Road again. Cross this gravel road and connect with the singletrack on the other side, completing the loop back to your vehicle.

**6.5** Arrive at your vehicle.

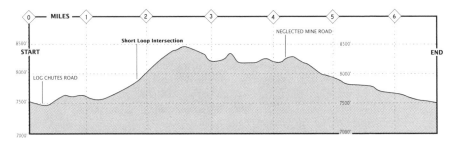

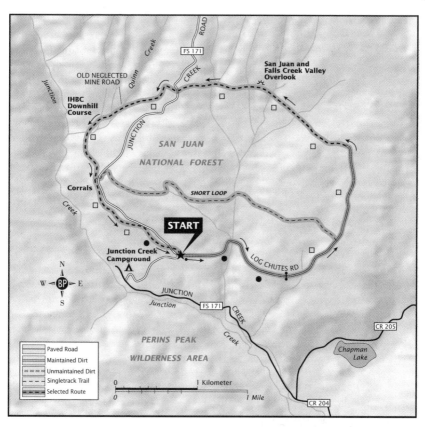

Letting it all hang out.

Jim Mayer and his younger brother Tom grew up along the tracks leading to Silverton. Jim was an engineer on the Durango to Silverton line. Tom was an avid cyclist. One day in the early 1970s, Tom challenged his brother Jim to a race—Tom on his steel 10-speed; Jim and his iron horse. The first one to reach Silverton, 47 miles and 5,500 feet later, was the winner. As the train neared their house, Jim blew the steam-engine whistle, sounding the start of the race. And the first unofficial run of the Iron Horse Bicycle Classic was initiated. When word reached Durango that Tom had actually started winning these races, all of Durango was abuzz for bicycling.

In 1972, 36 riders came out for the first official Iron Horse Bicycle Classic. More than 25 years later, still racing the iron horse, the race continues to draw a crowd. The Classic, held annually on Memorial Day weekend, has grown to include a number of other bicycle events as well. Circuit races, road races, tours, BMX races, trials, and mountain bike races all have their place in Durango's Iron Horse Bicycle Classic. Although occupying its own rightful place within the Iron Horse Classic, the Log Chutes Trail is one of Durango's lesser celebrated trails—a trail, nevertheless, made more intriguing by its relative anonymity among the giants of Durango's trail system.

The Log Chutes Trail begins as a moderate climb up a dirt road over relatively rocky terrain. The singletrack begins once you connect with the more difficult, long-loop Chutes Trail. The trail begins as an easy climb through tall stands of ponderosa and lodgepole pine. The singletrack here features hard packed forest earth with a variety of exposed rocks. At 2.4 miles, the trail begins to level out, offering westerly views of Durango, the San Juans, and the hidden valley of Falls Creek. Here, the sand of the trail is intermingled with rocky, hard terrain, as it passes through intermittent fields of scrub oak and aspen glens.

By mile 4.1 you intersect with the old Neglected Mine Road, the highlight to the Log Chutes Trail. As part of the Iron Horse Bicycle Classic downhill course, this trail is rocky and fast and offers many dips over which to hop. The speedy descent winds through overgrown sagebrush and tight, exposed root sections. Upon reaching the old corrals, the route continues to descend through a mixed conifer forest and crosses Junction Creek Road at mile 6.4. From the road it's a short stretch of singletrack back to your vehicle.

San Juan views from an all but forgotten Durango Trail.

# Ride Information

## 🔵 Trail Contacts:
San Juan Mountains Association, Durango, CO; (970) 385-1210 • Durango Cyclery, Durango, CO; (970) 247-0747 • San Juan-Rio Grande National Forests, Columbine Ranger District, Bayfield, CO; (970) 884-2512

## 🕐 Schedule:
May to October

## ❓ Local Information:
Durango Area Chamber Resort Association, Durango, CO; (970) 247-0312 or 1-800-525-8855 • San Juan National Forest, Supervisor's Office, Durango, CO; (970) 247-4874 • Purgatory Resort, Durango, CO; (970) 247-9000 or 1-800-525-0892 • Durango, CO – for information visit www.durango.com • Animas Ranger District, Durango, CO; (970) 385-1283

## 📍 Local Events/Attractions:
Durango & Silverton Narrow Gauge Railroad, Durango, CO; (970) 247-2733 or 1-888-872-4607 • Iron Horse Bicycle Classic, in May, Durango, CO – contact the Durango Area Chamber Resort Association at (970) 247-0312 or 1-800-525-8855 • Trimble Hot Springs, 6 miles north of Durango on U.S. 550, Trimble, CO; (970) 247-0111

## 🛏 Accommodations:
Strater Hotel, 699 Main Avenue, Durango, CO; (970) 247-4431 or 1-800-247-4431 or www.strater.com

## 👥 Organizations:
San Juan Mountains Association, Durango, CO; (970) 385-1210 • Trails 2000, Durango, CO; (970) 259-4682

## 🍴 Restaurants:
Lady Falconburgh's Barley Exchange, Durango, CO; (970) 382-9664 or www.falconburgh.com • Stonehouse Subs, Durango, CO; (970) 247-4882 • Nature's Oasis, Durango, CO; (970) 247-1988

## 🚴 Tours:
Fat Tire Downhill, Durango, CO; (970) 385-1778 • Southwest Adventures, Durango, CO; (970) 259-0370 • Durango Singletrack Tours, Durango, CO; (970) 385-7489 or 1-888-336-8687

## 🏕 Camps:
Durango Mountain Bike Camp, Durango, CO; (970) 259-0238 or (970) 259-0481

## 🚲 Local Bike Shops:
Durango Cyclery, Durango, CO; (970) 247-0747 • Pedal the Peaks, Durango, CO; (970) 259-6880 or www.big-mountain.com/pedalpks • Mountain Bike Specialists, Durango, CO; (970) 247-4066 • Hard Line Sports, Durango, CO; (970) 259-9141 • Hassle Free Sports, Durango, CO; (970) 259-3874

## Ⓝ Maps:
USGS maps: Durango West, CO • Trails Illustrated map: #504, Durango, Silverton, Telluride, Pagosa Springs, and Cortez • Bicycle on Public Lands of Southwest Colorado Routes Map – available at area bike shops

# Sand Canyon Trail

## Ride Summary

Constructed in 1993 by volunteers for Outdoor Colorado, the Sand Canyon Trail links the lower canyon trail to Sand Canyon Pueblo at the northern end of the canyon. Sand Canyon Pueblo is one of the largest Anasazi pueblos ever discovered. Weaving through the plastered ruins of a once thriving ancient Anasazi culture, the Sand Canyon Trail strikes a fun course through desert sands and over patches of slickrock. There is no water available anywhere along the trail, so bring ample amounts of water. Also, riding in exposed desert terrain requires sunscreen, sunglasses, and a wide-brimmed hat.

## Ride Specs

**Start:** From the Sand Canyon Trailhead
**Length:** 7.2-mile out-and-back
**Approximate Riding Time:** Advanced riders, 45–60 minutes, Intermediate riders, 1½–2 hours
**Technical Difficulty Rating:** Technically easy to moderate due to the well-maintained trail which rolls over relatively smooth hard-packed dirt and slickrock. Some of the trail, however, does include switchbacks and rockier sections.
**Physical Difficulty Rating:** Physically easy to moderate. Although there is very little elevation gain, the hot climate of this semi-arid region takes its toll on the body.
**Terrain:** Singletrack. This trail weaves its course through a semi-arid, desert environment. Types of terrain encountered include sand, slickrock, hard packed earth, cacti, and cryptobiotic crust.
**Elevation Gain:** 1,214 feet
**Nearest Town:** Cortez, CO
**Other Trail Users:** Hikers, equestrians, geologists, and anthropologists
**Canine Compatibility:** Not dog friendly—*due to the dry, hot climate and the lack of water in this area*

## Getting There

**From Cortez:** Drive west on U.S. 160 (Main Street) from the Cortez Visitors Center and Chamber of Commerce. After 1.2 miles, bear left by the Burger King, following signs for U.S. 160 South and U.S. 666 South. Now on U.S. 160 South, pass a Phillips 66 Truck Stop & Gas Station on your left and bear right onto Montezuma County Road G (McElmo Canyon Road) at mile 3.8, passing the airport sign. At mile 5.0, pass the Cortez Municipal Airport on your left. After crossing McElmo Creek at 16.2 miles, via a steel bridge, drive for another 0.6 miles to the Sand Canyon Trailhead. Park your vehicle at the Sand Canyon Trailhead on the right side of McElmo Road at mile 16.8.
***DeLorme: Colorado Atlas & Gazetteer.*** Page 84, B-2

The Sand Canyon Trail lies in the Four Corners Region of the country, where the borders of Colorado, Utah, New Mexico, and Arizona all converge at right angles. Here, in this plateau country of Colorado, the landscape begins to take on the ruddy-colored, bone-dry features more commonly associated with Utah and New Mexico. Water is limited and towns are separated by large stretches

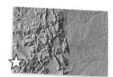

First Anasazi dwelling.

of flat, windswept desert and canyon. It is here, among this dry and seemingly barren landscape, that the Four Corners Region's first known inhabitants, the ancient Anasazi Indians, thrived.

The early Anasazi Indians ("anasazi" being Navajo for "The Ancient Ones") first settled the area around 450 AD. This period is commonly referred to as the "Modified Basketmaker Period" (from 450 to 750 AD). These so-called "basketmakers" hunted

Trailhead.

## **Miles**Directions

**0.0 START** from the Sand Canyon trailhead and begin your ride by heading north over the slickrock. Cairns atop the slickrock mark the route.

**0.2** Reach the Sand Canyon Trail sign to your left. Continue riding in a northeasterly direction, passing the sign.

**1.1** Arrive at your first Anasazi ruin off to your left (west).

**1.9** Reach the top of a juniper and piñon field, across from which lie two Anasazi ruins imbedded in a natural amphitheater. Descend four technically moderate switchbacks to this juniper and piñon field and arrive below these two ruins.

**2.9** Arrive at the fourth and largest of all the cliff dwellings in this area. This site has been roped off due to erosion. Access to this ruin is pending stabilization.

**3.6** Arrive at a sign that reads "The next mile is rocky and steep. Recommended for foot traffic only." Turn around here and return the way you came to your vehicle. [You may wish to stash your bike and hike the three miles to Sand Canyon's northern trailhead and the Sand Canyon Pueblo. You may opt to bike the three miles. Be advised that half of these next three miles include a very sandy dried up creek bed and some thirty switchbacks which rise steeply from the creek bed to the northern end of Sand Canyon—thus making riding virtually impossible.]

**7.2** Reach your vehicle.

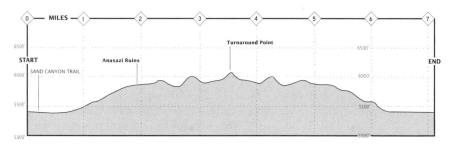

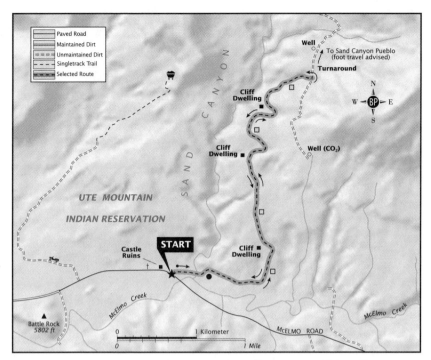

with spears and gathered desert plants to survive. Their dexterous craftsmanship is evidenced in what we find of their woven baskets. The Anasazi began to evolve, trading their spears for bows and arrows, creating pottery, growing yellow flint corn, and building underground pit houses. These pit houses were shallow, saucer-like dwellings topped with logs bounded by fibrous yucca plant strips and chinked with mud mortar. They served as ceremonial meeting places—forebears to today's conference halls. Between 750 and 1100, their achievements would finally culminate in the building and establishing of large communal dwellings, virtual cities of stone and adobe built into the sand-blasted cliff sides. This period marked the emergence of the "Pueblo" culture. The Cliff Palace in Mesa Verde National Park is a perfect example of the ancestral Puebloans' architectural mastery.

The Sand Canyon Trail passes a number of these cliff-dwellings, as it leads to one of the largest pueblos ever built, the Sand Canyon Pueblo. The trail begins on slickrock, with cairns marking the route to the wide singletrack. Rolling over hard-packed desert sand, it passes through piñon-juniper forests and sagebrush. There are a number of playful dips and natural velodromes highlighting the beginning portion of the trail. The trail also passes one of the desert's most unique and important, but very fragile, life forms—cryptobiotic crust.

Appearing as a miniature city of dark sand castles, cryptobiotic crust is actually a living organism. The crust has anti-erosional and nitrogen-enriching qualities that prepare the ground for future plant life. Growing on barren ground and requiring little nutrition from the soil, cryptobiotic crust is a self-sustaining biological unit, a critical part of the desert's soil-building processes. Since it can take as long as 100 years to mature—and less that one revolution of a bicycle tire to be destroyed—it is imperative that you avoid disturbing this organism and only admire it from the trail.

# Ride Information

**Trail Contacts:**
Offices of the San Juan National Forest and the Bureau of Land Management San Juan Research Area, Durango, CO; (970) 247-4082 or (970) 247-4874

**Schedule:**
April to October

**Local Information:**
Crow Canyon Archeological Center, Cortez, CO; 1-800-422-8975 • Cortez Area Chamber of Commerce and Colorado Welcome Center, Cortez, CO; (970) 565-3414 • Mesa Verde Country Visitor Information Bureau, Cortez, CO; (970) 565- 8227 or 1-800-253-1616 or www.swcolo.org

**Local Events/Attractions:**
Mesa Verde National Park, CO; (970) 529-4461 or www.mesaverde.org • Ute Mountain Tribal Park, Towaoc, CO; (970) 565-3751 (ext. 282) or 1-800-847-5485 • Hovenweep National Monument, c/o Mesa Verde National

Park, CO; (970) 749-0510 or www2.educ.ksu.edu/projects/hovenweep/hovenhome.html • Anasazi Heritage Center Museum, Dolores, CO; (970) 882-4811 • Cortez CU Center, Cortez, CO; (970) 565-1151 or www.fone.net/~cucenter

**Tours:**
Crow Canyon Archeological Center, Cortez, CO; 1-800-422-8975

**Restaurants:**
Main Street Brewery, Cortez, CO; (970) 564-9112 • Francisca's, Cortez, CO; (970) 565-4093

**Local Bike Shops:**
Kokopelli Bike & Board, Cortez, CO; (970) 565-4408

**Maps:**
USGS maps: Battle Rock, CO; Woods Canyon, CO • Trails Illustrated map: #504, Durango, Silverton, Telluride, Pagosa Springs, and Cortez

Within two miles, you pass four ancestral Puebloan cliff-dwellings. Sand Canyon is unique in that it offers the mountain biker a chance to examine these ruins more intimately than you could otherwise at places like Mesa Verde National Park (where bicycles are restricted to paved and designated roads). These ruins have a certain presence about them, one that envelops the entire canyon with an air of arcane inventiveness. Donald G. Pike writes in his book *Anasazi:* "The old cities have weathered well, retreating only slightly, and then only into a more harmonious union with the face of the land. They, like the earth, abide in a quiet strength, a presence that betokens an assurance of permanence." This lasting power is testimony to the ancestral Puebloans' craftsmanship, as well as their understanding of the land. The droves of cacti growing before most of these ruins act as a warning to unwary travelers who might think to disrespect these ancient dwellings.

Just over half-a-mile from the fourth cliff-dwelling is the turnaround point. From this point, riding your bike to Sand Canyon's northern end may prove more foolhardy than adventurous, as the trail becomes considerably sandier, rockier, and steeper, combining no less than thirty switchbacks on its way to the top of the canyon. A better option would be to hike these last remaining three miles to the canyon's northern end and the Sand Canyon Pueblo.

In cooperation with the Bureau of Land Management, research and excavation at the Sand Canyon Pueblo was first conducted in 1983 by the Crow Canyon Archeological Center staff. The Sand Canyon Pueblo is believed to have been inhabited in the latter part of the 13th Century and may well have been a social and ceremonial center. A community of an estimated 735 residents once occupied this area. No less than 420 rooms, 90 kivas (underground rooms used for ceremonial and social gatherings), and 14 towers make up the village. Most of the excavations are being backfilled for preservation, so aside from pueblo mounds and room outlines, there are few structures to view from afar. Thus, a tour of the Sand Canyon Pueblo is best suited for people with a serious archeological interest, as opposed to those having only a casual interest in archeology.

No one knows with any real certainty why these ancestral Puebloans mysteriously disappeared around 1300 AD. A long drought in the area (from 1276 to 1299 AD) may have been the cause of their sudden departure. Others hold that raiding Shoshonean hunters, who had begun to roam the plateau at that time, forced the ancestral Puebloans to leave. Researchers at the Sand Canyon Pueblo hope to uncover the answers to this and other questions that have gone unanswered for nearly 700 years, regarding the life and culture and customs of these "Ancient Ones."

Sandstone rock formation.

## Southwest Colorado

Compiled here is an index of great rides in the Southwest region that didn't make the A-list this time around but deserve recognition. Check them out and let us know what you think. You may decide that one or more of these rides deserves higher status in future editions or, perhaps, you may have a ride of your own that merits some attention.

### (C) Portland Creek Trail

Its been called the "Switzerland of America" and for good reason. Ouray, Colorado, is quite possibly one of the most beautiful places in Colorado. Nestled safely in an alpine cathedral at the bottom of the treacherous Red Mountain Pass, in the heart of one of America's most scenic drives, The San Juan Skyway, Ouray offers jaw-dropping views of towering San Juan peaks. Coupled with Ouray's head-tilting scenery are the many waterfalls that veil its walls. The dramatic waterfalls of Box Canyon, Cascade, Bear Creek, and Twin Falls in Yankee Boy Basin are all testimony to the town's relation to Switzerland. In winter, these falls turn to an ice climber's paradise. Ouray recognizes this boasting the world's only manmade ice park in existence. Among these highest of heights lies the Portland Creek Trail, a short, but sweet ride.

As one of the Amphitheater trails, the Portland Creek Trail is a great acclimatization ride for travelers. With views of the Amphitheater cliffs and peaks to the west and south of Ouray, this trail travels directly above America's Switzerland. If you were to travel south through the town on U.S. Route 550, you'd bear left just after passing the turnoff for Box Canyon and follow the signs for Cascade Falls. After turning left, make your first right where you'll see the sign for the Portland Trail to your left.

For more information contact Ouray Mountain Sports at (970) 325-4284 or the Ouray County Chamber of Commerce at 1-800-228-1876. **DeLorme: Colorado Atlas & Gazetteer:** Page 66, D-4

## (D) Ute Mountain Ute Tribal Park

The Ute Mountain Ute Tribal Park offers riders a unique look into early Native American culture. Personal tour guides will inform riders about regional archeology, history, rock art, geological land formations, artifacts, and dwellings. The Utes of Ute Mountain (the Weenuche band) are one of the seven original Ute bands who once thrived throughout all of Colorado.

Following an old jeep road along the Mancos River, riders descend 800 feet to a group campground 13 miles later. The route passes by several Anasazi archeology ruin sites, which can be accessed by short side hikes. The riding is remote, with spectacular Mancos River valley views, but the area offers no water or food, so riders should carry their own.

Due to the extensive Ute artifacts and dwellings, the Ute Mountain Ute Tribe strictly controls trips into the Tribal Park. Riders must first call and reserve their space. Bike tours may be arranged by calling the Tribal Park at 1-800-847-5485. For a full day tour the cost is $30. For a half day tour it's $17. To reach the Ute Mountain Ute Tribal Park, drive south on Main Street from the Mancos Visitors Center at the intersection of U.S. Route 160 and Colorado 184 in downtown Mancos, Colorado. Main Street will shortly merge with County Road 41. Drive on County Road 41 for 10 miles to a sign identifying the Ute Mountain Tribal Park. Park your vehicle here.

*DeLorme: Colorado Atlas & Gazetteer:* Page 85, C-6

# North Central Colorado

*WYOMING*

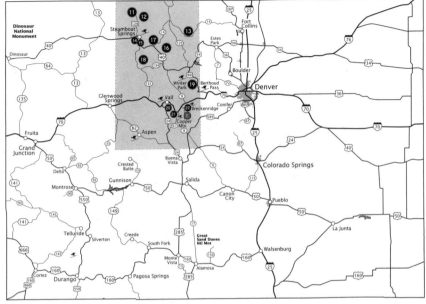

*NEW MEXICO*

N orth Central Colorado is likely the state's principal destination, receiving the most visitors than any other region. It's where more people go to play when visiting Colorado, as it typifies the Colorado mountain experience.

Lying to the northwest is the Yampa River Valley, a vast expanse of rolling green mountains. Here the traditional ranching and cowboy communities of Hahns Peak Village, Clark and Steamboat Springs coalesce with a burgeoning recreational destination to deliver western congeniality with first-rate recreation. One of the premier rides in the area, the Nipple Peak Loop challenges the hardiest of riders. Moving east into Steamboat Springs, the Yampa Valley comes alive with a vast network of trails guaranteed to delight. Try soaking your bum in the hot springs of Strawberry Park or marvel at the 90-meter long jump sliding precipitously down Howelsen Hill.

The area east of Rabbit Ears Pass and the Continental Divide is more appropriately known as North Park, the moose viewing capital of Colorado. Just west of Cameron Pass lies the Bockman Campground Loop, offering great moose viewing potential. The stark and sheer face of the Nokhu Crags is breathtaking. Here the landscape is marked by towering ponderosa and lodgepole pine. During the autumn months, golden aspen appear as a patchwork in North Park's mountains.

Centrally located in this region lies the town of Winter Park, in the Fraser Valley. With over 600 miles of maintained trails for every ability level and the most extensive trail system in the Colorado high country, its no surprise that Winter Park and the Fraser Valley bill themselves as "Mountain Bike Capital USA™." Typifying the riding in this area, the Tipperary Creek Loop offers soft singletrack, fast descents and moderate climbs.

Just south of Winter Park and the Fraser Valley are the bustling Summit and Eagle counties, the modern heart of Colorado. With Interstate 70 running straight through Colorado's heart, Summit and Eagle counties are among the most accessible mountain regions in the state. Since Summit and Eagle counties have the highest concentration of ski resorts of any other area in the state (Vail was even host to the 1999 World Alpine Ski Championship), they provide a treasure of lift-accessible mountain bike terrain after the winter snowmelt. That's not to say, however, that the trails described herein offer easy and immediate access to the top. Far from it. We earn our turns here. Vail's famed Grand Traverse Trail passes by views of the Holy

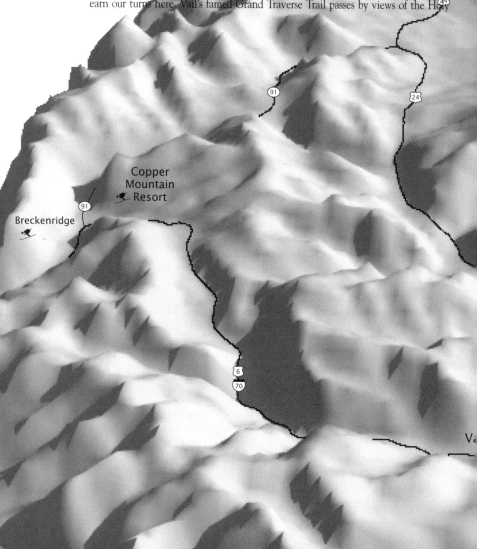

Copper
Mountain
Resort

Breckenridge

Cross Wilderness and the Gore, Sawatch and New York mountain ranges, while Breckenridge's Wise Mountain Trail is one of the most impressive stretches of the 470-mile long Colorado Trail. Some of the area's other highlights include the historic gold mining town of Breckenridge, which is surrounded by the Tenmile mountain range; the Vail Valley, and the Colorado Ski Museum and Hall of Fame and the Dillon Reservoir.

# Nipple Peak Loop

## Ride Summary

By all accounts, the Nipple Peak Loop is a stellar trail, but not for the faint-hearted. It requires advanced skills in climbing and descending. Covering 20.5 miles, this loop offers an elevation gain of roughly 3,000 feet, with the highest elevation topping off at 9,600 feet. Bring lots of sandwiches for this ride and expect to be out most of the day. The challenging climbs and incredibly fast and technical singletrack places this trail on equal par with any of Colorado's finest. Although area locals seem to prefer riding it clockwise, the loop can be done just as enjoyably counter clockwise. If ridden counter clockwise, the climbing comes early, but makes for more hike-a-bike sections up the steeper and rockier sections of trail. Also, riding it counter clockwise allows the rider to return to his or her vehicle via easier gravel roads. If ridden clockwise, the rider descends more technically challenging sections but will also have to contend with much of the climbing toward the end of the loop. This ride follows the loop clockwise.

## Ride Specs

**Start:** At the Nipple Peak Loop trailhead
**Length:** 20.5-mile loop
**Approximate Riding Time:** Advanced Riders, 3 – 3½ hours; Intermediate Riders, 4 – 4½ hours
**Technical Difficulty Rating:** Technically moderate to challenging due to the variety of roots, rock, and ruts
**Physical Difficulty Rating:** Physically challenging to demanding due to the taxing climbs at high elevations
**Terrain:** Paved road, dirt road, doubletrack, and singletrack—includes thick roots, loose rock, and steep inclines and offers soft, pine-needled surfaces, muddy sections, and sandy patches
**Elevation Gain:** 3,823 feet
**Nearest Town:** Hahns Peak Village, CO
**Other Trail Users:** Hikers, equestrians, backpackers, and motorcyclists
**Canine Compatibility:** Dog friendly

## Getting There

**From Steamboat:** Drive west on U.S. 40. Turn right onto Elk River Road (CR 129), just after the 7-Eleven. Drive on Elk River Road for 32.5 miles, passing through the towns of Clark, Hahn's Peak Village, and Columbine. At 30.5 miles, Elk River Road turns to dirt and changes its name to FS 129. After 32 miles, look to your right for the brown Nipple Peak East/Trail 1147 sign. Just beyond the sign, turn left onto the Fire Road. Cross the cattle guard and pass through the gate before parking your vehicle. *DeLorme: Colorado Atlas & Gazetteer:* Page 16, A&B 1-2

### FYI...

- *More than half of Colorado's 104,651 square miles is public land.*

The Nipple Peak Loop takes its name from the protruding promontory located in the northernmost reaches of Routt National Forest, near the Wyoming border. Nestled roughly 15 miles to the northwest of Hahns Peak, the wind-scoured mountain visible from downtown Steamboat Springs, Nipple Peak is far less distinguished than its neighbor is. That's not to say, however, that area locals don't appreciate Nipple Peak. On the contrary, Nipple Peak is, perhaps, even more appreciated, if only for its association with that particular body part. Although some may argue that

Nearing the top of the first ridge climb to views of Sawtooth Mountain and California Park.

referring to a mountain peak as a nipple is brash at best, I wonder what those same people would think if it were known that the nipple in question actually belonged to someone at one time.

"Maggie's Nipple" (the one-time name of Nipple Peak) was named after Maggie Baggs, the common-law wife of George Baggs (who lent his name to Baggs, Wyoming). According to the cowhands on the Baggs' Double Eleven Ranch, Maggie enjoyed belittling and bossing the hired help, and on occasion, would take certain less-than-honorable liberties with them. One can only imagine the sport made of Maggie behind her back.

On a routine roundup, cowhand Jack Farrell referred to the infamous peak as "Maggie's Nipple." When word reached Maggie that her honor was attacked she had Jack publicly horsewhipped. Otherwise unaffected by the slur, Maggie ran off to California with a red-haired, freckle-faced cowboy named Mike Sweet. After the money from her divorce settlement was exhausted, Sweet skipped out of town. When last anyone heard, Maggie was managing "rooming apartments" as a "social matron" in Galveston, Texas. Maggie Baggs' story notwithstanding, the Nipple Peak Loop remains one of the most sought after mountain bike trails in all of Northwest Colorado.

Nipple Peak stands within close range of Hahns Peak, its slightly more dignified neighbor. The Ute Indians (the so-called Top-of-the-Mountain People) were the first to appreciate Hahns Peak—which they called "Old Baldy." They would use the peak's massive 10,839-foot crown as a lookout. From atop the peak, scouts could see well into what today are Wyoming, Utah, and Colorado.

Hahns Peak owes its present name to the German immigrant Joseph Hahn who came to Colorado in 1860 prospecting gold and finding it in the Hahns Peak Basin. Delayed by the Civil War, Hahn returned to the area in 1865 with William Doyle and Captain George Way. Together they established the Hahns Peak Mining District. Having left Hahn in camp one summer day, Doyle and Way climbed to the yet-unnamed peak's summit with a waterproof Preston and Merrill baking powder tin. Inside the tin Doyle had placed a scrap of paper upon which he had written: "This is named Hahns Peak by his friend and comrade, William A. Doyle, August 27, 1865." The tin was left atop the peak, anchored in stones.

Although the Hahns Peak Mining District failed to strike the mother load, the town did occupy the county seat for 35 years and remains Routt County's oldest permanent town. As for Hahns Peak, perhaps its greatest distinction came in 1912,

## **Miles**Directions

**0.0 START** at the Nipple Peak Loop trailhead. Return to Elk River Road and ride back (south) toward Columbine.

**2.5** Elk River Road turns to pavement.

**3.0** Pass through the town of Columbine.

**4.0** Bear right onto FS 488.

**5.5** A singletrack trail veers off to the left of FS 488. This is the trailhead for TR 1156 (Prospector Trail) and the beginning of the singletrack for the Nipple Peak Loop. Bear left here onto TR 1156 and descend through a stand of aspen.

**8.2** Cross FS 487 and continue on the singletrack on the other side, following the sign for TR 1156.

**9.4** Reach the top of the ridge and take in the stunning views of Sawtooth Mountain and California Park directly in front of you.

**11.3** TR 1156 intersects with TR 1147 (Nipple Peak Trail). Bear right onto TR 1147.

**12.3** Cross the two forks of Oliver Creek and begin your long grunt of a climb through the aspens.

**14.1** Reach the junction of TR 1147 and TR 1192 (Burton Creek Trail). Continue climbing on TR 1147, passing TR 1192 to your left.

**15.3** Reach the top of the ridge, elevation 9,410 feet.

**17.7** Reach the scree section, offering views of Nipple Peak.

**17.9** Cross FS 488 and pick up the final stretch of trail on the other side.

**18.6** The trail intersects with a doubletrack trail. Veer right, continuing your descent to your vehicle.

**20.5** Reach your vehicle.

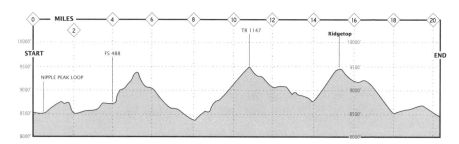

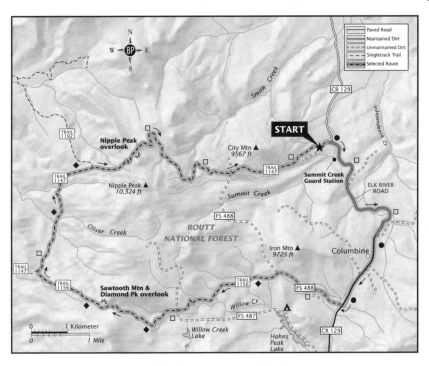

Hahn's Peak and Hahn's Peak Lake.

# Ride Information

## 📞 Trail Contacts:
**Sore Saddle Cyclery**, Steamboat Springs, CO; (970) 879-1675

## 🕐 Schedule:
July to October

## ❓ Local Information:
**Routt National Forest**, Steamboat Springs, CO; (970) 879-1870 • **Hahns Peak Ranger District**, Steamboat Springs, CO; (970) 879-1870

## 💡 Local Events/Attractions:
**Strawberry Park Hot Springs**, Steamboat Springs, CO; (970) 879-0342 • **Tread of Pioneers Museum**, Steamboat Springs, CO; (970) 879-2214 • **Steamboat Lake State Park**, North of Steamboat Springs along FS 129, CO; (970) 879-7019 • **A Walking Tour of the Springs of Steamboat**, Steamboat Springs, CO; (970) 879-2214 – *pick up area map at Tread of Pioneers Museum*

## 🍴 Restaurants:
**Harwigs**, Steamboat Springs, CO; (970) 879-1980 • **Steamboat Brewery & Tavern**, Steamboat Springs, CO; (970) 879-2233

## 👥 Organizations:
**Routt County Riders Bicycle Club**, Steamboat Springs, CO; (970) 879-1735

## 🚲 Local Bike Shops:
**Sore Saddle Cyclery**, Steamboat Springs, CO; (970) 879-1675 • **Ski Haus**, Steamboat Springs, CO; (970) 879-0385 • **Ski Kare**, Steamboat Springs, CO; (970) 879-9144

## 🅝 Maps:
**USGS maps:** Elkhorn Mountain, CO; Hahns Peak, CO; Meaden Peak, CO; Shield Mountain, CO • **Routt National Forest vicinity map** – *available at the Routt National Forest office* (970) 879-1870

when Washington, D.C. authorized the Routt National Forest to build one of the first fire lookout stations in the Rocky Mountain Region. It seems fitting that after all the digging and scrambling for gold over its rocky slope, Hahns Peak had become once again a lookout. In a way, Chief Colorow, the stubborn Ute Indian who fought to keep his tribe's mountain from being exploited, finally succeeded in securing "Old Baldy" for his Top-of-the-Mountain People.

With a nod to Chief Colorow, modern-day guardians of the mountain pedal their way to surrounding heights scouting for prospective singletrack. And considering the singletrack of Nipple Peak Loop, they have hit pure pay dirt.

The route begins by heading south on County Road 129. From County Road 129 you connects with Forest Service Road 488 and begin to climb moderately. Views of Hahns Peak lie to the east. Once you pick up the singletrack Trail 1156 (Prospector Trail), the terrain offers fast, root- and rock-filled descents through tall aspen and lodgepole pine. After two short climbs, you cross Willow Creek, before arriving at a large area of deadfall. The climb from out of the deadfall area is beset with steep and rutted terrain.

Once you cross Forest Service Road 488, be prepared for a long grunt of a climb through aspens and hillside meadows. Here's a good place to fuel up for the long climb ahead. At the top of the ridge, gorgeous views of Sawtooth Mountain await the diligent climber. Your climb to this overlook is rewarded with three miles of prime, rocky real estate. From here, it's a 3-mile assault on some very steep and technical terrain through old-growth forests. The singletrack eventually drops you onto a service road at 10.3 miles. Cross the road and continue descending down the singletrack.

After crossing the forks of Oliver Creek, a tough sandy section awaits, as well as a grueling climb through the aspens ahead. After climbing sharply for roughly one mile, the forest turns to pine and the pitch begins to level off as the trail snakes over rocks and roots. From the top of this ridge at 15.3 miles, the trail descends rapidly over technical root sections, through a couple of creeks, and past the south side of an old logging area. Sections of trail hug the hillside rather precariously, sometimes causing you to slip a little. Careful. Once you cross Forest Service Road 487, pick up the singletrack on the other side. This final descent is sandy, so take care when ripping around corners and over berms. Continue descending, bearing right at all junctions, to your vehicle.

# Diamond Park to Scott's Run

## Ride Summary

Diamond Park to Scott's Run is a great ride through densely wooded terrain. Combining climbs, smooth descents, and a number of creek crossings, this ride is sure to please. Although moderate in length, it's not too technical, so riders of any ability would enjoy Diamond Park to Scott's Run. The ride passes by the pristine Hinman Lake, resting in the middle of an aspen forest—which makes for a great autumn excursion. One of the highlights to this trail is the optional ride to views of Mount Farwell—great backcountry ski terrain.

## Ride Specs

**Start:** From the Diamond Park Road parking lot
**Length:** 17.5-mile loop
**Approximate Riding Time:** Advanced Riders, 2 hours; Intermediate Riders, 3–4 hours
**Technical Difficulty Rating:** Technically moderate to challenging due to a variety of steep climbs, offering much in the way of rocks and roots
**Physical Difficulty Rating:** Physically challenging due to its higher elevations, 8,000-8,800 feet
**Terrain:** Gravel road, 4WD road, and single-track mostly over rolling terrain. Typical lower montane forest.
**Elevation Gain:** 1,935 feet
**Nearest Town:** Clark, CO
**Other Trail Users:** Hikers, equestrians, campers, and four-wheelers
**Canine Compatibility:** Dog friendly

## Getting There

**From Steamboat Springs:** Drive west on I-40 out of town, turn right onto FS 129 (Elk River Road) toward the tiny town of Clark. Drive through Clark. Just after passing the Glen Eden Guest Ranch in Clark, bear right onto Seed House Road (FS 400), roughly 19 miles from Steamboat Springs. Drive east on Seed House Road for another 8.5 miles to FS 431 (Diamond Park Road), which will be on the left side of the road just before crossing the Middle Fork of the Elk River at mile 27.6. Park on the right, just after turning up FS 431—Diamond Park parking lot. *DeLorme: Colorado Atlas & Gazetteer:* Page 16, B-3

Diamond Park to Scott's Run is located just 8.5 miles outside the town of Clark, a tiny community whose backdoor opens to the Mount Zirkel Wilderness Area. Though it boasts a 72,500-acre backyard, Clark is rooted in humility. With a simple beginning as a stage stop in the early 1880s, Clark became a way station for eager pioneers and prospectors, all looking for ranching and mining opportunities. By the early 1900s, Clark had become a flourishing community, fitted with all the requirements for life on the range. The building that housed the community general store, post office, and telephone exchange still stands on the banks of the Elk River at the Glen Eden Bridge.

Just across the bridge lies Seed House Road. It owes its name to a now defunct Forest Service seed house that stands alongside the road. Built in 1910, the Seed House served the Forest Service as a replenishing station for fire-torn forests around

Author carrying his gear over deadfall.

the world. During the Seed House's operation, forestry employees searched out squirrel caches of conifer cones and brought them in big sacks and baskets back to the Seed House. The cones were laid across large screens and dried with wood fires. The warmed cones would release their seeds into wooden trays. The seeds were then packaged and stored. Eventually the seeds would be distributed across the world in order to re-seed forests devastated by fire.

Shortly after the Seed House, the trail begins a gradual ascent into a silent stand of aspen trees. At mile 1.4 the trail divides. Bear right, following the sign to Diamond Park and immediately cross English Creek. After negotiating through a half-mile-long section of rocky terrain, cross Lost Dog Creek. The creek gets its name from an old hunting story told by one of Steamboat Springs' founding fathers. While out bear hunting on this tributary of the Elk River, John Crawford, son of the first family to settle in Steamboat Springs, lost his hunting dogs. The "lost" dogs found their way home. James Crawford, John's father, then had to send out a search party for his lost son. In jest, old James named the creek "Lost Dog"—even though "Lost Son" would have been more appropriate.

The author wakes up for a morning ride.

## **Miles**Directions

**0.0 START** from the Diamond Park parking lot and head back onto Seed House Road riding east, crossing the Middle Fork of the Elk River.

**0.1** The Seed House is to your left.

**0.9** The singletrack begins. Bear left into an aspen grove onto TR 1101 (the Wyoming Trail).

**1.4** Bear left at the "T" intersection and follow the sign to Diamond Park.

**5.0** Arrive at a footbridge that crosses the North Fork of the Elk River, after having ridden through rocky singletrack, open meadows awash with wildflowers, and lush lodgepole pine forests.

**5.6** Arrive at Diamond Park. From here, riders can take a break from their saddles and access many hiking trails that lead into the Mount Zirkel Wilderness Area—no bikes allowed in Wilderness Areas.

**6.0** Ford Trail Creek.

**6.3** TR 1101 meets with FS 431 (Diamond Park Road). Bear right and follow the sign to Mount Farwell.

**6.5** TR 1177 (Hinman Creek Trail) will be to your left. This is the trail to Scott's Run.

**9.6** After riding through canyons and meadows, come upon smooth needle-covered singletrack as you make your way down to Hinman Creek.

**10.0** Cross Hinman Creek.

**11.5** Come to TR 1188A (the Cutover Trail). Pass this trail and continue heading south on TR 1177, which will eventually run into Scott's Run.

**12.5** Reach Hinman Lake.

**13.5** Bear left as you come upon the barbwire and private property. Cross Hinman Creek and pick up FS 430.

**14.6** FS 430 connects with Seed House Road. Turn left.

**17.0** Reach the Diamond Park parking lot.

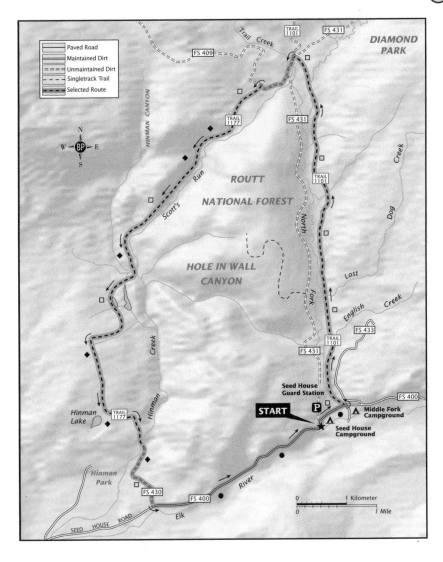

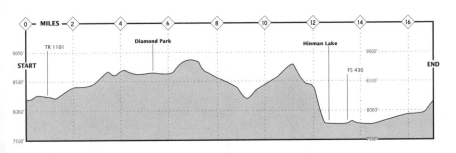

# Ride Information

**Trail Contacts:**
**Sore Saddle Cyclery**, Steamboat Springs, CO; (970) 879-1675

**Schedule:**
Late June to October

**Local Information:**
**Routt National Forest**, Steamboat Springs, CO; (970) 879-1722 • **Hahns Peak Ranger District**, Steamboat Springs, CO; (970) 879-1870 • **City of Steamboat Springs**, Steamboat Springs, CO; (970) 879-2060 or *www.ci.steamboat.co.us* • **Steamboat Springs Chamber Resort Association**, Steamboat Springs, CO; (970) 879-0880 or *www.steamboat-chamber.com*

**Local Events/Attractions:**
**The Seed House** • **Mount Zirkel Wilderness**, Routt National Forest (970) 879-1870 • **Steamboat Lake Steamboat State Park**, North of Steamboat Springs along FS 129, (970) 879-7019

**Restaurants:**
**Harwigs**, Steamboat Springs, CO; (970) 879-1980 • **Steamboat Brewery & Tavern**, Steamboat Springs, CO; (970) 879-2233 • **Clark Store & Touring Center**, Clark, CO; (970) 879-3849

**Organizations:**
**Routt County Riders Bicycle Club**, Steamboat Springs, CO; (970) 879-1735

**Local Bike Shops:**
**Sore Saddle Cyclery**, Steamboat Springs, CO; (970) 879-1675 • **Ski Haus**, Steamboat Springs, CO; (970) 879-0385 • **Ski Kare**, Steamboat Springs, CO; (970) 879-9144

**Maps:**
**USGS maps:** Steamboat Springs, CO; Rocky Peak, CO; Mad Creek, CO • *Trails Illustrated* **maps:** # 117, Clark, Buffalo Pass; #118, Steamboat Springs, Rabbit Ears Pass • **Routt National Forest Map** – *available at Routt National Forest Office (970) 879-1722*

Continue riding through wide-open meadows, lush valleys, and cool, dark forests. At mile 5.0 you come to a footbridge that crosses the North Fork of the Elk River. A short, but steep climb waits to the north. Diamond Park, named for the diamond shaped grove of evergreens in its center, sits just over a half of a mile from the bridge. Cross the park and continue to follow the signs for Trial 1101. At this point the singletrack turns to dirt road. Trail Creek lies at mile 6. From June to mid-July a portage is normally required. Cross the creek and pass around the gate. Head straight along the dirt road. Trail 1101 divides again at mile 6.3—this is Forest Service Road 431 (or Diamond Park Road). Bearing left and riding for four miles will deliver you to the Diamond Park parking lot. To reach Scott's Run, bear right onto Forest Service Road 409 and look for the Trail 1177 (Hinman Creek Trail) sign on the left just before a short hill.

This section includes very technical and rocky singletrack. Begin descending along the north side of Scott's Run, passing through a couple of small creeks and by several beaver ponds. At mile 9.6 the trail turns to a smooth, pine-needled surface before steeply descending south to Hinman Creek. In the late 1800s, the area surrounding Scott's Run ran wild with big game, so much so, that big game hunter President Teddy Roosevelt found himself hunting these parts. The run's namesake didn't exactly fare that well in his now-infamous hunting adventure. In 1875, a hunter by the name of Scott was found lying dead in this creek. It seems that after wounding a grizzly bear and attempting to flee, Scott was mauled to death by the wounded animal. That's one way to attach your name to a creek.

Upon reaching a low-lying saddle, the trail becomes a sweet cruise through the aspens on sensational, smooth-running singletrack. Continue descending south, passing Trail 1188A (the Cutover Trail) at mile 11.5. After riding about a mile past Trail 1188A, you'll notice an unmarked trail to your right just after a short steep descent. This unmarked trail leads to incredible views of Hinman Lake.

After soaking your senses, if not your self, in Hinman Lake, double back from the lake and continue descending south on Trail 1177. Here the forest battles the singletrack in an effort to reclaim what was once whole. Crowded on both sides by lush vegetation, this section of singletrack offers you a limited field of vision and innumerable blind turns. Know your line and stick to it, or else you too will be trying to reclaim what was once whole.

Near mile 13.5 is a barbwire fence. Bear left here and splash into Hinman Creek. Enter into a dark and dense pine forest—the perfect setting for a Tolkien novel. A variety of camping sites exist, none of which would make Bilbo Baggins the least bit uncomfortable. Pick up Forest Service Road 430 and continue riding south until reaching Seed House Road at mile 14.6. Turn left onto Seed House Road and pedal for another 2.5 miles back to the Diamond Park parking lot.

Roadside maintenance.

# Bockman Campground Loop

## Ride Summary

Linking the Cache La Poudre-North Park Scenic and Historic Byway and old logging roads, the Bockman Campground Loop offers a mostly mellow ride with two miles of somewhat difficult climbing over 10,000 feet. The loop introduces the rider to pristine North Park, the Moose Viewing Capital of Colorado. The many logging roads make for a variety of mountain bike options; although, know that many of the logging roads have gone unused for years and bear the effects of strong winters. Caution should be observed when riding these roads. Some of the routes depicted by the Colorado State Forest State Park mountain bike map are not accurate (e.g. The Grass Creek Loop does not connect to Colorado 14 anymore). The Bockman Campground Loop is a great loop to do during the week, when motor traffic is considerably reduced. Be sure to carry insect repellent, as the mosquitoes in the North Park can be dreadful.

## Ride Specs

**Start:** From the turnout for Lake Agnes, approximately 2.5 miles from the summit of Cameron Pass on the south side of CO 14
**Length:** 19.9-mile loop
**Approximate Riding Time:** Advanced Riders, 1½ hours; Intermediate Riders, 2½–3 hours
**Technical Difficulty Rating:** Technically easy, since the trail travels over a forest service road
**Physical Difficulty Rating:** Physically moderate. Although most of this ride is a casual cruise through North Park, portions are quite steep and travel over 10,000 feet.
**Terrain:** Surface includes paved highway, improved dirt roads, and rougher jeep roads. The rougher jeep roads have sections of considerable washout, owing to the area's harsh winters. There are a number of ruts with which to contend; otherwise, mostly easy going.
**Elevation Gain:** 1,988 feet
**Nearest Town:** Walden, CO
**Other Trail Users:** Equestrians, campers, anglers, four-wheelers, hikers, and picnickers
**Canine Compatibility:** Dog friendly

## Getting There

**From Fort Collins:** Take U.S. 287 north to CO 14 west. Drive on CO 14 for 61.9 miles, passing through the Poudre Canyon and going over 10,276-foot Cameron Pass, before turning left into the Lake Agnes turnout. The Lake Agnes turnout is approximately 2.5 miles west of Cameron Pass. Park your vehicle here and begin by riding west on CO 14. **DeLorme: Colorado Atlas & Gazetteer.** Page 18, D 2-3

The Bockman Campground Loop is nestled in the northern reaches of Colorado's North Park. Within the state forest's 70,768 acres lie endless logging roads on which to observe area wildlife and explore the region's rich logging history.

North Park stretches along the west side of the Medicine Bow Mountains and into the north end of the Never Summer Range.

Bull Mountain.

Originally called "Bull Pen" by native Ute Indians, North Park provided a natural grazing environment for large herds of buffalo. With the buffalo long since removed from Colorado's active reserve list, the "Bull Pen" now boasts the highest concentration of moose in Colorado.

Though native to Colorado, moose were rarely seen in North Park until the late 1970s when the Colorado Division of Wildlife (DOW) decided to establish a moose herd here. In March of 1978, 12 moose were rounded up near the Bear River in Utah. Financed by private donations, the moose were tranquilized, removed by helicopter and transported in cattle trucks to North Park. Having been tested for disease, the moose were released on the upper end of North Park's Illinois River.

Due to its ideal habitat of willow-lined streams, North Park is now home to an estimated 550 to 600 moose. In recognition of the proliferation of moose in the area, the Colorado Senate in 1995 designated North Park and the nearby town of Walden as the Moose Viewing Capital of Colorado.

Bull Mountain overlooking North Michigan Reservoir.

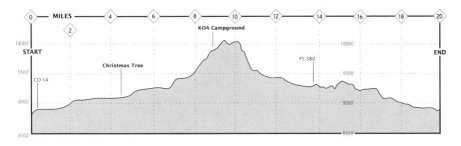

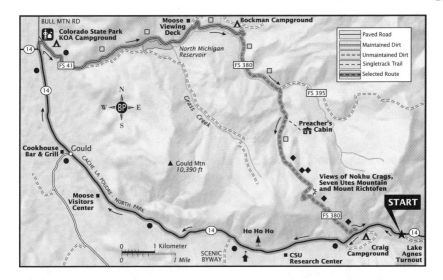

## **Miles**Directions

**0.0 START** at the Lake Agnes Turnout. Head back onto CO 14 and continue riding west down the highway.

**3.0** The Colorado State Research Center is to your left.

**4.5** Christmas Tree is to your right.

**5.6** The Moose Visitors Center for the Colorado State Forest is to your left.

**6.2** Enter the tiny town of Gould.

**7.0** The Cookhouse Bar & Grill will be to your left. Make note of it, as you may wish to swill some suds after the ride's end.

**8.9** Turn right into the KOA campground and the Colorado State Park and immediately bear left onto CO 41. Stop at the Ranger Station and purchase your $2 daily pass. The general store at the KOA campground is a good place to stock up on snacks for the rest of the ride.

**10.2** CO 41 forks. Take the left fork, following signs for the Bockman Campground and the Moose Viewing deck.

**12.6** CO 41 forks again. Veering off of CO 41, take the right fork, following signs to Bockman Campground. The left fork leads to the Moose Deck Viewing Area.

**13.8** Again, the road forks. The left fork leads you over a cattle guard to Bockman

Campground, while the right fork leads you to CO 14 along FS 380. Bear right onto FS 380.

**14.5** FS 380 intersects with FS 390, which leads to Montgomery Pass and the Montgomery Pass Yurt. Continue riding straight on FS 380, following signs for CO 14.

**15.3** FS 380 intersects with FS 395. Continuing on FS 380, blast through the North Fork of North Michigan River and resume your Bockman Campground Loop.

**16.0** FS 380 forks again. Bear left. The right side only leads to a locked gate. From here the going gets a lot tougher, all the way to the top at 17.6 miles. Expect rutted roads and washouts.

**17.6** As you near the top, there's a clearcut off to the left. Hike through it and take in the views of the Nokhu Crags to your south, Bull Mountain to the north, and the farthest stretches of the Mount Zirkel Wilderness Area due west.

**17.8** Come to an intersection. Continue left on FS 380.

**19.1** FS 380 connects with CO 14. Bear left and ride the last 0.8 miles to the Lake Agnes turnout and your vehicle.

**19.9** Arrive back at your vehicle.

# Ride Information

## 📞 Trail Contacts:
**Colorado State Parks**, North Region Office, Fort Collins, CO; (970) 226-6641 **Colorado State Forest State Park**, Walden, CO; (970) 723-8366

## 🕐 Schedule:
Late June to October

## 💲 Fees/Permits:
$2 daily park pass is required for each bicycle entering the Colorado State Forest State Park; $4 daily park pass is required for any motorized vehicle to enter the Colorado State Forest

## ❓ Local Information:
**North Park Chamber of Commerce**, Walden, CO; (970) 723-4600 • **U.S. Forest Service Visitor Information Center**, Fort Collins, CO; (970) 498-2770

## 💡 Local Events/Attractions:
**The North Park Pioneer Museum**, Walden, CO; (970) 723-8371 or (970) 723-4212 or (970) 723-4711 – *located behind the Jackson County courthouse*

North Park Fair, Walden, CO; (970) 723-4600 • **Yurts of Never Summer Nordic**, Fort Collins, CO; (970) 482-9411 or *www.nsnyurts.com*

## 🚲 Local Bike Shops:
**Rock 'n Road Cyclery**, Fort Collins, CO; (970) 223-7623 – *Fort Collins is about 62 miles away, however* • **Lee's Cyclery**, Fort Collins, CO; (970) 482-6006 or 1-800-748-BIKE; second location Fort Collins, CO; (970) 226-6006 • **The Freewheeler Bicycle Shop**, Fort Collins, CO; (970) 224-3262

## Ⓝ Maps:
**USGS maps:** Gould, CO; Clark Peak, CO • *Trails Illustrated* **map:** #112, Poudre River & Cameron Pass and #114, Walden & Gould, CO • **Never Summer Nordic Mountain Bike Trail Map** – *available in Fort Collins from Yurts of Never Summer Nordic (970) 482-9411 and R.E.I (970) 223-0123*

The descent: Remnants of the old logging days with views of the Nokhu Crags, Mount Richthofen, and seven Utes Mountain.

The Bockman Campground Loop is an ideal introduction to this celebrated area. The first nine miles of the 19.9-mile route pass over the 101-mile Cache La Poudre-North Park Scenic and Historic Byway. The route passes the band-saw spires of the 12,400-foot Nokhu Crags—that's NO-koo, a corruption of the original Arapahoe word "Neaha-no-xhu" meaning "eagle's nest"—and leads through the Colorado State Forest. Then it's on to the site of the largest logging camp ever to have operated in Colorado.

The first 1.5 miles is a fast cruising descent past the Nokhu Crags and the Seven Utes Mountain. At mile 0.8, Forest Service Road 380 will be to your right. Here is where the Bockman Campground Loop reconnects with the highway. Heading toward the tiny town of Gould, you pass on your right the never-out-of-season Christmas Tree—a pine tree that's decorated year-round with garland and ornaments—and to your left, the Ranger Lakes Campground, the Moose Visitors Center, and the Cookhouse. Once you officially enter the state forest, the route turns onto Colorado 41, a dirt road.

Passing through a densely populated lodgepole pine forest, Colorado 41 forks just after mile 10. Bear left, following the signs to Bockman Campground, and ride along the north rim of North Michigan Reservoir. Traveling along the willow-lined banks of the North Michigan drainage, you'll encounter perfect moose viewing settings. As you ride away from the reservoir, the great expanse of Bull Mountain lies directly in front of you.

Heading toward the Bockman Campground, the route pierces the heart of North Park's prosperous logging tradition. By 1949 the Bockman Lumber Camp, now the Bockman Campground, was Colorado's largest operating logging camp. Derelict log loading ramps and sawdust piles—relics of old logging days gone by—are all that remain of the camp's former glory. Albeit to a lesser degree, logging continues to be an important source of revenue for the state forest.

Starting from the Bockman Campground, Forest Service Road 380 threads its way through the forest and travels over 10,000 feet. You may notice the forest beginning to thin to your left at roughly 14 miles into your ride. A plaque here commemorates a boy scout, who in order to receive the highest rank of Eagle Scout, had to organize and conduct a community project. The project here was to thin the forest. Thinning forests is a means of regeneration whereby competition among existing trees is lessened, thereby adding to the natural diversity of the forest.

After passing the Eagle Scout's community project, the route becomes increasingly tougher. At mile 15.3, Forest Service Road 380 intersects with Forest Service Road 395 (Montgomery Pass Road). Continue on Forest Service Road 380 and splash through the North Fork Michigan River. By mile 16.5 the steepest section of the route begins, ending only after a lung-busting one-mile climb to the top. At mile 17.6, Forest Service Road 380 levels. Lying in stark contrast to the otherwise thick forest, a large clearcut lies to your left. Hike through the clearcut to the very top and take in the beautiful views of the Nokhu Crags and Seven Utes Mountain to the south, Bull Mountain to the north, and the Mount Zirkel Wilderness Area to the west.

From here it's a speedy and steep descent to Colorado 14. You'll come to an intersection at mile 17.8. An unidentified road leads off to the right. Continue left, however, along Forest Service Road 380 as it drops you past gray slab piles of logging remains and through a lush green meadow replete with aspen, lupine, and thistle. Descend onto Colorado 14 and bear left for the 0.8-mile return to your vehicle.

# Hot Springs to Mad Creek to Red Dirt Trail Loop

## Ride Summary

Mountain bike riders in Steamboat Springs are tough. When one trail isn't long enough to fill up the space of a day, local riders combine two or more trails. The Hot Springs to Mad Creek to Red Dirt Trail Loop is more than just a ride—it's three rides combined. A favorite among area locals, this loop spotlights the Strawberry Park Hot Springs, the steep-walled canyon of Mad Creek, and the quiet solitude of the Red Dirt Trail. Each one of these rides can be ridden separately or fashioned into shorter loops.

## Ride Specs

**Start:** From the corner of 3rd Street and Fish Creek Falls Road, by the Steamboat Springs Post Office

**Length:** 24.3-mile loop, with options to shorten

**Approximate Riding Time:** Advanced Riders, 2–2½ hours; Intermediate Riders, 3–3½ hours

**Technical Difficulty Rating:** Technically moderate. Most of the trail rolls over smooth, hard-packed singletrack, though there are a couple of challenging rocky sections (predominately on the Hot Springs segment of the route).

**Physical Difficulty Rating:** Physically moderate to challenging. The climb to the top of the Hot Springs is challenging, and the road is steep in sections and climbs to heights above 8,000 feet.

**Terrain:** Paved road, improved dirt road, and singletrack. Riders encounter rocky singletrack, sand, creek crossings, ruts, and soft forest singletrack.

**Elevation Gain:** 3,481 feet

**Nearest Town:** Steamboat Springs, CO

**Other Trail Users:** Hikers, campers, equestrians, and bathers

**Canine Compatibility:** Dog friendly

## Getting There

**From downtown Steamboat Springs:** Drive east on CO 40 (Lincoln Avenue) to 3rd Street. At the light, make a left by the Steamboat Springs Post Office and Norwest Bank. Drive for one block and intersect Fish Creek Falls Road. Park your vehicle and begin riding up Fish Creek Falls Road.

**DeLorme: Colorado Atlas & Gazetteer:** Page 26, A-3

To reach the Hot Springs, riders pass through a long and verdant meadowland surrounded by expansive views of Steamboat Ski Resort and Buffalo Pass. This area is known as Strawberry Park (formerly called Sheddeger Park). From 1900 to 1916, Strawberry Park bore fields of commercially grown strawberries. The area was named after the Kansas farmer Lester J. Remington who first noticed the marketability of the strawberries that grew in his hay meadows at the base of Buffalo Pass. The berries were harvested and then shipped to Denver. The newly built railroad afford-

Strawberry Hot Springs.

ed Remington accessibility to Denver's affluent market. Denver's lavish hotel and restaurant, the Brown Palace, became one of Strawberry Park's first accounts. Remington learned that his berries would continue to grow long after plants at lower elevations had stopped bearing fruit. Spurring the town's first economic boon, Strawberry Park became site to two flourishing general stores and provided Steamboat Springs with 16 years of fruitful strawberry production. Area old-timers speak of Remington's strawberries as too big to fit into a drinking glass, and as sweet as they were large. Rising competition among other berry growers, coupled with a killing frost in the early summers of 1915 and 1916, would ultimately cause Strawberry Park to cease its operations for good.

Long before strawberries blanketed this meadowland, summering Ute Indians used the open meadows to dry the roots of the yampa plant (a turnip-like plant that grows along the banks of the Yampa River) for winter storage. As winter approached, they would set camp near the Hot Springs, basking in its warmth and bathing in its curative geothermal waters. Elk, too, would often descend from the higher elevations to drink from these waters and warm themselves, providing Ute Indians all the more

## **Miles**Directions

**0.0 START** at the junction of 3rd Street and Fish Creek Falls Road, by the Steamboat Springs Post Office. Bear right and begin riding up Fish Creek Falls Road, passing above the Steamboat Springs Health and Recreation Club on your right.

**0.3** Bear left onto Amethyst Drive, following signs for Buffalo Pass, Perry Mansfield, and the Hot Springs. Once on Amethyst, after passing through the first block of residential homes, pass Spring Creek Trail to your right (another great ride). From the Spring Creek Trail, continue climbing on Amethyst through a residential neighborhood before passing the Steamboat Springs high school at 1.3 miles.

**2.0** Amethyst Drive intersects CR 36. Continue riding on CR 36 in a northerly direction, through Strawberry Park, following signs for the Hot Springs. Pass CR 38 to your right and the sign for Dry Lake Campground, 3 miles; Buffalo Pass, 11 miles; Fish Creek Reservoir, 16 miles; and CO 14, 32 miles.

**3.7** CR 36 turns into a dirt road. Cross Soda Creek via Soda Creek Bridge and continue riding along CR 36.

**5.9** As the road cuts sharply to the left, you're offered one of the best views of Mount Werner (the Steamboat Springs ski mountain). This point marks the end of the climb. The road weaves its way through dense aspen before descending to the Strawberry Park Hot Springs.

**7.3** Arrive at the Strawberry Park Hot Springs. Ride through the red iron gate, entering the hot springs area, and ride down the hill. A private dirt road will be immediately to your right. Pass this road and pass another turnoff to your left that leads down to the hot springs. Continue riding straight ahead to the singletrack, toward the outhouse.

**7.4** Reach the trailhead for the Hot Springs 1169 singletrack.

**9.9** Arrive at the junction of the Hot Springs 1169 trail and Red Dirt Road. Here, the rider has a number of options from which to choose. **Option One:** (which we are featuring in this chapter) Bear left onto Red Dirt Road and descend to the paved CR 129 (Elk River Road). Once on CR 129, bear right and head for the singletrack climb up through Mad Creek Canyon. **Option Two:** Bear right onto Red Dirt Road and climb to high alpine meadows. Reach the Mad House (Forest Service Guard Station), and ride down either the Mad Creek or Red Dirt trail to CR 129. **Option Three:** Bear left onto Red Dirt Road and descend to the paved CR 129 (Elk River Road). Once on CR 129, bear left again and return to Steamboat Springs.

**10.7** After following Option One, the Mad Creek trailhead will appear to your right. Ride into the Mad Creek parking lot and begin riding up the singletrack of Mad Creek Canyon, following signs for Mad Creek and Swamp Park.

**12.2** Arrive at a gate and go through it. Continue riding straight ahead, along the wooden fence, and toward the Mad House.

**12.4** Mad Creek Trail intersects with the Saddle Trail 1140. Bear left onto the Saddle Trail 1140. The Saddle Trail heads in a southwesterly direction and eventually connects with the Red Dirt Trail.

**13.5** The Saddle Trail 1140 intersects with the Red Dirt Trail 1171. Bear left onto the Red Dirt Trail, as it descends back down to CR 129 (Elk River Road). Bearing right will lead you into the Mount Zirkel Wilderness Area.

**15.4** Red Dirt Trail 1171 intersects with CR 129 (Elk River Road). Bear left (south) onto CR 129.

**21.0** The Steamboat Springs Airport is to your right. Pass the airport and ride down a speedy descent to U.S. 40.

**22.2** CR 129 intersects with U.S. 40. Bear left (east) onto U.S. 40 and return to Steamboat Springs to complete the loop.

**23.4** Enter into the town of Steamboat Springs. Ride through town on Lincoln Avenue (U.S. 40) and turn left at 3rd Street.

**24.3** Arrive at the intersection of 3rd Street and Fish Creek Falls Road and your vehicle.

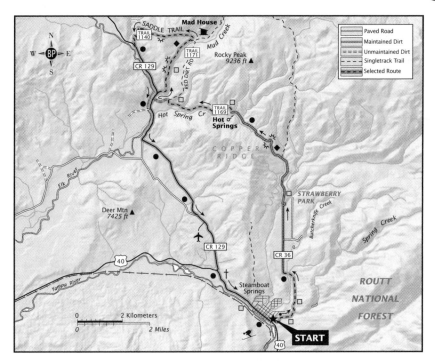

reason to camp near the springs. Oftentimes after battle, Indians would visit these springs to rejuvenate their strength and vitality. For the Utes, these springs were sacred ground, under which manitou, the supernatural force pervading the natural world, resided. Elaborating on this idea of the spiritual force beneath the ground, Dr. R.E. Jones writes, "Mineral Springs are magical in their charm for man. All people have an abiding faith in nature and the mysterious workings that are constantly taking place in her unseen laboratories deep below the earth's surface."

It wasn't long before Europeans discovered the curative powers of hot springs. During Colorado's rise as a health spa paradise in the latter part of the 1800s, bathers were known, not only to soak in the hot springs' mineral-rich waters, but they would also drink from them. Lulita Crawford Pritchett, daughter of Steamboat Springs' founding father, describes the delicious taste of "iron water lemonade" in her book, *The Cabin at Medicine Springs*. A 1946 article in the Steamboat Springs paper, the *Pilot*, tells of a peculiar pastime among area residents. They would march down to the hot springs with picnic baskets and tea pots containing a few spoonfuls of tea. They

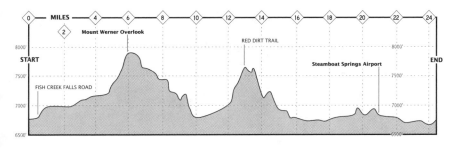

would first boil their eggs in their tea pots full of spring water. After the eggs were boiled, a cup of tea was made from the leftover water to wash the eggs down.

From the Strawberry Park Hot Springs, riders descend along the north edge of Hot Springs Creek. In many places the trail slopes precipitously to the creek. While this segment of trail isn't overly technical, there are a number of short technical sections that require advanced bicycle handling skills. With Hot Springs Creek to your left, the trail weaves in and out of lodgepole pine and aspen forests before letting out onto Red Dirt Road and the second part of the ride.

As you pedal north up the Mad Creek drainage along the wide, sometimes sandy and rocky trail, you'll notice the crashing waters of Mad Creek directly below. The nerve-jarring echoes from Mad Creek Canyon suggest why this creek is "Mad." Deriving its name, as you might assume, from its fast flowing waters, Mad Creek has taken its fair share of casualties. In 1877 a weary traveler narrowly escaped drowning in its current. His horse, not so lucky, was beaten to death on the rocks. So take pains not to get too close to the trail's edge, as it tightly hugs an east-facing slope on its way to the Mad House (a Forest Service Guard Station).

On the morning of October 25, 1997, easterly winds blowing over the Continental Divide and traveling in excess of 120 mph razed roughly 20,000 acres of trees surrounding the Mad House. A wall of wind nearly five miles wide and 30 miles long destroyed over four million of Routt National Forest's Engelmann spruce and subalpine fir. One of the hardest hit areas of this Routt Divide Blowdown included the Mad Creek drainage. Although this route through Mad Creek Canyon lies to the south of the drainage's hardest hit areas, riders should, nevertheless, use caution when cornering around blind curves. The Forest Service is responding to this crisis by implementing salvage logging programs, conducting impact research projects, organizing trail rerouting procedures, and analyzing insect infestation probabilities.

Views of Steamboat's ski resort.

# Ride Information

## 🛈 Trail Contacts:

**Medicine Bow-Routt National Forest**, Steamboat Springs, CO; (970) 879-1870 • **Sore Saddle Cyclery**, Steamboat Springs, CO; (970) 879-1675 • **Medicine Bow-Routt National Forest (Blowdown Hotline)**, Steamboat Springs, CO; (970) 870-2192 or *www.fs.fed.us/mrnf*

## 🕐 Schedule:

Mid June to early October

## ❓ Local Information:

**City of Steamboat Springs**, Steamboat Springs, CO; (970) 879-2060 or *www.ci.steamboat.co.us* • **Steamboat Springs Chamber Resort Association**, Steamboat Springs, CO; (970) 879-0880 or *www.steamboat-chamber.com*

## 📍 Local Events/Attractions:

**Strawberry Park Hot Springs**, Steamboat Springs, CO; (970) 879-0342 • **A Walking Tour of the Springs of Steamboat, CO** – *pick up area map at Tread of pioneers Museum* • **Tread of Pioneers Museum**, Steamboat Springs, CO; (970) 879-2214 • **Steamboat Springs Health & Recreation Center**, Steamboat Springs, CO; (970) 879-1828 • **Steamboat Lake State Park**, North of Steamboat Springs along FS

129, CO; (970) 879-7019 • **Sweet Pea Tours**, Steamboat Springs, CO; (970) 879-5820 – *Hot Springs tours* • **Peak Experience Tours**, Steamboat Springs, CO; (970) 879-1873 – *Hot Springs tours*

## 🏢 Organizations:

**Routt County Riders Bicycle Club**, Steamboat Springs, CO; (970) 879-1735

## 🍴 Restaurants:

**Harwigs**, Steamboat Springs, CO; (970) 879-1980 • **Steamboat Brewery & Tavern**, Steamboat Springs, CO; (970) 879-2233

## 🚲 Local Bike Shops:

**Sore Saddle Cyclery**, Steamboat Springs, CO; (970) 879-1675 • **Ski Haus**, Steamboat Springs, CO; (970) 879-0385 • **Ski Kare**, Steamboat Springs, CO; (970) 879-9144

## 🅽 Maps:

**USGS maps:** Steamboat Springs, CO; Rocky Peak, CO; Mad Creek, CO • *Trails Illustrated* maps: # 117, Clark, Buffalo Pass; #118, Steamboat Springs, Rabbit Ears Pass • **Routt National Forest Map** – *available at the Medicine Bow-Routt National Forest office (970) 879-1870*

---

Escaping the mad-running waters and the wind-torn forests, one finally finds sanctuary in the peaceful solitude of the Saddle Trail. After connecting onto the Saddle Trail, dense rows of golden aspen run alongside the singletrack and bow overhead like drawn swords at a West Point wedding. Riding through this peaceful, gold-leafed gauntlet, you pass rows of beautiful pearly everlasting (anaphalis margaritacea) before intersecting with the Red Dirt Trail.

The Red Dirt Trail combines exquisite hard-packed singletrack through some of the area's most undisturbed terrain. As you ride through varying aspen and fir forests, you're delivered a cool and quiet ride. You're thrown from your blissful reverie at mile 14.3, when washboard ruts 12 inches deep and wide jostle the unsuspecting rider. Once you've connected with Elk River Road (Route County Road 129), bear left for the mellow highway ride back to Steamboat Springs.

# Howelsen Hill Loop 6

## Ride Summary

As a skiing hill, Howelsen Hill has already been the proving grounds for 37 Olympians, 14 members of the Colorado Ski Hall of Fame, and six members of the National Ski Hall of Fame—and has sent more skiers to international competition than any other area in the nation. As a mountain biking hill, Howelsen Hill offers great singletrack riding immediately accessible from downtown Steamboat Springs. Billed as a quick ride to squeeze in before work, the Howelsen Hill Loop climbs 2.3 miles to a rock quarry before ripping down incredibly steep, rocky, and hard-packed singletrack.

## Ride Specs

**Start:** From the base of Howelsen Hill by the Tow House
**Length:** 4.1-mile loop
**Approximate Riding Time:** Advanced Riders, 45 minutes; Intermediate Riders 1–1½ hours
**Technical Difficulty Rating:** Technically moderate to challenging. There are a couple of tough rocky and steep sections with which to contend, but the majority of the route follows over hard-packed dirt singletrack and improved dirt road.
**Physical Difficulty Rating:** Physically moderate due to a short but steep section of road
**Terrain:** Improved dirt road, doubletrack, and singletrack. The terrain includes sandy and rocky sections, creek-crossings, and hard-packed dirt through meadows and aspen and fir forests.
**Elevation Gain:** 1,240 feet
**Nearest Town:** Steamboat Springs, CO
**Other Trail Users:** Hikers, joggers, and equestrians
**Canine Compatibility:** Dog friendly

## Getting There

**From Steamboat Springs:** Drive east on U.S. 40 (Lincoln Avenue) and turn right onto 5th Street. Cross the 5th Street Bridge and Yampa River. Turn right by the Rodeo Grounds and drive toward the softball fields. Bear left by the softball fields and park in the Howelsen Hill parking lot. Begin your ride by the Tow House at the base of Howelsen Hill.
***DeLorme: Colorado Atlas & Gazetteer.*** Page 26, A 2-3

H owelsen Hill is holy ground—though you wouldn't necessarily know it, given its "other side of the tracks" heritage. Riders from downtown Steamboat Springs access the trails to Howelsen Hill by crossing the Yampa River via the 5th Street Bridge. Dividing the north from the south sides of Steamboat Springs, the Yampa River flows directly through the middle of town. Back in the early 1900s, the 5th Street Bridge was more commonly referred to as the "Brooklyn Bridge"—more for its corrupt city-like connotations than for any physical similarity to the famous New York City bridge. As riders head toward Howelsen Hill via the 5th Street

Bridge, they cross over into what was Steamboat Springs' red light district. While the north end of town had its bible thumpers, the south end of town enjoyed all the comforts whiskey, women, and cards could afford. Given this history, it seems unlikely that anything holy could arise from this side of the tracks.

Howelsen Hill gets its name from the Norwegian ski jumping champion Carl Howelsen, who came to America in 1905. Barnum and Bailey Circus first discovered Howelsen while working as a stone mason in Chicago. A makeshift ski jump was set up inside arenas from Chicago to New York. Howelsen would descend this slick ramp on his skis and soar through the air, not unlike the way he used to do as a boy growing up in Norway. His daring flights through the air, covering over 80 feet, thrilled audiences in New York City's Madison Square Garden. Having played the star attraction for the "Greatest Show on Earth," Howelsen found it not nearly as gratifying as the simple pleasures of living in Ski Town, U.S.A. Howelsen moved to Steamboat Springs in 1913. Although he would never become an Olympian, Howelsen would become legend.

Almost immediately after arriving in Steamboat Springs, Howelsen was jumping and performing for the local crowds. In 1914, he organized the town's first Winter Carnival on Woodchuck Hill (the present site of Colorado Mountain College). This is not to say that the people of Steamboat didn't know what skiing was prior to Howelsen's arrival. As early as the 1880s, men like George Wren and Elmer Brooks would ski to Morrison Creek to meet the mail carriage and ski the mail back to town. Among the Steamboat people, Howelsen found the same passion for skiing that he had. This is the connection he had been missing in the concrete jungles of Chicago and New York City.

In the summer following the first Steamboat Springs Winter Carnival, Howelsen helped organize the Steamboat

Carl Howelsen, circa 1920.

131

Group photo atop the quarry. Steamboat Springs ski resort and town in the background.

Springs Winter Sports Club, the first nationally recognized ski club west of the Mississippi. By this time Howelsen recognized the need for a first class jumping hill, so by 1915 Howelsen had a Winter Carnival Committee cutting underbrush and timber to make way for the first ski jump below Emerald Mountain. By February of 1917, during the 4th Annual Winter Sports Carnival, the new ski jumping hill was officially christened Howelsen Hill.

Howelsen continued to promote ski jumping throughout Colorado. Enthusiasm for ski jumping grew by leaps and bounds. Howelsen's reward came in 1921 when he won the National Professional Ski Championships at Gennesee Mountain. Perhaps it was this final achievement that prompted Howelsen to return to the "old country" in the fall of that same year. Howelsen soon married a fellow Norwegian and lived out the remainder of his days in his homeland—no doubt on a pair of skis.

Left without their "Flying Norseman," the people of Steamboat Springs continued skiing. By the late 1930s, Howelsen Hill included not only a ski jump, but slalom

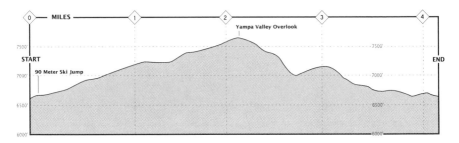

## **Miles**Directions

**0.0 START** riding on the doubletrack by the Tow House at the base of Howelsen Hill, following signs for Loops 1 through 6 and Howelsen Hill Hiking Trail. Bear right around the Tow House and ride up in front of the 90-meter ski jump.

**0.2** After a brief descent, the doubletrack intersects with a singletrack. Bear left onto this singletrack, following signs for Loops 1-6. This singletrack immediately connects with another dirt road. Bear left onto the dirt road and continue climbing.

**0.4** This dirt road intersects with another dirt road. Bear right here, continuing in a southerly direction, riding on the same road on which you started.

**0.8** Arrive at a fork, noticeable by a squat wall of river stone encased within wire. A single-track trail bears to the right as the road continues to the left. Bearing left here leads you to trail signs for Loops 1-6, while bearing right on the singletrack leads you to another dirt road. Either fork will lead you to the top and the beginning of Loop 6. At this junction, bear right onto the singletrack, passing the wall of river stone and continue climbing.

**0.9** The singletrack intersects with another dirt road. Veer left onto this dirt road. This road leads you to the top of Howelsen Hill, passing signs for Option Meadows cross-country and Loops 2-6.

**1.3** Pass the beginning of Loop 2.

**1.5** Pass the beginning of Loop 3.

**1.7** Pass the beginning of Loop 4.

**2.0** Pass the beginning of Loop 5.

**2.3** Reach the top of Loop 6. Begin your descent by ripping down the shale-torn singletrack, past the Loop 6 sign on the right. The initial descent on Loop 6 heads straight for the road that delivered you to the top. Approximately 25 feet before you reach this road again, another singletrack trail veers off to the right (at 2.4 miles). Veer right onto this singletrack. It drops you in a north-easterly direction through a forest of scrub oak.

**3.1** The Loop 6 singletrack intersects with a rough doubletrack. Bear left onto this double-track, heading in a northwesterly direction. If you look down this doubletrack, you'll notice

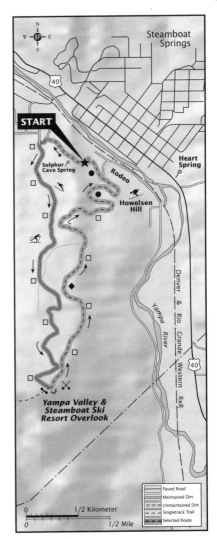

a point where the trail reaches a short crest. Just over this crest is a singletrack that bears off to the right. Bear right onto this single-track. It passes a couple of beaver ponds.

**3.5** Bear right onto a singletrack, following signs for the Base Area. Howelsen ski hill will be to your left. Notice the chairlifts.

**3.8** Bear right again onto the singletrack. It will lead to a dirt road directly behind the Rodeo Grounds. Once on this dirt road, bear left and descend to the parking lot.

**4.1** Reach the base of Howelsen Hill and your vehicle.

# Ride Information

### 📞 Trail Contacts:
**Howelsen Hill**, (970) 879-8499 • **Steamboat Springs Parks & Recreation Department**, Steamboat Springs, CO; (970) 879-4300

### 🕐 Schedule:
June to early October

### ❓ Local Information:
**City of Steamboat Springs**, Steamboat Springs, CO; (970) 879-2060 or *www.ci.steamboat.co.us* • **Steamboat Springs Chamber Resort Association**, Steamboat Springs, CO; (970) 879-0880 or *www.steamboat-chamber.com*

### 🔦 Local Events/Attractions:
**Strawberry Park Hot Springs**, Steamboat Springs, CO; (970) 879-0342 • **Tread of Pioneers Museum**, Steamboat Springs, CO; (970) 879-2214 – *offers a walking tour map* • **Steamboat Lake State Park**, North of Steamboat Springs along FS 129, CO (970) 879-7019

### 👥 Organizations:
**Routt County Riders Bicycle Club**, Steamboat Springs, CO; (970) 879-1735

### 🍴 Restaurants:
**Harwigs**, Steamboat Springs, CO; (970) 879-1980 • **Steamboat Brewery & Tavern**, Steamboat Springs, CO; (970) 879-2233

### 🚲 Local Bike Shops:
**Sore Saddle Cyclery**, Steamboat Springs, CO; (970) 879-1675 • **Ski Haus**, Steamboat Springs, CO; (970) 879-0385 • **Ski Kare**, Steamboat Springs, CO; (970) 879-9144

### Ⓜ Maps:
**USGS maps:** Steamboat Springs, CO • **Trails Illustrated maps:** # 118, Steamboat Springs, Rabbit Ears Pass

and downhill courses as well. By 1934, a "boat tow," powered by a car motor, pulled skiers to the top of Howelsen Hill via cable and two sleds. The 1940s saw the construction of a log ski lodge at the base of Howelsen Hill, another rope tow and one of the United states' longest ski lifts at that time, running from the hill's base to the top of Emerald Mountain. During the 1950s, a 90-meter ski jump was built and is still in use today.

In fact, all of Howelsen Hill is still being enjoyed, making it one of the oldest jumping complexes in the nation. Today, Howelsen Hill is an official city park and is managed by the Steamboat Springs Parks and Recreation Department. Just as the mountain brought the Steamboat Springs community together through skiing, it now brings people together through mountain biking as well.

It wasn't until 1998 that the first mountain bike trail signs appeared on Howelsen Hill. Prior to that, the trails were there; they just weren't marked. Today, the Parks and Recreation Department has marked six loop rides for added convenience. Loop 6 (the area's longest official ride) takes us to the top of Howelsen Hill and delivers us to the Rodeo Grounds. To access Loop 6, riders begin from the Tow House and pedal past the 90-meter jump before reaching the dirt access road. As the road climbs to the south, views of the Sleeping Giant lie to the west. Looking from the east, the mountain resembles a giant sleeping on his back, his knees drawn up. This road eventually takes you to the beginning of Loop 6 and a beautiful overlook. From the overlook, panoramic views from east to west include Mount Werner, Fish Creek Canyon, Buffalo Pass, Soda Mountain, Hahns Peak, and the Mount Zirkel Wilderness Area.

Loop 6 descends rapidly over rocky and sometimes steep terrain. After passing through intermittent forests of pine and aspen, the trail descends through a number of meadows before reaching the cow ponds. Once past the cow ponds, bear left to finish your ride with a narrow and steep descent to the Rodeo Grounds and the base of Howelsen Hill.

Making short work of the "Hill's" singletrack.

# Arapaho Ridge Trail

## Ride Summary

This Continental Divide-brushing ride, bordering on the Routt and Arapaho National Forests, is great for anyone seeking an awe-inspiring 360-degree view, coupled with a savage descent. Although the view and descent do come at a price, the climb to the top of the Divide shouldn't deter any dreamy-eyed mountain biker. Once you reach the top, you're rewarded with a narrow, rutted, rocky, and switch-backing singletrack descent. The trail continues its vertical fall over rocky hillsides, through creeks, meadows, ponds, and evergreen forests before entering into the lower elevations and increasingly smoother singletrack. Speed was never so pretty.

## Ride Specs

**Start:** From the trailhead for the Arapaho Ridge Trail and Hyannis Peak Trail 1135
**Length:** 12.2-miles out-and-back
**Approximate Riding Time:** Advanced Riders, 2–2½ hours; Intermediate Riders, 3–4 hours
**Technical Difficulty Rating:** Technically demanding due to the amount of rocky, rutted, and sloping terrain upon reaching the higher elevations
**Physical Difficulty Rating:** Physically challenging to demanding due to grueling climbs
**Terrain:** Singletrack. Travels over soft, forest earth, coupled with exposed rocks and roots; sloping, marshy meadows; rocky and rutted tundra-like terrain; and a number of creek crossings.
**Elevation Gain:** 3,487 feet
**Nearest Town:** Kremmling, CO
**Other Trail Users:** Hikers, campers, anglers, and motorcyclists
**Canine Compatibility:** Dog friendly

## Getting There

**From Kremmling:** Drive west on U.S. 40 for 15.6 miles before turning right onto CR 27 (Chimney Rock Road), following signs for Chimney Rock. After six miles (from when you turned onto CR 27) enter into the Arapaho National Forest. CR 27 becomes FS 103. Drive on FS 103 for another four miles before bearing right onto FS 700. Soon thereafter, FS 700 intersects with FS 104. Bear left at this intersection and continue on FS 700 for another five miles before FS 700 forks again. Bear right at this fork and continue on FS 700. Drive for another four miles to the trailhead for the Arapaho Ridge Trail. After crossing the Middle Fork Arapaho Creek, the trail will be to your right, marked by a bulletin board. *DeLorme: Colorado Atlas & Gazetteer:* Page 27, A 6-7

he Arapaho Ridge Trail remains one of Colorado's most anomalous trails. Located in the Routt National Forest, the trail leads to the top of the Continental Divide—the geographical dividing line of the Platte River watershed, which flows to the Atlantic Ocean, and the Colorado River watershed, which flows to the Pacific Ocean. The Divide also marks the boundary between the Arapaho and Routt National Forests. Although the Arapaho National Forest includes land on both sides of the Continental Divide, a vast majority of its land lies near the high population communities of the Front Range. As such, the Arapaho National Forest is one of Colorado's most visited national forests.

Taking care of business along the trail's rockier sections.

The 1,126,346-acre Routt National Forest, on the other hand, lies on Colorado's western slope and receives far less traffic. Of the trails within the Routt National Forest, the one that receives perhaps the least number of visits is the Arapaho Ridge Trail, as it lies along the forest's easternmost boundary. While Front Range cyclists enjoy most of the Arapaho National Forest east of the Continental Divide, mountain bikers of the Routt National Forest tend to enjoy the more interior trails west of the Colorado Divide. Since the Arapaho Ridge Trail lies on the cusp of each of these forests, it typically gets overlooked by both camps. As a result, the Arapaho Ridge Trail remains relatively unused, hidden in a kind of "No Man's Land" amidst the wilds of Colorado's western slope. With neither Front Range, nor western slope riders claiming the Arapaho Ridge Trail as their own, the trail would certainly remain an orphan were it not for its close proximity to Kremmling, a tiny town nestled in a valley at the confluence of the Colorado and Blue rivers.

Kremmling seems a fitting surrogate for this orphaned trail since its own birth shares a similar kind of isolation. Kremmling's first settlement, and later its first business, rose from a cave located on the banks of the Muddy River, just north of the town's present location. James Crawford settled alone into the cave in 1873 with hopes of securing a place to live for his family. Before he'd move his family into what was then a wild and inhospitable country, Crawford would lead a relatively solitary life, mostly tending his cattle. He made his way out from the cave only to carry milk to his family whom he'd left in Hot Sulphur Springs. On these few and infrequent occasions, Crawford would load a wooden sled and drag it himself the 15 miles to Hot Sulphur Springs. Deciding that a cave was no place to raise a family, Crawford moved west to Steamboat Springs, this time bringing his family with him.

A sigh of relief...

## **Miles**Directions

**0.0 START** at the Arapaho Ridge and Hyannis Peak trailhead. Begin riding in a southerly direction through a dense evergreen forest, climbing moderately over hilly terrain.

**1.4** Arrive at a beaver bond, lying to the southwest. Bear right, riding around the pond.

**2.1** Cross Arapaho Creek for the first time and again at 2.2 miles.

**2.6** Cross Arapaho Creek for the third time. After riding out of the drainage, the route leads across a hillside. This hillside is marked by slippery, exposed rock.

**3.4** Enter into a hillside and meadow, and ride toward the Forest Service sign for "Carter Creek – 5 miles." Here is a good spot to rest and re-fuel, as the toughest part of the route begins from this point on.

**4.6** A rocky technical section awaits. Here the tight and rocky route descends into a small gully, before cutting sharply to the right at bottom and rising steeply from the gully to the top.

**6.1** Reach the top of Arapaho Ridge and the Continental Divide. Return the same way you came.

**12.2** Arrive at your vehicle.

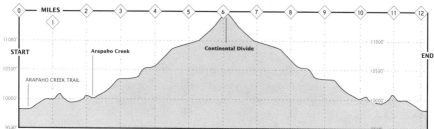

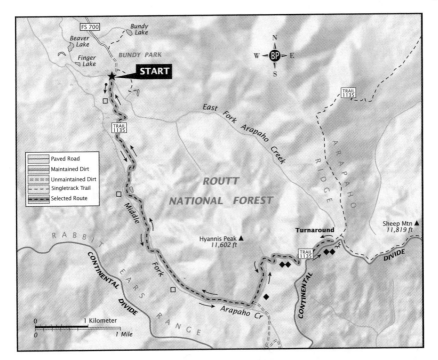

With the cave now vacant, and somewhat of a curio by now, Rudolph Kremmling, a retail businessman from Dillon and Kremmling's founding father, decided that the cave would make an excellent shop. In 1874 the town of Kremmling had its first business. Run by the Dillon retailer, the cave became a supply store for settlers traveling west. With the promise of the coming Denver, Northwestern, and Pacific railroad and the good ranch land available in the area, Kremmling found it necessary to move his shop to a bigger location. In 1875 his outfitter shop moved to its present site, now the Dan Hoare Village Smithy building, north of the Town Square. Out of this new location grew his business and eventually the town's first post office. By 1900 Kremmling became a town on the rise, with 270 people building for a promising future.

When the railroad arrived in 1906, Kremmling had already established itself as one of the Colorado West's premier social towns, complete with eight libation stations. And who could ask for a better setting. The town is surrounded by the peaks of the Gore Range to the south; to the west by Gore Canyon's steep crevasse, through which flows the Gore River; to the north by the monolithic cliffs; and to the east by the William's Fork Range and the Continental Divide. Today, Kremmling is poised as one of Colorado's premier playgrounds.

We begin exploring the playground on the Arapaho Ridge Trail's hard-packed singletrack through a densely mixed conifer forest. As the route climbs moderately over hilly terrain, the trail courses through the best of Colorado woodlands. During the summer, the Arapaho Indians frequently hunted these woodlands, perhaps following this same trail as it courses through prime elk, moose, and deer real estate. After crossing Arapaho Creek three times, you reach the Carter Creek sign.

# Ride Information

### 📞 Trail Contacts:
**Medicine Bow-Routt National Forests**, Steamboat Springs, CO; (970) 879-1870 • **Motion Sports**, Kremmling, CO; (970) 724-9067

### 🕐 Schedule:
July to mid October

### ❓ Local Information:
**Kremmling Chamber of Commerce and Information Center**, Kremmling, CO; (970) 724-3472

### 💡 Local Events/Attractions:
**Junction Butte**, Kremmling, CO – called "Elk Mountain" by locals, it's located south of town and features the outline of a buck on its north face • **Gore Canyon**, located roughly five miles southwest of Kremmling, CO – offers Class IV and V whitewater rafting on the Colorado River. For details contact AdventureQuest.com, Colorado Blue Adventures (970) 724-9419, or Monarch Guides (970) 653-4210 or 1-888-463-5628 • **Green Mountain Reservoir**, 12 miles south of Kremmling on Colorado 9. For more information, contact the Kremmling Chamber of Commerce and Information Center (970) 724-3472 • **Wolford Reservoir**, just six miles north of town, off of U.S. 40 – offers some of the area's best gold medal fishing. For more information, contact the Kremmling Chamber of Commerce and Information Center (970) 724-3472. • **Annual Roadkill Supper**, in October, Kremmling, CO; (970) 724-3472 – an all-you-can-eat dinner featuring wild game • **Middle Park Fair & Rodeo**, in September, Kremmling, CO; (970) 724-3436 – children's games, food and crafts • **Kremmling Days**, in June, Kremmling, CO; (970) 724-3472 – parade, kids' games, crafts, family activities • **Fire at the Cliffs**, July 4, Kremmling, CO (Close to Junction Butte), (970) 724-3472 – fireworks display

### 🛏 Accommodations:
**Hotel Eastin**, Kremmling, CO; (970) 724-3261 or 1-800-546-0815 • **Stagecoach Country Inn**, Hot Sulphur Springs, CO; 1-800-725-3919

### 🚲 Local Bike Shops:
**Motion Sports**, Kremmling, CO; (970) 724-9067

### 🅝 Maps:
**USGS maps:** Hyannis Peak, CO; Buffalo Peak, CO • **Trails Illustrated map:** #106 • **Routt National Forest map** – available at the office of Medicine Bow-Routt National Forests (970) 879-1870. • **Kremmling Area Mountain Bike Map** – available at Chamber of Commerce. This map incorporates the Arapaho Ridge Trail as part of the larger "Continental Divide Loop;" however, locating the "jeep road" off of the Arapaho Ridge Trail to connect the loop is an ascetic's lesson in patience, if not futility.

Although not particularly technical to this point, the trail becomes increasingly so after you leave the sign. After four miles, the trail begins to climb significantly over tight and gravely singletrack. As you near the timberline, at about 4.5 miles, the trail opens up onto an east-facing slope. Here the trail climbs sharply to the north. Loose rock, deep ruts, narrow singletrack, and high elevations all take their toll on your struggling body—but never your will.

As the route dips into an enormous valley, trees fall from view as surrounding Hyannis Peak (11,602 feet) rises like the sun. Here, all is mountain. If the trail were the thread and the route, the stitching, you'd find yourself nothing more than a spec of lint in the huge pocket of a mountainous coat. A south-facing gully provides easy access into the deepest recesses of this pocket before delivering you to the last remaining switchback to the top.

Although the climb to the top is very demanding, the views upon reaching the Continental Divide are unbelievably well worth the strain. The panoramic view offers up the Mount Zirkel Wilderness to the north, the Gore Range to the south and west, and the Never Summer Wilderness to the east. The view will no doubt delay your descent for a time.

# Base Camp to Mountain View Trail

## Ride Summary

The Base Camp to Mountain View Trail incorporates one of Routt County's newest trails. Starting from Rabbit Ears Pass, riders travel over steep, rocky descents and ascents; through fast, smooth high alpine meadows and bone-chilling creeks on their way to the top of the Steamboat Springs Ski Resort. Commanding views of the Yampa Valley and Routt National Forest reward the tireless rider as he or she approaches the resort. From the top of the resort there are a variety of trail options to the bottom, ranging from technical singletrack (described herein) to dirt service roads.

## Ride Specs

**Start:** From the Rabbit Ears Trailhead
**Length:** 26.5-mile point-to-point
**Approximate Riding Time:** 3–4 hours
**Technical Difficulty Rating:** Technically moderate to challenging due to rocky and rutted terrain.
**Physical Difficulty Rating:** Physically challenging due to long miles and extended climbs at higher elevations.
**Terrain:** Improved dirt roads, singletrack, and doubletrack. You'll pass a number of lakes and cross a variety of creeks, traveling mostly in dense woodlands. The ride extends over very mountainous terrain.
**Elevation Gain:** 2,397 feet
**Nearest Town:** Steamboat Springs, CO
**Other Trail Users:** Hikers, campers, anglers, back-country skiers, and snowmobilers
**Canine Compatibility:** Dog friendly

## Getting There

**From Steamboat Springs:** Drive east on U.S. 40 toward Rabbit Ears Pass. Turn left (north) onto FS 315, two miles before Rabbit Ears Pass—a sign for Dumont Lake marks the entrance. Follow FS 315 for nearly two miles as it winds its way eastward. Just beyond the Dumont Lake Campground, on the north (left) side of the road, you'll notice a large boulder monument commemorating the Rabbit Ears Pass. Turn here and drive into the parking lot. Begin your ride through the wooden gate (not the trail to the right of it) and onto FS 311, Base Camp Road.
***DeLorme: Colorado Atlas & Gazetteer.*** Page 27, A-4
**Shuttle Required:** Leave one vehicle parked in the municipal parking lot on the corner of Mount Werner Circle and Ski Time Square. Park the second vehicle at the Rabbit Ears Trailhead, at the start of Base Camp Road.

Base Camp Trail to Mountain View Trail is located at the top of Rabbit Ears Pass in the Routt National Forest. Riders typically access this trail from the Steamboat Springs Ski Resort at the top of Mount Werner; however, starting, as this ride does, from Rabbit Ears Pass allows the rider to explore a network of trails along the Continental Divide, while testing his or her climbing strength.

Rabbit Ears Pass takes its name from an enormous rock formation located to the north of the pass. Rabbit Ears Peak, as it's called, consists of twin 100-foot pinnacles, which bear a striking resemblance to a pair of rabbit ears. The "ears" are actually a single volcanic plug split in half. This lava-filled artery is all that remains of a pre-Cambrian that has since been done in by time and erosion. The cementing of broken volcanic material with reddish lava has given the formation its mahogany-colored shadings. Iron oxide remains the dominant color influence. The base of the

Rabbit Ears' south face is steeped in this agglomerate rock. Since this rock's consistency closely resembles that of cooled cinders, hikers to the peaks make sport of jumping down the Rabbit Ears' south face as if it were a snow-covered hillside. One can literally "ski" down the south face in the summertime, redefining the sport of ski jumping.

Just west of Rabbit Ears Peak lies the Meadows Campground, an early Ute Indian campsite. On a larger scale, the area surrounding the Base Camp Trailhead used to be a general meeting ground for a variety of Native Americans. The mountain tribes of the Arapahoes and Gros Ventres, the Great Plains tribes of the Sioux and Cheyenne, and the Colorado and Great Basin tribes of the Utes would travel the great natural wilderness highways to partake of the area's excellent hunting and fishing.

Rabbit Ears Pass saw little more than foot traffic until 1914, when, funded by private investors, it saw its first highway. Dedicated as a memorial to those who lost their lives in World War I, the Victory Highway (now U.S. Route 40) provided the first transcontinental link between New York and San Francisco. In the early days of the Victory Highway, a well was placed in the Meadows Campground to aid the boiling radiators of vehicles ambitious enough to cross.

Beginning at 9,573 feet, Base Camp Road climbs to a modest 10,320 feet within the first four miles—a good warm up by anyone's standards. The well-worn jeep road meanders through thick evergreen forests and past open meadows and marshes, offering stunning views of Rabbit Ears Peak and Dumont Lake. Although the terrain is physically and technically moderate, it should take approximately 45 minutes to arrive at the Base Camp Trailhead.

There are a number of tricky dips on the Base Camp Trail, with a fair amount of rocky, technical sections. The trail eventually dances its way out of the forest to meet with the siren song of Fishhook Lake—a sub-alpine lake whose banks caress the heart of the forest in the shape of a fishhook. From Fishhook Lake the trail climbs through thick rows of evergreens and polished aspen until arriving at the junction of the Percy Lake Trail (FS 1134), the Wyoming Trail (FS 1101, which runs along the Continental Divide to Buffalo Pass), and the beginning of the Fish Creek Falls Trail (FS 1102). Known to local riders as the 7-Eleven spot, this junction's only edible treats come in the way of huckleberry bushes. Continue riding west on the Fish Creek Falls Trail to Long Lake.

Once you arrive at Long Lake—a century-old watershed at the head of Fish Creek—the singletrack gives way to a service road. Avoid the unmarked, bush-whacked trail to the left which crosses a Long Lake tributary near a solar-paneled post. Bear right and continue on the Fish Creek Falls Trail as it flanks the north side of the lake. Eventually the road forks, and you notice a sign for the Fish Creek Falls Trail, directing you to the left. Continue on this trail for a mile until arriving at the Mountain View Trail.

The Mountain View Trail begins with a steep but short climb until eventually lev-eling off in the thick of the woods. From here, the trail winds its way through dense stands of pine and aspen and past meadows and beaver ponds. Just past the beaver ponds, at roughly 14.1 miles, the sun-warmed scree off to the right of the trail pro-vides a great spot to dry wet socks and warm cold feet. The toughest climbing of the day begins here.

You'll encounter two switchbacks at the trail's steepest gradient. Northern views of Buffalo Pass, western views of Hahns Peak and the Lost Ranger Peak, and south-ern views of the Never Summer Mountain Range surround you and compliment the dizzying sensation one experiences while climbing at altitudes in excess of 9,000 feet. The trail eventually crests and offers outstanding views of the Flat Tops Wilderness Area and the Yampa Valley. Follow the trail as it makes its way to the top of Storm Peak, passing through stellar wintertime backcountry skiing terrain.

At 17.5 miles you arrive at the top of Storm Peak. From here, there are a variety of options to reach the bottom: Pete's Wicked to Duster to ZigZag or Creekside is a fine option. From the top of Mount Werner, plan on taking at least an hour to reach the bottom, covering roughly nine miles in the process.

Views from the top of Pete's Wicked Trail.

# Ride Information

## 🕿 Trail Contacts:

**Medicine Bow-Routt National Forest**, Steamboat Springs, CO; (970) 879-1870 • **Sore Saddle Cyclery**, Steamboat Springs, CO; (970) 879-1675

## ⏰ Schedule:

July to early October

## ❓ Local Information:

**City of Steamboat Springs**, Steamboat Springs, CO; (970) 879-2060; *www.ci.steamboat.co.us* • **Steamboat Springs Chamber Resort Association**, Steamboat Springs, CO; (970) 879-0880; *www.steamboat-chamber.com*

## 💡 Local Events/Attractions:

**Steamboat Ski Area**, Steamboat Springs, CO; (970) 879-6111 or *www.steamboat-ski.com* • **Strawberry Park Hot Springs**, Steamboat Springs, CO; (970) 879-0342 • **Tread of Pioneers Museum**, Steamboat Springs, CO; (970) 879-2214

## ➖ Accommodations:

**Steamboat Bed And Breakfast**, Steamboat Springs, CO; (970) 879-5724 • **Rabbit Ears Motel**, Steamboat Springs, CO; (970) 879-1150 or *www.toski.com/rabbitears/summer*

## 🍴 Restaurants:

**Harwig's**, Steamboat Springs, CO; (970) 879-1980 • **Steamboat Brewery & Tavern**, Steamboat Springs, CO; (970) 879-2233 or *www.steamboat.-tavern.com*

## 👥 Organizations:

**Routt County Riders Bicycle Club**, Steamboat Springs, CO; (970) 879-1735

## 🚲 Local Bike Shops:

**Sore Saddle Cyclery**, Steamboat Springs, CO; (970) 879-1675 • **Ski Haus**, Steamboat Springs, CO; (970) 879-0385 • **Ski Kare**, Steamboat Springs, CO; (970) 879-9144

## Ⓝ Maps:

**USGS maps:** Rabbit Ears Peak, CO; Mount Werner, CO • *Trails Illustrated map: # 118*, Steamboat Springs and Rabbit Ears Pass, CO • **Steamboat Springs Ski Resort Bike Map**–*available at the Steamboat Ski Area*

# **Miles**Directions

**0.0 START** on Base Camp Road.

**1.4** "Little Snowbird" is to your right—a popular back country skiing site for Steamboat Springs locals.

**4.3** On your right, leading into the forest due north, is the start of the singletrack. Notice the sign for FS 1102. This is the Base Camp Trailhead. There may be vehicles parked here.

**6.5** Here the trail intersects. A short hike will bring you to Lost Lake. Bear left, however, and continue on Base Camp Trail, following signs for Lake Elmo.

**8.8** The Base Camp Trail meets the junction of the Wyoming Trail (FS 1101, the

Continental Divide Trail), the Percy Lake Trail (FS 1134), and the Fish Creek Falls Trail (FS 1102). Bear left and continue westward on Trail 1102, now the Fish Creek Falls Trail, for about a mile until arriving at Long Lake.

**9.8** Arrive at Long Lake. Bear right following the Fish Creek Falls Trail signs.

**10.7** The Mountain View Trail starts to your left as it splits from the Fish Creek Falls Trail and immediately begins to climb.

**17.5** Reach the top of Storm Peak and intersect the Storm Peak Challenge Trail. Veer right heading for Pete's Wicked Trail. Just past the top of the Storm Peak Express Lift, veer

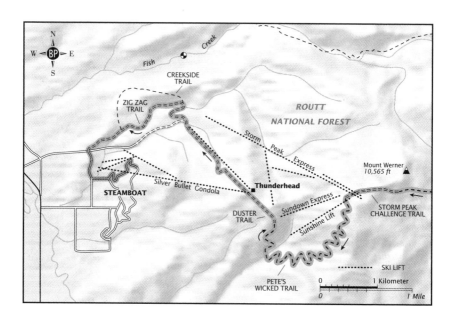

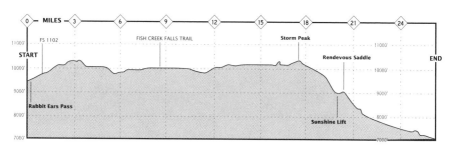

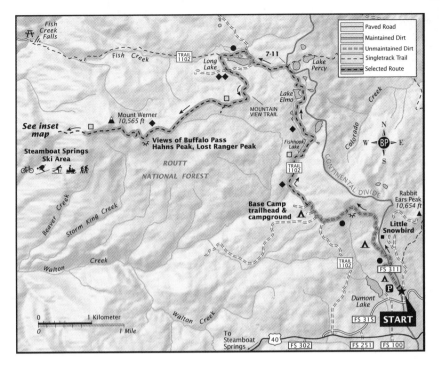

right onto the singletrack of Pete's Wicked Trail. With the exception of one short climb at the bottom of the Sunshine lift, it's all down hill from here.

**20.2** Arrive at the bottom of the Sunshine Lift. Continue climbing up the road until you reach the Rendezvous Saddle, where refreshments are available. At this point, Pete's Wicked Trail ends. Take "Duster," a long and fast cruise with luscious views of the valley.

**21.5** Arrive at the Rainbow Saddle. Take the middle of three roads to your left and climb for approximately three-tenths of a mile. Come to a "slow" sign on your right. Veer right onto this doubletrack, which is now the ZigZag Trail. ZigZag will immediately come to an abrupt

fork. Take the fork hard to the right. It winds down to the Arrowhead Lift Line, where the trail once again turns to dirt road. In just six-tenths of a mile dive left onto a singletrack trail that eventually leads out onto another service road.

**24.2** This road winds past the bottom of the Storm Peak Express Chairlift until reaching the Creekside Trailhead on the right. Continue on the doubletrack of ZigZag, but be careful to check your speed as dips across the trail make for hazardous high speed travel.

**26.5** Once you reach the bottom of the ski resort, you'll find tasty margaritas at the Dos Amigos and frothy micros at the Heavenly Daze.

# Muddy Slide
# Morrison Divide Trail

## Ride Summary

The Muddy Slide Trail is one of Routt County's oldest and best trails. The trail leads riders to the geological oddity after which this ride is named. Atop Green Ridge lies a mountain with half of its side missing. The trail was built expressly to deliver tourists to this particular view, and it has been doing so for some 75 years. Due to its age and its historical and geological significance, the Muddy Slide Trail is eligible to be listed on the National Register of Historic Places. By the summer of 1999, a two-panel interpretive sign will be constructed atop Green Ridge and will include geological and historical accounts of the muddy slide. The Rocky Mountain Youth Corps (an organization designed to foster leadership and teamwork in high risk Junior and High School-aged youths) in partnership with the Routt National Forest Service, has maintained the trail's integrity by building a number of "turnpikes" (banked sections of trail designed to prevent erosion) through its muddier sections. By all counts, the Muddy Slide Trail just gets better with age.

## Ride Specs

**Start:** From the trailhead of Morrison Divide Trail 1174

**Length:** 20.2-mile loop

**Approximate Riding Time:** Advanced Riders, 2–2½ hours; Intermediate Riders, 3–3½ hours

**Technical Difficulty Rating:** Technically moderate to challenging due to off-camber terrain, roots, and rocks

**Physical Difficulty Rating:** Physically moderate to challenging due to extended climbs over rougher terrain

**Terrain:** Improved dirt road, doubletrack and singletrack—portions include ruts, mud, tree roots, and rocks; however, most of the route runs over hard-packed forest earth

**Elevation Gain:** 2,815 feet

**Nearest Town:** Yampa, CO

**Other Trail Users:** Equestrians, hikers, and campers

**Canine Compatibility:** Dog friendly

## Getting There

**From Steamboat Springs:** Travel east on U.S. 40. Turn right onto CO 131, heading south. Drive for 7 miles before turning left onto CR 14, just beyond the brown sign for Stagecoach State Park. Drive for another seven miles on CR 14 before turning left onto CR 16, following signs for Lynx Pass. Drive around Stagecoach Reservoir and turn left by the Eagles' Nest condominiums (approximately 2 miles from where you turned onto CR 16). Still on CR 16, bear right at the Yield sign and drive for approximately 10 miles. The sign for Trail 1174 and Morrison Divide will be on your right. Park on the right just beyond this sign, before the bulletin board. **DeLorme: Colorado Atlas & Gazetteer.** Page 26, C-3

Though officially dubbed the Morrison Divide Trail 1174 by the Routt National Forest, area locals more affectionately refer to this trail as "Muddy Slide." The trail takes its provincial name from the geological wonder high atop the east slope of Green Ridge. There, surrounded by the shimmering greens of tight-fitting lodgepole pine trees, lies in stark contrast the remains of a mountain with half of its side missing…Muddy Slide.

Making their speedy retreat from the top.

To reach this surreal sight, riders first pedal up Routt County Road 16 to Lynx Pass. Paralleling the road, Morrison Creek flows north from Lynx Pass some 15 miles to its confluence with Stagecoach Reservoir just east of Oak Creek in Stage Coach State Park. Legend has it that Morrison Creek was named by James Harvey Crawford, Steamboat Springs' founding father and first permanent settler.

In 1878 some local Ute Indians reported having spotted a starving "crazy man" along the banks of the creek. James Crawford organized a search party to find the lost man. When the men found Joe Morrison, he was near death and cooking his last remaining stores of food: the tails of his burros. When asked how he had gotten lost, the crotchety old prospector told Crawford that he had been looking for the Phantom Gold Pillar, a finger-like rock of almost pure gold believed to be in an area just east of Lynx Pass. In those days, any hint of the existence of gold would have sparked any

Taking a breather from the steeps.

## **Miles**Directions

**0.0 START** at the Morrison Divide Trail 1174 (Muddy Slide) trailhead. From the trailhead, begin riding southerly down CR 16 through Morrison Valley to Lynx Pass.

**6.5** After passing the sign for Morrison Divide/1174, veer right onto the service road. Ride up this service road for roughly 0.1 miles before turning right onto the Muddy Slide singletrack, just beyond the bulletin board.

**8.8** Cross a dirt road and continue along the singletrack on the other side.

**10.4** The trail will let out onto a dirt road. Bear left onto the fire road and begin a steady descent. There will be a locked iron gate to your right.

**12.7** Reach the junction of the Morrison Divide Trail 1174. Bear right onto the singletrack.

**13.5** The trail will let out onto another dirt road. Bear left onto it, following signs for TR 1174 as you head to the "Slide."

**14.6** Reach the Slide. Pass beyond the red iron gate and ride southwest along the rim of the Slide on the fire road.

**15.0** The fire road will intersect with the Muddy Slide singletrack. Bear right onto the singletrack.

**17.5** Encounter a root and rock section.

**19.8** The trail lets out into a wide meadow. Follow the trail through the meadow as it delivers you to your vehicle.

**20.2** Arrive at your vehicle.

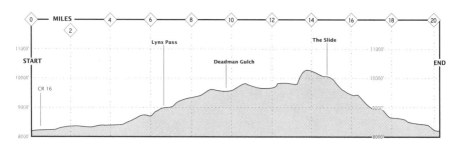

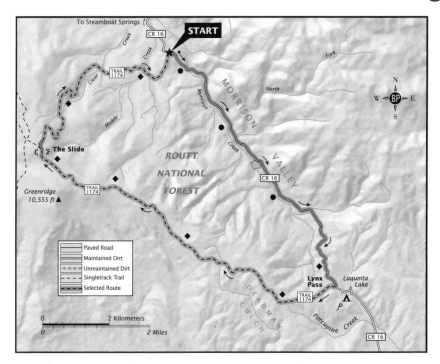

would-be prospector's curiosity, and Morrison was no exception. After Morrison's return to town, news of the pillar's existence spread fast throughout the Yampa Valley. As many people back then were wont to do, living in the milieu of gold fever, area would-be prospectors sought to find the Phantom Gold Pillar for themselves. Although several prospectors returned from their searches claiming to have found the pillar, no one ever produced any evidence of its existence, nor could any one find their way back to where they allegedly had found it. The Phantom Gold Pillar's location and existence remain a mystery.

Continuing along the banks of Morrison Creek, westerly views reveal Muddy Slide high atop Green Ridge. Once on Lynx Pass, the Muddy Slide singletrack begins. Within the first 0.5 miles, two short, but steep climbs await you. The trail then levels out, snaking its way in and out of logging areas and through thick stands of pine and aspen on smooth, hard-packed terrain.

The trail climbs steadily on its way to Muddy Slide. As the trail passes through sandy, rocky, and rooty sections, riders are offered small, intermittent dashes of downhill delight. One such descent comes after passing under a set of power lines at 9.4 miles. After veering onto the dirt road a mile later, the route gradually disintegrates into a rough doubletrack and offers a fast and rocky descent to its intersection with the continuation of the Muddy Slide singletrack. Once reconnecting with the singletrack, the trail climbs through an open hillside meadow awash with wildflowers. This section of the route, which is sometimes severely rutted, eventually delivers you onto some off-camber singletrack through an aspen grove. At this point, you're only two miles from Muddy Slide and the beginning of your savage descent. Having persevered this grueling singletrack climb, follow the road to Muddy Slide and spend a few moments taking it in.

The Slide is unlike anything you've ever seen. It overlooks the entire Morrison Valley, with northeasterly views of Rabbit Ears Peak, northwesterly views of Hahns Peak, and southeasterly views of the Eagles Nest Wilderness and the Gore Range. Consisting of mostly glacial out-wash, the Muddy Slide debris was part of the Alluvial Valley formed by the uplifting of the nearby Flat Tops Mountains millions of years ago. This uplift deposited large amounts of unconsolidated rock directly in the path of slow-moving glaciers. During glaciation, which carved the Morrison Valley, loose rock was pushed to the tops of steep, high valley walls. Over time, the effects of wind, water, and erosion caused this rock to slide all at once in a large scale rotational slump, referred to in geological circles as a "mass movement."

Taking a powder after grunting to the Slide. Dig the shirt?

# Ride Information

## 📞 Trail Contacts:
**Medicine Bow-Routt National Forests,** Yampa Ranger District Office, Yampa, CO; (970) 638-4516

## 🕐 Schedule:
Mid June to early October

## ❓ Local Information:
**Medicine Bow-Routt National Forest,** Steamboat Springs, CO; (970) 879-1870 • **Stagecoach State Park,** Oak Creek, CO; (970) 736-2436 • **City of Steamboat Springs,** Steamboat Springs, CO; (970) 879-2060 or *www.ci.steamboat.co.us* • **Steamboat Springs Chamber Resort Association,** Steamboat Springs, CO; (970) 879-0880 or *www.steamboat-chamber.com*

## 📍 Local Events/Attractions:
**Steamboat Springs Health & Recreation Center,** Steamboat Springs, CO; (970) 879-1828 • **Tread of Pioneers Museum,** Steamboat Springs, CO; (970) 879-2214 • **Steamboat Lake State Park,** North of Steamboat Springs along FS 129, CO; (970) 879-7019 • **Flat Tops Trail Scenic Byway,** connecting the towns of Yampa and Meeker, (970) 638-4516

## 👥 Organizations:
**Routt County Riders Bicycle Club,** Steamboat Springs, CO; (970) 879-1735 **Rocky Mountain Youth Corps.,** Steamboat Springs, CO; (970) 879-6960

## 🍴 Restaurants:
**Harwigs,** 911 Licoln Avenue, Steamboat Springs, CO; (970) 879-1980 • **Steamboat Brewery & Tavern,** Steamboat Springs, CO; (970) 879-2233

## 🚲 Local Bike Shops:
**Sore Saddle Cyclery,** Steamboat Springs, CO; (970) 879-1675 • **Ski Haus,** Steamboat Springs, CO; (970) 879-0385 • **Ski Kare,** Steamboat Springs, CO; (970) 879-9144

## 🗺 Maps:
**USGS maps:** Green Ridge, CO; Gore Mountain, CO; Lynx Pass, CO • **Trails Illustrated map:** # 119 Yampa, Gore Pass • **Routt National Forest Map** – *available at Routt National Forest Office and Medicine Bow-Routt National Forests (970) 638-4516*

From the Slide's highest point, 10,240 feet above sea level, layers of different colored rock—tan, gray, yellow and pink—mark the passing of Earth's billion-year-old history. Looking down from the top of the Slide, a gash nearly 800 feet long and a quarter-mile wide breaks almost perpendicularly from Green Ridge. At its base lies Muddy Creek. Continually receiving eroded soil from the Slide, Muddy Creek stays murky the whole year through and delivers more silt to the upper Yampa River than any other waterway in the county.

From the Slide, the trail begins as a fast descent through mixed conifer forests. The five-mile descent from the Slide is technically challenging and offers many thrills, if not spills, for the weary rider. Crossing over sloped-singletrack, roots, rocks, and ruts, the trail weaves its way through creeks and meadows before letting out by your vehicle. Although the push to the top of Green Ridge is a considerable effort, the descent from the Slide is well worth the pains taken to reach the top.

# 19

# Tipperary Creek Loop

## Ride Summary

The Tipperary Creek Loop is a shorter version of the famed Tipperary Creek Classic (the main attraction at the Winter Park Mountain Bike Festival). Though it doesn't include the entire Classic route, the Tipperary Creek Loop does include the legendary Tipperary Creek Trail, and it provides access to a number of other Fraser Valley and Winter Park singletrack trails. Though not overly technical or physically demanding, the Tipperary Creek Loop exemplifies how neat and clean singletrack riding can be—something Mountain Bike Capital, USA™ takes pride in. Its soft, smooth-running singletrack will delight, as well as excite a playfulness in the spirit of any mountain biker.

## Ride Specs

**Start:** From Elk Creek Road, heading west past the Safeway Center
**Length:** 20.4-mile loop
**Approximate Riding Time:** Advanced Riders, 1½–2 hours; Intermediate Riders 2½–3 hours
**Technical Difficulty Rating:** Technically easy to moderate, due to smooth-running singletrack
**Physical Difficulty Rating:** Physically moderate. Although there is some climbing involved, it isn't very long, and it doesn't travel over too rough terrain.
**Terrain:** Paved road, dirt road and singletrack. Most of the singletrack is very smooth, not much in the way of rocks and roots
**Elevation Gain:** 2,535 feet
**Nearest Town:** Fraser, CO
**Other Trail Users:** Equestrians, hikers, and campers
**Canine Compatibility:** Dog friendly

## Getting There

**From Denver:** Travel west on I-70, taking Exit 232 onto U.S. 40 west. Follow the signs to Winter Park. Drive over Berthoud Pass and into Winter Park. From Winter Park drive west to the town of Fraser and turn left at the light by the Safeway Center. This will be Elk Creek Road (CR 72). Park your vehicle in the Safeway Center parking lot and begin your ride heading west on Elk Creek Road under the railroad tracks. **DeLorme: Colorado Atlas & Gazetteer.** Page 38, A 3-4

One of the largest living organisms in the world is a grove of aspen trees. A stand of aspens shares a single root system.

With over 600 miles of marked, mapped and maintained mountain biking trails, the town of Winter Park and the area surrounding the town, Fraser Valley, enjoy one of the world's largest trail systems. Add to that, its legendary 30-mile point-to-point Tipperary Creek Classic racecourse, voted one of the world's best, and you begin to see why Winter Park and the Fraser Valley's trademarked "Mountain Bike Capital, USA™" is far from hyperbole.

What sets the Fraser Valley and Winter Park apart from other mountain biking destinations is, in large part, the lay of the land. The Fraser Valley is very open and fairly level, while Winter Park's mountains rise gradually above the valley to the top of the Continental Divide—yin to Telluride's yang.

On the slick Tipperary Creek Trail.

From its earliest beginnings, the Fraser Valley and Winter Park were destined for mountain biking greatness. Ute and Arapaho Indians held the Fraser Valley as a favorite hunting ground. They created within the valley a network of unidentified hunting and game trails, which area locals estimate to travel well over 2,400 miles. When pioneers began settling the Valley in 1850, railroad and logging industries started to flourish. These industries proved to be the impetus behind Mountain Bike Capital, USA™.

David H. Moffat spearheaded the building of a transcontinental railroad line that extended from Denver to Salt Lake City and the west coast. The line over Rollins Pass, which lies roughly seven miles to the east of Fraser atop the Continental Divide, was completed in 1905 and remained in service until 1928 when the 6.2-mile Moffat Tunnel was opened. The tunnel provided a safer and more direct alternative to crossing over the western slope mountains. Winter Park now sits at the west portal of the Moffat Tunnel.

As the railroad pushed farther west, it provided easier access for boomtowns to acquire timber. The forests west of the Continental Divide provided ample stores of timber for burgeoning cities. By providing Denver with valuable raw materials, Fraser Valley's logging industry helped secure Denver's state capital status. And the Fraser Valley, for its part, had begun bidding for capital claims of its own—that is, becoming America's mountain bike capital. The many logging roads and trails which were being created to supply Denver with timber would eventually evolve into one of the world's largest mountain biking trail systems.

Since Mountain Bike Capital, USA™ grew in response to the needs of the people, it seems fitting that its trails remain intimately connected with the people. Names of trails reflect the sacrifices made to construct them, as well as recognize the industries upon which the Fraser Valley's strong mountain biking foundation was laid. Twisted Ankle, Northwest Passage, Flume, Chainsaw, and WTB (named for trail-builders Wade, Todd, and Bill), all attest to the close relationship the Fraser Valley residents share with their mountain biking.

The Fraser Valley's local Forest Service branch is one of the only branches to employ a full-time mountain bike ranger in the summer, while Winter Park's Adopt-A-Trail program has fostered the adoption of more than 300 miles of trails by local bike shops, hotels, and restaurants. The fantastic condition of area trails speaks for each of their success in trail maintenance.

While the Tipperary Creek Loop incorporates part of the Tipperary Creek Classic racecourse, it also includes a number of other fine area singletrack. Funded with Colorado Lottery dollars, the Givelo Trail, for instance, runs alongside County Road 73 over nap-worthy earth. Here bicycles are so heralded that they adorn nearby trees. Retired bicycles literally hang like ornaments on nearby evergreens. Passing these now ornamental war horses, you connect with the Northwest Passage Trail.

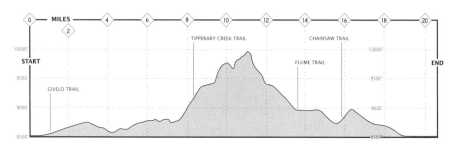

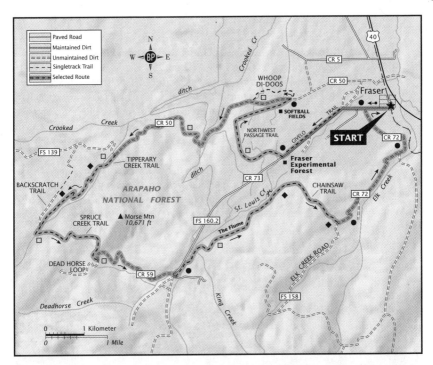

## MilesDirections

**0.0 START** at the Safeway Center parking lot. Ride west on Elk Creek Road (CR 72) and head under the railroad tracks. Once having gone underneath the railroad tracks, immediately bear right onto Fraser Parkway. There will be a tubing hill off to your left.

**1.0** Fraser Parkway intersects with CR 73. Cross CR 73 and bear left onto the Givelo Trail, as it parallels CR 73.

**2.6** The Givelo Trail will let out onto CR 73. Travel on CR 73 for roughly 0.1 miles before turning right onto the Northwest Passage Trail, just before the Fraser Experimental Forest sign.

**4.6** Northwest Passage Trail connects with CR 50. Bear left and ride on CR 50 for approximately 3.5 miles before arriving at the Tipperary Creek trailhead.

**8.3** After passing over a cattle guard, pick up the Tipperary Creek Trail off to the left side of CR 50, as it cuts sharply to the right.

**10.5** Reach the junction of Tipperary Creek Trail and Back Scratch Trail. Continue heading straight, passing the Back Scratch Trail to your right. Now the Tipperary Creek Trail becomes the Spruce Creek Trail.

**12.1** Reach the junction of Spruce Creek Trail and Deadhorse Loop. Pass the Deadhorse Loop and continue descending the Spruce Creek Trail.

**13.4** Spruce Creek Trail drops to the St. Louis Creek Road. Turn right onto St. Louis Creek Road and immediately turn left onto CR 59.

**13.6** Veer left onto the Flume Trail.

**15.8** Reach the junction of the Flume Trail and the Chainsaw Trail. Connect onto the Chainsaw Trail and begin a steady climb to Elk Creek Road.

**18.0** Reach the junction of Chainsaw Trail and Elk Creek Road. Turn left onto Elk Creek Road and follow the road back to your vehicles.

**20.4** Arrive back at your vehicle in the Safeway Center parking lot.

The Northwest Passage Trail delivers two miles of tacky, soft-forest earth through thick stands of lodgepole pine. Rest assured, Henry Hudson and the Half Moon never had it this good. An easy, woodsy trail with two major creek crossings, the Northwest Passage Trail eventually connects with an access road at 3.8 miles. Follow this road straight past the old softball fields to connect with County Road 50. Once you pass the old, red log cabin on your right, the softball fields should follow immediately.

Once on County Road 50, you can either ride for 3.5 miles to the Tipperary Creek trailhead or pedal up the short "Whoop-Di-Doos" singletrack paralleling County Road 50 on the right. The "Whoop-Di-Doos" trail eventually leads back onto County Road 50 after 0.5 miles.

At the Tipperary Creek Trail fork, bear right, crossing Tipperary Creek. Begin a slow and steady climb to Morse Pass. With Tipperary Creek to your left, ride through alternating forests of aspen and pine on relatively smooth singletrack. The ridge across Morse Pass travels up to 10,351 feet before descending 1,000 feet over fast and rocky terrain to St. Louis Creek Road.

On the Giuelo Trail.

# SUBSCRIBE!

**YES, I want *OUTSIDE*! Start my subscription at the term I've checked below:**

Best Offer

○ **Send me 36 issues for $38**

○ **Send me 24 issues for $30**

○ **Send me 12 issues for $18**

Name _____

Address _____

City _____

State/Province _____ Zip/PC _____

**E-Mail Address (optional)** Please send me notification of special offers from *Outside Magazine* and other carefully selected sources via email.

Canada: CDN $32 for 1 year, $49 for 2 years (includes GST).
Others: $45 for 1 year, $79 for 2 years. U. S. funds prepaid.
Visit us at www.outsidemag.com

# Ride Information

### ○ Trail Contacts:

**Winter Park Sports Shop, Ltd.**, Winter Park, CO; (970) 726-5554 or 1-800-222-7547 or www.winterparkbike.com

### ○ Schedule:

July to October

### ○ Local Information:

**Winter Park/Fraser Valley Chamber of Commerce**, Winter Park, CO; (970) 726-4118 or 1-800-903-7275 or www.winter-park-info.com • **Winter Park Resort**, Winter Park, CO; (970) 726-5514 or 1-800-729-5839 or 1-800-977-6195 or www.skiwinterpark.com • **Arapaho National Forest**, Sulpher Ranger District, Granby, CO; (970) 887-3331

### ○ Local Events/Attractions:

**King of the Rockies Off-Road Stage Race and Mountain Bike Festival**, August, Winter Park, CO; (970) 887-2519 • **The American Red Cross Fat Tire Classic**, June, Winter Park, CO; (970) 722-7474

### ○ Mountain Bike Tours:

**Adventure Works Mountain Bike Guide Service**, Winter Park, CO; (970) 726-9192 • **The Winter Park/Fraser Valley Chamber of Commerce**, Winter Park, CO; (970) 726-4118 or 1-800-903-7275 – *offers free guided town rides, acquainting riders with the trails of Winter Park and the Fraser Valley*

### ○ Organizations:

**Winter Park Fat Tire Society (FATS)**, Winter Park, CO; (970) 726-8044 or 1-800-521-BIKE – *offers free town rides*

### ○ Local Bike Shops:

**Winter Park Sports Shop, Ltd.**, Winter Park, CO; (970) 726-5554 or 1-800-222-7547 or *www.winterparkbike.com* • **Powder Tools**, Winter Park, CO; (970) 726-1151 • **Powder Play Sports**, Winter Park, CO; (970) 726-5359 or 1-800-266-5359 • **Viking Bike Shop**, Winter Park, CO; (970) 726-8885 or 1-800-421-4013

### ○ Maps:

**USGS maps:** Bottle Pass, CO; Fraser, CO • *Trails Illustrated* **map:** # 503, Winter Park/Grand Lake, CO • **Chamber of Commerce Mountain Bike Trail Map:** Winter Park & Fraser Valley – *available at the Winter Park/Fraser Valley Chamber of Commerce (970) 726-4118 or 1-800-903-7275*

---

The Flume Trail, named after the water flume that loggers once used to transport timber to Fraser in the early 1900s, passes through lodgepole pine forests and meadows. Although it has some rooty and rocky sections, the Flume Trail is mostly smooth and delivers you to a serene meadow at 15.7 miles, offering views of Byers Peak. From there, the Chainsaw Trail delivers some tough climbing but features the quietness of a dark forest. By 17.7 miles you'll arrive at the junction of the Chainsaw Trail and the Zoom Trail. Continue riding on the Chainsaw Trail to Elk Creek Road. Bear left onto Elk Creek Road and ride the two miles back to your vehicle.

Historian Margaret Cole describes this home of the ancient Arapaho Indians as a "boundless land," where there were "always opportunities to test their independence by racing their ponies wildly across the plains, whooping and hollering, far away from the security of the village." Who can't appreciate the connection between we modern-day Arapaho and our horse-backed predecessors?

# Grand Traverse and Cougar Ridge Trail

## Ride Summary

This ride incorporates the widely popular Grand Traverse Trail on Vail Mountain to access the more obscure Cougar Ridge Trail to Minturn. Via the Village Trail, riders get an overview of the Vail Ski Resort, as it winds its mellow way from the base of the Vista Bahn Express Lift to the top of Eagle's Nest. From there, two miles along the Grand Traverse Trail deliver stellar views of the Sawatch Range and the Mount of the Holy Cross. After picking up the unpatrolled Cougar Ridge Trail, the rider is afforded a blasting descent to Minturn before connecting with U.S. 24 and the Vail Bike Path back to your vehicle.

## Ride Specs

**Start:** From the base of the Vista Bahn Express Lift
**Length:** 21-mile loop
**Approximate Riding Time:** Advanced Riders, 2–2½ hours; Intermediate Riders, 3–3½ hours
**Technical Difficulty Rating:** Technically easy to moderate, with a few short, challenging sections along the Cougar Ridge Trail
**Physical Difficulty Rating:** Physically moderate to challenging due to the elevation gained from the base of Vail Ski Resort to its summit
**Terrain:** Dirt access road, paved road, paved bicycle path and singletrack. Most of the terrain is smooth and non-technical, however, the Cougar Ridge portion offers a variety of roots, rocks and washboards.
**Elevation Gain:** 4,917 feet
**Nearest Town:** Vail, CO
**Other Trail Users:** Equestrians, hikers, anglers, rafters, and kayakers
**Canine Compatibility:** Dog friendly

## Getting There

**From Denver:** Travel west on I-70 to Vail. At 29.5 miles past Silverthorne, take Exit 176 and turn left onto Vail Road, crossing under I-70. At the circle, bear right onto the South Frontage Road for roughly 0.5 miles. Park at the Lionshead parking lot, just before the Vail Valley Tourism & Convention Bureau. From the Lionshead parking lot, ride your bicycles east on West Meadow Drive, which will turn into East Meadow Drive. Make a right onto Bridge Street through Vail Village to the Vista Bahn Express Lift. Begin your ride from the base of the Vista Bahn Express Lift. *DeLorme: Colorado Atlas & Gazetteer.* Page 37, C-D 6-7

**Public Transportation:** From Beaver Creek and Edwards, take the Eco-Transit shuttle bus to the Lionshead gondola.

Described as a jewel, the Grand Traverse is Vail's hallmark mountain bike trail. What most people know of the Grand Traverse is that it offers mountain bikers rolling singletrack past Vail's hyped back bowls. What many do not know is that the Grand Traverse—by way of unmarked singletrack—links with the Cougar Ridge Trail, a five-mile stretch of unmaintained and unpatrolled, descending singletrack that ends in the quirky old railroad town of Minturn. Aside from dirt, dust, and endless delight, these two seemingly unrelated trails share in the unmistakable presence of higher power.

"Sawatch," a derivative of a Native American word meaning "water of the blue earth," is the name given to the range that overlooks the Grand Traverse and the

Cougar Ridge Trail. The first recorded use of the name dates back to 1853, when it originally identified a large lake in the San Luis Valley. How this range came to acquire the name is a mystery, as is much of the history surrounding its mountains. Steeped in legend and lore, the Sawatch Mountains demand reverence. The Mount of the Holy Cross is, perhaps, the Sawatch Range's most prominent mountain and sits within view of the Grand Traverse and the beginning of the Cougar Ridge Trail. Although the stories of the Mount of the Holy Cross tend to stem from legend rather than life, they provide meaning for the holy land upon which your wheels tread.

One such legendary story recalls the tale of a friar who had been part of the expedition led by the Spanish explorer Hernando de Soto. After having explored much of America's interior and claimed much of the explored land for Spain, de Soto finally concluded his expedition along the banks of the Mississippi River. Upset that the expedition had come to an end, the Franciscan friar questioned de Soto's decision. As penalty for his insolence, the Franciscan friar was stripped of his holy habit and crucifix by an angry soldier of de Soto. Ashamed for his actions, the friar set out alone, continuing his travels through America's interior. A Chickasaw brave who had witnessed the event at the Mississippi River decided that he would follow the friar. Having thought himself alone for several days since his falling out with de Soto, the friar, no doubt, was surprised upon seeing that he had been followed by the brave. The friar drew a cross in the sand to show the brave that his intentions were peaceful. Seeing this, the Chickasaw Indian led the friar to his tribe to join them in the Mississippi Delta.

## **Miles**Directions

**0.0 START** at the base of the Vista Bahn Express Lift. Begin riding on the Village Bike Path toward Eagle's Nest.

**1.0** The Village Bike Path intersects with Gitalong Road. Although both lead to the top, the Gitalong Road follows much of Vail's ski routes; whereas, the Village Bike Path follows the eastern route to the top of Eagle's Nest. Cross under the Vista Bahn Express Lift and continue riding up the Village Bike Path.

**3.2** Encounter the first little descent of the Village Bike Path. Ride past the gate and around Chairlift 10, the Highline Lift. From the Highline Lift, the Village Bike Path begins to climb more steadily.

**5.6** Reach Mid-Vail and the top of the Vista Bahn Express Lift. As the trail levels out, continue riding across the mountain to Eagle's Nest.

**6.8** Arrive at Eagle's Nest, where you're offered food, drink and recreation amid a beautiful alpine setting. Bear left around Eagle's Nest, following the sign for The Grand Traverse.

**8.4** Cross under the Vail Ski Area boundary ropes.

**8.7** Grand Traverse cuts sharply to the left, as it climbs to Wildwood, Vail's westernmost summit (10,950 feet). Here is where you break from the Grand Traverse and pick up the Cougar Ridge Trail. As the Grand Traverse cuts sharply left, continue straight along the singletrack heading into the pine forest. This junction is marked by two blue signs: one

pointing in the direction from which you came and designating the way back to Eagle's Nest via the Grand Traverse, the other pointing to Wildwood and the continuation of the Grand Traverse. Note: there is no designation for the Cougar Ridge Trail at this junction.

**8.9** Reach the trailhead to the Cougar Ridge Trail. Marked by a red sign, the Cougar Ridge Trail breaks right from the trail you are on.

**11.3** Reach the Lionshead overlook of Minturn.

**13.4** Connect with the Game Creek Trail. Cross the Game Creek and head left down the Game Creek Trail.

**13.9** Come to the end of the Game Creek Trail and to its trailhead. Veer left onto the gravel/dirt road, and ride alongside the railroad tracks, keeping them to your right. Cross the tracks and ride around the old depot, now the International Trade Center.

**14.6** Intersect with U.S. 24. Bear right onto U.S. 24, and ride north to the intersection with I-70 and the Vail Bike Path.

**16.5** Having crossed underneath I-70, reach the Vail Bike Path. Bear right onto the Bike Path, crossing the Eagle River, heading east back to Vail.

**18.0** Pass Stephens Park to your right, a local watering hole.

**21.0** Reach the Eagle Bahn Gondola and Clock Tower of Lionshead. Walk through the square to your vehicle at the Lionshead parking lot.

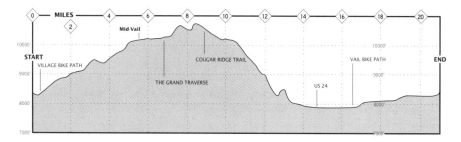

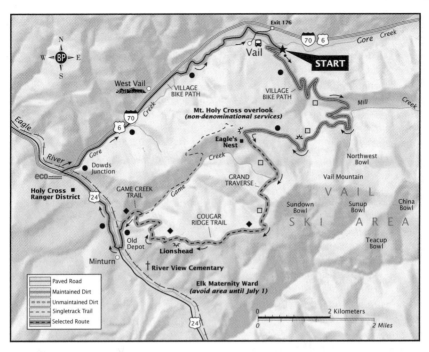

On the Cougar Ridge Trail, backdropped by the Mount of the Holy Cross.

163

# Ride Information

## Trail Contacts:
**Wheel Base** (two locations), Vail, CO; (970) 479-0913 or (970) 476-5799 • **Mountain Pedaler of Vail**, Minturn, CO; (970) 827-5522

## Schedule:
July to October

## Local Information:
**Vail**, Vail, CO; (970) 476-5601 or www.snow.com • Vail **Valley Tourism & Convention Bureau**, Vail, CO; (970) 476-1000 • **Summit County Chamber of Commerce**, Frisco, CO; (970) 668-2051 • **White River National Forest**, Holy Cross Ranger District, Minturn, CO; (970) 827-5715 • **Vail Information Booth**, Vail, CO; (970) 479-1394

## Local Events/Attractions:
**Colorado Ski Heritage Museum** (in the Vail Village Transportation Center), Vail, CO; (970) 476-1876 • **Taste of Vail**, early April, Vail, CO; (970) 476-1000

## Restaurants:
**Cougar Ridge Café**, under the Lionshead Rock in Minturn, Minturn, CO; (970) 827-5609 – the best pizza in Minturn, highlighted by New Belgium Brewing Company's Fat Tire Amber Ale

## Local Bike Shops:
**Wheel Base** (two locations), Vail, CO; (970) 479-0913 or (970) 476-5799 • **Mountain Pedaler of Vail**, Minturn, CO; (970) 827-5522

## Maps:
**USGS maps:** Vail East, CO; Vail West, CO; Minturn, CO; Red Cliff, CO • **Vail & Eagle Valley Mountain Biking & Recreation map** by Latitude 40 – available at select bicycle shops • **Vail & Beaver Creek Summer Biking & Hiking maps** – available at the ticket office

While living with the Chickasaw, the friar came upon a spattering of de Soto's army. Included among the rambling few was the soldier who had stripped the friar of his vestments. Trying to disguise himself from the friar, the soldier had now been dressed in the friar's own garb. Enraged, the friar stabbed the soldier, killing him instantly. Ashamed with what he had done, the friar left the Chickasaw in search for divine forgiveness. His search led him west, towards the Rocky Mountains. With his strength failing, the friar knelt in prayer upon a fog-covered mountainside. As he asked for forgiveness one last time, the fog lifted, revealing a snow-white cross imbedded in a dark mountainside—a sign of spiritual redemption.

This story and others like it spawned a massive pilgrimage campaign to seek out this most blessed place. Mountain men and early fur traders sought furiously after this snowy symbol of Christianity. It wasn't until the Hayden Survey Team of 1873 that the site's exact location was documented in photographs taken by the famed western photographer William H. Jackson. Legend had turned to life, and life would shortly thereafter turn to art.

Impressed with Jackson's photographs, the famed English artist Thomas Moran visited the mountain in 1874. On his return, Moran painted a variety of pictures of the Mount of the Holy Cross, the most famous of which now hangs in England and measures 6'10"x6'. The American poet Henry Wadsworth Longfellow also immortalized the mountain in his poem "The Cross of Snow."

> There is a mountain in the distant West
> That, sun-defying, in its deep ravines
> Displays a cross of snow upon its side.

With this kind of exposure, it's no wonder that in 1912 three Episcopal priests held Eucharist on the summit of nearby Notch Mountain, precedent for the famous Mount Holy Cross pilgrimages. What began with three priests in 1912, grew to two thousand visitors by 1932. Colorado became the American version of Canterbury, as tales of miraculous healings were reported by returning pilgrims.

By today's standards, the cross in the mountainside can best be understood, perhaps, as a vertical couloir, running 15-hundred feet long and 25 to 50 feet wide. An outward-sloping shelf runs across and near the top of this couloir, collecting more snow on its flatter surface than what would normally collect on the mountain's steeper sides. When snow fills the couloir and collects atop the shelf, the two combine to offer the appearance of a downy white cross on the northeast peak of the Mount of the Holy Cross. This geological explanation, however, hasn't detracted from the spiritual air surrounding the Mount of the Holy Cross. Riders reaching the top of Vail Mountain, near the Eagle's Nest restaurant and concession stand, are offered a dazzling view of this sacred mountain. An overlook nearby is site to nondenominational sunrise services.

Returning from this natural altar, the Grand Traverse invites the rider to reflect on the grandness that is the Sawatch Range. For two miles the Grand Traverse rolls over moderate rolling terrain before connecting with the Cougar Ridge Trail. The unmanaged singletrack of the Cougar Ridge Trail recalls the hardships earlier explorers and traders had to endure in their search for truth. Today, however, truth is yours and found among pools of blue columbine and organ-jarring descents. Like life in the high country, this trail is definitely not for everybody. Those expecting a smooth ride, should look elsewhere. Those who enjoy a bit of pounding, will relish in this trail's unmaintained terrain.

Since this is an unmaintained trail, expect a lot of low-lying tree branches and rutted singletrack. The first mile descent travels west from Vail Mountain and offers expansive views of the Sawatch Range and the Mount of the Holy Cross. One short burst of a hill climb comes at roughly 10 miles. From there the singletrack runs its course through intermittent stands of pine and aspen, offering a beautiful view atop the Lionshead rock formation above Minturn and a fast switchback descent to the Game Creek Trail. The Game Creek Trail provides some tricky rocks before picking up U.S. Route 24 in Minturn. Turn right onto U.S. Route 24 and connect with the Vail Bike Path back to the Lionshead parking lot and your vehicles.

# The Tenth Mountain Division

Colorado's vast hut systems provide backcountry bikers solitude and peace of mind in the deepest reaches of the Colorado's wilderness. It's interesting that these huts were borne of a threat to our national security.

To combat the growing threat of Nazi infiltration in Europe during World War II, the United States established in 1942 a winter training facility for an elite corps of champion skiers, mountain climbers, and European mountaineers—a group known as the Tenth Mountain Division, America's only mountain winter warfare unit. Just one year after the bombing of Pearl Harbor, Camp Hale (elevation 10,000 feet) was established along Leadville's northern boundaries in Pando, Colorado, just south of Vail Pass in Alpine Valley. Camp Hale (nicknamed Camp Hell) was home for over 14,000 mountain soldiers trained to battle the Nazis in the snow-covered mountainous regions of Europe.

Donning coveralls of all white, carrying over 90 pounds of gear in their army-issued rucksacks, and skiing on 7½ foot-long hickory boards, these soldiers trained at altitudes in excess of 13,000 feet on nearby Copper Hill and atop Passes Tennessee and Vail. Temperatures would sometimes fall 40 degrees below zero. These "phantoms of the snow" honed their fighting skills by engaging in alpine military tactics under the most severe and strenuous conditions imaginable—and yet, great pains were taken to make these conditions as bearable as possible. The first snowmobile, the first motorized toboggan, and the first snow cat were all created for the ski troops.

Their skills would eventually be brought to bear on the night of February 18, 1945, near Florence, Italy. The Tenth Mountain Division climbed the 2,000 vertical-feet escarpment of Riva Ridge in a single file line in the dead of night. By 5 A.M. the next morning, the Tenth reached the top of the ridge. In the dense fog that had enshrouded the entire ridge, the Tenth Mountain Division ambushed the Germans, taking Riva Ridge. The next day, the Tenth Mountain Division stormed Mount Belvedere. Their assault on Riva Ridge and Mount Belvedere proved to be turning points in the war.

After their tour was over, many of the men of the Tenth Mountain Division returned to Colorado to take up permanent residence. Two such corps members, Pete Seibert and Earl Eaton, took what they learned from training and living in the farthest reaches of Colorado's backcountry and established Colorado's first ski resort, at Loveland Pass. Pete Seibert also played a pivotal role in developing the Vail Valley's ski industry. Larry Jump, a Tenth Mountain veteran, established Arapahoe Basin in 1946. In all, 2,000 Tenth Mountain men became ski instructors, and 62 American ski resorts were either founded, managed, or had their schools directed by members of the Tenth Mountain Division.

Of course, not all of the former members of the Tenth Mountain Division pursued a life in the ski industry. David Brower became the first executive director of the Sierra Club. Fritz Benedict created the Tenth Mountain Hut & Trail System. Paul Petzoldt founded the National Outdoor Leadership School. Bob Lewis created the "Braille Trail"—the first hiking trail for the blind. Bill Bowerman, the track coach for the University of Oregon, was introduced to a new fitness exercise while his team was competing in New Zealand. The Kiwis called it "jogging." Bringing the idea back to the States, Bowerman began making jogging shoes. His waffle iron became the inspiration for a sole that wouldn't pick up mud. He called these shoes "The Waffle" and would later call his new shoe company Nike®.

In 1988 the Tenth Mountain Division helped create the International Federation of Mountain Soldiers, a worldwide alliance of mountain troops dedicated to world peace. Germans included. On February 18, 1995, 50 years after their assault on Riva Ridge, a group of these septuagenarian mountain men climbed the ridge again. At the top, the Germans joined them in peace. Of the 14,300 Tenth Mountain men, 992 were killed and more than 4,000 were wounded. A memorial to these 992 men stands at the top of Tennessee Pass.

Today, the Tenth Mountain Trail Association Hut System, established in 1980, offers backcountry thrill seekers 34-square-miles of adventure within the White River and San Isabel national forests. Aside from the 13 huts in the Tenth Mountain Hut System, Colorado boasts over 40 other established huts and yurts throughout the state, most of which are accessible by mountain bikes.

# 21

# Searle and Kokomo Pass Trail

## Ride Summary

This portion of the Colorado Trail delivers you above timberline via the beautiful Guller Gulch. On the other side of Copper Mountain Ski Resort, the singletrack passes high above Janet's Cabin to Searle Pass and onto Kokomo Pass. This entire area proved to be an invaluable resource to America during World War II. You'll pass by an area where soldiers of the Tenth Mountain Division once trained for wintertime warfare. Visible from Searle Pass, the Climax Molybdenum Mine supplied the Allied Forces with most of their Molybdenum, an element used to reinforce steel alloys, which was critical to the war effort. With incredible singletrack over smooth and rocky terrain leading well above timberline, the Searle/Kokomo Passes trail is a true Rocky Mountain gem.

## Ride Specs

**Start:** At the Union Creek parking lot in the Copper Mountain Ski Resort

**Length:** 13.6-mile out-and-back from Searle Pass – 19.6-mile out-and-back from Kokomo Pass

**Approximate Riding Time:** Advanced Riders, 2½–3 hours; Intermediate Riders, 3–3½ hours

**Technical Difficulty Rating:** Technically moderate to challenging due in large part to the rockiness of much of the trail, particularly above treeline, and the commonness of tree roots.

**Physical Difficulty Rating:** Physically moderate to challenging since the trail starts at 9,877 feet and reaches its height at 12,320 feet

**Terrain:** The route begins with a short stint on a paved bicycle path before connecting to singletrack. The singletrack includes rocky terrain and many roots.

**Elevation Gain:** 5,515 feet

**Nearest Town:** Silverthorne, CO

**Other Trail Users:** Equestrians, hikers, backpackers, and backcountry skiers

**Canine Compatibility:** Dog friendly

## Getting There

**From Denver:** Drive west on I-70 over the Eisenhower Tunnel and into Silverthorne. From Silverthorne continue traveling west on I-70 for 10 miles before taking Exit 195 for Copper Mountain Resort. Turn right at Copper Road and drive through the Resort. After 1.8 miles from where you turned onto Copper Road, turn right at Beeler Place. The Telemark Lodge will be to your right and Club Med, to your left. Drive up Beeler to the Union Creek parking lot. *DeLorme: Colorado Atlas & Gazetteer:* Page 48, A-1

- *Steamboat Springs, CO, has produced more Winter Olympians than any other town in the country.*
- *Crested Butte, CO, is home to the Mountain Biking Hall of Fame.*
- *Bailey, CO, is home to the World Bicycle Polo Federation.*

Located at the base of Copper Mountain Ski Resort, the Searle/Kokomo Passes trail is one of the most easily accessible routes of the entire 470-mile Colorado Trail. The trail's somewhat boring beginning along the paved bike path of Vail Pass quickly redeems itself once it connects with the singletrack to Searle Pass. The singletrack winds its way under Interstate 70, crossing Guller Creek a number of times. Split-log footbridges span these creek crossings, a challenge to ride no matter how fat your tires. Winding its way through Guller Gulch, a beautiful willow-filled valley, the trail

snakes over varied terrain of root and rock. After 2.5 miles, the drainage opens widely, offering expansive views of Elk Ridge. Dilapidated cabins, left over from an old
sawmill, dot the first four miles of Guller Gulch. After negotiating a series of sharp
climbing switchbacks, you reach the head of the gulch, marked by a wooden bench
and fire ring. Just barely in sight, at the end of this long gulch, is Janet's Cabin, trophy to the Summit Huts Association.

Although quite far away, a sharp eye can make out the black tin roof of Janet's
Cabin, as it sits hidden in a stand of trees. Named after Janet Boyd Tyler, an icon
among the Colorado ski scene, Janet's Cabin was built in 1990 and sits at 11,610 feet.
In response to the growing popularity of hut-to-hut skiing, the Breckenridge-based
Summit Huts Association began work on its own hut system. With Janet's Cabin as

Atop Searle Pass.

## **Miles**Directions

**0.0 START** from the Union Creek parking lot. Begin riding on the paved bike path beyond the bulletin board, passing the horse stables to your right and following West Ten Mile Creek upstream.

**0.7** Veer left over the bridge at the Colorado Trail sign. Look for the Searle and Kokomo Pass sign once over the bridge. Here begins the singletrack portion of the route.

**2.2** Pass a collapsed cabin and horse trail to your left. Once you pass these, bear right and continue along the Colorado Trail.

**3.8** A series of lodgepole pine trees have fallen and lay across the trail. Carefully maneuver around them and continue your ride on the other side.

**4.3** Encounter switchbacks and a tougher section of the climb.

**5.2** The trail becomes very smooth and soft through forest.

**6.4** Reach Janet's Cabin.

**6.8** Reach the top of Elk Ridge—Searle Pass is actually below this point. You have the option of turning around here.

To continue to Kokomo Pass: Veer right and traverse in a southwesterly direction along Elk Ridge for roughly three miles. A number of switchbacks bring you to the route's high point. Turn around here—Kokomo Pass is actually below this point.

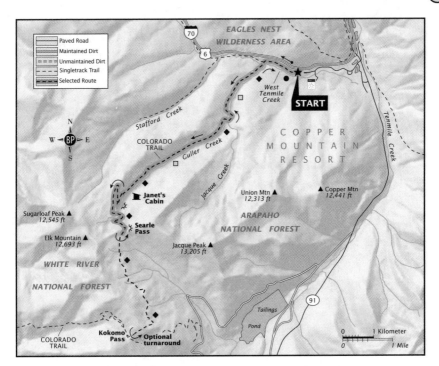

its inaugural hut, the Summit Huts Association began its plan to connect eastern and western Summit County via a network of backcountry huts. Janet's Cabin stands as a skillfully crafted and luxurious retreat for back country skiers and winter enthusiasts. In addition to a wood burning stove, cookware, and other requisite backcountry hut amenities, Janet's Cabin includes a $10,000 toilet, solar-heated showers, and the Nancy Dayton Memorial Sauna, which had to be airlifted in.

Continue riding through thick stands of lodgepole pine and blue spruce. Here begins the final push to Searle Pass. After crossing a wide mountain runoff at 5.5 miles, cairns mark the rest of your way above and beyond timberline. Both oxygen depleted air and rocky terrain makes the going rough. Take care to stay on the trail, though. The tundra-like environment above the timberline is a very fragile ecosystem and may retain irreparable damage if heavily treaded. The trail winds its way left above Janet's Cabin. With a sneering, contemptible heart for the luxuries that lie below, continue onto Searle Pass.

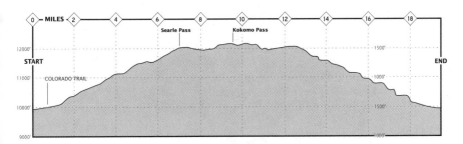

# Ride Information

### 🕒 Trail Contacts:
**Wildernest Bike Shop**, Silverthorne, CO; (970) 468-8519

### 🕐 Schedule:
July to September

### ❓ Local Information:
**Arapaho National Forest**, Dillon Ranger District, Silverthorne, CO; (970) 468-5400

### 📍 Local Events/Attractions:
**Janet's Cabin**, Summit Huts Association, Breckenridge, CO; (970) 925-5775 – *Janet's Cabin is not rented out for the summer*

### 📖 Other Resources:
*The Colorado Trail: The Official Guidebook* by Randy Jacobs, Westcliffe Publishing, Englewood, CO

### 🚲 Local Bike Shops:
**Wildernest Bike Shop**, Silverthorne, CO (970) 468-8519

### 🅽 Maps:
**USGS maps:** Vail Pass, CO; Copper Mountain, CO • *Trails Illustrated* maps: #108, Vail Pass, and #109, Breckenridge South, CO

---

Once atop Searle Pass, bask in the luxury that only eyes can afford. To the southeast lie the spirey peaks of the Tenmile Range and 13,205-foot Jaque Peak. On all other sides remain the Gore and Holy Cross ranges. Via mountain bike, you've just accessed the one-time winter training grounds for the U.S. Army's Tenth Mountain Division.

Notice the dirt roads and pools of water to the south and below Searle Pass. These are the remains of the Climax Molybdenum Mine—once the world's largest underground mine, producing 1.9 billion tons of molybdenum. Nearby Bartlett Mountain provided the world's single largest deposit of molybdenum. As mountain bikers, we owe a debt of gratitude to this hard gray metallic element that is used to reinforce steel alloys. It was molybdenum that added the "moly" to chro-moly bicycle frames.

During World War II, the Climax Mine worked feverishly, supplying roughly 72% of the world's molybdenum stock needed for the war effort. Sadly, the ponds you see below Searle Pass are remnants of the billions of tons of mill tailings that the Climax Mine has dumped into Tenmile Valley over the years. In fact, the Climax Mine dumped enough mill tailings in the valley to literally bury the sites where the one-time 1880s silver-mining camps of Recene and Kokomo once stood—a fitting end to these silver-mining camps. There is presently a program underway to cover these tailings.

From Searle Pass, veer right and traverse upward along Elk Ridge to reach Kokomo Pass. The ride ends once you arrive at Elk Ridge's high point—Kokomo Pass is actually below this point. The trail does continue, however, to Kokomo Pass—taking you on to Camp Hale, the site of the original winter camp for the Tenth Mountain Division.

From either Searle or Kokomo Pass, it's a wild ride back down. Starting from above timberline, the trail descends with surprising speed over rough terrain. The first section after returning to the trees is full of tight switchbacks and smooth-running singletrack. Snaking through intermittent spans of forest and meadow, the trail crosses over some tricky rock and root sections. The last three miles of singletrack offer more than enough occasion for speed, but they also include an assortment of technical, rocky terrain.

Passing over Guller Creek and under Interstate 70, the singletrack once again meets with pavement. This time, however, the bike path offers more in the way of remission than resistance. Like a fine sipping whiskey, the bike path back to your vehicles makes for a mellow and smooth finish to your feast of a ride.

Keeping a low profile.

# Wise Mountain/ The Colorado Trail

## Ride Summary

On top of offering the whole enchilada, this section of the Colorado Trail smothers it in green chili. Sink your knobby teeth into this: mellow cruising along Breckenridge's Tiger Road, roaring descents on smooth-like butter singletrack and climbs that would impress even Sir Hilary. This trail is particularly well suited for mountain biking novitiates and anyone you're hoping to recruit to the sport. One word of caution, the switchbacks at the end of the ride descend quite steeply, so watch your speed. If you haven't ridden this trail yet, you don't know what you're missing.

## Ride Specs

**Start:** From the Gold Hill Trailhead
**Length:** 24.8-mile loop
**Approximate Riding Time:** Advanced Riders, 2½ hours; Intermediate Riders, 3–3½ hours
**Technical Difficulty Rating:** Technically moderate; although, a number of severe switchbacks do challenge even the most technical of riders.
**Physical Difficulty Rating:** Physically moderate to challenging due to the length, altitude and amount of climbing involved
**Terrain:** Improved dirt roads and singletrack. Singletrack is very smooth, most of which is made up of soft, forest earth; some roots and rocks with which to contend, but nothing that would pose too technical a challenge to the intermediate mountain biker
**Elevation Gain:** 5,391 feet
**Nearest Town:** Frisco, CO
**Other Trail Users:** Hikers, equestrians, backpackers, campers, and anglers
**Canine Compatibility:** Dog friendly

## Getting There

**From Denver:** Travel west on I-70 through the Eisenhower Tunnel. Take Exit 203 to CO 9 south. Once on CO 9 drive south for 6.4 miles, passing through the town of Frisco, then turn right onto CR 950 and park at the Gold Hill Trailhead, just off the paved bike path. **DeLorme: Colorado Atlas & Gazetteer:** Page 38, D-2

**Public Transportation:** From Frisco, take the Summit Stage Breckenridge bus to the intersection of CO 9 and CR 950. Ride west on CR 950 to the Gold Hill Trailhead.

This 25-mile section of the Colorado Trail may be the finest example of singletrack ecstasy ever to be experienced within the limits of law (divine or otherwise)—a kind of hedonism, basking within the gray shades that separate the spiritually holy from the sinisterly evil. Even the most stoic mountain bikers have succumbed to fits of frenzy before the base of Wise Mountain—and understandably so, owing to the trail's close proximity to that brain-beleaguered town of Breckenridge.

You might say Breckenridge hangs in the balance of a hybrid identity. Owing to its earliest scrambles for gold, Breckenridge is home to the largest gold nugget ever unearthed in Colorado—the 13-pound, 7-ounce "Tom's Baby." Of more recent fortune, Breckenridge boasts a relatively new, multi-billion dollar ski industry and offers the dreamy-eyed tourist Colorado's largest historic district—over 250 authentically

maintained structures. Its quaint 1890s Victorian downtown offers a charming first impression, thanks to its ski industry economy. But ride down any one of a number of its back streets and you'll see the dilapidated remains of its notorious 19th Century gold mining history.

The Colorado Trail leads the historically-minded mountain biker down one such back street. Adhering to the maxim "a spoon full of sugar helps the medicine go down," the trail passes alongside the world's only publicly owned Jack Nicklaus-designed golf course before offering the rider views of the area's more sinister past.

Littered alongside Tiger Road and the banks of the Swan River, and indeed throughout Summit County, are miles of river stone churned up by dredging boats that operated in the area from 1898 to 1942. The first of nine dredging boats to operate in Colorado was brought here by Ben Stanley Revett. Revett's boats, weighing as much as 500 tons and measuring 100 feet long by 30 feet wide, ripped through surrounding river valleys in an effort to mine gold. These massive wooden boats dredged the river beds to depths of 50 feet, in a swell 200 feet wide. The tons of dredged glacial rock were separated from the river bed's finer sands and tossed to the banks. With the river stones laid aside, these mechanical miners could easily wash the gold deposits from the separated sands.

Today, the glacial rocks that were left behind and piled high atop one another, now lie like exposed sores along the otherwise verdant slopes of the Swan River Valley. Painstaking efforts are being made, however, to rid the valley of these sores. Stones are being collected, loaded onto trucks, and driven to mills where they're pulverized and added to cement mixtures. As you near three miles into your trip, an abandoned Buckcyrus Erie model dredger, the kind once used for dredging the Swan River, sits in a still pond surrounded by some exhumed river stone.

Your cathartic 8.9-mile ride along the dirt roads eventually leads you to the salvation of the Colorado Trail singletrack. This trail takes you over rolling terrain along the base of Wise Mountain. As smooth as a buttered baby's bottom, and on occasion, every bit as tacky, the singletrack descends to the North Fork of the Swan River, snaking its way through switchback-laden hillside meadows and past crowded stands of pine.

After crossing the Swan River, the trail will veer sharply to the left, before a camping site, at mile 11.5. A cairn marks the way to the left, while a Colorado Trail marker validates the move soon thereafter. Here begins your long grunt of a climb to West Ridge. This climb is not for the faint of heart, but it can be ridden without having to walk your bicycle. Stay on the main trail at all junctions—you'll pass two singletrack trails to your right that drop you to Keystone Mountain Ski Resort. With Keystone now lying across the valley on the East Ridge, the trail levels out, offering smooth-running singletrack through a pine forest.

At mile 16, the trail starts descending fast. Although this section invites speed, there are a number of tight switchbacks with which to contend. After descending for approximately four fast miles, you cross Horseshoe Gulch Road and begin the final climb of the ride. The trail eventually forks right into a meadow, offering expansive views of the Ten Mile Range. After roughly two miles of moderate climbing, the trail's final descent through several tight switchbacks leads you to the Tiger Run RV Resort. The switchbacks above the resort are not easily managed and should not be taken lightly. Ride quickly and quietly to the front of the resort. Cross Colorado 9 and turn right on the paved bike path back to your vehicle.

# Ride Information

### ⓒ Trail Contacts:
**Knorr House**, Breckenridge, CO; (970) 453-2631

### ⓢ Schedule:
July to October

### ❓ Local Information:
**Breckenridge Resort Chamber**, Breckenridge, CO; (970) 453-2913 or (970) 453-6018

### 👥 Organizations:
**Summit Fat Tire Society**, Breckenridge, CO; (970) 949-8057 • **Breckenridge Fat Tire Society**, Breckenridge, CO; (970) 453-5548 or (970) 453-INFO, push #FATT

### ⓣ Other Resources:
*The Colorado Trail: The Official Guidebook* by Randy Jacobs, Westcliffe Publishing, Englewood, CO

### ⓖ Local Bike Shops:
**Knorr House**, Breckenridge, CO; (970) 453-2631

### Ⓝ Maps:
USGS maps: Boreas Pass, CO; Keystone, CO; Frisco, CO • *Trails Illustrated* map: #104

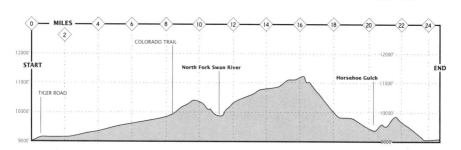

176

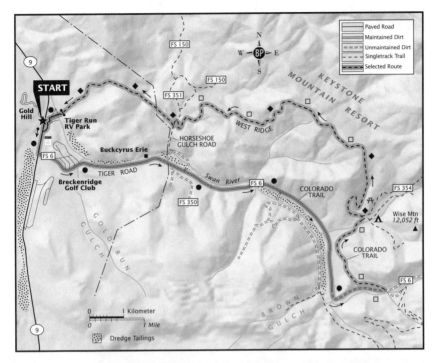

## **Miles**Directions

**0.0 START** at the Gold Hill Trailhead. Travel south on the bike path, heading toward Breckenridge.

**0.7** Cross CO 9 and turn left onto Tiger Road (by the Breckenridge Golf Club).

**3.3** The abandoned Buckcyrus Erie dredging boat is on your left.

**5.4** There's a dilapidated mine off to your right.

**6.5** Reach the junction of North and Middle Fork roads. Turn right onto the Middle/South Forks Road.

**7.0** Reach the junction of Middle and South Fork roads. South Fork Road bears to your right and heads over Georgia Pass. Continue riding straight on the Middle Fork Road.

**8.9** Two entrances to the Colorado Trail will be on both sides of the road. Turn left onto the Colorado Trail singletrack. (The right fork climbs steeply to Georgia Pass, and the main road climbs above timberline, eventually dropping into Montezuma.)

**11.1** Cross the North Fork of the Swan River. There are a number of picnic and camping sites here. Noticeable are the manmade log foot bridges.

**11.5** Cross the North Fork Road, which climbs to a high alpine valley. The trail continues across the road. After crossing the North Fork Road, the trail will cross over a stream and come to another road and a log fence. Cross through the log fence area and continue on the trail.

**13.7** Arrive at a fire line. Keystone Ski Resort will be to your right. Notice the chair lift.

**14.5** The trail will fork. The right fork will lead into Keystone Ski Resort. Bear left, continuing on the Colorado Trail.

**17.9** Pass through a gate.

**20.7** Cross Horseshoe Gulch Road, underneath the power lines, and continue on the trail directly in front of you, climbing over the hill.

**22.0** Enjoy the final fast descent, ending with a number of very tight switchbacks as the trail descends onto Tiger Run RV Resort.

**24.8** Reach your vehicle.

# Honorable Mentions

## North Central Colorado

Noted below is one of great rides in the North Central region that didn't make the A-list this time around but deserves recognition nonetheless. Check it out and let us know what you think. You may decide that it deserves higher status in future editions or, perhaps, you may have a ride of your own that merits some attention.

### E Baker's Tank Loop

Located in the heart of Summit County, Baker's Tank Loop is accesses by climbing up Boreas Pass Road. Named after the god of wind, Boreas Pass Road connects with many shorter singletrack trails, one of which is the Baker's Tank Loop. This moderately challenging 5.5-mile loop gains little elevation, only traveling between 10,360 and 10,850 feet. The attraction riders have to this trail is its relatively "hidden" location within one of Colorado's more recognized mountain areas. From the road the singletrack descends through dense pine forests on an old 4WD road to Baker's Tank, site of one of the earlier mining operations in Summit County. From Baker's Tank, riders intersect with the singletrack on the left that begins near a fence. This section of trail clings to a steep slope, so riders beware. Due to its predominately shaded route, this trail may remain too wet to ride until late June.

With views of Bald Mountain (13,684 feet), this trail is a gem of a ride in the heart of outdoor Colorado. To access the Baker's Tank Loop, drive south through Breckenridge on Colorado 9. After the stoplight on the south end of town, bear left onto Boreas Pass Road. Drive for 3.5 miles on Boreas Pass Road until the pavement ends. Park your vehicle here in a pullout on the left and begin riding up the road. For more information on this ride and other Summit County rides contact the Knorr House at 303 S. Main St., Breckenridge, Colorado, (970) 453-2631; or the Breckenridge Resort Chamber in Breckenridge, Colorado, at (970) 453-2913 or (970) 453-6018. ***DeLorme: Colorado Atlas & Gazetteer:*** Page 48, A-3

# South Central Colorado

*WYOMING*

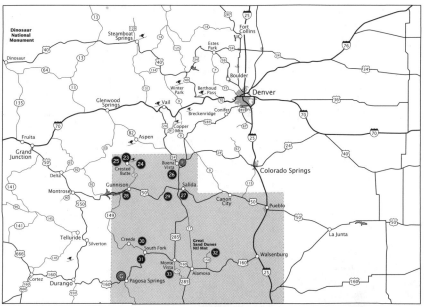

*NEW MEXICO*

Colorado owes much to its South Central region. Many of the state's "firsts" happened here. Founded in 1849, Garcia is Colorado's first and oldest town. Our Lady of Guadalupe (built in the town of Conejos during the early Spanish settlements of the 1800s) is the state's oldest church. Fort Garland, established in 1858 by Kit Carson, is Colorado's oldest military post. Colorado mountain biking was first discovered in Crested Butte, 1976. Aside from these "firsts," however, South Central Colorado also enjoys a rich geography.

This region is truly a land of contrasts. The San Luis Valley, one of the largest alpine valleys in the world, is surrounded by the 14,000 foot peaks of the Sangre de Cristo mountains to the east, the San Juan mountains to the west and the Sawatch mountains to the north. Colorado's tallest mountain, Mount Elbert (14,433 feet), is located at the northern tip of this region. Northeast of the town of Alamosa, near the region's eastern flank, lie the Great Sand Dunes, a veritable 700-foot-high mountain range of sand, the tallest in North America.

Owing to its sun-drenched terrain, the San Luis Valley provides a longer riding season than most other areas in Colorado. Ironically, however, the valley remains relatively unknown as a mountain biking destination. The Zapata Falls Trail is a fun, stacked singletrack loop and offers incredible views of the Great Sand Dunes and the Sangre de Cristo mountains. Traveling west, near the little known town of South Fork, the Cat Creek Trail provides an intermediate ride through tall stands of spruce and fir. In the winter of 1999, lynx were reintroduced into this area. As one heads north toward Salida and the 14ers region of Chaffee County, the landscape does an acrobatic turnaround, providing 15 of Colorado's 54 14ers (mountains which are 14,000 foot or higher). Typifying the riding of this area is the Colorado classic, Monarch Crest Trail. To the northwest of Salida, lies the birthplace of Colorado mountain biking—Crested Butte, Colorado. Crested Butte is considered by many to have the best riding in all of Colorado.

From exploration, to agriculture, to mining, South Central Colorado's cultural influences are as varied as its landscape. To the credit of Colorado's first explorers, this region is steeped in Spanish influences. In 1596, Juan de Zaldivar, on behalf of the Don Juan de Onate expedition into New Mexico, came into Colorado through the San Luis Valley to track troublesome Indians. This early exploration into the valley laid the groundwork for a region founded on ancient Spanish culture and tradition.

The fertile San Luis Valley turns into a veritable sea of green in the spring. With a growing agricultural economy, the San Luis Valley owes much of its success to the Rio Grande del Norte. Flowing through the middle of the valley, this river is the agricultural lifeblood to the economy of the San Luis Valley.

Further north, in towns like Crested Butte, Buena Vista and Salida, mining was the area's mainstay, that is, before giving way to mountain thrill seekers. Remnants of the bygone mining days can still be seen throughout the mountainsides. Today, however, these mountainsides serve better to wow the crowds with steep singletrack descents and jaw-dropping views.

Mt Elbert
El. 14,433

# Deer Creek Trail

## Ride Summary

With the Gunnison National Forest blanketing nearly 85 percent of the entire county, Crested Butte is a mountain biker's town. The Deer Creek Trail is one of the town's most celebrated trails. This trail has one of the longest stretches of singletrack of any single trail in Crested Butte and offers incredible views after a grueling, but short climb through the aspens. Since the Deer Creek Trail is open for cattle grazing toward the latter end of the mountain biking season, the trail does tend to become "ripped up," particularly near the end as you ride through the meadows into Gothic. Because of this, it's a good idea to do this trail around mid-season. The trail features hard-packed singletrack, tight aspens, and rutted and rocky ascents and descents. It's a Crested Butte favorite.

## Ride Specs

**Start:** From the Alpineer bicycle shop in downtown Crested Butte

**Length:** 28.9-mile loop

**Approximate Riding Time:** Advanced Riders, 3–4 hours; Intermediate Riders, 4–5 hours

**Technical Difficulty Rating:** Technically moderate to challenging with some demanding sections. Some route segments combine steep singletrack grades (both ascending and descending) with exposed roots and rocks.

**Physical Difficulty Rating:** Physically moderate to challenging due to the significant climbing at high altitude

**Terrain:** Paved state road, dirt forest road, and singletrack. The terrain includes tough-climbing dirt road and singletrack. Most of the route travels over mountainous terrain at higher elevations and rolls over a number of rocks and roots.

**Elevation Gain:** 4,329 feet

**Nearest Town:** Crested Butte, CO

**Other Trail Users:** Hikers and equestrians

**Canine Compatibility:** Dog friendly

## Getting There

**From Gunnison:** Drive north on CO 135 into Crested Butte. Once in Crested Butte, drive through the all-way stop intersection at 0.2 of a mile to the next four-way stop at 0.4 of a mile. Turn left into the shopping complex before the Bullion King sign. Park your vehicle in the lot just outside the Alpineer, Crested Butte's ski and bike shop. *DeLorme: Colorado Atlas & Gazetteer.* Page 58, A-2

Just rewards after the long climb.

Although mountain biking has saturated many of Colorado's mountain towns, one town remains relatively untracked by the mountain biking masses, and curiously, it offers some of the state's best singletrack trails. Crested Butte enjoys clandestine cranking like Durango and Moab could only dream of. Virtually endless trails weave their sinuous courses through the region's highest terrain (above timberline), to its lowest (the high desert sands). Among Crested Butte's best and most beloved rides is the Deer Creek Trail.

The Black Hole Trail skirts to the right with Crested Butte Ski Resort behind.

As you begin riding south out of town on Colorado 135, you pass through the shadow of 12,516-foot Whetstone Mountain—just as the miners did who worked the Bulkley Mine over 100 years ago. During the winter months, miners, clothes darkened from the bituminous coal, formed long processionals on their way to the mine. The scene looked like a trail of chucked coffee on virgin snow as the miners slogged single-file from Crested Butte to the Bulkley Mine through waist-deep drifts. When the lead miner would get tired from breaking trail, he'd hand off the duty to the second-in-line and fall to the rear for his rest. This would continue until it was his turn again.

Situated along the steep sides of Whetstone Mountain, the Bulkley Mine was quite susceptible to avalanches. In 1912 an avalanche ripped over the head house of the mine, carrying six men 500 feet before burying them alive. Workers quickly began their search for the buried men. All of the men were eventually found, but not before the avalanche claimed one of the men.

After reaching the ominous shadow of Whetstone Mountain, riders intersect with Brush Creek Road. Here the mood lightens considerably, as high alpine valleys and expansive views of the 1,700,000-acre Gunnison National Forest greet you. The first big climb of the day comes after roughly eight miles. This climb features steep grades and rocky terrain, before topping out at mile 9.5. Having connected to the singletrack, the second big climb arrives after crossing Deer Creek. Luckily, this climb lasts only half a mile, as it passes through a beautiful aspen glen. Steep grades, ruts, and exposed root sections make this climb physically demanding and technically challenging. Upon reaching the top, you're offered expansive westerly views of the Ruby Range, the West Elk Wilderness, and Mount Crested Butte's ski resort. In full prominence stands the 12,392-foot Mount Emmons. This mountain is home to the Red Lady Bowl, and one of Crested Butte's most heated disputes.

## **Miles**Directions

**0.0 START** from the Alpineer bike shop in downtown Crested Butte and begin riding south on CO 135, heading out of town.

**2.0** Bear left onto FS 738 (Brush Creek Road), by the Crested Butte Country Club sign, heading toward the airport.

**2.6** FS 738 turns into an improved dirt road. Continue riding on the road. The Crested Butte Golf Course is to your left.

**3.9** After crossing a second cattle guard, the Upper Upper Loop Trail is to your left. Pass this trail and descend on FS 738.

**4.5** The Brush Creek trailhead is on your left. Continue riding on FS 738.

**6.6** Cross Brush Creek.

**7.7** FS 738 reaches a trail intersection marked by a sign that reads "Deer Creek Trail 568 – 3 miles" and the "Teocalli Ridge Trail 557 – 5 miles." Bear left here and climb up the rough doubletrack, heading in a northeasterly direction en route for the Deer Creek Trail.

**8.6** Arrive at another trail intersection marked by a sign that reads "Deer Creek Trail 568 – 2 miles," and "Teocalli Ridge Trail 557 – 4 miles." Bear left at this trail intersection and head in a northwesterly direction, following signs for Deer Creek Trail 568.

**9.5** Pass through a gate (closing it behind you) and descend quickly into an aspen and lodgepole pine forest.

**9.7** The trail forks. Bear left at this fork, following signs reading "Deer Creek. Stay on Trail."

**10.1** Intersect the Deer Creek singletrack and continue riding in a northwesterly direction.

**11.0** Cross Deer Creek and begin a slow grunt of a climb through the aspens.

**11.6** Arrive at the crest and a beautiful vista. From here, descend through slope-side meadows, past a slide area, and into a dense aspen forest.

**13.4** Arrive at a stock tank. Pass around the tank and continue riding due west.

**13.7** Cross over the barbwire fence via a step ladder and descend through Dry Basin.

**14.1** Cross Perry Creek and climb up another hillside meadow through another stand of aspen.

**15.1** Top out and descend through meadows and aspen glens to the town of Gothic.

**17.1** The trail meets with a barbwire fence and a cattle tank. Continue riding due west on the trail with the barbwire fence running alongside the trail to your left.

**19.6** After crossing underneath the telephone

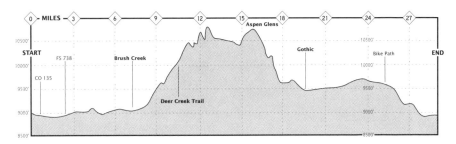

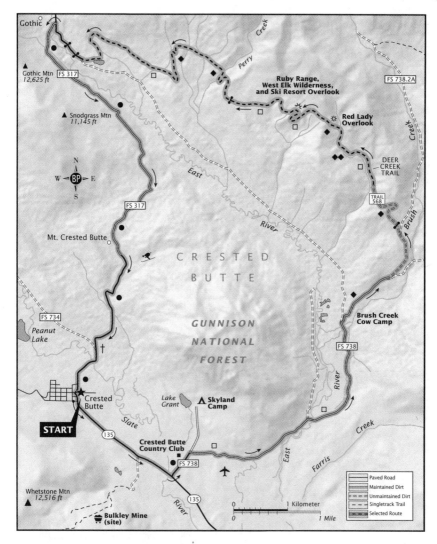

lines, arrive at the west Deer Creek trailhead and a dirt road. Bear right onto the dirt road, heading toward the town of Gothic.

**19.8** Pass through an orange gate and continue up the dirt road.

**20.0** Pass through another orange gate and continue up the dirt road.

**20.3** After passing through a couple of gates, the dirt road intersects with an improved dirt road in Gothic. Bear left onto this improved dirt road and cross the East River to FS 317.

**20.4** Bear left onto FS 317 and ride south, back to Crested Butte.

**24.0** Reach Mt. Crested Butte. FS 317 becomes paved and turns into Gothic Street. Ride on Gothic Street through Mt. Crested Butte to the paved bicycle path.

**24.4** Intercept the bike path and ride back to Crested Butte and your vehicle.

**28.0** Pass the Crested Butte Cemetery to your left.

**28.8** Pass the Crested Butte Chamber of Commerce to your left

**28.9** Arrive at your vehicle.

# Ride Information

## 📞 Trail Contacts:
The Alpineer, Crested Butte, CO; (970) 349-6292 or www.alpineer.com

## 🕐 Schedule:
Mid-June to October

## ❓ Local Information:
The Crested Butte/Mt. Crested Butte Chamber of Commerce, Crested Butte, CO; (970) 349-6438 or 1-800-545-4505 • Gunnison National Forest and Bureau of Land Management, Gunnison Resource Area, Gunnison, CO; (970) 641-0471 • High Country Citizens' Alliance, Crested Butte, CO; (970) 349-7104 or www.sni.net/hcca

## 📍 Local Events/Attractions:
Mountain Bike Hall of Fame & Museum, Crested Butte, CO; (970) 349-6817 or 1-800-454-4505 • Crested Butte Mountain Heritage Museum, Inc., Crested Butte, CO; (970) 349-1880 • Fat Tire Bike Festival, in June, Crested Butte, CO; (970) 349-6438 or 1-800-545-4505. • Annual Wildflower Festival, in July, Crested Butte, CO; (970) 349-6438 or 1-800-545-4505 • One World Music Festival, in September, Crested Butte, CO; (970) 349-6438 or 1-800-545-4505 • Rendezvous Gallery, Crested Butte, CO; (970) 349-6804

## 👥 Organizations:
Crested Butte Mountain Bike Association (C.B.M.B.A), Crested Butte, CO; (970) 349-5517 or (970) 349-6817

## 🛏 Accommodations:
Irwin Lodge, Crested Butte, CO; (970) 349-9800 or 1-888 GO-IRWIN • Crested Butte International Hostel LLC, Crested Butte, CO; (970) 349-0588 or 1-888-389-0588 or www.gunnison.com/~hostel/

## 🍴 Restaurants:
Idle Spur, Crested Butte, CO; (970) 349-5026 • Donita's Cantina, Crested Butte, CO; (970) 349-6674 • Wooden Nickel, Crested Butte, CO; (970) 349-6350

## 🚴 Tours:
No Limits Center, Crested Butte, Mt. Crested Butte, CO; (970) 349-4247 or 1-888-954-4247 • Pioneer Guide Service, Crested Butte, CO; (970) 349-5517 or www.pioneer@crestedbutte.net • Paddle Trax & Sngltrax, Crested Butte, CO; (970) 349-1100 • Alpine Outside, Crested Butte, CO; (970) 349-5011 or 1-800-833-8052; Almont, CO; (970) 641-1303 or 1-888-761-FISH or www.3riversresort.com

## 🚲 Local Bike Shops:
The Alpineer, Crested Butte, CO; (970) 349-6292 or www.alpineer.com • XTC Cycles, Crested Butte, CO; (970) 349-6776 • Crested Butte Sports Ski & Bike Shop, (Next to the Nordic Inn at the Ski Area), Mt. Crested Butte, CO; (970) 349-7516 or 1-800-301-9169 • Christy Sports Ltd., Crested Butte, CO; (970) 349-6601 • Pinnacle Cycles, Crested Butte, CO; (970) 349-2237

## 🗺 Maps:
USGS maps: Crested Butte, CO; Gothic, CO • Trails Illustrated map: #133 • Crested Butte Bike Trails Map – available at the Alpineer • Aspen, Crested Butte, Gunnison Recreation Topo Map, Latitude 40° Inc. – available at select bike shops

Frank Orazem, a Crested Butte elder, recalled first seeing the bowl: "...I saw the red ore glowing in what we call Mount Emmons Basin. Then I saw her, shaped by the ore or shadows or a trick of light...an Oriental empress...her kimono was bright red...I called her the *Red Lady* because that's what the basin looked like to me." Needless to say, the locals take their mountains quite seriously.

In 1977 the Cyprus-Amax Mining Company discovered the world's largest known molybdenum deposit approximately 1,200 feet below Red Lady Bowl and threatened to mine it. The molybdenum deposit, with a diameter of 2,500 feet and

Tight singletrack leading into Aspens. Grueling climb after crossing Deer Creek.

an average thickness of 300 feet, is estimated to have a market value of $7 billion. Amax's proposal included not only the building of the molybdenum mine, but also the building of a mill and a sludge pond, all to be located on surrounding national forest and ranch land. The town of Crested Butte rallied against the proposal and formed the High Country Citizens' Alliance. The dispute was described by the *High Country News* on December 8, 1997 as "a classic David vs. Goliath battle." The article went on to say that the "residents of the ski-resort town of Crested Butte, Colorado chased the world's largest mining conglomerate out of their valley."

Now, over 20 years later, the battle rages on. In an attempt to supply the would-be mine with water, Cyprus-Amax has filed in Colorado Water Court for rights to tap the Slate River. If approved, Cyprus-Amax's access to water would mark the first step to molybdenum mining atop Red Lady, a project whose current estimates propose mining 6,000 tons (with the ability to extend) of molybdenum a day. In their continued fight against Cyprus-Amax, the members of the High Country Citizen's Alliance worry that a mine of this proportion might deliver negative environmental, social, and economic blows to Crested Butte. Presently, the High Country Citizen's Alliance, in cooperation with local volunteers, is gathering more information about mining and molybdenum. They're conducting educational lectures on what a mine would mean to Crested Butte, showing slide shows of previous mining activity and hiking to the proposed site below Red Lady Bowl. Lawyers for the High Country Citizen's Alliance are fighting Cyprus-Amax's appeal for water rights.

From the site of this bone of contention, you descend through hillside meadows and aspens where large herds of elk are frequently bugling. Skirting the rim of the "black hole" (a large slide out area) you continue into a sun-drenched, tightly packed aspen grove. From here the trail descends through a variety of meadows to Perry Creek. Climb from Perry Creek and top out approximately at mile 15. Starting at the top of this climb lies the most technical riding of the entire route. As you pass through intermittent meadows and aspen glens, steep ruts and large rocks mark your way into the town of Gothic at the base of Gothic Mountain (12,625 feet). From Gothic it's a fast descent through Mount Crested Butte to the town of Crested Butte and to your vehicle.

# Deadman's Gulch

## Ride Summary

The Deadman's Gulch Trail is one of Crested Butte's finest, running the gamut for Rocky Mountain riding. Burning climbs, savage descents, technical singletrack (both up and down), and the famed Deadman's switchbacks all contribute to this trail's legendary status. The views of the Elk Mountains, where innumerable clashes between Ute Indians and the early prospecting parties of the 1860s and 1870s occurred, are fantastic. Since most of Crested Butte's trails are multi-use, some sections may be rutted from motorcycles—particularly the climb from Deadman's Gulch. Due to the preponderance of creeks that flow throughout the area, this trail is best ridden during the later half of the season.

## Ride Specs

**Start:** From the Deadman's Gulch Trailhead
**Length:** 20.1-mile loop
**Approximate Riding Time:** Advanced Riders, 3–3½ hours; Intermediate Riders, 4–5 hours
**Technical Difficulty Rating:** Technically challenging to demanding due to a variety of exposed roots and rocks. The numerous switchbacks down Deadman's Gulch to your vehicle are particularly technical.
**Physical Difficulty Rating:** Physically challenging to demanding due to sustained climbs at high elevations over rough terrain.
**Terrain:** Dirt forest road, logging road, and singletrack. Types of terrain over which you'll be riding include steep ascending and descending singletrack, large amounts of exposed roots and rocks, slippery creek-side moss-covered roots and rocks, tough switchbacks, hard packed dirt, sand, and ruts.
**Elevation Gain:** 4,048 feet
**Nearest Town:** Crested Butte, CO
**Other Trail Users:** Hikers, equestrians, motorcyclists, campers, and anglers
**Canine Compatibility:** Dog friendly

## Getting There

**From Crested Butte:** Drive south on CO 135 for 6.9 miles (from the Alpineer bike shop) before turning left onto Gunnison CR 740 (Cement Creek Road). At 7.8 miles the pavement ends. Cross a cattle guard at 8.9 miles. CR 740 (Cement Creek Road) forks at mile 10.3. Continue straight (left) here, passing a sign for Cement Creek. Enter into the Gunnison National Forest at 10.6 miles. Pass the Mad Creek Ranch to your right at mile 11.6. At mile 14 bear right into the Deadman's Gulch Trailhead. ***DeLorme: Colorado Atlas & Gazetteer.*** Page 58, B-A 3

fter the Big Mine closed in 1952, effectively putting an end to coal mining in Crested Butte, a new breed of settlers started to move into town. There were the summer vacationers—among them Dick Eflin and Fred Rice, co-founders of the Crested Butte Ski Resort. And there were the hippies. By the late 1960s and early 1970s, Crested Butte had become a skiing commune

This footbridge is a good landmark for knowing you're on the Bear Creek Trail.

for nature lovers. Surrounded by three wilderness areas and over a million acres of national forest, Crested Butte offered a good deal of elbow room. Skiing would prove to be too limited an endeavor upon which to build a recreation paradise, and so the sport of mountain biking soon arrived to fill the void.

Mountain biking came to Crested Butte, and indeed the rest of Colorado, in the summer of 1976. Before then, town bikes were nothing more than a means of transport, from the market to the post office to home. Local fire fighters, after the threat of summer fires had passed, would return from their mountain posts on their town bikes. After ripping down rough mountain roads at hair-raising speeds (helmetless, of course), they'd drop into Crested Butte and skid to a stop at the local watering hole. Well, in 1976, a group of motorcyclists from Aspen rode their bikes over Pearl Pass (12,705 feet) and descended upon Crested Butte. Before the dust from their bikes had settled, the bikers were already bragging of their high alpine accomplishments. Not to be outdone, the firefighters decided to cross Pearl Pass and descend into Aspen with their town bicycles. The passage took two days and featured a Deadheaded campout in Cumberland Basin. The riders descended upon Aspen and set themselves up at the Hotel Jerome, their bikes piled in a clunking heap outside. This has since become an annual event. What began on a cold September morning with only 15 fat-tire faithfuls has today evolved into a multi-million dollar industry. We owe a certain debt of gratitude to Crested Butte for its accomplishments and its continued support of the sport.

Seven years after the "birth of mountain biking" in Colorado, Crested Butte formed the Crested Butte Mountain Bike Association, a volunteer, nonprofit organization designed to preserve and protect trails and the surrounding ecosystem, while informing and educating users on proper trail etiquette. In 1988 Crested Butte founded the country's first Mountain Biking Hall of Fame and Museum (MBHOF). The MBHOF preserves and displays vintage bicycles, classic photos, and numerous press clippings. Since its inception as a nonprofit corporation, the MBHOF has inducted 66 of the sport's major players.

A major player in its own right, the Deadman's Gulch Trail is one of Crested Butte's rowdier rides. The ride begins by paralleling the rushing Cement Creek. It continues its way through the steep rock walls of Cement Canyon. After crossing Cement Creek, you climb moderately and are offered views of Crystal Peak and Mount Tilton. The space between the two mountains is where a rush of Leadville prospectors descended in 1879 and 1880. Their silver discovery prompted the building of the Red Cloud, Tilden, Moonlight, and Climax mines near the headwaters of Cement Creek. The inaccessibility of the mines eventually led to their downfall. But a prospector's misfortune is a mountain biker's gain. You'll appreciate this as you continue riding to the top of Reno Divide.

## **Miles**Directions

**0.0 START** from the Deadman's Gulch trailhead and begin riding up FS 740 (Cement Creek Road).

**1.0** Pass a small hillside waterfall to your left and continue riding up the rocky road through narrow Cement Creek Canyon.

**1.3** FS 740 crosses Cement Creek. Continue riding up the road. Pass a singletrack trail to your left before crossing the creek and a campground to your right after crossing the creek.

**2.2** FS 740 intersects with FS 759 (Reno Divide Road). Bear right onto the FS 759, following signs for Reno Pass.

**3.5** Pass a dilapidated cabin to your left.

**4.2** The climb begins to level somewhat.

**5.9** Reach the summit of Reno Divide. As you bear right (east) atop the ridge, pass through the gate and ride to the junction of Italian Creek Road and the Flag Creek Trail 422.

**6.0** Reach the Flag Creek 422 trailhead. A sign here marks "Spring Creek – 4 miles" and "Bear Creek – 6 miles." Continue riding on the singletrack of the Flag Creek Trail, heading in an easterly direction.

**8.9** Cross an eroding wooden footbridge and continue descending the Flag Creek Trail.

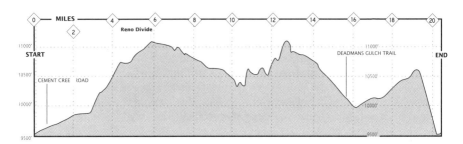

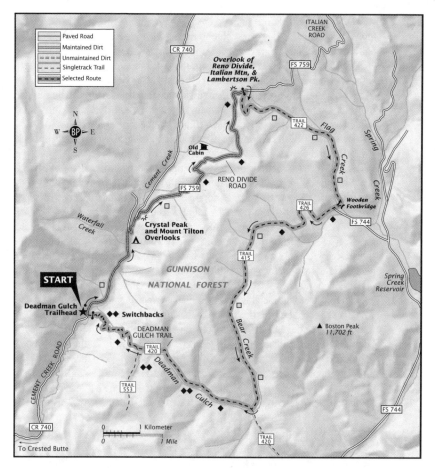

Legend:
- Paved Road
- Maintained Dirt
- Unmaintained Dirt
- Singletrack Trail
- Selected Route

**9.1** Arrive at the intersection of Trail 426 and the Spring Creek Trail. Bear right at this intersection, following the sign for Trail 426 and "Bear Creek – 9.1 miles." Immediately after bearing right here, notice a sign posted on a lodgepole pine tree for "Deadman's Gulch – 7 miles" pointing you in the right direction. Cross Flag Creek and continue riding due west.

**11.4** After climbing through a meadow, the trail intersects with an old logging road. Bear left onto this old logging road and continue riding in a southerly direction. Be sure not to cross this logging road to connect with the continuation of the singletrack on the other side.

**12.0** The logging road forks. Bear right to the intersection of Bear Creek Trail 415, passing

signs for "Deadman's Gulch – 4 miles" and "Spring Creek – 7 miles." Continue riding on Bear Creek Trail 415 as it heads in a southerly direction through a meadow.

**12.3** Cross a wooden footbridge.

**13.4** Cross Bear Creek.

**15.4** Reach the intersection of Bear Creek Trail and Deadman's Gulch Trail. Bear right (west) onto Deadman's Gulch Trail 420.

**17.8** Reach the top of the Deadman's Gulch climb and descend the switchbacks to your vehicle.

**18.9** Reach a beautiful aspen forest.

**19.8** Pass a private home to your left, as the trail parallels a barbed wire fence.

**20.1** Arrive at your vehicle.

The Reno Divide Road climbs steeply via switchbacks through a dense conifer forest and passes an old miner's cabin to the left. In 1892 Reno Divide served as a halfway station for freighters of local area mines. Views of Italian Mountain (13,378 feet) and Lambertson Peak lie to the north. From Reno Divide, connect with the Flag Creek Trail, which offers the first of several great descents. After crossing Flag Creek, you may notice a singletrack spur that breaks left. This is not the trail. Continue straight on the main trail for a mile before reaching a very sandy, rooty, and rocky section, which climbs steeply through dense forest.

Once you connect with the Bear Creek Trail, the ride descends rapidly through a meadow and crosses a wooden footbridge. After crossing Bear Creek, you have to descend through sections of tricky, technical sand and rock. After this tricky descent, the trail becomes a fast and smooth tour through the pines. With Bear Creek flowing to your left, you ride along a precipitous west-facing slope, with slippery rocks and roots. From here, the trail opens up onto a beautiful high alpine valley. The singletrack through this valley is fast and smooth and leads to Deadman's Gulch. The gulch received its foreboding name in 1859, when Ute Indians massacred six miners here who had trespassed on their land in search of gold. Today, however, the gulch's killer climb may better serve to identify the spot.

Although most of this climb is manageable, save the last 200-300 yards where the climbing gets considerably steeper, it does arrive late in the ride—around mile 15.4. Its late arrival makes this final push that much more challenging. Once you reach the top, the dark pine tree forest offers cool relief after a burning climb. From the top of Deadman's Gulch, descend down the famed switchbacks through tight aspens and over large exposed rocks. After ripping the switchbacks, you pass a private home before descending steeply to Cement Creek. The trail travels upstream for 100 yards. A large, fallen tree with notched stairs carved into its ends lies across the creek. Cross the creek via the tree and climb to your vehicle.

Making their way to the top of Deadman's Gulch and the switchbacks.

# Ride Information

## 📞 Trail Contacts:
The Alpineer, Crested Butte, CO; (970) 349-6292 or www.alpineer.com

## 🕐 Schedule:
Mid July to October

## ❓ Local Information:
The Crested Butte/Mt. Crested Butte Chamber of Commerce, Crested Butte, CO; (970) 349-6438 or 1-800-545-4505 • Gunnison National Forest and Bureau of Land Management, Gunnison Resource Area, Gunnison, CO; (970) 641-0471 • High Country Citizens' Alliance, Crested Butte, CO; (970) 349-7104 or www.sni.net/hcca

## 💡 Local Events/Attractions:
Mountain Bike Hall of Fame & Museum, Crested Butte, CO; (970) 349-6817 or 1-800-454-4505 • Crested Butte Mountain Heritage Museum, Inc., Crested Butte, CO; (970) 349-1880 • Fat Tire Bike Festival, in June, Crested Butte, CO – contact the Crested Butte/Mt. Crested Butte Chamber of Commerce at (970) 349-6438 or 1-800-545-4505 • Annual Wildflower Festival, in July, Crested Butte, CO – contact the Crested Butte/Mt. Crested Butte Chamber of Commerce at (970) 349-6438 or 1-800-545-4505 • One World Music Festival, in September, Crested Butte, CO – contact the Crested Butte/Mt. Crested Butte Chamber of Commerce at (970) 349-6438 or 1-800-545-4505 • Rendezvous Gallery, Crested Butte, CO; (970) 349-6804

## 👥 Organizations:
Crested Butte Mountain Bike Association, Crested Butte, CO; (970) 349-5517 or (970) 349-6817

## 🛏 Accommodations:
Irwin Lodge, Crested Butte, CO; (970) 349-9800 or 1-888 GO-IRWIN • Crested Butte International Hostel LLC, Crested Butte, CO; (970) 349-0588 or 1-888-389-0588 or www.gunnison.com/~hostel/

## 🍴 Restaurants:
Idle Spur, Crested Butte, CO; (970) 349-5026 • Donita's Cantina, Crested Butte, CO; (970) 349-6674 • Wooden Nickel, Crested Butte, CO; (970) 349-6350

## ♿ Tours:
No Limits Center, Crested Butte, Mt. Crested Butte, CO; (970) 349-4247 or 1-888-954-4247 • Pioneer Guide Service, Crested Butte, CO; (970) 349-5517 or www.pioneer@crestedbutte.net • Paddle Trax & Syngltrax, Crested Butte, CO; (970) 349-1100 • Alpine Outside, Crested Butte, CO; (970) 349-5011 or 1-800-833-8052; Almont, CO; (970) 641-1303 or 1-888-761-FISH or www.3riversresort.com

## 🚲 Local Bike Shops:
The Alpineer, Crested Butte, CO; (970) 349-6292 or www.alpineer.com • XTC Cycles, Crested Butte, CO; (970) 349-6776 • Crested Butte Sports Ski & Bike Shop, (Next to the Nordic Inn at the Ski Area), Mt. Crested Butte, CO; (970) 349-7516 or 1-800-301-9169 • Christy Sports Ltd., Crested Butte, CO; (970) 349-6601 • Pinnacle Cycles, Crested Butte, CO; (970) 349-2237

## 🗺 Maps:
USGS maps: Cement Mountain, CO; Pearl Pass, CO; Italian Creek, CO • Trails Illustrated map: #133 • Crested Butte Bike Trails Map – available at the Alpineer • Aspen, Crested Butte, Gunnison Recreation Topo Map, Latitude 40° Inc. – available at select area bike shops

# Dyke Trail

## Ride Summary

The Dyke Trail Loop is another trail in Crested Butte's long list of incredible rides. Combining long climbs, lakeside views, towering mountains, fast singletrack, and aspen forests, the Dyke Trail is sure to please. With the exception of the road climb to Kebler Pass and the short distance from Irwin Lake to Dyke Trailhead, this ride is comprised mostly of unbeatable singletrack. Even though your ride takes you to the top of Kebler Pass, don't be fooled that the way from Irwin Lake is all downhill. There are a couple of steep, rocky, and sandy climbs en route to Horse Ranch Park, one of which arrives just as you near the dyke.

## Ride Specs

**Start:** From the Horse Ranch Park
**Length:** 14-mile loop
**Approximate Riding Time:** Advanced Riders, 2 hours; Intermediate Riders, 3 hours
**Technical Difficulty Rating:** Technically moderate to challenging due to a number of steep-walled creek crossings
**Physical Difficulty Rating:** Physically moderate to challenging due to the climbing involved at higher elevations. As you reach the middle of the ride there is one long sustained climb that travels steeply through the aspens.
**Terrain:** Improved dirt road and singletrack. This trail runs its mountainous course along hard-packed forest earth. There are a number of exposed roots and rocks with which to contend. Several creek crossings, coupled with one major rock field, round out this ride's terrain.
**Elevation Gain:** 2,415 feet
**Nearest Town:** Crested Butte, CO
**Other Trail Users:** Hikers, equestrians, and picnickers
**Canine Compatibility:** Dog friendly

## Getting There

**From Crested Butte:** Drive west on CO 135 from the Alpineer store to the four-way stop intersection at Elk Avenue. Bear left on Elk Avenue, passing the sign for Crested Butte Business District and Kebler Pass. At mile 0.5, bear left onto 1st Avenue, passing the sign for Kebler Pass Road. Make your next immediate right onto Whiterock Avenue. Whiterock Avenue turns into Gunnison CR 12 (Kebler Pass Road). At mile 1.8 the pavement ends. Bear left at mile 2.4, passing the sign for Kebler Pass. Continue on CR 12. Bear left (still on CR 12) at the Irwin Lake intersection (mile 7.2), passing the sign for Kebler Pass. Reach Kebler Pass at mile 7.9. Begin your descent to Horse Ranch Park. At mile 12.5 bear right into Horse Ranch Park. Park your vehicle here. ***DeLorme: Colorado Atlas & Gazetteer.*** Page 58, A-B 1-2

As you begin riding up Kebler Pass Road to Kebler Pass, views of the Anthracite Range are to the south (right), with Ohio Peak (12, 271 feet) standing out most prominently. The ruddy looking Anthracite Range takes its name and its color from the hard natural coal found in abundance in its mountains. In Crested Butte's early mining days, fired coal from the surrounding mountains filled the crisp alpine air with a glow reminiscent of a city under siege. Lewis Lathrop, a Rio Grande engineer, recalled: "Both anthracite and soft coal poured in never-ending

Irwin Lake with Ruby Peak, Mount Owen, and Purple Peak in the background.

streams from the surrounding mountains…Long banks of coke ovens made the night sky lurid with leaping red flames and the sickening-sweet odor of coal being baked into coke hung heavily over the snow-covered town." Although these now dilapidated coke ovens can be dismissed as nothing more than a minor pox on an otherwise unblemished Colorado landscape, they, nevertheless, whisperingly bespeak of the fortunes, foibles, strengths, and triumphs of the human spirit. This spirit now lies quietly captured in the Irwin Cemetery atop Kebler Pass.

Dejected, penniless, and disgusted after not having reaped the benefits of a 12-year prospecting venture, A.T. Gilkerson decided to pack what little belongings he had and move his impoverished family back across the Great Plains. After his mule gave out, Gilkerson left his family with some provisions and went out in search of work. Gilkerson paused one day for lunch. There, on that warm July afternoon in 1879, in a ledge laid bare by horses' hooves, Gilkerson discovered Ruby Gulch, a deposit rich in ruby and wire silver.

Word of Gilkerson's discovery soon spread—perhaps by none louder than Richard P. Irwin, a well-respected prospector who had prospected the entire length of the Rocky Mountains from Canada to Mexico. Miners and prospectors descended upon Ruby Gulch in record numbers in the spring following Gilkerson's discovery, causing a mushroom of competing mining towns. Perhaps no other mining town grew as aggressively in the area as did the town of Irwin.

With the town speedily coming of age, an ambitious printer from the town of Rosita saw his chance to set up Irwin's first newspaper. After arriving in Gunnison on March 3, 1880, John E. Phillips awaited the arrival of a Washington hand press he had sent for from Chicago. In the interim, Phillips walked the 30 miles to Irwin in 10 feet of snow and bought himself a lot—which also happened to be under 10 feet of snow. When the press equipment arrived, Phillips organized a team of freighters equipped with homemade snowshoes to transport the goods to Irwin. George Crofutt, author of *Crofutt's Grip-Sack Guide of Colorado*, best described their journey over Ohio Pass and the descent into Irwin as being "in a style peculiarly western, . .

## **Miles**Directions

**0.0 START** from Horse Ranch Park. Bear left back onto Kebler Pass Road and begin riding in an easterly direction back to Kebler Pass.

**3.0** Cross over Ruby Anthracite Creek.

**4.7** Reach Kebler Pass (10,007 feet). To your left is the Irwin Cemetery. Descend from Kebler Pass to the intersection with Irwin Lake.

**5.3** Bear left onto FS 826, following signs for the Lake Irwin Campground.

**5.5** FS 826 intersects with Gunnison CR 826 2A. Bear left here, continuing on FS 826, following signs for Lake Irwin.

**7.7** Enter the Gunnison National Forest. Continue riding on FS 826, passing alongside Lake Irwin's western banks.

**7.8** Pass the "Fisherman Parking" to your right.

**7.9** Pass the Lake Irwin Campground to your right.

**8.3** FS 826 breaks hard to the right. Bear left onto the dirt road that heads due west, by the brown signs to Dyke Trailhead and Dead End Road. The road to the right continues on to Irwin Lodge.

**8.5** The Dead End Road forks. Bear left at the fork and follow the sign for the Dyke Trail (Trail 837).

**8.6** The Dyke Trail singletrack begins. Descend swiftly in a southerly direction on the Dyke Trail through a meadow.

**8.8** Descend into a thick lodgepole pine forest. Notice the black and white Dyke Trail marker pointing you to the right. Bear right here and descend steeply to a creek.

**11.3** Descend along a sloping and rocky section of trail to a rock field (the dyke). From the rock field area, a long and arduous climb through the aspens awaits.

**12.5** The Dyke Trail intersects the Raggeds Wilderness Area. Bear left (south), continuing on the Dyke Trail and following signs for Horse Ranch Park. Descend savagely to Horse Ranch Park.

**13.8** Arrive at Horse Ranch Park and the trailheads for Dark Canyon Trail 830, Oh-Be-Joyful Pass 9, and Erickson Springs 13. Bear left onto the dirt Horse Ranch Park road and ride back to your vehicle.

**14.0** Reach your vehicle.

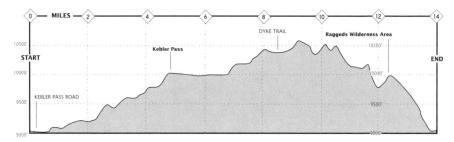

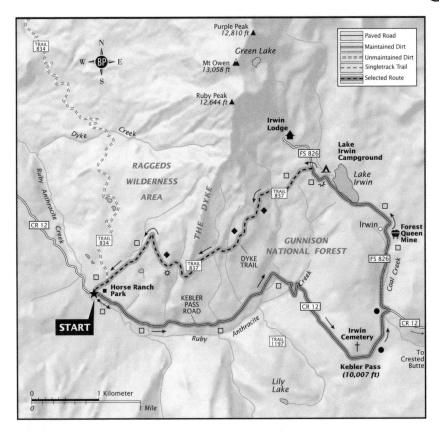

. American in the extreme." Irwin's first newspaper press was set up in a cabin without doors, windows, or a floor—the town had no milled lumber yet. The first edition of the *Elk Mountain Pilot*, dated June 17, 1880, was displayed atop a whiskey barrel in the middle of the street and auctioned off at $56, along with the whiskey in the barrel. "American in the extreme," indeed.

The town flourished through the summer of 1880 and grew from a population of 50 to 100 times that number in just two months. Early miners built their cabins from trees felled just above the snowline, since digging through the snowline to the bottom of the trees proved to be too labor-intensive for miners eager to strike it rich. As a result, Irwin's first cabins sat 10 feet above the ground, on top of the snowpack. As the snows melted and the cabins sank some 10 feet to the ground, the cabins began to look like those which could have been built by the procurer of the town's first newspaper edition. Large quantities of snow like this and the failure to obtain a railroad, eventually led to the demise of Irwin. Its boom only lasted from 1879 to 1881. By the late 1880s, most of the area mines had been shut down. All that remains of this once bustling boomtown is the Irwin Cemetery.

Take a moment to tour through the cemetery upon reaching Kebler Pass. There's a footpath that weaves past a number of old headstones. Passing the old Irwin Cemetery to your left, descend toward Lake Irwin and the intersection with the Dyke Trail.

Surrounded by Ruby Peak (12,644 feet), Mount Owen (13,058 feet), and Purple Peak (12,810 feet), Lake Irwin bears peaceful testimony to the strength of will and depth of courage exhibited by the now-vanished community of Irwin. From the lake, you ride to the Dyke Trail. A fast initial descent through a hillside meadow delivers you to the first of many steep-walled creek beds. After descending through thick aspen and lodgepole pine forests and scurrying across a sloping rock field, you arrive at the bottom of the dyke. The large igneous rocks you see before you are the cooled remains of liquid magma forced through narrow vertical slits in a mountainside. Resembling a backbone, this natural dyke runs down the southern shoulder of Ruby Peak and terminates in the forests just before crossing the trail.

The descent from the dyke leads you to the junction of the Raggeds Wilderness Area and the Dyke Trail. The descent from this junction is savage, as the trail runs over a variety of mountainous terrain on its way through a pristine aspen forest. This section of the trail is very sinewy, so hip-steering is a must. Upon reaching the Dark Canyon Trailhead, bear left and descend to your vehicle.

# Ride Information

## Trail Contacts:
The Alpineer, Crested Butte, CO; (970) 349-6292 or www.alpineer.com

## Schedule:
Mid-June to October

## Local Information:
The Crested Butte/Mt. Crested Butte Chamber of Commerce, Crested Butte, CO; (970) 349-6438 or 1-800-545-4505 • Gunnison National Forest and Bureau of Land Management, Gunnison Resource Area, Gunnison, CO; (970) 641-0471 • High Country Citizens' Alliance, Crested Butte, CO; (970) 349-7104 or www.sni.net/hcca

## Local Events/Attractions:
Mountain Bike Hall of Fame & Museum, Crested Butte, CO; (970) 349-6817 or 1-800-454-4505 • Crested Butte Mountain Heritage Museum, Inc., Crested Butte, CO; (970) 349-1880 • Fat Tire Bike Festival, in June, Crested Butte, CO; (970) 349-6438 or 1-800-545-4505. • Annual Wildflower Festival, in July, Crested Butte, CO; (970) 349-6438 or 1-800-545-4505 • One World Music Festival, in September, Crested Butte, CO; (970) 349-6438 or 1-800-545-4505 • Rendezvous Gallery, Crested Butte, CO; (970) 349-6804

## Organizations:
Crested Butte Mountain Bike Association (C.B.M.B.A), Crested Butte, CO; (970) 349-5517 or (970) 349-6817

## Accommodations:
Irwin Lodge, Crested Butte, CO; (970) 349-9800 or 1-888 GO-IRWIN • Crested Butte International Hostel LLC, Crested Butte, CO; (970) 349-0588 or 1-888-389-0588 or www.gunnison.com/~hostel/

## Restaurants:
Idle Spur, Crested Butte, CO; (970) 349-5026 • Donita's Cantina, Crested Butte, CO; (970) 349-6674 • Wooden Nickel, Crested Butte, CO; (970) 349-6350

## Tours:
No Limits Center, Crested Butte, Mt. Crested Butte, CO; (970) 349-4247 or 1-888-954-4247 • Pioneer Guide Service, Crested Butte, CO; (970) 349-5517 or www.pioneer@crestedbutte.net • Paddle Trax & Syngltrax, Crested Butte, CO; (970) 349-1100 • Alpine Outside, Crested Butte, CO; (970) 349-5011 or 1-800-833-8052; Almont, CO; (970) 641-1303 or 1-888-761-FISH or www.3riversresort.com

## Local Bike Shops:
The Alpineer, Crested Butte, CO; (970) 349-6292 or www.alpineer.com • XTC Cycles, Crested Butte, CO; (970) 349-6776 • Crested Butte Sports Ski & Bike Shop, (Next to the Nordic Inn at the Ski Area), Mt. Crested Butte, CO; (970) 349-7516 or 1-800-301-9169 • Christy Sports Ltd., Crested Butte, CO; (970) 349-6601 • Pinnacle Cycles, Crested Butte, CO; (970) 349-2237

## Maps:
USGS maps: Oh-Be-Joyful, CO; Mount Axtell, CO; Marcellina Mountain, CO; Anthracite Range, CO • Trails Illustrated map: # 133 • Crested Butte Bike Trails Map – available at the Alpineer • Aspen, Crested Butte, Gunnison Recreation Topo Map, Latitude 40° Inc. – available at select bike shops

# Mount Princeton to Raspberry Gulch

## Ride Summary

The Mount Princeton to Raspberry Gulch ride offers a great introduction into Colorado's 14er Region. Incorporating sections of the Colorado Trail, this ride provides fat tire enthusiasts with great views of the Arkansas Valley and the Sawatch Range's Collegiate Peaks. Although the ride is both technically and physically challenging, a soak in the Mount Princeton Hot Springs at the trail's end is inspiration enough to grunt up Raspberry Gulch Road. The singletrack portion of the ride provides challenging access to two of the Sawatch Range's most dominant peaks: Mount Princeton and Mount Antero. You'll enjoy passing through gorgeous stands of aspen and mixed conifer forests.

## Ride Specs

**Start:** From the parking lot of the Mount Princeton Hot Springs, begin your ride on County Road 162.

**Length:** 19.6-mile loop

**Approximate Riding Time:** Advanced Riders, 2–2½ hours; Intermediate Riders, 3–3½ hours

**Technical Difficulty Rating:** Technically moderate: Though seven miles of the route pass over paved county road, there are some rough sections of singletrack, offering near impossible switchbacks and rocky descents.

**Physical Difficulty Rating:** Physically moderate to challenging due to lung-busting steep climbs over rutted and off-camber terrain

**Terrain:** Paved highway, county roads, forest roads, and singletrack. Forest Service Road 273 becomes very rutted and rocky as it nears its end. The singletrack includes it all: nearly impassable rock sections, softened forest earth, and sand.

**Elevation Gain:** 2,522 feet

**Nearest Town:** Buena Vista, CO

**Other Trail Users:** Hikers, campers, backpackers, and equestrians

**Canine Compatibility:** Dog friendly

## Getting There

**From Buena Vista:** Drive south on CO 24 until you intersect U.S. 285 at around mile 2.3. Continue traveling south on U.S. 285. Just after the town of Nathrop, turn right onto CR 162 at mile 8.1, by the Mount Princeton Hot Springs Resort sign. Drive 4.5 miles before turning left into the resort parking lot at mile 12.6. Park here and begin riding east on CR 162. *DeLorme: Colorado Atlas & Gazetteer.* Page 60, C 1-2

The Mount Princeton to Raspberry Gulch trail is located in the heart of Colorado's 14ers Region (the highest concentration of 14,000-foot peaks in the continental United States). Fifteen Colorado peaks, all reaching over 14,000 feet, lie within a region no larger than 30x20 miles. Here the impressive Sawatch Mountains stretch across the west side of the Arkansas Valley from southwest of Salida north to Leadville. The Mount Princeton to Raspberry Gulch Trail snakes its way along the

Mount Princeton.

base of two of the Sawatch Range's most prominent peaks, Mount Princeton and Mount Antero. Of these 15 peaks, four (including Mount Princeton) are typically referred to as the Collegiate Peaks.

At 14,197 feet, Mount Princeton is the second highest of the Collegiate Peaks— second only to Mount Harvard. The Collegiate Peaks include Mount Princeton, Mount Harvard (14,420 feet), Mount Columbia (14,073 feet) and Mount Yale (14,196 feet). Each peak gets its name from the institution that sponsored its study and survey in the mid to late 1800s. Of the four Collegiate Peaks, and perhaps of all the mountains in the Sawatch Range, Mount Princeton remains as one of the most striking. Looking west from the Arkansas Valley, Mount Princeton displays an almost perfect symmetry, with two smaller peaks flanking the central summit. But Mount Princeton's symmetry is not all that attracts the eye. No doubt your curiosity will be sparked by the mountain's south sloping escarpment.

## **Miles**Directions

**0.0 START** from the Mount Princeton Hot Springs and bear right onto CR 162, riding east.

**0.7** CR 162 intersects with CR 270. Bear right onto CR 270.

**4.5** Cross a cattle guard

**4.7** CR 270 intersects with CR 272. At the "T" intersection, bear right onto dirt CR 272 following the signs for Browns Creek.

**5.6** Cross a cattle guard and enter into the San Isabel National Forest. Camping is available once you pass into the national forest.

**6.9** Arrive at the junction of CR 272 and FS 274. CR 272 turns left (south). Bear right onto FS 274.

**7.2** FS 274 intersects with FS 273 (Raspberry Gulch Road). Bear left onto FS 273 and climb steadily over rocky and rutted terrain. You'll climb over 1,000 feet in two miles. As the FS 273 nears its end, the trail becomes increasingly narrow, to the point of it becoming a wide doubletrack.

**9.4** From this point on, FS 273 is closed to motor vehicle travel. A few yards beyond the rusted "Road Closed to Motor Vehicles" sign lies the singletrack. Signs here indicate Browns Creek to be two miles to the south and Chalk Creek, three miles to the north. Bear left here onto the Colorado Trail and head in a southerly direction, following signs for Browns Creek.

**10.5** Arrive at the intersection of the Colorado Trail (Trail 1776) and Trail 1430 (Little Browns Creek Trail). The Colorado Trail spurs left and also continues straight ahead,

while the Trail 1430 bears right. The spur directly in front of you will eventually start leading south, crossing Browns Creek, while the spur to your left follows a northerly route back to the Mount Princeton Hot Springs. Bear left, following the Colorado Trail in a northerly direction.

**11.8** The Colorado Trail drops to a flat pine-forested meadow. The trail is fast here.

**12.2** Cross an old 4WD road and continue straight ahead on the Colorado Trail. From the meadow, beautiful views of the Sawatch Range and Chalk Cliffs are offered.

**12.8** Cross Raspberry Gulch Road, just before the beautiful stands of aspen, and continue climbing up the other side of the hill.

**14.3** Cross another 4WD road and begin a steep singletrack climb.

**15.1** Here are the best views of the Chalk Cliffs.

**15.4** Catch some great views of Mount Princeton. From here, follow the trail in a westerly direction over some loose rocky terrain.

**16.5** Cross the dirt road and continue on the Colorado Trail, heading toward Chalk Creek.

**16.9** Cross over Chalk Creek and turn right onto CR 291, heading east through Chalk Creek Canyon.

**18.2** Arrive at the junction of CR 291 and CR 162. CR 291 ends where CR 162 begins. Continue on CR 162 east to the Mount Princeton Hot Springs and your vehicle.

**19.6** Arrive at the Mount Princeton Hot Springs and your vehicle.

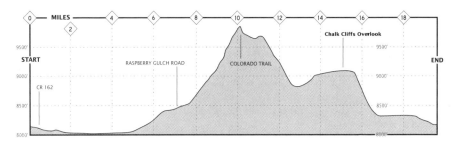

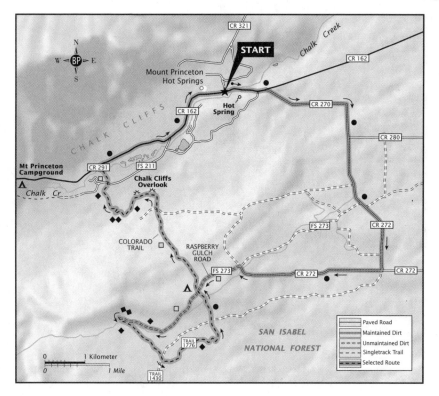

As if someone took a giant cleaver to the mountain, Mount Princeton's south slope falls abruptly from the mountainside to form the Chalk Cliffs. Though chalk-like in appearance, the white, crumbly composition of these cliffs is actually an admixture of quartz, K-feldspar, and plagioclase called white quartz monzonite. Strikingly unique, these cliffs have developed, over the years, an identity and a history that are almost independent of the mountain to which they cling.

One story tells of a band of Spaniards who raided a nearby Ute village 200 years ago. With the stolen booty in hand, the Spaniards headed for the sanctuary of the Chalk Cliffs. Undeterred by the Spaniards' dangerous route, the Ute Indians followed. Sensing the Utes hot on their trail, the Spaniards buried the booty somewhere in the Cliffs. The Utes finally caught up with the thieves, but the Spaniards wouldn't say where they hid the stolen possessions. The Utes summarily killed the raiders. According to legend, the treasure still remains buried somewhere in the dusty recesses of the Chalk Cliffs.

With the Chalk Cliffs to the north (left), pedal your way from the Mount Princeton Hot Springs to Mount Antero and back. The hot springs once served as a mining camp for the Hortense Mine, located on the southern peak of Mount Princeton. The Hortense Mine, one of the most productive silver mines in the Sawatch Range, drew much attention from itinerant traffic, and consequently, so too did the Mount Princeton Hot Springs.

By 1915 the hot springs had a 100-room hotel, complete with stained glass windows and a gigantic ballroom. The market crash of 1929 dealt a serious blow

Mt. Princeton hot springs.

to the hot springs' popularity, and by 1930 the hotel was re-opened as the Antero Hotel (named after the nearby mountain). It too would struggle, until 1950 when the wrecking ball destroyed the opulent hotel and laid to waste what little semblance of luxury and refinement these Colorado wilds could afford. Today, the Mount Princeton Hot Springs is back in business. With the Princeton Club dining room, three separate lodging units, convention facilities, and packaged recreational activities, the Mount Princeton Hot Springs recaptures much of its Roaring Twenties grandeur.

From the hot springs, the trail skirts the westernmost border of the Arkansas Valley on its way to Mount Antero. Mount Antero takes its name from Chief Antero, the one-time leader of the Uintah band of Ute Indians. Chief Antero was among those who signed the 1878 treaty that allotted portions of Ute land in the San Juans to the silver-mining camps of the day. An advocate for peace, Chief Antero quelled many Indian uprisings and kept his own tribe at peace during the White River Utes' uprising in 1879.

Mount Antero is one of Colorado's most mineral-rich 14ers. Aquamarine, topaz, and clear and smoky quartz crystals color all of Antero's 14,269 feet. To preserve and display the mountain's mineral wealth, the Colorado Mineralogical Society created the Mount Antero Mineral Park on August 1, 1949. A bronze plaque imbedded in a granite boulder marks Mount Antero as North America's highest mineral site.

As you approach Mount Antero along Forest Service Road 273, you pass through flat, open stands of lodgepole pine before climbing steeply to the point where forest road closes to motor vehicles. The singletrack that connects this point to the Colorado Trail delivers short, rocky sections; smooth-tracking terrain; and tight

# Ride Information

## ☎ Trail Contacts:
**Greater Buena Vista Area Chamber of Commerce**, Buena Vista, CO; (719) 395-6612 or *www.fourteenernet.com*

## ⏱ Schedule:
Late April to early October

## ❓ Local Information:
**Free Visitors' Guide** call 1-800-831-8594 or visit *www.colorado.com* • **FourteenerNet**, a website detailing 14er Country at *www.vtinet.com/14ernet*

## 📍 Local Events/Attractions:
**Buena Vista Heritage Museum**, Buena Vista, CO; (719) 395-8458 – *open daily June, July, August, and part of September* • **Mount Princeton Hot Springs Resort**, Nathrop, CO; 1-888-395-7799 or *www.mtprinceton.com* • **Gold Rush Days and Music Festival**, August, Buena Vista, CO; (719) 395-6612

## 🍽 Restaurants:
**Casa del Sol**, Buena Vista, CO; (719) 395-8810 – *reservation advised* • **Bongo Billy's**, Buena Vista, CO; (719) 395-2634 or (719) 395-4991

## 🚵 Mountain Bike Tours:
**Buffalo Joe River Trips**, Buena Vista, CO; 1-800-356-7984 or (719) 395-8757

## 🏢 Organizations:
**Banana Belt Fat Tracks Club**, Salida, CO; (719) 539-6704

## 🚲 Local Bike Shops:
**The Trailhead**, Buena Vista, CO; (719) 395-8001 • **Coast to Coast**, Buena Vista, CO; (719) 395-8067 • **Otero Cyclery**, Salida, CO; (719) 539-6704 • **Capricorn Sports**, Salida, CO; (719) 539-3971 • **Headwaters**, Salida, CO; (719) 539-4506

## 🗺 Maps:
**USGS maps:** Mount Antero, CO; Nathrop, CO • **Trails Illustrated map:** # 130 Salida, St. Elmo, Shavano Peak • **14ers Region Mountain Bike Guide** – *available for free from the chambers of commerce (719) 395-6612*

turns. Once on the Colorado Trail, the route descends over very technically challenging rocky terrain before opening up to fast runs through mixed conifer forests and sandy meadows.

Once you cross Forest Service Road 273, the trail passes through a small aspen glen and winds its way up a hillside laden with pine saplings and scrub oak. This section of the route offers incredible views of the Chalk Cliffs. Meadows of roundleaf bluebell (campanula rotundifolia), Indian paintbrush (castilleja miniata), scarlet bugler (penstemon centranthifolius), and Richardson's geranium (geranium richardsonii) dot the landscape around Mount Antero. You'll cross a 4WD road at mile 14.3, where technically steep singletrack over rocks, sand, and silt await the tireless rider.

In another mile, the trail begins its descent into Chalk Creek and runs over incredibly demanding technical sections, requiring most riders to dismount. Once across Chalk Creek, it's a smooth coast through Chalk Creek Canyon back to your vehicle and a 105-degree geothermal soak in the Mount Princeton Hot Springs.

# Bear Creek to Methodist Mountain

## Ride Summary

The Bear Creek to Methodist Mountain Trail is part of the annual Banana Belt Mountain Bike Loop Race, one of the most time-honored mountain biking traditions in Salida, if not in Colorado. The non-sanctioned race pays tribute to the grassroots beginnings of mountain biking by including riders of all ability levels to participate in the festivities. A favorite of Salida locals, the Bear Creek to Methodist Mountain Trail travels up the beautiful Bear Creek drainage into the San Isabel National Forest to its intersection with the famed Rainbow Trail. This route incorporates a section of the 100-mile Rainbow Trail. The Rainbow Trail, itself, extends from the Continental Divide, southwest of Salida, to Music Pass and travels along the east side of the Sangre de Cristo mountain range.

## Ride Specs

**Start:** From the USDA Forest Service Office, Salida Ranger District, in downtown Salida
**Length:** 20-mile loop
**Approximate Riding Time:** Advanced Riders, 2–2½ hours; Intermediate Riders, 3–3½ hours
**Technical Difficulty Rating:** Technically moderate due to a number of rocky and sandy sections
**Physical Difficulty Rating:** Physically moderate to challenging due to its extended climbing over 8,000 feet
**Terrain:** Paved highway, county road, 4WD road, and singletrack. The route passes through semi-arid terrain along the Arkansas River to narrow, high mountain valleys lined with wildflowers. Expect smooth-running singletrack, pavement, and exposed rocks and roots. After crossing Rock Creek, the terrain becomes somewhat gravely and sandy.
**Elevation Gain:** 3,456 feet
**Nearest Town:** Salida, CO
**Other Trail Users:** Hikers, campers, and equestrians
**Canine Compatibility:** Dog friendly

## Getting There

**From Poncha Springs:** Drive east on U.S. 50 for 3.1 miles to the USDA Forest Service Office, Salida Ranger District, which is to the right. Park your vehicle and begin riding east on U.S. 50 through Salida. **DeLorme: Colorado Atlas & Gazetteer:** Page 60, D-3

Woodlawn Cemetery below Methodist Mountain.

elcome to Colorado…*the way it Used to Be*," touts the welcoming sign to 14er Country's southern-most town. Surrounded by the Collegiate Peaks to the west, the Mosquito Range to the east, and the Sangre de Cristo Mountains to the south, Salida typifies the Colorado experience, yesterday and today. Owing to its prime location and the genuine warmth of its

Rainbow singletrack with views of Methodist Mountain.

people, Salida inspires awe and provides thrills galore for those seeking to play in and around its majestic mountains. Grounded in every John Denver colloquialism, Salida sets the standard by which all other outdoor oriented Colorado towns are judged.

Members of the Colorado Historic Preservation Review Board determined that downtown Salida has not only one of the largest, but also one of the finest collections of historically significant buildings in all of Colorado. Receiving its listing in the National Register of Historic Places in July of 1984, Salida recalls much of the state's old world charm. The relatively private location of its historic district—located behind the motels, chain restaurants, and gas stations lining U.S. routes 50 and 285—attests to the unassuming nature of Colorado's past. Downtown buildings stand in quiet memorial to the dreams and determinations of the city's earliest inhabitants.

In 1880 the town of Salida (originally named South Arkansas) was established along the track beds of the Denver & Rio Grande Railroad. As the railroad grew, expanding its services to the nearby mining districts of Monarch and Turrent, so too did Salida grow. Salida's farmers and ranchers profited off of supplying produce and meat to railroad and mining crews. The town mushroomed in the early half of the 1880s. But as it grew, Salida was dealt its share of blows when major fires ripped through its downtown in both 1886 and 1888. Not to be slowed by this unfortunate turn of events, residents created Salida Fire Blocks, an ordinance requiring all new downtown buildings to be built of brick. From Front Street (now Sackett) to

## **Miles**Directions

**0.0 START** from Salida Ranger Station in downtown Salida and head east on U.S. 50 through Salida.

**0.5** Pass the sign for Methodist Mountain, elevation 11,655 feet.

**3.7** U.S. 50 intersects with CR 101. Bear right (south) onto CR 101 and ride over the cattle guard.

**4.6** Cross the Chaffee/Fremont County line. (Here Chaffee CR 101 becomes Fremont CR 49.)

**6.9** Cross over the cattle guard and enter into the San Isabel National Forest. (Here Fremont CR 49 becomes FS 101.3).

**9.1** FS 101.3 intersects with Tail 101A on the left. Pass by Trail 101A and continue climbing straight ahead.

**9.4** Ford Bear Creek. After crossing Bear Creek, head up a short, but rocky climb before arriving at the Rainbow Trail singletrack.

**9.5** Arrive at the trailhead for the Rainbow Trail (Trail 1336) on your right. There'll also be signs for "Howard Creek – 3 miles" and "Methodist Mountain – 6 miles." Bear right onto the Rainbow Trail, following signs for Methodist Mountain.

**9.9** Cross a 4WD road where a sign on the left reads "Bear Creek – 0.25 miles" and "Methodist Mountain – 6 miles." Pass the sign and continue heading west along the Rainbow Trail.

**10.2** Cross Bear Creek again.

**11.4** Cross Rock Creek and begin a short climb through a gravely and sandy section. As the trail continues heading north through fields of scrub oak, see the meadow across the gully through which you've just ridden.

**12.4** Cross another 4WD road and continue riding on the Rainbow Trail.

**14.3** Arrive at another beautiful hillside meadow, offering the best views of Salida and the San Isabel National Forest. Notice the "S" on the hillside. A collection of white painted rocks, "S" marks the spot for the town of Salida and offers yet another area ride, known simply as the "S" Trail. Here's a great spot to have a snack and take in the view. Continue riding through the meadow and descend on plush singletrack through the pine forest.

**15.4** Arrive at FS 108, the road that leads to the top of Methodist Mountain. Bear right onto FS 108 and descend to U.S. Highway 50.

**17.0** FS 108 becomes a graded, two-lane road, as you leave the San Isabel National Forest. Here FS 108 becomes CR 107. Bear right, heading down CR 107.

**18.7** Woodlawn Cemetery is off to your left. Pass the old cemetery and continue heading for U.S. 50.

**19.4** CR 107 intersects with U.S. 50. Bear left (west), heading back to your vehicle.

**20.0** Reach your vehicle at the Salida Ranger Station.

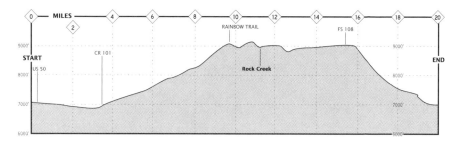

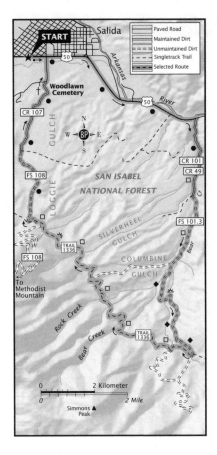

Fourth Street and between C and H Streets, Salida Fire Blocks now make up Salida's historic district.

The Corner Stone Pub (formerly known as Club Rio) is believed to be Salida's oldest commercial building. Once a flourishing general store, the building's original wooden frame got its brick face-lift in 1883 from proprietors Edward W. Corbin and Elias H. Webb. It later became a tavern and currently holds the distinction of having Colorado's second oldest liquor license. A huge mural inside the tavern depicts the history of Salida. Joe "Kidd" Orr, champion boxer and one-time owner of the club, named the bar "Club Rio" in honor of his father Ralph Edward Orr. Dad's initials, phonetically at least, provided Kidd with "Rio."

After the passing of the Denver & Rio Grande Railroad and the mining booms and busts of the early 1970s and 1980s, Salida turned itself into a thriving recreational community, rallying mostly around mountain biking and river boating. The people of Salida now commemorate themselves through shared outdoor activities.

Located within the so-called "Banana Belt," Salida and the towns of Buena Vista and Poncha Springs enjoy a unique environment that's highly conducive to outdoor recreation. Guarded by a veritable wall of 14ers and nestled in the relatively low-lying Arkansas Valley (6800-8500 feet), these three towns receive a mere 10 to 12 inches per annum of rainfall. What little precipitation does find its way over the Sawatch range, is usually evaporated in the drier, warmer atmosphere of the Arkansas Valley. Just 35 miles north of these towns, in the mountains surrounding the town of Leadville (10,430-feet), snowfall arrives in excess of 10 feet a year—while in Salida, Buena Vista, and Poncha Springs conditions remain remarkably dry. People can literally ski a peak and ride a trail in a single day all within an area of 35 miles. Leading this outdoor-rec lifestyle is the Salida-based Banana Belt Fat Tracks Club.

In an effort to bring the community together in a sharing and healthy environment, the Banana Belt Fat Tracks Club organized the first Banana Belt Mountain Bike Loop Race in 1989. That year 76 local riders turned out to enjoy the festivities. Since then, the number of participants has grown to well over 150. In response to the many high profile mountain biking events throughout Colorado, the Banana Belt Mountain Bike Loop Race remains a non-sanctioned, grassroots memorial to the community and welcomes every rider, regardless of the ability level.

# Ride Information

## 🕐 Trail Contacts:
**Heart of the Rockies Chamber of Commerce**, Salida, CO; (719) 539-2068 • **San Isabel National Forest**, Salida Ranger District, Salida, CO; (719) 539-3591

## 🕐 Schedule:
Late April to late September

## ❓ Local Information:
For a free Visitors Guide call 1-800-831-8594 or visit *www.colorado.com* • For a website detailing 14er Country try FourteenerNet at *www.vtinet.com/ 14ernet*

## 💡 Local Events/Attractions:
**Salida Hot Springs Aquatic Center**, Salida, CO; (719) 539-6738 • **Banana Belt Mountain Bike Loop Race**, in September, Salida, CO; (719) 539-2068

## 🛏 Accommodations:
**The Piñon and Sage**, Salida, CO; (719) 539-3227 or 1-800-840-3156 – *run by mountain bikers for mountain bikers*

## 🍴 Restaurants:
**The Flour of Life Bakery, Coffeehouse, Pizzeria and Pub**, Salida, CO; (719) 539-0999 – *Guinness on tap* • **Cornucopia**

**Bakery & Cafe**, Salida, CO; (719) 539-2531 • **First Street Café**, Salida, CO; (719) 539-4759 • **Il Vicino Pizzeria & Brewery**, Salida, CO; (719) 539-5219

## 🏢 Organizations:
**Banana Belt Fat Tracks Club**, Salida, CO; (719) 539-6704

## 🚵 Mountain Bike Tours:
**Buffalo Joe River Trips**, Buena Vista, CO; 1-800-356-7984 or (719) 395-8757

## 🚲 Local Bike Shops:
**Otero Cyclery**, Salida, CO; (719) 539-6704 • **Headwaters**, Salida, CO; (719) 539-4506 • **Capricorn Sports**, Salida, CO; (719) 539-3971 • **The Trailhead**, Buena Vista, CO; (719) 395-8001 • **Coast to Coast**, Buena Vista, CO; (719) 395-8067

## Ⓝ Maps:
**USGS maps:** Salida West, CO; Salida East, CO; Wellsville, CO; Poncha Pass, CO • **14ers Region Mountain Bike Guide** – *available free at local bike shops and Chambers of Commerce*

The Bear Creek to Methodist Mountain Trail covers a large portion of the race's course and invites you to become part of the community. From downtown Salida, ride east on U.S. Route 50 to its intersection with County Road 101. County Road 101 is bordered east and west by private property, so stay on the road. Once in the San Isabel National Forest, the road becomes the single-lane Forest Service Road 101.3. This road will fork at mile 7.1. Bear right and continue climbing. The road becomes steep, rocky, and rutted, with views of the peaks Simmons and Hunts through the trees at mile 8.

Once on the singletrack of the Rainbow Trail, the riding becomes generally smooth with only a few exposed rocky sections, making the trail moderately technical as it cuts across pine-filled hillsides in a westerly direction. Views of the surrounding San Isabel National Forest and Salida lie to the northwest.

Rather than providing sustained lengths of high speed, the Rainbow Trail mixes short, rocky sections with blind curves and small hill climbs, making for a colorful ride.

From Forest Service Road 108, the descent is steep and rocky. Almost immediately you're thrown a sharp hairpin turn to the right, where after the road becomes steep and rocky. This rough section lasts for about two miles until Forest Service Road 108 becomes a graded two-lane road. Once becoming a graded two-lane road, the route gets speedy. You'll be able to fly down this section to your vehicle, making up for any lost time on the climb.

# Hartman Rocks

## Ride Summary

The Hartman Rocks area offers high desert riding in a 6,000-acre basin. Funky granite formations, slickrock, sand, and sage add to this geological curiosity's appeal. The Rocks, as Gunnison locals call it, is a mountain biking area replete with interconnecting trails. This route skirts the perimeter of the Hartman Rocks area and follows, in part, the Rage in the Sage course, Gunnison's annual mountain bike race. Although the trails throughout Hartman Rocks can get confusing, this shouldn't deter you from riding the "Rocks," as efforts are continually being made to distinguish the right from the wrong way. Take notice of smaller rocks or sticks imbedded in the ground across a trail, signifying a wrong way. Observe branches lying parallel to a trail, seemingly pointing the right way. In general, look for "natural" reference points, which might otherwise seem out of place: a stacked pile of rocks (cairns), orange tape, painted arrows, or even arrows drawn in the sand.

## Ride Specs

**Start:** From the Hartman Rocks parking lot

**Length:** 18.5-mile loop – with many options to either shorten or lengthen

**Approximate Riding Time:** Advanced Riders, 2½–3 hours; Intermediate Riders, 3–4 hours

**Technical Difficulty Rating:** Technically moderate with a few tight rocky sections. Most of the singletrack is smooth.

**Physical Difficulty Rating:** Physically moderate. There are some steeper climbs, coupled with sandy sections that make for a tough ride in spots.

**Terrain:** Jeep road and singletrack. The trail rolls over hilly terrain and through sagebrush meadowland. Much of the terrain is hard-packed, but there are a number of rocky and sandy sections. Some sections go through riparian areas. The area offers seemingly endless miles of singletrack and dirt road that break off in every direction.

**Elevation Gain:** 2,044 feet

**Nearest Town:** Gunnison, CO

**Other Trail Users:** Campers, hikers, motorcyclists, rock climbers, and picnickers

**Canine Compatibility:** Not dog friendly – due to exposed terrain and vehicular traffic in the area

## Getting There

**From Gunnison:** Drive west on U.S. 50 for 1.5 miles before bearing left on Gunnison CR 38 (south). CR 38 is also called Gold Basin Road. After crossing Tomichi Creek, drive for another mile before turning right onto CR 56 and into the Hartman Rocks' parking lot at mile 4.0. *DeLorme: Colorado Atlas & Gazetteer:* Page 58, D-2

Gunnison, Colorado, offers you a sandy twist to your everyday trip through the timbers. Located in the southwestern region of the state, the town of Gunnison sits at nearly 8,000 feet. But don't let its elevation fool you into believing that Gunnison is your typical mountain town. On the contrary, its nearest mountain is located roughly 25 miles north in Crested Butte. Gunnison, rather, sits on a plateau and features high-plains desert riding, as opposed to high-mountainous alpine riding. As such, the dwarfed colonies of chaparral, the sandy mesas, and the

red, 100-foot undulating granite formations that make up the lunar landscape, all contribute to Gunnison's overall feeling of eerie otherworldliness.

Gunnison began its life as a mining town, resting at the northern edge of the San Juan mining district. The town took its name from a Captain John Gunnison of the Army Topographical Engineers. In 1853 Congress enlisted Gunnison to survey the central railroad route between the 38th and 39th parallels, in order to settle the debate over which would be the best route between the East and West via a transcontinental railroad. Departing from Fort Leavenworth, Kansas, on June 15, Gunnison, an experienced explorer with 11 years of wilderness surveying to his credit, was put in charge of 32 mounted riflemen, 16 six-mule wagons, a four-mule drawn carriage full of instruments, and a four-mule medical supply carriage. By September, the team crossed Cochetopa Pass (10,032 feet) and the Continental Divide in Southcentral Colorado. They camped near what is today the town of the Cochetopa Pass. Gunnison and his team continued west until on October 25, 1853, while seeking winter quarters near Sevier Lake in Utah, Gunnison and his men were attacked and killed by marauding Paiute Indians. Few escaped to tell of the horrid events that transpired that day.

# **Miles**Directions

**0.0 START** by riding west on CR 58 from the Hartman Rocks' parking lot.

**0.2** As CR 58 veers sharply to the right, bear left through the yellow gate and continue riding up a rough dirt road. Bear right onto Hartman Rocks Road (Kill Hill) and begin your steep, granny gear ascent into Hartman Rocks heading in a northerly direction.

**0.6** Upon reaching the crest of this initial climb, Hartman Rocks Road comes to a "T" intersection. Bear left at this intersection, crossing a yellow cattle guard.

**0.7** Just after crossing the cattle guard, notice the large pullout area to your right. Bear right into this pullout and onto a smooth doubletrack, following the brown trail marker sign, as the trail descends northerly through a sage-filled meadow. The doubletrack eventually disintegrates to sandy singletrack, eventually leading out onto a rough, 4WD road.

**0.9** Bear right onto the road and begin climbing, following the brown trail marker sign.

**1.6** The road cuts sharply to the left (west) alongside a barbwire fence. Bear right passing through this barbwire fence, following the brown trail marker sign.

**2.0** The road starts to level out, as it crosses a field of imbedded slickrock. Riding in an easterly direction across the slickrock, intersect with the singletrack on the other side.

**2.5** The singletrack intersects with another jeep road. Here, bear right onto this road, following the trail marker sign. Ride in a northerly direction.

**3.1** The road intersects with the Luge Trail. Bear right onto the smooth singletrack of the Luge and descend in a northerly direction.

**4.8** The Luge Trail breaks sharply to the left.

Continue due west alongside a barbwire fence. Bear left at this point, riding to the right of the fence. Soon thereafter, notice another brown trail marker sign that directs you to ride away from this fence. As you make your way from the fence, descend into a beautiful riparian segment of the route.

**5.6** After descending speedily through this riparian ecosystem, the Luge Trail forks. Bear left here and begin climbing in a southerly direction. The right fork reaches down to the Gunnison River and private property.

**6.1** Descend to a treatment plant and the very northwest corner of the loop. Bear left here, climbing moderately and heading due south, as the trail continues alongside another barbwire fence to your right.

**6.8** Veer right, passing through an opening in the fence. Now the fence is on your left, as the trail continues in a southerly direction, passing a trail marker. Continue climbing to the crest of the hill.

**7.1** Reach the crest. From here, a jeep road passes through the fence to your left and descends steeply to McCabe Lane to your right. Bear right here and rip steeply down this rough jeep road to the junction with McCabe Lane and CR 32B.

**7.6** Reach CR 32B and bear left onto it, continuing in a southward direction.

**9.2** From CR 32B, bear right (west) onto the singletrack identified by the brown trail marker. Climb up a short ridge. Follow past the trail marker sign and descend over some moderately technical rocky terrain and through a flat, sage-filled meadow.

**10.4** Having descended past some large rocks on either side of the trail, arrive at

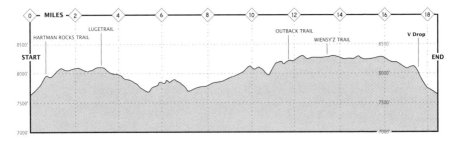

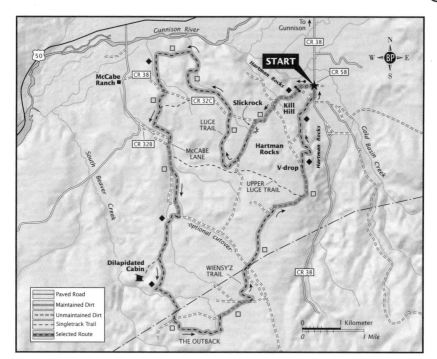

another dirt road. Bear left onto this dirt road, following the brown trail marker sign.

**10.8** The road intersects with a rough jeep trail that descends to the right. An old motorcycle trail marker signals the jeep trail. Bear right onto this trail and descend sharply. *[**Option:** You can forgo the jeep trail and continue straight on the current road. If you do this, you'll rejoin the main course in about a mile and avoid approximately one mile of moderate climbing.]*

**11.1** After passing the long and deep rut cutting through the center of this jeep trail, bear left (east) onto another singletrack, following a brown trail marker sign. If you encounter a gate and a dilapidated cabin, you've gone too far. Turn around and ride back to intersect with the singletrack now on your right.

**11.5** The trail arrives at a gate and a barbwire fence. Pass through the gate and veer right (south), following the singletrack to the left of the barbwire fence.

**11.7** Cross under the power lines and continue on the singletrack of the Outback Trail. Ride on the Outback Trail to this route's southernmost location.

**13.5** The Outback Trail's singletrack intersects with a road. Bear right onto this road, riding in an easterly direction through a vast, open plateau of sagebrush before bearing left onto the Wiensy'z Trail.

**13.6** Bear left onto the Wiensy'z Trail and continue riding in a northerly direction.

**14.5** Cross under the power lines again and bear right onto the 4WD road. Riding directly under the power lines, you're now back on the Rage in the Sage course. Continue riding in an easterly direction, following the brown trail marker signs.

**14.7** Once you pass through the barbwire fence gate, veer left, following the brown trail marker sign. From here you're offered a view of the Hartman Rocks.

**16.4** The 4WD road forks into a variety of directions. Bear left, and continue toward Hartman Rocks, passing the entrance to the "Upper Luge."

**17.2** Bear right onto the singletrack of "V-Drop" for an exciting technical descent to the Hartman Rocks parking lot.

**18.5** Arrive at your vehicle.

Rider of the purple sage.

As if naming a town after a man slaughtered by Indians isn't enough to put the voodoo on you, the town of Gunnison would again be haunted 20 years later, this time by one of Colorado's most notorious acts of barbarism. During the winter of 1873-74, Alferd Packer set out from Provo, Utah, to prospect a new gold strike in Breckenridge. (Yes, it's "Alferd." A tattoist misspelled his name and Packer happened to like it.) Upon reaching the Uncompahgre Valley, Ute Indian Chief Ouray advised Packer and his party not to continue, for the snowfall had been especially heavy that winter. Not to be bothered by Ouray's concerns, Packer pressed on, leaving the morning of February 9th and taking only seven days worth of provisions. Packer expected to reach the Los Pinos Indian Agency in the Cochetopa mountains, just southeast of present-day Gunnison.

Sixty-six days passed without word from Packer or anyone in his party. Then, on the morning of April 6th, agency officials spotted the bedraggled Packer walking alone through Los Pinos. Lost and with frostbitten feet, Packer spoke of being abandoned by his party and forced to fend for himself. Curiously unaffected by his traumatic ordeal, Packer continued on to Saguache, still intent on reaching Breckenridge. While in Saguache, Packer began to arouse suspicion. He had been carrying a Winchester rifle that belonged to a member of his prospecting party, as well as a skinning knife that belonged to another. And some noted that he was looking a little too rosy-cheeked for a man who had endured such privation. Placed in the Saguache jail pending investigation, Packer managed to escape on August 8, 1874. For nine years he roamed free, with no one having a clue as to his whereabouts.

On March 11, 1883, Packer was spotted in Cheyenne, Wyoming, living under the alias John Schwartze. After returning to Saguache for trial, Packer was found guilty of murder and cannibalism. While awaiting sentence in the Gunnison jail, Packer's attorneys seized upon a technicality in the trial, explaining that these horrific crimes occurred on Ute land when Colorado was still a territory, so Packer should not have been tried under state law, but instead, territorial law. Appealing his conviction to the Colorado State Supreme Court on October 10, 1885 under this grandfather clause, Packer's attorneys successfully spared their client the noose. As a result, the State Supreme Court threw out the case—striking the record clean. Interestingly, Colorado had become a state inbetween the murders and his first trial, so Packer could now be tried again, under newly appointed state laws, since he, in effect, had never been tried for these crimes under state law. So on August 5, 1886, Parker was tried in Gunnison and once again found guilty, his sentence now upheld by the Colorado Supreme Court. Sentenced to 40 years in prison, Packer was paroled in 1901. He died six years later—his death certificate reading: "of senility - trouble & worry." In 1989 a forensic team led by James Starrs located the bodies of Packer's party on a bluff above the Lake Fork River. Among their findings were crushed skulls (thought to be struck while the men were sleeping), signs indicating a struggle, and chipped bones—all indicating that these men hadn't been murdered without a struggle.

Careful not to chip any bones, cross over imbedded slickrock at mile 2.0, where beautiful views of Gunnison lie to the north. Views of the Hartman Rocks give you a perspective of how far you've come. From here you skirt alongside the rocks them-

# Ride Information

## 📞 Trail Contacts:
**Tune Up Ski & Bike Shop**, Gunnison, CO; (970) 641-0285

## 🕐 Schedule:
May to September

## ❓ Local Information:
**Gunnison Country Chamber of Commerce**, Gunnison, CO; (970) 641-1501 or 1-800-274-7580 or www.gunnison-co.com • **Gunnison National Forest and Bureau of Land Management**, Gunnison Resource Area, Gunnison, CO; (970) 641-0471 • **Gunnison River Territory**, Gunnison, CO; 1-800-323-2453

## 💡 Local Events/Attractions:
**Black Canyon of the Gunnison**, Montrose, CO; (970) 249-1915 • **Rage in the Sage**, in May, Tune Up Ski & Bike Shop, Gunnison, CO; (970) 641-0285 • **Blue Mesa Reservoir and the Dillon Pinnacles** – for information contact the Gunnison Chamber at (970) 641-1501 or 1-800-274-7580 • **Gunnison Pioneer Museum**, Gunnison, CO; (970) 641-4530 • **Hinsdale County Museum**, Lake City, CO; (970) 944-9515 – boasts most extensive collection of Alferd Packer memorabilia

## 🛏 Accommodations:
**Hylander Inn**, Gunnison, CO; (970) 641-0700 • **Mary Lawrence Inn**, Gunnison, CO; (970) 641-3343

## 🍴 Restaurants:
**Café Silvestre**, Gunnison, CO; (970) 641-4001 – closed Tuesdays • **Firebrand Deli**, Gunnison, CO; (970) 641-6266 • **W. Café**, Gunnison, CO; (970) 641-1744

## 🎒 Tours:
**Gunnison Valley Adventure Guides**, Gunnison, CO; (970) 641-5541

## 🚲 Local Bike Shops:
**Tune Up Ski & Bike Shop**, Gunnison, CO; (970) 641-0285 • **Tomichi Cycles**, Gunnison, CO; (970) 641-9069 • **Rock 'n Roll Sports**, Gunnison, CO; (970) 641-9150 or 1-800-659-3707

## 🗺 Maps:
**USGS maps:** Gunnison, CO; Iris NW, CO • **Trails Illustrated** map: #132 • **Gunnison Area Mountain Bike Map** – available at Tune Up Ski & Bike Shop • **Aspen, Crested Butte, Gunnison Recreation Topo Map**, Latitude 40° Inc. – available at select area bike shops

selves. The Hartman Rocks area is one of only five igneous ring dykes in the world. Millions of years ago lava-injected magma cooled several miles below the earth's surface. Over time, this magma formed into granite. A subsequent series of uplifts forced the granite through the earth's surface, forming the Hartman Rocks. The porous nature of granite allows Douglas fir, ponderosa pine, and juniper to grow in an area that otherwise would be too dry. This gives the area a surreal feel.

From these rocks, you intersect with the Luge Trail, one of the Rage in the Sage's highlights. Its fast and smooth course offers many banked turns on which to rip before dropping you into one of the area's most unique features: a beautiful riparian segment of the ride. Thick cottonwoods and tall plants abound, as the rushing of the Gunnison River can be heard just to the right, behind the trees.

Once you've connected with the Outback Trail, you're offered sweet slickrock with variable sandy sections through hard-packed, sagebrush meadows. From the meadows, return back to the "Rocks" and descend the harrowing "V-drop" back to your vehicle.

# Monarch Crest Trail

## Ride Summary

Epic is the only word for it. The Monarch Crest Trail is considered the premier mountain bike ride in the entire 14ers Region. Touted by *Bicycle Magazine* as one of the top five rides in the United States, the trail covers roughly 40 miles of descending singletrack over tundra-like terrain, across talus fields, through old-growth forests and high plains desert. This ride is one not to be missed, an impressive addition to anyone's mountain biking resume.

## Ride Specs

**Start:** From atop Monarch Pass on the Continental Divide Trail

**Length:** 35.1-mile point-to-point (shuttle required) – many break-off points allow for shorter rides

**Approximate Riding Time:** Advanced Riders, 3–4 hours; Intermediate Riders, 4–5 hours

**Technical Difficulty Rating:** Technically challenging due to the route's rocky terrain, sloping trail, and steep grades

**Physical Difficulty Rating:** Physically challenging to demanding due to the trail's length, altitude, and extended climbs

**Terrain:** Singletrack, 4WD Road, improved dirt road, and highway. The terrain includes mountaintop granite and quartz, tundra, talus fields, dark forest, and high plains desert.

**Elevation Gain:** 3,712 feet

**Nearest Town:** Pagosa Springs, CO

**Other Trail Users:** Hikers, equestrians, backpackers, and sightseers

**Canine Compatibility:** Not dog friendly. Due to the length of this ride and the harsh terrain over which it travels, bringing a dog is ill advised.

## Getting There

**To Reach Monarch Pass:** From Poncha Springs and the intersection of U.S. 285 and U.S. 50: Drive west on U.S. 50 for 18.4 miles, passing the Monarch Pass Ski Resort at 16.7 miles, to Monarch Pass (11,312 feet).
*DeLorme: Colorado Atlas & Gazetteer.* Page 69, A-7

**Shuttle Point. From Buena Vista:** Drive south on U.S. 24 until it intersects with U.S. 285. Continue driving south on U.S. 285 for approximately 22 miles before entering into the town of Poncha Springs. In Poncha Springs, bear left and continue on U.S. 285 south for another 0.7 miles before turning left into the High Valley Center. *DeLorme: Colorado Atlas & Gazetteer.* Page 60, D-2

The Monarch Crest Trail descends an Odyssean 3,500 feet, from high atop Monarch Pass (11,312 feet) to the ride's lowest point at U.S. Route 285. The trail leads around Mount Peck and reaches its highest point at 12,145 feet. As you near Mount Peck, three distinct peaks come into view: Mount Ouray (13,971 feet), named after Chief Ouray; Chipeta Mountain (12,050 feet), named after Ouray's wife; and Pahlone Peak (12,667 feet), named after their son.

Born in 1833, Chief Ouray was the first U.S. appointed Chief of the Ute Nation. As such, Chief Ouray acted as liaison between the government of the United States

and the Ute Nation. Many hold Chief Ouray out to be a hero, but there are just as many who consider him as a sell-out. Chief Ouray's "political" career began with the Tabeguache Treaty of 1863, which first recognized Ouray as head of all the Utes. The treaty forced the Utes back from the Eastern Slope of the Rockies and the San Luis Valley, resulting in the loss of significant amounts of Ute land. Since not all of the Utes abided by the Tabeguache Treaty, Chief Ouray was asked to visit Washington again for another treaty.

After some tough bargaining at the Treaty of 1868 (or the Hunt Treaty), the first definitive boundaries were set for the Utes' territorial relocation. Essentially, the Utes were limited to 15,120,000 acres (approximately the western third of Colorado). This move called for them to abandon the San Luis Valley, the Yampa River Valley, and the Middle and North Parks. In exchange, the United States briefly halted white settlement in the Ute's ancestral lands of the San Juan Mountains or "The Shining Mountains." At the treaty's signing, Chief Ouray expressed his people's helplessness: "The agreement an Indian makes to a United States treaty is like the agreement a buffalo makes with his hunter when pierced with arrows. All he can do is lie down and give in."

Today, regardless of any negative opinions, Chief Ouray is considered one of Colorado's founding fathers. High in the rotunda of Colorado's Capital Building hang stained glass portraits of the 16 most highly regarded pioneers of the state. Of these, Chief Ouray is the only Native American. Moreover, Ouray was the only one to receive a unanimous vote.

As you ride atop this seemingly barren alpine tundra, take time to smell the wildflowers. Their squat, fibrous stems are well adapted to the harsh and unpredictable weather experienced above timberline. Tiny, hair-like fibers create an air space around the stems that help the plants retain the requisite moisture in this windy environment. Alpine primrose (primula angustifolia), Western yellow paintbrush

## **Miles**Directions

**0.0 START** at the top of Monarch Pass (11,312 feet). Begin riding up the single-lane FS 906 under the Monarch Scenic Tramway.

**0.3** At the sign reading "South Fosses Creek – 5 miles, Green Creek – 6 miles, Little Cochetopa Creek – 8 miles and Marshall Pass – 10 miles," bear right onto the single-track of the Continental Divide Trail, heading toward Marshall Pass.

**1.0** The Continental Divide Trail intersects with a 4WD road. Bear right onto this 4WD road and head under the power lines, following signs for the Continental Divide Trail, South Fosses Creek – 4, and Marshall Pass – 9.

**1.5** After two switchbacks, continue climbing on the 4WD road heading into the trees. Bear right onto the singletrack Continental Divide Trail.

**5.0** Arrive at the junction where the Continental Divide Trail and the Colorado Trail 1776 merge and continue to share the same route to Marshall Pass and the Rainbow Trail. Continue on the Continental Divide Trail, heading in a southeasterly direction.

**6.5** Arrive at the hunting cabin. Pass the sign for the Green Creek Trail and continue on the Continental Divide Trail.

**7.9** Pass a sign for the Little Cochetopa Creek Trail to your left and continue on the Continental Divide Trail.

**10.7** Arrive at the Marshall Pass trailhead. Toilet facilities are located here. Bear right onto the Old Denver & Rio Grande Railroad grade, now FS 200. *[**Option**. Bear left onto the Old Denver & Rio Grande Railroad Grade*

*(FS 200) and follow this graded road to Gray's Creek, just over a mile after crossing the Chaffee-Saguache county line sign. Continue down the embankment on the right to O'Haver Lake. Ride along the lake's southern rim and leave the campground on FS/CR 202. After one half mile, you'll ride through an intersection. Continue riding for another mile before arriving at another "T" with a stop sign. Bear left, heading in an easterly direction onto CR 200 to U.S. 285. This is a very easy cruise back to U.S. 285 and will shorten the entire length of the ride by eight miles.]*

**11.0** FS 200 forks. Bear left (now FS 203), following Colorado Trail signs. Continue on FS 203. After a short climb, pass two trails on your left, as you continue heading straight.

**11.1** FS 203 intersects with FS 486 by the gate. Bear left onto the singletrack trail marked by a sign reading "Silver Creek – 3 miles, Continental Divide Trail, Colorado Trail and Saguache – 28 miles." Begin climbing up this singletrack on your way to the Silver Creek and Rainbow trails.

**13.5** The singletrack intersects with an old logging road. Bear left onto this logging road, following signs for Silver Creek.

**13.9** The singletrack of the Silver Creek/Rainbow trails veers off to the right from this road. The words "Silver Creek" and "Rainbow Trail" are spray-painted yellow on a placard to the left of the trail. The logging road descends to the left. Bear right onto this singletrack, following signs for the Silver Creek and Rainbow trails.

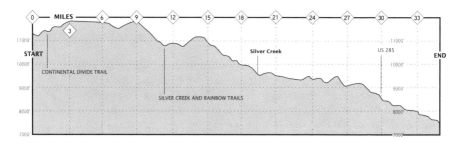

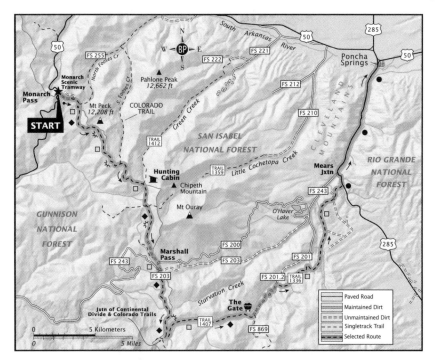

**14.7** Reach the trailhead for the Silver Creek Trail 1407. Bear left (east) onto the Silver Creek Trail 1407.

**19.0** Pass the Kismuth Mine to your right and cross Silver Creek. Ride past a Silver Creek Trail 1407 sign before connecting with 4WD road 201.2 (Silver Creek Road).

**19.2** Come to the intersection of Silver Creek Road and Toll Road Gulch (FS 869). Bear left, continuing on the Silver Creek Road, passing Toll Road Gulch (FS 869) on the right.

**19.3** Come to the intersection of the Silver Creek Road and the continuation of the singletrack Rainbow Trail 1336. Bear right onto the famed Rainbow Trail. *[**Option**. You can choose to continue descending on the Silver Creek Road (now CR 201) to U.S. 285. Although CR 201 to U.S. 285 is a faster and easier alternative, both options cover roughly nine miles each. For tired riders, choosing CR 201 to U.S. 285 is the best option. Its smooth and fast downhill run is accentuated by many dips across the road. Riders should,*

*however, be aware of the vehicular traffic on this road. After 4.5 miles from the intersection of the Silver Creek Road and the Rainbow Trail, you'll arrive at a spot known as Shirley, the junction of CR 200, CR 201, CR 203, and CR 243. At this junction, continue on CR 243 to U.S. 285.]*

**25.9** Cross a dirt road and pass a sign for "Highway 285 – 3 miles," continuing on the singletrack of the Rainbow Trail. This marks the beginning of a short, grunt of a climb, as the trail passes through a number of hillside meadows.

**28.6** The Rainbow Trail singletrack intersects with an old 4WD road. Passing a Rainbow Trail sign reading "Silver Creek 7.5" and "Highway 285 1.5" on your left, continue down the steep singletrack descent to U.S. 285.

**30.0** Arrive at U.S. 285. Bear left (north) onto U.S. 285 and return to your vehicle at the High Valley Center in Poncha Springs.

**35.1** Arrive at your vehicle.

(castilleja occidentalis), white marsh marigold (caltha leptosepala), snow buttercup (ranunculus adoneus), and rock primrose (androsace septentrionalis) are all endemic to the Rockies and may be found along the Monarch Crest Trail.

From this alpine tundra, descend 400 feet into a mixed conifer forest until reaching a hunting cabin. The cabin marks the beginning of the ride's last major climb. The climb, which may get bogged down in wet weather, eventually rejoins the crest, but not before testing your technical skills with some short, rocky sections. Cross Agate Creek and descend through the trees before arriving at a bone-jarring talus field at 8.5 miles. Ride over this field and descend to a 4WD road (CR 234.2G).

The 600-foot descent to Marshall Pass offers a number of dips over which to either bunny or bonk. Pass an old mine to your right and cross a cattle guard before connecting with the Old Denver & Rio Grande Railroad grade. Marshall Pass (10,846 feet), located on Mount Ouray's southern flank, is the lowest crossing of the Sawatch Range. In a race to rail link Colorado's East and West slopes via the mighty Sawatch Range, the Denver South Park & Pacific Railroad bored a third-of-a-mile tunnel through the range, while the Denver & Rio Grande Railroad opted for the Marshall Pass route. Although longer, the Marshall Pass route did not require a tunnel bore, and so, proved the better. On August 8, 1881, the Denver & Rio Grande Railroad made it into Gunnison via Marshall Pass, beating the Denver South Park & Pacific Railroad by nearly a year. For 70 years afterward, the Marshall Pass line was a featured addition to "The Scenic Line of the World," a collection of the world's most scenic railroad lines. The Marshall Pass route remained in use until 1954 when coal mines in Crested Butte ceased operations.

From Marshall Pass connect with the Silver Creek 1407 / Rainbow Trail. The descent is wicked. Beginning with steep and rocky switchbacks through a sloping meadow awash with wildflowers, the trail runs its scree-filled course through intermittent stands of pine and aspen on its way to the Kismuth Mine.

From the trail's intersection with the 4WD road (Silver Creek Road 201.2), riders connect with the Rainbow Trail. Resembling a rainbow in shape, the trail was blazed by settlers of the Upper Arkansas River and Wet Mountain Valley. As the need for timber grew, foot-beaten trails provided access into surrounding mountains. Similarly, miners and prospectors carved their own trails to mines like the Kismuth. Other trails owe their existence to foraging animals. In 1912 a program to connect these trails was implemented, resulting in the present-day 100-mile-long Rainbow Trail.

Celebrating a ride atop the Continental Divide.

# Ride Information

### ☎ Trail Contacts:
**Heart of the Rockies Chamber of Commerce**, Salida, CO; (719) 539-2068 • **Poncha Springs Chamber of Commerce**, Poncha Springs, CO; (719) 539-7055 • **San Isabel National Forest**, Salida Ranger District, Salida, CO; (719) 539-3591

### ⊟ Monarch Crest Shuttle Service:
**Mountain Bike Shuttle**, High Valley Center, Poncha Springs, CO; 1-800-871-5145 or (719) 539-6089 • **Headwaters**, Salida, CO; (719) 539-4506

### ⏱ Schedule:
July to September

### $ Fees/Permits:
Shuttle costs $11.50

### ❓ Local Information:
**FourteenerNet**, a website detailing 14er Country – *www.vtinet.com/14ernet*

### ♀ Local Events/Attractions:
**Salida Hot Springs Aquatic Center**, Salida, CO; (719) 539-6738 • **Monarch Crest Scenic Tram**, Salida, CO; (719) 539-4789 or (719) 539-4091

### 🛏 Accommodations:
**The Piñon and Sage**, CO; (719) 539-3227 or 1-800-840-3156 – *run by mountain bikers for mountain bikers*

### 🍴 Restaurants:
**Subway**, on U.S. Route 50, Monarch Pass, CO - *the world's highest Subway franchise* • **The Flour of Life Bakery, Coffeehouse, Pizzeria, and Pub**, Salida, CO; (719) 539-0999 – *Guinness on tap* • **Cornucopia Bakery & Cafe**, Salida, CO; (719) 539-2531 • **First Street Café**, Salida, CO; (719) 539-4759 • **Il Vicino Pizzeria & Brewery**, Salida, CO; (719) 539-5219

### 🏢 Organizations:
**Banana Belt Fat Tracks Club**, Salida, CO; (719) 539-6704

### 🚵 Mountain Bike Tours:
**Buffalo Joe River Trips**, Buena Vista, CO; 1-800-356-7984 or (719) 395-8757

### 🚲 Local Bike Shops:
**Otero Cyclery**, Salida, CO; (719) 539-6704 • **Headwaters**, Salida, CO; (719) 539-4506 • **Capricorn Sports**, Salida, CO; (719) 539-3971 • **The Trailhead**, Buena Vista, CO; (719) 395-8001 • **Coast to Coast**, Buena Vista, CO; (719) 395-8067

### Ⓝ Maps:
**USGS maps:** Bonanza, CO; Poncha Pass, CO; Pahlone Peak, CO; Mount Ouray, CO; Salida West, CO • **14ers Region Mountain Bike Guide** – *available free at area locations and chambers of commerce*

As the Rainbow Trail rolls in and out of hillside gullies, the scene is something out of Kauai's Na Pali Coast. In contrast to the stark landscape near Mount Peck, the Rainbow Trail winds its way through gardens ripe with evergreens, aspens, creeks, wildflowers, and ferns. The lush old-growth forests of the Rainbow Trail occasionally give way to hillside meadows, where surrounding rocky peaks offer dimension to the distances already traveled. The last three miles before intersecting with U.S. Route 285 offer a fast and rocky technical descent as Douglas fir and lodgepole pine eventually give way to oak and piñon-juniper woodlands. Once on U.S. Route 285, it's a smooth five-mile coast back to your vehicle in Poncha Springs.

# Wheeler Monument

## Ride Summary

Located in Mineral County (95 percent of which is national forest public access land), the Wheeler Geologic Area is truly one of Colorado's most unique and fascinating attractions. The result of numerous volcanic ash flow eruptions, this geological phenomenon has shaped itself into a city of spiny pinnacles and dark-seated caverns. Its towering spires and sheer cliff walls, rising directly from the middle of the forest like petrified trees, give the impression of a ghost's castle. But as with anything worthwhile, the way to the Wheeler Monument is not an easy one. The route begins at 10,840 feet and climbs to 12,000 feet and includes tough climbs, fast descents, deep ruts, and large rocks. Mountain bikers must leave their bicycles outside of the Wheeler Geologic Area, but a short half-mile hike delivers you to this bizarre geological wonder.

## Ride Specs

**Start:** From Hanson's Mill on FS 600
**Length:** 28.9-mile out-and-back
**Approximate Riding Time:** Advanced Riders, 3½–4 hours; Intermediate Riders, 4½–5 hours
**Technical Difficulty Rating:** Technically moderate due to the 4WD road—rocky and rutted in sections
**Physical Difficulty Rating:** Physically challenging, as you're riding just below timberline, between 10,840-12,000 feet
**Terrain:** 4WD road—most of which is quite manageable, though there are a number of steep rock and rooty sections
**Elevation Gain:** 5,058 feet
**Nearest Town:** Creede, CO
**Other Trail Users:** Hikers, campers, and backpackers
**Canine Compatibility:** Not dog friendly. FS 600 receives a good deal of vehicular traffic.

## Getting There

**From Creede:** Drive south on CO 149 for 7.6 miles. After crossing the Rio Grande River, turn left onto FS 600 (Pool Table Road/Spring Gulch), following signs for Hanson's Mill. Drive on FS 600 for roughly ten miles before reaching the site of the old Hanson's Mill at mile 17.5. Pass the big sawdust pile on your left and pull up to the bulletin board for the "Wheeler Area" and "Wheeler Trail 790." The route begins here. **DeLorme: Colorado Atlas & Gazetteer:** Map 78-79, B 3-4

San Juan's Badlands. That's how one leaflet describes the Wheeler Geological Area. Nestled in a remote region of the San Juan Mountains, occupying 60 acres of the Rio Grande National Forest, the Wheeler Geological Area is, if not badlands, certainly bad-ass. From the 40-million-year-old remains of violent volcanic eruptions rise fiendish spires and ghoulish mounds, which Dante himself could never have envisioned. As if the Great Creator forgot to put away His plans for the netherworld, the Wheeler Geological Area leaves us with a hint of what Hades must look like.

Forming the largest volcanic region in Colorado, the San Juan Mountains proved the perfect setting for this geological ghost town. Lava from erupting volcanoes coa-

San Juan's "Badlands."

lesced to form a rise 4,000 feet thick and 9,000 square miles wide. After lying dormant for one million years, these volcanoes erupted again, with ash flows accumulating to depths of 3,000 feet.

The volcanic debris thrown from these eruptions, consisting of dust particles and pebbles, settled on the ground in layers called volcanic tuff. Occasional rock fragments (breccia), sometimes as large as three feet in diameter, were also spat from erupting volcanoes and found perches on these relatively soft tuff beds. Since tuff particles have weak bonds, they became more susceptible to wind and rain erosion. Over time, the wind and rain cut away at the volcanic tuff, leaving behind spindly minarets topped precariously with breccia. The pinnacles regularly developed vertical cracks, which soon widened as erosion took its toll to form towering legions of stony specters, silently standing abreast.

In December of 1908 President Theodore Roosevelt proclaimed the site a National Monument in honor of George M. Wheeler, a member of the U.S. Army Corps of Topographical Engineers. Although Wheeler conducted extensive geological research in the area from 1873 to 1884, it's unclear whether he ever actually visited the site. Due to its remoteness and coupled with a lack of funds, the Wheeler National Monument lost its designation on August 3, 1950.

Cañon Fernandez and a dotted landscape.

## **Miles**Directions

**0.0 START** riding on FS 600 across from the "Wheeler Area" and "Wheeler Trail 790" bulletin board.

**0.4** A sign for the Wheeler Geologic Area is to your right, with views of the San Juans to the west.

**3.4** Arrive at a large meadow. Climb eastward through the meadow.

**4.5** Come to the junction of FS 600 and FS 600/3A. FS 600/3A goes right to Agua Ramon Tie. Bear left, continuing on FS 600 in a northwesterly direction.

**6.0** Cross Trujillo Creek.

**9.9** Pass through Canon Fernandez.

**11.2** Pass through Canon Nieve.

**12.5** A brown Wheeler arrow sign is to your left.

**13.3** Come to the junction of FS 600 and FS 790 (Wheeler Trail).

**14.4** Reach the Wheeler Geologic Area and Trailhead. No bicycles are allowed. When you've finished looking around, turn around and retrace your tracks back to the start.

**28.9** Arrive back at your vehicle.

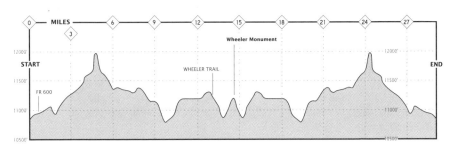

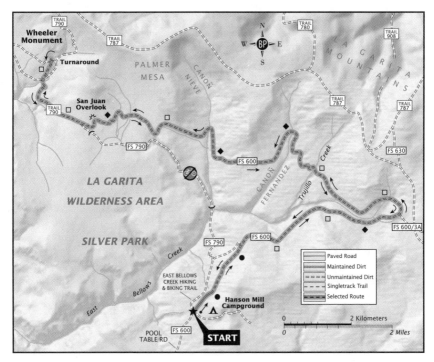

For a time the Wheeler Geologic Area remained in the custody of the Forest Service and the Rio Grande National Forest. Fortunately in 1993, with the passing of the Colorado Wilderness bill, the area was protected by its inclusion in the La Garita Wilderness Area. Today the Wheeler Geologic Area enjoys complete wilderness protection, preventing any and all logging, mineral exploration, road building, new water diversion structures, or mechanized travel—yes, mountain bikes included.

Twenty miles west of the Wheeler Geologic Area, on the north side of the San Luis Peaks, lies Mineral County's only town: the quirky, onetime mining camp of Creede. During its silver mining heyday, Creede was notorious for its wild goings-on. As one visitor once wrote: "I couldn't sleep with all the noise…hollering, yelling, horses galloping, wagons chuckling, hammering, pounding, sawing, shooting."

Three of Colorado's most notorious characters were Creede residents McGinty, Jefferson Randolph "Soapy" Smith, and Bob Ford. McGinty, whom the rest of Colorado knew as the "Solid Muldoon," was a seven-foot figure cast out of Portland cement and passed off as a petrified man. By 1842, this Missing Link became one of Creede's most profitable attractions. Jefferson Randolph "Soapy" Smith, a con man of the highest order, duped the Creede townspeople but chose to put his earnings into building churches and helping the poor. His altruism also extended to the canine population, as he would frequently befriend lost dogs.

Bob Ford, perhaps Creede's most infamous citizen, was the proprietor of the Ford Exchange saloon. Ford rocketed into infamy when on April 3, 1882 he sneaked in and shot the famous outlaw Jesse James in the back. Ten years later, a wandering cowboy named Ed O'Kelley moseyed into Creede and returned the favor, killing Ford in

229

his saloon. Although little is known of O'Kelley's background or his motive, his comment to the arresting officer after he had turned himself in for murder was: "I don't rob and I don't insult women, but I kill rats like Bob Ford." During O'Kelley's trial, the court received thousands of letters asking for a pardon of James' avenger. These letters were all postmarked from James' home state of Missouri, where James had retired just prior to his death, vowing to lead an honest life.

The road to discovery is beset by toil and pain, and so too is the road to the Wheeler Geological Area. The ride begins on Forest Service Road 600—not on the singletrack of the Forest Service Road 790 (Wheeler Trail), which begins immediately from the bulletin board. (Forest Service Road 790 descends for 2.5 miles to East Bellows Creek, across from which lies the La Garita Wilderness Area. After the East Bellows Creek, the trail is open to horses and hikers only, as it makes its way to the Wheeler Monument. No bikes!) Riders need to ride Forest Service Road 600 to reach the Wheeler Monument. The route's first half runs its rutted and rocky course for 14.4 miles at elevations exceeding 11,000 feet. Passing through montane and subalpine bio-geographic zones, the route offers long stretches of intermittent climbs and descents through high alpine meadows and evergreen forests.

At these higher bio-geographic zones, the terrain is very fragile and damaged if trodden upon needlessly. Though fragile and, at times, inhospitable, the terrain at these higher elevations does offer an abundance of life. The hardy, yet beautiful northern fairy candelabra (androsace septentrionalis), whose bunches of flowers resemble tiny star bursts; the spring beauty (claytonia lanceolata), whose hurried attempts to flower will usually give rise to its location along the receding snowline; and the subalpine buttercup (ranunculus eschscholtzii), whose cups are the largest of any North American species—all reside at these higher elevations. After you climb through the first meadow and cross East Bellows Creek at mile 4.3, you arrive at the intersection of Forest Service Road 600 and Forest Service Road 6003A.

Descend through another high alpine meadow to Trujillo Creek and climb moderately for one mile. Here, surrounding mountain walls pulsate with the echoes of howling coyotes. By mile 7.2, a two-mile descent delivers you through another high alpine meadow and Canon Fernandez. The only good thing about climbing out from Canon Fernandez is the thought of savagely ripping down its rock-torn road on your return.

Downtown Creede welcomes you.

# Ride Information

### 🏔 Trail Contacts:
**South Fork Visitors Center**, South Fork, CO; (719) 873-5512 or 1-800-571-0881

### 🕐 Schedule:
FS 600 to the Wheeler Monument usually opens the last week in May (or the first week in June) and closes the first week in October, all depending on the snow pack.

### ❓ Local Information:
**South Fork Interpretive Center**, South Fork, CO; (719) 873-5836 or 1-800-571-0881 • **Creede-Mineral County Chamber of Commerce**, Creede, CO; (719) 658-2374 or 1-800-327-2102 or *www.creede.com* • **U.S. Forest Service**, Creede Ranger District, Creede, CO; (719) 658-2556

### 🔍 Local Events/Attractions:
**Silver Thread Colorado Scenic and Historic Byway.** *Beginning in South Fork on CO 149, the byway weaves 75 miles through the historic communities of South Fork, Creede, and Lake City; and through the Gunnison and Rio Grande National Forests.* • **Creede Underground Mining Museum**, Creede, CO; (719) 658-0811 • **Creede Repertory Theater**, Creede, CO; (719) 658-2540

### 🚴 Mountain Bike Tours:
**Mountain Man Tours Highway**, Creede, CO; (719) 658-2663

### 🏢 Organizations:
**Creede Mountain Bike Club**, Creede, CO; (719) 658-2351

### 📖 Other Resources:
*Creede: A Quick History by Leland Feitz* – *retells much of Creede's quirky history, from its founding as a town to its present-day distinction as a tourist town*

### 🔧 Local Bike Shops:
**San Juan Sports**, Creede, CO; (719) 658-2359

### 🗺 Maps:
**USGS maps:** Wagon Wheel Gap, CO; Pool Table Mountain, CO; and Half Moon, CO • *Trails Illustrated* map: #142, South San Juan/Del Norte, CO • **Chamber of Commerce Wheeler Geological Area map** – *available at Creede-Mineral County Chamber of Commerce (719) 658-2374 or 1-800-327-2102*

---

After passing the brown Wheeler arrow sign at mile 12.5, ride for another half-mile to a beautiful overlook with views to the west of the San Juan Mountains. A cursory glimpse reveals the seemingly out-of-place formations of the Wheeler Geologic Area. From here descend to the southern boundary of the Wheeler Geologic Area, where you'll have to park your bicycle and hike a half a mile to the Wheeler site.

The return trip has you climbing almost immediately. By mile 17.7, however, all that changes. A fast and rocky descent just below timberline delivers you to Canon Fernandez at mile 18.9. From Canon Fernandez, climb steadily. A few short descents keep you from going mental. Cross Trujillo Creek and head for the intersection of Forest Service Road 600 and Forest Service Road 600/3A at mile 24.4. Once atop the last meadow, enjoy the fast descent to your vehicle.

# Trout Creek Trail

## Ride Summary

The Trout Creek Trail is a great date ride. A short 4.5 miles up and over two hills delivers you to an idyllic picnic setting in the meadows surrounding Trout Creek. Comprised entirely of smooth singletrack, the trail is lined on either side by wild raspberry bushes, and the meadows of Trout Creek offer droves of wild mint. The enormous rock outcroppings near Trout Creek have great bouldering potential. Although not particularly technical, there are brief sections of rocky, off-camber trail, and moderate switchbacks that add an element of surprise to this predominately user-friendly trail. Trout Creek Trail is great for those interested in a short and sweet ride.

## Ride Specs

**Start:** From the Trout Creek #831 Trailhead
**Length:** 9-mile out-and-back
**Approximate Riding Time:** Advanced Riders, 1–1½ hours; Intermediate Riders, 2–2½ hours
**Technical Difficulty Rating:** Technically moderate due to the smooth-running singletrack that passes over only a few rocky sections
**Physical Difficulty Rating:** Physically moderate due to shorter hill climbs at relatively low elevations
**Terrain:** Singletrack and doubletrack—mostly smooth-running over two hills and through thick pine/aspen forests. There are a few tough rocky sections.
**Elevation Gain:** 2,029 feet
**Nearest Town:** South Fork, CO
**Other Trail Uses:** Hikers, picnickers, and equestrians
**Canine Compatibility:** Dog friendly

## Getting There

**From Monte Vista:** Drive west on U.S. 160 to South Fork. Once in South Fork, continue driving on U.S. 160 to its intersection with CO 149. From this intersection (location of the South Fork Visitor Center), continue southwest on U.S. 160 for three more miles. After three miles, a gravel parking lot will be on the right side of the road. Pull into this parking lot. There you'll notice a sign for the Trout Creek Trail 831. *DeLorme: Colorado Atlas & Gazetteer*: Pages 78-79, C-D 3&4

Put on your finest silver because we're going for a ride on Colorado's Silver Thread Scenic & Historic Byway. And the first stop is South Fork, Colorado. Just five miles from the Trout Creek trailhead lies the small timbering town of South Fork. Located at the junction of the Rio Grande River and its south fork, where U.S. Route 160 abuts Colorado 149, South Fork is the gateway to one of Colorado's most scenic and historic roads.

The Silver Thread Scenic & Historic Byway extends over 75 miles, following the winding Rio Grande River to its headwaters in the San Juan Mountains of Southwestern Colorado. It crosses the Gunnison and Rio Grande National Forests on its way through the quaint historic towns of South Fork, Creede, and Lake City. The present-day route follows the old toll roads Del Norte & Antelope Park and Antelope Park & Lake City, roads instrumental in developing the forbidding San Juan Mountains in the 1870s.

Picnic Meadow along Trout Creek.

Interested in securing the "gateway city" title over the rich mining discoveries being made near Bakers Park in the upper Animas Valley, the town of Del Norte, neighbor to South Fork, started building the Del Norte & San Juan Toll Road in 1873. The road stretched 55 miles from Del Norte up the Rio Grande River to Antelope Park. From Antelope Park, it continued up Crooked Creek, over Stoney Pass, and through Cunnigham Gulch into Bakers Park. To further increase its stronghold on mining discoveries, Del Norte constructed a second road called the Antelope Park & Lake City Toll Road.

The Antelope Park & Lake City Toll Road split from the Del Norte & San Juan route at Antelope Springs (then a stage stop). From the Springs, this new road skirted past Mirror Lake and over the Continental Divide, eventually dropping into the Lake Mining District, where in 1874 the town of Lake City was established. These early roads to the rich San Juan mines were hardly paved with gold—in fact, they weren't paved at all. One early traveler remarked: "With a pitch and a jolt and a jerk, and a jerk and a jolt and a pitch, down, down you go till you think you have reached the bottom of all things. Down, down till the bottom of all things seems an elevated peak, and down, down till you lose all sense of every thing, but the awful downwardness of life—and here you are at Lake City, the very heart of the San Juan mines."

The rich mining exploits of Creede and Lake City caught the attention of the Denver & Rio Grande Railroad. Up until the arrival of the railroad in 1882, South Fork existed simply as a stage stop along the Del Norte & San Juan Toll Road. With the arrival of the railroad, cheap and reliable transportation was brought into the Animas Valley. South Fork could now exploit its vast stores of timber.

Sawmills started popping up like bubbles in boiling water. Timber from surrounding mountains (which today make up nearly two million acres of national forest) were brought down and processed through these mills. The refined timber was then shipped to the more populated areas of Denver and Durango. In addition, the wood processed by these sawmills provided the building materials for mines and miners' homes and supplied ties to the railroad boom of the late 1880s through the early 1900s.

## **Miles**Directions

**0.0 START** from the Trout Creek Trail 831 trailhead. Pass through the wooden gate and ride due west.

**1.2** Reach the top of the first climb, which offers a nice campsite and a fire ring off to the left. Cross over the white, nylon cord gate and begin your first descent.

**2.3** Cross a tributary of Trout Creek after your first descent.

**2.7** Pass through the barbwire gate, closing it behind you.

**3.2** The second hill climb tops out.

**4.0** Arrive at FS 831 (more like a rough doubletrack) and bear right onto FS 831.

**4.5** Reach the private property fence. Turn around.

**5.0** The singletrack Trout Creek Trail 831 begins to your left.

**5.8** Reach the top of the first hill on the return trip and descend.

**6.3** Pass through the gate and descend to a creek tributary.

**6.7** Cross the creek tributary and begin the second climb of the return trip.

**7.8** Reach the top of the second climb. Cross over the nylon rope gate and descend.

**9.0** Arrive at your vehicle.

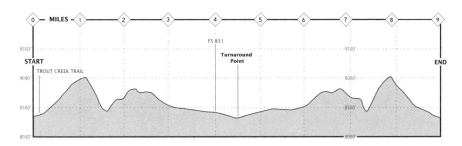

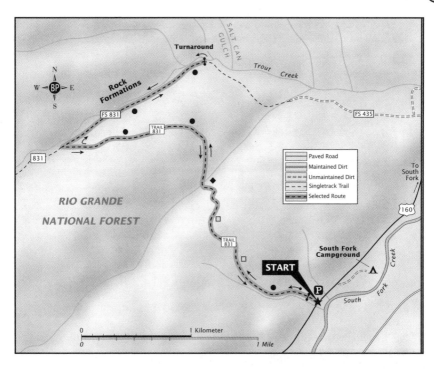

Trout Creek trailhead.

# Ride Information

## Trail Contacts:
**San Luis Valley Cycling Club**, Kristi Mountain Sports, Villa Mall, Alamosa, CO; (719) 589-9759 • **Rio Grande Country Information**, Monte Vista, CO; (719) 852-0660 or 1-800-884-7609

## Schedule:
Late Spring to early Autumn

## Local Information:
**South Fork Visitor Center**, South Fork, CO; (719) 873-5512 or 1-800-571-0881 **Rio Grande Country Information**, Monte Vista, CO; (719) 852-0660 or 1-800-884-7609 • **Rio Grande National Forest Supervisor's Office**, Monte Vista, CO; (719) 852-5941

## Local Events/Attractions:
**Logger Days**, 3rd weekend in July, South Fork, CO – *for information contact the South Fork Visitor Center at (719) 873-5512 or 1-800-571-0881* • **Silver Thread Colorado Scenic and Historic Byway.** *Beginning in South Fork on CO 149, the byway weaves 75 miles through the historic communities of South Fork, Creede, and Lake City; and through the Gunnison and Rio Grande National Forests.*

## Organizations:
**San Luis Valley Cycling Club**, Kristi Mountain Sports, Villa Mall, Alamosa, CO; (719) 589-9759

## Local Bike Shops:
**Kristi Mountain Sports**, Villa Mall, Alamosa, CO; (719) 589-9759

## Maps:
**USGS maps:** South Fork West, CO • **Colorado's San Luis Valley Mountain Bike Guide** – *available at Kristi Mountain Sports* • **National Forest's Best Trails of Colorado's San Luis Valley** – *available at the Rio Grande National Forest Supervisor's Office (719) 852-5941* • **Rio Grande National Forest Map** – *available at Rio Grande National Forest Supervisor's Office (719) 852-5941*

The brothers Orville and Charlie Galbreath owned and operated the O.S. Galbreath Tie & Timber Company, the area's most productive timber company. Providing South Fork with a hotel, post office, and company store, the O.S. Galbreath Tie & Timber Company provided the life-blood for the "company town" of South Fork. Its influences stretched so far as to control the lumber interests of South Fork, Del Norte, Pagosa Springs, and Juanita. Workers for the company were paid with script, forbear to our modern-day coupons. Scripts were written documents, essentially, IOUs, which entitled workers to receive goods for their exchange. The script, however, was only redeemable at the company store. How's that for owning your soul?

Today South Fork, still a vibrant timber town, remains a hub for tourism, offering up for show its colorful past. One of the town's most notable tourist attractions is a 24-foot tall lumberjack called "Biggin." Carved out of a 450-year-old Douglas fir by

Ron McDowel in the summer of 1987, Biggin stands at the junction of U.S. Route 160 and Colorado 149. Positioned at the extreme southern end of the Silver Thread Scenic & Historic Byway, Biggin marks the beginning of a 75-mile journey past such attractions as the spiraling rock towers of the Palisades on the east side of the Rio Grande River, the stagecoach travelers' inscriptions on Post Office Rock, the important stage stop of Antelope Springs, and the incredible views of the mountain peaks surrounding Lake City at Windy Point Scenic Overlook. Toll roads and byways aside, the real area attraction for mountain bikers is the Trout Creek Trail.

Located at the base of Wolf Creek Pass, the Trout Creek Trail offers a fun out-and-back ride comprised of eight parts. The first mile switchbacks up a hillside and delivers views of the next hill to climb. From there you descend for roughly one mile through intermittent stands of lodgepole pine and aspen, catching as much air off of the dips strewn about the trail. The switchbacks at mile 2.5 include loose sand and rocks, offering a little challenge to this otherwise smooth ride.

By mile 3.2, the trail starts to bear south, as it begins its second descent to Trout Creek. Before reaching Trout Creek, however, the trail forks, with a left spur climbing up the west-facing slope. Pass this spur to the left and continue descending in a southerly direction. Once on Forest Service Road 831, the trail continues in a northeasterly direction along the banks of Trout Creek. Upon reaching the fence, turn around and begin your return to your vehicle.

## Stephen's Trail Bars

*Nothing quite satisfies a hunger on the trail like a wholesomely delicious snack. My trail bars have wowed crowds from backcountry hut trips to backyard Bar-B-Qs. They will wow you too.*

½ cup whole wheat flour
½ cup white flour
¼ cup wheat germ
½ cup dry milk powder
3½ cups of uncooked oatmeal
½ cup honey
1 cup margarine
1 egg
½ cup nuts
1 cup raisins or dates
2 cups strawberry jam

*Mix both kinds of flour, wheat germ, dry milk powder, and oatmeal in a large bowl. In a smaller bowl, melt margarine. Add honey and beat in the egg. Combine the two mixtures thoroughly. Stir in nuts and raisins (or dates). Pour into a greased 13"x9" pan. Press slightly as you spread it around. Form a smooth layer—this will keep it from becoming too crumbly. Bake at 300° for 40 to 50 minutes. After cooling, cut the 13"x9" mixture in half. Spread the strawberry jam on one half and place the other half on top. Cut into squares. Eat!*

# Zapata Falls

## Ride Summary

The Zapata Falls Trail offers a short but scenic tour of the San Luis Valley, the Great Sand Dunes, and the Sangre de Cristo Mountains. An easy, stacked-loop ride, the Zapata Falls Trail is a great family ride, offering four to 10 miles of well-maintained singletrack—an excellent trail for the beginner mountain biker. Although the Zapata area is comprised of four distinct numbered loops, the loop described here actually includes sections of each loop—introducing the rider to all four. It's best to consult interpretive area map signs when deciding which loops to add or subtract from this description. A short quarter-mile hike beginning at 9,000 feet delivers you to Zapata Falls. The falls are 50 feet high and enter into an open aired cavern. To reach the falls, you must hike through the Zapata Creek bed upstream—be prepared to get your feet wet. But once there, the falls and cavern offer chilling relief from even the most sweltering of summer days.

## Ride Specs

**Start:** From the trailhead for Loop 1 at Zapata Falls

**Length:** 2.5-mile loop – with at least four miles of trail that you can ride without duplication

**Approximate Riding Time:** Advanced Riders, 20 minutes; Intermediate Riders, 30 minutes

**Technical Difficulty Rating:** Technically easy due to its mellow singletrack terrain

**Physical Difficulty Rating:** Physically easy due to its lack of elevation gain

**Terrain:** Singletrack—mostly hard-packed earth that weaves through piñon pine and juniper forests and scrub oak trees; a few rocky sections

**Elevation Gain:** 640 feet

**Nearest Town:** Alamosa, CO

**Other Trail Users:** Hikers, picnickers, and gold panners

**Canine Compatibility:** Dog friendly

## Getting There

**From Alamosa:** Drive east on U.S. 160 for 15 miles. Turn left onto CO 150 (Great Sand Dunes Road) and drive for another 11 miles. After driving roughly 26 miles, look for the brown, wooden Zapata Falls Recreation Area sign to your right. Bear right onto the gravel road by the sign and drive up it for roughly 3.5 miles. Pass the first pullout parking area at 28.4 miles and continue up the road for another mile. Park your vehicle at the second pullout parking area to your left at 29.4 miles. This is the trailhead for Loop 1. *DeLorme: Colorado Atlas & Gazetteer.* Page 81, D-6

I f contradiction and contrast are the realities of life, then the San Luis Valley—home to the Great Sand Dunes National Monument, the Sangre de Cristo Mountain Range, and Zapata Falls—is truly alive.

Just five miles north of the Zapata Falls trailhead is the entrance to the Great Sand Dunes National Monument. President Herbert Hoover designated the Great Sand Dunes a National Monument in 1932. The snowcapped Sangre de Cristos provide a unique backdrop to the teeming sands below. Lieutenant Zebulon Pike (of Pike's Peak fame) came upon the Great Sand Dunes while leading an expedition to the southwestern borders of the Louisiana Purchase. His journal

One of many views of the Great Sand Dunes with the peaks of the Sangre de Cristos in the background.

entry of January 28, 1807 describes the encounter: "We discovered sandy hills...Their appearance was exactly that of a sea in a storm except as to color..."

The San Luis Valley's prevailing southwest winds wash these desert sands to heights rising above 14,000 feet. During spring and fall, winds that blowing in excess of 40 mph funnel sand from the valley's floor through three low-lying Sangre de Cristo passes—Mosca, Music, and Medano. As these winds sweep up over the mountains, they deposit sand along the western foothills of the Sangre de Cristo Range.

The sand is comprised of mostly rounded grains of quartz and metamorphic rocks from the San Juan Mountains, giving the dunes a darker color than one might expect. Since darker surfaces absorb solar radiation more readily than lighter surfaces, these dunes can reach temperatures in excess of 140 degrees. In the early 1970s, Jim Ryan, the famous Kansas miler, ran to the top of the high dune and back in 30 minutes— no doubt encouraged by the burning sands.

Blanca Peak enshrouded in clouds.

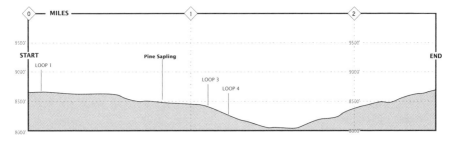

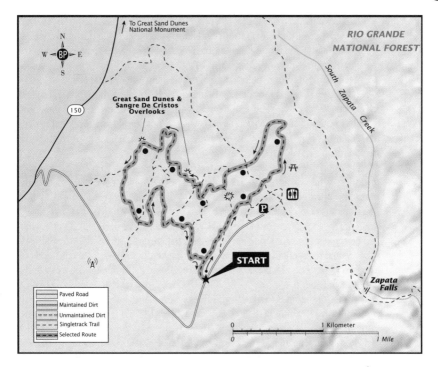

## **Miles**Directions

**0.0 START** at the trailhead for Loop 1. Go through the wooden fence and immediately bear right at the fork marked by an island of rocks. This is the beginning of Loop 1.

**0.2** Arrive at a second fork. Bear left here.

**0.5** The trail starts descending moderately, heading in a southwesterly direction.

**0.8** Connect with the north rim of Loop 2. At this point, veer right. A pine sapling in the middle of a rock island marks the intersection.

**1.1** Connect with Loop 3 as it travels north. Bear right, directly behind the Zapata Falls area trail map sign.

**1.2** Arrive at the junction of Loop 3 and Loop 4. Bear right onto Loop 4, heading west.

**1.4** Loop 4 forks. Bear left, heading for the connection with Loop 3.

**1.8** Connect with Loop 3 and cut sharply to the left.

**2.0** Reach the intersection of Loop 3 and Loop 2. At this junction, veer right, heading south on Loop 2.

**2.2** Loop 2 forks. Bear right.

**2.3** Loop 2 intersects with Loop 1. Bear right, heading south on Loop 1.

**2.5** At intersection, veer right and ride south back to your vehicle.

These winds, functioning in a cycle that has been repeating itself for over 12,000 years, have deposited sand accumulating to depths of 750 feet and covering 39 square miles. Sheltering this continent's tallest sand dunes from erosion is the patriarch of the Sangre de Cristos, the 14,345-foot massif Blanca Peak. The fourth highest mountain in Colorado, Blanca Peak towers over Zapata Falls as well. The series of lesser summits surrounding Blanca Peak help create the geological hierarchy that has since become synonymous with the Sangre de Cristo Mountains. "Such a beautiful subordination of parts we had not seen before anywhere among the mountains of Colorado," wrote Franklin Rhoda in 1875 when mapping the region for the Hayden Survey.

The Sangre de Cristo's history stands apart from most other Centennial-mountain histories. While other ranges have their stories of harrowing exploits during the Anglo mining rushes of the 1800s, the story of the Sangre de Cristo Range had to be translated from its original language: Spanish.

After the founding of Santa Fe in 1609, Spanish missionaries traveled north, naming prominent geographic features. The name Sangre de Cristo (or "Blood of Christ") is attributed to an unknown missionary who apparently witnessed the reflection of a crimson sunset upon its peaks. Moved by this divine sight, the missionary gave the range its religious name.

As the southernmost range in the Rocky Mountain chain, running for roughly 200 miles from south of Salida well into New Mexico, the Sangre de Cristo Mountains became sought after as a sanctuary for many Mexicans. When Mexico declared its independence from Spain in 1820, the new government issued large parcels of land along its northern frontier. The Sangre de Cristo Grant included

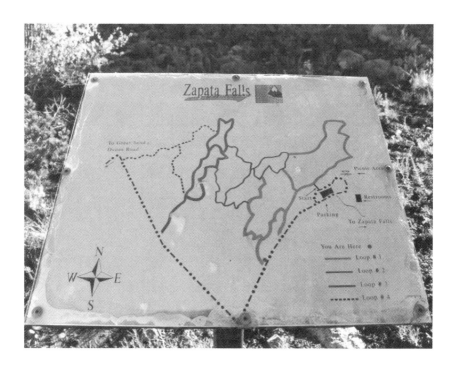

## Ride Information

### 🌣 Trail Contacts:

**Kristi Mountain Sports**, Villa Mall, Alamosa, CO; (719) 589-9759 • **Conejos Ranger District**, La Jara, CO; (719) 274-8971

### 🕗 Schedule:

May to October

### ❓ Local Information:

**Conejos Ranger District**, La Jara, CO; (719) 274-8971 • **Bureau of Land Management**, Alamosa, CO; (719) 598-4975 • **Alamosa Visitor Information Center**, Cole Park, Alamosa, CO; (719) 589-4840 or www.alamosa.org • **Alamosa County Chamber of Commerce**, Cole Park, Alamosa, CO; 1-800-589-3681 • **U.S. Forest Service, Monte Vista**, CO; (719) 852-5941

### 🌣 Local Events/Attractions:

**Great Sand Dunes National Monument**, Mosca, CO; (719) 378-2312 or www.nps.gov/grsa/ • **Alamosa/Monte Vista National Wildlife Refuge Complex**, Alamosa, CO; (719) 589-4021

### 🚹 Organizations:

**San Luis Valley Cycling Club**, Kristi Mountain Sports, Villa Mall, Alamosa, CO; (719) 589-9759

### 🚲 Local Bike Shops:

**Kristi Mountain Sports**, Villa Mall, Alamosa, CO; (719) 589-9759

### 🅝 Maps:

**USGS maps:** Zapata Ranch, CO; Twin Peaks, CO • **Colorado's San Luis Valley Mountain Bike Guide** – available at Kristi Mountain Sports

much of the southeastern San Luis Valley. With Mexicans moving into the valley in hopes of creating new lives for themselves, the new Mexican government stood a better chance at maintaining their presence in the recently annexed area.

Settlement began in the valley in 1849. By 1851 the community of San Luis (Colorado's oldest) was founded. Today, thanks to the Colorado Wilderness Bill of 1993, 226,455 acres of the Sangre de Cristos—the length of the range from south of Salida to the Great Sand Dunes National Monument—is a protected Wilderness Area.

Respectfully skirting the protected domain of the Great Sand Dunes National Monument, Blanca Peak, and the Sangre de Cristo Range is the Zapata Falls Trail. Named after the spectacular 50-foot waterfall located on the west slope of the Sangre de Cristo Range, the Zapata Falls Trail offers scenic views of the San Luis Valley, the Great Sand Dunes, and the Blanca Wetlands.

Beginning as a nicely manicured and hard-packed singletrack trail, the Zapata Falls Trail loops its way through piñon pine and juniper forests and over a few short rocky sections. This stacked-loop trail system exhibits the docile side of mountain biking. Four clearly marked loops lead you through the entire Zapata Falls area. Four miles of trail can be ridden without duplication.

The 2.5-mile route described here includes portions of each loop. Longer or shorter loops can be made if desired. Since the area is somewhat limited in terms of rideable miles, it's best to combine hiking, picnicking, and riding into your day.

# Cat Creek Trail

## Ride Summary

Since a vast majority of the route passes through dense stands of aspen, the Cat Creek Trail makes for a great autumn ride. With a total elevation gain of 1,400 feet, this ride is moderately difficult. If done at a conservative pace, nearly anyone in good physical condition can enjoy this ride. Forest Service Road 271 can get quite muddy after a rainstorm, making its steeper sections a grueling challenge, if not a chore. Nevertheless, the easterly views of the San Luis Valley more than make up for a little mud in the face. The singletrack is smooth and fast and virtually unused, but it does see a fair share of deadfall, so be aware when ripping around blind turns. Views of Blowout Pass display a wind-eroded cup-shaped hollow in the side of a mountain.

## Ride Specs

**Start:** From the junction of FS 271 and Cat Creek Trail # 704

**Length:** 14.4-mile loop

**Approximate Riding Time:** Advanced Riders, 1½ hours; Intermediate Riders, 2–2½ hours

**Technical Difficulty Rating:** Technically moderate with a few minor rocky and root sections

**Physical Difficulty Rating:** Physically moderate to challenging, due to the climbing on the rutted FS 271

**Terrain:** Forest road and singletrack through high alpine meadows and aspen forests. Though predominately smooth, parts of the route include steeper climbs and descents over rocks and roots.

**Elevation Gain:** 1,886 feet

**Nearest Town:** Monte Vista, CO

**Other Trail Users:** Hikers, equestrians, and anglers

**Canine Compatibility:** Dog friendly

## Getting There

**From Monte Vista:** Drive south on CO 15 for roughly 12.7 miles. Bear right onto FS 250, by the bulletin board. Heading west, cross a cattle guard at mile 19.4, and enter into the Rio Grande National Forest. To your right will be a brown sign for Cat Creek, Cat Creek Park, and Deer Creek. At mile 19.9, turn right onto FS 271 and drive approximately 4.5 miles to the intersection of FS 271 and the Cat Creek Horse Trail. The Cat Creek Horse Trail is off to your left. Park your vehicle here. You have traveled 24.3 miles from Monte Vista. *DeLorme: Colorado Atlas & Gazetteer.* Map 89, A-7

Cat Creek Trail lies south of Monte Vista in the 1,852-acre Rio Grande National Forest. Located on the eastern slope of the Continental Divide in Southern Colorado, the Rio Grande National Forest is composed of four major interrelated land forms: the San Juan Mountains, the Sangre de Cristo Mountains, the San Luis Valley, and the Rio Grande del Norte. The elevation within the forest ranges from 7,500 feet to over 14,000 feet, and the average yearly precipitation can vary from under eight inches to over 50 inches. As the natural depository of all this potential precipitation, the San Luis Valley is a fertile basin for agriculture.

Located in the heart of the San Luis Valley, Monte Vista enjoys all the spoils that the world's largest alpine valley can offer. An area the size of Connecticut, the San

The beginning of the Cat Creek singletrack through the Aspens.

Luis Valley is bordered on the east by the Sangre de Cristo Mountains and along the west by the San Juan Range. At the valley's southern tip lies the town of Monte Vista. Since the valley's southern section lies above its northern section, precipitation in the south drains to the north. Were it not for the desert-like climate of the northern stretches of the San Luis Valley, the naturally-closed basin of the north would have certainly become a lake by now—and indeed, it almost did.

In 1880 ambitious valley farmers constructed large canals in an effort to divert water from Rio Grande tributaries into the northern half of the valley. Ultimately, these canals would prove to be ill-conceived. When the water table rose to the surface of the ground, fields flooded. Farmers were forced to move south to Monte Vista to cultivate their crops.

Passing a lonely barn on the way to the trail.

Hardship would again strike the farmers, this time in the form of a long drought beginning in the early 1930s. Runoff continued to fall below normal levels until as late as 1955. Desperate, farmers turned to subsurface water, drilling wells into the valley floor. The trough-shaped San Luis Valley floor, in concert with porous gravel and impenetrable layers of clay, ash, and lava, provided farmers with artesian wells. Today, more than 7,000 artesian wells exist throughout the valley.

Monte Vista enjoys a fertile agricultural economy, relying on these wells to irrigate its fields. Potatoes, head lettuce, peas, and cauliflower are all cultivated in and around Monte Vista. And according to W.H. Odin, a state agricultural official, Monte Vista's future looks secure. "We have the soil, the altitude, the climate, and the irrigation that insures quality in our mountain truck crops and vegetables."

## **Miles**Directions

**0.0 START** at the junction of FS 271 and the Trail 704 (Cat Creek Trail). Notice the squat stone wall behind the trail sign and begin riding up FS 271.

**3.2** Intersect with FS 236 and Cat Creek Park to your right. Continue heading west on FS 271.

**6.6** FS 271 connects with the singletrack of Trail 703 (Alamosa/Rock Creek Trail). Follow Trail 703 into aspen timber.

**8.2** Reach the Blowout Pass overlook.

**9.4** Come to the junction of "Alamosa River, 2 mi.; South Rock Creek, 3 mi.; Blow Out Pass, 5mi.; and South Cat Creek, 5mi.." From Trail 703, bear left onto Trail 704, heading east. Caution: Do not miss this turnoff, as Trail 704 will deliver you right to your vehicle.

**14.4** Arrive at to your vehicle.

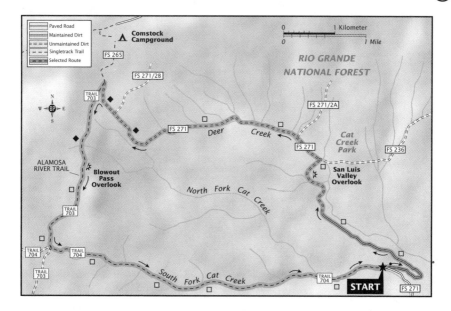

With its green fields surrounded by snow-covered mountains, Monte Vista sits like an emerald in snow, a rare Colorado gem inspiring many to appreciate its people, its places, and its potatoes. The Cat Creek Trail facilitates this appreciation. From its intersection with Forest Service Road 271, begin the route with a moderate climb up the road, passing large open meadows that lie to the northwest.

Besides intersecting with Forest Service Road 236 at 3.2 miles, Forest Service Road 271 crosses only two other roads: one at 3.7 miles, where Forest Service Road 271/2A veers off to the right; and the second at 5.1 miles, where Forest Service Road 271/2B veers off to the left. At either location, continue straight ahead in a north-westerly direction.

After five miles, the road steepens, climbing through pine forests and meadows. Once you reach the road's highest point at mile 6.6, you'll need to look for the connecting singletrack of the Alamosa/Rock Creek Trail 703. It lies out of plain view and is hidden among a stand of thick aspens. After 6.6 miles, Forest Service Road 271 levels off through a small meadow, continuing through it before descending to the town of Comstock. If you start descending after reaching this meadow, you've gone too far. Before reaching the end of the meadow, start looking for the Alamosa/Rock Creek Trail 703 after the road levels. It will be marked by a "No Vehicles - More Than 40

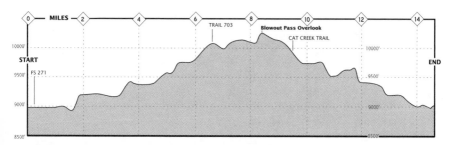

247

View from Blowout Pass.

## Ride Information

### 🕐 Trail Contacts:
**Kristi Mountain Sports**, Villa Mall, Alamosa, CO; (719) 589-9759

### 🕐 Schedule:
June to October

### ❓ Local Information:
**Rio Grande National Forest Supervisor's Office**, Monte Vista, CO; (719) 852-5941 • **Monte Vista Chamber of Commerce**, Monte Vista, CO; (719) 852-2731 • **San Luis Valley Information Center**, Monte Vista, CO; (719) 852-0660 or 1-800-835-7254 • **Rio Grande Country Information**, Monte Vista, CO; (719) 852-0660 or 1-800-884-7609

### 💡 Local Events/Attractions:
**Monte Vista National Wildlife Refuge**, on CO 15, six miles south of Monte Vista, CO – for information, contact the U.S. Fish and Wildlife Service, Alamosa, CO; (719) 589-4021 • **Monte Vista Crane Festival**, during February and March, Monte Vista, CO; (719) 852-3552 – more

than 20,000 sandhill cranes migrate through the Monte Vista National Wildlife Refuge • **Sky High Stampede**, in July, Monte Vista, CO; (719) 852-2731 – Colorado's oldest pro rodeo

### 👥 Organizations:
**San Luis Valley Cycling Club**, Kristi Mountain Sports, Villa Mall, Alamosa, CO; (719) 589-9759

### 🚲 Local Bike Shops:
**Kristi Mountain Sports**, Villa Mall, Alamosa, CO; (719) 589-9759

### 🇳 Maps:
**USGS maps:** Greenie Mountain, CO; Jasper, CO • **Colorado's San Luis Valley Mountain Bike Guide** – available at Kristi Mountain Sports • **National Forest's Best Trails of Colorado's San Luis Valley** – available at the Rio Grande National Forest Supervisor's Office (719) 852-5941

Inches Wide" sign. The trail begins 50 feet to the left of Forest Service Road 271 and disappears into aspen timber, following in a southerly direction.

Once on Alamosa/Rock Creek Trail 703, climb over wide and soft singletrack through aspen and pine forests. After crossing the north fork of Cat Creek, the climbing becomes more severe. By mile 7.5, the trail starts descending rapidly along narrow, rock and root-filled terrain to the Blowout Pass overlook. Ride west over the cracked shale and descend to a fork at mile 8.5.

The left fork crosses a barbwire fence and leads into a meadow, while the right fork climbs through a stand of aspens. Bear right. After crossing Cat Creek, pass through a barbwire fence and begin a fast and smooth cruise down to the junction of Cat Creek Trail 704.

Cat Creek Trail 704 offers smooth, soaring descents past aspen and mixed conifer forests, through creeks and across marvelous meadows. At mile 10.4, the trail hugs a sloping south face as it switchbacks into the aspen-lined drainage of Cat Creek's south fork. Here the singletrack becomes rockier.

At mile 12.8, pass through another lush meadow—although this time the meadow is surrounded by sky-piercing granite walls. From here, it's a final rocky descent past a wooden gate and beaver ponds to your vehicle.

# In Addition

# Colorado's Off-Road Wheelchair Riding

Jackie Robinson did it for African-Americans and baseball in 1947 when he first took the field as a Brooklyn Dodger. Roberta "Bobbi" Gibb did it for women and marathon racing when she broke the "men-only" Boston Marathon rule in 1966. John Davis did it for off-road riders and mountain biking in 1991 when he wheeled himself to the starting gate of a NORBA-sponsored mountain bike race, becoming the sport's first wheelchair athlete.

No one can contest the significance of Jackie Robinson's actions, nor can anyone question the contribution of Bobbi Gibb—such is the luxury of hindsight. It may be too soon to tell, but Michael Whiting, manager of Team Phoenix and owner of Denver-based Wildernet—a designing and manufacturing company of off-road wheelchairs—realizes the significance of Davis' actions. For Whiting, Davis' bold move in 1991 was the necessary first step in the evolution of off-road wheelchair competition in the National Off-Road Biking Association (NORBA).

Davis rode on a "Cobra" hardtail, the original off-road wheelchair designed by John Castellano specifically for Davis. Since the "Cobra" was custom fit to Davis, an elite athlete, its design hampered the development of off-road wheelchairs for the average rider.

"The first time I met David Noonan," remembers Whiting, speaking of the man who inspired him to create his first off-road wheel-chair, "he had just wheeled himself into my mountain bike shop. We started talking about mountain biking, and he told me of his frustrations with his inability to do the things he used to do prior to his injury, so we started kicking around the idea of building an off-road wheelchair."

Whiting began by making a list of performance parameters for a person in a wheelchair. The chair would need a suspension system that would enable a 150 to 200-pound individual to mock down a rough stretch of trail in excess of 50 mph without being bounced out. It would also need a braking system that offered four-times the braking power of traditional bicycles, as well as a frame that would be light enough and strong enough to handle the rigors of mountain racing. What he came up with was the "Phoenix"—named after the mythical bird that rose from its own ashes and took to flight.

Today, Wildernet offers two different off-road wheelchairs: the "Phoenix," a full-suspension downhill racing bike with hydraulic brakes and independent dual-wishbone suspension; and the "Razor," a suspended cross-country chair and Wildernet's first production model. The "Razor" offers an unprecedented amount of adjustments which enable the rider to get a dialed-in fit without paying top dollar. These two off-road wheelchairs provide the fire power for Team Phoenix, Colorado's only off-road wheelchair racing team.

Team Phoenix's mission statement focuses on enhancing and highlighting ability rather than compensating for disability. In 1994 Team Phoenix built and raced the first full-suspension wheelchair in the world. In 1995 Team Phoenix member Gretchen Schaper became the first disabled woman to compete in a NORBA event and was the recipient of the first NORBA medal for a disabled person. The first quadriplegic mountain biker ever to race in a NORBA downhill raced with Team Phoenix. In the summer of 1997, Team Phoenix hosted the first off-road wheelchair race with a cash purse at Winter Park, Colorado. The team gained international exposure at the 1997 All Japan Mountain Bike Cup, Japan's largest mountain bike event.

Ultimately, Whiting sees mountain biking as a form of self-expression, and his adaptive off-road wheelchair technology offers the disabled person an opportunity to express him or herself. "People with disabilities," says Whiting, "need their own way of self-expression, and every time someone sees our product, it changes the size of the planet for them."

Off-road wheelchair mountain biking is well on its way to becoming the next niche in the mountain bike racing scene. In fact, off-road wheelchair racing has already furnished the mountain biking community with its own list of major players: Matt Feeny of Winter Park, Colorado; Gerard Morano of Los Angeles, California; and H.D. Baily—off-road wheelchair racing's own Iggy Pop.

The concerns of latter-day mountain bikers arguing over the gram weights of little nuts and bolts fade from view when confronted by questions like "How is an off-road wheelchair going to enhance my life?" and "What will I be able to do now that I couldn't do before?" These questions demand a shift in perspective from the mountain biking community, a perspective heretofore missing in the endless gram-debates.

# Honorable Mentions

## South Central Colorado

Compiled here is an index of great rides in the South Central region that didn't make the A-list this time around but deserve recognition. Check them out and let us know what you think. You may decide that one or more of these rides deserves higher status in future editions or, perhaps, you may have a ride of your own that merits some attention.

### (F.) Old Midland Railroad Grade

The "14ers Region" of Chaffe County is a veritable home to the giants—including four of Colorado's five highest peaks—but you don't have to be a colossus to enjoy the Old Midland Railroad Grade. This intermediate, eight-mile ride is one of Buena Vista's most popular trails and has had a long-standing reputation as a favorite among visitors. In fact, the Midland is the 14ers Region's, and the San Isabel National Forest's, first designated mountain bike trail. In cooperation with the Bureau of Land Management and the town of Buena Vista, the U.S. Forest Service began construction on the trail in 1990. It connects riders to a number of other area rides as well, most notably, the Lenhardy Cutoff and the Buena Vista River Road.

The Old Midland Railroad grade follows the historic and long-abandoned Midland rail line. Old ties, hillside cuts, and telegraph poles remind us of a bygone era whose pioneers conquered many hardships to establish flourishing communities. One look around and these hardships are colorfully brought to bear in the views of the surrounding Sawatch Range's Collegiate Peaks: Mount Princeton, Mount Harvard, and Mount Yale. The grade is very rideable, with only a few difficult stretches where the cut walls have collapsed. These tougher sections serve as a good introduction to technical singletrack.

Although short, this trail will require a shuttle. Park your shuttle vehicle at the Shield's Gulch trailhead. To reach Shields Gulch, drive south on U.S. Route 24 from Buena Vista to Johnson Village. Bear left onto U.S. Route 285 in Johnson Village and drive east for five miles to Forest Service Road 315. Turn left (north) onto Forest Service Road 315 and drive for another half a mile. The trailhead will be to your left. Leave your second vehicle at the trail's end, at the Arkansas River footbridge at the end of Buena Vista's East Main Street. For details on this and other rides, contact the Greater Buena Vista Area Chamber of Commerce at 343 U.S. Route 24 South, Buena Vista, Colorado, (719) 395-6612, or visit *www.fourteennet.com*. Or try The Trailhead at 707 U.S. Route 24 North, Buena Vista, Colorado, (719) 395-8001. *DeLorme: Colorado Atlas & Gazetteer:* Page 60, B-2

## (G) Reservoir Hill

Reservoir Hill is Pagosa Springs' centrally located trail system. On land owned by the town, this system combines singletrack and dirt road routes of varying difficulty. The annual "Gone to the Hill" mountain bike race is held here every September. The area boasts two main bike routes up the hill: a moderate-grade singletrack and an even mellower road. The singletrack delivers you to the water tower on top, while the road leads you to a cabin where it forks. Riders can go in either direction from the fork. From the top a network of mellower terrain abounds. Upon returning from the top of the hill, riders can descend the west side of the hill on either one of two options, the road or the singletrack. There are also descents off the hill's north and east sides, but these routes won't bring you directly to your vehicle and are considerably steeper.

The hill, however, includes more than just bicycling, as this trail system is located near the Town Park, Visitor Center, and the Hot Springs. These springs serve up warm relief after a day's ride and are as a much a part of the town as its residents. Indeed, "Pagosa" hails from the Ute Indian name meaning "Healing Waters." Hot springs aren't the only attraction, however. Pagosa Springs' country also boasts a number of waterfalls such as Treasure Falls, Piedra Falls, and Four Mile Falls. To reach Reservoir Hill, drive south through Pagosa Springs to the stoplight at the center of town. Turn southeast on Hot Springs Boulevard toward the Visitor Center. After crossing the San Juan River, bear left onto San Juan Street. Drive for another block before turning right onto a gravel road, climbing a short hill, to the parking area and the trailhead.

For more information on this ride and the surrounding area, contact the Pagosa Springs Area Chamber at 402 San Juan St., Pagosa Springs, Colorado, 1-800-252-2204 or (970) 264-2360. Also check out Juan's Mountain Sports at 155 Hot Springs Blvd, Pagosa Springs, Colorado, (970) 264-4730; or try Pedal the Peaks at 300 E. Pagosa Street, Pagosa Springs, Colorado, 1-800-743-3843. *DeLorme: Colorado Atlas & Gazetteer:* Page 88, B-1

# Front Range

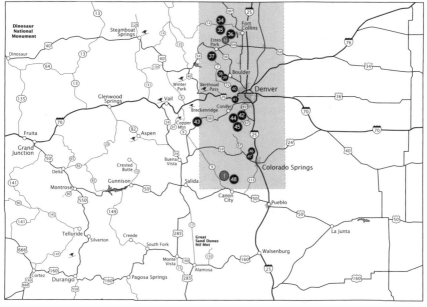

T he length of Rocky Mountain foothills running south from Fort Collins to Colorado Springs, where amber waves of grain meet the purple mountains' majesty, is generally referred to as the Front Range. It is Colorado's most populated region (home to nearly 80% of the state's population). The Front Range's terrain is predominately semi-arid and rocky. Offering cacti, steep grades and loose rocks, the Front Range delivers some of the most technical riding in the state. Although the views are not as dramatic as the ones found in Colorado's inner Rocky Mountains, the trails here are just as good, albeit somewhat more crowded.

Unlike most major metropolitan areas, those found along the Front Range—Fort Collins, Boulder, Golden, Denver, Colorado Springs—are all within an easy 30 minutes' drive of incredible riding. Since trails along the Front Range typically receive a higher volume of use, their routes tend to be considerably easier to follow. That's not to say, however, that Front Range riding is all user-friendly. Front Range trails oftentimes travel through rattlesnake and mountain lion habitats, something to consider if ever riding alone. Moreover, the Front Range's semi-arid terrain is an ideal growing environment for the weed commonly referred to as "Goathead" or "Puncturevine" (Tribulus terrestris). The fruits which these weeds produce are also known as goatheads. After these goatheads fall from their host weeds, they harden and dry (with the seed of the weed inside). Becoming a three-pointed, thorn-like enemy on the trail, goatheads have an uncanny ability of finding their way into your tires. Their pervasion throughout the Front Range demands riders to ride with thicker and/or spare tubes, pump and stocked patch kit.

To the north, Fort Collins lies in the Cache la Poudre River Valley. Here, riders enjoy over 20 miles of multi-use recreational trails, over 3,000 acres of open space and over 80 miles of designated bikeways, including paved trails, bike lanes, and bike routes. The Poudre Canyon, Horsetooth Reservoir and Lory State Park offer the best in area mountain biking. Just south of Fort Collins lies Rocky Mountain National Park. With 410-square-miles of forests, meadows, tundra and opaline ponds, in addition with Trail Ridge Road, the country's highest continuos highway reaching above timberline into the tundra, Rocky Mountain National Park is a must see.

Roughly 60 miles south of Fort Collins, Boulder is, perhaps, the region's reigning recreational town. With the sheer granite walls of the Flatirons as a backdrop, Boulder provides a healthy lifestyle. To accommodate the number of bicycle commuters in Boulder (which, incidentally, is 7 times greater than the national average), the town boasts 60,000 acres of open space and 150 miles of trails. Moreover, the International Mountain Bicycling Association (IMBA) has its headquarters in Boulder. The Walker Ranch Loop, as well as the Sourdough Trail, are two of Boulder's classic rides. To the south of Boulder, near Golden, White Ranch offers a venous network of trails, accommodating riders of every ability.

Although Denver, Colorado's capital, provides all the art, shopping and dining as any other city, it also contributes to Colorado's health-conscious attitude. Bicycling Magazine rated Denver City Number 6 in its "Best Bicycling Cities" feature for cities whose populations were greater than 100,000. The Hogback, boasting technical

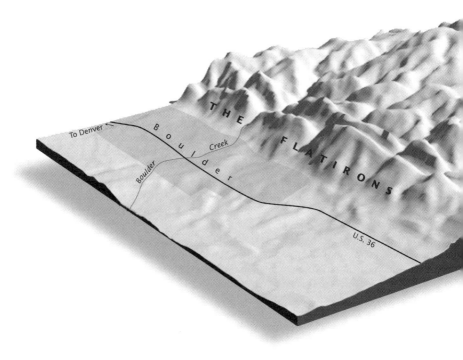

descents and offering incredible views of the geological phenomenon of Red Rocks Amphitheater, is a great ride and just 20 minuets from downtown Denver. Waterton Canyon is another Denver riding destination and marks the beginning of the 470-mile Colorado Trail.

Just an hour's drive south of Denver is Colorado Springs, home to Pikes Peak. Colorado Springs also does its part in keeping up with Colorado's active lifestyle. Although a major city in its own right, Colorado Springs, nevertheless, is home to USA Cycling (888-405-7223), the national governing body of bicycling, which includes the National Off-Road Mountain Biking Association (NORBA), the national governing body for mountain bike racing. Colorado Springs is also home to the US Olympic Training Center. Some of the better rides in the area include Rampart Reservoir Shoreline Loop and Waldo Canyon. Each trail features single-track lined with Pikes Peak granite, which helps in the absorption of water, keeping trails drier and extending the riding season.

# Hewlett's Gulch

## Ride Summary

Hewlett's Gulch is a favorite among mountain bikers in and around Fort Collins. Its fast single-track, big drop-offs, creek crossings, killer climbs, and one very rocky descent will satisfy any mountain biker's idea of a good ride. Although technically and physically moderate to challenging, the ride serves first-time mountain biker's well, as it can be ridden at any pace. For those who like to grab air, there's a great spot at the 2.3-mile mark where the trail dips into a small gully. With enough speed, you'd swear you were flying.

## Ride Specs

**Start:** From Poudre Canyon, just past Poudre Park

**Length:** 8.5-mile loop (with an additional 4 miles added if you opt for the out-and-back)

**Approximate Riding Time:** Advanced Riders, 1½ hours; Intermediate Riders, 2½ hours.

**Technical Difficulty Rating:** Technically challenging, due to a very rocky and steep descent on the return.

**Physical Difficulty Rating:** Physically moderate to challenging due to an extended climb midway through the ride.

**Terrain:** Rough doubletrack and singletrack. This trail crosses many creeks and enters in and out of mixed conifer forests before climbing up through a meadow. Though generally manageable, there are big drop-off sections, as well as one of the rockiest singletrack descents in all of the Front Range.

**Elevation Gain:** 1,135 feet

**Nearest Town:** Poudre Park, CO

**Other Trail Users:** Hikers, campers, equestrians, and hunters

**Canine Compatibility:** Dog-friendly

## Getting There

**From Fort Collins:** Head north on U.S. 287. Turn left onto CO 14 following signs for the Poudre Canyon. Drive 10 miles. After passing the tiny town of Poudre Park, you'll spot a bridge to the north spanning the Cache la Poudre River. The bridge is blocked by an iron bar, but biking is allowed. Park on either side of CO 14—additional parking is located 100 yards down the road on the right. Respect residents of the Poudre Canyon by not parking in front of their driveways or mailboxes. *DeLorme: Colorado Atlas & Gazetteer:* Page 19 C-7

### Did you know...

*The term "champagne powder" was coined in Steamboat Springs, CO.*

As the crashing waves of the Cache la Poudre River blaze through the Poudre Canyon in Roosevelt National Forest, the echoes of a distant pioneering past resound from its granite walls. The very name of the canyon (and more specifically the river) recalls the struggles that the early pioneers had to endure in order to come to terms with this western wilderness.

The story goes that a party of French-Canadian trappers and traders, led by Antione Janis of John Jacob Astor's American Fur Company, was en route to a pre-scribed rendezvous on the Green River when bad weather hit. It was November of 1836. The snowstorm made it impossible for the company to safely ford the Poudre

Canyon's river, so Janis gave the order to lighten the wagon loads. The men dug a large pit, lined it with pine boughs and animal skins, and filled it with what could be spared from each wagon. After back-filling the pit, the trappers burned a large fire on top of the pit to disguise the site. They feared the supplies would be taken by the native Arapaho and Cheyenne Indians. Included in the buried supplies were several hundred pounds of gunpowder. The French-speaking trappers called this place, "cache la poudre" ("the hiding place of the powder"). Some months later, the party returned to the Poudre Canyon and recovered all of their supplies. The name stuck.

Typical of the mountain biking trails of Colorado's Front Range, the Hewlett's Gulch run delivers smooth, fast-riding singletrack; rocky, non-negotiable climbs and descents; and a dizzying array of creek-crossings. The trail begins as an overgrown doubletrack, which soon turns to singletrack within half a mile. There are four creek-crossings within the first mile of the trail. Erosion logs have recently been placed across the trail for the first two to three miles, making for some steep drop-offs and tough, taco-bending hill hops. The erosion logs have effectively made Hewlett's Gulch more technical than ever before.

Catching sick air at "Sick Air."

Within the first mile, you encounter the remnants of Horace Huleatt's old homestead. Huleatt settled the gulch in 1870 on land he later found out was sacred Ute Indian land. When word passed to Horace that his claim rested upon ancient ground, he quickly moved on, leaving his homestead as a parting gift. Today a stone chimney and a concrete foundation are all we have of old Horace Huleatt, but his name lives on, though slightly corrupted, in Hewlett's Gulch. Legions of wild lilac and poppy surround the old homestead—evidence that Huleatt landscaped his claim with native Colorado flora. After the homestead the trail leads into a lush pine-covered sanctuary awash with thousands of wild purple poppies. This is a great place to string a hammock and blow the soul out of your saxophone.

The author splashes down, though he claims to have managed the big rocky drop behind him "brilliantly."

## **Miles**Directions

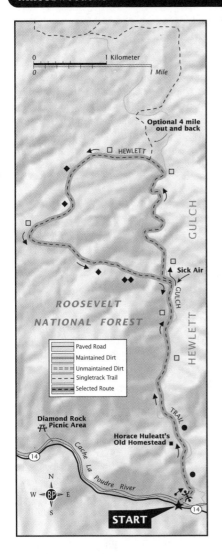

**0.0 START** from CO 14. Cross the gated, wooden-planked bridge. The Cache la Poudre River is below you. Ride up the road.

**0.1** Bear left onto a rough doubletrack, and enter Roosevelt National Forest. (A right will take you to private homes).

**0.4** The singletrack begins.

**1.1** Here the trail crosses its fourth creek and leads into a lush pine forest carpeted with wild poppies. This is a great place for a picnic or resting spot.

**2.3** Sick Air. The trail comes to a "T." Bear right.

**3.3** An extremely difficult and rocky descent delivers you to a broad and grassy two-mile hill climb.

**4.2** Don't be fooled. This is a false summit, albeit an ideal resting spot for those in the need.

**4.3** A short, but fast stretch of singletrack, highlighted by a couple of rocky sections, rewards the patient hill climber.

**5.3** The trail leads into a deep gully. You'll need your speed getting out of it. The trail continues up a steep, but short ascent. At the top of this short climb, come to a "T" in the trail. Bearing right offers a four-mile out-and-back option, while bearing left continues on the main trail. Bear left here, toward your eventual descent.

**5.4** Begin a rugged, sick descent.

**6.2** Arrive at the bottom where you caught the sick air. Bear right and backtrack the remaining 2.3 miles of the first and last part of Hewlett's Gulch.

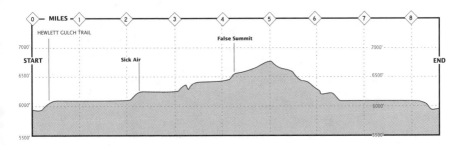

The trail continues through intermittent fields and groves of cedar and pine. The canyon narrows here. Sheer granite walls climb the sides of the canyon in a vain attempt to pierce the sky. The surroundings become more rugged, save the yellow flowering cacti—a bittersweet reminder of the agony and ecstasy through which we mountain bikers put ourselves.

After about two miles into the ride, the trail comes to a "T" before a big gully, offering the opportunity for sick air. Bear left and climb the side of the hill. The hit is on the right side of the trail as you scream up the other side of the gully. From there the trail meanders through alternating stands of lodgepole pine and spruce, offering occasional short, rocky, and steep climbs. After one such climb the trail lets out onto a broad grassy hill completely devoid of trees. A half-mile to the north of this hill stands a beautiful house boasting an even better southerly view. Turn around and enjoy an inspiring view of the canyon through which you've just ridden.

Trailside maintenance.

# Ride Information

## Trail Contacts:

Diamond Peaks Mountain Bike Patrol, Timnath, CO; (970) 482-6006 ext. 22 or DPMBP@aol.com

## Schedule:

April to November

## Local Information:

Forest To Grassland Information Center, Fort Collins, CO; (970) 498-2770 • Forest Supervisor Office: Arapaho and Roosevelt National Forests & Pawnee National Grassland, Fort Collins, CO; (970) 498-1100 • Fort Collins Website: www.fortnet.org

## Local Events/Attractions:

Mishawaka Amphitheater, Fort Collins, CO; (970) 482-4420 – a point of reference for anyone traveling the Poudre Canyon, the first digit of a four-digit address (or the first two digits of a five-digit address) marks the distance from the start of the canyon to the residence. For instance, Mishawaka Amphitheater, at 13714 Poudre Canyon, is 13 miles up the canyon.

## Restaurants:

Rio Grande, Fort Collins, CO; (970) 224-5428 – best margaritas you'll ever drink. • CooperSmith's Pub & Brewing, Fort Collins, CO; (970) 498-0483

## Organizations:

Friends of the Poudre, Fort Collins, CO; (970) 221-2957

## Local Bike Shops:

Lee's Cyclery, Ft. Collins, CO; (970) 482-6006 and 1-800-748-BIKE or (970) 226-6006 • Rock 'n Road Cyclery, Fort Collins, CO; (970) 223-7623 • Brave New Wheel, Fort Collins, CO; (970) 416-0417

## Maps:

USGS maps: Poudre Park, CO • Trails Illustrated map: #101, Cache La Poudre & Big Thompson • Arapaho and Roosevelt National Forests map – available at the Forest Supervisor Office.

The two-mile climb to the top of this hill is deceiving, as there is a false summit at mile 4.8. This false summit does, however, offer a great opportunity to dismount and take in the views. Although Hewlett's Gulch does have its challenging, short, steep climbs, it rewards the persistent rider with incredible rocky singletrack descents. After arriving at the second gully, the trail once again comes to a "T." Here you have the option to bear right for a rugged four-mile out-and-back, or simply bear left and continue on the main trail.

The descent from this point is famed for its technical riding. Complete with steep grades and loose, football-size rocks, all sidelined with thorny cacti and this-tle, this descent has some of the sickest singletrack descents on Colorado's Front Range. Once you arrive at the bottom, bear right and backtrack for the remaining 2.3 miles.

# Young Gulch

## Ride Summary

Young Gulch is a great ride to do for those who like to get wet. During the spring thaw, the trail crosses a number of larger creeks. Since this ride travels through mixed conifer forests and under thick canopies, the trail remains quite cool, so don't expect to be warm and dry too quickly. In fact, it's best that you bring a towel and an extra pair of shoes and socks. There are a few rocky and steep technical sections, but for the most part, this out-and-back is well suited for the beginner and intermediate rider. The advanced rider will find some of the steeper, rockier sections a challenge and the descent back to his or her vehicle, an absolute thrill.

## Ride Specs

**Start:** Young Gulch Trailhead. From the south side of CO 14, at milepost 109, 3.2 miles from Poudre Park
**Length:** 10.3-mile out-and-back
**Approximate Riding Time:** Advanced Riders, 1½ hours; Intermediate Riders, 2½ hours
**Technical Difficulty Rating:** Technically moderate to challenging due to its rocky, but short climbs and descents
**Physical Difficulty Rating:** Physically moderate due to its mellower elevation gain: 5,800-7,040 feet
**Terrain:** Singletrack, traveling through a gulch. As such, there are many creek crossings under forest cover.
**Elevation Gain:** 1,519 feet
**Nearest Town:** Poudre Park, CO
**Other Trail Users:** Campers, hikers, and equestrians
**Canine Compatibility:** Dog friendly

## Getting There

**From Fort Collins:** Head north on U.S. 287. Turn left onto CO 14, following signs for the Poudre Canyon. Drive on CO 14 for 13 miles. The dirt road turnoff to Young Gulch is 3.2 miles past the tiny town of Poudre Park and will be on the left, at milepost 109. Drive up the dirt road to the parking area and trailhead. A wooden and wired gate marks the beginning of the trail. After entering the gate, please be sure to close it behind you.
***DeLorme: Colorado Atlas & Gazetteer.*** Page 19, C-7

The Young Gulch trail is located in Roosevelt National Forest's beautiful Poudre Canyon. In 1918, the Forest Service granted the town of Fort Collins permission to develop Young Gulch as a place where people could picnic, camp, and hike. Three years later Young Gulch was opened. Today it stands as a reminder of Colorado's early commitment to mountain recreation.

Convict labor built the original road leading to Young Gulch—now Colorado 14. The Poudre Valley Good Roads Association constructed a masonry fireplace to celebrate the completion of the road to that point. Located just beyond the turnoff for Young Gulch, the fireplace was left for others to use in the future.

Splashing through one of the many creeks.

Just before coming to the old fireplace, one notices the Forest Service's sign marking the Cache la Poudre River as a "Wild and Scenic River System." Seventy-five miles of the Poudre, from Poudre Park to Rocky Mountain National Park, have been preserved for future generations. The Poudre was the first river in Colorado to receive protection under the National Wild and Scenic River Act. Covering an estimated 150 miles, the Poudre River originates from Poudre Lake (an alpine lake located high in the mountains of Rocky Mountain National Park) and extends to the South Platte River, just east of the town of Greeley.

The Poudre Canyon is dedicated to a variety of outdoor activities: mountain biking, hiking, camping, rock climbing, four-wheeling, kayaking, and rafting. Local citizen groups, like Friends of the Poudre, are currently working together to develop boat chutes at diversion structures on the river so kayakers and rafters can run the entire river in the lower canyon without having to portage their crafts. These chutes are estimated to cost between $200,000 to $300,000 each—further evidence of Colorado's commitment to recreation and healthy living.

Just three miles up Colorado 14 from the Young Gulch trailhead stands the Mishawaka Inn, a laid back, riverside amphitheater serving locally brewed beer. The Inn is a summer venue for the likes of Merle Saunders, The Radiators, Arlo Guthrie, The Ugly Americans, Robert Bradley's Blackwater Surprise, Bella Fleck and the Flecktones, and the David Grisman Quintet—to name but a few. In February of 1916, Walter S. Thompson, a musician from Fort Collins, purchased the surrounding land with the intent of operating a self-supporting home. Within three years, Thompson had built himself a very comfortable house, several cabins,

# Ride Information

## 📞 Trail Contacts:
**Diamond Peaks Mountain Bike Patrol**, Timnath, CO; (970) 482-6006 ext. 22 or e-mail at *DPMBP@aol.com*

## 🕐 Schedule:
April to November

## ❓ Local Information:
**Forest To Grassland Information Center**, Fort Collins, CO; (970) 498-2770 • **Forest Supervisor Office: Arapaho and Roosevelt National Forests & Pawnee National Grassland**, Fort Collins, CO; (970) 498-1100 • **Fort Collins Website**: *www.fortnet.org*

## 💡 Local Events/Attractions:
**Mishawaka Inn Amphitheater**, Fort Collins, CO; (970) 482-4420

## 🍴 Restaurants:
**Rio Grande**, Fort Collins, CO; (970) 224-5428—*great margaritas* • **Cooper Smith's Pub & Brewing**, Fort Collins, CO; (970) 498-0483

## 🧍 Organizations:
**Diamond Peaks Mountain Bike Patrol**, Timnath, CO; (970) 482-6006 ext. 22 or e-mail at *DPMBP@aol.com* • **Friends of the Poudre**, Fort Collins, CO; (970) 221-2957

## 🚲 Local Bike Shops:
**Lee's Cyclery**, Ft. Collins, CO; (970) 482-6006 and 1-800-748-BIKE or (970) 226-6006 • **Rock 'n Road Cyclery**, Fort Collins, CO; (970) 223-7623 • **Brave New Wheel**, Fort Collins, CO; (970) 416-0417

## 🅝 Maps:
**USGS maps**: Poudre Park, CO • *Trails Illustrated* **map**: #101, Cache La Poudre & Big Thompson • **Arapaho and Roosevelt National Forests map** – *available at the Forest Supervisor Office: Arapaho and Roosevelt National Forests & Pawnee National Grassland (970) 498-1100*

a general store, and a dance hall. More than 80 years later, the music continues to play throughout the Poudre Canyon, keeping time with the rocking and rolling of our bikes through Young Gulch.

Rocking and rolling do well to describe this trail. Young Gulch offers a vast array of terrain for any level mountain biker. Its steep-sided, narrow, and rocky terrain offers challenges for even the best riders, while its many creek-crossings allow the novice mountain biker many chilling thrills. The creek-crossings, along with dense forests, make this trail ideal for those hot summer days. Unfortunately the heavy forest cover causes the snow at Young Gulch to melt late, creating a potentially cold and wet environment late into spring. These spring conditions can be tricky to ride in. Deep creek crossings, wet rocks, and slippery roots are all factors of significant braking power loss.

At mile 1.4, the trail will lead to a rocky impasse, over which you'll have to portage your bike. The remaining three miles of Young Gulch are smoother and wider, making for a fast descent on your way back. Take care on your return, as rocky approaches into creeks come up on you fast. The rocky downhills can be hairy if not approached carefully—but oh the fun.

## **Miles**Directions

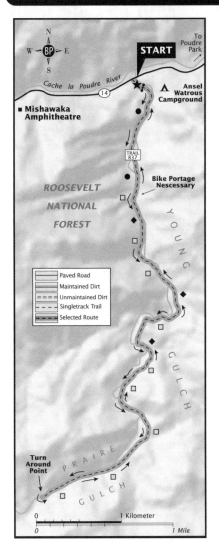

**0.0 START** from the gate at the trailhead. Begin riding through the thickly forested gulch.
**0.6** Arrive at a sweet, shaded spot, just to your right—ideal for a quick rest or snack. Blooming cacti abound, creek-side.
**1.3** Reach one of two short, but technical climbs. Climb this section with thoughts of your returning descent. Picking the line to your right on your return is probably best.
**3.5** Fallen trees blocked the trail here at time of this writing. Pick up the trail by walking up creek for approximately 50 feet. From here the gulch widens out, letting up on some of the rocks and roots.
**5.0** The trail merges with a 4WD road heading up the hillside to you left. Climb for another 0.2 miles to reach the turnaround point. As the top of this climb levels out, bear an immediate right for a short grind to the top of a knob of stone. From here, there is a good view of the gulch and Stove Prairie Road. After resting, backtrack and enjoy the fast and rocky descent.
**10.3** Arrive back at your vehicle.

### Check the Address First:

*As a point of reference for anyone traveling the Poudre Canyon, the first digit of a four-digit address (or the first two digits of a five-digit address) marks the distance from the residence to the start of the canyon. For instance, the Mishawaka Inn Amphitheater, at 13714 Poudre Canyon, is 13 miles up the canyon.*

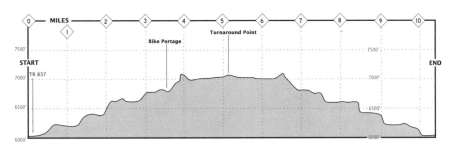

# Mill Creek Trail

## Ride Summary

Lory State Park/Horsetooth Mountain Park is prime real estate for some of the area's best mountain biking. The Mill Creek Trail is one of the most technically and physically challenging rides in all of Fort Collins. Riders climb into the semi-arid woodlands of Colorado's Front Range, the first step into the Rocky Mountains. Aside from gorgeous views of Colorado's Eastern Plains, this route offers rolling terrain alongside Horsetooth Reservoir, a burly climb to Horsetooth Mountain, and a steep and rocky descent down the Mill Creek Trail.

## Ride Specs

**Start:** From the entrance to Lory State Park, at the guard station, just beyond the stop sign
**Length:** 13.3-mile loop
**Approximate Riding Time:** Advanced Riders; 1½–2 hours; Intermediate Riders; 2½–3 hours
**Technical Difficulty Rating:** Technically moderate to challenging due to its rocky and steep singletrack descents.
**Physical Difficulty Rating:** Physically moderate to challenging due to 3 miles of steep and arduous hill climbing.
**Terrain:** Rocky and rolling terrain on both singletrack and dirt road surfaces
**Elevation Gain:** 1,899 feet
**Nearest Town:** Fort Collins, CO
**Other Trail Users:** Hikers, campers, equestrians, and water recreationalists
**Canine Compatibility:** Dog-friendly (but beware the equestrians)

## Getting There

**From downtown Fort Collins:** Drive north on College Avenue (from the junction of College Avenue and Mountain Road) for 6.3 miles, heading toward La Porte and Lory State Park. After you pass La Porte, veer left onto CR 52E. Drive on CR 52E for approximately one mile before making a left on CR 23, by the red, flagstone Bellvue Senior Center. At 8.7 miles, turn right onto CR 25G and follow signs to Lory State Park. Drive another 1.6 miles to the entrance of Charles A. Lory State Park. Leave your vehicle outside of the park, as you will begin your ride by the guard station.
***DeLorme: Colorado Atlas & Gazetteer:*** Page 20 D-1

The 4,500 acres that comprise Lory State Park and Horsetooth Mountain Park boast a venous network of trails. This network, running along the transitional ecology of the Rocky Mountain foothills, weaves its way through a variety of terrain and vegetation: unique rock outcroppings, sandstone hogbacks, grassy open meadows, cacti-laden hillsides, and ponderosa pine forests. To the northwest, Arthur's Rock (6,780 feet) marks the high-point in Lory State Park and overlooks the town of Fort Collins. Its jutting granite foundation stands as a memorial to the strength of will and the indomitable character of the people of Fort Collins.

On July 29, 1997, Fort Collins' local newspaper, the *Coloradoan*, ran the headline: "Torrential rain floods city." That same morning, City Manager John Fischbach declared Fort Collins under a state of local emergency. In a five hour span, Fort Collins received 8.41 inches of rain. The ensuing flood washed trains off their tracks.

Ninety-two mobile homes were destroyed; 145 houses and 116 apartments were damaged; and five lives were lost. The town suffered millions of dollars in damages. Historically, it was Fort Collins' worst natural disaster to date.

The deluge dropped in excess of 10 inches of rain on nearby Lory State Park, wreaking havoc on the park's trails. By September of 1997 a massive reconstruction effort of the park's trails was underway, involving the efforts of the Diamond Peaks Mountain Bike Patrol, trail design professionals from the International Mountain Biking Association (IMBA), and local residents and riders.

Prior to becoming a state park in 1967, Lory State Park was primarily ranch land. The trails in the park most likely started as game trails. Over the years, and after much use, they've evolved into mountain bike trails. Unfortunately, the trails had never received proper attention, not in the way of erosion-proofing or trail system design. And so, when the flood of '97 hit, Lory State Park's trail system sustained incredible damage. Since the flood, a concerted effort has been lodged into redesigning and preserving these natural trails.

Through a great deal of hard work, the Diamond Peaks Mountain Bike Patrol, the IMBA, and local residents and riders have rectified much of the damage brought on by the flood of '97. The lower stretches of trail—those hardest hit by the flood—which lie just west of Horsetooth Reservoir in Lory State Park's valley, offer ideal riding conditions for beginners practicing their techniques. Advanced riders wanting to increase their heart rates will enjoy it as well. The first 4.7 miles of Valley Trail meander through rolling, open meadows and past a number of Horsetooth Reservoir's coves and bays.

## **Miles**Directions

**0.0 START** on the singletrack by the ranger station, just beyond the stop sign. Drinking water is available here. Note that the singletrack weaves itself onto the main road on occasion, but it's clear to the rider where and when to reconnect with the singletrack. Follow the singletrack.

**0.3** Ride right into the Timber Trail group area and pick up the singletrack of the Timber Trail to the left of the sign. Follow it as it climbs. Within 0.2 miles from where Timber Trail started, the singletrack comes to a "Y." Bear left at the "Y" onto Valley Trail. (Timber Trail continues to the right—where bikes are not allowed.) Valley Trail crosses a number of other trails that lead into the hills. Be sure not to veer right on any offshoots.

**2.3** Valley Trail connects to the Lory State entrance road. Cross the road and ascend to the sign that marks the trailheads for Bridal Trail and Arthur's Rock Trail. Continue riding south, beyond the sign. From here, there are a number of routes that branch left to coves at Horsetooth Reservoir. Following the rolling terrain of Valley Trail, continue through the meadow, paralleling the sandstone hogbacks of Horsetooth Reservoir to your left.

**4.7** Reach the junction of Valley Trail and Sawmill Trail. Look for a frog pond to your right. Head right and climb up Sawmill Trail. Sawmill Trail is a rough service road and marks your entrance into Horsetooth Mountain Park.

**7.1** Having climbed 2.4 miles, and having passed the tempting singletrack of the Stout, Loggers, and East Ridge trails, the trailhead to Mill Creek Trail begins to your right. Note: there are a number of offshoots to your left, which lead down the west side of Horsetooth Mountain. Reserve taking any of these trails for another day.

**9.1** Reach the junction of Loggers Trail and Mill Creek Trail. Veer left and continue on Mill Creek Trail.

**10.2** Arrive at a red gate, which marks your reentrance into Lory State Park. Close the gate behind you and enjoy the views of Fort Collins and Horsetooth Reservoir to the east. Ride for 0.1 miles to the sign for "Arthur's Rock," "Horsetooth Mountain," and "Parking Area." Ride straight ahead, past the sign.

**10.8** Arrive at the sign that marks the trailheads for Bridal and Arthur's Rock trails. From here, either return via the road or via the singletrack to your vehicle.

**13.3** Reach the entrance of Lory State Park and ranger station.

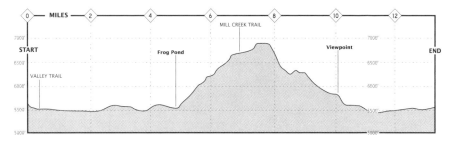

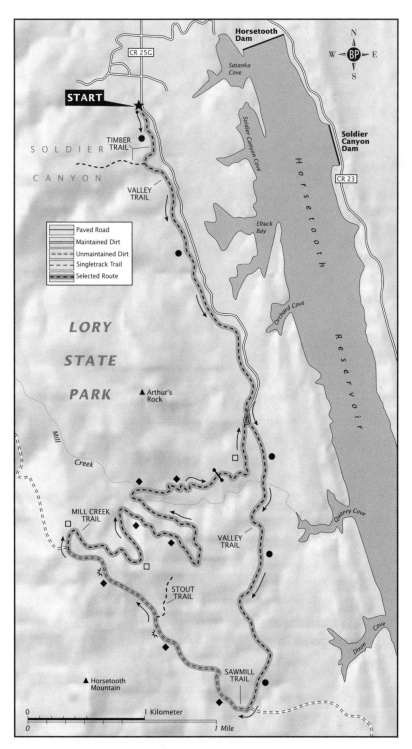

Original trappers lodge in LaPorte, Colorado

There's Santanka Cove, named for the red sedimentary formations in the area; and Soldier Cove, located at the base of Soldier Canyon—so called because a skeleton and three U.S. Army buttons were found there. Eltuck Bay was named after Elton Collins, who with the help of Tuck (J. Morris) Howell helped build the reservoir, as part of the Colorado-Big Thompson Irrigation Project in the late 1940s. Before the waters of the reservoir swept in to cover them Quarry Cove was a sandstone quarry and Orchard Cove, a cherry orchard.

Once you arrive at the service road in Horsetooth Mountain Park (a.k.a. Sawmill Trail), you begin your 2.4-mile climb to the top of Horsetooth Mountain—the Front Range's answer to those lung-busting climbs of the Colorado high-country interior. While climbing, you pass beneath Horsetooth Rock, from which the mountain receives its name. According to an Arapaho Indian legend, Horsetooth Rock is the heart of the Great Red Warrior who was killed by the Great Black Warrior in a long and bitter struggle in the heavens. The blood shed in the battle is said to have stained the rock red. So how did it get its name? A not so careful inspection will reveal its striking resemblance to a horse's molar.

With the grind of capping this tooth accomplished, it's time for a sick ride down the singletrack of the Mill Creek Trail. The trail begins through a dense ponderosa pine forest. Heading south, as you hug the east face of Horsetooth Mountain, you'll have to negotiate your line through some steep and rocky sections, all within the first mile of starting the Mill Creek Trail. Remember, the straightest line is always your strongest line. At mile 9.6, you cross Mill Creek—so-called because the Latham Mill once operated on it, behind Horsetooth Reservoir. The mill provided lumber for bridges in the early history of Larimer County. Nothing of the mill remains.

As you cross the creek and begin your climb out, notice the cool, little wading pond to your left. If you don't cool off here, the next leg of the trail may toss you. Just 0.2 miles ahead is the tight switchback section of the trail. Although the approaches to each switchback can be ridden quickly, check your speed, as the switchbacks come up quickly. The remaining descent through Lory State Park to your vehicle comes complete with short, rocky sections and smooth-running singletrack.

# Ride Information

## Trail Contacts:
Diamond Peaks Mountain Bike Patrol, Timnath, CO; (970) 482-6006 ext. 22 or *DPMBP@aol.com* • **Friends of Lory Trails,** Lory State Park, Bellvue, CO; (970) 493-1623

## Schedule:
April to November

## Fees/Permits:
$2.00 individual park pass must be purchased before entering the park. Prices are subject to change.

## Local Information:
Lory State Park, Bellvue, CO; (970) 493-1623 • **Larimer County Parks and Open Lands Department**, Loveland, CO; (970) 679-4570 • Fort Collins website: *www.fortnet.org*

## Local Events/Attractions:
Horsetooth Reservoir, contact Larimer County Parks and Open Lands Department, Loveland, CO; (970) 679-4570 • **Horsetooth Mountain Park,** contact Larimer County Parks and Open Lands Department, Loveland, CO; (970) 679-4570 • **Lory State Park,** Bellvue, CO; (970) 493-1623

## Restaurants:
**Rio Grande Rio Grande,** Fort Collins, CO; (970) 224-5428 – *the best margaritas you'll ever drink* • **CooperSmith's Pub & Brewing,** Fort Collins, CO; (970) 498-0483

## Organizations:
Diamond Peaks Mountain Bike Patrol, Timnath, CO; (970) 482-6006 ext. 22 or *DPMBP@aol.com* • **Friends of Lory Trails,** Lory State Park, Bellvue, CO; (970) 493-1623

## Local Bike Shops:
**Lee's Cyclery,** Ft. Collins, CO; (970) 482-6006 and 1-800-748-BIKE or (970) 226-6006 •**Rock 'n Road Cyclery,** Fort Collins, CO; (970) 223-7623 • **Brave New Wheel,** Fort Collins, CO; (970) 416-0417 • **Horsetooth Mountain Bikes,** (Inlet Bay) Fort Collins, CO; (970) 225-9674

## Maps:
**USGS maps:** Horsetooth Reservoir, CO • *Trails Illustrated* **map:** # 101 • **Lory State Park:** Colorado State Parks maps – *available from the park office* (970) 493-1623 • **Larimer County Parks Department map:** Horsetooth Mountain Park – *available from Larimer County Parks and Open Lands Department* (970) 679-4570

# House Rock to Pierson Park

## Ride Summary

House Rock to Pierson Park follows a primitive jeep road. There are a number of steep switchbacks, both up and down, which will test your bike handling skills. The ride also offers a good amount of fast, flat tracking, particularly around House Rock. The descent into Pierson Park is fast and under dense forest cover. Although close to popular Estes Park, this ride sees little traffic, therefore offering riders a generally undisturbed experience. Though the riding is not particularly technical, the fast and rocky descent to Pierson Park may try to throw you, so beware.

## Ride Specs

**Start:** From the first gate after turning onto FS 119 off of Cabin Creek Road
**Length:** 8.4-mile point-to-point (with options to explore the Homestead Meadows area via the Lion Gulch Trail from Pierson Park Trailhead)
**Approximate Riding Time:** Advanced Riders, 2 hours; Intermediate Riders, 2½–3 hours
**Technical Difficulty Rating:** Technically easy to moderate. Some rocky sections test your mountain biking skills.
**Physical Difficulty Rating:** Physically moderate to challenging due to sustained climbs at higher elevations.
**Terrain:** Forest Service fire roads with rocky and sandy patches. Most of the route leads through thick ponderosa pine and aspen forests.
**Elevation Gain:** 2,143 feet
**Nearest Town:** Estes Park, CO
**Other Trail Users:** Hikers, campers, motorcyclists, and equestrians
**Canine Compatibility:** Dog friendly

## Getting There

**To the start:** Drive south on CO 7 (The Peak-to-Peak Highway) from Estes Park for 11.5 miles. Turn left onto Cabin Creek Road (CR 82). After a mile, Cabin Creek Road comes to a "T." Bear right following signs for Larimer CR 82 east. Cross a gate. After roughly one mile turn left onto FS 119 and follow signs for Pierson Park. Park your vehicle at the first gate you come to and begin your ride ascending FS 119. *DeLorme: Colorado Atlas & Gazetteer.* Page 29, C-6

**To shuttle point:** Drive east on U.S. 36 from Estes Park to Fishcreek Road (just past Lake Estes). Turn right and drive 2.8 miles to Little Valley Road (dirt road) on left. Take Little Valley Road and follow the forest access signs for 1.5 miles up a number of switchbacks before parking your vehicle at Pierson Park. The ride will end here. *DeLorme: Colorado Atlas & Gazetteer.* Page 29, B-7

H ouse Rock to Pierson Park is a scenic ride that winds its way along dirt roads originally used by the areas first homesteaders. With views of Mount Meeker and Long's Peak, this route offers much climbing and descending around the 11,428 feet Twin Sisters Peaks. The area is a veritable web of primitive jeep roads. For those wanting to extend their day's outing, there's plenty of camping on the south side of House Rock, so bring a tent if you like.

The route begins as you ascend Forest Service Road 119. The climbing here is not as technically difficult as it is physically challenging. At 8,160 feet even the widest of

dirt roads becomes a struggle. At the half-mile mark you may notice a stand of very young aspen trees surrounded by much larger and more mature ponderosa pines—a sight demanding investigation. In place of Nature's regenerative method (that is to say, fire), aspen stands are often clearcut to preserve the forest habitat. Over-mature aspen trees are removed to allow young, healthier trees to grow and add more diversity to the forest. This thinning process also encourages the growth of low-lying shrubs, which as a food source benefits livestock and wildlife.

House Rock framed by green trees.

The beautiful St. Malo Church along the Peak to Peak Highway with Mount Meeker in the background.

The trail climbs gradually for the next four miles. Although this trail is not highly technical, it does offer a sense of serenity that can be found only in the deepest of covers. All too often, that serenity is broken when one is beleaguered with choices of which line to take and at what speed to take it. After four miles of gradual climbing and descending, the trail begins to descend very rapidly. This section of trail is perhaps the fastest mile you'll ride.

Standing stone cold in the middle of an idyllic meadow, House Rock stands monumental, a tribute to the area's earliest homesteaders who struggled to survive in some of the most rugged, yet remarkably beautiful country known to anyone. "We used what we had for medicines," remembered Nina Boren in a 1992 interview at the age of 99. "If someone had a cough, we'd put drops of coal oil on a teaspoon of sugar. It cut the phlegm in your throat; 'course it just about killed you too."

All of the homes in the Homestead Meadows area have stories to tell about early pioneer life. Names of past inhabitants are carved into the log walls of the Brown Homestead of 1918, and some of its original furniture remains inside. The Irvin Homestead of 1917 is still in good condition and boasts a barn, springhouse, and bunkhouse. The Walker Homestead of 1914 sleeps in an ocean of tall grass. Because

276

## MilesDirections

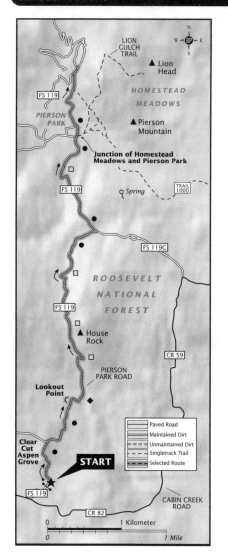

**0.0 START** at the first gate of FS 119, off of Cabin Creek Road.

**0.5** Reach the aspen clearcut. FS 119 ascends for four miles through thick forest cover. There are a number of offshoots from FS 119—don't take any of them.

**4.0** Reach the view of Mt. Meeker to west and its neighbor Long's Peak.

**5.0** FS 119 intersects with FS 119C. Veer left, continuing on FS 119.

**6.0** The route begins to climb again as it wraps its way around House Rock, named after its house-like appearance.

**6.8** Reach the junction of Pierson Park, Homestead Meadows, and Lion Gulch. FS 119 forks at this point. To reach your vehicle parked at Pierson Park, take the left fork. Another option is to head towards the Homestead Meadows Area and Lion Gulch Trail. These sections begin as singletrack. However, unless you have prearranged for a vehicle to be at the Lion Gulch Trailhead, continue on FS 119.

**8.4** Arrive at the Pierson Park parking lot after descending a fast section of FS 119.

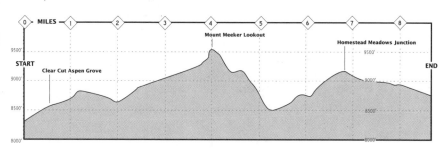

of what it can teach us, and has taught us, about the settling of the American West, Homestead Meadows was placed on the National Register of Historic Places on October 4, 1990. Since none of the surviving structures have been properly buttressed, take care when exploring in and around them.

Over 100 years ago, the promise of abundant game, rich pastures, and crystal clear waters lured hearty homesteaders to the lush, albeit isolated, meadows of this valley. These pioneers made their livelihood primarily in cattle ranching and timber harvesting. As a result of the depression of the 1930s and the declining price of cattle and timber in the 1950s, many of those early pioneers were forced to sell their homesteads. Some just picked up and left. The result: individual homesteads were consolidated and sold. The Holnholz family bought what is today Homestead Meadows. In 1978 the U.S. Forest Service purchased the land and made it available for public use.

From the junction of Forest Road 119 and Homestead Meadows, take the left fork and begin your last 1.6 miles to your vehicle at Pierson Park. Having traveled along roads that once felt the weight of a "wagon load" and whose dusty sands tasted the fears and dreams in a cattle farmer's sweat, we mountain bikers may begin to appreciate the tougher climbs, welcome the narrower descents, and relish in the harrowing escapes that make up a day in the saddle.

## Ride Information

### 🌐 Trail Contacts:

**Colorado Bicycling Adventures,** Estes Park, CO; (970) 586-4241 or *www.coloradobicycling.com* – *they also run mountain bike tours*

### 🕐 Schedule:

June to October

### ❓ Local Information:

**Roosevelt National Forest,** Estes Park Ranger Station, Estes Park, CO; (970) 586-3440 • **Estes Park Chamber of Commerce,** Estes Park, CO; (970) 586-4431 or 1-800-44-ESTES

### 📍 Local Events/Attractions:

**Rocky Mountain National Forest:** (970) 586-1333 *(pre-recorded message)*; (970) 586-1206 *(general information)*; For additional information or correspondence, please write to Superintendent, Rocky Mountain National Park, Estes Park, CO 80517; For backcountry permit information: During the summer months, permits cost $10. Reservations are recommended. For reservations or bivouac permits call (970) 586-1242.

### 🚲 Local Bike Shops:

**Colorado Bicycling Adventures,** Estes Park, CO; (970) 586-4241 or *www.coloradobicycling.com*

### 🅽 Maps:

**USGS maps:** Allens Park, CO; Panorama Peak, CO; Raymond, CO • **Trails Illustrated maps:** #101, Cache La Poudre and Big Thompson, CO; #200 Rocky Mountain National Park, CO • **Boulder County Mountain Bike Map by ZIA Maps** – *available at many bicycle shops*

## The Homestead Act of 1862

Much of America's expansion West relied upon the willingness of pioneers to pick up their lives and their meager belongings and resettle in the rugged, unfenced, and unbroken lands leading west. The incentive to draw these people west had to be either money or land. Well, the government owned plenty of land.

Under the Homestead Act of 1862, Congress encouraged expansion to the west by opening up its public lands to agricultural settlement. Contrary to what you might imagine, homesteads were not just given to any Joe with a traveling bone. There were qualifications to meet—albeit rather inclusive qualifications.

An individual had to be a United States citizen—or at least intend to become one. He or she had to be older than 21 years of age and own no more than 159 acres of land—not a great problem for most Americans. And that's it. You're qualified! But here's the rub. To acquire title to the property, you had to build a house within five years, occupy the land for at least six months out of the year, make an income related to the property, and cultivate a portion of the land—then it's yours...to buy. Yes, after six months you held the option to buy the land for $1.25 an acre—not a bad deal. After you homesteaded the land for five years, the title would be granted in full for the mere filing fee of $15—not quite the deal you had in mind, but still pretty darn cheap.

Under the Homestead Act of 1862, Homesteaders could acquire as much as 320 acres. This program ended in 1976 in all states except Alaska—which continued its program until 1986.

Inside the Cherry Tree.

# Sourdough Trail

## Ride Summary

The Sourdough Trail skirts the fringes of the beautiful Indian Peaks Wilderness Area. The drive alone from Boulder to the trailhead is reason enough to head for the Sourdough Trail. While travelling along the Boulder Canyon, multi-sport adventurers can stop to enjoy great climbing and hiking opportunities, before continuing on Colorado's famed Peak-to-Peak Highway. Once on the trail, however, the fun really starts. The Sourdough Trail is almost entirely covered beneath a thick forest canopy, providing cool, shaded relief the whole ride through. Although the climb to Brainard Lake is challenging (but enjoyable), the descent is what you ride it for. A fast and smooth descent through a thick emerald forest will have you screaming: "There's no place like here and now."

## Ride Specs

**Start:** Sourdough Trailhead off of County Road 116, (the road to the University of Colorado Research Station)

**Length:** 12.2-mile out-and-back (with an optional 13.2-mile loop)

**Approximate Riding Time:** Advanced Riders, 2-2½ hours; Intermediate Riders, 3-3½ hours

**Technical Difficulty Rating:** Technically moderate due to a relatively smooth trail with little in the way of rocks. There are, however, a few switchbacks that make the riding moderately technical.

**Physical Difficulty Rating:** Physically moderate to challenging due to the extended climbing to Brainard Lake Road

**Terrain:** Singletrack, plus some paved and dirt road if optional loop is taken

**Elevation Gain:** 2,284 feet

**Nearest Town:** Ward, CO

**Other Trail Users:** Hikers, campers, skiers, and snowshoers

**Canine Compatibility:** Dog friendly

## Getting There

**From Boulder:** Drive west on Canyon Boulevard to the town of Nederland. Canyon Boulevard will eventually become a single-lane highway (CO 119), winding its way through the steep-walled Boulder Canyon. Before reaching Nederland, you'll drive alongside Barker Reservoir and be offered stunning views of Eldora Ski Resort. From Nederland, take CO 72 east (a.k.a. the Peak-to-Peak Highway) toward Ward for 7.5 miles until seeing the sign for the University of Colorado Research Station on the right side of the road. Turn left immediately after the sign onto CR 116 and drive another half of a mile. The trailhead is on the right. *DeLorme: Colorado Atlas & Gazetteer.* Page 29, D-6

The Sourdough Trail is one of Boulder County's last remaining single-track routes and one of its most popular. It's located just half a mile west of the majestic Peak-to-Peak Highway, between the historic tungsten and gold mining towns of Nederland and Ward. The trail brings together rolling climbs with a number of narrowly negotiable switchbacks through densely mixed forests of lodgepole pine, Douglas fir, and aspen. The forest opens occasionally to reveal outstanding views of the Continental Divide above, the foothills of the Front Range below, and the Great Plains to the east. As you near the Peace Memorial Bridge, the canopy of the forest

flatters its Northwestern cousins by mimicking the lush woodland of Oregon and Washington. When many of the other trails in the foothills area turn sandy as the summer nears its end, the Sourdough Trail, owing to its superb tree coverage and high altitude, remains ideal with smooth-running, hard-packed singletrack.

The Sourdough Trail begins at 9,220 feet and stretches to a dizzying 10,280 feet, with an elevation gain of 1,240 feet. The trail provides some of the highest alpine mountain biking you'll find near Boulder and Denver. With elevations such as these, it's hard to believe that Sourdough's sinewy path skirts only the base of the Indian Peaks—a congeries of jagged mountain summits, ragged arêtes, windswept tundra uplands, and cirque glaciers. The range stretches southward for 27 miles and consti-

The general store at Ward.

## **Miles**Directions

**0.0 START** at the Sourdough trailhead.

**0.3** Crossing the footbridge begins a short climb through a thick pine forest

**1.4** After negotiating a challenging climb with a number of switchbacks, the forest opens and the trail continues under a stretch of power lines, offering views of the Peak-to-Peak Highway to the east—a good resting spot before attempting a short, technical section of trail.

**1.9** Arrive at a sign that reads "Sourdough Trail" and "Red Rock Trailhead." Follow the "Sourdough Trail."

**2.7** Cross the Peace Memorial Bridge.

**5.7** Sourdough Trail arrives at a trail intersection. Bearing left will take you to the Little Raven Ski Trail and Brainard Lake. Continuing

straight will deliver you to Brainard Lake Road via Sourdough Trail.

**6.1** Arrive at Brainard Lake Road. At the time of this writing, workers were clear-cutting the forest to create a cross-country ski trail. At this point, you can either bear right onto Brainard Lake Road and do the loop or simply backtrack to your vehicles, going the way you came. I suggest backtracking and enjoying the Sourdough's fast singletrack descent.

**To do the loop:** Turn north onto Brainard Lake Road and follow it to the Peak-to-Peak Highway where you'll ride west along the paved highway for 6.5 miles until once again arriving at CR 116. Turn right onto CR 116 and ride for another 0.5 miles to your parked vehicle.

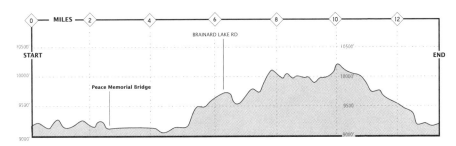

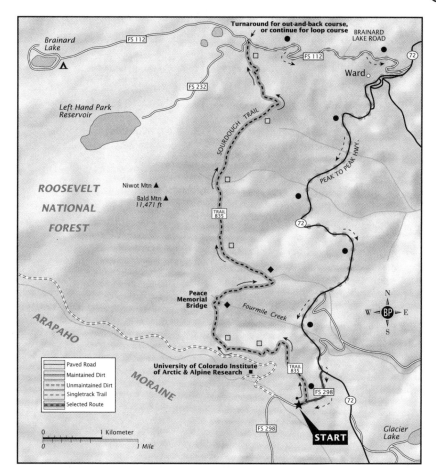

tutes the crest of the Continental Divide in this part of Colorado.

For years Ellsworth Bethel (1863-1925), a Denver high school botany teacher, enjoyed a view of the peaks from his classroom. Moved by them, Bethel and his students went about naming each of them after various Native American tribes from Colorado's history. Though Bethel didn't succeed with all of his suggestions, he did secure approval from the United States Board on Geographic Names for seven tribe names on seven Front Range peaks—which constitute the Indian Peaks.

South and North Arapaho Peaks (13,397 and 13,502 feet, respectively) are so called for the tribe whose name means "our people" and who are part of the Algonquin family of Native Americans. Mount Neva (12,814 feet) is the principal summit on the western skyline and is named in honor of an Arapaho Indian who once hunted in the area. Arikaree Peak (13,150 feet) recalls the story of the tribe who migrated to this area of Colorado from North Dakota after having been exiled by the United States Army in 1823 for attacking a party of fur traders heading up the Missouri River. Shoshoni Peak (12,967 feet) is named after the "Sentinels of the Rockies," a tribe who eventually settled themselves in naturally fortified mountain

# Ride Information

**Trail Contacts:**

**Happy Trails & Cool Beans Espresso,** Nederland, CO; (303) 258-3435 • **Boulder Area Trails Coalition (BATCO),** Boulder, CO; (303) 441-5262 • **Boulder Off-road Alliance (BOA),** Boulder, CO; (303) 441-5262

**Schedule:**
May to October

**Local Information:**

**Roosevelt National Forest,** Boulder Ranger District, Boulder, CO; (303) 444-6600 • **Boulder Area Trails Coalition (BATCO),** Boulder, CO; (303) 441-5262 • **Boulder Off-road Alliance (BOA),** Boulder, CO; (303) 441-5262 • **Front Range Mountain Bike Association,** Boulder, CO; (303) 674-4862 • **Trail Mix-Nederland Area, Nederland,** CO; (303) 258-3435

**Local Events/Attractions:**
**Eldora Mountain Resort,** Nederland, CO; 1-888-2-ELDORA or Denver Direct: (303)

440-8700 • **Peak-to-Peak Highway,** CO 7, CO 72 and CO 119 offer a beautiful drive, connecting Estes Park and the Black Hawk/Central City gambling district.

**Accommodations:**
**Sundance Lodge & Stables,** Nederland, CO; (303) 258-3797 or 1-800-817-3797

**Local Bike Shop:**
**Happy Trails & Cool Beans Espresso,** Nederland, CO; (303) 258-3435

**Maps:**
**USGS maps:** Ward, CO • *Trails Illustrated* map: #102, Boulder • *Boulder County Mountain Bike Map* by Mary Morrison and Jim Robb, Boulder, CO • **ZIA Maps** – *available at select Mountain Bike shops.*

positions from which they battled their enemies. Pawnee Peak (12,943 feet) honors the Pawnees of Eastern Colorado whose name translates to "horn." The Pawnees would stiffen their hair with berry juices and bear grease, making it stand up like a horn and would dare their enemies to touch their scalps. North and South Arapaho Peaks mark the southern end of the Indian Peaks Group and cradle the Arapaho Glacier, the largest snowfield in Colorado and the site of incredible backcountry skiing opportunities. The Arapaho Glacier furnishes about 10 percent of the city of Boulder's water supply.

The snowfields and glaciers of the Indian Peaks are some of the most studied alpine environments in the world. Just north of the Sourdough trailhead lies the University of Colorado's Institute of Arctic and Alpine Research. Modest and cramped huts—some of them secured to the mountainside with cables as thick as a man's wrists—form the offensive line of this world-renowned field station. Rustic buildings resembling early trapper homesteads are tucked among trees just below timberline, camouflaging modern laboratories which house state-of-the-art meteorological equipment. Studies and classes are conducted on topics such as acid precipitation, climatic patterns, and alpine flora.

Just a few miles from the Sourdough Trail, amid the cutting edge technology of the University of Colorado's Institute of Arctic and Alpine Research, are the small, one-time mining communities of Nederland and Ward. Just 12 miles from Boulder, Nederland was originally named Brownsville after its first founder. Its close proximity to Boulder prompted Brownsville to be called Middle Boulder. When a homesick Dutch Company bought the tungsten mill, the town was renamed Nederland—an archaic spelling for Netherlands. From 1900 to 1918, Nederland produced $23 million worth of tungsten, making Boulder County the largest tungsten producer in the United States. The town of Ward also boasts a prosperous mining heritage. During Ward's heyday (1860 to 1900), the mining district's population peaked at 5,000 and was the greatest mining camp in Northern Colorado. With five hotels, eight lodges, and seven saloons—not to mention the $5 million in gold reserves—Ward achieved a certain Vegas status among Colorado mining towns of the late 1800s and early 1900s.

From state-of-the-art weather tracking devices to tungsten mines, the Sourdough Trail hangs in the balance between the new and the old. As such, it is a pleasure to ride and an education to experience.

Sourdough Trail through a dense pine forest.

# Walker Ranch Loop

## Ride Summary

The Walker Ranch Loop is a popular ride among Boulder mountain bikers. It's initial singletrack descent to South Boulder Creek is amazing. During the spring thaw, South Boulder Creek is an impressive torrent of white water—an exhilarating sound to hear while riding along its banks. This ride weaves in and out of mixed conifer forests and offers a number of rocky singletrack sections. There is one section of the trail that requires you to portage down a steep cliff section—a section which some area riders consider the Walker Ranch Loop's best or worst feature. Mountain lions have been spotted in the area, so pay attention to the mountain lion warning signs.

## Ride Specs

**Start:** From the parking lot of Walker Ranch Open Space, at the South Boulder Creek Trailhead

**Length:** 8-mile loop – with other options to ride in Walker Ranch

**Approximate Riding Time:** Advanced Riders, 1 hour; Intermediate Riders, 2 hours

**Technical Difficulty Rating:** Technically moderate to challenging due to smooth, fast singletrack coupled with tough rocky sections. Note: There is a section of trail called "Cliff Conditions," which requires you to portage your bicycle down steep steps and over rock faces. Take care.

**Physical Difficulty Rating:** Physically challenging due to the variety of climbing involved

**Terrain:** Singletrack with patches of rocks and sand; improved dirt road

**Elevation Gain:** 1,369 feet

**Nearest Town:** Boulder, CO

**Other Trail Users:** Hikers, anglers, picnickers, equestrians, and climbers

**Canine Compatibility:** Dog friendly

## Getting There

**From Boulder:** Drive west on Baseline Road to Flagstaff Mountain Road. Baseline turns into Flagstaff after Chautauqa Auditorium (on your left). Stay on Flagstaff Mountain Road for about 8 miles, as it winds its way up and over Flagstaff Mountain. The road is crisscrossed heavily by hiking trails, so keep an eye out for pedestrians and cyclists. Following the signs for Walker Ranch, drive past the sign for the Flagstaff Mountain Amphitheater and Green Mountain Lodge, after roughly four miles. Flagstaff Mountain Road eventually "tops out" before descending down the other side of Flagstaff Mountain. Pass the Meyers Homestead Picnic Area and trailhead on the right. From there, Walker Ranch is roughly half of a mile on the left. Pull into the dirt road and drive up the short distance to the South Boulder Creek Trailhead and parking lot. *DeLorme: Colorado Atlas & Gazetteer.* Page 39, A-7 & Page 40, A-1

N ear Flagstaff Mountain and just west of Boulder is an area that evokes a love/hate relationship among many mountain bikers. Walker Ranch's cliff-like descent from the South Boulder Creek Trail to South Boulder Creek has the reputation of being one of the more hazardous portages in Colorado. This section of trail—loved for its uniqueness, hated for its vertigo-inducing incline—has summoned many a masochist. The portage notwithstanding, Walker Ranch offers some exciting singletrack mountain biking and beautiful scenery, set amidst a rich local history.

On the climb to Crescent Meadows.

In 1869, James Walker, with only $12 in his pocket and suffering from a life-threatening illness, traveled from Missouri to Boulder on the advice of his physician. Colorado's high, dry climate would prove to be Walker's salvation. His health dramatically improved. Having reclaimed his health, Walker, along with his wife Phoebe, would reclaim their lives together by filing a homestead claim to 160 acres in 1882.

By 1883, Walker Ranch—consisting of a ranch house, barn, blacksmith shop, root cellar, granary, smokehouse, springhouse, chicken and turkey houses, corn storage house, and pig barn—afforded James and Phoebe the self-sufficient lifestyle with which they both would eventually fall in love. With various corrals, fenced pastures, and 160 acres, Walker Ranch was one of the largest cattle ranches in this region and is listed on the National Register of Historic Places. Not bad for a sick tiger with only $12 to his name.

Today, posted signs of "mountain lion" territory greet the would-be mountain biker at the South Boulder Creek's trailhead. The route begins on the South Boulder Creek Trail, contouring to the south of Langridge Dyke and descending to Tom Davis Gulch and South Boulder Creek at mile 1.0. There are a number of great fly-fishing holes along this patch of the creek. The route to this point is fast on rock-riddled singletrack with varying patches of sand. A number of switchbacks and dips prevent the rider from going too fast. Once it reaches South Boulder Creek, the trail smoothes to soft forest singletrack blanketed with pine needles. Ride upstream to a footbridge that crosses the creek at mile 1.5, whereupon the trail divides. Bear left here and continue your ride. For those requiring a bit of a dip, riding straight ahead will deliver you to a cool wading pond about 50 yards up.

After bearing left, the trail climbs out of the drainage to the Crescent Meadows trailhead at mile 2.7, offering views of the Grande Western Railroad. The climb to Crescent Meadows is a grunt but one well worth undertaking. It climbs to 7,300 feet and offers a beautiful view of Gross Dam and snowcapped peaks to the west. Ride east on the Crescent Meadows Trail, as it parallels Eldorado Canyon State Park to the right. Mountain bikes are prohibited beyond the county boundary in Eldorado Canyon State Park.

This section of the route begins as a moderate descent through meadows awash with wildflowers and then becomes considerably steeper as it drops to South Boulder Creek. This may be the best section of the entire route. After dropping some big rocky hits, arrive at a sign at mile 4.8 that reads "Danger: Cliff Conditions." Dismount and carefully climb down the very technical terrain to South Boulder Creek. Once at its shores, scramble over the boulder field directly downstream, and head to the bridge that crosses the creek.

After crossing the bridge, the Crescent Meadows Trail connects with the Eldorado Canyon Trail. (Note: Mountain bikers are prohibited from entering Eldorado Canyon State Park via the Eldorado Canyon Trail from lower Walker Ranch.) Climbing through Martin Gulch, the Eldorado Canyon Trail intersects with the

## MilesDirections

**0.0 START** at the South Boulder Creek trailhead. As the trail contours south of Langridge Dyke, descend the switchbacks into Tom Davis Gulch, to South Boulder Creek.

**1.0** Descend to South Boulder Creek. Follow the creek upstream.

**2.7** Reach Crescent Meadows (7,300 feet). From here you can see Gross Dam due west.

**5.0** Reach the Cliff Area. Dismount and portage your bike down to South Boulder Creek carefully.

**6.1** Meet the junction of Columbine Gulch Trail and Crescent Meadows Trail. The Columbine Gulch Trail will return you to your

vehicles, but the trail is not recommended for bicycles. Continue straight to the Ethel Harold Picnic Area and trailhead for the Eldorado Canyon Trail.

**6.3** Reach the Ethel Harold Picnic Area and trailhead for the Eldorado Canyon Trail. Ride straight out of the parking lot and turn left onto Pika Road.

**7.6** Reach a stop sign and the intersection of Pika Road and Flagstaff Mountain Road. Bear left onto Flagstaff Mountain Road.

**8.0** Reach the South Boulder Creek trailhead and Walker Ranch parking lot. You're at your vehicle.

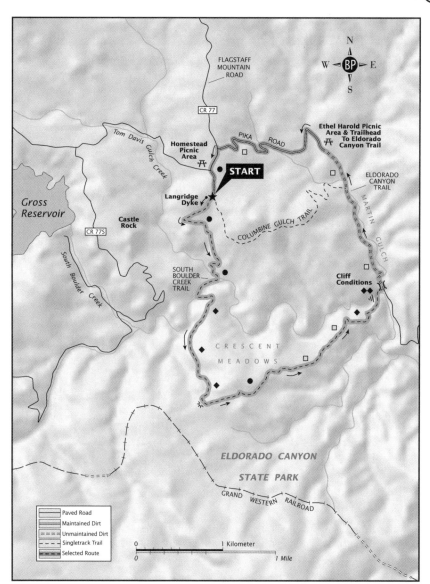

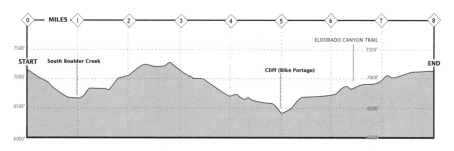

# Ride Information

### 🕐 Trail Contacts:
**Boulder County Parks and Open Space Department**, Boulder, CO; (303) 441-3950

### 🕐 Schedule:
May to October

### ❓ Local Information:
**Boulder Mountain Parks and Recreation**, Boulder, CO; (303) 441-3408 • **U.S. Forest Service**, Boulder District, Boulder, CO; (303) 444-6600 • **Boulder Convention and Visitors Bureau**, Boulder, CO; (303) 442-2911

### 💡 Local Events/Attractions:
**Walker Ranch Tours**. Contact: Boulder County Parks and Open Space Department, Boulder, CO; (303) 441-3950

### 👥 Organizations:
**International Mountain Biking Association (IMBA)**, Boulder, CO; (303) 545-9011 • **Boulder Bicycle Commuters**, Boulder, CO; (303) 499-7466 • **Boulder Off-Road Alliance**, Boulder, CO; (303) 447-9378 or (303) 441-5262 • **Boulder Old Wheelers**, Boulder, CO; (303) 444-0801

### 🚲 Local Bike Shops:
**University Bicycles**, Boulder, CO; (303) 444-4196 • **Full Cycle**, Boulder, CO; (303) 440-7771

### 🅝 Maps:
**USGS maps:** Eldorado Springs CO • **Walker Ranch:** Boulder County Parks and Open Space map • *Boulder County Mountain Bike Map*, by ZIA Maps – available at select mountain bike retailers

Columbine Gulch Trail at mile 6.1. Here you have the option of veering left onto the Columbine Gulch Trail and shortcutting over the 1.5-mile trail back to the South Boulder Creek trailhead and to your vehicle. Or, you can continue straight ahead to Pika Road, past Ethel Harold Picnic Area.

The Columbine Gulch Trail climbs for 400 feet via a number of steep switch-backs—testimony to this trail's designation as one "not recommended for mountain bikes." For those seeking the challenge of tough singletrack climbing, this part of the route, which ascends under thick forest cover, delivers all you'll ever want. For the spinners who prefer constant pedaling over intermittent singletrack, ride straight past the Columbine Gulch Trail to the Ethel Harold Picnic Area. Pass the gate, ride out of the parking lot, and intercept Pika Road to the left. Pika Road offers 1.3 miles of gradual "cool down" climbing before intersecting with Flagstaff Mountain Road. Turn left onto Flagstaff Mountain Road and ride to your vehicle atop the dirt road at the South Boulder Creek trailhead.

## Mountain Lions

The mountain lion (felis concolor)—sometimes called cougar, panther, or puma—is one of North America's biggest cats and inhabits much of Colorado, including the Front Range, residing in areas of piñon pine, juniper, mountain mahogany, ponderosa pine, and oak brush. For this reason, it's not uncommon to see mountain lion warning signs at many mountain bike trailheads. Although encounters are rare, due to the big cat's calm, quiet, and elusive nature, they are on the rise as a consequence, in part, of increased mountain biking in lion habitat. In fact, a standoff involving a mountain lion and a mountain biker occurred on October 22, 1997 at one of Boulder County's most popular mountain biking areas, Walker Ranch.

Varying from seven to eight feet in length and 90 to 150 pounds, the mountain lion is much larger than other wild cat species in Colorado. According to Division wildlife experts, a mountain biker may run a higher-than-normal risk of being attacked. A mountain biker's lowered head posture may spark a lion's curiosity. Also, to a lion, a mountain biker riding through the forest may look like fleeing prey, stimulating its predatory attack response. When bicycling in mountain lion habitat, keep the following suggestions in mind.

- Ride in groups
- Make noise during times of prime mountain lion activity—dawn and dusk.

If you should encounter a mountain lion:
- Never approach a lion, but keep your bicycle between yourself and the lion.
- Stay calm. Speak calmly but firmly to the animal.
- Back away from the lion slowly, facing the lion and standing upright. Do not turn and run and chance stimulating the lion's predatory instincts.
- Make yourself larger in appearance: raise your arms, open your jacket if you're wearing one.
- If the lion becomes aggressive, throw stones or branches, trying not to crouch down too often or turn your back.
- If the lion attacks, fight back and avoid falling to the ground.

To report mountain lion sightings or encounters, immediately contact the Colorado Division of Wildlife. Their hours are Monday to Friday, 8 A.M. to 5 P.M. Here are the regional offices.

Northeast Region and Denver
Service Center
6060 Broadway
Denver, CO 80216
(303) 291-7230

West Region and Grand Junction
Service Center
711 Independent Avenue
Grand Junction, CO 81505
(970) 248-7175

Southeast Region and Colorado Springs Service Center
2126 North Weber Street
Colorado Springs, CO 80907
(719) 473-2945

For more information on mountain lions, refer to Harley G. Shaw's excellent book Soul Among Lions: The Cougar as Peaceful Adversary, 1989, Johnson Books, Boulder CO; or Sandra Chisholm Robinson's The Wonder Series: Mountain Lion, A Story and Activities, Denver Museum of Natural History.

# 40

# White Ranch

## Ride Summary

White Ranch offers grueling climbs, steep and narrow descents, and tight switchbacks. The route described here includes all of these features but is still only a small sampling of what White Ranch has to offer. With steep grades, loose rock and plastic erosion bars strewn across the trail, the initial climb from the parking lot is one of the toughest on the Front Range. From there, riders are offered fast descents along precipitously sloping terrain and through mixed conifer and piñon forests. Though close to Golden, Boulder, and Denver, White Ranch is seldom crowded, largely due to its being viewed as a more advanced area to mountain bike.

## Ride Specs

**Start:** From the parking lot off Pine Ridge Road
**Length:** 8.4-mile loop – with many options to add and/or subtract from this distance.
**Approximate Riding Time:** Advanced Riders, 1½ hours; Intermediate Riders, 2-2½ hours
**Technical Difficulty Rating:** Technically moderate to challenging due to its steep and rocky climbs and descents with many tight switchbacks
**Physical Difficulty Rating:** Physically challenging due to the climbing involved in very exposed and hot terrain
**Terrain:** Singletrack and doubletrack which runs over very rocky terrain, as well as very smooth, forested terrain
**Elevation Gain:** 1,835 feet
**Nearest Town:** Golden, CO
**Other Trail Users:** Hikers, equestrians, campers, picnickers, and marksmen
**Canine Compatibility:** Dog friendly – but bring plenty of water for the pooch

## Getting There

**From Boulder:** Drive south on CO 93 (Broadway) for 17.4 miles (from the intersection with Canyon) until you see the "White Ranch Open Space" sign to your left. Before the sign turn right onto 56th Avenue. Drive approximately one mile on 56th Avenue before turning right onto Pine Ridge Road. Pine Ridge Road will lead you to the White Ranch parking lot. *DeLorme: Colorado Atlas & Gazetteer.* Page 40, B-1

Down the Longhorn Trail.

Once a cattle operation, today White Ranch is a 3,040-acre Open Space Park. Taking its name from a local homesteader, Paul R. White, the park includes roughly 18 miles of multi-use trails. Only a half-mile northwest of Golden, White Ranch offers mountain bikers living in the Denver metro area a great escape from the city grind.

The majority of the park is exposed, particularly the east side which traverses a steep slope, and so for this reason, White Ranch receives ample amounts of sunlight—making it one of the first mountain bike areas of Colorado's higher foothills region to open for the mountain biking season. Because of the jump on the season,

Racing man's best friend down Belcher Hill Trail.

White Ranch tends to get sandy toward the end of summer. Because of the exposure, you'd be well advised to bring plenty of water with you while riding the Ranch.

From advanced riding to novice riding, White Ranch offers it all. Rugged and rocky steep climbs challenge even the best of riders, while smooth and gentle meadow shots tempt weary neophytes to release the death grip on the brakes. From the many vantage points in the park, mountain bikers are offered sweeping views of the Great Plains and the Denver skyline.

The first part of the route ascends a steep, sandy and rocky doubletrack. Even the best riders will feel the burn after 2.4 miles of this kind of climbing. Luckily, the singletrack descent of Mustang Trail to Longhorn Trail offers a brief respite. After passing the continuation of the Longhorn Trail and continuing to climb up the Shorthorn Trail, the route winds its way through a dense pine forest. The terrain of the singletrack here is narrow and smooth. The trail eventually exits the forest and winds its way north along an east-facing slope.

## MilesDirections

**0.0 START** from the parking lot at the trail-head of Belcher Hill Trail. Pass through two gates and cross Van Bibber Creek via a foot-bridge within the first half-mile. Please close both gates behind you and begin climbing up Belcher Hill Trail after crossing the creek.

**1.8** Arrive at the junction of Longhorn (to your right) and Belcher Hill trails. You will eventually return via Longhorn Trail, but for now, forgo turn-ing right onto Longhorn Trail and continue pedal-ing west up Belcher Hill Trail. To your east, views of the Denver skyline sprawl out before you.

**2.4** Belcher Hill Trail intersects with Mustang Trail. Here is a good place to rest, as your initial climb has ended—not to mention there's a bench seat to sit on. Hang a right, now descend-ing on the singletrack of the Mustang Trail.

**3.0** Arrive at the junction of Mustang and Longhorn trails. Veer left onto the Longhorn Trail, which within a quarter of a mile "Y"s: Longhorn to your right, Shorthorn to your left. Continue left and begin climbing, now on the Shorthorn Trail.

**4.3** Arrive at the northern junction of Shorthorn and Longhorn trails. Bear right onto the Longhorn Trail.

**6.0** Arrive at the southern junction of Shorthorn and Longhorn trails. Bear left, con-tinuing your ride on Longhorn. Within three-tenths of a mile you will once again arrive at the junction of Mustang and Longhorn. Continue on Longhorn for another tenth of a mile before arriving at the junction of Longhorn and Belcher Hill trails. Veer left onto Belcher Hill Trail and descend—along what previously you had climbed—back to the parking lot.

**8.4** Arrive at the parking lot.

## Ride Information

**Trail Contacts:**
Jefferson County Open Space, Golden, CO; (303) 271-5925

**Schedule:**
April to November

**Local Information:**
Jefferson County Open Space, Golden, CO; (303) 271-5925

**Local Events/Attractions:**
**Coors Brewing Company Tours**, Monday-Saturday, 10 A.M.-4 P.M., Golden, CO (303); 279-6565 • **Hakushika Sake Tours**, Monday-Friday, 10 A.M.-3 P.M., Golden, CO; (303) 278-0161

**Local Bike Shops:**
**Foothills Ski & Bike,** Golden, CO; (303) 526-2036

**Maps:**
**USGS maps:** Golden, CO; Ralston Buttes, CO • **Trails Illustrated map:** # 102 • **White Ranch Park Map**, Jefferson County Open Space – *available at the trailhead*

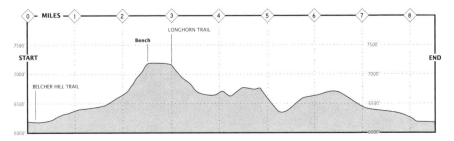

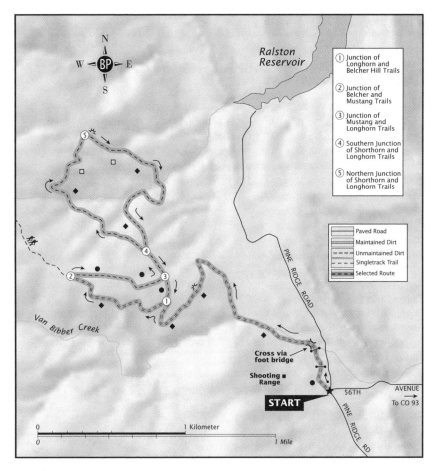

Along the slope you'll find patches of what is more commonly referred to as Indian T.P. (toilet paper). Botanists would probably rather you call the plant by its proper name, mullein (also spelled "mullen"). The plant's wide leaves account for the nickname. Tea made from brewing mullein leaves is said to relieve respiratory problems—a great thing to know when riding at higher altitudes.

At mile 4.3, the northern junction of Shorthorn and Longhorn trails marks the beginning of your return. The most challenging part of this entire route begins once you turn onto the Longhorn Trail. At mile 5.0, the route hits a steep and rocky descent, followed by tight switchbacks and big drop-offs, eventually delivering you to the bottom of a steep-walled drainage. What follows is a steep and rocky ascent up the other side, with tight switchbacks. From here, it's a fast race back to the Belcher Hill Trail and an even faster race back to the parking lot.

With elevations raging from 6,150 feet to 8,000 feet (atop Belcher Hill), White Ranch offers some tough climbing but rewards you with bombing singletrack. One note of caution: because of the many narrow trails leading around blind curves, it's likely that you may run into someone. Control your speed while descending.

# The Hogback:
## Dakota Ridge & Red Rocks Trail

## Ride Summary

The Hogback is a popular mountain bike ride within easy reach of Denver or Golden. From its highest points, you can see stunning views of Red Rocks Amphitheater. The ride demands sound legs and technical skills. With some of the most technically challenging terrain in the Front Range, the Hogback is not for the faint of heart. Its rocky drop-offs and narrow single-track, tightening atop a steep ridge of tilted strata, have left many cyclists crying "mommy." Once you descend from the hogback, the ride continues within Red Rocks Park and among its beautiful sanguine rocks.

## Ride Specs

**Start:** From the Village Walk parking lot in the Matthews/Winters Park

**Length:** 6.5-mile loop

**Approximate Riding Time:** Advanced Riders, 1 hour; Intermediate Riders, 2 hours

**Technical Difficulty Rating:** Technically moderate to challenging due to steep, sandy drop-offs and climbs.

**Physical Difficulty Rating:** Physically moderate to challenging due to some short, but steep climbs.

**Terrain:** Singletrack, dirt road, and paved highway. The terrain is very rocky and sandy in spots. This is a good early season ride, as it tends to get too sandy after long dry spells. Not recommended as an autumn ride.

**Elevation Gain:** 1,129 feet

**Nearest Town:** Golden, CO

**Other Trail Users:** Hikers, marksmen, concert-goers, and picnickers

**Canine Compatibility:** Dog-friendly—but watch out for the rattlesnakes

## Getting There

**From Denver:** Head west on I-70 to Exit 259, following signs to Morrison. Exit at 259 and turn left, driving under I-70. Now on CO 26, turn right into Matthews/Winters Park, marked by a brown sign on the right side of the road. Park in the Village Walk parking lot. *DeLorme: Colorado Atlas & Gazetteer.* Page 40 C-1

D akota Ridge is part of the Dakota Group, a 14-mile long ridge of steeply sloping, tilted strata—otherwise known as a "hogback." The ridge extends from Golden to Roxborough Park and is comprised of Lower Cretaceous rock units. Formed roughly 66 million years ago, the hogback is the result of the upward thrust of the Rocky Mountains' Front Range. Due to the abundance of Jurassic dinosaur fossils this area has yielded, the section of the Dakota Hogback stretching from Interstate 70 to the town of Morrison has recently been renamed "Dinosaur Ridge," a geologically famous national landmark.

Dinosaur discoveries near Morrison date back as early as 1877 when Arthur Lakes, a part-time professor at what later became the Colorado School of Mines, found a stegosaurus vertebra with a 33-inch circumference. Aside from offering up the first dinosaur fossils found in the western United States, many of the discoveries near Morrison were the first of their kind.

With fossilized remains of Jurassic dinosaurs, millions of years old, tucked in its geological folds, the hogback invites the mountain biker not with the terrors of a *Jurassic Park* but with a subtlety that whispers the secrets of the ages. Riders begin their journey with an instant lung-buster to the top of the hogback and onto the Dakota Ridge Trail. From this knife-like ridge, sweeping views of the High Plains lie to the east, marked distinctly by Green Mountain and Denver. The Rocky Mountains lie to the west, with Mount Morrison and Red Rocks Park in plain view. The crest is marked by plentiful patches of sand and rock, remnants of a 135 million-year-old sea moving westward across Colorado.

## **Miles**Directions

**0.0 START** at the Village Walk parking lot in the Matthews/Winters Park. Ride back out of the parking lot and cross CO 26. Begin ascending the rock and sand-laden dirt road to the top of Hogback Park.

**0.3** Bear right at the gate onto the Dakota Ridge Trail. Do not ride beyond this gate, as there is a firing range on the other side of the hogback.

**0.7** Reach the top of the hogback. To your right is I-70, leading west into the mountains. There are some big drop-offs from here until you reach a killer, but short climb.

**1.0** Reach the killer, but short climb. What makes this climb difficult is its steep pitch coupled with large waterbars strewn across the trail.

**2.2** The trail comes to a "Y" intersection. Hang a left. (By continuing straight, you end up having to duck under a gate to get back onto the main trail.) Ride down the trail with

caution. Arrive at a staircase and bear right onto the paved road (Dinosaur Ridge). Ride to where the road curves to the right and cross over the cement barricade to rejoin the trail on your left. Climb briefly and then descend sharply.

**3.0** After riding down a fast singletrack, the trail once again lets out onto a paved road (CR 93). Be cautious here and stay in control, as the trail leads you right onto the road. Bear right here again and follow signs for the Red Rocks Trail. Cross the paved road and hang an immediate left onto an access into the Red Rocks Park. Pedal for 0.2 miles and bear right onto the singletrack Red Rocks Trail.

**4.2** Reach the junction of Morrison Slide Trail and Red Rocks Trail. Bear right here, continuing on the Red Rocks Trail.

**6.5** Arrive back at the Village Walk parking lot in the Matthews/Winters Park.

400-foot "Creation Rock" on the left, "Shiprock" to the right, and "Rock of Mnemosyne" in the center.

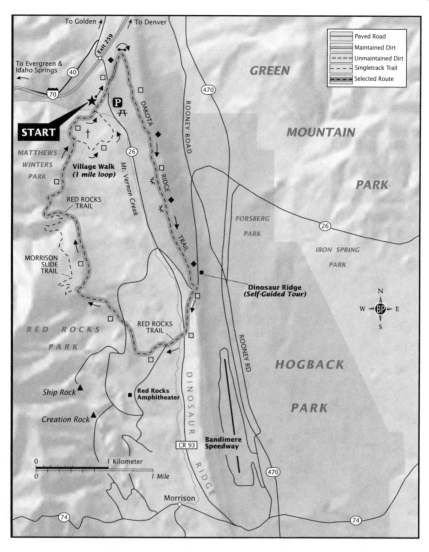

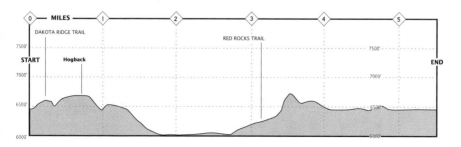

The trail snakes atop the hogback for roughly two miles. Rattlesnakes are occasionally spotted here, though they typically stick to the rock piles and tall grasses that dot Dakota Ridge. It's recommended that riders carry—and know how to use—a snake bite kit. If you stick to the trails, it's unlikely you'll have an encounter, but better safe than sorry. The southern end of the Dakota Ridge Trail delivers some of the trickiest rocky sections found along the entire route. At mile 2.1 there's a rock face embedded in the ground. The line to the left requires deft technical skills, particularly since it cuts sharply to the right along the edge of a big drop-off. The center line is attractive but delivers a strong blow to your front tire, not to mention your ego.

Ride for another mile before entering Red Rocks Park, en route to the Red Rocks Trail. The town of Morrison opened the park as "The Garden of the Titans" in 1906. Students studying mythology at nearby Episcopal College imagined the park to be the Titans' playground and ascribed fitting names to each rock formation.

One of the smooth tracks of the Hogback.

## Ride Information

**Trail Contacts:**
Jefferson County Open Space, Golden, CO; (303) 271-5925

**Schedule:**
April to November

**Local Information:**
Jefferson County Open Space, Golden, CO; (303) 271-5925, fax (303) 271-5955

**Local Events/Attractions:**
Dinosaur Ridge, Morrison, CO; (303) 697-3466 or www.dinoridge.org • **Red Rocks Park and Amphitheater** (303) 697-6486 or www.red-rocks.com • **Bandimere Speedway,** Morrison, CO; (303) 697-6001

**Restaurants:**
The Fort, Morrison, CO; (303) 697-4771 – specializes in big game entrées

**Organizations:**
Friends of Dinosaur Ridge, Morrison, CO; (303) 697-3466 or www.dinoridge.org

**Local Bike Shops:**
Foothills Ski & Bike, Golden, CO; (303) 526-2036

**Maps:**
USGS maps: Morrison, CO • Matthews/Winters Park Map: Jefferson County Open Space – available at the Village Walk trailhead

To the north of the stage of the Red Rocks Amphitheater stands the 400-foot monolith Creation Rock. Facing Creation Rock is Shiprock, so named because it looks like a sinking ship. The formation behind the stage is the Rock of Mnemosyne, named for the Greek goddess of song and memory. Iron oxide deposits, left over from the vast inland sea that once engulfed Red Rocks Park, hardened as the ancient waters receded and are responsible for the many shades of red.

Today, Red Rocks Park is best known for its naturally formed amphitheater. Nestled between two 400-foot high red sandstone formations, the amphitheater provides near perfect acoustics. The 9,200-seat theater provides concert-goers with an intimate listening experience—complete with a 30-mile panoramic view of hued plains and the stunning Denver city lights.

Once on the Red Rocks Trail, be sure to keep bearing right (north) at all trail crossings. The Red Rocks Trail offers rolling hills and mild climbs, mixed with some smooth descents. At mile 5.8 the Red Rocks Trail once again intersects with the Morrison Slide Trail at Cherry Gulch. Taking the Morrison Slide Trail on your left for 1.2 miles adds about a half-mile and some more climbing to your route. Continue on the Red Rocks Trail until you reach the intersection of the Village Walk. This is a one-mile loop that will lead you back to your vehicles, whichever way you decide to turn.

# Waterton Canyon

## Ride Summary

Waterton Canyon is a favorite trail among Denver-area residents. As such, it may be crowded during the weekends. The trail begins on a wide, dirt service road, as it travels through the canyon. Following the South Platte River, this section of the trail offers a mellow cruise, a great family ride. The trail, however, becomes increasingly more difficult, with steeper climbs and moderate switchbacks, as one nears the trailhead and beginning of the 470-mile Colorado Trail. Reaching this junction of the Colorado Trail and the Roxborough Connection, riders continue on the Roxborough Connection. Note: the beginning of the Roxborough Connection is very thick and overgrown, so control your speed. This section of trail offers a screaming singletrack descent, complete with steeps and creek crossings, before letting out into Waterton Canyon.

## Ride Specs

**Start:** From the trailhead of the Colorado Trail in Waterton Canyon

**Length:** 17.5-mile loop—with options to continue on the Colorado Trail. (Note: if you do decide to continue on the Colorado Trail, special arrangements for your return must be considered, as these routes will not lead you back to your vehicle at the mouth of Waterton Canyon.)

**Approximate Riding Time:** Advanced Riders, 1½ hours; Intermediate Riders, 2-2½ hours

**Technical Difficulty Rating:** Technically moderate. The first six miles offer an easy, scenic ride along the South Platte River on an improved dirt road. The singletrack of the Roxborough Connection offers some tight ascending switchbacks, with sudden tight twists along the trail on the descent.

**Physical Difficulty Rating:** Physically moderate. Although there is no significant elevation gain, there are a number of tough steep climbs.

**Terrain:** Singletrack, doubletrack, and improved dirt road. The singletrack and doubletrack offer a variety of terrain: sand, rocks, and softened forest growth.

**Elevation Gain:** 1,902 feet

**Nearest Town:** Littleton, CO

**Other Trail Users:** Hikers, equestrians, anglers, campers, and picnickers

**Canine Compatibility:** Not dog friendly. Dogs are not allowed in the canyon because they may contaminate drinking water, as well as disturb the resident herd of big horn sheep.

## Getting There

**From Denver:** Take I-25 south to Exit 207B. Exit and drive south on U.S. 85, which will "Y" shortly after exiting I-25; stay to your left. Take U.S. 85 south for 10 miles until you reach CO 470. Veer right onto CO 470, and head west. Drive west on CO 470 for a few miles before exiting at Wadsworth Boulevard, following signs for Waterton Canyon. After exiting at Wadsworth, bear left, driving under CO 470 and pick up CO 121 south. Drive south on CO 121 for roughly 4.5 miles before turning left into Waterton Canyon State Park. The parking lot will be on your left. ***DeLorme: Colorado Atlas & Gazetteer***. Page 50, A 1-2

Negotiating a switchback up the Colorado Trail.

If you're looking for testament to Denver's metropolis status, you need only look to the Denver Broncos, the Colorado Rockies, the Denver Nuggets, and the Colorado Avalanche, but that wouldn't present the whole picture. Consider the $4.3 billion Denver International Airport, the $76 million refurbished Central Library, and the yearly loss of 90,000 acres of farmland to development, and you've got one *hell* of a megalopolis. But what distinguishes Denver from other large U.S. cities isn't its sports teams, or even the fact that its airport rests on a site larger than Manhattan, but rather that it's only minutes away from some of the sweetest stretches of single-track in all of Colorado.

The eastern-most trailhead of the 470-mile Colorado Trail begins on an improved dirt road in Waterton Canyon. Following the former railroad bed of the Denver, South Park, and Pacific railroads through Waterton Canyon, the first six miles of this route are a mellow cruise along the South Platte River—admittedly, not the most excitingly technical. What the first six miles through Waterton Canyon lacks in technical challenge, it delivers in natural beauty and historical significance.

On July 6, 1820, Stephen H. Long (remembered in the naming of Long's Peak) led an expedition to the mouth of what is now Waterton Canyon. As a member of the U.S. Engineering Corps, Long was instructed to find the headwaters of the Platte, Arkansas, and Red rivers. His expedition camped at the site where the South Platte River emerges from the mountains. His camp would become the town of Waterton, and even later the location of the Denver Union Water Company, forbear of the Denver Water Department—the largest water district for the entire Front Range.

## **Miles**Directions

**0.0 START** at the parking lot of Waterton Canyon State Park. Ride back out of the parking lot and cross the road. The Colorado Trail sign marks the beginning of the ride into Waterton Canyon. Follow the trail around as it weaves itself onto the improved dirt road and into Waterton Canyon.

**2.2** Pass an abandoned mine to your left.

**3.3** Reach Marston Diversion Dam.

**4.3** Cross Mill Gulch Bridge.

**6.1** Reach Strontia Springs Dam and Reservoir. Beware the big horn sheep that descend from the tall canyon walls, making their way to the Colorado Trail. A herd of 20 to 35 bighorn sheep lives in the canyon, remaining at low elevation all year.

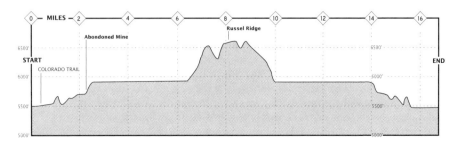

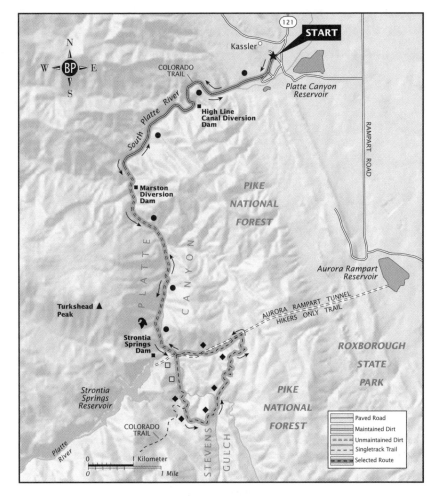

**6.3** Reach the junction of the Roxborough Connection and the Colorado Trail. Here is where the route lets out. For now, keep heading west, ascending straight on.

**6.6** Reach the start of the Colorado Trail singletrack, on the left side of the road. From this point, the maintained dirt road is closed to public use.

**8.0** Reach the top of Russell Ridge, the route's high point. At this point, the Colorado Trail continues heading southwest all the way to Durango. Instead, bear left (east) onto the singletrack marked by the Roxborough State Park sign.

**10.3** Here the singletrack "T"s. Bear left and head toward Waterton Canyon. This way will lead you back to the improved dirt road on which you began your ride, just above the Strontia Springs Dam in Waterton Canyon. (Bearing right will lead you to the Roxborough State Park and Visitor Center— however, this section of trail is off limits to bikes.)

**11.2** You're back on the improved dirt road of the Colorado Trail in Waterton Canyon. From here, bear right and return to your vehicle the way you came.

305

# Ride Information

### 🌀 Trail Contacts:
**Pike National Forest**, South Platte Ranger District, Morrison, CO; (303) 275-5610

### 🕐 Schedule:
Although Waterton Canyon is open daily from 4 A.M. to 9 P.M. year-round, riding the Roxborough Connection may only be reasonable between the months of May and October.

### ❓ Local Information:
**Colorado Division of Wildlife**, Denver, CO; (303) 297-1192 • **South Platte Ranger District**, Morrison, CO; (303) 275-5610 • **Chatfield State Park**, Littleton, CO; (303) 791-7275 • **U.S. Army Corps of Engineers**, Omaha District, Tri-Lakes Project Office, Littleton, CO; (303) 979-4120 • **The Colorado Trail Foundation**, American Mountaineering Center, Golden, CO; (303) 384-3729, ext. 113 • **Roxborough State Park**, Littleton, CO; (303) 973-3959 • **Pike National Forest**, Pueblo, CO; (719) 545-8737

### 💡 Local Events/Attractions:
**Roxborough State Park**, Littleton, CO (303); 973-3959 • **Chatfield State Park**, Littleton, CO; (303) 791-7275

### 👫 Organizations:
**Chatfield Environmental Education Resource System (CHEERS)**, a group of agencies within Chatfield Basin that share educational opportunities and deliver recreational resources for residents. Contact the Chatfield State Park, Littleton, CO; (303) 791-7275

### 📖 Other Resources:
*The Colorado Trail: The Official Guidebook* by Randy Jacobs—publisher, Westcliffe Publishing, Englewood, CO

### 🚲 Local Bike Shops:
There are none within the immediate vicinity, but the Denver-metro area offers a wide assortment of bike shops.

### 🗺 Maps:
**USGS maps**: Kassler, CO; Platte Canyon, CO • *Trails Illustrated* **map**: 135 Deckers & Rampart Range, CO • **Waterton Canyon Map**, Denver Water—available at the trailhead or through the U.S. Army Corps of Engineers; (303) 979-4120

---

The initial six miles through Waterton Canyon is a hydrologist's dream. In 1912, the Kassler Treatment Plant, located at the mouth of Waterton Canyon, became the first English slow-sand water filtration plant west of the Mississippi. At the time, the English slow-sand water filtration system was the newest technological advancement in the area of water filtration. Only two other towns could boast being equipped with this latest filtration process: Albany, New York, and Ashland, Wisconsin (on Lake Superior).

The process at the Kassler Treatment Plant involved diverting water from the South Platte River into large beds of sand. These beds can still be seen today. Underneath these sand beds were perforated pipes. The English slow-sand water filtration process allowed for water to flow through the sand and into the pipes.

As the water sifted through the sand, debris and sediment would collect on the sand's top layer. Once the filtered water reached the perforated pipes, chlorine would be added, and delivered to Denver as drinking water. From time to time, the top layer of these sand beds would have to be skimmed to keep them clean, a very labor-intensive process. In 1979 the plant became a national Waterworks Landmark. One hundred years earlier, the High Line Canal (just over a mile into the canyon), constructed by an English-Scottish land development company, was supplying irrigation water to plains settlements east of Denver. Marking the start of the High Line Canal, the original rock and timber diversion dam is visible from the trail.

About three miles from the trailhead and the mouth of the canyon, the Platte Canyon Intake Dam and the Marston Diversion routes South Platte and Blue River water to Marston Reservoir. At mile 6.1 the Strontia Springs Dam skies 243 feet above the South Platte stream bed and diverts water into a 3.4 mile-long tunnel under the mountains to the Foothills Water Treatment Plant. This massive tunnel project, and others like it in Colorado, is necessary because the state only receives 14 inches of annual precipitation. An even larger tunnel (23 miles long and 10 feet wide) connects the South Platte River with a Dillon reservoir. This particular conduit, bored through the Front Range, is one of the world's longest such tunnels.

As you head west from the Strontia Springs Dam, the road begins to climb. Within a mile, the Colorado Trail's singletrack will begin to your left. From here the trail rises out of the canyon to Russell Ridge (6,560 feet). The singletrack to this point offers a moderately challenging climb to the top. Among this section's highlights are smooth-running singletrack, thick ponderosa pine forests, and switchbacks (which deserve special attention). Intermediate riders can manage the switchbacks with careful balance and control, while advanced riders can spin their way to the top with minimal effort. The last switchback, which breaks right before summating Russell Ridge, is beset with rocks. Keep spinning, don't forget to smile, and you'll make it with relative ease.

Atop the ridge, the Colorado Trail will continue southwest to Durango. To begin your return of the Waterton Canyon route, you'll have to turn off of the Colorado Trail at this point and follow the sign marking Roxborough State Park.

The singletrack of this section of trail is sweet. Thick overgrowth at the section's beginning makes for very narrow and tight paths. The trail weaves its way through cool forests and offers riders a number of screams. One such scream comes at mile 8.2. The singletrack descent is steep and narrow as it hugs the slope of the ridge. For an added element of fear, a tree at this section's bottom welcomes any would-be tree-hugger. The trail winds through forests, over creeks, and through one meadow before delivering another tight spot at mile 10.8. A rocky and big drop off invites you to take it down the center.

From here, ride for another mile using "The Force" as you go. The forest once again struggles to engulf the trail and impede visibility. Having finished the Roxborough Loop, the feeling with which one is left is a kind of pleasant amazement: How can such sweet singletrack be so close to a city? Arrive at the road where you started your ride. Bear right and top-ring it back to your vehicle.

# Kenosha Pass to Georgia Pass

## Ride Summary

The Kenosha Pass to Georgia Pass ride is mack-daddy. On top of plush terrain and the rich groves of aspen, the trail includes awe-inspiring descents through hillside meadows and dense forests, as well as technical rocky and rooty climbs. Views from the top of Georgia Pass and Continental Divide are breathtaking, including the entire South Park Valley below. The town of South Park, incidentally, was the inspiration for the quirky fictional town in Comedy Central's popular cartoon series "South Park." South Park City, a restored mining town located in South Park, also offers a glimpse into life of a 19ᵗʰ Century Colorado mining town.

## Ride Specs

**Start:** From the trailhead for the Colorado Trail atop Kenosha Pass

**Length:** 23.8-miles out-and-back

**Approximate Riding Time:** Advanced Riders, 3 hours; Intermediate Riders, 4 hours

**Technical Difficulty Rating:** Technically moderate to challenging due to the abundance of exposed roots and rocks

**Physical Difficulty Rating:** Physically moderate to challenging due to the higher elevations at which you're riding

**Terrain:** Singletrack and doubletrack. Most of this route rolls over smooth, soft forest earth. There are, however, a few rougher sections of roots and rocks. Aspen and evergreen forests, high alpine valleys, and mountain passes form the backdrop to this incredible ride.

**Elevation Gain:** 4,389 feet

**Nearest Town:** Fairplay, CO

**Other Trail Users:** Hikers, bikepackers, equestrians, and backpackers

**Canine Compatibility:** Dog friendly

## Getting There

**From Denver:** Drive west on U.S. 285, passing through the town of Bailey at approximately 43 miles. Continue for another 19 miles to Kenosha Pass (10,000 feet). Once atop Kenosha Pass, turn right (west) into the Kenosha Pass Campground lot. Park in the designated area marked by Colorado Trail parking signs. Bike into the campground. Drinking water and toilet facilities are available. The Colorado Trail begins just to the left of these facilities. *DeLorme: Colorado Atlas & Gazetteer.* Page 49, A-4

A plaque on the west steps of the capitol building in downtown Denver marks a spot exactly 5,280 feet above sea level. Standing on the 18th step, you are exactly one mile high— which explains Denver's "Mile-High City" nickname.

Situated at the western end of the Pike National Forest, the trail begins atop the 10,001-foot Kenosha Pass and continues to the 11,585-foot Georgia Pass, the Continental Divide. Green and gold Q-tipped aspens crowd the trail along its westerly route like bristles in a mountainous brush, lending a special quality found only in Colorado's highest places.

As home to this kind of Colorado quality, it's fitting that the Pike National Forest should enjoy the respectable history it does. After the private Front Range timber stores were savagely depleted for the mining and railroad industries in the

late 1800s, cutters turned to scouring public lands to obtain their valuable timber. As a result, large tracks of public forestland were rubbed out along the Front Range. In response to growing concerns for Colorado's depleting natural resources, Congress passed an act in 1891 delegating President Benjamin Harrison the authority to create timber reserves. These reserves, forebears to our national forests, were large tracts of forestland that were set aside and protected from further depletion.

In 1892 the Plum Creek, South Platte, and Pikes Peak reserves southwest of Denver were among Colorado's earliest timber reserves. In August of 1898, William Kreutzer was appointed ranger for the Plum Creek Reserve, marking him the United States' first Forest Ranger. As one might expect, the early years of Kreutzer's appointment were beset with timber bootleggers, scalpers, and poachers—oftentimes calling for dangerous confrontations with Kreutzer himself. Overcoming these corrupting pressures, Kreutzer stayed true to his duties as Forest Ranger and eventually moved on to become supervisor for all of Colorado's national forests.

Comprised of the Plum Creek, South Platte, and Pikes Peak Reserves, the Pikes Peak Forest Reserve was created in 1905. Later that year, the Department of Agriculture and the newly-formed Forest Service took over as managers of the Reserve. As part of President Theodore Roosevelt's conservation program, Pikes Peak Forest Reserve was designated the Pike National Forest in 1907. Now under management of the Forest Service, the Pike National Forest expanded its services to include the preservation of all natural resources, not just timber. Today, the Pike National Forest contains a whopping 1,105,704 acres.

## **Miles**Directions

**0.0 START** at the Trail 1776 (the Colorado Trail) trailhead atop Kenosha Pass. Begin riding through serene groves of aspen and pine on smooth and hard-packed singletrack.

**2.5** Cross Guernsey Creek and continue riding on the singletrack into a muddier section of the trail.

**4.3** Cross Deadman Creek and continue riding in a westerly direction, negotiating through a tough root section, before intersecting with a doubletrack. Bear right onto this doubletrack at mile 4.6. The doubletrack soon disintegrates into singletrack, as it winds its way up a hillside marked by a miniature forest of pine saplings.

**5.1** Pass through a gate, closing it behind you, and continue riding through a moderately technical rocky singletrack section.

**5.8** After closing the gate behind you, descend through lush forests of pine and aspen before arriving at FS 401 (Jefferson Creek Road). Cross FS 401 and Jefferson Creek, continuing on the Colorado Trail to Georgia Pass. Just after crossing Jefferson Creek, ride to where the singletrack intersects with a doubletrack. Bear right onto this doubletrack, following signs for the Colorado

Trail and Georgia Pass. Roughly 0.1 miles from where you picked up this doubletrack, notice the continuation of the Colorado Trail singletrack bearing left into the pine forest. Another sign on the right reads "West Jefferson Trail 643, Jefferson Creek Campground, and Georgia Pass via Trail 643." Following signs for the Colorado Trail and Georgia Pass, veering left onto the singletrack. At this point, you're about six miles from Georgia Pass.

**7.7** The Colorado Trail intersects with the Michigan Creek Road Trail. Continue on the Colorado Trail in a northerly direction, passing the Michigan Creek Road Trail on your left (west).

**10.5** Near the timberline, with views of Mount Gugot and Bald Mountain immediately to your left. Continue climbing over tundra-like terrain to Georgia Pass. Since the area is treeless, cairns mark the way of travel.

**11.9** Arrive at FS 400. Bear left and ride for roughly 100 yards to the top of Georgia Pass. Turn around here and retrace your tracks back to your vehicle.

**23.8** Arrive back at your vehicle.

Returning from lightning strikes atop Georgia Pass.

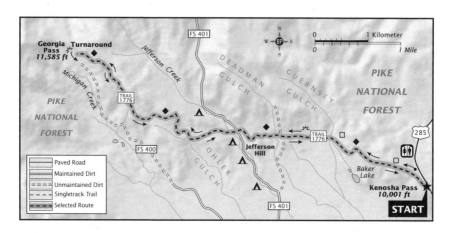

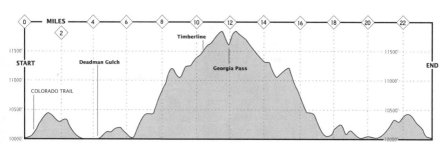

The real-life "South Park."

The first mile of the trail climbs moderately over very smooth terrain. Riders are coddled between a feeling of peaceful quietude descending from the thick canopy above and the snap, crackle, and pop of a tire's first meeting with a fallen pine needle below. The first technical section arrives within the first two miles. After descending very rapidly through a meadow and into an aspen grove, the trail switches back sharply to the left and over a group of large rocks, adding a nice wake-up call to the drowsily smooth singletrack. After roughly 2.4 miles, the singletrack exits the forest and opens up onto a hillside meadow awash with wildflowers. In view are the Continental Divide and Mount Gugot (13,370 feet), both straight ahead. Georgia Pass (11,585 feet) lies to the northwest, while the entire South Park Valley opens to the south.

The South Park Valley is an expansive 900-square-mile island in a sea of rolling mountains. In its center lies the small town of South Park. After gold was discovered here in 1859, eager prospectors flocked to the South Park Valley in droves. Within months, the unblemished valley floor became freckled with the mining camps of Tarryall, Leavick, Eureka, and Buckskin Joe. With increased development and trade, these rough-and-tumble mining camps metamorphosed into flourishing communities until all the gold was gone. With no gold to dig, miners found little reason to stay, and the mining camps, in turn, crumbled. These camps and the spirit that fueled their development had all but been forgotten until 1957.

In 1957, South Park City restoration project was conceived. By 1959, with 34 original buildings housing over 60,000 artifacts, South Park, the one-time boom-

# Ride Information

## 🌣 Trail Contacts:
**Pike National Forest**, South Park Ranger District, Fairplay, CO; (719) 836-2031

## 🕐 Schedule:
July to September

## ❓ Local Information:
**Park County Tourism Office**, Fairplay, CO; (719) 836-4279 or *www.idirect.com/~showcase* • **Colorado Trail Foundation**, Lakewood, CO; (303) 526-0898 [info] or (303) 384-3729, ext. 113 [bus]

## ⚲ Local Events/Attractions:
**South Park City Museum**, Fairplay, CO; (719) 836-2387 • **Forest Service Mountain Bike Trails**, Fairplay, CO; (719) 836-4279 • **Fairplay Beach Recreation Area**, Fairplay, CO; (719) 836-4279

## ⚙ Local Bike Shops:
**The Trailhead**, Buena Vista, CO; (719) 395-8001 • **Coast to Coast**, Buena Vista, CO; (719) 395-8067 • **Bike Shop Bill's**, Conifer, CO; (303) 816-0449 or 1-800-682-9282 or *www.bikeshopbills.com*

## Ⓝ Maps:
**USGS maps:** Jefferson, CO; Boreas Pass, CO • **Trails Illustrated map:** #105, Bailey and #109, Breckenridge. **Pike National Forest Map** – *available at Pike National Forest, South Park Ranger District, (719) 836-2031*

---

town of the late 1800s, was again a functioning town. The year also marked the centennial anniversary of Colorado's first gold rush. The restored mining camp of South Park City features the industries that made life in 19th Century Colorado livable. This recreation of a Colorado boomtown invites you to take a step back in time and listen for the slightly out-of-tune piano heard from Rache's Place. Farther up the street you'll notice the Simpkins General Store, the Garo School, and Merriam's City Drug Store. Complete with all the early-day tinctures, remedies, and poultices, Merriam's may provide temporary relief from the pains of climbing to Georgia Pass.

After crossing Deadman Creek, the trail becomes very narrow as it runs its course over large exposed roots. As you begin the last six-mile push to Georgia Pass, the route climbs steadily. Upon reaching Forest Service Road 400, bear left and pedal for roughly 100 yards to Georgia Pass. The descent from Georgia Pass to Jefferson Creek Road is fast and rocky. After crossing Deadman Creek for the second time, begin a tough climb through the meadow to the gate. From the gate, it's a fast and smooth descent through clustered aspens to the floor of South Park Valley.

The final 1.5 miles to Kenosha Pass and your vehicle is perhaps the most exhilarating. Smooth-running singletrack through quiet stands of aspen and pine offer the weary rider a certain peace-in-motion. The trail's narrow width, its smooth running course, and the close-standing trunks of pine and aspen offer the rider inclusion into the forest's high society. Riders silently track their tires into the soft belly of the earth, revealing unto no one but themselves and the surrounding forest, the simple pleasures shared by two.

# 44

# Baldy Trail to Gashouse Gulch Trail

## Ride Summary

The Buffalo Creek Area includes a network of outstanding singletrack within an hour's drive of Denver. Most of the riding rolls through thick forests over smooth and tacky singletrack. Some sandy sections appear along the way, but they don't last long. Charred trees mark the path of a forest fire that devastated much of this area. Despite the burn scars, the Buffalo Creek Area remains a mountain biker's playground. A variety of campsites dot the region in case you want to turn your day ride into an overnighter.

## Ride Specs

**Start:** From the junction of FS 550 and FS 543

**Length:** 7.7-mile loop—with options to connect to a host of other singletrack trails

**Approximate Riding Time:** Advanced Riders, 45-60 minutes; Intermediate Riders, 1½ hours

**Technical Difficulty Rating:** Technically easy to moderate due to occasional sandy and rocky sections

**Physical Difficulty Rating:** Physically easy to moderate due to short mileage and some moderate climbing

**Terrain:** Improved dirt roads, doubletrack, and singletrack. Consists of mostly smooth-running singletrack, but there are a number of sandy patches, particularly at the route's onset. Two small rocky sections along the Gashouse Gulch Trail offer a challenge.

**Elevation Gain:** 942 feet

**Nearest Town:** Conifer, CO

**Other Trail Users:** Hikers, campers, anglers, and picnickers

**Canine Compatibility:** Dog Friendly

## Getting There

**From Denver:** Take U.S. 285 west to Conifer. At the light in Conifer make a left onto Pine Valley Road and go 13.9 miles. Turn right onto FS 550, roughly 4 miles past the town of Buffalo Creek, and travel another 5 miles before parking your vehicle at the junction of FS 550 and FS 543. Park your vehicle on the right side, alongside Buffalo Creek. The route begins on FS 543 after crossing Buffalo Creek. *DeLorme: Colorado Atlas & Gazetteer:* Page 49, B-7

J ust 30 miles southwest of Denver lies a mini metro-mountain biking mecca. Commonly referred to as the "Buffalo Creek Area," this part of the Pike National Forest provides a vast network of fine singletrack. Along with being one of several put-ins for the 470-mile Colorado Trail, the Buffalo Creek Area is also home to the Baldy and Gashouse Gulch trails. Acclaimed for its smooth and negotiable singletrack, the 7.7-mile Baldy to Gashouse Gulch route provides as much satisfying sweetness as a short stack of flapjacks on a breezy camper's morning.

The route begins with a fast and cool descent on Forest Service Road 543, following Buffalo Creek downstream. After a mile, you come upon the chilling remains of a once thriving forest. Thrown from your mountain biking reverie, the bitter reality of Nature's destructive and regenerative forces is brought immediately to bear. Before you lies the charred remains of the 1996 Buffalo Creek forest fire.

On Saturday, May 18, 1996, a campfire left for dead atop Gashouse Gulch turned itself into a wind-whipped wildfire. Within hours, the flames had grown from the confines of a rock-lined fire pit to a 10,000-acre furnace. Ten miles long and two miles wide, the fire raged for five days and destroyed 12,000 acres at a cost of $2.8 million. The effects of such an inferno take on a whole new reality after one enters into its devastating path. Beginning at mile 1.5, the Baldy Trail weaves its singletrack course in between the standing corpses of ponderosa pine. As the Baldy Trail scratches its sandy way to higher ground, staccato islands of roundleaf bluebell (campanula rotundifolia) and mullein (verbascum thapsus) reaffirm Nature's recuperative powers.

Portions of this route's 7.7 miles remain remarkably unscathed by fire and are full of life. After two miles into the ride, the trail enters into a wonderful ponderosa pine forest and climbs gradually. The singletrack narrows, and the forest through which you're riding widens a bit. The trees here seem taller and less crowded—a welcomed contrast to the soot-caked skeletons that introduced your ride.

As you near the summit and the junction of Baldy and Gashouse Gulch trails, the singletrack exits the forest and enters onto a huge rock face. Pushing its way into overlying metamorphic rocks, this granite batholith remains as a tremendous intrusion of molten magma. Continue your fire-ride by scaling this formerly-molten magma and then veer to the left. By mile 3.7 the forest has been overtaken by boulders. A natural grotto to your left provides a dry respite from the area's sudden and regular thunderstorms.

From this point, the trail takes you over grassy knolls and though meadows and flat-surfaced forests before exiting to the Gashouse Gulch Trail. Beginning as a dirt road, the Gashouse Gulch Trail eventually disintegrates into a rough-looking doubletrack before connecting to a singletrack trail leading off to the left. The Gashouse Gulch singletrack offers fast descents, tight switchbacks, creek crossings, and one very technical rocky section at mile 5.8. Riders can choose to complete the loop where the Baldy trail singletrack begins, but this description foregoes part of that connection because of the many non-negotiable blowdowns that litter the trail. Instead, proceed to the Gashouse Gulch trailhead, pass through its wooden gate, and enjoy a fast ride on the road to Forest Service Road 550, hitting as many jumps as possible. From there, Forest Service Road 550 takes you back to your vehicle.

## **Miles**Directions

**0.0 START** from the gate at FS 543. Go under the gate and begin your ride, with Buffalo Creek to your right. A beautiful alpine log home sits to your left. Fashioned after the Euro-style log homes of old, this private residence backs up to a collection of enormous rocks.

**0.4** Go around another gate and cross Buffalo Creek a second time.

**1.3** Arrive at the sandy bottom. A re-vegetation project along the banks of Buffalo Creek is to your left. Approximately 50 yards past this project, still following FS 543 downstream, is a large sandy area to your left. Strewn across this area are four large rocks imbedded in the sand. Veer left off of FS 543, riding between these rocks. Continue through the sand and head into the burned forest. The singletrack begins to your left shortly thereafter, marked by the Gashouse Gulch trail sign.

**1.5** Reach the junction of the Gashouse Gulch and Baldy trails. Veer right onto Baldy Trail.

**2.3** A fallen pine tree obstructs the trail. Carefully walk your bike under it and continue your ride. Be aware of blowdowns.

**3.7** Cross wire gate. The area here is distinct for its large rock formations—a great place to mix bouldering in with your day of riding. If you scurry to the tops of the boulders to your right, you'll be treated to a killer view of Baldy Peak.

**4.5** Reach the junction of the Gashouse Gulch and Baldy trails. Gashouse Gulch leads both to the right and to the left. Take the left route. At this point the trail becomes a rough-looking dirt road.

**5.1** The rough doubletrack/dirt road intersects with a singletrack veering off to the left. Veer left onto this singletrack.

**6.1** Cross another wire fence.

**6.8** Arrive at FS 550. Veer left onto FS 550 and cross the cattle guard at mile 6.9.

**7.2** FS 550 intersects with FS 543 to your right. Bear left and continue on FS 550.

**7.7** Arrive at your vehicle.

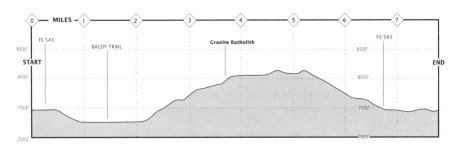

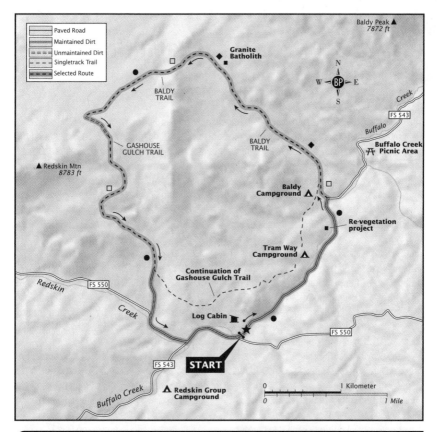

# Ride Information

**📞 Trail Contacts:**
Pike and San Isabel National Forests, Pueblo, CO; (719) 523-6591

**🕐 Schedule:**
May to October

**❓ Local Information:**
Colorado Trail Foundation, P.O. Box 260876, Lakewood, CO 80226

**💡 Local Events/Attractions:**
Colorado Trail, 470-mile trail from Denver to Durango

**🍴 Restaurants:**
Coney Dog Stand, Conifer, CO; (303) 838-4210

**📖 Other Resources:**
*The Colorado Trail: The Official Guidebook* by Randy Jacobs, Westcliffe Publishing, Englewood, CO

**🚲 Local Bike Shops:**
Bike Shop Bill's, Conifer, CO; (303) 816-0449 or 1-800-682-9282; *www.bike shopbills.com—beside the Coney Dog Stand*

**Ⓝ Maps:**
USGS maps: Green Mountain, CO •
*Trails Illustrated:* map: # 135 Deckers & Rampart Range, CO

# Jackson Creek Trail

## Ride Summary

The Jackson Creek Trail is a mellow ride through some of metro-Denver's most remote woodlands and mountains. Combining relatively easy road ascents, ridge rides of touring ease, fast and furious descents, and steady climbs through mountain flanked canyons, this route offers the most bang for your buck. The descent toward Watson Park and Jackson Creek is a blast, delivering sandy sections, rooty sections, and a number of dips, while the climb from Jackson Creek to your cars will have you churning your pedals. For those packing a lunch, the optional out-and-back spur will lead you to Watson Park, a great place for a picnic. Should your visit to Jackson Creek include camping, this ride passes Jackson Creek Campsite at mile 11.2.

## Ride Specs

**Start:** From the junction of Rampart Range Road (FR 300) and Jackson Creek Road (FR 502). Begin your ride from the Pike National Forest Campground: Jackson Creek sign and ascend the Rampart Range Road.

**Length:** 12.8-mile loop (with many options to explore a vast network of fire roads)

**Approximate Riding Time:** Advanced Riders, 1 hour; Intermediate Riders, 1½–2 hours

**Technical Difficulty Rating:** Technically easy, due to the well-maintained forest road. There are some sandy and rooty sections, but none that are overly technical.

**Physical Difficulty Rating:** Physically easy to moderate. Although there is little elevation gain, the last half-mile climb to your vehicle is relatively tough.

**Terrain:** Forest Service and jeep roads, which are typically smooth; however, some sections include sand, roots, and larger rocks, along with a variety of dips and washouts.

**Elevation Gain:** 1,470 feet

**Nearest Town:** Sedalia, CO

**Other Trail Users:** Hikers, campers, motorcyclists, and equestrians

**Canine Compatibility:** Dog-friendly

## Getting There

**From Denver:** Take I-25 south to Exit 207B (U.S. 85 South). Stay in the left three lanes of U.S. 85 South, since it splits soon after exiting onto it. Drive for 21 miles before turning right onto CO 67 West in Sedalia. After about a mile, turn left onto CO 105 South. CO 105 turns into Perry Park Road. At mile 28.5, turn right onto Jackson Creek Road (CR 38). After two miles, Jackson Creek Road will turn to dirt. At mile 33 the road forks. Head right, continuing on Jackson Creek Road. Drive 4.5 miles from the fork, and come to a stop sign, where Jackson Creek Road merges with Rampart Range Road. Veer left, continuing on Rampart Range Road. At mile 40.3, come to a 3-sided wooden sign in the middle of the road. Bear right, following signs to Woodland Park. At mile 45.1, arrive at the junction of Rampart Range Road (FS 300) and Jackson Creek Road (FS 502). Park your vehicle behind the Pike National Forest: Jackson Creek Campground sign. *DeLorme: Colorado Atlas & Gazetteer:* Page 50 C-2

ou'll want to ride Jackson Creek Loop more for what it is *not* than for what it actually *is*. What it is not is overpopulated or technically frustrating or physically demanding—making it a purely enjoyable ride for those who simply want to spend the day spinning in one of Colorado's hidden treasures. A ride the whole family can enjoy, Jackson Creek Loop offers the perfect mellow, out-of-town ride.

From the trailhead parking, you begin the route by climbing the moderately pitched Rampart Range Road. This road was built by the now defunct Civil Conservation Corps (CCC) in the 1930s, during America's Great Depression. Part of President Franklin Roosevelt's New Deal project to jumpstart the American economy, the CCC provided employment for out-of-work, physically fit, unmarried men between the ages of 18-25. The bivouacking workers each received a weekly salary of $30–$25 of which had to be sent home to family members. All told, the corps constructed 41,000 bridges, 3,982,000 dams, and 44,475 buildings in 31 states. By building shelter beds, fire lanes, trails, and rural roads, the CCC enabled three times the number of visitors to visit the state parks in 1936.

Much like the Appalachian Trail and the Pacific Crest Trail, the Rampart Range Road remains a symbol of the old "pull-yourself-up-by-the-bootstraps" work ethic. A monument to its builders who camped along its 60 miles and braved the mountain elements, Rampart Range Road is still in use today and invites mountain bikers to choose the road less traveled. Dotting much of the road are the CCC's original handmade rail fences.

Pedaling alongside Jackson Creek with wonderful bouldering possibilities behind.

The route along Rampart Range Road continues for 2.7 miles before intersecting with Forest Road 563.

Veer left onto Forest Service Road 563 and begin a fast half-mile descent. This descent provides a number of embankments for you to ride high on—along with an engineering safety net so that mountain bikers can scream around curves while minimizing the threat of crashing. The route eventually climbs through a densely populated lodgepole pine forest. If you're looking for a brief respite from the thick forest travel, the route passes by a vista with views of Castle Rock and the Front Range High Plains to the east. From this point (about four to 4.5 miles) the trail descends again. Here you're offered a chance to practice your bunny-hop, as a number of "whoop-di-doos" cross your path.

After mile 6.5, Forest Service Road 563 intersects with Forest Service Road 503. Veer left onto Forest Service Road 503. This section of the Jackson Creek Loop is the steepest part of the entire route. Luckily, it's all down hill. Forest Service Road 503 does have some thick, sandy sections, so take care at warp speeds. At mile 7.0, Forest Service Road 503 comes to a "Y." (Veering left here and riding for a half-mile will deliver you to Watson Park, an idyllic picnicking point.) Jackson Creek Loop, however, continues to the right as it drops to Jackson Creek. After you cross Jackson Creek, veer left onto Jackson Creek Road (Forest Service Road 502) and follow the creek upstream.

This section of the loop follows through a canyon with ghoulish-looking rock formations to your right—the most prominent of which taking its name and its image from the master of the netherworld. The hike to Devil's Head Mountain via the Devil's Head Trailhead is a great one. The mile-and-a-quarter hike is moderately challenging. Once at the summit, scale the steps to the top of the fire lookout tower and breathe in one of Colorado's best panoramic views of the Front Range.

Devil's Head Mountain will be to your right after passing the Jackson Creek Campground. Since a number of motorcycle trails run through this area, it offers campers a wide selection of trails and roads on which to mountain bike. From the campground, Forest Service Road 502 begins to gradually ascend with the last half-mile being a bit of a grunt. The last push to your vehicles, though not particularly breezy, won't leave you discouraged for having completed the entire Jackson Creek Loop.

## Ride Information

### ☎ Trail Contacts:

**Pike and San Isabel National Forests,**
1920 Valley Drive, Pueblo, CO; (719) 523-6591

### ⊙ Schedule:

April to November

### ♀ Local Events/Attractions:

**Devil's Head Tower and Trail** – *Backtrack 4.8 miles on Rampart Range Road from where you parked your car. Bear right at the 3-sided wooden sign in the middle of the road and head toward Devil's Head Campground and trailhead.*

### ☞ Local Bike Shops:

*Unfortunately, the nearest bike shop is in Denver, which is 45 miles away. So plan ahead.*

### Ⓝ Maps:

**USGS maps:** Devil's Head, CO; Dakan Mountain, CO • *Trails Illustrated* **map:** #135, Deckers, Rampart Range, CO

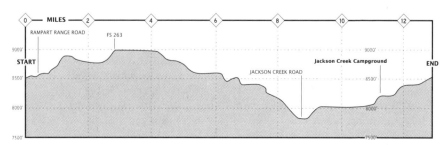

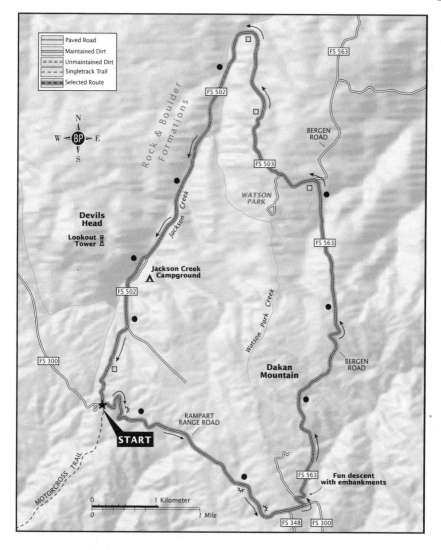

## **Miles**Directions

**0.0 START** at the junction of Jackson Creek Road (FS 502) and Rampart Range Road (FS 300). The route begins as a gradual ascent along the Rampart Range Road.

**2.5** FS 300 meets with FS 348. Ride straight ahead on FS 300, climbing the short hill in front of you.

**2.7** Reach the junction of FS 300 and FS 563. Veer left onto FS 563.

**6.5** Reach the junction of FS 563 and FS 503. Veer left onto FS 503

**8.6** Reach the junction of FS 503 and FS 502 (Jackson Creek Road). Veer left onto FS 502.

**11.2** Jackson Creek Campsite is to your left. Continue riding upstream.

**12.8** Arrive at your vehicle.

# Rampart Reservoir Shoreline Loop

## Ride Summary

The Rampart Reservoir Shoreline Loop offers mountain bikers of any ability the chance to test their skills on a variety of terrain. From sand to gravel to rocks and soft forest earth, the loop delivers it all. Within a stone's throw of the reservoir and under the watchful eye of Pike's Peak, this trail follows the shoreline all the way around, providing opportunities for fishing access and picnicking. A favorite among locals, the Rampart Reservoir Shoreline Loop can get crowded on the weekends. It's best that mountain bikers ride the trail in a clockwise direction, so as not to come upon riders unexpectedly around the many tight and rocky curves.

## Ride Specs

**Start:** From the Rampart Reservoir Shoreline Loop trailhead
**Length:** 15.3-mile loop
**Approximate Riding Time:** Advanced Riders, 1½ hours; Intermediate Riders 2–2½ hours
**Technical Difficulty Rating:** Technically moderate to difficult due to a few tight rocky sections
**Physical Difficulty Rating:** Physically moderate, due to a modest elevation gain
**Terrain:** Improved dirt road and singletrack. The singletrack is covered in Pike's Peak granite (pebble-like rocks that absorb water), which keeps the trails in good shape during wet weather. These rocks are like ball bearings under your tires, making it tough to get out of steeper climbs.
**Elevation Gain:** 1,179 feet
**Nearest Town:** Woodland Park, CO
**Other Trail Users:** Hikers, anglers, picnickers, boaters, equestrians, campers, and ski tour groups
**Canine Compatibility:** Dog friendly

## Getting There

**From Colorado Springs:** Take I-25 to Exit 141. After exiting, continue heading west on U.S. 24 to Woodland Park. Drive west on CO 24 for 17.8 miles before reaching the "Welcome to Woodland Park" sign on your right. Turn right onto Baldwin Street, which takes you behind McDonald's. Passing the Woodland Park High School on your right, Baldwin Street becomes Rampart Range Road. After 2.9 miles from when you turned onto Baldwin Street, Rampart Range Road forks. Take the right fork and then turn right again onto the dirt road and the continuation of Rampart Range Road at 4.4 miles, following signs to the reservoir. After 6.8 miles (from when you turned onto Baldwin Street), the trailhead appears on your left side. Pull into the lot for the Rampart Reservoir Shoreline Loop and begin your ride beyond the wooden gate.
***DeLorme: Colorado Atlas & Gazetteer:*** Page 62, A-3

D ue in large part to the eye-catching pink granite pebbles blanketing this trail's 12-mile stretch of singletrack, the Rampart Reservoir Trail is a popular mountain biking ride among Colorado Springs riders. This trail's singletrack is made of the same stuff as Pike's Peak— namely, Pike's Peak granite. The rock consists of interlocking crystals of glass-like quartz, flat-surfaced white and pink feldspar, and a dash of black flaky mica. For those mountain bikers with a less than roadside knowledge of geology, the presence of these cute pink pebbles on the trail requires a more practical interpretation.

Peace in motion...

Pike's Peak granite absorbs a great deal of water. For this reason, the Rampart Reservoir Trail sheds water easily, keeping the trail dry and in good shape, even after the wettest of weather. This feature allows the loop to remain active nearly twice the measly three-month, prime-time window Colorado typically affords mountain bikers. But Pike's Peak granite isn't necessarily always working in the mountain biker's best interest.

Its pebbly form acts as a kind of geological ball bearing. A collection of these pesky pink pebbles can throw even sequoia-like limbs into a tizzy. With the Rampart Reservoir's many roller coaster dips, up and around protruding boulders, and in and out of a variety of creek beds, the Pike's Peak granite singletrack does make for a physically challenging ride.

The ride begins at the Rampart Reservoir Shoreline Loop Trailhead. As you cross the wooden gate, the trail begins with a fast, easterly 1.5-mile run through stands of quaking aspen to the pipeline spillway and the bridge. Bear left and continue on the north side of the spillway. Now on your right side, the spillway brings water from mountain runoff to Rampart Reservoir.

Rampart Reservoir and Pikes Peak in the distance.

After four miles, you cross a creek and confront huge granite formations along the banks of the reservoir. For all you lounge lizards, here's a great place to take your rest and bask in pleasant warmth. Just beyond these rocks is a thick evergreen forest, complete with coiling roots and moist earth. This section quickly fades as the trail dries and leads into a tricky rocky section before offering a beautiful view of Pike's Peak. Part of the Rampart Reservoir Trail's appeal is its flirtatious skirting around huge boulders and through tight rocky sections. Pick your lines carefully and watch the noggin.

By mile 8.4 the trail leads to what local riders call "The Dip." Large boulders lie in front of you as the trail descends to meet the banks of the reservoir. When the water is high, you'll have to take the left spur of the singletrack, traversing up and over these rocks. If the water level is low, after carefully negotiating the tight rocky section just before these boulders, lift your bicycle and scramble over the rocks to rejoin the trail above. Just beyond this section is the "Triple Squeeze"—three tight rocky sections that are very technical but can be done. These tight rocky sections keep you honest on a trail as user-friendly as this. Once you reach the dam, absorbing views of Pike's Peak await. Be careful here, as vehicles readily use this road.

## **Miles**Directions

**0.0 START** at the trailhead located to the left of the parking lot. Go through the wooden gate and begin riding on the fast descending Rampart Reservoir Shoreline Road to the spillway.

**0.7** Reach the spillway and bear left over it. The trail continues after crossing the pipeline spillway. Continue riding downstream, now with the spillway on your right.

**1.5** Reach a footbridge. This footbridge also marks the point to which you'll be returning. Pass the bridge and keep heading straight—we're going clockwise. (You have the option of riding the trail in a clockwise or counterclockwise direction. But there are three good reasons to ride the trail clockwise. **1.** Logic and courtesy dictate that you travel in a clockwise direction, so as to avoid colliding with

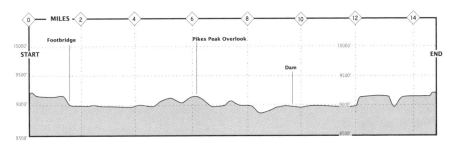

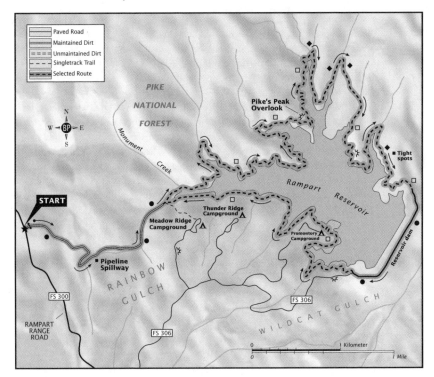

other trail users around the many blind curves. **2.** It's more ridable in a clockwise direction. **3.** Your drive train will usually be hanging downhill if ridden in a clockwise direction, minimizing the chances of damaging it.)

**1.7** The singletrack begins

**2.3** Reach a marshy area. Cross this marshy area via footbridge.

**5.4** Encounter technical, rocky section. The middle line offers the best results. Since this trail does have some tight rocky sections, pick your lines carefully.

**6.3** Beautiful place to take your rest and take in the view of Pike's Peak.

**6.8** The trail divides here, leading into another marshy, forested area. The tendency is to follow the trail to the left, which will soon thereafter lead into a meadow, ultimately dead-ending. Instead, bear right, scouting out the trail and cross the creek.

**8.4** Reach the Dip. Here a rock wall blocks immediate passage. You'll have to portage your bicycle up and around this wall.

**9.7** Reach the dam. Cross dam and pick up the singletrack on the other side.

**10.4** Come to the Wildcat Wayside Sign (Pike National Forest). The singletrack trail continues 10 yards past the sign, on the right, just beyond the parked cars. At this point, you can take the road back to your vehicles. Although far less technical, this option does add some mileage to your ride, as well as a significant amount of climbing. Bear right onto the singletrack. Note that this section of the trail has a higher level of foot traffic, so be cautious.

**11.6** Reach a sweet picnic spot, offering picnic tables and water spigots. Here the trail will "Y." A hiking trail will veer to the left and split the two picnic tables, as the Rampart Reservoir loop trail veers to the right, passing the picnic table with the large boulder behind it.

**13.8** Reach the bridge. Veer left and climb back up the road the way you came to your vehicle.

**15.3** Arrive back at your vehicle.

As a holding tank, Rampart Reservoir supplies Colorado Springs with water via a 12-foot wide tunnel. A Swedish engineering firm bored Rampart Reservoir's shaft and its connecting tunnel. They bet city planners that the shaft and the tunnel would connect within one inch of spec. The Swedes hit it right on the nose, an impressive display of engineering acuity if you consider the 20 miles the tunnel had to travel.

After rejoining the Rampart Reservoir singletrack just beyond the Wildcat Wayside Pike National Forest sign, continue through the ponderosa pine forest. Cross a stone culvert before arriving at Picnic Peninsula—a picnic area offering tables, water spigots, and shoreline views. Continue on the singletrack, veering right as it passes in front of the picnic table with the large boulder backdrop. This area contains many offshoots from the main trail. Know that the shoreline loop generally runs the course of the land contour through here. Passing through Picnic Peninsula, you're rewarded with a fast and smooth singletrack descent to the bridge. Veer left by the bridge and return to your vehicles.

## Huckleberry Bread Pudding

*Wild huckleberries thrive in upper montane and subalpine forests, often growing for miles as a solid carpet under spruce and fir trees. The berries have an almost nut-like flavor and are extremely juicy—perfect pie potential. The leaves can be stewed to make a kind of back-country tea. Just imagine.*

*American Indians valued the berry highly, combining huckleberries boiled in bear grease with dog flesh for their feast meal. Cherokee women would encase huckleberries in cornmeal dough and deep-fry them in bear fat. These dishes are still showcased at the annual feast of Cherokee foods held in Cherokee, North Carolina.*

*Huckleberries were so much a part of early American life that they were adopted into the vernacular. Since huckleberries are tiny, plentiful, and common, a "huckleberry" became early nineteenth-century slang for a person of little consequence—undoubtedly inspiring Mark Twain to dub his most memorable literary character Huckleberry Finn.*

*When you do come across a patch of wild huckleberries, be sure to pick a shirt-full, as you can travel for miles and never see any. I should also add: BE SURE YOU'RE PICKING HUCKLEBERRIES! The following recipe has the charm of an old railway carriage and the staying power of a great American classic.*

*8 thin slices of white bread*
*4 cups huckleberries*
*butter*
*½ to ¾ cup sugar*
*bourbon*

*Butter each slice of bread lightly and line a round four to five-cup bowl with the slices. Fill in the small spaces with bread so that the bowl is completely covered, sparing one slice for the crown. Cook the huckleberries with the sugar and a 1/3 cup of water for 10 minutes. Add bourbon to taste. Then, pour the mixture into the bread-lined bowl. Place a slice on top and fold the edges over to meet. Place a saucer on top and press down. Serve excess liquid with pudding. Chill for five hours and then serve with heavy cream. Enjoy.*

# Ride Information

## Trail Contacts:
**Team Telecycle,** Woodland Park, CO; (719) 687-6165 or 1-800-894-8961 or *www.teamtelecycle.com*

## Schedule:
April to November

## Local Information:
**Woodland Park Chamber of Commerce,** Woodland Park, CO; (719) 687-9885 or *www.woodland-park-co.org* • **Colorado Springs Chamber of Commerce,** Colorado Springs, CO; (719) 635-1551 **Pike's Peak Ranger District,** Colorado Springs, CO; (719) 636-1602

## Local Events/Attractions:
**Florissant Fossil Beds National Monument,** Florissant, CO; (719) 748-3252 – *$2 to $4 admission fee* • **Garden of the Gods,** Colorado Springs, CO; (719) 634-6666 – *admission is free*

## Restaurants:
**Grandmother's Kitchen,** Woodland Park, CO; (719) 687-3118 • **The Donut Mill,** Woodland Park, CO; (719) 687-9793 • **Tres Hombres,** Woodland Park, CO; (719) 687-0625

## Mountain Bike Tours:
**Challenge Unlimited,** Colorado Springs, CO; 1-800-798-5954 or (719) 633-6399 or *www.pikespeak.com/challenge*

## Organizations:
**Friends of the Peak,** Colorado Springs, CO; (719) 570-8958

## Local Bike Shops:
**Team Telecycle,** Woodland Park, CO; (719) 687-6165 or 1-800-894-8961 or *www.teamtelecycle.com* • **Old Town Bike Shop,** Colorado Springs, CO; (719) 475-8589

## Maps:
**USGS maps:** Woodland Park, CO; Cascade, CO • **Trails Illustrated map:** # 137, Pike's Peak & Canon City, Colorado • **Team Telecycle map** – *available at Team Telecycle bicycle shop* • **Selected Colorado Hiking Trails:** Pike's Peak Series – *available at Pike's Peak Ranger District, Colorado Springs, (719) 636-1602*

Otis, our fearless leader.

# Waldo Canyon

## Ride Summary

The Waldo Canyon Trail, although primarily a hikers trail, does invite gonzo-minded mountain bikers to strut their stuff. What makes this trail particularly appealing to tough riders is its steep climbs out of creek beds and its fast and rocky descent—added to this is the variety of terrain Waldo Canyon delivers. Views from its highest point include Pike's Peak, Colorado Springs, and NORAD. Its location right beside U.S. Route 24 makes for a speedy assault of the trail for those in transit. For those of you whose riding mentality is one fry short of a happy meal, try tackling the stairs on your return.

## Ride Specs

**Start:** From the trailhead to Waldo Canyon
**Length:** 7-mile loop
**Approximate Riding Time:** Advanced Riders, 1 hour; Intermediate Riders, 1½–2 hours
**Technical Difficulty Rating:** Technically moderate to challenging due to the many rocky sections and big drop-offs
**Physical Difficulty Rating:** Physically challenging due to the variety of climbing and having to portage your bicycle over rocky creeks
**Terrain:** Singletrack. Although this trail is all singletrack, it covers a variety of different terrain: various kinds of rock surfaces, hard-packed dirt, wet forest earth, large roots, and Pike's Peak granite.
**Elevation Gain:** 3,126 feet
**Nearest Town:** Colorado Springs, CO
**Other Trail Users:** Primarily day-hikers—a good reason not to mountain bike in this area on the weekends
**Canine Compatibility:** Dog friendly

## Getting There

**From Colorado Springs:** Take I-25 to Exit 141 and U.S. 24 west. Drive west on U.S. 24 for 7.8 miles before reaching the turnoff for Waldo Canyon to your right. Park your vehicle here. You'll have to portage your bicycle up two sets of stairs to the registration box and the trailhead before beginning your ride.
**From Woodland Park:** Head east on U.S. 24 toward Colorado Springs, starting from the intersection of U.S. 24 and Baldwin Street. At 9.9 miles, arrive at the turn off for the Waldo Canyon trailhead, which is to your left. The trailhead is to the north side of U.S. 24, so you'll have to cross U.S. 24's westbound traffic. (Should you miss this opportunity to cross U.S. 24's westbound traffic, another turnoff will be to your left. Stay in the left lane. Turn left at 11.0 miles and backtrack westbound on U.S. 24. Drive for 1.1 miles from when joining onto westbound traffic and bear right into the Waldo Canyon parking lot). **DeLorme: Colorado Atlas & Gazetteer:** Page 62, A-B 3

At its worst, Waldo Canyon is a crowded thoroughfare for weekend hikers. At its best, it's a grunt of a climb to some of the area's best unobstructed views of Pike's Peak. The tireless mountain biker is rewarded with a singletrack descent of titillating switchbacks, past a veritable smorgasbord of geological timetables and drop-offs.

To help maintain and operate the district system trails, a donation of $1 is asked of every user and is collected at the bottom of the wooden stairs leading to the trail's registration box and the start of your ride. If not paralyzed with quizzical angst, wondering why you just carried yourself and your bike up these steep

wooden steps, begin riding up the switchbacks. The trail parallels the U.S. Route 24 for roughly a mile and then climbs steadily, your tires relentlessly spinning through the ball-bearing-like Pike's Peak granite that blankets the trail. On a softer note, patches of lavender mullein (Verbascum thapsus) and roundleaf bluebell (Campanula rotundifolia) stand alongside of these unrelenting granite pebbles. They're called to arms each spring and summer to passively assert Waldo Canyon's soft beauty among the harshness of semi-arid sand and rock. As the trail turns away from the highway, you're given your last look at civilization for awhile. Views of the city of Colorado Springs vanish as you descend farther into this sun-splashed foothill oasis.

Riding through tall stands of leafy greens, surrounded by the smell of summer camp, you descend into a cool meadow area, complete with campfire rings. If you plan to camp and need a campfire, it's best that you use these campfire rings, so as not to scorch the earth any further than necessary. Once you arrive at the "Waldo Canyon Loop, 3½ miles" sign, bear left. In so doing, you'll be riding the loop in a clockwise direction, choosing to climb in the shade rather than in the more exposed areas of Waldo Canyon. From here the work begins.

A mile of steep climbing awaits you. The large rocks, knotty tree roots, and creek-crossings make it a grunt by anyone's standards—a true trial rider's dream. By mile 2.5, the trail "Y"s before sending you up another set of wooden stairs. This time, the stairs are a bit more manageable, as long as you hug the left side—anyone less than advanced might find this difficult to ride. Bear right at the Waldo Canyon sign and continue ascending through the ponderosa and fir forest. Areas of this trail are severely loaded with rocks, so be aware on the approach. By the third mile the trail levels out and offers incredible views of 14,110-foot Pike's Peak along the east rim of Waldo Canyon.

In 1929, Bill Williams rolled a peanut to the top of Pike's Peak using his nose. His performance lasted 20 days.

By mile 3.4 you come upon an example of the "Great Unconformity"—a term coined by the "Father of Geology" James Hutton. The Great Unconformity refers to a break in the geologic record in which two kinds of rock are found in abnormal succession. In this case, Precambrian metamorphic rock (granite) sits directly beneath Pennsylvanian red sandstone, with no sign between of the Ordovician, Silurian, Devonian, or Mississippian periods. With 500 million years of time apparently lost, a crucial piece in Earth's geological jigsaw puzzle remains missing. Possible explanations for this mysterious absence are severe erosion and folding and faulting.

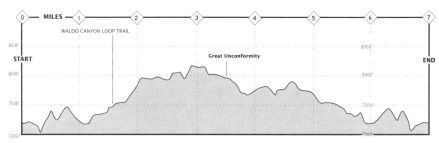

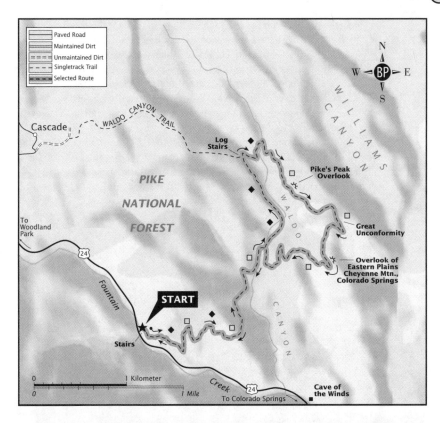

**Miles**Directions

**0.0 START** at the registration tower and box at the top of the stairs.

**0.1** Waldo Canyon Trail will bear left. To the right will be an overlook of U.S. 24 and a description of the composition of Pike's Peak granite.

**0.8** Cross the ridge and begin descending into clearing.

**1.6** Arrive at a brown sign reading "Waldo Canyon Loop, 3½ miles." Bear left here. You'll eventually return to this spot after completing the loop.

**2.5** Reach the set of log stairs leading to the trail's intersection. Veer right, as the left route will lead you out of Waldo Canyon and to the town of Cascade.

**3.4** Here's a good example of the Great Unconformity.

**4.9** Begin your switchback descent.

**5.3** Arrive at the creek and the Waldo Canyon sign.

**7.0** Arrive back at the trail register box and tower.

## "Pike's Peak" the Hot Drink

*Ingredients: ½ oz. Peppermint Schnapps, ½ oz. Kahlua, and 5 oz. coffee. Pour into a coffee mug and top with a dollop of whipped cream. Mmmm.*

From the site of the Great Unconformity, the trail traverses the sun-exposed hills above Williams Canyon before snaking its way back down into Waldo Canyon. Williams Canyon cuts through the hillside in which the Cave of the Winds is located. The only limestone cavern in Colorado developed as a tourist attraction, Cave of the Winds deposits its dissolved limestone along the roadside leading through Williams Canyon. Cave of the Winds is a dazzling network of rooms and passageways encrusted with limestone stalactites, stalagmites, and flowstone curtains. The cave is one of the nation's oldest show caves. In 1881 two young brothers, picnicking with their church, decided to explore the area. What they discovered was a 200-million-year-old geological phenomenon. Today, Cave of the Winds is one of Colorado's leading attractions. Open year round (10 A.M. to 5 P.M. in the winter and 9 A.M. to 9 P.M. in the summer), the cave offers a variety of tours, from the casual walker to the hardcore spelunker, and puts on an outstanding laser-light show.

# Ride Information

## 🛈 Trail Contacts:
**Team Telecycle,** Woodland Park, CO; (719) 687-6165 or 1-800-894-8961 or *www.teamtelecycle.com* • **Old Town Bike Shop,** Colorado Springs, CO; (719) 475-8589

## 🕐 Schedule:
May to October

## ❓ Local Information:
**Woodland Park Chamber of Commerce,** Woodland Park, CO; (719) 687-9885 or *www.woodland-park-co.org* • **Colorado Springs Chamber of Commerce,** Colorado Springs, CO; (719) 635-1551

## 💡 Local Events/Attractions:
Cave of the Winds, Manitou Springs, CO; (719) 685-5444 • **Florissant Fossil Beds National Monument,** Florissant, CO; (719) 748-3252 • **Garden of the Gods,** Manitou Springs, CO; (719) 634-6666. *It's free!*

## 🍴 Restaurants:  .
**Grandmother's Kitchen,** Woodland Park, CO; (719) 687-3118 • **The Donut Mill,** Woodland Park, CO; (719) 687-9793 • **Tres Hombres,** Woodland Park, CO; (719) 687-0625

## 🚲 Mountain Bike Tours:
**Challenge Unlimited,** Colorado Springs, CO; 1-800-798-5954 or (719) 633-6399 or *www.pikes peak.com/challenge*

## 🏢 Organizations:
**Friends of the Peak (FOTP),** Colorado Springs, CO; (719) 570-8958

## 🔧 Local Bike Shops:
**Team Telecycle,** Woodland Park, CO; (719) 687-6165 or 1-800-894-8961 or *www. teamtelecycle.com* • **Old Town Bike Shop,** Colorado Springs, CO; (719) 475-8589

## 🅝 Maps:
**USGS maps:** Woodland Park and Cascade, CO • **Trails Illustrated map:** # 137, Pike's Peak & Canon City, CO

Riding high above Williams Canyon, the trail passes gorgeous views of the Eastern Plains, Colorado Springs, and the hollowed-out Cheyenne Mountain—home to NORAD (North American Aerospace Defense). The underground city housing NORAD monitors foreign aircraft, missiles, and space systems that could threaten U.S. security. Aside from the vast array of antennae protruding from its scalp, Cheyenne Mountain is virtually indistinguishable from any other mountain in Colorado. The trail from this point is packed with dirt and thick with overgrowth as it begins its descent back into Waldo Canyon.

This descent is fast and fun, as it travels over a variety of terrain, keeping you on your toes if not putting you on your noggin. Manitou limestone-sprinkled switchbacks, precipitously sloping Sawatch sandstone, crowded Peerless (better known as "Fearless") dolomite sections, and carvable Pike's Peak granite turns—all question the standards of your ANSI and SNELL head. Riders are afforded a crash-course in geology as a host of interpretive signs explains the geology of each of these sections.

By mile 5.3 you arrive at a tributary of Fountain Creek and the "Waldo Canyon Loop, 3½ miles" sign. Bear left and return to your vehicles. After a short climb out of this valley, the descent to your vehicle is sweet and fast, offering blind corners and a number of rocks. You'll arrive at the trail register at 7.0 miles. If you're feeling lucky, try doing the stairs down to the parking lot.

# Shelf Road

## Ride Summary

The Shelf Road is a historic stagecoach toll road that connects Canon City with the gold mining camps of Cripple Creek and Victor. The Shelf travels precipitously along the limestone cliffs of Helena Canyon and then descends into the canyon, revealing incredibly tall red rock walls. Here is a mellow ride that offers a lot of spinning. It's a cool ride to combine with a day of gambling in Cripple Creek. The Banks-Shelf Road area is also world-renowned for its rock climbing. For those who want something a little more laid-back than Cripple Creek, make tracks to Victor, a traditional turn-of-the-century mining town that doesn't allow gambling. Bighorn sheep abound within Helena Canyon and most often can be spotted drinking from Fourmile Creek at dusk. Helena Canyon is a "hard hat" zone, meaning: loose rock will occasionally give in to gravity. The return from Cripple Creek or Victor is fast, offering a number of blind curves and washboard sections of road, with the last push to the Banks-Shelf Road parking area one burley climb.

## Ride Specs

**Start:** From the Banks-Shelf Road parking area. Take the right fork (Shelf Road).
**Length:** 27.2-mile out-and-back
**Approximate Riding Time:** Advanced Riders, 3½ hours; Intermediate Riders, 4½–5 hours
**Technical Difficulty Rating:** Technically easy, there are no major obstacles
**Physical Difficulty Rating:** Physically easy to moderate due to some degree of climbing
**Terrain:** Shelf Road Trail follows an old wagon and stagecoach toll road; aside from the occasional washboard effect, the road is relatively smooth; at times it is very exposed
**Elevation Gain:** 4,115 feet
**Nearest Town:** Cripple Creek, CO
**Other Trail Users:** Equestrians, hikers, four-wheelers, bighorn sheep viewers, climbers, and gamblers
**Canine Compatibility:** Not dog friendly, as there is vehicular traffic on Shelf Road

## Getting There

**From Canon City:** Drive east on U.S. 50. Make a left onto Dozier Avenue—near the Wal-Mart. In a half of a mile, Dozier turns west and becomes Central. Continuing on Central (Dozier), drive north for 1.6 miles before turning right onto Fields Avenue. Fields Avenue turns into a dirt road at 11.6 miles. Continue on Fields for another 2.3 miles before arriving at the Banks—a limestone cliff area located near the beginning of Shelf Road and known internationally for its incredible sport climbing. Park here and begin your ride, taking the right fork (Shelf Road). *DeLorme: Colorado Atlas & Gazetteer:* Page 62, D-B 1

As part of Colorado's Gold Belt Tour and the Bureau of Land Management's designated National Backcountry Byway system, Shelf Road recalls much of the Old West. Originally built in 1892 as a wagon and stagecoach toll road, Shelf Road connected the Arkansas River Valley community of Canon City with the turn-of-the-century gold camps of Cripple Creek and Victor. Today the road offers the relaxed mountain biker a chance to experience Colorado history from the seat of his or her mountain bike.

Finger Rock.

Colorado in the 1890s was home to America's last great gold rush. Towns like Cripple Creek, Victor, Florence, McCourt, Adelaide, and Wilbur (towns included within the Cripple Creek Mining District), all shared in the spoils that gold could afford. Gold offered these towns a chance to make a name for themselves—or as with the case of Cripple Creek, a new name. When Bob Womack discovered gold in October of 1890 in a high-country cow pasture west of Pike's Peak, the town of Poverty Gulch officially changed its name to Cripple Creek.

Bighorn sheep abound in Helena Canyon. Notice the family of sheep at the top of the photo.

Throughout its gold mining days, Cripple Creek enjoyed a standard of living never before seen in Colorado. By 1893, Cripple Creek had unearthed $3 million in gold ore. That figure grew to $59 million by 1899, and by the end of the gold rush (circa 1903), area gold mines within the Cripple Creek Mining District had produced $432 million—making it the fourth largest gold producing camp in the world.

Cripple Creek established itself as a social center as well. Grand opera houses were built. A variety of musicians performed for the area residents. Jack Dempsey drew huge crowds for his boxing bouts in town. Even President Teddy Roosevelt visited Cripple Creek, and while squatting and rubbing elbows with fellow miners, panned for gold.

## **Miles**Directions

**0.0 START** at the Banks-Shelf Road parking area. Take the right fork and begin climbing up Shelf Road.

**2.0** Riding along the steep limestone walls of Helena Canyon, you'll notice an old abandoned cabin from the late 1800s on the canyon floor.

**4.0** Shelf Road eventually widens and leads into the floor of Helena Canyon, affording additional parking to climbers and those who would like to forgo the initial, narrow descent to the canyon bottom. (The crags behind you offer great climbing opportunities and can be accessed via a variety of foot trails.)

**5.0** The remains of an old stone home are on your right.

**8.1** Come to an old abandoned mine shaft to your right.

**10.0** Take in the beautiful vista of the Sangre de Cristo Mountains off to the west.

**11.4** Cross Cripple Creek.

**11.8** Shelf Road forks. Here signs of Cripple Creek point to the left fork, while signs for Victor point to the right fork. Take the left fork and ride toward Cripple Creek. Pass the Scenic Byway sign, marked by a Colorado Columbine.

**13.3** Shelf Road connects to CO 67. At the stop sign, bear left onto CO 67 and ride into Cripple Creek.

**13.6** Reach the corner of 2nd Street and Bennett Avenue, downtown Cripple Creek. Turn around here and return the way you came.

**27.2** Arrive at your vehicle.

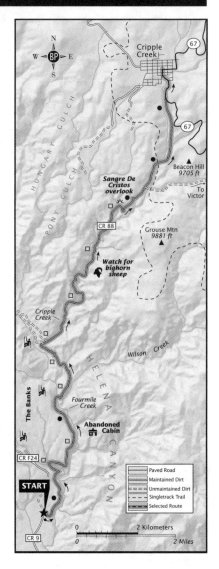

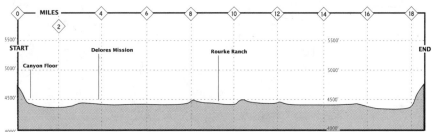

Today, Cripple Creek continues to grow by offering limited-stakes gambling. Other than housing an estimated 2,200 new jobs, many of Cripple Creek's original brick buildings now merely serve as vintage facades to the glittering casinos within. Though meant to maintain the city's National Historic District designation, Cripple Creek casinos can't help but lend an element of gross excess. Its buzzing bells, neon lights, and reeling pace all but erase any semblance of Cripple Creek's old west charm.

Six miles from Cripple Creek lies the gold mining town of Victor. Known as the City of Mines, Victor is the heart of the great Cripple Creek Mining District, and by point of pride, still remains true to its roots. Its century-old streets offer a quiet, non-gambling relief from Cripple Creek, while retaining much of the area's 1890s authenticity. The original brick buildings, built by residents after a fire destroyed their town in 1898, still stand. Even the hillsides are dotted with original miners' homes, visual echoes recalling the town's illustrious past.

Connecting Colorado's past with its present is Shelf Road. Six hundred feet above Fourmile Creek, Shelf Road cuts through Helena Canyon's limestone cliff walls. The initial four miles is perhaps the most dramatic section of the entire route. If you fear heights or are prone to vertigo, this section could be difficult. Shelf Road skirts dangerously above Helena Canyon, oftentimes offering only a car width's margin of error.

As you descend to the canyon floor and the banks of Fourmile Creek, a feeling of peace overcomes you as the exposed road gives way to hosts of juniper, legions of scrub oak, and a spattering of lush cottonwoods. Behind you remain the limestone crags whose allure has attracted many a rock climber. From here, one begins the extended 10-mile push to Cripple Creek. Shelf Road gradually climbs as it winds its way across and back Fourmile Creek.

The descent.

# Ride Information

## Trail Contacts:
**Bike Tech**, Canon City, CO; (719) 269-3825

## Schedule:
April to October

## Local Information:
**Canon City Chamber of Commerce**, Canon City, CO; (719) 275-2331 • **Cripple Creek Chamber of Commerce**, Cripple Creek, CO; (719) 689-2169 or 1-800-526-8777 • **Canon City District Office**, Canon City, CO; (719) 269-8500 **Bureau of Land Management**, Royal Gorge Resource Area, Canon City, CO; (719) 269-8538

## Local Events/Attractions:
**Donkey Derby Days**, last full weekend of June, Cripple Creek, CO; (719) 689-2169 or 1-800-526-8777 – *donkey races, greased pigs and lots of fun* • **Mardi Gras Conga**, June 7th, Canon City, CO; 1-888-333-5597 – *a conga parade across the Royal Gorge Bridge (the*

*world's highest suspension bridge in Canon City)* • **Limited-stakes Gambling**, Cripple Creek, CO; (719) 689-2169 or 1-800-526-8777 – *slot machines, poker and blackjack tables* • **Gold Rush Days**, third weekend of July, Victor, CO; (719) 689-3553 or (719) 689-3211 • **Gold Belt Tour**, year-round, Canon City, CO; (719) 275-2331

## Other Resources:
*A Mountain Bike Tour Guide for Canon City, Colorado* by Carol Boody's, Mountain Bike Tour Guides, 1989

## Local Bike Shops:
**Bike Tech**, Canon City, CO; (719) 269-3825

## Maps:
**USGS maps:** Cooper Mountain, CO; Cripple Creek South, CO • *Trails Illustrated* map: # 137, Pike's Peak & Canon City, CO

By mile 6.0, the steeper part of the climbing begins and leads you through forests of lodgepole pine by mile 8. These elegant and slender tree trunks were used by American Indians as poles for their teepees, hence the name. Like smoke from a fire ring, your eyes are drawn upward to the tips of these trees and onward toward the tops of the canyon walls.

After passing a number of abandoned mines between miles 10.0 and 11.4, Shelf Road eventually forks at mile 11.8. Victor is to the right, and Cripple Creek, to the left. Here remnants of the El Paso mine remain. After veering left, your solitary bicycle ride quickly fades as you become absorbed in the bustle of Cripple Creek. Veer left once again onto Colorado 67 at mile 13.3 and you come to downtown Cripple Creek, home to the largest population of free-roving donkeys—some the direct descendants of those used during Cripple Creek's gold mining glory.

Your return trip is fast and bumpy. Be cautious of your speed, as the descent on Shelf Road offers many tight turns. The many washboards are sure to test your shocks, and for those without shocks, your patience. Enjoy the ride.

# Honorable Mentions

# Front Range Colorado

Compiled here is an index of great rides in the Front Range region that didn't make the A-list this time around but deserve recognition. Check them out and let us know what you think. You may decide that one or more of these rides deserves higher status in future editions or, perhaps, you may have a ride of your own that merits some attention.

## (H) Crosier Mountain Loop

Located just outside of the gateway town for Rocky Mountain National Park, the Crosier Mountain Loop is quite possibly Estes Park's best kept secret. This trail's layout is almost entirely all singletrack. Complete with rocks, water, and switchbacks, the trail winds around the northeastern slope of Crosier Mountain before briefly intersecting with Devil's Gulch Road, and then it's back to your vehicle. The trail is roughly 10 miles long and reaches above 9,000 feet, which accounts for its physically and technically challenging rating.

Estes Park, set before the towering peaks of Rocky Mountain National Park, offers its own brand of alpine entertainment. Resident elk herds continually descend upon area lawns and gardens, unabashed by staring visitors. It's no surprise to see and hear a herd of elk bugling in someone's backyard. While in town, check out the Stanley Hotel. Built in 1909 the hotel served as an inspirational setting for Stephen King's *The Shining*.

To reach the Crosier Mountain Loop, drive north on Devil's Gulch Road from downtown Estes Park. The road winds around the Stanley Hotel before bearing northeast to Glen Haven. Park your vehicle in Glen Haven and begin riding here. For more information, contact Colorado Bicycling Adventures at Estes Park, 184 East Elkhorn, Estes Park, Colorado, 1-800-607-8765 or visit *www.coloradobicycling.com*; or contact the Estes Park Chamber of Commerce at 500 Big Thompson Highway Avenue, Estes Park, Colorado, (970) 586-4431 or 1-800-44-ESTES. *DeLorme: Colorado Atlas & Gazetteer:* Page 29, A-7

## (C) Deer Haven Ranch

Offering stunning views of the Sangre de Cristo Mountains and set in the semi-arid region of Canon City, Colorado, Deer Haven Ranch is a diamond in the rough. Although limited to a minimal amount of rideable miles—five to seven miles of mostly doubletrack and dirt roads—Deer Haven Ranch is an isolated and relatively unknown mountain biking destination.

Located about 25 miles northwest of Canon City, Deer Haven Ranch is a relatively new acquisition of the Bureau of Land Management. In 1992 a private foundation purchased the 4,840-acre ranch for $650,000 and presented it to the Bureau of Land Management as a gift. Since that time, the BLM, in conjunction with the Medicine Wheel (a mountain bike advocacy group from Manitou Springs) and a local equestrian group, has worked on developing a trail system for Deer Haven Ranch. As of the summer of 1998, three miles of singletrack were added to the ranch.

With grassy rolling meadows, an abundance of wildlife, an isolation factor of 10, and the BLM's continued commitment to developing a trail system, Deer Haven Ranch remains a diamond in the rough, but one whose edges increasingly becoming smoother. Look to Deer Haven Ranch as an up-and-coming success story for the mountain biking community.

To reach Deer Haven Ranch, travel west on U.S. Route 50 from the First National Bank in downtown Canon City, on the corner of 9th Street and Royal Gorge Blvd. (U.S. Route 50 West). Drive west on U.S. Route 50 for 9.7 miles. Turn right onto Colorado 9 North and drive for nine miles before turning right onto County Road 11 (a.k.a. Scenic Byway: Gold Belt Tour)—cross the creek after the red, ranch house and barn. Drive on County Road 11 for 5.3. After a long and gentle descent, make a right into Deer Haven Ranch (marked by the Deer Haven Ranch sign) and drive on County Road 69 (dirt road) for just under a mile before turning right onto a rough-looking doubletrack. Marked by the "Thompson Mountain" and "Dead End" signs, drive on this doubletrack for roughly one mile. After 0.3 of a mile, you'll need to go through a fenced gate. Be sure to close it behind you. After passing through this first gate, continue driving for 0.5 miles to the Deer Haven Ranch trailhead, marked by another gate and a bulletin board.

For more information, contact the Bureau of Land Management at Royal Gorge Resource Area, 3170 E. Main Street, Canon City, Colorado, or call (719) 269-8538. *DeLorme: Colorado Atlas & Gazetteer:* Page 61, D-7

**49.** Picket Wire Canyonlands

# Eastern Plains

**Honorable Mentions**
**J.** Pawnee National Grasslands

**WYOMING**

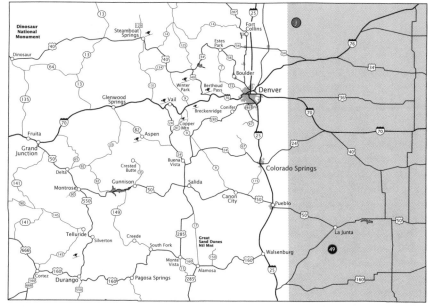

*NEW MEXICO*

The Eastern Plains provide a stark contrast to the mountainous terrain typically thought of when referring to Colorado's landscape. Although the rocky mountains do cast an ominous shadow over these amber waves of grain, these behemoths still cannot darken all of the eastern plains, an area covering nearly half of Colorado's acreage.

Commonly referred to as "Colorado's Outback," the Eastern Plains marks the western terminus of the high plains of the midwest. Across these plains came droves of pioneers during America's great expansion out west. Peppered by old forts, wagon trails and former farm settlements, Colorado's Outback is a treasure trove of the pioneering spirit. Roughly ten miles east from the town of La Junta, near the southern end of this region, lies Bent's Old Fort National Historic Site.

Although today, Bent's Old Fort may seem to lie in the middle of nowhere, it was unquestionably the epicenter of the frontier during America's expansion out west. Built in 1833, the fort lies on the north bank of the Arkansas River (then the U.S./Mexican border). As the only trading post between Missouri and Santa Fe, New Mexico, Bent's Old Fort catered to all walks of pioneer: prospectors and fur traders from the mountains, Native Americans and soldiers from the plains and Mexican and Anglo merchants arriving via the Mountain Branch of the Santa Fe Trail.

The Santa Fe Trail was a major thoroughfare for explorers, pioneers and homesteaders making their way across the American frontier. Following a direct line along the Arkansas River, the Sante Fe Trail offered frontiersmen like Kit Carson and John C. Fremont passage into the Rockies. Following limestone posts marking the route, historian buffs can follow twenty-two miles of the Santa Fe Trail along U.S. Highways 350 and 160, as it runs its course through the Comanche National Grasslands.

The Comanche National Grasslands occupy 435,707 acres just south of La Junta. Not only were they a major thoroughfare for early pioneers, but these grasslands continue to be a major fly way zone for some 275 different species of birds migrating in the spring and fall. Ranging in topography from deep cut canyons with vertical walls to gently rolling slopes and flatlands, the Comanche National Grasslands offer great recreational opportunities. Picket Wire Canyonlands offers a great ride past ancient Native American art, old homesteads and North America's longest recorded set of pre-Cambrian dinosaur tracks. Other areas of interest include Vogel Canyon, Picture Canyon and Carrizo Canyon.

The northern Eastern Plains is home to Colorado's other national grassland: Pawnee National Grasslands. Roughly 30 miles east of Fort Collins, near Briggsdale, CO, the Pawnee National Grasslands occupies an area of 193,000 acres. Its flat and gently rolling landscape is predominately composed of a wide expanse of blue grama and buffalo grass. These grasslands are distinguished, however, by a pair of buttes (Pawnee Buttes). These islands in the sky rise to 5,500 feet, 600 feet above the prairie's surface. The buttes support over 296 species of birds, a bird watches paradise. While riding to the base of these buttes is prohibited, there is a short hiking trail to the buttes. A scenic and relaxing ride through the grasslands includes traveling the Auto Bird Tour.

Other riding possibilities include traveling the famed Overland Trail. During America's expansion, the Overland Trail became the most heavily used pioneer route to the West. Established in 1862, this route avoided the Native American uprisings which were occuring on the Oregon Trail farther north through central Wyoming. The Overland Trail Museum, located in the town of Sterling, east of the Pawnee National Grasslands, showcases a reproduction of an old fort, provides details on the trail's route and displays a vast array of historical memorabilia. East of Sterling, in the town of Julesburg, lies the Fort Sedgwick Depot Museum. Here is where the 14-year-old Buffalo Bill Cody signed on with the Pony Express, Colorado's sole Pony Express stop.

# Picket Wire Canyonlands

## Ride Summary

Picket Wire Canyonlands takes you far away from Colorado's high country and delivers you near-ly to Kansas. Roughly 80 miles from the state line, Picket Wire Canyonlands is oftentimes over-looked by many Coloradoans, but remains, most certainly, one of its treasures. The initial 500-foot drop into the canyon is steep and rock-laden—the only technically challenging section of the entire ride. The rest of the ride travels over a worn jeep road that has since been reclaimed by doubletrack. While passing outcroppings of blocky limestone engraved with Native American art-work, the route delivers you to the banks of the Purgatoire River and to North America's longest recorded set of pre-Cambrian dinosaur tracks.

## Ride Specs

**Start:** From the Picket Wire Canyon Trailhead, by the pipe gate

**Length:** 18.2-mile out-and-back

**Approximate Riding Time:** Advanced Riders, 1½–2 hours; Intermediate Riders, 2–2½ hours

**Technical Difficulty Rating:** Technically easy to moderate: the first and last 500 feet of this out-and back trail offer some steep, rock- and sand-laden terrain as you begin by descending and end by climbing this portion of the trail. The route between rolls over relatively flat ter-rain with some climbs and descents thrown in.

**Physical Difficulty Rating:** Physically easy to moderate: although the route meanders at a considerably lower elevation (4,660 feet) than most mountain bike trails in Colorado, the heat and dryness of the desert bottom will tax your body's hydration tanks. Bring as much water as you can carry. It'd be a good idea to bring a water filter as well, since filtered water can be obtained throughout the ride from the Purgatoire River.

**Terrain:** Doubletrack and dirt road on desert terrain with sand and rocks

**Elevation Gain:** 1,098 feet

**Nearest Town:** La Junta, CO

**Other Trail Users:** Hikers, tour groups, and equestrians

**Canine Compatibility:** Dog-friendly—however, you will be riding through a desert, with exceedingly hot temperatures. Fortunately, there is the Purgatoire River.

## Getting There

**From La Junta:** Drive south on CO 109 for 13 miles. Turn right onto CR 802 (dirt road) and continue for eight miles. Turn left (south) on CR 25 and drive for six miles before turning left (east) again at FS 500.A. Drive on FS 500.A for one mile and pass the wire gate. (FS 500.A is not maintained and may be haz-ardous driving for anyone without a high clear-ance 4WD vehicle, particularly after a strong rain.) Continue following this dirt road for two miles until the road forks. Take the left fork. Drive to the parking sign and park your vehi-cle. For those unable to make it on this road, you may park your vehicle at the start of FS 500.A, at the bulletin board, and start your ride there. **DeLorme: Colorado Atlas & Gazetteer:** Page 100, B-3

Marveling at the natural arch on the way to the Rourke Ranch.

Not all of Colorado's open spaces have been overrun by urban sprawl, as many would have you believe. The Canyonlands' 16,000+ acres, surrounded by the 400,000-acre Comanche National Grassland, offer room to spare in a remarkably beautiful and sun-drenched landscape.

Picket Wire Canyonlands may never have received its protective status had it not been for two Colorado legislators, Senator Timothy Wirth and Representative Hank Brown. Their proposal to shift the land's management from the U.S. Army to the Forest Service passed in 1991. The one-time training site became expressly our own. Today it's one of our most treasured inheritances. The Canyonlands' boiling desert sands and scorched canyon walls remain patient attendants to this desert solitaire. The winding Purgatoire River is its only relief—and ours.

**FYI...**

*Since ranching is a primary means of livelihood in this area, please close all gates behind you and do not disturb livestock. Sunscreen, sunglasses, hat, insect repellent, and first aid kit are highly recommended.*

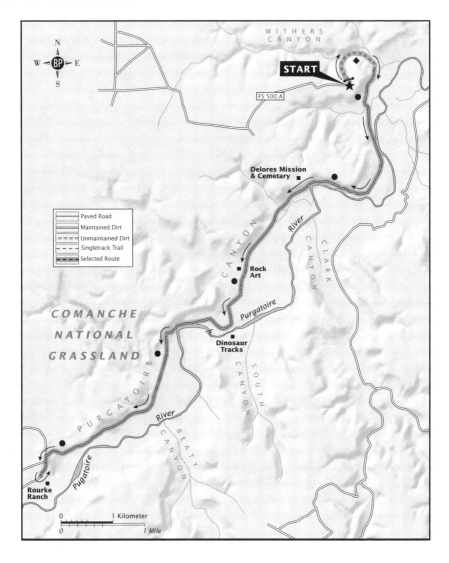

## **Miles**Directions

**0.0 START** at the trailhead to Picket Wire Canyonlands.

**0.1** Reach a pipe gate. Pass beyond the pipe gate and begin your ride by descending 500 feet through Withers Canyon to the canyon floor.

**3.0** First views of the Purgatoire River, as the trail rolls over mellow doubletrack through a meadow.

**4.0** You come to the remains of the Delores Mission.

**5.6** The trail "Y's." Bearing left will take you to the banks of the Purgatoire River and site of the longest recorded set of dinosaur tracks in North America.

**9.1** Reach Rourke Ranch and return the way came.

Mountain bikers must access Picket Wire Canyonlands by descending Withers Canyon via the Picket Wire Trail. Picket Wire Trail leads you on a journey through time. About 150 million years ago, long-necked gentle giants like the Brontosaurus and four-ton carnivores like the Allosaurus walked along the banks of the Purgatoire. Evidence of this is their footprints. Roughly 10,000 years ago, ancient Anasazi Indians passed through the canyon, leaving their mark on its surrounding walls. By the mid 14th Century, Picket Wire Canyonlands saw the exploration of the Spaniards—most notably of whom Francisco Vasquez de Coronado, whose search for gold led him throughout Southeast Colorado, including Picket Wire Canyonlands. Today, mountain bikers imbed their own tracks into Picket Wire sands, searching too for something within the blazing confines of the canyonlands.

With a pucker-rating of 9+, the 500-foot doubletrack descent through Withers Canyon is steep and rocky. Prickly pear, cholla cactus, prairie rattlesnakes, scorpions, tarantulas, badgers, and lizards—the poetry of natural selection—all await your arrival. Since temperatures are 10 degrees hotter on the canyon floor than atop the prairie and since summer temperatures range from 90 to 105 degrees, riders ought to bring a gallon of water per person. To cut down on the weight of a gallon of water, consider filtering your water from the Purgatoire River.

Once on the canyon floor, Picket Wire Trail becomes a doubletrack, with the semblance of a dirt road, and snakes its way through the Purgatoire Canyon in a south/southwesterly direction. Following along an old telegraph line—one still standing—the first five miles of trail lead past historic adobe ruins, probably left over from when migrant Spaniards roamed this area, and through thick and tall stands of vegetation. The latter will have you questioning your line of travel, as any semblance of earth beneath you becomes lost in a sea of green.

As you exit these tall grasses, the flat-faced vertical rocks to your right contain a number of prehistoric Anasazi petroglyphs. Although not much is known about these ancients, archeologists speculate that they were a nomadic people who tracked migrating game. Studies of these ancient petroglyphs reveal some to be 4,500 years old. Native Americans left markings of themselves hunting game in the canyon walls.

The hunger for food wasn't the only driving force behind human exploration of Purgatoire Canyon. In 1540, Francisco Vasquez de Coronado, a prospector for the Spanish crown, set out with 340 fellow Spaniards, 300 Native American allies, and

After a rift occurred between two leaders of Francisco Vasquez de Coronado's army during his search for gold in 1540, the expedition split into two camps, one of which was later found dead along the banks of what is today the Purgatoire River. Because the men died without having been given last rites, the river became known as the "River of Purgatory."

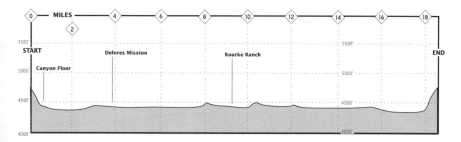

# Ride Information

## 📞 Trail Contacts:
Comanche National Grassland, La Junta, CO; (719) 384-2181

## 🕐 Schedule:
Picket Wire Canyonlands stays open from dawn to dusk and is best visited between March and November.

## ❓ Local Information:
Comanche National Grassland, La Junta, CO; (719) 384-2181 • **Rocky Ford Chamber of Commerce**, Santa Fe Depot, Rocky Ford, CO; (719) 254-7483 **Otero County Sheriff Office**, La Junta, CO; (719) 384-5941 or 911

## 💡 Local Events/Attractions:
**Annual Arkansas Valley Fair** held each August in Rocky Ford, CO—*contact the Rocky Ford Chamber of Commerce at (719) 254-7483*

## 🍴 Restaurants:
Café Grandmere, La Junta, CO; (719) 384-2711

## 🍲 Camping:
No overnight camping is allowed in Picket Wire Canyonlands.

## 🚲 Local Bike Shops:
Joey's Bike Shop, La Junta, CO; (719) 384-6575

## 🅝 Maps:
**USGS maps:** Riley Canyon, CO; Beaty Canyon, CO; O V Mesa, CO

1,000 slaves (both Indian and African) in search of gold in this region. Finding none, the Purgatoire Canyon remained unsettled for some time. However, as a result of Coronado claiming for Spain all the land through which he explored, this area has since become steeped in Spanish and Mexican culture. If legend holds true, the name of the Purgatoire River recalls the unfortunate deaths of a few Spanish fortune seekers who ventured into this canyon and eventually died of exposure. Since the deceased died before receiving their last rights—seeing as no priests were present— the Spanish religious faithfuls named the river "El Rio de Las Animas Perdidas en Purgatorio" (The River of Lost Souls in Purgatory). French trappers wandering into the canyon during the 18th Century would later rename the river Purgatoire.

At mile 4.0 lies the Delores Mission and Cemetery, built sometime between 1871 and 1889 when Mexican pioneers first began permanent settlement in this valley. Proof that offertories never go out of style, a rusting pot still hangs from a beam in the mission. Decorating the mission's small courtyard are the crumbling headstones of these early pioneers.

Just 1.6 miles from the Delores Mission and Cemetery lie the 150 million-year-old footprints of Brontosaurus and Allosaurus. Imbedded in the limestone rock along the banks of the Purgatoire River are 1,300 visible dinosaur tracks that extend for a quarter-mile. Imagine two-stepping with a 33-ton, 16-foot-tall, 70-foot long lizard. Watch the toes! The majority of tracks (about 60 percent) were left by the Allosaurus. The sharp claw prints of the three-toed Allosaurus sink deep into the antediluvian mud of the Purgatoire River.

Having feasted your eyes on these enormous tracks and cooled your caboose in the Purgatoire River's waterfall, continue south along the trail over the relatively easy terrain of rock and sand and past a natural arch. At mile 9.1 your route ends at the Rourke Ranch—only a fenced-off house and a shed remain. Built in 1871 by Eugene Rourke, the Rourke Ranch remained in the Rourke family for 100 years, three generations. When it was sold in 1971, the Rourke Ranch was known as one of the oldest and most successful operations in Southeast Colorado. Its acreage had grown from Eugene's original settlement of 40 acres to well over 52,000. With that kind of aged wealth, it's no wonder why the Rourke Ranch was known as the "Wineglass Ranch." From the Rourke Ranch, turn your mountain bike around and return back to the future.

# Honorable Mentions

## Eastern Plains Colorado

Noted below is one of great rides in the Eastern Plains region that didn't make the A-list this time around but deserves recognition nonetheless. Check it out and let us know what you think. You may decide that it deserves higher status in future editions or, perhaps, you may have a ride of your own that merits some attention.

### (J) Pawnee National Grasslands

Although Colorado's lowlands tend to get overlooked for their more sloping terrain, one of Colorado's flat-landed areas demands attention. Located 90 miles northeast of Denver and 30 miles east of Fort Collins, the 193,000-acre Pawnee National Grasslands has turned many a back to the mountains for the expansive grasslands east of Interstate 25. The most striking feature of these grasslands are the sandstone towers of the Pawnee Buttes. Each of the three buttes stands one half mile apart and rises 350 feet above the plains to an elevation of 5,375 feet. Since cliffs along the buttes are a preferred nesting area for larger birds of prey, riders are restricted to ride on a designated road. Access to these buttes is by foot-travel only. Users should know that these birds breed and nest from March through June, so hikers are encouraged to stay on designated trails.

The Pawnee Buttes is one of the finest sites in the world for vertebrate fossils. A number of horse species (including three-toed and dwarf versions), rhinoceros, ancient swine, and camel (a hippopotamus-like animal) have all been unearthed here. The Buttes also have a link to America's westward expansion, as a pioneer trail led straight across the Pawnee National Grasslands. To reach the Pawnee National Grasslands, drive north from Denver on Interstate 25 for roughly 60 miles. Turn right (east) onto Colorado 14, following signs for Ault. Drive on Colorado 14 for roughly 30 miles to the grasslands. For more information, contact Pawnee National Grassland at 660 "O" Street in Greeley, Colorado, (970) 353-5004. *DeLorme: Colorado Atlas & Gazetteer*: Page 94, B-2

# The Great Escape

## Telluride to Moab

### Two Wheels and Seven Days

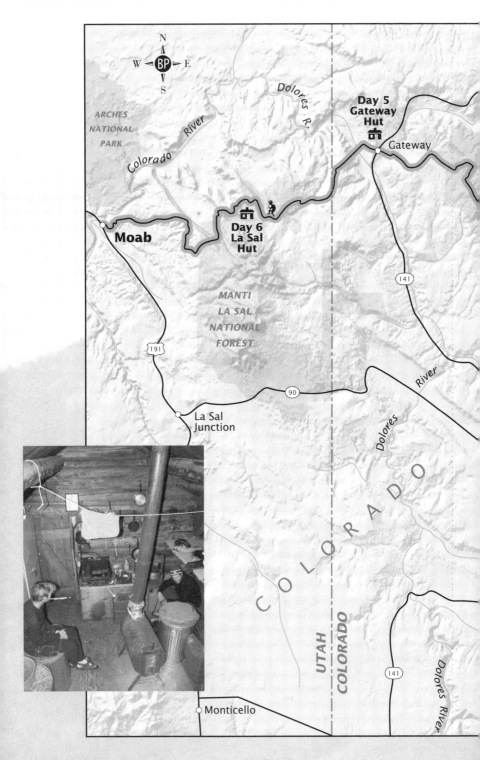

N
W ← BP → E
S

ARCHES
NATIONAL
PARK

Dolores R.

Day 5
Gateway
Hut

Gateway

Colorado River

Moab

Day 6
La Sal
Hut

141

MANTI
LA SAL
NATIONAL
FOREST

191

Dolores River

90

La Sal
Junction

COLORADO

UTAH
COLORADO

Dolores River

141

141

Monticello

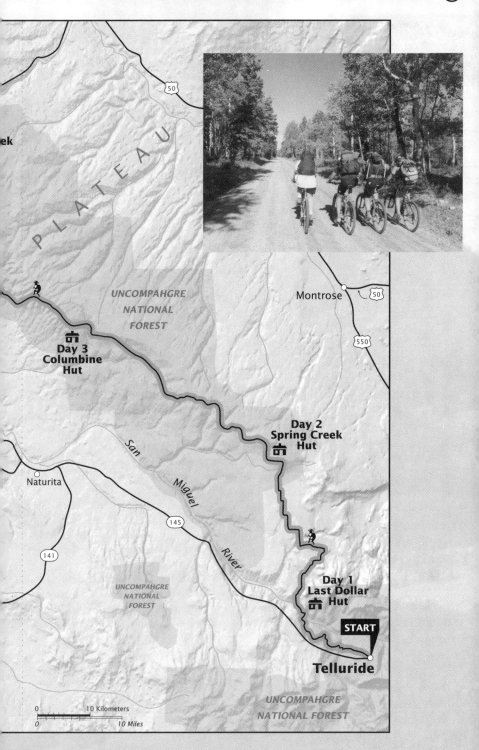

U.S. 50

PLATEAU

ek

UNCOMPAHGRE
NATIONAL
FOREST

Montrose

50

550

Day 3
Columbine
Hut

Day 2
Spring Creek
Hut

San

Miguel

Naturita

145

River

141

UNCOMPAHGRE
NATIONAL
FOREST

Day 1
Last Dollar
Hut

START

Telluride

UNCOMPAHGRE
NATIONAL
FOREST

0        10 Kilometers
0                10 Miles

# 50

# Telluride to Moab Hut to Hut

Packing up for the great escape.

Riders taking part in the San Juan Hut System's Telluride to Moab bicycle tour are in for an epic adventure. Expect to be treated to the 14,000-foot, snow-capped peaks of the San Juans, the 100-mile-long Uncompahgre Plateau, the awe-inspiring canyons of the Dolores River Valley, the rugged La Sal Mountains rising high above the red plain deserts of Moab, and the surreal red-rocked canyons and mesas of Moab. Save for the few singletrack trails that spur from the main route, the trip from the one-time tent-city of Telluride to the outlaw-town of Moab is more a test of stamina than of mountain bike handling skills.

Riders travel for seven days, mostly along U.S. Forest Service and Bureau of Land Management roads in the Uncompahgre and Manti-La Sal national forests, staying in a different hut each night. Situated along the route, these huts stand anywhere from 13 to 38 miles apart and include all the comforts of home. The six huts are equipped with eight padded bunks, a propane cook stove, propane lights, a wood-burning stove (except for the Gateway and La Sal huts), firewood (usually), and kitchen facilities. Although there is no running water, all huts include a water supply for drinking and cooking. The hut is stocked with dry and canned goods, some fresh fruit and vegetables, spices, drinking water, and sleeping bags. Note: riders have found occasions where huts were lacking certain food and/or cooking items, i.e. jelly, Gatorade, pizza and propane, so make sure your hut is stocked properly by contacting the San Juan Hut System.

Mike Turrin and Joe Ryan, Telluride locals, started the San Juan Hut System and their Telluride to Moab Hut to Hut trip in 1988. Since then, this trip has amassed classic status among fat tire enthusiasts. Riders receive three meals a day, lodging, and miles of jaw-dropping views. And if that doesn't sell you, try adding a 7,000-foot vertical drop from the Last Dollar Hut, atop Last Dollar Pass, and a cold glass of beer at the Moab Brewery into the mix. All this and more can be yours for just $395 per person. That's $56.42 per day.

Although riders are given a minimum-suggested equipment list and route descriptions, this hut tour is designed to be self-guided. And so, riders are expected to be in good physical shape and have knowledge of backcountry safety, first aid, and bicycle repair. A consideration often overlooked when assessing one's physical ability is the extra weight one may be carrying along this trip. Since this route travels through remote mountain territory, expect the unexpected, particularly weather—which can range from sweltering heat to snowstorms. You'll need to equip yourselves with a bicycle repair kit, first aid kit, hydration system or at least three large bottles of water, rain gear, a full layering system (shirt, hat, gloves, socks, separate pair of shoes), and bug repellent. The added weight of these items, coupled with the length and elevations of some of the day's rides, may greatly reduce an individual's stamina. Please know your limits.

Bike Creek Cabin and bikes.

From Telluride, the Victorian mining town tucked deep in the corner of a San Juan box canyon, riders ascend Last Dollar Pass along the western edge of the Sneffels Range. From there, it's a savage descent to Buck Canyon and Howard Flats before connecting with the Uncompahgre Plateau, a massive mesa whose sides are cut by massive gorges. Riding west atop the entire length of the Plateau's spine, riders descend via a knuckle-wrenching road into the Dolores River Valley. From deep in the heart of the valley, a long and arduous climb up John Brown Canyon awaits, as riders head toward the Utah border and the La Sal Mountains. From the La Sal Mountains, it's a fast-paced ride down into Moab, where millions of years of wind, water, and erosion have carved some of this country's most startling landscapes.

## Ride Information (General)

**Schedule:**
June 1 to October 1

**Fees/Permits:**
Through the San Juan Hut System, it's $395 per person for a seven-day, self-guided hut-to-hut tour from Telluride to Moab.

**Maps:**
*DeLorme Colorado Atlas & Gazetteer:*
Page 76, A 2-3; Page 66, D-B 1-2; Page 65, B-A 7-4; Page 55, D 4; Page 54, D-C 4-1—continued in *DeLorme Utah Atlas*—Page 41, D 6-4; Page 31 A 5-3 • **Uncompahgre National Forest Map and the Manti-La Sal National Forest Map** – *available at San Juan Hut System, Easy Rider Mountain Sports, 101 Colorado Ave., Telluride, CO; (970) 728-6935 or www.telluridegateway.com/sjhuts*

Just desserts atop Last Dollar Pass.

# Ride Information (In Telluride)

## 📞 Trail Contacts:

**San Juan Hut System**, Easy Rider Mountain Sports, 101 Colorado Ave., Telluride, CO; (970) 728-6935 or *www.telluridegateway.com/sjhuts*

## ❓ Local Information:

**Telluride Visitor Center**, 666 W. Colorado Ave., Telluride, CO; (970) 728-6265 or 1-800-525-2717 • **Ridgway Chamber of Commerce**, Ridgway, CO; (970) 626-5181

## 💡 Local Events/Attractions:

**Telluride Bluegrass Festival**, in June, Telluride, CO – *contact Telluride Visitor Center (970) 728-6265 or 1-800-525-2717* • **Melee in the Mines Mountain Bike Races**, in July – *contact Telluride Visitor Center (970) 728-6265 or 1-800-525-2717* • **Wild Mushrooms Conference**, in August – *contact Telluride Visitor Center (970) 728-6265 or 1-800-525-2717* • **Film Festival**, in September – *contact Telluride Visitor Center (970) 728-6265 or 1-800-525-2717* • **Blues & Brews Festival**, in September – *contact Telluride Visitor Center (970) 728-6265 or 1-800-525-2717*

## 🛏 Accommodations:

**Town of Telluride Park & Camp**, Telluride, CO; (970) 728-2173 – *$11.00 per night camping, showers and toilet facilities available May 15 to October 15*

## 🍴 Restaurants:

**La Cocina De Luz**, 123 E. Colorado Ave., Telluride, CO; (970) 728-9355 – *Mexican take-out and catering company* • **Rustico Ristorante**, 114 East Colorado, Telluride, CO; (970) 728-4046 • **Smuggler's**, 101 W. San Juan Ave., Telluride, CO; (970) 728-0919 – *Telluride's only brewpub*

## 🚵 Tours Guides:

**Telluride Outside**, 1982 W. CO 145, Telluride, CO; (970) 728-3895 or 1-800-831-6230 or *www.tellurideoutside.com* • Back Country Biking, Telluride, CO; (970) 728-0861 • **Telluride Sports/Adventure Desk**, 150 W. Colorado Ave., Telluride, CO; (970) 728-4477 or 1-800-828-7547 • **Telski/Mountain Adventures**, Telluride, CO; (970) 728-6900

## 🚲 Local Bike Shops:

**Easy Rider Mountain Sports**, 101 Colorado Ave., Telluride, CO; (970) 728-4734 • **Paragon Ski & Sport**, 213 W. Colorado Ave., Telluride, CO; (970) 728-4525 • **Telluride Sports**, 150 W. Colorado Ave., Telluride, CO; (970) 728-4477 or 1-800-828-7547

## ✈ Shipping Bikes:

(if you want to ship your bike)
**Easy Rider Mountain Sports**, Telluride, CO; (970) 728-4734 – *contact Missy Smith*

---

This kind of mountain bike tour includes some momentous gems one might not otherwise consider. Conversations with riding companions range from the day's sorest bum to the unrivaled benefits of being in Colorado. The days tend to pass quickly as you ride, eat, sleep, and ride again. In between the rhythm of the days, you may find the time to harmonize with friends during a heated wood-chopping competition. Not seeing your own reflection for a week, enduring unexpected rain delays, and meeting the challenge of making a new and exciting meal at the end of each day are just a few of the interesting times shared by all.

# Ride Information (In Moab)

## 🗲 Trail Contacts:

**Poison Spider Bicycle Shop**, 497 N. Main street, Moab, UT; (435) 259-7882 or 1-800-635-1792 or *www.poisonspiderbicycles.com* • **Kaibab Mountain Bike Tours**, 391 S. Main Street, Moab, UT; (435) 259-7423 or 1-800-451-1133 or *www.kaibabtours@aol.com* • **Chili Pepper Bike Shop**, 702 S. Main Street, Moab, UT; (435) 259-4688 or 1-800-677-4688

## ❓ Local Information:

**Moab, Green River Visitors Center**, Moab, UT; 1-800-635-6622 • **Moab Chamber of Commerce**, Moab, UT; (435) 259-7814

## 💡 Local Events/Attractions:

**Canyonlands National Park**, (435) 259-7164 • **Arches National Park**, (435) 259-8161

## 🛏 Accommodations:

**Free camping along the Colorado River** • **Slickrock Campground**, 1301½ N. U.S. 191, (435) 259-7660 or 1-800-448-8873

## 🍴 Restaurants:

**Moab Brewery**, 686 South Main (next to McDonald's), Moab, UT; (435) 259-6333 • **Grand Old Ranch House**, 1266 N. U.S. Highway 191, Moab, UT; (435) 259-5753 • **La Hacienda**, 574 North Main, Moab, UT; (435) 259-6319 •

Eddie McStiff's, 57 South Main, Moab, UT; (435) 259-BEER • **Moab Diner**, 189 South, Moab, UT; (435) 259-4006 – *great milkshakes*

## 🍴 Tours Guides:

**Dreamride Tours**, Moab, UT; 1-888-MOABUTAH or *www.dreamride.com* • **Never Summer Western Spirit Cycling**, Moab, UT; 1-800-845-2453 • **Nichols Expedition**, 497 N. Main, Moab, UT; (801) 259-3999 or *www.NicholsExpeditions.com* • **O.A.R.S/North American River Expeditions**, 543 North Main, Moab, UT; 1-800-342-5938 or *www.oars.com/moab* • **Holiday Expeditions, Inc.**, 544 East 3900 South, Salt Lake City, UT; (801) 266-2087, 1-800-624-6323 or *www.bikeraft.com*

## 🚲 Local Bike Shops:

**Poison Spider Bicycle Shop**, 497 N. Main street, Moab, UT; (435) 259-7882 or 1-800-635-1792 or *www.poisonspiderbicycles.com* • **Kaibab Mountain Bike Tours**, 391 S. Main Street, Moab, UT; (435) 259-7423 or 1-800-451-1133 or *www.kaibabtours@aol.com* • **Chili Pepper Bike Shop**, 702 S. Main Street, Moab, UT; (435) 259-4688 or 1-800-677-4688 • **Rim Cyclery**, 1233 S. U.S. 191, Moab UT; (435) 259-5333

## 🔆 Other Resources:

*Mountain Bike America: Moab*, by Lee Bridgers, *www.outside-america.com*

Although most of the riding is non-technical, there are three great singletrack rides you can do: Spring Creek, Ute Creek, and Porcupine Rim. Consult with the San Juan Hut System for more information on these and other available alternatives. With the Telluride-to-Moab mountain bike tour becoming as popular as it is, would-be vacationers should reserve their spaces early, probably three to six months in advance. Reservations are made through the San Juan Hut System at (970) 728-6935.

## Hut-To-Hut Biking

There are hut-to-hut trips available throughout the country. Most, however, are booked six to 12 months in advance. Here is a short list of other hut-to-hut outfitters you might be interested in contacting.

**The Yurts of Never Summer Nordic**, Fort Collins, Colorado (970) 482-9411. May 1 to October 1. Situated on the eastern flank of North Park in the Colorado State Forest, the Never Summer Nordic yurts are canvas, tent-like structures. There are as many as five yurts to which you can ride. Although kitchen facilities are provided, you must bring your own food, water, and sleeping bags. Rates range from $45 to $75.

**10ᵗʰ Mountain Hut System**, Aspen, Colorado (970) 925-5775 or www.aspen.com/huts. Aspen to Vail, Colorado. July 1 to September 30. Surrounding the Holy Cross Wilderness Area, this system includes 11 huts between Aspen and Vail. $22 per person includes sleeping bunks and kitchen facilities. Riders must bring their own food. Guided tours are available.

**Galena Lodge Yurts**, Galena, Idaho (208) 726-4010. June 15 to September 15. The Galena Lodge Yurts include three summer yurts. These yurts are open every day of the week, except Thursday nights. $50 per night will get you one yurt with the capacity to sleep five or six. Each yurt includes a wood-burning stove, a propane burner, and kitchen facilities, but no running water. A water supply is included. Situated roughly 24 miles north of Ketchum/Sun Valley, Idaho, these yurts are roughly two to three miles from each other. You must bring your own food.

**Gunflint Trail Lodges**, Grand Marie, Minnesota 1-800-322-8327. July 9 to September 21. Located in Minnesota's Superior National Forest, the Gunflint Trail Lodges offer yurt-to-yurt mountain biking for $870. The package includes a guided five-day tour along the north shore of Lake Superior, with lodging and meals provided. Fall tours can also be arranged for $429 (September 18-21). Self-guided tours are also available.

# Day 1

# Telluride to Last Dollar Hut

## Ride Summary

One of the most scenic and most photographed Colorado back roads, the Last Dollar Road leads to the Last Dollar Hut. Last Dollar Hut overlooks the La Sal Mountains and Utah to the west, the Wilson Peaks and the Lizard Head Wilderness Area to the south, and the Silverton West Group of the San Juan Mountains to the east. While the route is not particularly long, it does climb steeply at high elevations, and it delivers challenging switchbacks as you near Last Dollar Pass at 11,000 feet. Once you reach the pass, you're greeted with a 300-vertical-foot hike-a-bike section to the hut itself. You can view this as your final payment for one of Colorado's most exquisite panoramic views.

## Ride Specs

**Start:** From downtown Telluride
**Length:** 13.7 miles
**Approximate Riding Time:** Advanced Riders, 2–3 hours; Intermediate Riders, 3–4 hours
**Technical Difficulty Rating:** Technically easy to moderate. Much of the route travels on well maintained paved and dirt roads. There are a couple of talus field crossings with which you'll have to contend.
**Physical Difficulty Rating:** Physically moderate to challenging due to the sustained and steep climbs at high elevations. The final approach to the Last Dollar Hut is particularly demanding.
**Terrain:** Paved bike path, paved road, and dirt road. The terrain encountered includes loose talus-field rock, sand, and dirt.
**Elevation Gain:** 2,915 feet
**Nearest Town:** Telluride, CO
**Other Trail Users:** Hikers, backpackers, sightseers, and photographers

## Getting There

**From Telluride:** Drive west on Colorado Avenue to Mahoney Drive. Turn left on Mahoney Drive, passing Prospect and Smuggler streets to your left, and bear right into the Coonskin parking lot at the base of the Coonskin Lift (Lift 7). Park your vehicle here and begin riding.

A t around 10 o'clock in the morning on June 24, 1889, Butch Cassidy, Tom McCarty, and Matt Warner robbed the San Miguel National Bank in Telluride, forever labeling this Telluride depository as the first bank Butch Cassidy ever robbed. After their successful gunpoint withdrawal, the "wild bunch" took to the hills with the loot. Destination? Moab, Utah. They were headed to Brown's Hole, located in a large valley, along the foot of Diamond Mountain, near the Green River of Utah. In his autobiography, Tom McCarty spoke of their first hit. "Our plans were accordingly laid very carefully to go to a certain bank [San Miguel

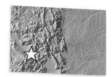

The crew setting out on Last Dollar Road.

National Bank of Telluride, which handled large mine payrolls] and relieve the cashier of his ready cash." The plan involved following a secret route from Telluride to Moab, with food and supplies located at key hideouts along the way. The threesome had even taken time to train the horses to stand perfectly still while each man vaulted into the saddle.

To aid in their getaway, Cassidy enlisted the services of his younger brother, Dan Parker. Parker served as supply runner. He'd travel ahead of the outlaws and drop stores of food and supplies at prearranged locations along the route—an important consideration if one hoped to cross the rugged San Juan and La Sal mountains successfully. No one doubted the Wild Bunch's ability to get away, even with a reputed $30,000 weighing them down—they were all accomplished riders—but Butch's little brother didn't fare so well. Parker was arrested while transporting the supplies. He was brought to Wyoming to answer to these and older charges. His subsequent arrest and imprisonment forced Cassidy, McCarty, and Warner to fend for themselves.

As for Butch and his gang, they were never found, nor was the stolen money. The posse employed to track the outlaws was not as enthusiastic about the chase as might be expected. The Wild Bunch were legendary gunmen whose pistol skills, no doubt, preceded them wherever they went. Telluride sheriff Beattie, masking his shame for never having captured the gang, resigned to boasting about the one thing he did manage to capture: Butch's horse. For years after the robbery, Sheriff Beattie delighted himself by riding around downtown Telluride on Butch Cassidy's horse, the only one who didn't get away.

A break in the action.

Today, riders can travel a similar route on their getaway from Telluride to Moab. By replacing saddlebags with panniers and horses with mountain bikes, riders can relive what it must have been like for Butch and his gang, riding from one food and supply hideout to the other. You begin your escape by riding up Telluride's Last Dollar Road, across the western corner of the Sneffels Range, to your first night's hideout, Last Dollar Hut. Although the 13.7-mile stretch from Telluride to the Last Dollar Hut is the shortest leg (in terms of miles) of the weeklong getaway, it climbs an impressive 2,800 feet to Last Dollar Pass (11,000 feet).

The Last Dollar Hut, the highest hut along the route and one of the first to be built in the San Juan Hut System, sleeps eight and sits atop a wind-beleaguered ledge, above the sheep-grazing meadows below. The Last Dollar Hut offers one of the most dramatic panoramic vistas in Colorado. From the perch you can take in views of the Silverton West Group of the San Juans, the La Sal Mountains in Utah (Day 6), and the Wilson Peaks (Mount Wilson, 14,246 feet and Wilson Peak, 14,017 feet). Of the three, the Wilson Peaks are perhaps the most prominent.

## **Miles**Directions

**0.0 START** from the Coonskin parking lot in downtown Telluride. Bear left onto Mahoney Drive and again on Colorado Avenue, riding west out of town. Intercept the paved Telluride Bicycle Path, and ride to Society Turn.

**3.0** Reach the intersection of Telluride Bicycle Path and Last Dollar Road by Society Turn. Cross CO 145 and bear right on Last Dollar Road (FS 638).

**5.1** Reach the intersection of the airport road and Last Dollar Road. Bear right at the top of the airport road (with the runway and hangers in sight to the left) onto the now dirt Last Dollar Road. A National Forest access sign and a stop sign (facing the opposite direction) mark this intersection.

**10.7** Enter into the Uncompahgre National Forest.

**11.2** Cross a talus field and continue riding through the aspen.

**11.4** Cross another talus field.

**12.8** Pass an old homestead to your left. Before crossing Summit Creek, a spring with water pouring from a black hose will be on your right. Begin climbing switchbacks as you near the final approach to the hut.

**13.3** Reach Last Dollar Pass. Bear right at the crest, following the steep and rocky road at the edge of the trees, and hike-a-bike the last quarter-mile up the ridge to the east. (Don't follow the road that darts left into the forest.) You'll be able to see the hut when you're within 50 feet of it.

**13.7** Arrive at the Last Dollar Hut.

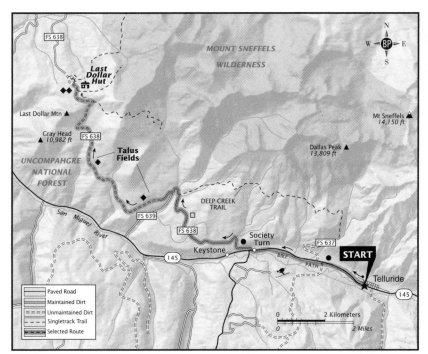

Mount Wilson and Wilson Peak were named after one man, the famed topographer of the Hayden Survey Team. To have even one of Colorado's 50-plus 14ers named after you would be an incredible honor, but to have two peaks bear your name is almost unimaginable. A.D. Wilson is so honored. Wilson's list of accomplishments include doing topographic work with Clarence King's 14th Parallel Survey, being the second to ascend Mount Rainier (within weeks of the first), and helping to organize the Hayden Atlas. The Hayden Survey Team was one of the first teams to accurately survey Colorado in the mid 1800s. Their extensive research and study was included in the *Hayden Atlas*. It was, however, primarily his work with the Hayden Survey Team that ensured Wilson his place among the highest peaks of the Colorado mountains.

As you rest by a blazing campfire outside the Last Dollar Hut and stare off across the canyon, you can't help but marvel at the grandness of the San Juans. Now nearly eye-level with these surrounding 14,000-foot peaks, you also can't help but marvel at the strength it took to reach this point in your own journey. Make sure you return from your reverie before too long, as another day awaits.

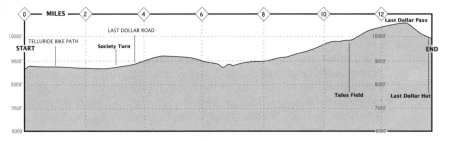

# Day 2

# Last Dollar Hut to Spring Creek Hut

## Ride Summary

Starting with one massive loss in elevation, this day's ride is perhaps the easiest of the tour. The ruddy complexion of Hastings Mesa offers a bit of insight into the kind of landscape into which you're heading (the lunar-scaped terrain of Moab, Utah), while the grandness of Howard Flats recalls visions of the galloping ponies Ute Indians once raced there. Once arriving at the Spring Creek Hut, riders can include some sideline riding on the Spring Creek Trail 116. The Spring Creek Trail 116 features some of the Uncompahgre Plateau's best singletrack. The 12-mile (one way) Spring Creek Trail 116 is mostly singletrack that passes through meadows, aspen groves, and creeks. Consult with San Juan Hut System for more information.

## Ride Specs

**Start:** From the Last Dollar Hut
**Length:** 27 miles
**Approximate Riding Time:** Advanced Riders, 2–3 hours; Intermediate Riders, 3–4 hours
**Technical Difficulty Rating:** Technically easy due to the well maintained dirt roads
**Physical Difficulty Rating:** Physically easy to moderate due to the large descent from the Last Dollar Hut. What moderate ascending there is comes at the end of the ride.

**Terrain:** Paved state road and well-maintained dirt road. Aside from a fast, sometimes loose, rocky descent from the Last Dollar Hut, the route to the Spring Creek Hut travels mostly through flat meadows, large valleys, and expansive plateaus.
**Elevation Gain:** -878 feet
**Nearest Town:** Montrose, CO
**Other Trail Users:** Sightseers, hunters, hikers, campers, anglers, and picnickers

The second day of your escape has all the makings of a fast getaway. You drop almost 3,000 feet to the paved Colorado 62 before eventually intersecting with Howard Flats—site of an old Ute horseracing track. Day two marks the beginning of your two-and-a-half day tour of the Uncompahgre Plateau, where Ute Indians once thrived. From Last Dollar Hut, continue riding on Last Dollar Road to Divide Pass and Colorado 62. En route, you'll descend through a forest of mixed aspens and conifers, passing old homesteads and paralleling Hastings Mesa. Once atop Hastings Mesa, you're treated to views of the Mount Sneffels Wilderness, including 14,150-foot Mount Sneffels. After intersecting Colorado 62 (the road that joins Placerville, in the southwest, with Dallas Divide and Ridgway, in the northeast), bear left onto Colorado 62 and speed down the paved highway. If you were to bear right onto Colorado 62, you'd soon reach the top of Dallas Divide and the town of Ridgway—which is perhaps next on Colorado's ever-dwindling list of mountain towns on the brink of massive discovery. Peter R. Decker's *Old Fences, New Neighbors*, The University of Arizona Press, Tucson, 1998 eloquently details Ridgway's burgeoning popularity.

After turning right off of Colorado 62, you ride up Buck Canyon and onto Howard Flats. Howard Flats used to be an old Ute horseracing track. Aside from its recreational use, the horse proved a formidable addition to the Utes' culture. Before the Spanish brought horses into North America, the Utes had led a primarily leaderless

and wandering existence. With the arrival of the horse, the Utes began to redefine themselves. They became individual, chief-led bands of hunters and warriors. They were also among the first tribes to maintain extensive domesticated horse herds. More horses meant more Ute Indians could hunt and raid more quickly and easily. Ute hunters gradually perfected their economy of motion. They would blitz into enemy Comanche-Arapaho territory and kill as many buffalo as they could, and still manage to make it back to their camps within half a moon's time (roughly 15 days). The efficiency with which Utes could now travel, enabled braves standing watch to react to enemy attacks with lightning speed. With their improved response, life inside Ute camps became more relaxed.

Horseracing became one of the Utes' most beloved pastimes. Whenever there was a social occasion, whether it be a wedding or a dance or a powwow, there was horse racing. The race became so much a part of Ute life that no camp was complete without its own racetrack. Before there was a Denver or a Mile-High Stadium, there was Howard Flats, home to the original big league broncos. If viewed from above, the Flats show long, straight sections of hoof-trodden earth, pinpointing the precise location where these races were held. Gambling eventually found its way into horse racing, and the scene began to spread, now starting to include white settlers. It was horseracing that would prove to be the gateway to a life of crime for men such as Butch Cassidy and his gang.

Cassidy first met Matt Warner, already an accomplished cattle rustler and horse racer, while at a horse race in Telluride in 1885. The young Cassidy, who worked as an ore hauler for one of the area mines, took a liking to Warner—despite the fact that

Spring Creek Hut.

## **Miles**Directions

**0.0 START** from the Last Dollar Hut. Bear left from the front door and walk (reducing further trail damage) your bicycle down the path located to the north side of the hut. This is not the way you came. When the path widens enough to allow a truck's passing, begin riding and descend from the pass on Last Dollar Road.

**0.4** Reach the intersection of the path and Last Dollar Road (FS 638). Bear right onto Last Dollar Road and descend the north side of Last Dollar Mountain.

**1.7** Arrive at a beautiful vista, on your left, with views of Hastings Mesa to the north, Wilson Peak to the south, and the La Sal Mountains to the distant west.

**4.4** After crossing two cattle guards, cross Alder Creek. Climb from Alder Creek onto Hastings Mesa and intersect CR 58P.

**6.0** Reach the intersection of Last Dollar Road, Sawpit Road, and CR 58P. Bear right onto CR 58P.

**8.4** Near San Juan Vista, pass an old ranch to the left. (This ranch was in the John Wayne movie "True Grit.")

**11.1** CR 58P intersects with the paved CO 62 at a stop sign. Bear left onto CO 62 and descend on pavement to CR 60X, passing CR 62X on the right.

**13.8** Reach the intersection of CO 62 and CR 60X. Bear right onto CR 60X, by an old ski cabin on the left. Begin climbing, moderately, up Buck Canyon into Howard Flats, site of an old Ute Indian horseracing track.

**17.2** Pass an old homestead, seen through a wide valley to your left.

**18.7** Reach the intersection of roads CR JJ6 and CR 59Z, by the San Juan Ranch gate and sign. Bear left onto CR JJ6.

**19.1** CR JJ6 will turn into CR 58.50 at a right curve. Bear right, continuing on CR 58.50.

**20.8** CR 58.50 connects with CR 11. Bear left on CR 11.

**21.0** Road 11 intersects with Dave Wood Road. Bear right onto Dave Wood Road, passing under power lines and descending moderately into a large valley.

**23.9** Reach the intersection of Sanborn Park Road (marked by a Sanborn Park sign) and Dave Wood Road. Bear right, continuing on Dave Wood Road, past the sign for Montrose. From here, the next and final three miles make up one long, steady climb to the Spring Creek Hut.

**24.6** Enter into the Uncompahgre National Forest.

**25.5** Pass the Johnson Spring on your right. This spring, fenced in by split aspen logs, features potable water pouring from a black hose.

**25.6** Reach the intersection of Dave Wood Road and Divide Road. A sign reads Columbine Pass, 31 miles. Bear left here onto the Divide Road (FS 402).

**25.9** Reach the intersection of the Divide Road and the Spring Creek Rim Road. Bear right onto the Spring Creek Rim Road and cross three cattle guards before turning left onto the path leading to the Spring Creek Hut.

**26.1** Cross the first cattle guard.

**26.4** Cross the second cattle guard.

**26.8** Cross the third cattle guard.

**27.0** Bear left, after a large water bar ditch, onto a path leading into the woods. An enormous cut section of a Douglas fir trunk lies to the left of the path. Follow this short path to the Spring Creek Hut.

**27.0** Arrive at the Spring Creek Hut.

Descending past the enormous cut Ponderosa stump to the Spring Creek Trail.

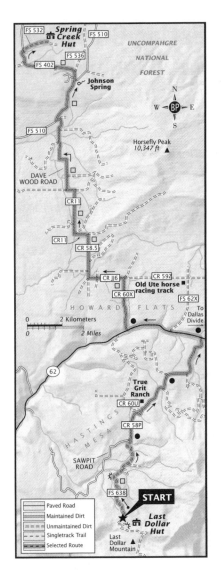

Cassidy had lost his savings to Warner in horse racing debts. And Warner, in turn, liked Cassidy, if for no other reason than Cassidy kept him in business. The two eventually became partners in their own horse racing business.

With their best horse Betty, and others like her, Butch and Matt managed to beat every horse in southern Colorado and Utah. While racing in Cortez, Matt met up with his brother-in-law Tom McCarty and invited him to join in their racing business. The three of them set out to become the area's most successful horse racing team. Butch, Matt, and Tom made names for themselves throughout the racing circuit of southern Colorado and Utah, so much so that, in time, only Indians would race against them.

At one such race, an Indian, who had lost his pony and a stack of blankets to the three men, launched a barrage of insults and threats, objecting to their win. Having been so affronted, Tom beat the Indian with a rawhide riding whip. The three quickly bolted from the scene to Tom's cabin. The next morning, Butch, Matt, and Tom awoke to the shrill cries of Indians howling. The Indians approached the cabin and demanded the return of their pony. When one of the Indians pointed a rifle at Tom, Tom quickly returned the idle threat by shooting the Indian off his horse, effectively ending the discussion.

From Howard Flats, you ride silently on, brooding over the possibility of a ghost-encounter with an envious Indian. Once beyond the Flats, you begin your two-and-a-half day journey across the Uncompahgre Plateau, Ute domain.

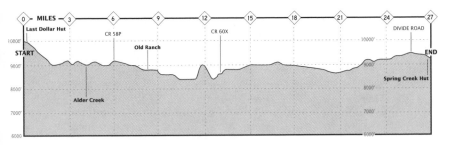

# Day 3

# Spring Creek Hut to Columbine Hut

## Ride Summary

Day three offers a pleasurably mellow cruise atop the Uncompahgre Plateau, traveling over gently rolling terrain on the Divide Road, the major southwest-to-northeast thoroughfare across the plateau. The Divide Road is thickly lined with old-growth evergreen forests, lending the riding an air of peaceful solitude. Although the trees enclose most of the way, there are three dramatic overlooks, evenly spaced along the route, which demand attention.

## Ride Specs

**Start:** From the Spring Creek Hut
**Length:** 34.8 miles
**Approximate Riding Time:** Advanced Riders, 3–3½ hours; Intermediate Riders, 4–5 hours
**Technical Difficulty Rating:** Technically easy. The route follows atop the relatively flat Uncompahgre Plateau via the well-maintained Divide Road.

**Physical Difficulty Rating:** Physically easy due to the minimal elevation gain
**Terrain:** Improved dirt road. The Uncompahgre Plateau offers a relatively flat, but densely forested ride.
**Elevation Gain:** -39 feet
**Nearest Town:** Montrose, CO
**Other Trail Users:** Anglers, hikers, hunters, and campers

The third leg of the journey travels through the heart of the Uncompahgre Plateau, summiting it atop Columbine Pass. From the Spring Creek Hut, the riding on the Divide Road features densely forested terrain. The day's riding is marked more by a sense of quiet solitude than by mind-blowing views. That's not to say there are no views. Quite the contrary. The first of three incredible overlooks arrives at mile 5.7, the Uncompahgre Overlook. To the east lie the peaks of Wetterhorn and Uncompahgre.

Wetterhorn Peak resembles a shark's nose. Named by the Wheeler Survey Team in 1874, the peak undoubtedly takes its name from the Swiss mountain of the same name, but finding a resemblance to the Swiss behemoth might require a bit of imagination. Just to the south of Wetterhorn Peak lies the Henson Creek Valley, a hotbed of mining activity. The chief city in the valley was Capitol City. (established in the mid 1870s). Its misleading name was purely intentional. George T. Lee, Capitol City founder and owner of the town's main economic draw, the Lee Mining and Smelting Company, had visions of relocating Colorado's capital at Capitol City. His scheme was so elaborate as to include building a two-story brick house, later dubbed "the Governor's Mansion," with bricks imported from Pueblo. Lee's capital dreams would eventually dissolve after silver prices dropped in 1893.

To the east of Wetterhorn Peak lies Uncompahgre Peak, the largest in the San Juan range. Towering over the Cimarron River and Big Blue Creek drainage, the Uncompahgre Peak is one of the San Juan's most prominent landmarks. The word "uncompahgre" (pronounced "Oon-cum-pa-gray") comes from the Shoshonean language, a dialect of the Uto-Aztecan language, and means "hot [unca] water [pah] spring [gre]." The Ute Indians found this San Juan precipice an ideal lookout. The name was officially given by the Hayden Survey Team during the latter part of the 1800s.

Sitting out a rain/hail storm.

During a massive study of the San Juans, Hayden Survey members A.D. Wilson and Franklin Rhoda made the first documented ascent of the peak in the summer of 1874. Once atop the peak, the two noticed markings in the ground. The markings turned out to be grizzly paw prints. Evidently, the area surrounding the Uncompahgre Peak was a favorite haunt among grizzlies. Given this, it seems no surprise that the Utes would convene here, as they held the bear in high regard, so much so that they called their most sacred and popular spring dance the Bear Dance. With thoughts of dancing bears aside, riders press on past the Uncompahgre Overlook to the Mount Sneffels Overlook.

The Mount Sneffels Overlook arrives at 10.3 miles into your ride. Mount Sneffels has been dubbed "Queen of the San Juans." It is one of those hallmark precipices that can hypnotize an observer for hours. Below this royal peak, reflecting its lofty throne, is the Blue Lakes Basin. During the Hayden Survey of 1874, a member of the team remarked that the basin reminded him of the absorbing hole described in Jules Verne's *Journey to the Center of the Earth.* Alluding to the Icelandic mountain located near the "hole" in Verne's novel, survey member Dr. Endlich exclaimed "There's Snaefell"—which in Icelandic translates to "snowfield." Today, we have sufficiently corrupted the spelling and pronunciation enough to give us Mount Sneffels.

Just under a mile from Columbine Pass and the top of the Uncompahgre Plateau, riders are offered their third and most dramatic scenic overlook: the Tabeguache Overlook, with views of the Dolores River Valley to the west. The Tabeguache (meaning "sunny side") were a band of Ute Indians who lived in the valleys of the Gunnison and Uncompahgre rivers. They lived in harmony with their natural surroundings. Of all the Tabeguache, perhaps no one was more prominent than Chief Shavano. The chief worked closely with Chief Ouray, leader of the Ute Nation, to help establish peaceful relations between the whites and the Utes. Chief Shavano's leadership was such that Chief Ouray, perhaps the greatest of all Ute chiefs, favored him his successor. In continued respect for his tireless efforts to bring about peace, Chief Shavano is one of only four Indians to have a Colorado 14er bear his name: Mount Shavano

## **Miles**Directions

**0.0 START** from the Spring Creek Hut. Ride up the path back to the Spring Creek Road. Bear right on the Spring Creek Road, heading back toward the Divide Road.

**0.2** Cross the first cattle guard.

**0.6** Cross the second cattle guard.

**0.9** Cross the third cattle guard.

**1.0** Reach the intersection of the Spring Creek Road and Divide Road (FS 402). Bear right (north) onto the Divide Road, toward Columbine Pass.

**5.7** Reach the Uncompahgre Overlook, to your left (east). There are views of Precipice Peak (13,144 feet), Uncompahgre Peak (14,309 feet), and Wetterhorn Peak (14,015 feet).

**8.3** Reach the intersection of the Divide Road and the Spring Creek trailhead, the Uncompahgre Plateau's premier singletrack. Continue riding on the Divide Road.

**10.3** Mount Sneffels Overlook is to your left (east). There are views of Mt. Sneffels (14,150 feet), Lizard Head (13,113 feet), Wilson Peak (14,017 feet), and Mount Wilson (14,246 feet).

**15.6** Reach the intersection of the Divide Road and CO 90 (FS 540). CO 90 will be to your right. Continue on the Divide Road, following signs for Columbine Pass.

**16.1** Pass Iron Springs Campground, on your left.

**16.6** Pass Transfer East Road, to your right.

**17.3** The intersection for Transfer Road and Olathe 27 will be to your right, as you continue riding on the Divide Road

**18.8** Pass West Antone Springs 559, to your left.

**19.9** Pass Pool Creek Trail 113, to your right.

**20.6** Pass Delta/Nucla Road, to your left.

**21.8** Pass Pool Creek Trailhead, to your right.

**22.2** Pass West Pool Creek Trail, to your right.

**23.4** Pass East Bull Creek, to your right.

**31.7** Tabeguache Overlook is on your left.

**32.5** Reach Columbine Pass and bear right onto FS 503.

**33.3** Reach Columbine Campground. Toilet facilities are available. Good drinking water is available from the spring.

**33.7** Pass the now-defunct Columbine Ranger Station and arrive at the intersection for FS 402 and FS 503. Bear left (west), following FS 402 (still the Divide Road) toward Windy Point.

**34.5** Pass a dirt road leading off to the left.

**34.7** Bear left onto this second dirt road leading into the woods. Follow this small non-gravel road for roughly 200 yards to the hut.

**34.8** Arrive at the Columbine Hut.

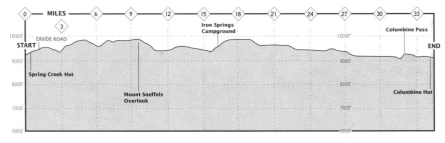

(14,229 feet). Today, descendants of the Tabeguache, along with members of the Grand, Yampa, and Uintah bands, comprise the Northern Utes. They live on the Uintah-Ouray Reservation, with their headquarters in Fort Duchesne, Utah.

From the Tabeguache Overlook, riders pass over Columbine Pass (where potable water is available) and continue in the direction of Windy Point, before arriving at the Columbine Hut.

Taking in the views.

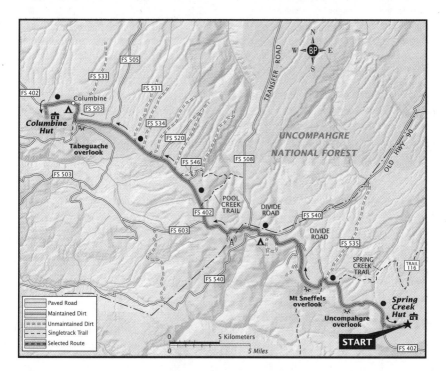

# Day 4

# Columbine Hut to Big Creek Cabin

## Ride Summary

Day four is perhaps the journey's most spectacular leg. As you near the end of your two-and-a-half day tour of the Uncompahgre Plateau, you ride down the western edge of the Plateau over the rolling Divide Road. En route, vertigo-inducing views of the La Sal Mountains and the high deserts of Southeastern Utah mesmerize your visual senses. Fear not the hypnotic trance in which you may find yourself. Let it carry you through to the Big Creek Cabin. A turn-of-the-century rancher's cabin, Big Creek Cabin is constructed of notched logs chinked with mortar. Poised among quaking aspens in a far corner of the Craig Ranch, overlooking a horse corral, Big Creek's idyllic setting only serves to enhance the buzz already acquired from the day's viewtiful ride.

## Ride Specs

**Start:** From the Columbine Hut
**Length:** 36.9 miles
**Approximate Riding Time:** Advanced Riders, 2½–3 hours; Intermediate Riders, 3½–4 hours
**Technical Difficulty Rating:** Technically easy due to traveling on mildly undulating terrain, along the well maintained Divide Road
**Physical Difficulty Rating:** Physically easy due to the little ascending involved, roughly 1,600 feet
**Terrain:** Improved dirt road. The route travels atop the densely forested Uncompahgre Plateau, with open views as you near the Plateau's western edge.

**Elevation Gain:** 3,100 feet
**Nearest Town:** Gateway, CO
**Other Trail Users:** Hikers, hunters, campers, anglers, and sightseers

For further reading: *Uncompahgre: A Guide to the Uncompahgre Plateau*, by Muriel Marshall, Valley Books, 3rd edition, 1998, 328 East Main Street, Montrose, CO 81401, (970) 249-1841.

For two-and-a-half days you've been riding on the Uncompahgre Plateau. Day 4 marks the final leg of your travels on the Divide Road and the Plateau. But what exactly is this Uncompahgre Plateau, and where does it fit in the grand scheme of things? Unlike the San Juan Mountains, whose high alpine peaks were formed 10 to 40 million years ago by volcanic upheaval and glaciation, the Uncompahgre Plateau was formed by a series of massive uplifts caused by internal disturbances of the earth's crust. Mysteriously, the Uncompahgre Plateau somehow escaped the geological turmoil which swept across the west to form the Sierra Nevadas, the ranges of Nevada and Utah and lastly the Rocky Mountains.

The Uncompahgre Plateau is located on the Colorado Plateau Province's eastern border. This province encompasses the vast area of flat-lying sedimentary rock extending into Utah, Arizona, and New Mexico. The Uncompahgre Plateau stretches in a southeast-to-northwest direction from the San Juan Mountains to the Utah-border southwest of Grand Junction. A virtually flat mesa stretching 25x100 miles, the Plateau, when viewed from a distance, is far less striking than its neighboring San Juan and West Elk mountains. This paling-by-comparison situation has allowed the

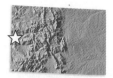

Plateau a certain degree of anonymity. Nevertheless, the Uncompahgre Plateau is, indeed, part of the ancestral Rocky Mountains and deserves attention. Its existence stems from the Uncompahgria uplift, the ancient range lifted high by faulting 310 million years ago A series of lesser uplifts, occurring roughly one million years ago, gave the Plateau its present formation.

Although archeological evidence suggests that people have been living on the Uncompahgre Plateau for at least 10,000 years, its recorded history did not start until the late 1770s. In 1776 two Spanish priests Silvestre Velez de Escalante and Francisco Antanasio Dominguez, accompanied by a Ute guide, led a party from Sante Fe, New Mexico, across the Uncompahgre Plateau in search of safe passage to the missions of California. As winter approached, the two decided to call off their tired search and head back to Santa Fe.

Fifty-two years later, Antoine Robidoux, who had been operating a fur trapper supply business in St. Louis, built a trading post near the present town of Delta, Colorado. In response to the recent popularity of the top hat (which was made of beaver pelts), many trappers flocked to the Uncompahgre in search of beaver. Robidoux's Fort Uncompahgre, functioning as a supply station for trappers and Indians alike, became a meeting ground for these two very different peoples. The fort was significant in that it provided an arena where trappers and Indians would meet; otherwise, these two groups would seldom see each other outside of the trading room. Not only this, but Fort Uncompahgre was significant in that it was one of only two white settlements in all of Colorado. This would change, however, when in 1850 the U.S. laid claim to all of western Colorado.

In 1853, Congress ordered Captain John Gunnison to explore the new territory and report on its potential. His travels took him from the Great Plains to the San Luis Valley, over Cochetopa Pass, down the Gunnison River, and into the Uncompahgre Valley. Gunnison would happen upon the ruins of Fort Uncompahgre, which had been set ablaze by Ute Indians shortly after it was built. Gunnison wrote of a savage and rugged Colorado, one that did not sound entirely hospitable. But to his credit, he did detail information that proved particularly helpful in future expeditions, like the Wheeler and Hayden surveys.

Wheeler and Hayden discovered the Uncompahgre Plateau to be rife with minerals. Once the news of this got out, countless miners and prospectors flocked to the Plateau to set up shop. As the Plateau mining increased, resident Utes were pushed farther and farther from their settlements. The mushrooming mining towns became the economic, social, and political lifeline of the Uncompahgre country and paved the way for other industries to move in. By the 1880s it was no surprise when tens of thousands of cattle were grazing on the Plateau. The large number of cattle, coupled with loose grazing regulations, eventually tuned many large tracks into barren wastelands. This resulted in the turn-of-the-century establishment of federal land reserves, precursors to our national forests.

## **Miles**Directions

**0.0 START** from the Columbine Hut and backtrack to the Divide Road.

**0.1** Intersect with the Divide Road. Bear left (north) onto the Divide Road and start riding toward Windy Point.

**9.4** Reach Windy Point. A scenic overlook of the La Sal and Abajo (Blue) mountains faces west.

**13.0** You're offered the first view of the Grand Mesa, to your right (northeast), near the town of Grand Junction.

**13.9** Leave Montrose County and enter Mesa County.

**22.3** Pass the Uncompahgre Butte (9,732 feet), to your right.

**23.2** The La Sal Mountains vista is to the west.

**25.2** Pass Mesa Creek, to the left.

**27.6** To the northeast lies the largest view of the Grand Mesa.

**29.1** Pass the Ranger Station and the Cold Springs Work Center, on your right.

**33.3** Pass the Divide Forks Campground, on your left.

**33.5** Reach the junction of Divide Road (FS 402) and Uranium Road (FS 404). Continue straight (right) on the Divide Road toward Grand Junction.

**33.7** Pass the Big Creek Trail 656, on your left.

**36.6** Reach the intersection of Divide Road and the doubletrack on the left which leads to the cabin. Bear left onto this doubletrack (which bears the sign "Private Access Road") directly before the cattle guard which crosses the Divide Road. Follow the split-rail fence (which eventually turns to a wire fence) to the cabin. The Telephone Trail begins to the right, just over the cattle guard.

**36.9** Arrive at the Big Creek Cabin.

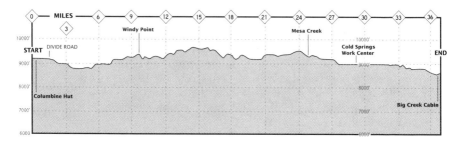

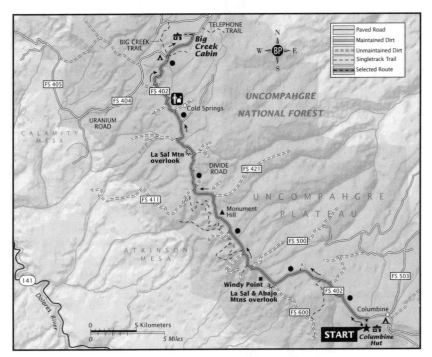

As you ride the former chuckwagon trail of the Divide Road, dodging perhaps 10 cattle, instead of tens of thousands, you can't help but appreciate our national forest system. That appreciation comes fully to bear when you arrive at Windy Point. Here the dramatic upward arching of the Plateau's rock layers is brought to view, as the Plateau, itself, drops precipitously nearly 2,000 feet in a collection of cliffs and slopes to Burro Creek. Looking northwest from Windy Point, you're offered a unique bird's-eye view of the Plateau's abrupt west face. A pair of eagles can often be seen soaring high above the Plateau's west face.

But eagles aren't the only birds to take up permanent residence on the Plateau. Located just after the turnoff leading to the Big Creek Cabin lies the nearby Telephone Trail—so called for the variety of nesting holes bored in the trail's tree trunks. The Telephone Trail makes for a great wind-down hike after you settle in at the cabin. The entire trail courses through a cavity-nesting bird habitat that's noted for its variety of uncommon birds which nest in holes burrowed into standing dead trees. Northern pygmy-owls (Glancidium gnoma), flammulated owls (Otus flammeolus), hairy woodpeckers (Picoides villosus), nuthatches (Sitta canadensis and Sitta carolinensis), and swallows (Tachycineta thalassina) all may be seen while hiking. If hiking after biking isn't your style, simply chill out at the cabin, a hideout with real character.

# Day 5

# Big Creek Cabin to Gateway Hut

## Ride Summary

Along with the mostly descending, nine-mile stretch of singletrack of the Ute Creek Trail 608, riders are treated to great views of the La Sal Mountains and the canyons of the Dolores River Valley. From the cool forests atop the western flank of the Uncompahgre Plateau, riders also descend along a six-mile shelf into the sandstone canyons of the Dolores River Valley. In total, the ride drops you 4,900 feet from the Big Creek Cabin to the Gateway Hut. The Gateway Hut is located in the tiny town of Gateway, Colorado. Unless you brought it with you, you've had no access to adult beverages in over four days. The Gateway Tavern can help. But take note: it's closed on Mondays, so plan your trip accordingly.

## Ride Specs

**Start:** From the Big Creek Cabin
**Length:** 28 miles
**Approximate Riding Time:** Advanced Riders, 2½–3 hours; Intermediate Riders, 3–4 hours
**Technical Difficulty Rating:** Technically easy to challenging. Most of this leg travels over well-maintained dirt road; however, the optional singletrack spur involves steep, rocky descents along sand and dirt packed trail. Also, there's a pulse-racing descent over rocky road from the top of the Uncompahgre Plateau into the Dolores River Valley.
**Physical Difficulty Rating:** Physically easy to moderate. The intermittent short, but tough, climbs of the singletrack spur, coupled with the more moderate climbs along the road, make this leg of the journey moderately physical.

**Terrain:** Improved dirt road, paved state highway, doubletrack and singletrack. Near the western edge of the Plateau, the thick, forested terrain gives way to rockier and sandier, semi-arid terrain. Sand, exposed rocks and roots are all to be expected along this route, particularly on the singletrack spur. As you enter into the Dolores River Valley and a flash flood zone, there are large sections of deep sand.
**Elevation Gain:** -4,010 feet
**Nearest Town:** Gateway, CO
**Other Trail Users:** Hikers, campers, four-wheelers, hunters, and sightseers

From Big Creek Cabin, riders return to the Divide Road and backtrack to its intersection with Uranium Road. As its name suggests, Uranium Road was once used to transport uranium from the many Plateau mines. Uranium was being shipped to Grand Junction as early as World War I, where it was used to aid in the war effort. The Uranium Road follows an old Ute trail that the Indians used frequently. This old Ute trail will eventually connect with one of the day's highlights, the singletrack of the aptly named Ute Creek Trail 608.

The Ute Creek Trail is an optional singletrack spur from the main route, but one well worth taking. The trail descends through thick aspens, over big rock drop-offs, into chilling creek beds, across sweeping meadows, and through piñon-juniper forests before letting out onto slickrock and sandstone. At mile 9.4 the views of the La Sal Mountains and John Brown Canyon are engulfing. Adding to the challenge of the

Descending down doubletrack into Dolores River Valley.

singletrack is the extra weight that bike touring necessitates. Panniers might be the way to go when touring on well-maintained forest roads, but their value is called into question when barreling down tight and rocky singletrack. The extra weight adds a new dimension to singletrack riding. After you intersect with the Snowshoe Trail, it's a short, grunt of a climb to Pine Mountain Road.

After riding roughly 1.5 miles from this intersection, the route unfolds to an overwhelming view of the Dolores River Valley. From the western flank of the Uncompahgre Plateau, you descend abruptly along a shelf road into the valley—a valley consisting of a maze of mesas and canyons. This is a hair-raising section of the ride. The shelf falls steeply from the Plateau with nothing to your right save a 300-foot drop to the canyon floor. This marks the beginning of a fast and furious descent into the Dolores River Valley and the town of Gateway.

The Dolores River received its name from the Spanish missionaries Dominguez and Escalante, who, in 1776, led an expedition across the Uncompahgre Plateau in search of safe passage to the missions of California. In order to reach the Ute Trail (Uranium Road), which crossed over the Uncompahgre Plateau, the expedition had to ford the, then unnamed, Dolores River. After realizing that they had passed the point where they should have crossed the river, Dominguez and Escalante hastily ordered their expedition to cross where they were. This decision proved costly, since Dominguez, Escalante and their expedition now found themselves entangled in thorny brush and standing before a steep canyon wall. They struggled to scale the

wall to the top of the Plateau, so much so that their horse's hooves started to bleed. Having endured such great pain and suffering in the crossing, the priests consequently named the river, appropriately enough, "dolores" or "pains."

In the 1880s gold was discovered on Mesa Creek Flats, located upriver, just four miles below the junction of the Dolores River and the San Miguel River. Soon thereafter, prospectors were panning for gold in Mesa Creek. However, there was one slight hitch to this endeavor; gold panning was limited to only the spring and early summer, since water flow from Mesa Creek was quite small. By mid-summer, in fact, Mesa Creek would run dry, effectively putting an end to gold panning in Mesa Creek Flats until the winter's snowmelt would again give rise to Mesa Creek. These circumstances inspired the Montrose Placer Mining Company, managed by Colonel N.P. Turner, to construct the San Miguel Flume, one of Colorado's greatest engineering achievements. The mining company believed that if enough water were to rush through Mesa Creek and into the Flats, millions of dollars worth of gold could be recovered from the soil all year through. Construction on the flume began in 1889 and was completed two years later. By 1891, this ambitious project began diverting water from the San Miguel River to Mesa Creek, a distance of roughly 12 miles.

Turner's intent was to mine Mesa Creek hydraulically, using pressurized water to sift the heavier gold particles from the river sediment. The water and sediment mixture would flow through a sluice box and over a riffle board. The sluice, which closely resembles a flume, was angled to allow the mixture to sift through. The riffles were small slats that ran perpendicular to the sides of the sluice box, much like venetian blinds might look if lain open in a shoebox. The riffles would catch the sand containing the heavier gold particles.

Turner's diversion plan called for an eight-mile long, four-foot deep, and six-foot wide flume running along the northern wall of the San Miguel Canyon. Workers were literally hung over the canyon wall, 250 to 500 feet below rim and 100 to 150 feet above the riverbed, all in order to secure the flume into the sandstone walls. Once completed, the flume ran a mile-and-a-half on the sandstone cliffs above the San Miguel River and six and a half miles on the canyon wall above the Dolores River. An estimated 1.8 million board-feet of lumber was used to construct the flume, which cost over $100,000 to build. Completed in 1891, the flume was an engineering success. It worked beautifully, delivering over 80 million gallons of water a day. But its true success was yet to be tested. Would it yield gold?

The gold found along the Mesa Creek Flats was known as "leaf gold" or, "flour gold," gold consisting of a very fine powder. Because of the gold's fine consistency, it washed straight through the sluice. Remaining suspended in the water, the gold flushed directly over the riffles in the flume, in effect, rendering them useless. It didn't take long for Turner, along with the Montrose Placer Mining Company stockholders, to realize that the entire project was a failure. With the entire investment in the flume lost, Turner became so dejected that he traveled to Chicago, rented a room and shot himself in the head. After Turner's horrific demise, the flume was soon abandoned, left only to the scavenging ranchers whose cabins and sheds and fences needed mending. Remnants of the flume still cling to sections of the canyon, near Uravan, roughly 25 miles south of Gateway.

Smiling on the Ute Creek singletrack.

Final approach into Dolores River Valley and Gateway.

## **Miles**Directions

**0.0 START** from the Big Creek Cabin and ride back up the doubletrack to Divide Road (FS 402).

**0.3** Reach the intersection of the doubletrack and Divide Road (FS 402). Bear right onto the Divide Road (FS 402), and return to the intersection of Divide Road (FS 402) and Uranium Road (FS 404).

**3.2** Pass the Bear Creek Trail, on your right.

**3.4** Reach the junction of Divide Road (FS 402) and Uranium Road (FS 404). Bear right onto Uranium Road (FS 404) and ride in a northwesterly direction.

**4.6** Pass the Big Creek Cutoff Trail, to your right.

**6.3** Pass the Rim Trail ("Wolf Hill – 2" and "Big Pond – 3"), to your right.

**6.7** Reach the intersection of Uranium Road and Ute Creek Trail 608. Bear right onto the Ute Creek Trail. [**Option.** *For those uninterested in riding the singletrack, you can continue on Uranium Road for roughly 14.6 miles, to the intersection of Uranium Road and CR 6.30/FS 405. At a sign marking the turnoff to the town of Gateway, bear right onto CR 6.30/FS 405 and descend to Indian Creek. Continue on CR 6.30/FS 405 at all other intersections and ride for roughly 6.5 miles to Calamity Basin. Rejoin the others at the Snowshoe trailhead. For more information: Contact the San Juan Hut System.]*

**7.7** Descend the rocky singletrack and ride straight through an opening in a barbed wire fence.

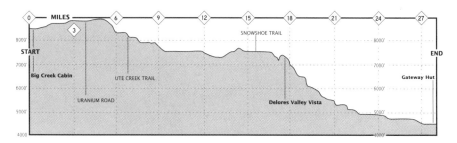

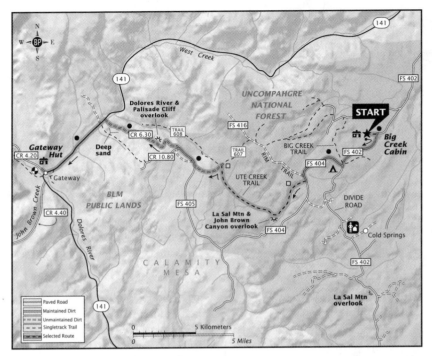

**8.5** The singletrack delivers a short, but rocky and sandy climb. Continue straight, through some scrub oak.

**9.4** Arrive at an incredible vista of the La Sal Mountains and John Brown Canyon. This is a great lunch spot and photo op.

**10.2** Arrive at another fence. Continue straight, passing through an opening in the fence, in a westerly direction between two pine trees. This marks the beginning of a very long and rocky descent.

**11.4** The singletrack turns into a doubletrack. Continue riding on the doubletrack, which is marked by iron fence posts, as it snakes its way through sage and scrub oak forests.

**14.5** Reach the intersection of Ute Creek Trail 608 and the Snowshoe Trail (Trail 607)—there are no trail signs at this intersection. Bear left onto the Snowshoe Trail, a rough-looking dirt road, and ride back to Pine Road and the main route.

**15.6** Reach the intersection of the Snowshoe Trail and CR 6.30/FS 405 (Pine Mountain Road). Bear right onto Pine Mountain Road.

**17.2** Reach the junction of Pine Mountain Road and CR 10 8/10. A sign for the town of Gateway will be to your right. Continue straight here, descending along the steep and rocky Pine Mountain Road (CR 6.30) into the Dolores River Valley.

**17.9** Descend to a cattle guard with vista of the Dolores River Valley. Views of Palisade Cliff are offered.

**21.3** Enter into a flash flood zone and patches of deep sand.

**23.1** Reach the intersection of Pine Mountain Road (CR 6.30) and CO 141, by a stop sign. Bear left (west), onto the paved highway, and descend into Gateway.

**27.1** Enter into Gateway and ride west through it.

**27.6** Bear right onto the dirt road, just before crossing the Dolores River via a steel bridge. Ride on this dirt road to the hut, with the Dolores River to your left.

**28.0** Arrive at the Gateway Hut.

# Day 6

# Gateway Hut to La Sal Hut

## Ride Summary

The route connecting the Gateway Hut with the La Sal Hut is probably the toughest leg of the entire journey. Riders climb over 4,000 feet and descend only 900 feet. Although the initial climb through John Brown Canyon is the steepest in the day, it also comes at the beginning of the day, so riders get the toughest part of the day over with first. The route crosses the Colorado boarder and enters into Utah near the Keesee Cow Camp. Since summertime temperatures in Gateway may exceed 100 degrees, it's strongly suggested that you get an early start on the day's riding, taking advantage of the morning's cooler temperatures. The La Sal Hut is the San Juan Hut System's newest hut. It was previously a yurt, until a local black bear clawed through its canvas walls. Gateway sits at 4,600 feet, while the La Sal Hut sits at 8,400 feet. You can do the math; it's a tough climb.

## Ride Specs

**Start:** From the Gateway Hut
**Length:** 22.3 miles
**Approximate Riding Time:** Advanced Riders, 3–4 hours; Intermediate Riders, 5–6 hours
**Technical Difficulty Rating:** Technically easy to moderate due to the route's well-maintained dirt roads. Some areas include washboard and sandy segments.
**Physical Difficulty Rating:** Physically challenging due to the hotter temperatures and the steep and long climb from the Dolores River Valley to the La Sal Mountains via John Brown Canyon.

**Terrain:** Paved highway and improved dirt road. The route's sandy and rocky in spots, as it makes its way through John Brown Canyon. Once above the canyon, loose gravel roads, along with rutted and sandy sections, make the climb to the La Sal Hut tough.
**Elevation Gain:** 5,027 feet
**Nearest Town:** Moab, UT
**Other Trail Users:** Sightseers, anglers, campers, and hikers

From the Gateway Hut, you start climbing almost immediately. The route through John Brown Canyon is a sandy—rutted in spots—road that cuts laboriously through the sheer, red sandstone canyon walls on its way to the La Sal Mountains. Only John Brown Creek, its accompanying cottonwoods, and the late-rising canyon sun provide any kind of relief from this torturous climb. Overhead, an old telegraph line suggests that there's a story of men who came long before you.

During America's early push west, these lines of communication proved to be a settlement's only link to the rest of the country. And it wasn't until 1897 that the link came into being. Due to this area's rugged and remote location, it didn't experience the relatively early colonization that Utah's Great Basin experienced. By 1847 Salt Lake City had already been established, but the areas surrounding the La Sal Mountains would not see any kind of settlement until the latter part of the 1870s. Although Spanish, Mexican, and American expeditions had passed through these parts as early as the 1760s, this area was considered far too remote

Crossing the state line into Utah!

and rugged to warrant settlement. In fact, the La Sal Mountains were one of the last areas in the continental United States to attract government explorers and survey teams.

For all intents and purpose, it wasn't until 1877, when gritty stockmen and their livestock first arrived in the area, that the La Sal Mountains were given much consideration. The first settlers to stake their claim to the area's large mineral and grazing resources were William Granstaff, an African-American, and a French-Canadian trapper, whose name has escaped historical records. The two prospected, grew vegetables, and raised cattle. The two eagerly claimed substantial portions of a major La Sal Mountain drainage. To the west of these claims, lies the Colorado River; to the south, the San Juan River; to the north, the Grand River and to the east, Mesa Verde country. Granstaff grazed his cattle in the drainage—which later became known as

Negro Bill Canyon, the canyon paralleling Porcupine Rim. During the next five years, cattle-ranchers continued their move into the La Sal region, establishing communities in Little Grand Valley, later to be renamed "Moab," Little Castle Valley, and on the south side of the La Sals. These early communities, nevertheless, remained particularly isolated from one another.

It wasn't until 1897 that J.N. Corbin organized the area's first telephone company, bringing service to Moab. Some of the more remote areas surrounding the La Sal Mountains, however, would remain without telephone service well into the 1920s. Following Corbin's lead, the newly created La Sal National Forest Service played a pivotal role in establishing the lines of communication in southeastern Utah. The La Sal Forest Reserve joined President Roosevelt's forest reserves relatively late—it wasn't created until January 25, 1906, roughly one year before all "reserves" became known as "national forests." As a latecomer, the La Sal National Forest Service was eager to establish itself as a viable institution.

With 128,960 acres in Utah and 29,502 acres in Colorado, it was crucial that the La Sal National Forest have the telephone communications to conduct its business. Foremost, the telephone lines would allow for speedy notification in case of fire. By 1910, phone lines ran through most of the La Sal National Forest and phone service, in turn, was made available to area locals. With these phone lines now in place, ranches and outlying settlements were now in contact with one another, paving the way for further settlement.

Climbing up John Brown Canyon.

Taking in the view to the La Sal Hut.

With old telegraph lines looming overhead, you can't help but feel, somehow, in touch with those who have traveled this road before. Heading up John Brown Canyon, you pass into an old uranium mining area. Take care to stay on the main road and stay out of the dilapidated mines. These mines have a tendency to cave-in and contain noxious and highly combustible gasses. Be thankful that your day's climbing is half over, with the steepest part of the climb behind you. Once you cross over into Utah, the La Sal Mountains seemingly pop up out from nowhere, looking curiously out of place.

Dubbed by early Spanish explorers the "mountains of salt," the La Sals are, quite visibly, an island range. Though the range never erupted, the core of the range began its life as a volcano. Over the years, erosion crumpled away the softer, volcanic rock on the outside and revealed the cooled volcanic core on the inside. This cooled core subsequently solidified the remaining range. What had at one time been a volcano, now remains exposed as the La Sal Mountains. With two prominent passes reaching over 10,000 feet, the La Sal Mountains are, indeed, no mere mounds of salt. The 11 peaks that make up the range have an average combined elevation of 11,930 feet. They are, from south to north: South Mountain (11,798 feet), Mount Tukuhnikivatz (12,483 feet), Mount Peale (12,721 feet), Mount Mellenthin (12,646 feet), Haystack Mountain (11,642 feet), Mount Tomasaki (12,230 feet), Manns Peak (12,273 feet), Gold Knob (11,055 feet), Mount Waas (12,331 feet), Horse Mountain (11,150 feet), and Grand View Mountain (10,905 feet). Their enormity only emphasizes the beauty of the mesas and valleys. The mountains and the mesas and the valleys, all make this one of the country's most striking landscapes.

Taking a dip at Hidden Lake en route to the La Sal Hut.

## **Miles**Directions

**0.0 Start** from the Gateway Hut. Return the way you came to CO 141.

**0.4** Bear right onto CO 141, crossing the Dolores River. The road bends left and leads to a sign for John Brown Canyon.

**0.9** Reach the junction of CO 141 and CR 4 4/10. Bear right onto CR 4 4/10, after passing sign for John Brown Canyon on left, and cross a cattle guard.

**1.4** The pavement ends. Here begins the climb through the steep and narrow-walled John Brown Canyon. The road through the canyon is called alternately State Line Road or Gateway Road.

**5.0** Begin to rise steeply out of the canyon.

**7.1** Enter into the historic uranium mining area. A warning sign marks your entrance. At this point you've already completed half of the days climbing, as you begin to notice taller pine trees along the road.

**7.2** Pass a BLM sign and a road to your left. Continue straight.

**8.0** Pass great views of John Brown canyon to your right.

**8.6** Arrive at an intersection. Bear left here, by the Gateway sign.

**9.8** Pass the Keesee Cow Camp in the valley, to your left, as you cross a cattle guard and the state line. Welcome to Utah.

**15.4** Enter into the La Sal Mountain State Forest. Bypass the road on the left and continue heading straight for the mountains.

**17.3** Arrive at a sign to your right reading: "5 Bar A," "Kirk's Basin – 9," and "Gateway – 16." Continue riding straight—do not bear left—as you continue to climb.

**19.3** Pass a sign indicating that you are leaving the La Sal Mountain State Forest. There will be another sign for the Taylor Livestock Company. Continue climbing.

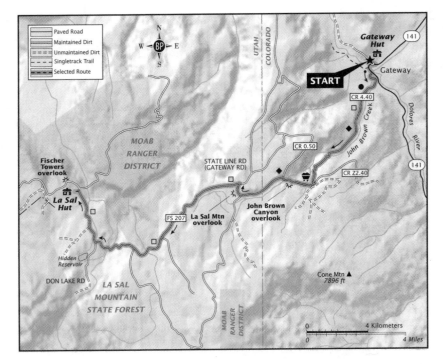

**19.7** Reach the Hidden Reservoir intersection by Don Lake Road and State Line Road. Pass Don Lake Road to your left and continue on State Line Road. *[Option: Bear left onto Don Lake Road at the sign for "Don Lake" and "Beaver Basin" to enjoy a refreshing dip in Hidden Reservoir. It's only a small diversion from the main route. To get to Hidden Reservoir: Travel along the Don Lake Road for approximately 0.5 miles. Bear right, down the 4WD road, just before the first cattle guard you come to.]*

**20.5** Pass the Manti-La Sal National Forest sign.

**22.3** Bear left (west), onto the 4WD road leading into a dense oak thicket. (If you've reached a "T" intersection bearing a sign for "Moab – 38," and "North Beaver Mesa – 4.5," you've gone too far. Turn around and backtrack roughly 500 feet south to the 4WD road, which will now be on your right.) Ride the 4WD road approximately 400 feet to the La Sal Hut.

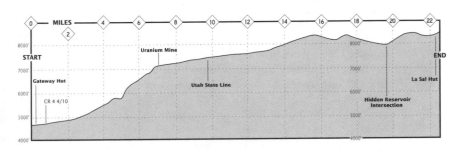

# Day 7

# La Sal Hut to Moab

## Ride Summary

Your final push to the end, in a way, encapsulates your entire seven-day odyssey. From the high alpine forests of the La Sal Mountains, through the sage-piñon fields of Moab's higher plateaus and mesas, to the surreal slickrock and sandstone formations of Moab's canyonlands, you descend an eye-popping 5,700 feet through a veritable time-capsule of natural history. The entire route overlooks Western Colorado and Eastern Utah, prominently displaying views of Fisher Valley, Fisher Towers, and Castle Valley. Although the main route of this final leg descends Sand Flats Road into Moab, a worthwhile alternative would be to break from this road at mile 28.1 and connect with the Porcupine Rim Trail, one of Moab's most incredible single-track trails.

## Ride Specs

**Start:** From La Sal Hut
**Length:** 38.4 miles
**Approximate Riding Time:** Advanced Riders, 3½–4 hours; Intermediate Riders, 4–5 hours
**Technical Difficulty Rating:** Technically moderate due to the variety of loose and exposed rocks, particularly once on Sand Flats Road
**Physical Difficulty Rating:** Physically moderate due to the hotter temperatures of Moab and the length of climbs
**Terrain:** Improved dirt road, 4WD road, and paved road. Slickrock and large, exposed loose rock make up the majority of the terrain. Sand and roots fill in the gaps. The sand and rock may cause unsteadiness on the more heavily weighted bicycles.

**Elevation Gain:** -4,131 feet
**Nearest Town:** Moab, UT
**Other Trail Users:** Hikers, sightseers, and four-wheelers

## Getting There

**From Moab, Utah:** Drive south on Main Street (U.S. 191) to 100 South Street. Turn right (west) onto 100 South Street (by the Arby's) and drive for a block and a half. Bear left into the municipal parking lot behind the police station and park your vehicle here.

Moab, Utah, seems a fitting finale to this weeklong getaway. It's been host, holdup, and hideout to a number of western outlaws—none more notable than Tom McCarty. Perhaps more than any other bad boy, Tom McCarty helped solidify Moab's outlaw mystique. The McCarty family rode into town in the late 1870s. The McCarty's were part of the vast migration of cattlemen and cowboys who were moving in to Southeastern Utah at the time. They were an independent lot, aggressive and adventurous. Of course, they had to be, given the area's unsettled terrain and remoteness. When the McCartys led their large herd of cattle across the Wasatch Mountains to roam in Moab's open ranges, no one thought to ask where they had gotten their cattle from; no one much cared.

Tom McCarty and his brother Bill operated their ranch near the La Sal Mountains. At the time, the ranch was situated on the best open range in Utah.

Climbing on the La Sal Mounain Loop Road.

Nevertheless, the two brothers sold it for $35,000 and turned, instead, to a life of crime. "My downfall commenced by gambling," Tom later wrote. "Horse racing was the first…" [see Day 2], followed by cattle rustling soon thereafter. From Moab, Tom took his cattle rustling on the road, traveling to Arizona, New Mexico, and Iowa.

While in Iowa he bought three of the fastest horses he could find. These horses would later provide transport for history's "Wild Bunch" (which included Butch Cassidy, Matt Warner, and, of course, Tom), as they made their getaway with $30,000 of Telluride's money [see Day 1]. As leader of another thieving troupe, the "Blue Mountain Gang," Tom would go on robbing in Utah and, indeed, throughout a major part of the American West for another four years. Sometime in the mid-to-late 1890s, Tom penned his autobiography and sent the manuscript to Matt Warner's father. Then he simply disappeared. The History of Tom McCarty was published in 1898.

With such notorious beginnings, it's curious that Moab acquired its name from the bible. In 1881, W.A. Pierce, an avid bible-reader (and minority by association thereof), gave the town its present name. Pierce recalled the stories of the "Far Country," a region distinguished for its remoteness and its flat-topped plateaus. This description of the biblical "Moab" closely resembled what he saw in Moab. Given what we know of Moab's raucous past, the name seems a fittingly formidable-sounding replacement for what Moab used to be called. "Little Grand Canyon" just doesn't have the punch Moab has; it's too contradictory to stand for that bold and independent town into which we now ride.

We ride into these canyonland badlands following the outlaw trail. High in the La Sal Mountains, we reach the Castle Valley Overlook at mile 9.3. Here one can view Castleton Tower, Castle Rock, and the entire Castle Valley. From our perch, the valley appears to resemble a large city of rock and sand, a city whose skyscrapers look like giant sandcastles. Situated prominently in the middle of the valley is Castle Rock. When viewed from the Porcupine Rim Trail, one notices the standing profile of a priest and two nuns—hence, Castle Rock is also known as Priest and Nuns.

About 300 million years ago, the Uncompahgre Uplift (a range in the Ancestral Rocky Mountains) caused thousands of cubic miles of earth to be washed down its western flanks. This earth moved over much of the area that now lies before you, compressing the area's salty bottom left behind by receding seas. As thousands of cubic miles of earth continued to cover this salty bed, the salt was forced to flow through pressure-alleviating fault blocks. Attaching themselves to these blocks, these massive bodies of salt and rock (some of which were 15,000 feet thick) would push their way upward towards the earth's surface. It would be nearly 290 million years later, however, that these blocks would finally reach the earth's surface in Castle Valley, known in geological circles as a "salt valley."

Castleton Tower.

Climbing with the Fischer Towers in the background.

Located within the Colorado Plateau, the vast area of flat-lying sedimentary rock that extends into almost half of Utah and smaller parts of Colorado, Arizona and New Mexico, Castle Valley offers an exceptional example of these one-time bodies of salt and rock. Under the pressures of tectonic plate shifting ten million years ago, the Colorado Plateau begun to rise. Rivers and streams, which had followed a relatively flat course across the Plateau, were now pouring through over a vertical mile of sedimentary rock. The layers of sedimentary rock, in turn, receded in cliffs, as further erosion carved a path for the valley's formation and exposed the massive bodies of salt and rock which had been forming since the Uncompahgre Uplift. Once these bodies were exposed to the elements, wind and water dissolved the salt, leaving behind the castles in the valley. Today, these formations are made up of mostly calcite, silica, gypsum and iron oxide, the latter of which giving rise to the castles' ruddy hue. This valley continues to undergo drastic erosion, as sandcastles made of sand will, ultimately, slip into the sea.

Don't let thoughts of cool ocean breezes trick you into thinking it's all down hill to Moab. From your seagull's perch above Castle Valley, descend briefly before climbing two switchback sections, five miles in length, to Sand Flats Road and the Porcupine Rim Trail. Once you turn onto Sand Flats Road, descend over loose sand and rock for roughly 11 miles, before intersecting with the Porcupine Rim Ride. If you're blown out at this point, I suggest finishing your seven-day tour on the Sand Flats Road. For those of you who have a bit more spunk left, bear right onto the Porcupine Rim Trail. Either way, enjoy—you got away!

## **Miles**Directions

**0.0 START** from the La Sal Hut. Backtrack to FS 207.

**0.1** Bear left onto FS 207, heading toward the "T" intersection.

**0.2** Arrive at the "T" intersection, marked by the sign for "Moab – 38," and "North Beaver Mesa - 4.5." Bear left (west), following signs for Moab.

**0.8** See incredible views of Fischer Towers off to your right.

**7.6** After a speedy descent, you leave Manti-La Sal Forest.

**8.1** Arrive at the head of Castle Valley, with a sign reading "Moab – 30 and La Sal Mountain Loop Road" and "Oowah Lake, Warner Campground, Moab." Bear left, onto the La Sal Mountain Loop Road, and begin climbing.

**9.3** Enjoy a fantastic view of Castleton Tower, to your right.

**10.1** Reach Harpole Mesa. Here begins a steady switchback climb on pavement.

**13.7** Reach the end of the pavement, as the road continues to climb moderately.

**14.3** Pavement begins again.

**16.6** Cross under the power lines. To your left are the communication towers. A fast descent to Moab awaits.

**17.0** Passing an "Oowah Lake" sign to your left, intersect with CR 67 (Sand Flats Road), to your right. Bear right onto Sand Flats Road, a rough 4WD road. Look to the distant west and see the Blues (or Abajos), the Henry's (the last mountains to be surveyed in the continental United States), and Navajo Mountain.

**20.6** Leave Manti-La Sal National Forest. Stay on Sand Flats Road, as it parallels a shallow rock canyon to the left, and reenter the National Forest.

**26.0** Pass the unmarked Porcupine Rim Cutoff Trail to your right.

**28.1** Pass the trailhead for Porcupine Rim, to your right, marked by stock troughs with water from a spring and continue down Sand Flats Road. [*Option. For those wanting to enjoy the great singletrack descent of Porcupine Rim, bear right here. This technically and physically challenging trail will eventually lead to UT 128 and the Colorado River. From there one may ride in a southwesterly direction to Moab or arrange to be picked up at the trail's terminus on UT 128. A good place for shuttle vehicles to park would be at the Negro Bill Canyon's trailhead, located off of UT 128, less than a quarter mile southwest of the Porcupine Rim Trail's terminus. Arranging to be picked up is highly recommended.]*

**34.2** Pavement begins.

**34.7** Pass the Slickrock trailhead to your right.

**37.2** Sand Flats Road turns to Mill Creek Drive.

**37.6** Reach the intersection of Mill Creek Drive and 400 East Street, by Dave's Corner Market. Bear right onto 400 East Street.

**37.9** Reach the intersection of 400 East Street and 100 South Street. Bear left onto 100 South Street.

**38.4** Reach the intersection of 100 South Street and Main Street. Continue for another one-and-a-half blocks west on 100 South Street to the municipal parking lot and your vehicle, ending your weeklong odyssey.

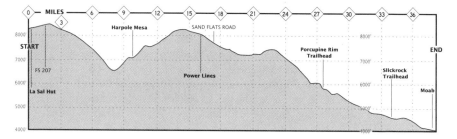

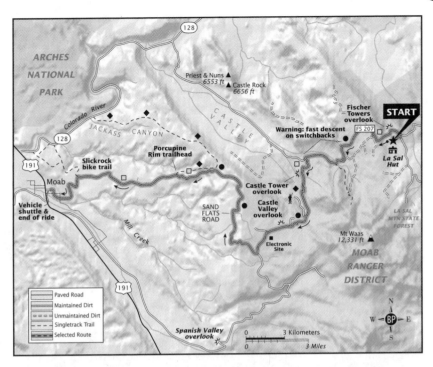

# Appendix

# Bicycle Clubs and Organizations

**Bicycle Camps, Clinics & Museums**
Barnett Bicycle Institution, 2755 Ore Mill Drive, Suite 14, Colorado Springs, CO 80904, (719) 632-5173.

**Carpenter/Phinney Mountain Bike Camp,** 2626 Baseline Rd., POB 252, Boulder, CO 80302, (303) 442-2371.

**Dirt Camp**
3131 Endicott, Boulder, CO 80303, (303) 499-3178 or 1-800-711-DIRT.

**Durango Mountain Bike Camp**
621 Columbine Road, Durango, CO 81301, (970) 259-0238.

**Mountain Bike Hall of Fame & Museum**
POB 845, Crested Butte, CO 81224, (970) 349-7382.

**Local Cycling Clubs**
Aspen Cycling Club, POB 4945, Aspen, CO 81612 (970) 925-7334.

**Banana Belt Fat Tracks Mountain Bike Club**
108 F St., Salida, CO 81201 (719) 539-6704 or (719) 539-5294.

**Bicycle Colorado**
POB 698, Salida, CO 81201 (719) 530-0051.

**Bicycle Racing Association of Colorado (BRAC),**
4615 E. 23rd Street, Denver, CO 80207 (303) 440-5366 or (303) 820-2453, a state-wide bicycling road racing association.

**Boulder Bicycle Commuters**
4820 Thunderbird Circle #108, Boulder, CO 80303 (303) 499-7466.

**Boulder Off-Road Alliance**
1420 Alpine Ave., POB 4954, Boulder, CO 80306 (303) 447-9378 or (303) 441-5262.

**Boulder Old Wheelers**
1740 Sunset Blvd., Boulder, CO 80304 (303) 444-0801.

**Boulder Women's Cycling Team**
Goes on road and mountain bike rides for women only. Boulder, CO (303) 497-8427.

**Breckenridge Fat Tire Society**
POB 2845, Breckenridge, CO 80424 (970) 453-5548; recorded info (970) 453-INFO, then push #FATT.

**Canon City Cycling Club**
1248 North Reynolds, Canon City, CO 81212 (719) 275-1963.

**City & County of Denver Bicycle Program**
200 W. 14th Ave., Rm. 302, Denver, CO 80204 (303) 649-BIKE.

**Colorado Bicycling Program**
4201 East Arkansas Ave., Rm. 225, Denver, CO 80222 (303) 757-9982.

**Colorado Heart Cycle Association**
POB 100743, Denver, CO 80210 (303) 267-1112.

**Colorado Off-Road Point Series**
222 N. Main St., Gunnison, CO 81230 (970) 641-1137.

**Colorado Plateau Mountain Bike Trail Association (COPMOBA)** POB 4602, Grand Junction, CO 81502 (970) 241-9561.

**Colorado Springs Cycling Club**
POB 49602, Colorado Springs, CO 80949-9602 (719) 594-6354, e-mail: CSCC@bikesprings.com.

**Colorado Velodrome Association**
4940 Meredith Way #305, Boulder, CO 80303 (303) 938-8679.

**Crested Butte Mountain Bicycling Association**
POB 845, Crested Butte, CO 81224 (970) 349-6817.

**Custer County Bicycle Club**
POB 352, Westcliffe, CO 81252 (719) 783-9231.

**Denver Bicycle Touring Club**
POB 101301, Denver, CO 80250-1301 (303) 756-7240.

**Diamond Peaks Mountain Bike Patrol**
P.O. Box 251, Timnath, CO 80547 (970) 482-6006 ext. 22or *DPMBP@aol.com*.

**Durango Wheel Club**
340 S. Camino Del Rio, POB 1389, Durango, CO 81301 (970) 259-4621.

**Fat Tire Week**
POB 782, Crested Butte, CO 81224 (970) 349-6817.

**Fort Collins Cycling Club**
Puts on social group rides. Fort Collins, CO (970) 482-6006.

**Front Range Mountain Biking Association**
POB 1003, Englewood, CO 80150 (303) 674-4862.

**Mountain Road Biking Association of Rocky Flats,**
8566 Cody Court, Westminster, CO 80005 (970) 422-2792; (303) 966-5135.

**Peak to Pub**
Fort Collins, CO (970) 226-6519 or (970) 266-1212.

**Pikes Peak Area Trails Coalition**
POB 34, Colorado Springs, CO 80901 (719) 633-6884.

**Ridefinders**
8 S. Nevada Ave., Ste. 401, Colorado Springs, CO 80903 (719) 471-7665 or 1-800-(719) RIDE.

**Rocky Mountain Cycling Club**
POB 101473, Denver, CO 80250-1473.

**Rocky Mountain Cycling Club**
Weekend road and training rides throughout the year. Denver, CO. *www.rmccrides.com*. No contact phone number available.

**Routt County Riders Bicycle Club**
POB 770094, Steamboat Springs, CO 80477-0094, President: Pete Wither (970) 978-1735.

**San Juan National Forest Association**
POB 2261, Durango, CO 81302 (970) 385-1210.

**San Luis Valley Cycling Club**
Kristi Mountain Sports, Villa Mall, 7565 W. Highway 160, Alamosa, CO 81101 (719) 589-9759.

**Summit County Mountain Bike Hotline**
Free 24-hour information source. Summit County, CO (970) 453-INFO, ext #FATT.

**Summit Fat Tire Society**
POB 5533, Breckenridge, CO 80424 (970) 949-8057.

**Team Evergreen Bicycle Club**
POB 3804, Evergreen, CO 80439 (970) 674-6048.

**The Medicine Wheel**
POB 685, Manitou Springs, CO 80829.

**Trails 2000**
1025 E. 5th Ave., Durango, CO 81301 (970) 259-4682.

**Tune-Up Ski & Bike Club**
222 N. Main St., Gunnison, CO 81230 (970) 641-0285.

**Vail Velo Club**
Social road or mountain bike rides. Vail, CO (970) 845-7928.

**Winter Park Fat Tire Society (FATS)**
POB 1337, Winter Park, CO 80482 (970) 726-8044 or 1-800-521-BIKE.

# National Organizations

### Alpine Snow Bicycle Association
620 South Knox Court, Denver, CO 80218 (303) 935-8494.

### American Alpine Club
Deals with mountain related activities and interests. Golden, CO (303) 384-0110.

### American Trails
POB 200787, Denver, CO 80220 (303) 321-6606, national trails advocacy organization.

### International Christian Cycling Club
7972 S. Vincennes Way, Englewood, CO 80112 (303) 290-9182.

### International Mountain Bicycling Association (IMBA)
POB 7578, Boulder, CO 80306 (303) 545-9011, works to keep public lands accessible to bikers and provides information of trail design and maintenance.

### National Off-Road Bicycling Association (NORBA),
One Olympic Plaza, Colorado Springs, CO 80909 (719) 578-4717, National governing body of US mountain bike racing.

### Outdoor Recreation Coalition of America
Oversees and examines issues for outdoor recreation. (ORCA), Boulder, CO (303) 444-3353, www.orca.org, info@orca.org.

### Rails-to-Trails Conservanacy
Organized to promote conversion of abandoned rail corridors to trails for public use. Washington, D.C. (202) 331-9696, www.railtrails.org.

### Trail Conservation Services
11694 W. Marlowe Pl., Morrison, CO 80465 (303) 932-1627.

### United States Cycling Federation
Governing body for amateur cycling. Colorado Springs, CO (719) 578-4581.

### United States Professional Cycling Federation
Governing body for professional cycling. Colorado Springs, CO (719) 578-4581.

### USA Cycling
One Olympic Plaza, Colorado Springs, CO 80909 (719) 578-4581.

### World Bicycle Polo Federation
POB 1039, Bailey, CO 80421 (303) 838-4878, manufactures and distributes equipment for official bicycle polo.

### Bicycle Advocacy Groups
Colorado Trail Foundation, POB 260876, Lakewood, CO 80226 (970) 526-0809.

### Greenway Foundation
1666 S. University Blvd., Suite B, Denver, CO 80210 (303) 698-1322.

### Trail Action Group
A trails' advocacy group. Contact Dawes Wilson of Pedal Power, Vail, CO (970) 845-0931.

### Peoples' Effort to De-emphasize Autos in Loveland (P.E.D.A.L).
Loveland, CO (970) 669-8858.

### Colorado Department of Transportation
Colorado Department of Transportation, Bicycle/Pedestrian Program, 4201 E. Arkansas Ave., Rm. 212, Denver, CO 80222 (303) 757-9982.

# The Perfect Guidebook Companions

*Tired of lugging your guidebook along on rides? Try CycoActive's BarMap or BarMap OTG. Simply photocopy the route map and ride cues, slip them into your BarMap, and leave that beautiful guidebook on the coffee table.*

The BarMap™ mapcase is a simple, lightweight solution to an age-old problem. Its soft mapcase, sewn of Cordura™ and clear vinyl, velcros easily to the handlebar. Those days of digging maps out of your fanny pack, unfolding, refolding, and stuffing them back in, are forever in the past. $7.95

The BarMap OTG™ (Of The Gods) carrying case goes a step further, allowing you to view an entire 8.5"x11" map, while still folding down to a compact 5"x6", wallet-size case that fits right on the stem. On the outside is a 4"x5" clear pocket for route maps; inside you'll find a mesh pocket for keys or money, and another pocket for energy bars, tools, and stuff. $19.95

# www.cycoactive.com

*CycoActive Products are designed and manufactured in Seattle, WA*

# Colorado Festivals

## April

**Fruita Fat Tire Festival,** Fruita, CO, Call Over the Edge Sports at (800) 873-3068. (Chapters 2 and 3).

**Peach Blossom Home Tour,** Palisade, CO; (970) 464-7458. (Chapters 2 and 3)

**Southwest Festival,** Grand Junction, CO; (970) 256-4060. (Chapters 2 and 3).

## May

**Annual Blossom Festival,** Canon City, CO; (719) 275-7234. (Chapter 49)

**Buena Vista Bicycle Festival,** Buena Vista, CO; (719) 594-6354. (Chapter 27 and 44).

**Capital Hill People's Fair,** Denver, CO; (303) 830-1651. (Chapters 41, 42, 43, 44, 45 and 46).

**Cinco de Mayo,** Grand Junction, CO; (970) 256-4060 (Chapters 2, 3 and 4).

**Colorado State Cowboy Championship,** Montrose, CO; (970) 249-5000. (Chapters 4 and 5).

**Iron Horse Bicycle Classic,** Durango, CO; (970) 259-4621. (Chapters 9 and 10).

**Jazz Festival and Art Walk,** Estes Park, CO; (970) 586-6104. (Chapters 38 and 39).

**Territory Days Celebration,** Colorado Springs, CO; (719) 471-0545. (Chapters 46, 47 and 48).

**Taste of Creede,** Creede, CO; (800) 327-658-2717. (Chapters 31 and 32).

## June

**Animas Music Festival,** Durango, CO; (970) 259-2606. (Chapters 9 and 10).

**Annual Yampa River Festival,** Steamboat Springs, CO; (970) 879-6249. (Chapters 12, 13, 15, 16, 17, 18 and 19).

**Backcountry Mountain Bike Festival,** Montrose, CO; (970) 249-5000 or (800) 923-5515. (Chapters 2, 3, 4 and 5).

**Breckenridge Music Festival,** Breckenridge, CO; (970) 453-2120. (Chapters 22 and 23).

**Bluegrass Festival,** Telluride, CO; (800) 525-3455. (Chapters 6 and 7).

**Colorado Brewers Festival,** Fort Collins, CO, (800) 274-FORT. (Chapters 14, 35, 36 and 37).

**Crested Butte Fat Tire Festival,** Crested Butte, CO; (802) 226-7411. (Chapters 24, 25, 26 and 29).

**Downtown Denver International Buskerfest,** Denver, CO; (303) 478-7878. (Chapters 41, 42, 43, 44, 45 and 46).

**Festival of Nations,** Avon, CO; (970) 476-9090. (Chapter 21).

**Fibark Boat Races and Festival,** Salida, CO; (719) 539-2068. (Chapter 28 and 30).

**Mardi Gras Conga,** Canon City, CO; (888) 333-5597. (Chapter 49).

**Norwest Art & Jazz Festival,** Grand Junction, CO; (970) 256-4060. (Chapters 2, 3 and 4).

**Rage in the Sage,** Gunnison, CO; (970) 641-0285. (Chapters 24, 25, 26 and 29).

**Strawberry Days,** Glenwood Springs, CO; (970) 945-6589. (Chapter 1).

**Sunshine Festival,** Alamosa, CO; (719) 589-6077. (Chapters 33 and 34).

**Taste of the Summit,** Dillon, CO; (970) 468-2403. (Chapters 22 and 23).

**Ute Mountain Rodeo Roundup,** Cortez, CO; (970) 565-4485. (Chapter 11).

**Western Heritage Days,** Estes Park, CO; (970) 586-6104. (Chapters 38 and 39).

## July

**American Music Festival,** Winter Park, CO; (800) 903-PARK. (Chapter 20).

**Annual Burro Days,** Fairplay, CO; (719) 836-4279. (Chapters 44 and 27).

**Annual New Old Fashioned Chaffee County Fair,** Poncha Springs, CO; (719) 539-2068 or (719) 395-6612. (Chapters 28 and 30).

**AT&T LODO Fest,** Denver, CO; (303) 892-1112. (Chapters 41, 42, 43, 44, 45 and 46.)

**Big Water Brew Fest,** Salida, CO; (719) 539-2068. (Chapters 27,28 and 30).

**Breckenridge Music Festival,** Breckenridge, CO; (970) 453-2120. (Chapters 22 and 23).

**Cattleman's Days,** Gunnison, CO; (800) 274-7580. (Chapters 24, 25, 26 and 29).

**Cherry Creek Arts Festival,** Denver, CO; (303) 355-ARTS. (Chapters 42, 43, 44, 45 and 46).

**Crested Butte Wildflower Festival,** Crested Butte, CO; (970) 349-2571. (Chapters 24, 25, 26 and 29).

**Deltarado Days,** Delta, CO; (800) 874-1741. (Chapters 2, 3 and 4).

**Downtown Boulder Art Fair,** Boulder, CO; (303) 449-3774. (Chapters 39, 40 and 41).

**Fairplay Burro Days,** Fairplay, CO; (719) 836-3155. (Chapters 27 and 44).

**Logger Days,** South Fork, CO; (719) 873-5512 or 1-800-571-0881. (Chapters 31 and 32).
**Melee in the Mines,** Telluride, CO; (970) 728-8666. (Chapters 6 and 7).
**Rainbow Weekend,** Steamboat Springs, CO; (970) 879-0880. (Chapters 12, 13, 15, 16, 17, 18 and 19).
**Ski-Hi Stampede,** Monte Vista, CO; (719) 852-2731. (Chapters 33 and 34).
**Vail Arts Festival,** Vail, CO; (800) 525-3875. (Chapter 21).
**Winter Park Jazz Festival,** Winter Park, CO; (800) 903-PARK. (Chapter 20).
**Wood Carvers Rendezvous,** Creede, CO; (800) 327-2102. (Chapter 31 and 32).

## August

**Arkansas Valley Fair,** La Junta, CO; (719) 254-7483. (Chapter 50).
**Avon Summer Fest.** Avon, CO; (800) 525-3875. (Chapter 21).
**Baily Day,** Baily, CO; (719) 836-4279. (Chapters 44 and 45).
**Breckenridge Music Festival,** Breckenridge, CO; (970) 453-9142 or (970) 453-2120. (Chapters 22 and 23).
**Downtown Boulder Fall Festival,** Boulder, CO; (303) 449-3774. (Chapters 39, 40 and 41).
**Garfield County Fair,** Rifle, CO; 970-625-2085 or 1-800-842-2085. (Chapter 1).
**Gold Rush Days,** Buena Vista, CO; (719) 395-6612. (Chapters 27, 28 and 30).
**New West Fest,** Fort Collins, CO; (970) 484-6500. (Chapters 14, 35, 36 and 37).
**Olathe Sweet Corn Festival,** Olathe, CO; (970) 323-6006. (Chapters 4 and 5).
**Palisade Peach Festival,** Palisade, CO; (970) 464-7458. (Chapters 2, 3, and 4).
**San Luis Valley Fair,** Monte Vista, CO; (719) 852-2731. (Chapters 33 and 34).
**Telluride Airmen's Rendezvous,** Telluride, CO; (970) 728-9525. (Chapters 6 and 7).
**Winter Park King of the Rockies,** Winter Park, CO; (970) 726-1590. (Chapter 20).
**Wild Mushrooms Festival,** Telluride, CO; (970) 728-6265 or 1-800-525-2717. (Chapters 6 and 7).

## September

**100 Years of the American Bicycle (1999),** Fort Collins, CO; (970) 221-6738, (970) 221-6735 and (970) 221-6243. Chapters (14, 35, 36 and 37).
**Annual Colorfest Arts & Crafts,** Cortez, CO; (970) 565-3414. (Chapter 11).
**Banana Belt Mountain Bike Loop Race,** Salida, CO; (719) 539-2068. (Chapters 27, 28 and 30).
**Coloradofest,** Colorado Springs, CO; (719) 275-7507. (Chapters 46, 47 and 48).
**Colorado Mountain Winefest,** Palisade, CO; (800) 704-3667.(Chapters 2, 3 and 4).
**Council Tree Pow Wow,** Delta, CO; (800) 874-1741. (Chapters 2, 3, 4 and 5).
**Early Settlers' Day,** La Junta, CO; (719) 384-7411. (Chapter 50).
**Middle Park Fair & Rodeo,** Kremmling, CO; (970) 724-3472. (Chapter 17).
**North Park Fair,** Walden, CO; (970) 723-4600. (Chapter 14).
**One World Festival,** Crested Butte, CO; (970) 349-6438 or (800) 545-4505. (Chapters 24, 25, 26 and 29).
**Telluride Blues & Brews Festival,** Telluride CO; (800) 525-3455. (Chapters 6 and 7).
**Telluride Film Festival,** Telluride, CO; (970) 728-6265 or 1-800-525-2717 (Chapters 6, 7 and 8).
**Celtic Festival & Highland Games,** Clifton, CO; (970) 256-4060 (Chapters 2, 3 and 4).

While campgrounds marked with a "Y" take reservations, those campgrounds marked with an "N" are on a first come, first serve basis. The term "GROUP" designates an area that limits the number of people allowed in a site. Group areas are usually larger recreational areas, providing boating, picnicking and camping. Daily fees for these Group areas vary widely, depending upon the amount of people in your group, and so, individual fees are generally unlisted. Terms, conditions, and fees are subject to change. Contact the respective ranger district for information on current terms, conditions and fees for individual campsites. Most of these campgrounds are open from Memorial Day through Labor Day. These campgrounds are listed by national forest and ranger district. For specific locations of any of these campgrounds, consult the corresponding national forest visitors map available at its respective national forest office. Reservations may be made by calling the National Recreation Reservation Service at (877) 444-6777 or online at: *http://reserveusa.com*. Reservations are accepted up to 240 days in advance of your stay but must be made prior to five days in advance. For further information, contact the U.S. Forest Service Rocky Mountain Region Headquarters, Lakewood, CO, at (303) 275-5350 or check its website at *www.fs.fed.us/r2*. *All of the information below was provided by the Colorado National Forest Service.*

### Arapaho & Roosevelt National Forest • (970) 498-2770
### Boulder RD • Boulder, CO • (303) 444-6600

Camp Dick, 8,650 feet, 41 Units, Y, $12 daily.
Kelly Dahl, 8,600 feet, 46 Units, Y, $12 daily.
Olive Ridge, 8,350 feet, 56 Units, Y, $12 daily.
Pawnee, 10,400 feet, 55 Units, Y, $12 daily.
Peaceful Valley, 8,500 feet, 17 Units, Y, $12 daily.
Rainbow Lakes, 10,000 feet, 16 Units, N, $6 daily.

### Clear Creek RD • Idaho Springs, CO • (303) 567-2901

Clear Lake, 10,000 feet, 8 Units, N, $9 daily fee.
Cold Springs, 9,200 feet, 38 Units, Y, $11 daily.
Columbine, 9,200 feet, 47 Units, N, $10 daily.
Echo Lake, 10,600 feet, 18 Units, Y, $10 daily.
Guanella Pass, 10,900 feet, 18 Units, Y, $11 daily.
Mizpah, 9,200 feet, 10 Units, N, $10 daily.
West Chicago Creek, 9,600 feet, 16 Units, Y, $9 daily.
Pickle Gulch, 9,100 feet, GROUP, Y.

### Canyon Lakes RD • Fort Collins, CO • (970) 498-2770

Ansel Watrous, 5,800 feet, 19 Units, N, $9 daily.
Aspen Glen, 8,660 feet, 8 Units, N, $8 daily.
Bellaire Lake, 8,600 feet, 26 Units, N, $12 daily.
Big Bend, 7,700 feet, 6 Units, N, $9 daily.
Big South, 8,440 feet, 4 Units, N, $7 daily.
Browns Park, 8,400 feet, 28 Units, N, $8 daily.
Chambers Lake, 9,200 feet, 52 Units, Y, $12 daily.
Dowdy Lake, 8,100 feet, 62 Units, Y, $10 daily.

Dutch George, 6,500 feet, 20 Units, N, $10 daily.
Grandview, 10,220 feet, 8 Units, N, $8 daily.
Jack's Gulch, 8,100 feet, 70 Units, N, $12 daily.
Kelly Flats, 6,600 feet, 23 Units, N, $9 daily.
Long Draw, 10,030 feet, 25 Units, N, $8 daily.
Mountain Park, 6,500 feet, 55 Units, Y, $12 daily.
Narrows, 6,400 feet, 9 Units, N, $7 daily.
North Fork Poudre, 9,200 feet, 9 Units, N, $8 daily.
Sleeping Elephant, 7,800 feet, 15 Units, N, $9 daily.
Stove Prairie, 6,000 feet, 9 Units, N, $10 daily.
Tom Bennett, 9,000 feet, 12 Units, N, $8 daily.
Tunnel, 8,600 feet, 49 Units, N, $10 daily.
West Lake, 8,200 feet, 29 Units, Y, $10 daily.
Jack's Gulch Group, 8,100 feet, GROUP, Y.
Mountain Park Group, 6,500 feet, GROUP, Y.

### Pawnee RD • Greeley, CO • (970) 353-5004

Crow Valley, 4,800 feet, 7 Units, N, $8 daily.
Crow Valley Overflow, 4,800 feet, GROUP.
Stewart J. Adams, 4,800 feet, GROUP.

### Sulphur RD • Granby, CO • (970) 887-4100

Arapaho Bay, 8,320 feet, 84 Units, Y, $12 daily.
Byers Creek, 9,360 feet, 6 Units, N, $8 daily.
Denver Creek, 8,800 feet, 25 Units, N, $10 daily.
Green Ridge, 8,360 feet, 81 Units, Y, $12 daily.
Horseshoe, 8,540 feet, 7 Units, N, $ 9 daily.
Idlewild, 9,000 feet, 26 Units, N, $8 daily.
Robbers Roost, 9,826 feet, 11 Units, N, $8 daily.
Sawmill Gulch, 8,780 feet, 5 Units, N, $10 daily.
South Fork, 8,940 feet, 21 Units, N, $10 daily.

**Stillwater,** 8,300 feet, 128 Units, Y, $12 daily.
**St. Louis Creek,** 8,900 feet, 18 Units, N, $8 daily.
**Sugarloaf,** 8,970 feet, 11 Units, N, $10 daily.
**Willow Creek,** 8,130 feet, 35 Units, N, $10 daily.
**Cutthroat Bay,** 8,400 feet, GROUP.

## Grand Mesa National Forest •
## (970) 874-6600
## Collbran RD • Collbran, CO •
## (970) 487-3534

**Big Creek,** 10,000 feet, 26 Units, N, $6 daily.
**Cottonwood Lake,** 10,000 feet, 42 Units, N, $8 daily.
**Jumbo,** 9,800 feet, 26 Units, N, $10 daily.
**Spruce Grove,** 9,900 feet, 16 Units, N, $8 daily.

## Grand Junction RD • Grand Junction, CO •
## (970) 242-8211

**Carp Lake,** 10,000 feet, 20 Units, N, $7.50 daily.
**Crag Crest,** 10,100 feet, 11 Units, N, $7.50 daily.
**Eggleston,** 10,100 feet, 6 Units, N, $7.50 daily.
**Fish Hawk,** 10,000 feet, 5 Units, N, FREE.
**Island Lake,** 10,300 feet, 41 Units, N, $7.50 daily.
**Kiser Creek,** 10,100 feet, 12 Units, N, FREE.
**Little Bear,** 10,200 feet, 36 Units, N, $8.75 daily.
**Trickle Park,** 10,000 feet, 5 Units, N, FREE.
**Twin Lake,** 10,300 feet, 13 Units, N, FREE.
**Ward Lake,** 10,200 feet, 27 Units, N, $8.75 daily.
**Weir & Johnson,** 10,500 feet, 12 Units, N, FREE.
**Eggleston Group,** 10,100 feet, GROUP, Y.

## Gunnison National Forest • (970) 874-6600
## Gunnison RD • Gunnison, CO •
## (970) 641-0471

**Almont,** 8,000 feet, 10 Units, N, $6 daily.
**Avery Peak,** 9,600 feet, 10 Units, N, FREE.
**Big Blue,** 9,600 feet, 11 Units, N, $4 daily.
**Cebolla,** 9,200 feet, 5 Units, N, $6 daily.
**Cement Creek,** 9,000 feet, 13 Units, N, $6 daily.
**Cold Spring,** 9,000 feet, 6 Units, N, $6 daily.
**Comanche,** 8,900 feet, 4 Units, N, FREE.
**Deer Lakes,** 10,400 feet, 12 Units, N, $8 daily.
**Dinner Station,** 9,600 feet, 22 Units, Y, $8 daily.
**Dorchester,** 9,800 feet, 10 Units, N, $8 daily.
**Emerald Lake,** 10,000 feet, 2 Units, N, FREE.
**Gold Creek,** 10,000 feet, 6 Units, N, $4 daily.
**Gothic,** 9,600 feet, 4 Units, N, FREE.
**Hidden Valley,** 9,700 feet, 3 Units, N, $6 daily.
**Lake Irwin,** 10,200 feet, 32 Units, Y, $8 daily.
**Lakeview,** 9,400 feet, 46 Units, Y, $10 daily.
**Lodgepole,** 8,800 feet, 16 Units, Y, $ 8 daily.

**Lottis Creek,** 9,000 feet, 27 Units, N, $10 daily.
**Middle Quartz,** 10,200 feet, 7 Units, N, $4 daily.
**Mirror Lake,** 11,000 feet, 10 Units, N, $6 daily.
**Mosca,** 10,000 feet, 16 Units, N, $8 daily.
**North Bank,** 8,600 feet, 17 Units, N, $8 daily.
**One Mile,** 8,600 feet, 25 Units, Y, $12 daily.
**Pitkin,** 9,300 feet, 22 Units, N, $10 daily.
**Quartz,** 9,800 feet, 10 Units, N, $6 daily.
**Rivers End,** 9,400 feet, 15 Units, N, $8 daily.
**Rosy Lane,** 8,600 feet, 20 Units, Y, $10 daily.
**Slumgullion,** 11,200 feet, 21 Units, N, $6 daily.
**Snowblind,** 9,300 feet, 23 Units, N, $6 daily.
**Soap Creek,** 7,700 feet, 21 Units, N, $8 daily.
**Spring Creek,** 10,900 feet, 12 Units, N, $8 daily.
**Spruce,** 9,300 feet, 9 Units, N, $6 daily.
**Taylor Canyon Tent,** 8,600 feet, 7 Units, N, $4 daily.
**Williams Creek,** 9,200 feet, 23 Units, N, $8 daily.

## Paonia RD • Paonia, CO (970) 527-4131

**Erickson Springs,** 6,800 feet, 18 Units, N, $8 daily.
**Lost Lake,** 9,600 feet, 11 Units, N, FREE.
**McClure,** 8,200 feet, 19 Units, N, $8 daily.

## Pike National Forest • (719) 545-8737
## Pikes Peak RD • Colorado Springs, CO •
## (719) 636-1602

**Colorado,** 7,800 feet, 81 Units, Y, $12 daily.
**Meadow Ridge,** 9,200 feet, 19 Units, $10 daily.
**Painted Rocks,** 7,900 feet, 18 Units, Y, $10 daily.
**South Meadows,** 8,000 feet, 64 Units, Y, $12 daily.
**Springdale,** 9,100 feet, 14 Units, N, $9 daily.
**The Crags,** 10,100 feet, 17 Units, N, $9 daily.
**Thunder Ridge,** 9,200 feet, 21 Units, Y, $10 daily.
**Trail Creek,** 7,800 feet, 7 Units, N, FREE.
**Wildhorn,** 9,100 feet, 9 Units, N, $9 daily.
**Wye,** 10300 feet, 21 Units, N, $9 daily.
**Pike Community,** 7,700 feet, GROUP
(1-800-416-6992)
**Red Rocks,** 8,200 feet, GROUP, Y.

## South Park RD • Fairplay, CO •
## (719) 836-2031 • (+) = $3.00 Parking Fee.

**Aspen (+),** 9,900 feet, 12 Units, N, $9 daily.
**Blue Mountain,** 8,200 feet, CLOSED.
**Buffalo Springs,** 9,000 feet, 17 Units, N, $9 daily.
**Cove (+),** 8,400 feet, 4 Units, N, $9 daily.
**Fourmile,** 10,800 feet, 14 Units, N, $9 daily.
**Happy Meadows,** 7,900 feet, 7 Units, N, $9 daily.
**Horseshoe,** 10,600 feet, 19 units, N, $9 daily.
**Jefferson Creek (+),** 10,100 feet, 17 Units, N, $9 daily.
**Kite Lake (+),** 12,000 feet, 7 Units, N, $5 daily.
**Lodgepole (+),** 9,900 feet, 35 units, N, $9 daily.
**Lost Park,** 10,000 feet, 13 Units, N, $7 daily.
**Michigan Creek,** 10,000 feet, 13 Units, N, $7 daily.
**Riverside (+),** 8,000 feet, 19 Units, N, $9 daily.
**Round Mountain,** 8,500 feet, 17 Units, N, $9 daily.
**Selkirk,** 10,500 feet, 15 Units, N, $7 daily.
**Spillway (+),** 8,500 feet, 24 Units, N, $9 daily.
**Springer Gulch (+),** 8,300 feet, 15 Units, N, $9 daily.
**Spruce Grove,** 8,600 feet, 26 Units, N, $9 daily.
**Twin Eagles Trailhead,** 8,550 feet, 9 Units, N, $5 daily.
**Weston Pass,** 10,200 feet, 14 Units, N, $9 daily.

## South Platte RD • Morrison, CO •
## (303) 275-5610

**Baldy,** 7,800 feet, CLOSED.
**Big Turkey,** 8,00 feet, 10 Units, N, $9 daily.
**Buffalo,** 7,400 feet, 21 Units, Y, $10 daily.
**Burning Bear,** 9,500 feet, 13 Units, N, $10 daily.
**Deer Creek,** 9,000 feet, 13 Units, N, $10 daily.
**Devils Head,** 8,800 feet, 21 Units, N, $10 daily.
**Flat Rocks,** 8,200 feet, 19 Units, N, $10 daily.
**Geneva Park,** 9,800 feet, 26 Units, N, $10 daily.
**Goose Creek,** 8,100 feet, 10 Units, N, $10 daily.
**Green Mountain,** 7,600 feet, 6 Units, N, $10 daily.
**Hall Valley,** 9,900 feet, 9 Units, N, $10 daily.
Handcraft, 9,800 feet, 10 Units, N, $10 daily.
**Indian Creek,** 7,500 feet, 11 Units, N, $10 daily.
**Jackson Creek,** 8,100 feet, 9 Units, N, $10 daily.
**Kelsey,** 8,000 feet, 17 Units, Y, $10 daily.
**Kenosha Pass,** 10,000 feet, 25 Units, N, $10 daily.
**Lone Rock,** 6,400 feet, 19 Units, Y, $10 daily.

**Meridian,** 9,000 feet, 18 Units, N, $10 daily.
**Molly Gulch,** 7,500 feet, 15 Units, N, $10 daily.
**Osprey,** 8,000 feet, 10 Units, N, $10 daily.
**Ouzel,** 8,000 feet, 13 Units, N, $10 daily.
**Platte River,** 6,300 feet, 10 Units, N, $10 daily.
**Tramway,** 7,200 feet, CLOSED.
**Whiteside,** 8,900 feet, 5 Units, N, $10 daily.
**Wigwam,** 6,600 feet, 10 Units, N, $10 daily.
**Meadows,** 7,000 feet GROUP, Y.

## Rio Grande National Forest • (719) 852-5941
## Conejos Peak RD • La Jara, CO •
## (719) 274-8971

**Alamosa,** 8,700 feet, 10 Units, N, FREE.
**Aspen Glade,** 8,500 feet, 34 Units, Y, $10 daily.
**Conejos,** 8,700 feet, 16 Units, N, $8 daily.
**Elk Creek,** 8,500 feet, 34 Units, Y, $10 daily.
**Elk Creek Overflow,** 8,500 feet, 10 Units, N, $5 daily.
**Lake Fork,** 9,500 feet, 18 Units, Y, $8 daily.
**Mix Lake,** 10,000 feet, 22 Units, N, $8 daily.
**Mogote,** 8,400 feet, 41 Units, Y, $10 daily.
**Spectacle Lake,** 8,700 feet, 24 Units, N, $8 daily.
**Stunner,** 9,700 feet, 10 Units, N, FREE.
**Trujillo Meadows,** 10,000 feet, CLOSED - Summer 1998
**Mogote Group,** 8,400 feet, GROUP.

## Divide RD • Creede, CO • (719) 658-2556

**Bristol Head,** 9,500 feet, 16 Units, N, $9 daily.
**Marshall Park,** 8,800 feet, 15 Units, Y, $10 daily.
**North Clear Creek,** 9,900 feet, 25 Units, N, $9 daily.
**Palisade,** 8,300 feet, 12 Units, N, $10 daily.
**River Hill,** 9,200 feet, 20 Units, Y, 410 daily.
**Silver Thread,** 9,500 feet, 11 Units, N, $9 daily.
**Thirty Miles,** 9,300 feet, 35 Units, Y, $10 daily.

## Divide RD • Del Norte, CO •
## (719) 657-3321

**Big Meadows,** 9,500 feet, 52 Units, Y, $11 daily.
**Cathedral,** 9,400 feet, 33 Units, N, FREE.
**Comstock,** 9,700 feet, 8 Units, N, FREE.
**Cross Creek,** 8,800 feet, 12 Units, N, $9 daily.
**Highway Springs,** 8,400 feet, 11 Units, N, $5 daily.
**Lower Beaver Creek,** 8,400 feet, 19 Units, N, $10 daily.
**Park Creek,** 8,500 feet, 16 Units, N, $10 daily.
**Rock Creek,** 9,200 feet, 23 Units, N, FREE.
**Tucker Ponds,** 9,600 feet, 16 Units, N, $8 daily.
**Upper Beaver Creek,** 8,500 feet, 15 Units, N, $10 daily.

## Saguache RD • Saguache, CO •
## (719) 655-2547

**Buffalo Pass,** 9,000 feet, 26 Units, N, $5 daily.
**Luders,** 9,900 feet, 6 Units, N, FREE.
**North Crestone,** 8,800 feet, 13 Units, N, $7 daily.
**Poso,** 9,100 feet, 11 Units, N, $5 daily.
**Stone Cellar,** 9,500 feet, 4 Units, N, FREE.
**Stormking,** 9,400 feet, 11 Units, N, $5 daily.

## Routt National Forest • (970) 879-1870
## Hahns Peak/Bears Ears RD • Steamboat
## Springs, CO • (970) 879-1870

**Dry Lake,** 8,000 feet, 8 Units, N, $10 daily.
**Dumont Lake,** 9,500 feet, 22 Units, N, $10 daily.
**Freeman Reservoir,** 8,800 feet, 17 Units, N, $8 daily.
**Granite,** 9,900 feet, 8 Units, N, $5 daily.
**Hahns Peak Lake,** 8,500 feet, 26 Units, Y, $10 daily.
**Hinman Park,** 7,600 feet, 13 Units, N, $10 daily.
**Meadows,** 9,300 feet, 30 units, N, $10 daily.
**Sawmill Creek,** 9,000 feet, 6 Units, N, $5 daily.
**Seedhouse,** 8,000 feet, CLOSED 1998.
**Summit Lake,** 10,300 feet, 16 Units, N, $10 daily.
**Walton Creek,** 9,400 feet, 16 Units, N, $10 daily.

## The Parks RD • Walden, CO •
## (970) 723-8204

**Aspen,** 8,900 feet, 7 Units, N, $10 daily.
**Big Creek Lakes,** 9,000 feet, 54 Units, Y, $10 daily.
**Grizzly Creek,** 8,500 feet, 12 Units, N, $10 daily.
**Hidden Lakes,** 8,900 feet, 9 Units, N, $10 daily.
**Pines,** 9,200 feet, 11 Units, N, $10 daily.
**Teal Lake,** 9,000 feet, 17 Units, N, $10 daily.

## Yampa RD • Yampa, CO • (970) 638-4516

**Bear Lake,** 9,600 feet, 29 Units, N, $10 daily.
**Bear River Dispersed,** 9,800 feet, 32 Units, N, $3 daily.
**Blacktail Creek,** 9,100 feet, 8 Units, N, $10 daily.
**Chapman Reservoir,** 9,400 feet, 12 Units, N, $5 daily.
**Cold Springs,** 10,400 feet, 5 Units, N, $10 daily.
**Gore Pass,** 9,500 feet, 12 Units, N, $10 daily.
**Horseshoe,** 10,000 feet, 7 Units, N, $10 daily.
**Lynx Pass,** 8,900 feet, 11 Units, N, $10 daily.
**Sheriff's Reservoir,** 9,800 feet, 5 Units, N, $5 daily.
**Vaughn Lake,** 9,500 feet, 6 Units, N, $7 daily.

## San Isabel National Forest •
## (719) 545-8737
## Leadville RD • Leadville, CO •
## (719) 486-0749

**Baby Doe,** 9,900 feet, 50 Units, Y, $12 daily.
**Belle of Colorado,** 9,900 feet, 19 Units, N, $11 daily.
**Dexter,** 9,300 feet, 24 Units, N, $8 daily.
**Elbert Creek,** 10,000 feet, 17 Units, N, $8 daily.
**Father Dyer,** 9,900 feet, 25 Units, Y, $12 daily.
**Halfmoon,** 9,900 feet, 22 Units, N, $8 daily.
**Lakeview,** 9,500 feet, 59 Units, Y, $9 daily.
**May Queen,** 9,900 feet, 27 Units, N, $11 daily.
**Molly Brown,** 9,900 feet, 49 Units, Y, $12 daily.
**Parry Peak,** 9,500 feet, 26 Units, N, $9 daily.
**Silver Dollar,** 9,900 feet, 43 Units, Y, $12 daily.
**Tabor,** 9,900 feet, 44 Units, N, $10 daily.
**Twin Peaks,** 9,600 feet, 39 units, N, $9 daily.
**Whitestar,** 9,300 feet, 68 Units, Y, $10 daily.
**Lakeview Group,** 9,500 feet, GROUP, Y.
**Printer Boy,** 9,900 feet, GROUP, Y.

## Salida RD • Salida, CO • (719) 539-3591

**Angel of Shavano,** 9,200 feet, 20 Units, N, $10 daily.
**Bootleg,** 8,400 feet, 6 Units, N, $2 daily.
**Cascade,** 9,000 feet, 23 Units, Y, $10 daily.
**Chalk Lake,** 8,700 feet, 21 Units, Y, $10 daily.
**Coaldale,** 8,500 feet, 11 Units, N, $6 daily.
**Collegiate Peaks,** 9,800 feet, 56 Units, Y, $10 daily.
**Cottonwood Lake,** 9,600 feet, 28 Units, N, $10 daily.
**Garfield,** 10,000 feet, 11 Units, N, $9 daily.
**Hayden Creek,** 8,000 feet, 11 Units, N, $8 daily.
**Iron City,** 9,900 feet, 15 Units, N, $9 daily.
**Monarch Park,** 10,500 feet, 38 Units, Y, $10 daily.
**Mt. Princeton,** 8,000 feet, 17 Units, Y, $10 daily.
**North Fork Reservoir,** 11,000 feet, 8 Units, N, $5 daily.

**O'Haver Lake,** 9,200 feet, 29 Units, Y, $10 daily.
**Angel of Shavano,** 9,200 feet, GROUP, Y.

## San Carlos RD • Canon City, CO •
## (719) 269-8500

**Alvarado,** 9,000 feet, 47 Units, N, $9 daily.
**Bear Lake,** 10,500 feet, 14 Units, N, $9 daily.
**Blue Lake,** 10,500 feet, 15 Units, N, $9 daily.
**Davenport,** 8,500 feet, 12 Units, N, $9 daily.
**Lake Creek,** 8,200 feet, 12 Units, N, $9 daily.
**Lake Isabel South Side,** 8,800 feet, 8 Units, Y, $9 daily.
**Lake Isabel La Vista,** 8,600 feet, 29 Units, Y, $9/14 daily.
**Lake Isabel St. Charles,** 8,800 feet, 15 Units, Y, $9 daily.
**Oak Creek,** 7,600 feet, 15 Units, N, FREE.
**Ophir Creek,** 8,900 feet, 31 Units, N, $9 daily.
**Purgatoire,** 9,800 feet, 23 Units, N, $9 daily.
**Ponderosa,** 8,800 feet, GROUP, Y.
**Spruce,** 8,800 feet, GROUP, Y.

## San Juan National Forest •
## (970) 247-4874
## Columbine RD • Bayfield, CO •
## (970) 884-2512

**Florida,** 8,500 feet, 20 Units, N, $10 daily.
**Graham Creek,** 7,900 feet, 25 Units, N, $10 daily.
**Middle Mountain,** 7,900 feet, 24 Units, N, $10 daily.
**Miller Creek,** 8,000 feet, 12 Units, N, $10 daily.
**North Canyon,** 7,900 feet, 21 Units, N, $10 daily.
**Old Timers,** 7,900 feet, 10 Units, N, $10 daily.
**Pine Point,** 7,900 feet, 30 Units, N, $10 daily.
**Pine River,** 8,100 feet, 6 Units, N, $6 daily.
**Transfer Park,** 8,600 feet, 25 Units, N, $10 daily.
**Florida Group,** 8,500 feet, GROUP, Y.

## Columbine RD • Durango, CO •
## (970) 247-4874

**Haviland Lake,** 8,000 feet, CLOSED - Summer 1998

**Junction Creek,** 7,500 feet, 34 Units, N, $10 daily.
**Kroeger,** 9,000 feet, 11 Units, N, $8 daily.
**Purgatory,** 8,800 feet, 14 Units, N, $8 daily.
**Sig Creek,** 9,000 feet, 9 Units, N, $8 daily.
**Snowslide,** 13 Units, N, $8 daily.
**South Mineral,** 10,000 feet, 26 Units, N, $10 daily.
**Chris Park,** 8,000 feet, GROUP, Y.

## Mancos/Dolores RD • Dolores, CO •
## (970)882-7296

**Burro Bridge,** 9,000 feet, 15 Units, N, $10 daily.
**Cabin Canyon,** 6,500 feet, 11 Units, N, $8 daily.
**Cayton,** 9,400 feet, 27 Units, N, $10 daily.
**Ferris Canyon,** 6,500 feet, 6 Units, N, $8 daily.
**House Creek,** 6,900 feet, 72 Units, Y, $12 daily.
**Mavreeso,** 7,600 feet, 14 Units, N, $10 daily.
**McPhee,** 7,100 feet, 73 Units, Y, $12 daily.
**Target Tree,** 7,800 feet, 25 Units, N, $10 daily.
**Transfer,** 8,500 feet, 12 Units, N, $10 daily.
**West Dolores,** 7,800 feet, 13 Units, N, $10 daily.
**House Creek Group,** 6,900 feet, GROUP, Y.
**McPhee Group,** 7,100 feet, GROUP, Y.

## Pagosa RD • Pagosa Springs, CO •
## (970) 264-2268

**Blanco River,** 7,200 feet, 6 Units, N, $8 daily.
**Bridge,** 7,800 feet, 19 Units, N, $8 daily.
**Cimarrona,** 8,400 feet, 21 Units, N, $8 daily.
**East Fork,** 7,600 feet, 26 Units, N, $8 daily.
**Lower Piedra,** 7,200 feet, 17 Units, N, $6 daily.
**Teal,** 8,300 feet, 16 Units, N, $9 daily.
**West Fork,** 8,000 feet, 28 Units, N, $8 daily.
**Williams Creek,** 8,300 feet, 67 Units, N, $9 daily.
**Wolf Creek,** 8,000 feet, 26 Units, N, $8 daily.
**Ute,** 7,200 feet, 24 Units, N, $8 daily.

## Uncompahgre National Forest •
## (970) 874-6600
## Grand Junction RD • Grand Junction, CO •
## (970) 242-8211

**Divide Fork,** 9,200 feet, 11 Units, N, FREE.
**Hay Press,** 9,300 feet, 11 Units, N, FREE.

## Norwood RD • Norwood, CO •
## (970) 327-4261

**Matterhorn,** 9,500 feet, 26 Units, N, $10/14 daily.
**Sunshine,** 9,500 feet, 15 Units, N, $10 daily.

## Ouray RD • Montrose, CO •
## (970) 240-3711

**Amphitheatre,** 8,400 feet, 30 Units, Y, $12 daily.

**Beaver Lake,** 8,800 feet, 11 Units, N, $8 daily.
**Big Cimarron,** 8,600 feet, 10 Units, N, $4 daily.
**Silver Jack,** 8,900 feet, 60 Units, N, $8 daily.

## White River National Forest •
## (970) 945-2521
### Aspen RD • Aspen, CO • (970) 925-3445
**Difficult,** 8,200 feet, 47 Units, Y, $12 daily.
**Lincoln Gulch,** 9,600 feet, 7 Units, N, $9 daily.
**Lost Man,** 10,700 feet, 10 Units, N, $9 daily.
**Portal,** 10,500 feet, 7 Units, N, $7 daily.
**Silver Bar,** 8,460 feet, 4 Units, Y, $12 daily.
**Silver Bell,** 8,490 feet, 5 Units, Y, $12 daily.
**Silver Queen,** 8,680 feet, 6 Units, Y, $12 daily.
**Weller,** 9,400 feet, 11 Units, N, $9 daily.
**Difficult Group,** 8,200 feet, GROUP, Y.

### Blanco RD • Meeker, CO •
### (970) 878-4039
**East Marvine,** 8,500 feet, 7 Units, N, $10 daily.
**Himes Peak,** 9,000 feet, 11 Units, N, $10 daily.
**Marvine,** 8,500 feet, 18 Units, N, $10 daily.
**North Fork,** 8,000 feet, 40 Units, Y, $11 daily.
**South Fork,** 8,000 feet, 16 Units, N, $10 daily.
**Trappers Lake Bucks,** 9,900 feet, 10 Units, N, $11 daily.
**Trappers Lake Cutthroat,** 9,900 feet, 14 Units, N, $11 daily.
**Trappers Lake Shepherds Rim,** 9,900 feet, 20 Units, N, $11 daily.
**Trappers Lake Trapline,** 9,900 feet, 13 Units, N, $11 daily.
**North Fork Group,** 8,000 feet, GROUP, Y.

### Dillon RD • Silverthorne, CO •
### (970) 468-5400
**Blue River,** 8,400 feet, 24 Units, N, $9 daily.
**Cataract Creek,** 8,600 feet, 4 Units, N, $4 daily.
**Davis Springs,** 8,000 feet, 7 Units, N, FREE.
**Eliot Creek,** 8,000 feet, 64 Units, N, FREE.
**Heaton Bay,** 9,100 feet, 72 Units, Y, $11 daily.
**Lowry,** 9,300 feet, 29 Units, Y, $10 daily.
**McDonald Flats,** 8,000 feet, 13 Units, N, $7 daily.
**Peak One,** 9,100 feet, 79 Units, Y, $11 daily.
**Pine Cove,** 9,100 feet, 55 Units, N, $8 daily.
**Prairie Point,** 8,000 feet, 44 Units, N, $7 daily.
**Prospector,** 9,100 feet, 108 Units, Y, $10 daily.
**Willows,** 7,950 feet, 35 Units, N, FREE.
**Windy Point,** 9,100 feet, GROUP, Y.

### Eagle RD • Eagle, CO • (970) 328-6388
**Coffee Pot Spring,** 10,160 feet, 15 Units, N, $6 daily.
**Deep Lake,** 10,460 feet, 45 Units, N, $6 daily.
**Fulford Cave,** 7,000 feet, 7 Units, N, $8 daily.
**Klines Folly,** 10,750 feet, 4 Units, N, $6 daily.
**Supply Basin,** 10,750 feet, 6 Units, N, $6 daily.
**Sweetwater Lake,** 7,700 feet, 10 Units, N, $8 daily.
**White Owl,** 9,500 feet, 5 Units, N, FREE.
**Yeomen Park,** 9,000 feet, 24 Units, N, $8 daily.

### Holy Cross RD • Minturn, CO •
### (970) 827-5715
**Blodgett,** 8,900 feet, 6 Units, N, $8 daily.
**Camp Hale Memorial,** 9,200 feet, 21 Units, Y, $9 daily.
**Gold Park,** 9,300 feet, 14 Units, N, $8 daily.
**Gore Creek,** 8,700 feet, 24 Units, N, $10 daily.
**Hornsilver,** 8,800 feet, 12 Units, N, $8 daily.
**Tigiwon,** 9,900 feet, 9 Units, N, $6 daily.
**Tigiwon Community House,** 9,900 feet, GROUP, Y.

### Rifle RD • Rifle, CO • (970) 625-2371
**Meadow Lake,** 9,600 feet, 10 Units, N, $9 daily.
**Three Forks,** 7,600 feet, 4 Units, N, $10 daily.

### Sopris RD • Carbondale, CO •
### (970) 963-2266
**Avalanche,** 7,400 feet, 13 Units, N, $10 daily.
**Bogan Flats,** 7,600 feet, 37 Units, Y, $11 daily.
**Chapman,** 8,800 feet, 84 Units, Y, $11 daily.
**Dearhamer,** 7,800 feet, 13 Units, N, $11 daily.
**Elk Wallow,** 8,800 feet, 7 Units, N, FREE.
**Little Mattie,** 7,800 feet, 20 Units, N, $10 daily.
**Little Maud,** 7,800 feet, 22 Units, N, FREE.
**Mollie B,** 7,800 feet, 26 Units, Y, $12 daily.
**Redstone,** 7,200 feet, 20 Units, Y, $15/17/22 daily.
**Ruedi Marina,** 7,800 feet, 5 Units, N, $8 daily.
**Bogan Flats Group,** 7,600 feet, GROUP, Y.
**Chapman Group,** 8,800 feet, GROUP, Y.

# Adventure Directory
## Outside America's Guide to Outdoor Adventure

If you're anything like us, one sport just won't do it. To give you an idea of what else is out there in the way of outdoor recreation, we at Outside America have created the Adventure Directory, your one-stop adventure-guide catalog. Since your mountain bike can't take you everywhere you'll want to go (it's virtually worthless on water), check out one of these guide companies and experience, under the direction of a local pro, the many facets of Colorado's great outdoors.

## Bicycling

**10th Mountain Hut System,** Aspen, CO (970) 925-5775, www.aspen.com/huts.

**Adventure Works Mountain Bike Guide Service,** POB 37, Winter Park, CO 80482 (970) 726-9192.

**Alpine Cycle Connection.** Coordinates your travel plans for mountain bike rides. Castle Rock, CO 1-800-875-6408.

**Alpine Vacations.** Guided mountain bike rides in the Fraser Valley. Winter Park, CO (970) 726-8822.

**Alpineer.** Guided mountain bike tours in Crested Butte and surrounding area. Crested Butte, CO (970) 349-5210.

**Back Country Biking.** Mountain bike tours in the San Juan mountains. Telluride, CO (970) 728-0861.

**Bicycle Tour of Colorado,** 3500 Wadsworth, # 201, Lakewood, CO 80235 (970) 985-1180 or 1-800-985-9399.

**Challenge Unlimited,** 204 S. 24 Street, Colorado Springs, CO 80904 (719) 633-6399 or 1-800-798-5954.

**Colorado Bicycling Adventures,** 184 E. Elkhorn Ave., POB 1301, Estes Park, CO 80517 (970) 586-4241 or 1-800-607-8765, www.coloradobicycling.com.

**Colorado Heartcycle Association,** POB 100743, Denver, CO 80210 (303) 267-1112.

**Colorado Trail Foundation,** POB 260876, Lakewood, CO 80226-0876, Info: (303) 526-0898, Bus.: (303) 384-3729, ext. 113.

**Dolores Mountain Bike Tours.** Guided mountain bike tours in the Four Corners region. Dolores, CO (970) 882-7203 or 1-800-842-8113.

**Durango Mountain Bike Camp.** Mountain bike tours throughout Durango. Durango, CO (970) 259-0481.

**Durango Singletrack Tours,** POB 3358, Durango, CO 81302, 888-336-8687, singletrack@big-mountain.com.

**Experience Plus Specialty Tours.** Guided mountain bike rides along the Front Range. Fort Collins, CO (970) 416-6389.

**Fat Tire Downhill.** Mountain bike tours in southwest Colorado. Durango, CO (970) 385-1778.

**Galena Lodge Yurts,** Galena, Idaho (208) 726-4010.

**Gunflint Trail Lodges,** Grand Marie, Minnesota 1-800-322-8327.

**Kaleidoscope Bicycle Tours.** Incredible on-road cycling in the Colorado Rockies. Greencastle, ID 1-800-401-BIKE (2453), www.wix.com/KBT.

**Life Cycle Tours,** 902 Hwy 133, Carbondale, CO 81623 (970) 963-1149 or 1-800-859-BIKE.

**Mountain Bike Specialists,** 949 Main Ave., Durango, CO 81301 (970) 247-4066.

**Mountain Bike Tour Guides,** 1248 North Raynolds, Canon City, CO 81212.

**Mountain Man Tours Highway,** 149 Main St., Creede, CO (719) 658-2663.

**Mountain Man Tours.** Guided mountain biking trips along old mining roads. Creede, CO (719) 658-2663.

**Paragon Guides.** Hut-to-Hut Mountain Biking. Vail, CO (970) 926-5299.

**Pedal the Peaks Bicycle Tour,** POB 3160, Littleton, CO 80161 (303) 979-7600 or 1-800-795-0898.

**Pike's Peak Mountain Bike Tours, Inc.,** Colorado Springs, CO (719) 635-3655.

**Pioneer Guide Service.** Fully supported camping and mountain biking trips in the Gunnison Valley territory. Crested Butte, CO (970) 349-5517.

**Roads Less Traveled.** Incredible backcountry mountain biking tours in the Rockies, Canyon Country and Southwest. Longmont, CO 1-800-488-8483.

**Rocky Mountain Bicycle Vacations,** 300 South Spring Street, Aspen, CO 81611 1-800-BIKE COLORADO.

**San Juan Hut System:** Telluride, CO (970) 728-6935, www.telluride-gateway.com/sjhuts.

**San Juan Mountain Bikes,** 925 Oceanwave Drive, Lake City, CO 81235 (970) 944-2274.

**Sherpa Tours,** Vail, CO 1-800-543-4417.

**Snow Mountain Ranch.** Guided mountain bike tours on over 600 miles of trails for all abilities. Winter Park, CO (970) 887-2152.

**Southwest Adventures Mountain Biking,** POB 3242, Durango, CO 81302 1-800-642-5389 or (970) 259-0370.

**Sports Rent,** 560 South Holly Street, Denver, CO 80222 (303) 320-0222.

**Talent Unlimited-Bike Down Pike's Peak** (719) 633-6399 or 1-800-798-5954.

**Telluride Outside.** Guided mountain bike trips in the San Juan mountains. Telluride, CO (970) 728-3895.

Teton Mountain Bike Tours, POB 7027, Jackson, WY 83002 1-800-733-0712, www.tetonmtbike.com.

The Yurts of Never Summer Nordic, POB 1983, Fort Collins CO, 80522 (970) 482-9411.

Timberline Bicycle Tours. Van-supported mountain bike tours throughout all of Colorado. Denver, CO 1-800-417-2453.

Trail Wise Guides. Mountain bike tours in the Vail Valley. Vail, CO (970) 827-5363.

Trails & Rails Downhill Mountain Bike Tours, POB 217 Georgetown, CO 80444 (970) 569-2403 or 1-800-691-4FUN.

Two Wheel Tours, POB 2655, Littleton, CO 80161 (303) 798-4601 or 1-800-343-8940.

Western Spirit Cycling: UT 1-800-845-2453.

Winter Park Fat Tire Society (FATS), POB 1337, Winter Park, CO 80482 (970) 726-8044 or 1-800-521-BIKE.

XTC Cycles. Guided mountain bike trips through the Gunnison National Forest. Crested Butte, CO (970) 349-6776 or 1-888-SNGLTRK.

## Mountain Biking at Ski Resorts

Aspen Ski Resort, POB 1248, Aspen, CO, 81612 (970) 925-1220 or 1-800-525-6200 www.skiaspen.com.

Beaver Creek Ski Resort, POB 7, Vail, CO, 81658 (970) 949-5750, www.snow.com.

Breckenridge Ski Resort, POB 1058, Breckenridge, CO 80424 (970) 453-5000 or 1-800-221-1091, www.snow.com.

Copper Mountain Resort, POB 3001, Copper Mountain, CO 80443 (970) 968-2882 or 1-800-458-8386.

Crested Butte Mountain Resort, POB A, Crested Butte, CO 81225 (970) 349-2333 or 1-800-544-8448, www.crestedbutteresort.com.

Keystone Resort/Arapahoe Basin, POB 38, Keystone, CO 80435 (970) 468-4208; 468-4245 or 1-800-222-0188; 1-800-438-7290.

Powderhorn Ski Resort, POB 370, Mesa, CO, 81643 (970) 268-5700 or 1-800-241-6997.

Purgatory-Durango Ski Resort, 1 Skier Place, Durango, CO 81301 (970) 247-9000 or 1-800-525-0892.

Silver Creek Ski Resort, POB 1110, Granby, CO, 80446 (970) 887-3384 or 1-800-754-7458.

Ski Sunlight, 10901 Rd 117, Glenwood Springs, CO, 81601 (970) 945-7491 or 1-800-445-7931.

Snowmass Ski Resort, POB 1248, Aspen, CO, 81612 (970) 925-1220 or 1-800-525-6200, http://skiaspen.com.

Steamboat Springs Resort, 2305 Mt. Werner Circle, Steamboat Springs, CO 80487 (970) 879-6111 or 1-800-922-2722, www.steamboat-ski.com.

Telluride Ski Resort, POB 11155, 565 Mountain Village Blvd., Telluride, CO 81435 (970) 728-3856 or 1-800-525-3455, www.telski.com.

Vail-Beaver Creek Resort, POB 7, Vail, CO 81638 (970) 476-5601; 476-9090 or 1-800-525-2257, www.snow.com.

Winter Park Resort, POB 36, Winter Park, CO 80482 (970) 726-5514 or 1-800-453-2525, www.skiwinterpark.com.

## Ski Resorts

Aspen, (970) 925-1220, www.skiaspen.com.

Breckenridge Ski Resort, POB 1058, Breckenridge, CO 80424, (970) 453-5000 or 1-800-221-1091, www.snow.com.

Copper Mountain Resort, POB 3001, Copper Mountain, CO 80443, (970) 968-2882 or 1-800-458-8386.

Crested Butte Mountain Resort, POB A, Crested Butte, CO 81225, (970) 349-2333 or 1-800-544-8448, www.crestedbutteresort.com.

Keystone Resort/Arapahoe Basin, POB 38, Keystone, CO 80435, (970) 468-4208; 468-4245 or 1-800-222-0188; 1-800-438-7290.

Purgatory-Durango Ski Resort, 1 Skier Place, Durango, CO 81301, (970) 247-9000 or 1-800-525-0892.

Steamboat Springs Resort, 2305 Mt. Werner Circle, Steamboat Springs, CO 80487, (970) 879-6111 or 1-800-922-2722, www.steamboat-ski.com.

Telluride Ski Resort, POB 11155, 565 Mountain Village Blvd., Telluride, CO 81435, (970) 728-3856 or 1-800-525-3455, www.telski.com.

Vail-Beaver Creek Resort, POB 7, Vail, CO 81638, (970) 476-5601; 476-9090 or 1-800-525-2257, www.snow.com.

Winter Park Resort, POB 36, Winter Park, CO 80482, (970) 726-5514 or 1-800-453-2525, www.skiwinterpark.com.

## Skiing & Winter Adventure

Aspen Skiing Company. Snowcat skiing in Aspen. Aspen, CO 1-800-525-6200, ext. 3720.

Chicago Ridge Snowcat Tours. Snowcat skiing tours at elevations exceeding 12,000 feet. Leadville, CO (719) 486-2277.

Crested Butte Nordic Center. Snowshoe, ski or skate in the Gunnison National Forest. Crested Butte, CO (970) 349-1707 1-800-215-2226, www.cbinyeractive.com/nordic-center/nordic. html.

Devil's Thumb Nordic Center. Colorado's most popular cross-country ski area. Tabernash, CO (970) 726-8231, www.rkymtnhi.com.devthumb.

Eldora Mountain Resort. Enjoy 45 kilometers of groomed cross-country ski trails. Nederland, CO (303) 440-8700.

Grand Lake Recreation District. 30 kilometers of cross-country ski trails offer views of Rocky Mountain National Park. Grand Lake, CO (970) 627-8008.

Great Divide Snowcat Tours. Offers some of Colorado's steepest snowcat skiing tours. Monarch, CO (719) 539-3573.

Irwin Lodge. Snowcat skiing within the Gunnison National Forest. Crested Butte, CO 1-888-464-7946.

Rocky Mountain Adventures Inc. Guided cross-country skiing and snowshoeing trips. Fort Collins, CO 1-800-858-6808.

Snow Mountain Ranch Nordic Center. Offering 100 kilometers of groomed cross-country ski trails.

Snowcat Tour Inc. Snowcat tours in the San Juan mountains. Durango, CO (970) 259-5680.

Steamboat Powder Cats. Snowcat skiing atop Buffalo Pass. Steamboat Springs, CO (970) 879-5188.

**Telluride Helitrax.** Ski and snowboard adventures in Colorado's San Juan Mountains by Colorado's only helicopter skiing operation. Telluride, CO 1-800-831-6230.

**The Bridgestone Winter Driving School at Steamboat.** Test your winter driving skills on a snow- and ice-covered track. Steamboat Springs, CO (970) 879-6104 or 1-800-WHY-SKID.

**Whistling Elk Ranch.** Offering 7,000 acres of private cross-country skiing. Rand, CO (970) 723-8311.

**Winter Park,** CO (970) 887-2152.

## Snowmobiling

**Alpine Expeditions.** Guided snowmobile tours in the Gunnison National Forest. Crested Butte, CO (970) 349-5011.

**Colorado Outback Adventures.** Snowmobile tours through the **San Juan mountains.** Durango, CO (970) 259-8797.

**Durango Snowmobile Adventures.** Guided snowmobile tours through the San Juan mountains. Durango, CO (970) 247-0271.

**Nova Guides.** Guided snowmobile tours in Eagle county. Vail, CO (970) 949-4232.

**Pagosa Power Sports.** High mountain snowmobile tours. Pagosa Springs, CO (970) 731-4320.

**Snowmobile Adventures Inc.** Guided tours on over 60 miles of trails at Purgatory Ski Resort. Durango, CO (970) 385-2141.

**Steamboat Lake Outfitters.** Provides snowmobiling tours in the Routt National Forest. Steamboat Springs, CO (970) 879-5878.

**Steamboat Snowmobile Tours.** Providing guide service over the Continental Divide. Steamboat Springs, CO (970) 879-6500.

**T Lazy 7.** Guided snowmobile tours in Aspen. Aspen, CO (970) 925-4614.

**Tiger Run Tours.** Runs snowmobile trips through the Arapaho National Forest. Breckenridge, CO (970) 453-2231.

**Timber Ridge Adventures.** Provides snowmobiling tours on 5,000 acres of historic mining area. 5 miles north of Copper Mountain Ski Resort, CO (970) 688-8349.

## Alpine Slides/Bobsledding

**Breckenridge Super Slide.** Summit County's famous alpine slide. Breckenridge, CO (970) 453-5000.

**Heritage Square Alpine Action.** Front Range's alpine slide. Golden, CO (303) 279-1661.

**Purgatory Ski Resort Alpine Slide.** Opens mid-June. Durango, CO (970) 247-9000 or 1-800-525-0892.

**Vail Associates Bobsledding.** Icy, one-minute run around 11 hairpin turns. Vail, CO (970) 476-9090.

**Winter Park Resort Alpine Slide.** The longest alpine slide in Colorado. Winter Park, CO (970) 726-5514.

## Sleigh Rides

**4 Eagle Ranch.** Horse-drawn sleigh rides in Eagle county. Vail, CO (970) 926-3372.

**Aspen Carriage Company.** Horse-drawn sleigh rides in Aspen. Aspen, CO (970) 927-3334.

**Aspen Lodge.** Horse-drawn sleigh rides in the gateway to Rocky Mountain National Park. Estes Park, CO (970) 586-8133.

**Buck's Livery Inc.** Horse-drawn sleigh rides with dinners served in an authentic miner's cabin. Durango, CO (970) 385-2110.

**Copper Mountain Stables.** Horse-drawn sleigh rides with food and drink. Copper Mountain, CO (970) 968-2232.

**Double Diamond Stable.** Hayrides & Bonfires. Bellvue, CO (970) 224-4200.

**Elk River Guest Ranch.** Horse-drawn sleigh rides in the Yampa Valley. Steamboat springs, CO (970) 879-6220.

**Mayday Livery & Carriage Rides.** Open sleigh rides. Hesperus, CO (970) 385-6772.

**Rapp's Guide Service.** Horse-drawn guided trips. Durango, CO (970) 247-8454.

**Sunset Ranch Inc.,** Winter sleigh rides and dinner. Steamboat Springs, CO (970) 879-0954.

**Sylvan Dale Guest Ranch.** Sleighrides and horseback riding along the Front Range. Loveland, CO (970) 667-3915.

## Snowshoeing

**Aspen Adventures.** Guided snowshoe tours in Aspen. Aspen, CO (970) 920-4386.

**Beaver Creek Cross Country Center.** Snowshoe guided tours. Beaver Creek, CO (970) 845-5313.

**Happy Trails Bike Shop.** Moonlit snowshoe walks. Nederland, CO (303) 258-3435.

**Steamboat Ski Touring and Snowshoeing Center.** Providing skate ski and snowshoeing opportunities. Steamboat Springs, CO (970) 879-8180.

## Horseback Riding and Pack Trips

**7W Guest Ranch.** Horseback riding with personalized western hospitality. Gypsum, CO 1-800-524-1286.

**A & A Horse Riding Stables.** Specializes in nightly moonlight rides. Idaho Springs, CO (303) 567-4808.

**Academy Riding Stables.** Guided horseback tours through the Garden of the Gods. Colorado Springs, CO (719) 633-5667.

**American Safari Ranch.** Guided or unguided horseback trips. Fairplay, CO (719) 836-2431.

**Aspen Canyon Ranch.** Horseback rides which lead into Vasquez Mountain wilderness. Parshall, CO 1-800-321-1357.

**Aspen Lodge Ranch Resort.** With Colorado's largest log lodge, Aspen Lodge Ranch Resort affords horseback riding on 36,000 acres of adjoining Ranch and Rocky Mountain National Park. Estes Park, CO 1-800-332-6120.

**Bar Lazy J Guest Ranch.** Along the Colorado River, daily horseback riding and breakfast rides.

**Bar Lazy L Ranch.** AllOseason sleigh/horse rides. Steamboat Springs, CO (970) 879-0095.

**Bill Dvorak River Expeditions.** Guided horseback riding tours. Nathrop, CO (719) 539-6851, www.vtinet.com/dvorak.

**C Lazy U Ranch.** Only guest ranch in the U.S. to receive the Mobil Five Star and AAA Five-Diamond Ratings. Granby, CO (970) 887-3344.

**Cherokee Park Ranch.** Horseback riding and various other activities. Livermore, CO 1-800-628-0949.

**Colorado Trails Ranch.** With over 37 years of specialization, Colorado Trails Ranch delivers great horseback rding int he San Juan mountains. Durango, CO 1-800-323-3883, www.colotrails.com.

**Coulter Lake Guest Ranch.** Provides horseback riding in White National Forest, in Rifle Mountain Park. Rifle, CO 1-800-858-3046.

**Deer Valley Ranch.** Christian family ranch welcomes horseback riders, fishers, hikers and rafters. Nathrop, CO 1-800-284-1708.

**Drowsy Water Ranch.** Provides horseback riding for all abilities. Granby, CO (970) 725-3456 1-800-845-2292.

**Echo Canyon Guest Ranch.** Located in the Sangre de Cristo mountains, Echo Canyon Guest Ranch offers a superb horse program. La Veta, CO 1-800-341-6603.

**Elk Mountain Ranch.** Provides horseback riding, whitewater rafting, fishing and trap shooting trips. Buena Vista, CO 1-800-432-8812.

**Fantasy Ranch Outfitters.** Horseback riding in the Gunnison national Forest. Crested Butte, CO (970) 349-5425.

**Focus Ranch.** A working cattle ranch with 1,000 to 1,500 steers on 100 square miles of National Forest. Slater, CO (970) 583-2410.

**Grand County Dude Ranches.** Offering six different family style dude ranches in Grand County. Grand County, CO, www.dude-ranch.com.

**Harmel's Ranch Resort.** Providing cabins along the Taylor River and horseback riding, mountain biking, river rafting and fishing. Almont, CO 1-800-235-3402.

**Hubbard Creek Outfitters.** Pack trips, tours, fishing and big game hunting. Hotchkiss, CO (970) 872-3818.

**King Mountain Ranch.** Horseback riding and gourmet meals. Granby, CO 1-800-476-KING.

**Lake Mancos Ranch.** Horseback riding, 4x4 trips and cookouts. Durango, CO 1-800-325-9462.

**Latigo Ranch.** Horseback riding, fishing and cross-country skiing. Kremmling, CO 1-800-227-9655.

**Lazy F Bar Outfitters.** Specializing in breakfast and dinner rides and overnight pack trips. Crested Butte, CO (970) 349-7593.

**Lazy H Guest Ranch.** Year-round riding. Allenspark, CO (303) 447-1388 1-800-578-3598.

• **Lost Valley Ranch.** 40,000 acres of riding for all

abilities. Sedalia, CO (303) 647-2311, www.ranchweb.com/lost.

**Lost Valley Ranch.** AAA-rated "4-Diamond" authentic working cattle ranch. Sedalia, CO (303) 647-2311, www.ranchweb.com/ lost.

**Many Ponies.** Horseback riding in telluride. Telluride, CO (970) 728-6278.

**North Fork Ranch.** Horseback riding, fly fishing and river rafting. Shawnee, CO 1-800-843-7895.

**Parshall, CO** (970) 725-3437 1-800-396-6279.

**Peaceful Valley Ranch.** Backcountry tours, hayrides and western dances. Lyons, CO (303) 747-2881.

**Powderhorn Guest Ranch.** Horseback riding, jeep trips and fishing. Powderhorn, CO 1-800-786-1220.

**Rainbow Trout Ranch.** Excellent riding, and fishing. Antonito, CO 1-800-633-3397.

**Rapp Guides & Packers.** Year-round horseback riding and pack trips. Durango, CO (970) 247-8454. ·

**Red Mountain Outfitters & Guides.** Pack trips, photography trips and big game hunts. Alamosa, CO (719) 589-4186.

**Ride with Roudy.** Horseback riding in he San Juan mountains. Telluride, CO (970) 728-9611.

**San Juan Guest Ranch.** Described by Jerry Hulse, Travel Editor for the L.A. Times, "The SJR is small with an intimacy that's contagious." Ridgway, CO 1-800-331-3015.

**Sky Corral Guest Ranch.** Intimate, year-round horseback riding. Bellvue, CO (970) 484-1362.

**Skyline Ranch.** Horseback riding in the San Juan mountains. Telluride, CO 1-888-754-1126, www.r anchweb.com/sky-line.glance.htm.

**Sundance Trail Guest Ranch.** A year-round family guest ranch. Red Feather Lakes, CO (970) 224-1222 1-800-357-4930.

**Sylvan Dale Guest Ranch.** Horseback riding, cattle drives, overnight pack trips. Loveland, CO (970) 667-3915.

**Tarryall River Ranch.** Horseback riding with a western flare. Lake George, CO 1-800-408-8407.

**The Historic Pines Ranch.** Horse programs for any ability through the Sangre de Cristo Mountains. Westcliffe, CO (719) 783-9261 1-800-446-9462, www.xpert.net/wedgwood/historic/.

**Triple G Outfitters.** Horseback riding in Vail. Vail, CO (970) 926-1234.

**Tumbling River Ranch.** Featured in both "Super Family Vacations" and "Great Resorts for Parents and Kids." Grant, CO 1-800-654-8770.

**Vista Verde Ranch.** Personalized, small and secluded. Steamboat Springs, CO 1-800-526-RIDE, www.vistaverde.com.

**Waunita Hot Springs Ranch.** Horseback riding, rafting and hot springs. Gunnison, CO (970) 641-1266.

**Whistling Acres Guest Ranch.** Horseback riding, jeeping and hayrides. Paonia, CO 1-800-346-1420.

**Wilderness Trails Ranch.** Horseback riding by skill level and cattle round up. Durango, CO 1-800-52-RANCH, www.wildernesttrails.com.

**Windwalker Tours.** Horseback riding in the Yampa Valley. Steamboat Springs, CO (970) 879-8065.

## Llama Trekking

**Antero Llamas.** Guided pack trips in the 14ers region. Salida, CO (719) 539-6405.

**Buckhorn Llama Company.** Guided pack trips throughout the San Juan mountains. Durango, CO 1-800-318-9454. Guided pack trips along the Front Range. Loveland, CO (970) 667-7411.

**Castle Llamas.** Pack trips into Colorado's Rocky Mountains. Fort Collins, CO (970) 484-3537.

**Columbine Llamas.** Guided pack trips in southwest Colorado. Durango, CO (970) 382-0026.

**Elk River Valley Llama Company.** Guided llama pack trips. Steamboat Springs, CO (970) 879-7531.

**Paragon Guides.** Llama backpacking in the Vail Valley. Vail, CO (970) 827-5363.

**Spruce Ridge Llamas Adventure Treks.** Guided llama treks in the San Isabel National Forest. Salida, CO (719) 539-4182 or 1-888-686-8735.

## Mountaineering and Climbing

**Access Fund,** Boulder, CO (303) 545-6772.
American Mountain Guides Association, Golden, CO (303) 271-0984, *www.amga.com.*

**Antoine Savelli's International Mountaineering Club.** Guided tours with instruction in climbing, trekking and mountaineering. Telluride, CO (970) 728-3705.

**Aspen Alpine Guides.** Multiday trips into the snowy backcountry. Aspen, CO (970) 925-6618.

**Aspen Expeditions, Inc.** Guides of ice and rock climbing and winter and ski mountaineering. Aspen, CO (970) 925-7625, *www.aspen.com/expeditions* or *climb@aspen.com.*

**El Diablo Alpine Guides.** Mountain and rock climbing instruction and guide service. Durango, CO (970) 385-7288.

**Fantasy Ridge Alpinism.** Guided climbing trips in Telluride. Telluride, CO (970) 728-3546.

**Faraway Adventure Program.** Offering adventure programs in climbing and mountaineering. Telluride, CO (970) 728-9386.

**International Mountaineering Center.** Guided mountaineering trips in the San Juan mountains. Telluride, CO (970) 728-3705.

**Lizard Head Mountain Guides.** Guided mountaineering tours in the San Juan mountains.

Telluride, CO (970) 728-4904.

**Mountain Quest Sports.** Climbing guides for the Vail Valley. Vail, CO (970) 926-3867.

**Ouray Victorian Inn,** located at the Ouray Ice Park, providing free breakfasts and guide services for ice climbers, Ouray, CO 1-800-84-OURAY, *www.ouray-lodging.com.*

**Paragon Guides.** Cave camping and hut tours in Eagle county. Vail, CO (970) 926-5299.

**Richard Rossiter Climbing Instruction and Guiding.** Guided climbing trips along the Front Range. Boulder, CO (303) 443-2439.

**Rocky Mountain Ventures.** Mixed ice and rock climbing trips. Steamboat Springs, CO (970) 879-4857.

**Southwest Adventures.** Guided mountaineering trips. Durango, CO (970) 259-0370.

**Vail Athletic Club.** Climbing guides for the Vail Valley. Vail, CO (970) 476-7960.

**Vail Rock Guides.** Climbing guides for the Vail Valley. Vail, CO (970) 471-1173.

## Hiking

**Black Mountain Ranch.** Guided wildflower hikes. Vail, CO (970) 653-4226.

**Cripple Creek Ghost Walk Tours.** Historically narrated hikes through the ghost towns around Cripple Creek. Cripple Creek, CO; (719) 689-3234.

**John Sir Jesse Herb Walker Tours.** Hiking with herbs. Telluride, CO; (970) 728-4538.

**Marcie Ryan Geology Tours.** Guided geology tours of the San Juan mountains. Telluride, CO; (970) 728-3391.

**Meadows Walking Tours.** Custom tailored hiking adventures. Colorado Springs, CO (719) 578-9155 or 1-800-462-WALK.

**Nova Guides.** Guided hikes in the Vail Valley. Vail, CO (970) 949-4232.

**San Juan Mountain Guides.** Guided hikes and climbs, from beginner to advanced levels, on the trails of the San Juan mountains. Ouray, CO (970) 325-4925.

**Shrine Mountain Adventure.** Guided hikes in the Vail Valley. Vail, CO (970) 827-5363.

**Sundance Adventures.** Organized Hikes along the Front Range. Boulder, CO (303) 665-5437.

## Boating

**A-1 Wildwater, Inc.** Guided raft and kayak trips. Fort Collins, CO (970) 224-3379, *www.A1wildwater.com.*

**Acquired Tastes Whitewater Rafting.** One, two or three day raft trips on the Arkansas River. Buena Vista, CO 1-800-888-8582.

**Adventure Bound River Expeditions.** Guided trips down the Colorado River: 2-7 day trips available. Grand Junction, CO 1-800-423-4668, *www.raft-colorado.com.*

**Alpine Kayak.** Guided kayaking tours on the Eagle River. Vail, CO (970) 949-3350.

**Arkansas River Tours.** Guided trips of the Arkansas River. Cotopaxi, CO 1-800-321-4352, *www.arkansasrivertours.com*.

**Bill Dvorak River Expeditions.** Guided kayak and raft trips of the Arkansas River. Nathrop, CO (719) 539-6851, *www.vtinet.com/dvorak*.

**Blazing Paddles/Snowmass Whitewater.** Guided river tours. Snowmass, CO 1-800-282-7238.

**Blue Sky Adventures.** Guided river tours. Glenwood Springs, CO (970) 945-6605.

**Boulder Outdoor Center.** Guided river trips. Boulder, CO (303) 444-8420.

**Buffalo Joe River Trips.** Guided river trips down the Arkansas River. Buena Vista, CO 1-800-356-7984, *www.netoasis.com/bj*.

**Canyon Marine Whitewater Expeditions.** Guided river trips down the Arkansas River. Salida, CO 1-800-643-0707.

**Centennial Canoe Outfitters.** Denver, CO (303) 755-3501.

**Clear Creek Rafting Company.** Guided trips along Clear Creek. Idaho Springs, CO 1-800-353-9901.

**Colorado Canoe and Kayak.** Glenwood Springs, CO (970) 928-9949.

**Colorado Riff Raft.** Guided river trips down the Roaring Fork, Colorado and Arkansas Rivers. Aspen, CO 1-800-759-3939, *www.riffraft.com*.

**Colorado River Runs.** Guided raft trips down the Colorado, Eagle and Arkansas Rivers, Bond, CO 1-800-826-1081.

**Colorado Whitewater Association.** Largest paddling club in the Rocky Mountain region. Englewood, CO (303) 430-4853.

**Confluence Kayaks, LLC.,** Denver, CO (303) 433-3676. Lessons, rentals, sales and outfitting.

**Denver Sailing Association.** Cherry Creek Reservoir. Denver, CO (303) 329-8100.

**Durango Rivertrippers.** Guided white water trips along the Animas and Dolores Rivers. Durango, CO 1-800-292-2885.

**Echo Canyon River Expeditions.** Guided trips down the Arkansas River. Canon City, CO 1-800-748-2953.

**Four Corners Rafting.** Guided raft trips along the Arkansas River. Buena Vista, CO (719) 395-4137, *www.pikes-peak.com/FourCorners*.

**Geo Tours.** Guided raft trips down Clear Creek and the Arkansas and Colorado Rivers. Denver, CO 1-800-660-7238.

**Good Times Rafting Tours.** Guided raft and duckie tours down the Arkansas, Blue, Colorado and Roaring Fork Rivers. Glenwood Springs, CO 1-800-808-0357.

**Lakota River Guides/Twin Lakes Expeditions.** Guided raft trips down the Arkansas, Eagle and Colorado Rivers. Vail, CO 1-800-274-0636.

**Lazy J Resort and Rafting.** Guided raft trips down the Arkansas River. Coaldale, CO (719) 942-4274.

**Mad Adventures.** Guided raft trips down the Arkansas River, Colorado River and Clear Creak. Winter Park, CO 1-800-451-4844.

**Mild to Wild Rafting.** Guided raft trips down the Rio Verde, Salt River, Upper and Lower Animas, Piedra and San Juan Rivers. Durango, CO 1-800-567-6745.

**Morrow Point Boat Tours.** Boat tours on Morrow Point Lake. Cimarron, CO (970) 249-4074.

**Mountain Man Rafting.** Guided raft trips down the Rio Grande River. Creede, CO (719) 658-2663.

**Mountain Quest Sports.** Kayaking trips in the Vail Valley. Vail, CO (970) 926-3867.

**Mountain Waters Rafting.** Guided raft trips down the Animas and San Juan Rivers. Durango, CO 1-800-748-2507.

**Noah's Ark Whitewater Rafting.** Guided raft tours down the Arkansas River. Buena Vista, CO (719) 395-2158.

**Peregrine River Outfitters.** Guided raft, duckie, kayak, paddle and oar boat trips down the Animas, Piedra, Dolores, San Juan and Gunnison Rivers. Durango, CO 1-800-598-7600, *www.peregrineriver.com*.

**Performance Tours.** Guided raft tours down the Arkansas, Colorado and Blue Rivers. Breckenridge, Buena Vista, Royal Gorge, CO (970) 453-0661 or 1-800-328-7238, *www.performancetours.com*.

**Poudre River Kayaks.** Guided kayak trips down the Poudre River. Fort Collins, CO (970) 484-8480.

**Raft Masters.** Guided raft trips down the Arkansas River. Canon City, CO (719) 275-6645 1-800-568-7238, *www.raftmasters.com*.

**Rapid Transit Rafting.** Guided raft trips down the Poudre River. Estes Park, CO (970) 586-8852.

**Raven Rafting.** Guided raft trips down the Arkansas River. Canon City, CO (719) 275-2890 1-800-332-3381.

**Rimrock Adventures.** Guided raft trips down the Colorado, Gunnison and Dolores Rivers Horseback, Hiking Fruita, CO (970) 858-9555.

**River Runners LTD.** Provides rafting and fishing trips down the Arkansas River. Salida, CO (800)-525-2081 *www.riverrunnersltd.com*.

**Rock Gardens Rafting.** Guided raft trips down the Colorado River. Glenwood Springs, CO (970) 945-6737 1-800-808-0357.

**Rocky Mountain Adventures Inc.** Guided rafting and kayaking trips along the North Platte, Arkansas, Poudre, Dolores and Colorado Rivers. Fort Collins, CO 1-800-858-6808.

**Rocky Mountain Outdoor Center.** Provides guided raft trips down the Arkansas River. Howard, CO (719) 942-3214 or 1-800-255-5784.

**Rocky Mountain Windsurfing Association.** Conducts clinics and races. Denver, CO (303) 973-9660.

**San Juan Rivers.** Guided kayak trips down the rivers of the San Juan mountains. Telluride, CO (970) 729-2579.

**Scenic River Tours.** Guided river tours down the Gunnison River. Gunnison, CO (970) 641-3131.

**Sheri Griffith Expeditions.** Guided paddle boat, duckie, J-rig trips down the Green, Colorado, Dolores and Yampa Rivers. Grand Junction, CO 1-800-332-2439.

**Telluride Flyfishing & Rafting Expeditions.** Guided whitewater raft trips in Telluride. Telluride, CO (970) 728-4477.

**Three Rivers Resort and Outfitting.** Guided raft, kayak and duckie trips down the Lake Fork, Taylor, Arkansas and Gunnison Rivers. Almont, CO (970) 641-1303, *www.3riversresort.com.*

**Timberline Tours.** Raft trips down the Eagle and Colorado Rivers and jeep tours Vail, CO 1-800-831-1414, *http://vail.net/timberline.*

**Wanderlust.** Provides rafting trips down the Poudre River. Fort Collins, CO (970) 383-1219 or 1-800-745-7238.

**Whitewater Adventure Outfitters.** Guided raft trips on the Arkansas River. Salida, CO 1-800-530-8212.

**Whitewater Rafting.** Provides raft and sit-on-top kayak trips down the Colorado, Roaring Fork Crystal Rivers. Glenwood Springs, CO (970) 945-8477.

**Whitewater Voyages.** Guided raft trips down the Arkansas River. Poncha Springs, CO 1-800-255-2585, *www.mtnspts.com.*

**Wilderness Aware Rafting, Inc.** Guided raft trips down the Arkansas River. Buena Vista, CO 1-800-462-7238, *www.inaraft.com.*

## Fishing

**AJ Brink Outfitters.** Outfitting guided fly-fishing trips in Vail. Vail, CO (970) 524-9301.

**Arkansas River Flyshop.** Guided fishing trips down the Arkansas River. Salida, CO (719) 539-FISH.

**Browner's Guide Service.** Guides for float fishing, alpine lake fishing, or walk-and-wade fishing. Salida, CO (719) 539-2214 or 1-800-288-0675.

**Buggywhips Fish & Float Service.** 1-4 day guided fishing trips. Steamboat Springs, CO (970) 879-8033.

**Chuck McGuire Fly Fishing.** Fly-fishing in the Vail Valley. Vail, CO (970) 949-0955.

**Colorado River Guides, Inc.** Guided fishing and rafting trips. Vail, CO 1-800-938-7238.

**Cottonwood Meadows Tackle & Grocery.** Guided fishing trips. Antonito, CO (719) 376-5660.

**Dilley's Guide Service.** Guided fishing trips in the San Juan mountains. Del Norte, CO (719) 657-2293.

**Dolores and Colorado Rivers.** Fort Collins, CO 1-800-858-6808.

**Don Oliver Fishing Guide.** Guided trips on the streams and lakes of the San Juan National Forest. Durango, CO (970) 382-0364.

**Dragonfly Anglers.** Providing fishing trips in Crested Butte. Crested Butte, CO (970) 349-1228.

**Duranglers.** Four Corners fishing guide and instruction. Durango, CO (970) 385-4081.

**Eagle River Anglers.** Guided fly-fishing trips on the Eagle River. Vail, CO (970) 328-2323.

**Elkhorn Outfitters Fishing Adventures.** Guided fishing trips along the Front Range. Fort Collins, CO (970) 484-6272.

**Inland Drifters Guided Rafting and Fishing.** Rafting and fishing tours down the Colorado River. Carbondale, CO (970) 96-DRIFT.

**Let It Fly.** Fly-fishing guide service. Pagosa Springs, CO (970) 264-3189.

**Mountain Man Rafting.** Guided fishing trips down the Rio Grande River. Creede, CO (719) 658-2663.

**Mountain Trails Outfitters.** Guided fishing trips in the San Luis Valley. Monte Vista, CO (719) 852-3870.

**River Runners LTD.** Provides rafting and fishing trips down the Arkansas River. Salida, CO (800)-525-2081 *www.riverrunnersltd.com.*

**Rocky Mountain Adventures Inc.** Guided fly fishing trips along the North Platte, Arkansas, Poudre.

**Rocky Mountain Fly Shop.** Providing guide service and instruction on rivers along the Front Range. Ft. Collins, CO (970) 221-9110.

**Steamboat Fishing Company.** Guided fishing trips on over 25 miles of private water. Steamboat Springs, CO (970) 879-6552.

**Straightline.** Guided fishing trips on Yampa and Elk Rivers. Steamboat Springs, CO (970) 879-7568.

**Telluride Angler.** Fly-fishing guide trips in the San Juan mountains. Telluride, CO (970) 728-0773.

**Trophy Flyfishing Adventures.** Guided fly-fishing trips in Telluride. Telluride, CO (970) 728-3439.

**Troutfitter Sports CO.** Guided fly-fishing trips throughout the Gunnison National Forest. Crested Butte, CO (970) 349-1323.

**Willowfly Anglers.** Offering Fly-fishing trips throughout the Gunnison River Territory. Crested Butte, CO 1-888-761-FISH.

## Thrills by Air

**Above It All Balloon Company.** Balloon rides over Aspen. Aspen, CO (970) 927-9606.

**Aspen Paragliding.** Paragliding instruction. Aspen, CO (970) 925-7635.

**Balloon Adventures of CB.** Balloon trips over the Gunnison National Forest. Crested Butte, CO (970) 349-6712.

**Balloon America.** Balloon trips over the Vail Valley. Vail, CO (970) 468-2473.

**Balloons Over Steamboat.** Balloon rides over the Yampa Valley. Steamboat Springs, CO (970) 879-3298.

**Big Horn Balloon Company.** Balloon rides over the Gunnison National Forest. Crested Butte, CO (970) 596-1008.

**Blue Sky Airplane/Balloon Adventures.** Plain and Balloon rides over the Fraser Valley. Winter Park, CO (970) 887-3001 or 1-800-696-1384.

**Camelot Balloons.** Balloon rides over Eagle County. Vail, CO 1-800-785-4743.

**Colorado Parachute Club.** Parachute trips along the northern Front Range. Fort Collins, CO (970) 498-9598.

**Durango Air Service Scenic Flights.** Scenic plain rides over the San Juan mountains. Durango, CO (970) 247-5535.

**Durango Soaring Club, Inc.** Offering scenic glider rides over the Animas Valley. Durango, CO (970) 247-9037.

**Fly Away Paragliding.** (303) 642-0849.

**Grand Adventure Balloon Tours.** Balloon rides over the Fraser Valley. Winter Park, CO (970) 887-1340.

**Life Cycle Balloon Adventures.** Balloon rides over the Front Range. Denver, CO (303) 759-3907.

**Mile-Hi Skydiving Center.** Colorado's largest drop zone. Longmont, CO (970) 702-9911.

**Mountain Breeze Ballooning.** Balloon rides over the Front Range. Masonville, CO (970) 482-0118.

**New Air Helicopters.** Charted helicopter flights over the San Juan mountains. Durango, CO (970) 259-6247.

**Owl Canyon Gliderport.** Glider tours atop Owl Canyon. Wellington, CO (970) 568-7627.

**Paraglide Telluride.** Learn to paraglide. Telluride, CO (970) 728-4098.

**Parasoft Paragliding School, Inc.** Paragliding school. Boulder, CO (303) 494-2820, www.parasoft. boulder.net.

**Pegasus Balloons.** Balloon rides over Steamboat Springs. Steamboat Springs, CO (970) 879-9191.

**Pterodactyl Paragliding.** Instruction and flights over the Gunnison National Forest. Crested Butte, CO (970)349-2836.

**Rocky Mountain Balloon Adventures.** Balloon rides over the San Juan mountains. Pagosa Springs, CO (970) 731-5315.

**San Juan Balloon Adventures.** Daily and year-round balloon rides over Ridgway, CO. Ridgway, CO (970) 626-5495.

**San Juan Balloons.** Balloon rides over Telluride. Telluride, CO (970)626-5495.

**Telluride Soaring.** Winter sail plane rides. Telluride, CO (970) 728-5424.

**The Cloud Base.** Offering sail plane rides above the Flatirons. Boulder, CO (303) 530-2208.

**Unicorn Balloons.** Balloon Rides over Snowmass. Snowmass, CO (970) 925-5752.

**Vail Valley Paragliding.** Paragliding instruction in the Vail Valley. Vail, CO (970) 845-4154.

**Wild West Balloon Adventures.** Balloon Rides throughout the Yampa Valley. Steamboat Springs, CO (970) 879-7219.

**Windtracker Balloon Adventures International.** Champagne Brunch served before every balloon ride. Fort Collins, CO (970) 482-4492.

## Multi-Sport Adventures

**A.J. Brink Outfitters.** Provides rafting, fishing, mountain biking and 4wd trips. Vail, CO (970) 524-9301.

**Adventure Quest.** Provides adventure travel excursions in scuba diving, sea kayaking, snowmobiling, snowshoeing, winter 14,000-foot summit climbs and ice climbing. Fraser, CO 1-888-782-4991, www.anadventurequest.com.

**Adventures Out West.** Provides balloon rides, raft trips, horseback riding and fishing tours. Colorado Springs, CO (719) 578-0935 or 1-800-755-0935.

**Adventures to the Edge.** Provides winter mountaineering and ice climbing tours. Crested Butte, CO (970) 349-5219 or atedge@crestedbutte.net.

**Alpine Outside.** Providing fishing, horseback riding, 4-wheeling, mountain biking and rafting trips in the Gunnison Valley territory. Crested Butte, CO (970) 349-5210.

**American Adventure Expeditions.** Ice climbing, rock climbing, rafting and fishing. Salida, Buena Vista and Canon City, CO 1-800-288-0675.

**American Wilderness Experience.** America's premier source for backcountry adventures. Boulder, CO (303) 442-2622 or 1-800-444-0099, www.gorp.com/awe.

**Colorado Adventure Training.** Eco-Quest adventure racing classes and training. Boulder, CO (303) 279-1429, www.adventuretraining.com, CAT@adventuretraining. com.

**Good Times, Inc.** Excellent snowmobiling, dogsledding and sleigh rides. Breckenridge, CO (970) 453-7604 or 1-800-477-0144.

**Gunnison Valley Adventure Guides.** Provides climbing and kayaking trips throughout the Gunnison Valley. Gunnison, CO (970) 641-9294.

**Headwaters.** Providing guided trips and instruction for mountain biking, rock climbing and kayaking. Salida, CO (719) 539-4506.

**MountainQuest Adventures.** Running, mountain biking, paddling, navigation and rope skills races. Fort Collins, CO (970) 225-2100, www.mountainquest.com.

**No Limits Center.** Providing instruction and guided trips for hiking, kayaking, rafting, rock climbing, horseback riding, wilderness camping and survival training. Crested Butte, CO. (970) 349-4247 or 1-888-954-4247.

**Nova Guides, Inc.** Provides guided jeep, fishing and mountain biking tours. Vail, CO (970) 949-4232 or 1-888-949-NOVA.

**Over The Hill Outfitters.** Specializes in horseback, horse supported trekking and multisport adventures in the Weminuche Wilderness.

**Rimrock Adventures.** Guided raft trips down the Colorado, Gunnison and Dolores Rivers, as well as guided horseback and hiking trips. Fruita, CO (970) 858-9555.

**Rocky Mountain Wilderness Adventures.** Bike, hike, raft, fish, backpack, climb, horseback ride, ski, snowmobile or snowshoe trips. State College, PA 1-800-US-ROCKIES (877-6254), www.gorp.com/rmwa.

**Steve Jones Guides and Outfitting.** Provides fishing, mountain biking and rafting trips in the Vail Valley. Vail, CO (970) 845-7770.

**Telluride Outside.** Flying, fishing, rafting, hiking, ballooning, dog-sledding and skiing trips. Telluride, CO 1-800-831-6230.

**Telluride Sports/Adventure Desk.** Offering kayaking, horseback riding, rafting, mountain biking, hiking, fishing, and glider tours. Telluride, CO (970) 728-4477.

## Ice Climbing

**Adventures to the Edge.** Guided ice climbing trips and instruction in the Gunnison National Forest. Crested Butte, CO (970) 349-5219.

**Lizard Head Mountain Guides.** Ice climbing in Telluride. Telluride, CO (970) 728-4904.

**Rocky Mountain Ventures.** Ice climbing in the Yampa Valley. Steamboat Springs, CO (970) 879-4857.

**Southwest Adventures.** Ice climbing in the San Juan mountains. Durango, CO (970) 259-0370.

## Dog-sledding

**Krabloonick.** Reliving the call of the wild in Aspen. Aspen, CO (970) 923-4342.

**Lucky Cat Dog Farm.** Dog-sledding runs through the Gunnison national Forest. Gunnison, CO (970) 641-1636.

**Mountain Mushers.** Mushing madness through Eagle county. Vail, CO (970) 328-PUPS (7877).

**Sunset Kennel Sled Dogs.** Dog-sledding tours in the San Juans mountains. Durango, CO (970) 588-3641.

## Paintball

**High Plains Paintball.** Provides recreational paintball games for groups and corporations. Denver, CO, 877-PAINTGAME or (303) 791-0741, www.paintgame.com.

**Lock & Load Paintball Fields.** Provides supplies and games for paintball. Colorado City, CO (970) 676-3517.

## Scuba Diving

**High Plains Scuba and Dive Club.** Runs scuba diving trips to some of the area high alpine lakes. Fort Collins, CO (970) 493-8562.

## Jeep

**4-Wheel Drive Tours of The Great Sand Dunes.** Guided 4x4 tours of the Great Sand Dunes. Mosca, CO (719) 378-2222.

**Alpine Express.** Guided 4-wheel drive tours to snow fields, alpine lakes, waterfalls and hikes. Crested Butte, CO (970) 349-5011.

**Bill Dvorak River Expeditions.** Guided 4x4 tours. Nathrop, CO (719) 539-6851, www.vtinet.com/dvorak. City, CO (970) 944-2780, www.coloradodirectory.com/rockytoplodge.

**Colorado West Jeep Tours & Rentals.** 4-wheel guided trips over the mountain passes of the San Juan range. Ouray, CO (970) 325-4014 or 1-800-648-JEEP.

**Dave's Historic Jeep Tours.** Guided jeep tours through Telluride's historic mining past. Telluride, CO (970) 728-9386.

**Henson Creek RV Park & Jeep Rentals.** Featuring the 4x4 Scenic Alpine Loop Byway. Lake City, CO (970) 944-2394.

**Mountain Wolf.** Jeep tours in the Vail Valley. Vail, CO (970) 949-1012.

**Nova Guide. Guided jeep tours in Vail.** Vail, CO (970) 949-4232.

**Pleasant View Resort & Rocky Mountain Jeep Rental.** Tours of old abandoned mining towns. Lake City, CO (970) 944-2275.

**Rocky Mountain High Tours.** Largest and oldest in Durango. Durango, CO (970) 247-0807 or 1-800-530-2022.

**Rocky Top Lodge & Hummer Adventure Tours.** Full day Hummer tours over Alpine Loop. Lake Silver Summit Jeep Rentals. More than 700 miles of Historic Jeep Roads. Silverton, CO 1-800-352-1637, www.silverton.org/silversummit.

**Switzerland of American Tours.** 4x4 guided trips through the "Switzerland of America," Ouray, CO.

**Texas Creek ATV Guided Tours.** Guided tours on mountain trails. Salida, CO (719) 275-8828 or 1-888-874-7824.

**Timberline Tours.** Jeep tours through he Rocky Mountains. Vail, CO 1-800-831-1414.

**Wilderness Journeys.** 4x4 tours, ghost town tours and archeology tours. Pagosa Springs, CO (970) 731-4081.

## Gambling

**Bullwhackers Casinos.** 1,250 slot machines and 23 blackjack and poker tables. Black Hawk/Central City, CO 1-800-GAM-BULL.

**Central Palace Casino.** Full-service restaurant and lounge with over 2,000 slots. Central City, CO 1-800-822-7466.

**Colorado Central Station Casino.** Features over 650 slot machines, 10 live blackjack and 9 live poker tables. Black Hawk, CO (303) 582-3000.

**Colorado Grande.** Features 193 slots, along with Maggie's Restaurant. Cripple Creek, CO (719) 689-3517.

**Creeker's Casino.** Offers over 250 slots and a progressive player's club. Cripple Creek, CO (719) 689-3239.

**Double Eagle Hotel & Casino.** A 6-story, 156-room hotel and casino. Cripple Creek, CO 1-800-711-7234.

**Harveys Wagon Wheel Hotel Casino.** Colorado's largest full-service hotel/casino. Central City, CO 1-800-WAGONHO.

**Imperial Casino Hotel.** Built in 1896 during the gold rush, the building boasts a 3-level casino, three restaurants and melodrama theater. Cripple Creek, CO (719) 689-7777 or 1-800-235-2922.

**Sky Ute Tribe Casino and Lodge.** Stay and play slots, poker, blackjack and bingo. Ignacio, CO (970) 563-3000.

**The Gilpin Hotel Casino.** Offering nearly 500 slots, poker and blackjack tables. Blackhawk, CO

(303) 582-1133.

**The Golden Rose Casino.** Offering 300 slots and 6 blackjack tables. Central City, CO 1-800-929-0255.

**Ute Mountain Casino.** The first tribal casino in Colorado and largest in the Four Corners area. Towaoc, CO 1-800-258-8007.

## Gold Panning

**Argo Gold Mine & Mill.** Over 105 years old and the world's longest haulage tunnel. Idaho Springs, CO (303) 567-2421.

**Bachelor-Syracuse Mine Tour.** Tour, pan and ride the train 3,350 feet into Gold Hill. Ouray, CO (970) 325-0220.

**Mollie Kathleen Mine.** Descend into a 1,000-foot shaft for guided tours of this turn-of-the-century gold mine. Cripple Creek, CO; (719) 689-2465.

**Old Hundred Gold Mine Tour.** Real gold mine tours and panning. Silverton, CO 1-800-872-3009.

**Phoenix Mine.** Runs gold mining tours, while real miners push tons of ore in small rail cars. Idaho Springs, CO (303) 567-0422, *www.mjordomos.com/goldmine*.

## Internet

We've done our best to list some of the more important online resources available, but as with most things Internet, addresses and names can change very quickly. If you discover a wrong address or if a web site has simply vanished into the ether, we'd love to know about it. Please send any changes to *editorial@outside-america.com*. Thanks.

### National Outdoor Websites:

*ActiveUSA.com* or *info@ActiveUSA.com* 1-800-932-2118, over 20,000 events and clubs in more than 50 sports; events, clubs and news updated daily; register online for events and clubs nationwide.

**Adventure Cycling Organization:** *www.adv-cycling.org*

**Adventure Travel Society:** *www.adventuretravel.com/ats.*

**Cyber Cyclery:** *www.cyclery.com*

**DirtWorld:** *www.dirtworld.com*

**Global Cycling Network:** *www.cycling.org*

**Great Outdoors Recreation Pages:** *www.gorp.com*

**Great Outdoors:** *www.greatoutdoors.com*

**Mountain Bike Info:** *www.mtbinfo.com*

MTB Review: *www.mtbr.com*

**On Sports Adventures:** *www.onsportsadventures.com*

**Out Your Backdoor:** *www.smen.com/~hoover*

**Outdoor Action Guide:** *www.princeton.edu/~rcurtis/outother.html*

**Outdoor Recreation Coalition:** *www.orca.com*

**Outside America:** *www.outside-america.com*

**Travelocity:** *www.travelocity.com*

**USA Cycling:** *www.usacycling.com*

**Velonet:** *www.cycling.org*

**Velonews:** *www.velonews.com/VeloNews*

### Local Outdoor Websites:

**Alcove Books:** Mountain Biking in South Central Colorado: *www.alcovebooks.com/PL1001.html.*

**American Trails:** *www.outdoorlink.com/amtrails/*

Bicycle Colorado email address: *info@bicyclecolo. org* or *www.bicyclecolo.org*

**Bicycling in Mesa Verde County:** *www.swcolo.org/Tourism/Recreation/Biking.html.*

**Colorado Mountain Bike Trails:** *www.webaccess.net/~cjevans/mtnbike/*

**Colorado Off-Highway Vehicle Coalition:** *www.cohvco.org.*

**Colorado Travel & Tourism Authority Website:** *www.colorado.com.*

**Front Range Mountain Biking Association:** *www.coloradosports.com/frmba.html.*

**Great Outdoor Recreation Pages:** *www.gorp.com/default.htm*

**Mountain Bike America Series:** *www.beachway.com/mtnbike*

**Mountain Biking in Durango, Colorado:** *www.creativelinks.com/recreat/mtnbike.htm.*

**Mountain Biking in Gunnison, Colorado:** *welcome.crestedbutte.net/bike.html.*

**Mountain Biking in Meeker Area:** *www.colorado-west.com/mtbike.html.*

**Mountain Biking in the United States:** *www.lvn.com/.local/mtb-usa2.html#Colorado.*

**Mountain Biking in Winter Park:** *www.digitalfrontier.com/wpf/recreation_guide/rafting.html.*

**Mountain Biking Near Purgatory:** *www.big-ountain.com/Purgatory/activities/biking.html.*

**Mountain Biking:** *www.vtinet.com/14ernet/Summer/mtnbike.htm.*

**Points West Map Guidebook Outfitters:** *pointswestoutfitters.com/cobike2.htm.*

**Rampart Reservoir:** *www.aalive.com/gonzo/rampart.html.*

**Rio Grande National Forest Cycling:** *www.gorp.com/gorp/resource/us_national_forest/colbik_riog.htm.*

**Rocky Mountain National Park Biking:** *www.gorp.com/gorp/resource/US_National_Park/co/bik_rock.htm.*

**Routt County Riders Website:** *www.cmn.net./~rcriders*

**Routt Mountain Biking:** *www.gorp.com/gorp/resource/us_national_forest/colbik_rou1.htm*

**Volunteers for Outdoor Colorado:** *www.voc.org., www.iBIKE.com*

---

***Dear Reader:*** *It's the very nature of print media that the second the presses run off the last book, all the phone numbers change. If you notice a wrong number or that a business has disappeared or that a new one has put out its shingle, we'd love to know about it. And if you run a guide company or have a favorite one and we missed it; again, let us know. We plan on doing our part to keep this list up-to-date for future editions, but we could always use the help. You can write us, call us, e-mail us, or heck, just stop by if you're in the neighborhood.*

**Outside America™**
300 West Main Street, Suite A, Charlottesville, Virginia 22903 • (804) 245-6800 • editorial@outside-america.com

# Repair and
## Mainte

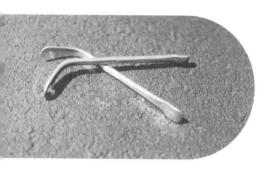

# FIXING A FLAT

## TOOLS YOU WILL NEED

- Two tire irons
- Pump (either a floor pump or a frame pump)
- No screwdrivers!!! (This can puncture the tube)

## REMOVING THE WHEEL

The front wheel is easy. Simply open the quick release mechanism or undo the bolts with the proper sized wrench, then remove the wheel from the bike.

The rear wheel is a little more tricky. Before you loosen the wheel from the frame, shift the chain into the smallest gear on the freewheel (the cluster of gears in the back). Once you've done this, removing and installing the wheel, like the front, is much easier.

## REMOVING THE TIRE

*Step one:* Insert a tire iron under the bead of the tire and pry the tire over the lip of the rim. Be careful not to pinch the tube when you do this.

*Step two:* Hold the first tire iron in place. With the second tire iron, repeat step one, three or four inches down the rim. Alternate tire irons, pulling the bead of the tire over the rim, section by section, until one side of the tire bead is completely off the rim.

*Step three:* Remove the rest of the tire and tube from the rim. This can be done by hand. It's easiest to remove the valve stem last. Once the tire is off the rim, pull the tubeout of the tire.

## CLEAN AND SAFETY CHECK

*Step four:* Using a rag, wipe the inside of the tire to clean out any dirt, sand, glass, thorns, etc. These may cause the tube to puncture. The inside of a tire should feel smooth. Any pricks or bumps could mean that you have found the culprit responsible for your flat tire.

*Step five:* Wipe the rim clean, then check the rim strip, making sure it covers the spoke nipples properly on the inside of the rim. If a spoke is poking through the rim strip, it could cause a puncture.

*Step six:* At this point, you can do one of two things: replace the punctured tube with a new one, or patch the hole. It's easiest to just replace the tube with a new tube when you're out on the trails. Roll up the old tube and take it home to repair later that night in front of the TV. Directions on patching a tube are usually included with the patch kit itself.

## INSTALLING THE TIRE AND TUBE
*(This can be done entirely by hand)*

*Step seven:* Inflate the new or repaired tube with enough air to give it shape, then tuck it back into the tire.

*Step eight:* To put the tire and tube back on the rim, begin by putting the valve in the valve hole. The valve must be straight. Then use your hands to push the beaded edge of the tire onto the rim all the way around so that one side of your tire is on the rim.

*Step nine:* Let most of the air out of the tube to allow room for the rest of the tire.

*Step ten:* Beginning opposite the valve, use your thumbs to push the other side of the tire onto the rim. Be careful not to pinch the tube in between the tire and the rim. The last few inches may be difficult, and you may need the tire iron to pry the tire onto the rim. If so, just be careful not to puncture the tube.

## BEFORE INFLATING COMPLETELY

*Step eleven:* Check to make sure the tire is seated properly and that the tube is not caught between the tire and the rim. Do this by adding about 5 to 10 pounds of air, and watch closely that the tube does not bulge out of the tire.

*Step twelve:* Once you're sure the tire and tube are properly seated, put the wheel back on the bike, then fill the tire with air. It's easier squeezing the wheel through the brake shoes if the tire is still flat.

*Step thirteen:* Now fill the tire with the proper amount of air, and check constantly to make sure the tube doesn't bulge from the rim. If the tube does appear to bulge out, release all the air as quickly as possible, or you could be in for a big bang.

When installing the rear wheel, place the chain back onto the smallest cog (furthest gear on the right), and pull the derailleur out of the way. Your wheel should slide right on.

# LUBRICATION PREVENTS DETERIORATION

Lubrication is crucial to maintaining your bike. Dry spots will be eliminated. Creaks, squeaks, grinding, and binding will be gone. The chain will run quietly, and the gears will shift smoothly. The brakes will grip quicker, and your bike may last longer with fewer repairs. Need I say more? Well, yes. Without knowing where to put the lubrication, what good is it?

### THINGS YOU WILL NEED
- One can of bicycle lubricant, found at any bike store.
- A clean rag (to wipe excess lubricant away).

### WHAT GETS LUBRICATED
- Front derailleur
- Rear derailleur
- Shift levers
- Front brake
- Rear brake

- Both brake levers
- Chain

## WHERE TO LUBRICATE

To make it easy, simply spray a little lubricant on all the pivot points of your bike. If you're using a squeeze bottle, use just a drop or two. Put a few drops on each point wherever metal moves against metal, for instance, at the center of the brake calipers. Then let the lube sink in.

Once you have applied the lubricant to the derailleurs, shift the gears a few times, working the derailleurs back and forth. This allows the lubricant to work itself into the tiny cracks and spaces it must occupy to do its job. Work the brakes a few times as well.

## LUBING THE CHAIN

Lubricating the chain should be done after the chain has been wiped clean of most road grime. Do this by spinning the pedals counterclockwise while gripping the chain with a clean rag. As you add the lubricant, be sure to get some in between each link. With an aerosol spray, just spray the chain while pedalling backwards (counterclockwise) until the chain is fully lubricated. Let the lubricant soak in for a few seconds before wiping the excess away. Chains will collect dirt much faster if they're loaded with too much lubrication.

# Index

# Index

# H

Hahn, Joseph, 108–10
Hahns Peak Village, 106
Harrison, Benjamin, 309
Hartman Rocks, 214
Hayden Survey, 242, 367, 373, 378
Hermosa, CO, 82
Hermosa Creek Trail, 82
Hewlett's Gulch, 258
Homestead Act of 1862, 279
Homestead Meadows, 276–78
Hoover, Herbert, 238
Hopi Indians, 48
Hot Springs to Mad Creek to Red Dirt Trail Loop, 124
House Rock, 276
House Rock to Pierson Park, 274
Howard Flats, 368–69

Howelsen Hill Loop 6, 130
Howelsen, Carl, 131–34
huckleberry bread pudding (recipe), 326
Huleatt, Horace, 260
Hunt, Alexander, 84
hut-to-hut biking, 363
Hutton, James, 330

# I

Indian Peaks, 281–84
Institute of Arctic and Alpine Research, 284–85
Iron Horse Bicycle Classic, 92
Irwin, CO, 197–99
Irwin, Richard P., 197

# J

Jackson Creek Trail, 318

Jackson, William H., 165
James, Jesse, 229–30

# K

Kassler Treatment Plant, 306–7
Kenosha to Georgia Passes, 308
King of the Rockies Off-Road Stage Race and Mountain Bike Festival, 159
Kokopelli Trail, 44–48
Kremmling, CO, 137–39
Kremmling, Rudolph, 139
Kreutzer, William, 310

# L

La Junta, CO, 346
La Sal Mountains, 389
Lee, George T., 372
legalities, 3–4
Liberty Mine avalache of 1902, 71
Littleton, CO, 302
Log Chutes Trail, 88
Long, Stephen H., 303
Longfellow, Henry Wadsworth, 165

# M

Mack Ridge, 45–46
maintenance, 15, 423–26
maps, 18
Marshall Basin, 77
Mayer, Jim and Tom, 92
McCarty, Bill, 392–94
McCarty, Tom, 364–65, 371, 392–93
McGinty, 229
McGuire, John, 50

# Euphoria...
# in many different states.

**The most beautiful, challenging and exhilarating rides are just a day-trip away.**

*Visit* **www.outside-america.com** *to order the latest guides for areas near you—or not so near.  Also, get information and updates on future publications and other guidebooks from Outside America™.*

*For more information or to place an order, call* **1–800–243–0495.**

# Meet the Author

Originally from Queens, NY, Stephen Hlawaty has since set camp in Colorado's Rocky Mountains. After receiving his Master of Arts degree in English from the University of Northern Colorado, Stephen embarked on his freelance writing career, publishing his work in *Rocky Mountain Sports Magazine, Outdoor, Skier, Steamboat Springs Magazine, Scene, Boulder Weekly,* and *Real Life.*

Struggling to make it as a writer, Stephen moved to Steamboat Springs, where his struggles lost most, if not all, of their potency. Finding peace in motion among the mountains of Steamboat Springs, Stephen has added to his outdoor resume over 2,500 miles of riding in a single season and in excess of 300 days of skiing in the last three years. An avid rider and telemarker, Stephen continues to find peace in riding 3,500-foot-vertical-gain mountain bike trails, as well as in heli-skiing among the glaciers of Valdez, Alaska. Although now living in Fort Collins, Stephen keeps in close contact with the mother ship, making frequent trips to Steamboat—summer, spring, winter, fall—and loving it all.